MANAGERIAL FINANCE

THIRD EDITION

MANAGERIAL FINANCE

J. FRED WESTON
UNIVERSITY OF CALIFORNIA, LOS ANGELES

EUGENE F. BRIGHAM
THE UNIVERSITY OF WISCONSIN

HOLT, RINEHART AND WINSTON

New York Chicago San Francisco Atlanta Dallas
Montreal Toronto London Sydney

Library of Congress Catalog Card Number: 69-16076
03-075580-8

Printed in the United States of America

123 22 9876

Preface

The field of finance has undergone significant change during the past few years. On the theoretical side, breakthroughs have been made both in the concepts of risk and uncertainty and in formally incorporating these concepts into such financial decision processes as capital budgeting, cost of capital, and working capital management. On the applied side, some of these new theories have already found application in business, and their use has spread as practicing financial managers continue to increase their use of more sophisticated concepts. To a large extent this trend dictated the revisions made in the third Edition of *Managerial Finance.*

In addition to introducing new materials into this edition, the revision also reflects our experience, and that of others, in teaching business finance. Organizational changes were made to provide for smoother flow and greater continuity; points that proved troublesome to students were clarified; a few outright errors were corrected; and, of course, descriptive materials dealing with such subjects as taxes were updated. In addition, the end-of-chapter questions, problems, and references were clarified and strengthened. The entire book was used in manuscript form at the introductory level in both undergraduate and MBA courses at several universities to facilitate this process.

Much of the specific content of the book is the result of our experience in executive development programs over a number of years. This experience, plus consulting with business firms on financial problems and policies, has helped us identify the most significant responsibilities of financial managers, the most fundamental problems facing firms, and the most feasible approaches to practical decision making. Some topics may be found difficult at places—but so are the issues faced by financial managers. Business managers must be prepared to handle complex problems, and finding solutions to these problems necessarily involves the use of advanced tools and techniques.

We have not sought to avoid the many unresolved areas of business financial theory and practice. The book could have been simplified in many places by avoiding the difficult issues, but we preferred to provide a basic framework that is based on the "received doctrine," then to go on (often in appendixes) to raise some of the questions that have plagued a number of important issues. It is hoped that our presentation, along with the additional references provided at the end of each chapter, will stimulate the reader to further inquiry, whether he follows an academic or a business career.

We acknowledge that the level and difficulty of the material is uneven. Certain parts are simply descriptions of the institutional features of the financial environment, and as such are not difficult for the student to understand. Other parts—notably the material on capital budgeting and the cost of capital—are by nature rather abstract, and as such are difficult for those not used to thinking in abstract terms. In some of the more complex sections, we have simply outlined procedures in the main body of the text, then justified the procedures in the chapter appendixes.

The appendixes permit great flexibility in the use of *Managerial Finance*. The book can be used in a basic course by omitting selected appendix topics. If instructors wish to cover selected topics from the appendixes, they may do so, and the more interested or mature student can go on to study these topics on his own. Alternatively, the book may be used in a two-semester course, supplemented as the instructor sees fit with outside readings or cases or both. We have used the basic chapters plus a very few appendixes in the introductory course, then referred to selected appendixes, as appropriate, in advanced courses, utilizing readings or cases. In fact, some of the appendixes were written specifically to help bridge the gap between basic texts and journal literature—Appendix A12, "The Gordon Model," is an example.

The end-of-chapter questions and problems have been revised and extended. In our opinion, practice with numerical problems is essential to an understanding of some of the basic principles, so we tend to emphasize the problems in our own courses. Cases are especially useful in this connection, but instructors in introductory courses frequently find it difficult to explore complex cases in the required depth and still have time to cover the necessary background material. Our own approach has been to use case problems from which all extraneous material has been removed, thus permitting the essential principles to be illustrated in a minimum amount of time. The problems in each chapter seek to illustrate the concepts presented in that chapter. Because the computations can be made quickly, students should have time to reflect on the generalizations illustrated by the problems and to fix in mind a method of attack for dealing with similar issues encountered in the future. With this objective, the *Study Guide* to *Essentials of Managerial Finance,* a briefer version of this book, has proved useful in putting the student on the right track in solving problems similar to the ones given in this book.

Reflecting both the introduction of new material and our experience in teaching with the previous editions, the book has been reorganized into eight major sections. Part I presents the nature of the economic and tax environment in which the firm operates, placing finance in its appropriate managerial-decision setting. Part II deals with the interrelated concepts of financial analysis, planning, and control. Part III presents the first portion of the analysis required for investment decisions. It deals with capital budgeting, taking into account uncertainty and utility theory. Part IV covers financial structure and the cost of capital, including dividend policy and alternative theories of the nature of the cost of capital functions. Part V extends decision models to working capital management, including cash and inventory decision models as well as the traditional materials on short- and intermediate-term financing instruments and institutions. Part VI focuses on the market for various types of long-term financing instruments and sources, including the theory and use of convertible securities and warrants. Parts VII and VIII deal with a range of financial strategies for stimulating and supporting the growth of the firm during various phases of its life cycle.

Although we have given much thought to the organization and structure of the book, we recognize that some instructors will prefer to take up the topics in a sequence different from the one used here. To facilitate this, we have made each chapter as self-contained as possible, and we have also provided a Glossary of terms at the end of the book.

Several reviewers suggested that it might be desirable to reduce the total length of the book. The idea was appealing, but we did not follow it for several reasons. First, such a reduction could be accomplished only (1) by reducing the scope of the book, (2) by eliminating some of the institutional material, (3) by eliminating some of the theory, or (4) by "being less verbose." There were compelling reasons for avoiding each of these approaches. We want the book to cover the entire field of business finance and to deal with all the functions of the financial manager. Eliminating institutional material and concentrating on theory and technique would give the student an unrealistic, sterile view of finance. Some of the more advanced theory and techniques could have been eliminated on the grounds that they probably would not be covered in basic courses, but it is useful to show where this material fits into the scheme of things and to provide the student with a bridge to the journal literature. Finally, our verbosity results to a large extent from adding statements, examples, and other matter, to clarify points that our students have found difficult; to eliminate these would have reduced the clarity of the book. These factors, together with the fact that the book is structured so that instructors do not have to assign all the material, caused us to forego a marked reduction in the book's length.

We are grateful to users of previous editions who have given us the benefit of their reactions and suggestions, and to our own students on whom we tested our ideas. We are particularly indebted to Professors William Beranek, Michael Adler, John Andrews, Robert S. Himes, Charles W. Haley, Gerald Pogue, Stewart Myers, William Frazier, Keith Smith, and William Sharpe for their careful reviews and criticisms of this and previous editions.

We would also like to express our appreciation to Messrs. Edward Altman, Robert Aubey, Barry Gertz, Craig Johnson, Richardson Pettit, Donald Kaplan, George Engler, and Timothy Nantell for aiding us in preparing the manuscript and in developing and checking the questions and the problems. For typing the manuscript and for reproducing drafts for classroom use, we are grateful to Misses Pauline Grossman, Rea Glazer, Cheri Abbott, and Virginia McGinnis.

The University of California and the University of Wisconsin, and our colleagues on these campuses, provided us with intellectual and material support in bringing this book to completion. To Ing. Leon Avalos Vez, we express thanks for the continued opportunity to test the ideas in a different institutional setting through the programs of the Instituto de Administracion Cientifica de las Empresas in Mexico. Finally, we are indebted to various other persons and organizations for the use of their materials as acknowledged in the text.

The field of finance will continue to experience significant changes and developments. It is stimulating to participate in these exciting developments, and we sincerely hope that the further development of the materials in *Managerial Finance* will contribute to a better understanding of the theory and practice of finance.

J. Fred Weston

Eugene F. Brigham

Los Angeles, California

Madison, Wisconsin

February 1969

Contents

PART SEVEN VALUATION IN MERGERS AND CORPORATE READJUSTMENT

PART EIGHT AN INTEGRATED VIEW OF FINANCIAL MANAGEMENT

PART ONE

INTRODUCTION

1

Financial Theory and Financial Decision Models

In recent years a revolution has been taking place in both the *theory* and the *practice* of finance. The theoretical concepts of finance now offer a challenging intellectual discipline, and daily articles in the financial press reflect the increasing importance of financial management in business firms.

Also, the nature of the firm's environment has changed, and new developments have had increased impact upon the management of business enterprise. The proper dimensions of the environment to which the business firm must adapt now include not only economic and technological developments, but also social and cultural and political ones as well. Clearly, the computer has provided a method of information processing and analysis that has permeated all aspects of business operations. In addition, a wide range of concepts and tools from the disciplines of mathematics, statistics, and the behavioral sciences has begun to be applied in business studies, including financial management. As a consequence, important advances have taken place in all areas of management.

To determine the significance of these developments for the nature of the finance field, it is useful to begin by examining a number of viewpoints from which finance has been considered. We summarize elements of four conceptual frameworks that provide insight into the nature of the finance function: (1) neoclassical management theory; (2) economic theory; (3) systems analysis; and (4) behavioral theory of the firm. This is a *summary* of some complex material with which the introductory student may not be familiar. Accordingly, it should be read with the idea of getting an over-all view of finance, not with the expectation of understanding the theories themselves. If some points are not clear on a first reading, they will perhaps become clearer as the student goes through the remainder of the book.

FINANCE IN THE NEOCLASSICAL MANAGEMENT APPROACH

The traditional view of finance is based on a management approach to the nature of the firm, and its rationale rests on the assumption that efficiency is increased by grouping activities. An organization chart shows a set of authority relationships among the executives in the firm. One way of grouping activities is by the traditional management functions, including finance. According to this older view, the determination of the total amount and structure of assets is the responsibility of nonfinancial executives, while the major responsibility of the financial manager is related to the financing of those assets. The finance function was viewed, in effect, as only the acquisition of funds.

The most important considerations in financing decisions involved liquidity and solvency; capital structure decisions called for balancing the current debt, any long-term debt, and the owner's capital to avoid problems of illiquidity and insolvency. Particular emphasis was placed on considerations of potential business recessions that would result in declines in asset values and in a reduction of cash inflows.

Developments modifying this emphasis occurred during the 1950s. These were years of economic expansion, but business was actively concerned about a major postwar recession paralleling those that had occurred in 1920–1921 and in 1929–1933. After the monetary accord of March 1951, a relative tightening in money market conditions took place. This scarcity of money, coupled with depressed stock prices during the early 1950s, led to an emphasis on the utilization of cash within the firm. Cash flow analysis and cash budgeting received increased attention. These developments marked, in effect, a concern with internal financial management procedures. The point of view stressed was that of the financial manager working within the firm. Internal financial controls contributing to cash conservation were further developed, and the consideration was directed to working capital management as well as to the acquisition of external funds and capital structure. Considerable weight was placed on the conservation and utilization of internal funds, as compared with the earlier emphasis on raising external funds.

In the 1960s, profit opportunities in mature industries appeared relatively limited, and seeking new investment opportunities became an important function. Accordingly, the responsibilities of financial managers were extended to fixed asset management and capital budgeting. Thus the scope of business finance was broadened to include effective utilization of funds in all aspects, including the generation of new investment opportunities. During this stage, increased progress was made in developing analytical concepts for evaluating alternative uses of funds. Some of these later developments are closely allied with the next new attitude to the role of finance, which is found in the economic theory of the firm.

THE ROLE OF FINANCE IN THE ECONOMIC THEORY OF THE FIRM

The economic theory of the firm in competitive markets postulates a given industry demand function and an industry supply function that is developed from the marginal cost functions of individual firms. In economic theory, the development of the cost functions for an individual firm begins with the production function, which relates factor inputs to product outputs. The cost functions are minimized by combining the optimal mix of input factors, which is achieved when the marginal rate of substitution between factor inputs is equal to the ratio of their costs (prices) to the firm. In equilibrium, the marginal revenue product of each factor will be equal to its unit input price. Also, the ratio of each pair of factors' marginal physical product is equal to the ratio of the factors' prices. By application of these criteria, the cost function is minimized for any given output.

Given the postulated competitive conditions in both the product and factor markets, the rate of output is determined by the point at which marginal cost (with respect to a given product) is equal to a market-determined price. In this framework, the money input, or interest cost, is regarded as any other input factor; the principles for determining the optimal amount of financing are based on the general principles of optimizing the combination of factor inputs.

Douglas Vickers has demonstrated that the treatment of finance in the economic theory of the firm just described is both erroneous and incomplete.[1] The theory treats money capital as a factor input, and Vickers shows that the theory is erroneous and explains that money capital should be more appropriately treated as a constraint than as a factor input.[2] He demonstrates that when money capital is a constraint, the marginal rate of substitution between the factors is changed, thus altering full equilibrium conditions.[3] Vickers goes on to point out that it is invalid to make capital budgeting decisions independent of financing decisions, or vice versa. The correct approach is a simultaneous solution in which equilibrium conditions for production, capital budgeting, and financing are all satisfied at the same time.

There are also important interactions between macroeconomic theory and financial decision-making in the firm.[4] This approach involves two important elements: (1) the role of money and capital markets and (2) the interaction between financial decisions of the firm and the aggregate level of economic activity. With regard to the first element, financial decisions are made within the environment of the financial sector of the economy, so the choice of financial structure, the forms and sources of financing, and the timing of new issues are all influenced by a complex of prices and conditions under which financing may be obtained as given by the characteristics of the money and capital markets.

The second element of the approach recognizes that the financial system is important both for the investment decisions and for the cost of capital conditions of the individual firm. When these functions are aggregated, they determine the position and shape of the investment function for the economy as a whole. Given that investment and financing decisions are interrelated and that maximizing capital values requires simultaneous solutions of both investment and financing decisions, the subject matter of finance is importantly influenced by, and has an impact on, investor behavior in the economy as a whole. Empirical studies of capital markets consider investor reaction to such factors as liquidity,

[1] Douglas Vickers, *The Theory of the Firm: Production, Capital, and Finance* (New York: McGraw-Hill, 1968).

[2] Vickers, pp. 138–169.

[3] Vickers, pp. 200–202.

[4] Basil J. Moore, *An Introduction to the Theory of Finance* (New York: Free Press, 1968).

leverage, and the general availability of funds, as well as the way these considerations affect the cost and availability of funds to the individual firm.

A SYSTEMS APPROACH TO THE FINANCE FUNCTION

The systems approach to the finance function, described by Moag, Carleton, and Lerner,[5] is a concept drawn from engineering that has become increasingly important in business operations in the last decade. For our purposes, a *system* is defined as "a collection of activities, operations, or elements that interact with one another."

The nature of such a system was illustrated by Moag, Carleton, and Lerner in the basic diagram reproduced in Figure 1–1. In their presentation, the *base system* represents the place at which physical transformations take place in the firm, that is, manufacturing operations. These transformations are brought about by a set of rules generated in the *metasystem,* which is a design and control mechanism that produces a set of rules, performance measures, and performance standards. The *environment* consists of two parts: the *endogenous environment,* consisting of all variables under control of the system, and the *exogenous environment,* reflecting influences over which the internal system has no control.

Systems analysis distinguishes among three types of flows within the firm: physical goods, information, and funds. In the Moag, Carleton, and Lerner development, the flows in a system are described in terms of three types of transformations—physical transforms, informational transforms, and value transforms.

Figure 1–2 illustrates these aspects of the systems approach, highlighting the role of the finance function. The three types of flows are distinguished—cash, physical, and information. Each is circular, and they all occur simultaneously. Materials, labor, and capital facilities flow into the manufacturing operations, where these inputs are transformed (via the production function) into outputs. Information flows include the quality of product, volume of sales, profit margins on sales, returns on investments, and cash flows. Reviews and analyses of information and cash flows influence the determinations reflected in budget con-

[5] Joseph S. Moag, Willard T. Carleton, and Eugene M. Lerner, "Defining the Finance Function: A Model-Systems Approach," *Journal of Finance,* XXII (December 1967), 543–555.

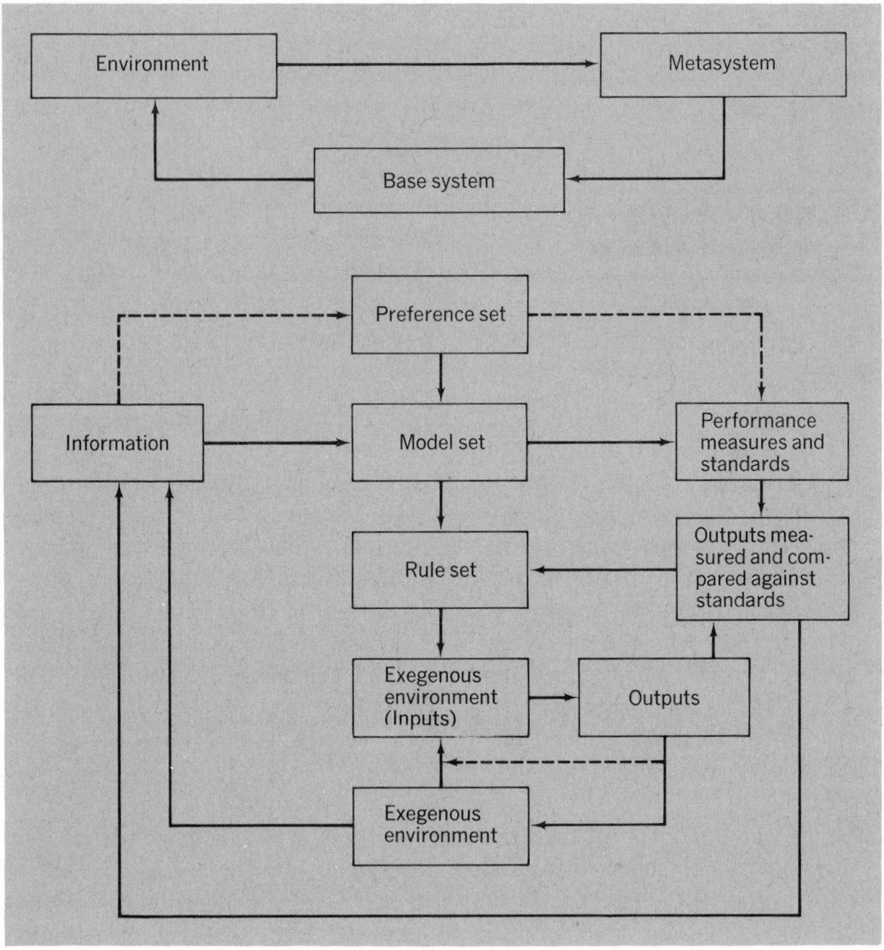

Figure 1–1 Basic Elements of Systems

SOURCE: Joseph S. Moag, Willard T. Carleton, and Eugene M. Lerner, "Defining the Finance Function: A Model-Systems Approach," *Journal of Finance*, XXII (December 1967), p. 545.

straints. Performance is compared to standards, and adjustments are made in both inputs and controls. The interaction of information flows, budget constraints, and determinations of the decision-making groups results in adjustments to the controls reflected in production, marketing, personnel, and financial policies. These, in turn, influence the nature and degree of the constraints provided by money-capital considerations.

The systems approach emphasizes four elements significant to the financial officer of the firm. One is the recognition of the simultaneous and interrelated flows of physical goods, information, and cash flows. The financial manager not only is responsible for controlling cash flows, but he also has an important role in structuring and controlling information and physical flows as well.

A second element is the interaction between financial decisions and other management functions. For the effective functioning of the total system, financial managers must take into consideration their influence on research and development activities; the stimulation of product development; manufacturing systems; production; marketing; planning and control; personnel requirements; and so on.

A third highlight relates to the nature of the firm as an adaptive mechanism. In interacting with its external environment, the firm represents an adaptive and learning mechanism. The planning and control functions are part of a feedback and correction system designed to achieve a fast reaction time to miscalculations and environmental changes.

The final characteristics of the finance function derived from the view of the firm as a system is the recognition of what Moag, Carleton, and Lerner have referred to as the "value transforms." Because the financial executives are ultimately responsible for the design and operation of both the information and cash flow systems for the firm, they are equally responsible for controlling the firm in its major profit centers, as well as from an over-all viewpoint. Financial executives are involved in the review, evaluation, and adjustment of all aspects of the firm's operations; their objective is to contribute to the maximization of the

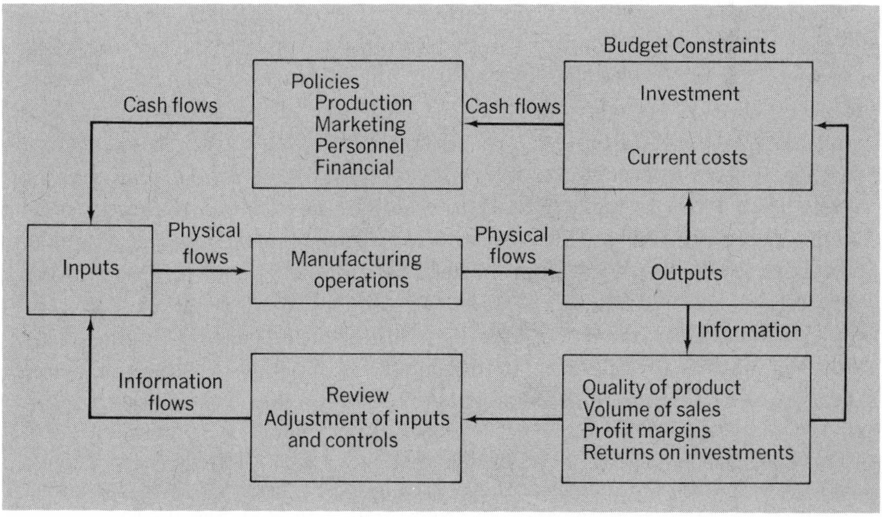

Figure 1–2 Systems Analysis of a Firm's Activities

value of the firm. Since all the firm's policies are ultimately reflected in value maximization, the theory of the firm may be viewed as a *financial theory* of the firm. Such a viewpoint is reflected in the emphasis in this book on viewing financial decisions not in isolation or in segments but as aspects of a simultaneous balancing of a variety of considerations that contribute to maximizing the value of the firm.

FINANCE IN THE BEHAVIORAL THEORY OF THE FIRM

The behavioral theory of the firm, rooted in psychological learning theory,[6] takes the systems approach a stage further by emphasizing the human behavioral aspects of organizations. The basic variables of the organization, or the firm, are goals, expectations, and choice. These are contrasted with the basic variables of the microeconomic theory of the firm—prices, quantities of inputs and outputs, returns. An analysis of organizational goals is similar to an analysis of the level of aspirations. Goals are compared with expectations of what will be accomplished by the firm, and this leads to an analysis of various alternatives for better achieving the goals or to a reformulation of goals.

A theory involves a system of variables and relations among them. In the behavioral theory of the firm, the relations among the basic variables—goals, expectations, choice—are analyzed in connection with the concepts of (1) conflict, (2) uncertainty, (3) search, and (4) organizational learning. The relations are analyzed by testing propositions with respect to quasi-resolution of conflict, uncertainty avoidance, a theory of problemistic search, and an analysis of organizational learning. The emphasis is on an adaptive process for improving organization performance. Figure 1–3 represents an extension of the previous diagrams of systems analysis by showing the interactions of the four relational concepts in the behavioral theory of the firm. The relationship among goals, feedback, search, evaluation, and decision rules is set out as an adaptive process.

The behavioral theory of the firm has some important implications for the nature of financial management. A number of the tools and processes in financial management involve the basic variables of the

[6] For an elaboration, see J. F. Weston, *The Scope and Methodology of Finance* (Englewood Cliffs, N.J.: Prentice-Hall, 1966), pp. 32–38, based on R. M. Cyert and James G. March, *A Behavioral Theory of the Firm* (Englewood Cliffs, N.J.: Prentice-Hall, Inc., 1963).

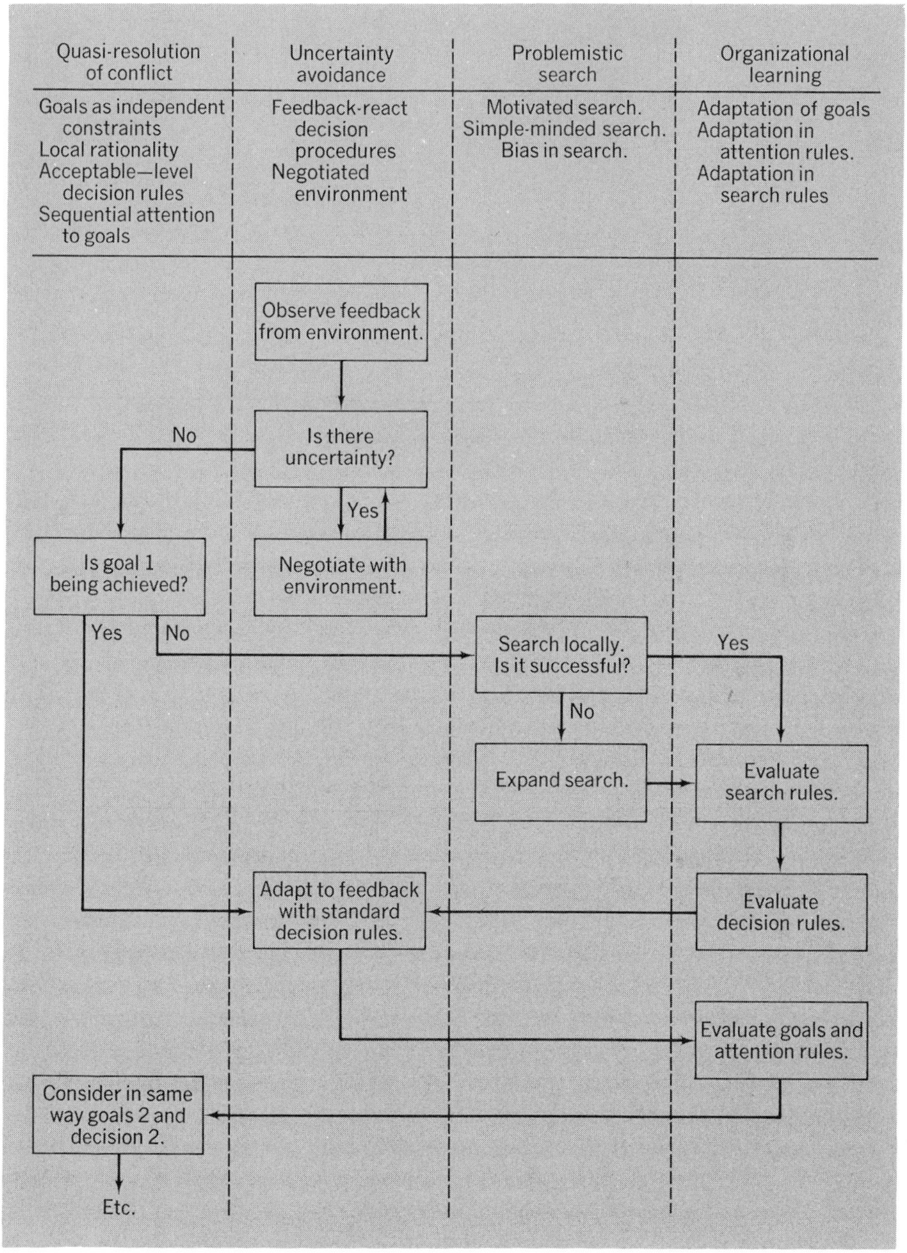

Figure 1–3 Organizational Decision Process in Abstract Form

SOURCE: Richard M. Cyert and James G. March, *A Behavioral Theory of the Firm* (Englewood Cliffs, N.J.: Prentice-Hall, 1963), p. 126.

behavioral theory—goals, expectations, and choice. Of particular significance is the detailed analysis of the adaptive process in improving the performance of the firm and the interaction among impersonal elements, such as physical, information, and cash flows, with the human, behavioral, and organizational aspects of the operations. These factors influence the effectiveness of financial ratio analysis, budgets, and other control devices. Further, theories of security valuation and capital structure involve management and investor attitudes toward risk and uncertainty, an important area of study in the behavioral theory of the firm. When the enterprise is viewed as a section of operations without regard to method of financing, the goal is stated as maximization of the value of the firm. Given that operating decisions have sought to maximize the value of the firm, financing decisions seek to maximize the present value of the ownership securities of the firm.

THEORY OF FINANCIAL MANAGEMENT

With a background comprised of four differing approaches to financial management, we may now focus attention on the nature of finance itself. Finance is not unique from other aspects of business operations in that it has a role, as do other management functions, in the optimization efforts of the firm. *Goals* are set, *decisions* are made, and *models* are used to help reach optimal decisions in terms of attaining these goals.[7] In the language of the behavioral theory of the firm, financial management involves goals, choices, and models.

The objective of this text is to develop a body of theory, as well as some decision models, that will help the financial officer to make an effective contribution to his firm. The idea is to substitute an emphasis on theory for the traditional description of finance functions. From the behavioral theory of the firm, it is recognized that we must begin with a consideration of goals; and the generally stated goal from the economic theory of the firm is profit maximization. The principal objection to profit maximization, as set forth in the economic theory of the firm, is that it fails to integrate the theory of production, or output determination, with the capital theory of profits as a stream over a projected

[7] This approach is spelled out and is the title of the second chapter of "Goals, Decisions, and Models," William Beranek, *Analysis for Financial Decisions* (Homewood, Ill.: Irwin, 1963), pp. 8–32.

period. Since profits, or net income, must properly be viewed as a stream over a projected time horizon, a consideration of the timing of flows must be taken into account.

A positive statement of the goals of the firm in modern financial literature has been expressed in terms of either the maximization of *value* (or wealth) or the maximization of expected *utility*. Consider the following three elements:

1. Alternative policies or decisions are related to alternative streams of earnings over some projected period.
2. An appropriate procedure for handling differences in timing of cash flows must be determined.
3. Investor attitudes toward risk must be determined, and ways of measuring risk and bringing it into the analysis must be developed.

We can recognize from this list that goals other than wealth or utility maximization have been set forth and that goals for different participants—stockholders, labor, customers, management, and so on—have been emphasized. Our judgment, however, is that the most relevant theories can be built on the principle of stockholder wealth maximization, and that the other goals should be taken as constraints limiting stockholder wealth maximization. In other words, corporate managers have their own personal goals as well as stockholder wealth maximization in mind when they make decisions. The managers of a firm may, for example, prefer to emphasize risk avoidance, the prestige that is attached to public service (as opposed to concentrating on running the business), and so on. Recognizing this, executive compensation plans emphasize incentives—bonuses, stock option plans, and so on—designed to stimulate management to operate in the stockholders' best long-run interests. At the same time, proxy fights, tender offers, and the like, present serious threats to a management that is not operating in the best interests of its stockholders. These pressures, we believe, serve to make stockholder wealth maximization a realistic, operational assumption in most situations.

The development of a body of theory starts with basic statements called *axioms* (or postulates), which are assumptions regarded as plausible for the subject under discussion. The axioms will be viewed as primary propositions to be left unproved by the present analysis. With the assumptions defined, propositions or theories can be first developed by a system of logical deduction and then tested in either of two ways. In pure theory, the propositions are stated in mathematical terms, and the test of a proposition is internal consistency within the model. For practical policy-making or real-world decision models, the test of a theory is its ability to predict or explain aspects of the real world.

A number of propositions or theories (we use propositions and theories synonomously) may be consistent with a given set of data. Thus, if a theory is tested by reference to empirical data and conformance between the two is found, the data or facts are said to be consistent with the theory. But the data may also be consistent with other theories, so a particular theory is not necessarily "proven" by a successful empirical test. However, if continued repetitions of the empirical tests are consistent with the theory, the degree of confidence in the validity of the theory is increased.

A good illustration from the finance field is provided by the Modigliani and Miller articles on the cost of capital.[8] These articles formulated a set of assumptions based on both the attitudes of the investors toward risks and on some aspects of economic theory. From these assumptions propositions were developed, and Modigliani and Miller conducted empirical studies and found the data to be consistent with their propositions. When empirical tests of the Modigliani and Miller propositions were repeated by others, some were consistent with their propositions or theories, and others were not. As a consequence, the validity of the Modigliani and Miller propositions, as compared with alternative propositions, remains a matter of dispute.

A distinction between *positive* (or descriptive) theory and *normative* (or prescriptive) theory is also made. Positive theory describes behavior. Normative theory sets forth models of what behavior ought to be. In business finance, then, we may generate models of how businessmen make decisions or how they should make decisions. In finance, it is most useful to make and test descriptive theories of *investor* behavior and then to use this information to develop normative theories to guide business decisions.

FINANCIAL POLICY DECISION MODELS

Financial decisions affect both the size of the earnings stream, or profitability, and the riskiness of the firm. These relationships are diagrammed in Figure 1–4. Policy decisions affect risk and profitability, and these two factors jointly determine the value of the firm.

The primary policy decision is that of choosing the industry in which to operate—the product-market mix of the firm. When this choice has been made, both profitability and risk are determined by decisions relat-

[8] Franco Modigliani and Merton H. Miller, "The Cost of Capital, Corporation Finance, and the Theory of Investment," *American Economic Review*, June 1958, pp. 261–297, and other articles listed at the end of Chapter 11.

Selected References

Anthony, Robert N., "The Trouble with Profit Maximization," *Harvard Business Review,* XXXVIII (November–December 1960), 126–134.

Curtis, Edward T., *Company Organization of the Finance Function,* AMA Research Study LV (New York: American Management Association, 1962).

Donaldson, Gordon, "Financial Goals: Management vs. Stockholders," *Harvard Business Review,* XLI (May–June 1963), 116–129.

———, "Financial Management in an Affluent Society," *Financial Executive,* XXXV (April 1967), 52–56, 58–60.

Marting, Elizabeth and Robert E. Finley (eds.), *The Financial Manager's Job* (New York: American Management Association, 1964).

Moag, Joseph S., Willard T. Carleton, and Eugene M. Lerner, "Defining the Finance Function: A Model-Systems Approach," *Journal of Finance,* XXII, (December 1967), 543–556.

Moller, George and George F. Plummer, "The Financial Executive," *The Controller,* XXX (January 1962).

Moore, John R., "The Financial Executive in the 1970s," *Financial Executive,* XXXV (January 1967), 28–29, 32–34, 36.

Sauvain, Harry, "Comment," *Journal of Finance,* XXII, 4 (December 1967), 541.

Solomon, Ezra, *The Theory of Financial Management* (New York: Columbia University Press, 1963).

———, "What Should We Teach in a Course in Business Finance?" *Journal of Finance,* XXI (May 1966), 411–415.

Vance, Jack O., "The Changing Role of the Corporate Financial Executive," *Financial Executive,* XXXI, 3 (March 1963), 27–29.

Weston, J. Fred, *The Scope and Methodology of Finance* (Englewood Cliffs, N.J.: Prentice-Hall, 1966).

———, "The Finance Function," *Journal of Finance,* IX (September 1954), 265–282.

——— (ed.), *Financial Management in the 1960s: New Challenges and Responsibilities* (New York: Holt, Rinehart and Winston, 1966), selection "The New Power of the Financial Executives," 2–8.

——— (ed.), *Readings in Finance from Fortune* (New York: Holt, Rinehart and Winston, 1958), selections 1, 3, 14, 15, and 16.

———, "The State of the Finance Field," *Journal of Finance,* XXII, 4 (December 1967), 539–540.

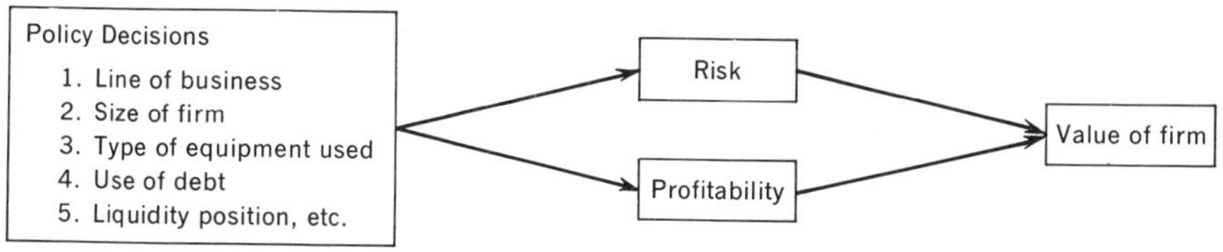

Figure 1–4 Valuation as the Central Focus of the Finance Function

ing to the size of the firm, the types of equipment that are used, the extent to which debt is employed, the firm's liquidity position, and so on.

These decisions generally affect both risk and profitability. An increase in the cash position, for instance, reduces risk; but since cash is not an earning asset, it also reduces profitability. Similarly, the use of additional debt will raise the rate of return or the profitability of the stockholders' net worth; at the same time, more debt means more risk. Financial analysis seeks to strike the particular balance between risk and profitability that will maximize the wealth of the firm's stockholders.

Business decision models have been designed to help solve various types of problems, including wealth maximization. Models are symbolic representations of some aspects of the world, and they consist of sets of variables and the relationships among them. In the most general terms, a model relates control variables and uncontrolled variables to output or performance. The solution to the model consists of determining the values of controllable variables that maximize performance (including minimizing cost).

When a decision rule is introduced into the optimizing value of the control variables, we have a decision-making model, or decision model, from which decision rules may be developed. For example, one decision model we shall discuss is the selection of the optimum quantity of inventory to carry. The model is solved to minimize inventory carrying costs. From this solution, we derive a decision rule for placing orders.

ORGANIZATION OF THE BOOK

The organization of this book reflects three elements: (1) theory, (2) the development of decision models, and (3) sufficient descriptive and institutional material to provide content for both the theory and the decision models.

Ideally, the theory should first be set out in its totality, thereby providing a method of analysis or framework for a systematic approach to decision models. However, both theory and decision models must be built upon at least some descriptive and institutional material. Because of this practical constraint, the organization of the book represents something of a compromise, blending together theories, decision tools, and descriptive materials as seems best for the subject at hand. This blend is reflected in our structuring the book into the following broad areas:

1. The tax environment
2. Financial analysis, planning, and control
3. Long-term investment decisions
4. Valuation and financial structure
5. Working capital management
6. Long-term financing
7. Valuation in mergers and corporate readjustment
8. An integrated view of financial management

Emphasis is given to theories related to value maximization. This, in turn, involves effective utilization of the techniques of planning and control and the important decision models involved therewith. Conceptually, we shall seek throughout to reflect the simultaneous optimization of output, capital budgeting, and financing decisions.

SUMMARY

Our emphasis in this book is placed (1) on defining the goals of a business firm, (2) on developing theories of how the actions of the firm interact with its environment, and (3) on providing models that help the firm optimize its decisions in the sense of making its operating results more closely approach it goals.

The modern theory of finance, which encompasses these three tasks, has developed as a blend of four separate but related disciplines: management theory, economic theory, systems analysis, and behavioral science. *Management theory* has made its principal contribution by defining the organization structure of the firm and the place of the finance function within this structure. *Economic theory* has contributed by specifying the conditions under which shareholder wealth will be maximized. *Systems analysis* involves the control process wherein goals are specified, actions are taken, feedback loops are employed to compare actual performance with specified standards, and modifications are made to the system when performance/target deviations exceed prescribed limits. The principal contribution of *behavioral science* has been to emphasize that decision-makers are humans, not automatons, and that human behavior

must be taken into account in the sense of properly motiv makers.

Modern financial theory, which draws upon these fo and overlapping areas, consists of both *positive* (descr and *normative* (prescriptive) theory. Descriptive models and tested to develop insights into the firm's environme models use the results of the descriptive theory to aid the ment in its task of maximizing shareholder wealth.

The two primary determinants of wealth are profitabi flows, and the riskiness inherent in these flows. Large increase wealth, but greater riskiness decreases it, and goals conflict in the sense that a decision which increases also increases the riskiness of the firm. In such situatio must strike a balance between the two goals, and much o will be related to how such conflicts are resolved.

QUESTIONS

1–1 Are financial decisions likely to be more crucial fo ness or for a successful, growing business? Woul executive officer, be more concerned about your fi in the failing firm or in the thriving firm?

1–2 What are the most important activities of the fi in terms of the importance of these activities to and the amount of the financial manager's time Are these relationships likely to be the same for small firms, (b) stable versus growing firms, and weak firms?

1–3 Would you expect the financial manager's role portant in a highly diversified, merger-minded c poration or in a single-product firm that is internal growth?

1–4 Finance may be thought of as having a number ternatively, as a topic that may be approached f different points of view. Discuss briefly how fin each of the following formats:
a. traditional management theory
b. economic theory of the firm
c. systems approach
d. behavioral theory

1–5 Having described the four approaches to finan in the preceding question, discuss how a theory make use of each of them to develop an operat financial management.

2

The Tax Environment[1]

The federal government is often called the most important stockholder in the American economy. This is not literally true, as the government does not "own" corporate shares in the strict sense of the word; it is, however, by far the largest recipient of business profits. Income of unincorporated businesses is subject to tax rates ranging up to 70 percent, and income of corporations is taxed at a 48 percent rate. State and sometimes city or county taxes must be added to these federal taxes, and dividends received by stockholders are subject to personal income taxes at the stockholders' individual tax rates.

With such a large percentage of business income going to the government, it is not surprising that taxes play an important role in financial decisions. To lease or to buy, to use common stock or

[1] This chapter has benefited from the assistance of Mr. R. Wendell Buttrey, tax attorney and lecturer on taxation at the University of California, Los Angeles.

debt, to make or not to make a particular investment, to merge or not to merge—all these decisions are influenced by tax factors. This chapter summarizes some basic elements of the tax structure relating to financial decisions.

OVERVIEW OF TAX AND EXPENDITURE PATTERNS

The overriding importance of governments—federal, state, and local—and the trend toward their increasing importance are shown by the figures in Table 2–1. In 1950, total tax revenues amounted to $68.7 billion, or 24.1 percent of that year's gross national product (GNP). By 1967, taxes had climbed to $227.3 billion, or 29 percent of GNP. The state and local governments' share of the total revenues rose somewhat more rapidly than that of the total governmental receipts—from 27.4 percent in 1950 to 33.3 percent in 1967.

TABLE 2–1 LEVEL OF GOVERNMENT RECEIPTS IN RELATION TO GROSS NATIONAL PRODUCT, 1950 AND 1967
(dollars in billions)

	1950		1967	
	Amount	Percent	Amount	Percent
Federal government receipts*	$ 49.9	72.6	$151.5	66.7
State and local government receipts*	18.8†	27.4	75.8	33.3
Total government receipts	$ 68.7	100.0	$227.3	100.0
Gross national product	$284.8		$785.1	
Government receipts as a percent of GNP	24.1		29.0	

* Based on the national income and product accounts.
† Federal grants-in-aid to state and local governments have been eliminated to avoid double counting.
SOURCE: *Economic Report of the President* (Washington, D.C.: U.S. Government Printing Office, 1968), pp. 214, 288.

Table 2–2 shows the principal sources of federal income for the years 1958 and 1967. Individual and corporate income taxes provided the bulk

TABLE 2–2 FEDERAL REVENUES BY SOURCES, FISCAL YEARS 1958 AND 1967
(dollars in billions)

	1958		1967	
	Amount	Percent	Amount	Percent
Individual income taxes	$34.7	43.6	$ 61.5	41.0
Corporation income taxes	20.0	25.2	34.0	22.7
Social security and related taxes	11.2	14.1	33.3	22.3
Excise taxes	10.6	13.3	13.7	9.2
Estate and gift taxes	1.4	1.8	3.0	2.0
Customs	.8	1.0	1.9	1.3
Other receipts	.8	1.0	2.2	1.5
Totals	$79.6	100.0	$149.6	100.0

SOURCE: *Economic Report of the President* (Washington, D.C.: U.S. Government Printing Office, 1968), pp. 280, 281.

of the revenues in each year; the percent contributed by corporate income taxes declined somewhat in relation to personal taxes, because personal incomes rose more than corporate incomes over the period. The relative importance of social security and other employment taxes has risen significantly.

The main source of state and local government revenue, shown in

TABLE 2–3 STATE AND LOCAL GOVERNMENT REVENUES BY SOURCES, FISCAL YEARS 1950 AND 1966
(dollars in billions)

	1950		1966	
	Amount	Percent	Amount	Percent
Property taxes	$ 7.3	34.9	$24.7	29.7
Sales and gross receipts taxes	5.2	24.9	19.0	22.8
Individual income taxes	0.8	3.8	4.8	5.7
Corporation net income taxes	0.6	2.9	2.0	2.4
Revenues from the federal government	2.5	12.0	13.1	15.7
Licenses, fees, and other revenues	4.5	21.5	19.4	23.7
Totals	$20.9	100.0	$83.0	100.0

SOURCE: *Economic Report of the President* (Washington, D.C.: U.S. Government Printing Office, 1968), p. 289.

Table 2–3, are licenses and other fees, property taxes, and sales taxes.[2] Income taxes, both personal and corporate, are of minor importance; transfers from the federal government, however, amounted to over 15 percent of state and local revenues in 1966. The most important change in the relative positions of the various sources of taxes is the decreased importance of the property tax and the increased importance of licenses, fees, and other revenues.

FISCAL POLICY

The federal government uses both monetary policy and fiscal policy to influence the level of economic activity. *Monetary policy,* which will be considered in a later chapter, deals with actions to influence the availability and cost of credit. *Fiscal policy* deals with altering the level and composition of government receipts and expenditures to influence the level of economic activity. Taxes constitute the primary receipt.

Three principle methods have been employed to change tax receipts: (1) changing tax rates, (2) changing methods permitted for calculating tax-deductible depreciation (accelerating depreciation), and (3) providing an investment tax credit for expenditures on new plant and equipment. Each of these points is discussed briefly in this section.

Changing Tax Rates

During periods of rapid and unsustainable economic expansion, and especially when such expansion has inflationary consequences, the federal government may attempt to dampen the level of economic activity by increasing income tax rates. When tax rates are raised, both personal disposable incomes and corporate profits after taxes are reduced. The reduction in personal disposable income reduces individuals' purchasing power and thereby decreases their demand for goods and services. The reduction in corporate after-tax profits reduces the profitability of new investments and, at the same time, reduces corporate funds available for investment. However, if the economy is depressed and requires some form of stimulation, tax rates can be reduced to provide both consumers and businesses with greater purchasing power and businesses with greater incentive to make investments in plant and equipment.

During the period 1966–1968 the economy was operating at a very

[2] It is important to note that these are *aggregate* statistics for all states and municipalities. There are considerable variations among governmental units, particularly with regard to the use of income taxes.

high level, and prices were increasing at a rate of 3 to 5 percent per year. Military expenditures associated with the Vietnam war were stimulating the economy, and a government deficit was adding to the inflationary pressure. The President, in January 1967, asked Congress to increase taxes by 10 percent. After an 18-month delay, Congress, in June 1968, did pass a 10 percent tax surcharge to be effective for the period January 1, 1968, through June 30, 1969, for corporations, and April 1, 1968, through June 30, 1969, for individuals.[3]

Tax rates have, in the past, been changed infrequently. Such changes must be made by the Congress, and congressional action on a decision with such a pervasive influence is not easy to obtain. Both economists and politicians have debated the idea of authorizing the President to change tax rates within certain prescribed limits, but it appears unlikely that Congress will be willing to give up this power. We expect, therefore, that in the foreseeable future tax rates will be changed infrequently.

Accelerated Depreciation

Depreciation charges are deductible when computing federal income taxes. Therefore, the larger the depreciation charge, the lower the actual tax liability. The tax laws specify the allowed methods for calculating depreciation for purposes of computing federal income taxes. If the tax laws are changed to permit more rapid or *accelerated* depreciation, this will reduce tax payments and have a stimulating effect on business investments.[4]

A number of different depreciation methods are authorized for tax purposes: (1) straight line, (2) units of production, (3) sum-of-years-digits, and (4) double declining balance. These methods are explained briefly in the appendix to this chapter. The last two methods listed are generally referred to as *accelerated depreciation methods;* ordinarily, they are more favorable from a tax standpoint than is straight-line depreciation.

The fiscal policy implications of depreciation methods stem from two factors: (1) using accelerated depreciation reduces taxes in the early years of an asset's life and thus increases corporate cash flows and makes

[3] The tax increase took the form of a surcharge. That is, taxes were computed under the rates given in the following pages of this book, then a surcharge equal to 10 percent of this amount was added to the calculated tax. At the time of this writing, there is a strong possibility that the 10 percent surtax will be extended beyond its scheduled expiration date.

[4] Federal tax statutes also consider the time over which assets must be depreciated. A reduction in the period over which an asset must be depreciated will have the same stimulating effect on the economy as would a change in permitted depreciation *methods* that increased depreciation expense for tax purposes.

more funds available for investment, and (2) faster cash flows increase the profitability, or rate of return, on an investment. This second point is made clear in Chapter 7, where capital budgeting is discussed.

Depreciation methods, like tax rates, are determined by the Congress and are altered on occasion to influence the level of investment and thereby stimulate or retard the economy. The most sweeping changes in permitted depreciation methods were made in 1954, when the accelerated depreciation methods listed above were first permitted, and in 1962, when the depreciable lives of assets for tax purposes were reduced.

Investment Tax Credit

The concept of an investment tax credit was incorporated into the federal income tax laws in 1962. Under the investment tax credit program, business firms could deduct as a *credit* against their income tax bills a specified percentage of the dollar amount of new investment in each of certain categories of assets. As a general rule, the tax credit amounts to 7 percent of the amount of new investment in assets having useful lives of eight years or more; two-thirds of 7 percent for assets having lives of six or seven years; one-third of 7 percent for assets having lives of four or five years; and no tax credit for assets having useful lives of less than four years.

The investment tax credit, like tax rates and depreciation methods, is subject to Congressional changes. During the boom in the early part of 1966, the investment tax credit was suspended in an effort to reduce investment; it was reinstated later in the year.

CORPORATE INCOME TAXES

Rate Structure

The first $25,000 of corporate taxable income is taxed at a 22 percent rate; all income over $25,000 is taxed at a 48 percent rate.[5] If a firm's taxable income was $100,000, for example, the tax would be computed as follows:

$$\begin{aligned} 22\% \times 25{,}000 &= \$\ 5{,}500 \\ 48\% \times 75{,}000 &= \underline{\ \ 36{,}000} \\ &\ \ \ \ \$41{,}500 \end{aligned}$$

[5] Technically, there is a "normal" corporate tax of 22 percent plus a surtax of 26 percent on all income over $25,000.

Table 2–4 shows that the average corporate income tax is moderately progressive up to $1 million, when it becomes virtually 48 percent.

This relatively simple tax structure has wide implications for business planning. Because the tax rate more than doubles when corporate income rises above $25,000, it clearly pays to break moderately sized companies into two or more separate corporations in order to hold the income of each unit under $25,000, and thus keep the tax rate at 22 percent.[6]

TABLE 2–4 MARGINAL AND AVERAGE TAX RATES OF THE CORPORATION INCOME TAX, 1968
(in percentages)

CORPORATE INCOME (IN DOLLARS)	MARGINAL TAX RATE*	AVERAGE TAX RATE†
0–25,000	22	22.00
25,001–26,000	48	23.00
26,001–32,000	48	27.69
32,001–38,000	48	30.89
38,001–44,000	48	33.23
44,001–50,000	48	35.00
50,001–60,000	48	37.17
60,001–70,000	48	38.71
70,001–80,000	48	39.88
80,001–90,000	48	40.78
90,001–100,000	48	41.50
100,001–150,000	48	43.67
150,001–200,000	48	44.75
200,001–500,000	48	46.70
500,001–1,000,000	48	47.35
1,000,001–5,000,000	48	47.87
5,000,001–10,000,000	48	47.94
10,000,001–100,000,000	48	47.99
100,000,001–500,000,000	48	48.00

* The *marginal tax rate* is the tax on each additional dollar of taxable income received. The tax on each of the first $25,000 is 22 cents; on each dollar over $25,000, the marginal tax rate jumps to 48 cents. The total taxes paid, when divided by the taxable income, gives the average tax rate.
† Applied to the upper limit of each class interval.

[6] This is less true today than it was prior to 1964. The Revenue Act of 1964 imposed an additional 6 percent tax on the first $25,000 of income of multiple corporations (1) when they are controlled by an individual or a group and (2) when they do not elect to file consolidated tax returns. In spite of this additional tax, in many cases there is still a tax advantage to forming multiple corporations.

We shall see later, however, that the income tax is not the only factor bearing on the decision whether or not to incorporate and the number of corporate entities to utilize.

THE 1968–1969 SURCHARGE. As was noted above, a 10 percent additional tax was imposed on corporations for the 18-month period beginning January 1968 and ending June 1969. The way this surtax works can be illustrated with the example used in the preceding section. A firm with $100,000 of taxable income has a $41,500 tax bill for 1969. Assume that the surcharge was in effect for six months in 1969, or for one-half of the year. This company's tax bill would be:

$$\begin{aligned} \text{Tax} &= \$41{,}500 + (10\%)(\$41{,}500)(50\%) \\ &= \$41{,}500 + \$2{,}075 \\ &= \$43{,}575 \end{aligned}$$

Corporate Capital Gains and Losses[7]

Corporate taxable income consists of two components: (1) profits from the sale of capital assets and (2) all other income, defined as *ordinary income.*

Capital assets are defined as assets, such as security investments, not bought and sold in the ordinary course of a firm's business. Gains and losses on the sale of capital assets are defined as capital gains, and under certain circumstances they receive special tax treatment. Real and depreciable property used in the business is not defined as a capital asset (Section 1221 of the Internal Revenue Code). However, Section 1231 of the code specifies that such property will be treated as a capital asset in the event of a net gain. In the event of a net loss, the full amount may be deducted from ordinary income without any of the limitations described for capital loss treatments.[8]

The sale of a capital asset held for six months or less gives rise to a *short-term* capital gain or loss; its disposal, when held for more than six months, produces a *long-term* gain or loss. Net short-term gains (gains minus losses) are added to the firm's ordinary income and taxed

[7] Corporate capital gains and losses (as well as most other tax matters) are subject to many technical provisions. This section and the others dealing with tax matters include only the most general provisions. For special cases the student is referred to *Federal Tax Course* (Englewood Cliffs, N.J.: Prentice-Hall, 1968), *passim.*

[8] This special treatment of depreciable properties should be kept in mind in connection with the material in Chapter 7 on Capital Budgeting. The difference between the book value of an asset and its salvage value or abandonment value, if lower than book value, can be deducted from ordinary income, and thus the full amount of this difference represents a form of tax shelter.

at regular corporate income tax rates. For long-term capital gains, the tax is limited to 25 percent. For example, if a corporation holds the common stock of another corporation as an investment for more than six months and then sells it at a profit, the gain is subject to a maximum tax of 25 percent. Of course, if income is below $25,000, regular tax rates of 22 percent will apply.

Depreciable Assets

If an asset, for example a machine tool, is subject to depreciation, its cost is defined as the original purchase price less accumulated depreciation. To illustrate, suppose a machine cost $10,000 and $5,000 of depreciation has been taken on it. Its book value, by definition, is $5,000 ($10,000 – $5,000).

If the company sells the machine for more than its book value, it may incur *either* a capital gain *or* ordinary income for tax purposes. If the gain is a recapture of depreciation, indicating that the firm had been depreciating the asset too rapidly (and charging off this depreciation as an expense to reduce ordinary income), the gain is ordinary income and is taxed accordingly. For example, if it sells the machine for $7,000, it incurs a $2,000 gain ($7,000 – $5,000). *This gain is not classified as a capital gain, however; it constitutes the recapture of depreciation and is taxed as ordinary income.*

The sale of a depreciable asset is subject to capital gains when the gain exceeds the amount of depreciation taken. To continue with the preceding example, if our machine had been sold for $12,000, then a total profit of $7,000 ($12,000 – $5,000) would have been incurred. Of this amount, $5,000 would represent the recapture of depreciation (since this amount of depreciation had been charged off) and would be taxed as ordinary income; the remaining $2,000 would be classified as a capital gain for tax purposes and would be taxed at a rate of 25 percent.

Finally, if the firm sells a machine for $3,000, it incurs a $2,000 loss ($5,000 minus $3,000 received). But this net loss can be deducted from ordinary income in full without any limitations.

Deductibility of Capital Losses

A net capital loss is not deductible from ordinary income. For example, if in 1967 a corporation had an ordinary income of $100,000 and a net capital loss of $25,000, it still paid a tax on the ordinary income at the normal rate of 22 percent on the $25,000 and 48 percent on the $75,000, a total tax of $41,500. The net capital loss may, however, be carried over for five years and used to offset capital gains during that period. For example, if this corporation has a net capital gain of $75,000 in 1968, its *taxable net capital gain* in that year is \$75,000 less the carry-over of \$25,000, or \$50,000. The tax on the net gain is 25 percent, or \$12,500, which is added to the tax on its ordinary income. The maximum period a corporate capital loss may be carried forward in this manner is five years. Corporate capital losses, short term or long term, can be carried forward five years and deducted from either short-term or long-term capital gains.

Dividend Income

Another important rule is that 85 percent of dividends received by one corporation from another is exempt from taxation.[9] For example, if corporation H owns stock in corporation S and receives \$100,000 in dividends from corporation S, it has to pay taxes on only \$15,000 of the \$100,000. Assuming H is in the 48 percent tax bracket, the tax is \$7,200, or 7.2 percent of the dividends received. The reason for this reduced tax is that to subject intercorporate dividends to the full corporate tax rate would, eventually, lead to triple taxation. First, firm S would pay its regular taxes. Then firm H would pay a second tax. Finally, H's own stockholders would be subject to taxes when they receive dividends. The 85 percent dividend exclusion thus reduces the multiple taxation of corporate income.

Payment of Tax in Installments

Before 1952, corporations paid their tax obligations in quarterly installments in the year *following* the year in which the income was earned. For example, if a corporation earned \$100,000 in 1949 and the tax payable on this income was \$50,000, the corporation paid \$12,500 in each of four quarterly installments on March 15, June 15, September 15, and December 15, 1950. Under the so-called Mills plan, beginning in 1952 corporations were moved toward a pay-as-you-go basis. By 1960, the larger corporations were paying 25 percent of their tax liability on each September 15 and December 15 of the year in which the income was earned (on an estimated basis), and 25 percent of the tax liability on each March 15 and June 15 of the year following that in which the liability was incurred. New provisions of the Internal Revenue Act

[9] If the corporation receiving the dividends owns 80 percent or more of the stock of the dividend-paying firm, it may file a consolidated tax return. In this case, there have been no dividends as far as the Internal Revenue Service (IRS) is concerned, so there is obviously no tax on dividends received. On the internal books of the related corporations there may be an accounting entry entitled "dividends" used to transfer funds from the subsidiary to the parent, but this is of no concern to the IRS.

of 1964 speed up collection even more, and by 1970 large corporations will be paying 25 percent of their estimated tax bill on the 15th of April, June, September, and December of the *current* year.

It will be seen in a subsequent chapter that the amount of taxes owed to the government constitutes an interest-free source of funds. As the movement toward pay-as-you-go corporate taxes progresses, new sources of financing must be found; thus planning for the speed-up in tax collections is important to American business.

Net Operating Carry-Back and Carry-Forward

For any year ending after December 31, 1958, any ordinary corporate operating loss can be carried back three years and forward five years. The law states that the loss must first be carried back to the earliest year, the remainder applied to the second earliest year, and so on. For example, an operating loss in 1969 may be used to reduce taxable income in 1966, 1967, 1968, 1970, 1971, 1972, 1973, and 1974; it *must* follow that sequence. The purpose of permitting this loss averaging is to avoid penalizing corporations whose incomes fluctuate widely.

To illustrate, suppose the Ritz Hotel made $100,000 before taxes in all years except 1969, when it suffered a $600,000 operating loss. The Ritz would use the *carry-back* feature to recompute its taxes for 1966, use $100,000 of the operating losses to reduce the 1966 profit to zero, and recover the amount of taxes paid in that year. Since $500,000 of unrecovered losses would still be available, Ritz would do the same thing for 1967 and 1968. Then, in 1970, 1971, and 1972, it would apply the *carry-forward* loss to reduce its profits to zero in each of these years.

The right to carry losses forward and backward has made some corporations attractive buys. For example, Atlas Corporation and Howard Hughes bought RKO Pictures because of a $30 million tax-loss credit. A corporation may acquire another firm that has had a tax loss, operate it as a subsidiary, and then present consolidated returns for tax purposes. In the RKO Pictures case, the $30 million loss would be worth $15 million to Atlas, assuming Atlas pays state and federal income taxes at a 50 percent rate. Newspapers frequently contain advertisements such as "Tax-Loss Corporation for Sale," "Attractive Tax Loss Available." The corporation may be a doubly attractive buy if the purchaser is able to operate the business effectively and turn it into a profitable corporation at the same time that he benefits from the tax-loss carry-forward.

The tax law of 1954 placed certain restrictions on this privilege: (1) If more than 50 percent of the stock changes hands within two years after the purchase and (2) if the old business is essentially abandoned, no loss carry-over is provided. The objective of the limitation is to prevent a firm from merging for the sole purpose of taking advantage of the tax law. If it merges for this purpose and files consolidated returns, the loss privilege may be disallowed. Moreover, deductions are denied where an acquisition appears to have been motivated largely by the prospects of such deductions.[10]

Improper Accumulation

A special surtax on improperly accumulated income is provided for Section 531 of the Internal Revenue Code, which states that earnings umulated by a corporation are subject to penalty rates *if the purpose e accumulation is to enable the stockholders to avoid the personal tax.* Of income not paid out in dividends, $100,000 is prima tainable for the reasonable needs of the business. This is a benefit l corporations. But there is a penalty rate on all amounts over 100,000 shown to be unnecessary to meet the reasonable needs of the business. The penalty rate is 27.5 percent on the first $100,000 of improperly accumulated taxable income shown on the balance sheet and 38.5 percent on all amounts over $100,000.

The 1954 law provides that the burden of proof of improper accumulation falls on the United States Treasury if the taxpayer files a statement supporting his accumulation. In other words, if the taxpayer presents a statement explaining why he is retaining the earnings, it is up to the Treasury to prove that his statement is not justified. Before 1954, the burden of proof was on the taxpayer to convince the Treasury and the courts that retention was justified.

Retained earnings are used to pay off debt, to finance growth, and to provide the corporation with a cushion against possible cash drains caused by losses. How much a firm should properly accumulate for uncertain contingencies is a matter of judgment. Fear of the penalty taxes that may be imposed under Section 531 may cause a firm to pay out a higher rate of dividends than it otherwise would.[11]

Sometimes Section 531 may stimulate mergers. A clear illustration is provided by the purchase of the Toni Company (home permanents) by the Gillette Safety Razor Company.[12] The sale was made early in

[10] Sylvan Tobolowsky, "Tax Consequences of Corporate Organization and Distributions," *Journal of Taxation,* XII (January 1960), 8–15.

[11] See materials in James K. Hall, *The Taxation of Corporate Surplus Accumulations* (Washington, D.C.: U.S. Government Printing Office, 1952), especially Appendix 3.

[12] See J. K. Butters, J. Lintner, and W. L. Cary, *Effects of Taxation, Corporate Mergers* (Boston: Harvard Business School, 1951). pp. 96–111. The lucid presentation

1948, when Toni's sales volume had begun to level off. Since earnings retention might have been difficult to justify, the owners of Toni, the Harris brothers, were faced with the alternatives of paying penalty rates for improper accumulation of earnings or of paying out the income as dividends. Toni's income after corporate taxes was $4 million a year; with the Harris brothers' average personal income tax of 75 percent, only $1 million a year would have been left after they paid personal taxes on dividends. By selling Toni for $13 million, they realized a $12 million capital gain (their book value was $1 million). After paying the 25 percent capital gains tax on the $12 million, or $3 million, the Harrises realized $10 million after taxes ($13 million sale price less $3 million tax). Thus, Gillette paid the equivalent of 3¼ years' after-corporate-tax earnings for Toni, while the Harris brothers received 10 years' after-personal-income-tax net income for it. The tax factor made the transaction advantageous to both parties.

Election of Legal Form for Tax Purposes

The broad aspects of the federal corporate income tax have now been covered. For many business decisions, the federal income tax on individuals is equally important, so the main outlines of this part of the tax system must be discussed. In the next section, the individual tax structure is examined and compared with the corporate tax structure, thus providing a basis for making an intelligent choice as to which form of organization a firm should elect for tax purposes.

PERSONAL INCOME TAX

Of some five million firms in the United States, over four million are organized as individual proprietorships or as partnerships. The income of businesses organized as individual proprietorships or partnerships is taxed as personal income to the owners or the partners. The net income of a proprietorship or a partnership is reported to provide a basis for determining the individual's income tax liability. Thus, as a business tax, the individual income tax may be as important as the corporate income tax.

---

by these authors has been drawn on for the general background, but the data have been approximated to make the illustration simple. The principle involved is not affected by the modifications of the facts.

Individual Income Tax Structure

The tax rates applicable to the single individual are set forth in Table 2–5, and rates applicable to married couples filing joint returns are shown in Table 2–6. Since joint returns are permitted whether or not one spouse earns the entire income, this privilege has the effect of lowering applicable tax rates.

TABLE 2–5 MARGINAL AND AVERAGE 1967 TAX RATES OF THE INDIVIDUAL INCOME TAX
(single taxpayers or separate returns)

	TAX CALCULATION			AVERAGE TAX RATE	
Taxable Income	Base Amount +	Marginal Tax Rate =	Tax*	Individual	Corporate
$0–$500	$0	14%	$70	14.0%	22.0%
500–1,000	70	15	145	14.5	22.0
1,000–1,500	145	16	225	15.0	22.0
1,500–2,000	225	17	310	15.5	22.0
2,000–4,000	310	19	690	17.3	22.0
4,000–6,000	690	22	1,130	18.8	22.0
6,000–8,000	1,130	25	1,630	20.4	22.0
8,000–10,000	1,630	28	2,190	21.8	22.0
10,000–12,000	2,190	32	2,830	23.5	22.0
12,000–14,000	2,830	36	3,550	25.3	22.0
14,000–16,000	3,550	39	4,330	27.0	22.0
16,000–18,000	4,330	42	5,170	28.7	22.0
18,000–20,000	5,170	45	6,070	30.3	22.0
20,000–22,000	6,070	48	7,030	31.9	22.0
22,000–26,000	7,030	50	9,030	34.7	23.0
26,000–32,000	9,030	53	12,210	38.1	27.7
32,000–38,000	12,210	55	15,510	40.8	30.9
38,000–44,000	15,510	58	18,990	43.1	33.2
44,000–50,000	18,990	60	22,590	45.2	35.0
50,000–60,000	22,590	62	28,790	48.0	37.2
60,000–70,000	28,790	64	35,190	50.3	38.7
70,000–80,000	35,190	66	41,790	52.2	39.9
80,000–90,000	41,790	68	48,590	54.0	40.8
90,000–100,000	48,590	69	55,490	55.5	41.5
100,000–150,000	55,490	70	90,490	60.3	43.7
150,000–200,000	90,490	70	125,490	62.7	44.8
200,000–500,000	125,490	70	335,490	67.1	46.7
500,000–1,000,000	335,490	70	685,490	68.5	47.4
1,000,000–5,000,000	685,490	70	3,485,490	69.7	47.9
5,000,000–100,000,000	3,485,490	70	69,985,490	70.0	48.0

* Based on upper limit of each class interval. Note also that the calculated tax must be adjusted upward to reflect the 1968–1969 surtax mentioned on page 23.

TABLE 2–6 MARGINAL AND AVERAGE 1967 TAX RATES OF THE PERSONAL INCOME TAX
(joint returns)

	TAX CALCULATION			AVERAGE TAX RATE	
Taxable income	Base amount +	Marginal tax rate =	Tax*	Individual	Corporate
$0–$1,000	$0	14%	$140	14.0%	22.0%
1,000–2,000	140	15	290	14.5	22.0
2,000–3,000	290	16	450	15.0	22.0
3,000–4,000	450	17	620	15.5	22.0
4,000–8,000	620	19	1,380	17.4	22.0
8,000–12,000	1,380	22	2,260	18.8	22.0
12,000–16,000	2,260	25	3,260	20.4	22.0
16,000–20,000	3,260	28	4,380	21.9	22.0
20,000–24,000	4,380	32	5,660	23.6	22.0
24,000–28,000	5,660	36	7,100	25.4	24.8
28,000–32,000	7,100	39	8,660	27.1	27.7
32,000–36,000	8,660	42	10,340	28.7	29.9
36,000–40,000	10,340	45	12,140	30.4	31.8
40,000–44,000	12,140	48	14,060	32.0	33.2
44,000–52,000	14,060	50	18,060	34.7	35.5
52,000–64,000	18,060	53	24,420	38.2	37.8
64,000–76,000	24,420	55	31,020	40.8	39.4
76,000–88,000	31,020	58	37,980	43.2	40.6
88,000–100,000	37,980	60	45,180	45.2	41.5
100,000–120,000	45,180	62	57,580	48.0	42.6
120,000–140,000	57,580	64	70,380	50.3	43.4
140,000–160,000	70,380	66	83,580	52.2	43.9
160,000–180,000	83,580	68	97,180	54.0	44.4
180,000–200,000	97,180	69	110,980	55.5	44.8
200,000–300,000	110,980	70	189,980	60.3	45.8
300,000–400,000	180,980	70	250,980	62.7	46.4
400,000–1,000,000	250,980	70	670,980	67.1	47.4
1,000,000–10,000,000	670,980	70	6,970,980	69.7	47.9
10,000,000–100,000,000	6,970,980	70	69,920,980	70.0	48.0

* Based on upper limit of each class interval. Note also that the calculated tax must be adjusted upward to reflect the 1968–1969 surtax mentioned on page 23.

For some decisions, the taxpayer will compare the marginal tax rates. If a taxpayer has income from other sources and is deciding on whether to set up a new venture as a proprietorship or a corporation, he will be concerned with the tax rate applicable to the additional income. In comparing the relative advantages of the corporate versus noncorporate form of business organization, he is likely to compare the personal individual income tax rates to which his income will be subject with the marginal corporate income tax rates.

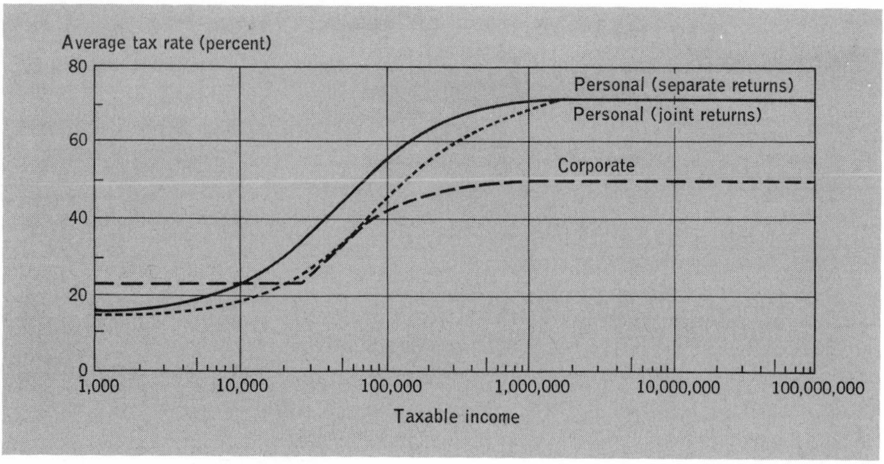

Figure 2–1 Comparison between Average Rates of Personal Income Tax and Corporation Income Tax (1967 Tax Rates)

When the taxpayer's income will be derived mainly from the enterprise he contemplates forming, he is more likely to compare the average rates of taxation. The relation between the average tax rates of the corporate income tax and the individual income tax is shown in Figure 2–1. For single returns, the individual rate rises above the corporate rate at about $10,000. For joint returns, the individual tax rises above the corporate after $54,000, at which point the amount of taxes on individual income is $19,320 and that on corporate income is $19,420. From this point on, the individual tax rate rises to 70 percent, while the corporate rate rises more slowly toward 48 percent.

Thus, for a firm with a net income of $1 million, there is no question but that the corporate form of business should be used. The tax advantage helps to explain why our largest businesses utilize the corporate form of organization. At incomes in the region of the $54,000 dividing line, whether the corporate or the noncorporate form will be most advantageous depends upon the facts of the case. If a firm finds it necessary to pay out a substantial part of its earnings, the noncorporate form is likely to be advantageous because the "double taxation" is avoided. However, the corporate form is satisfactory if the nature of the business operation makes it possible to set up a number of corporations for the purpose of keeping the tax rate at 22 percent.

THE 1968–1969 SURTAX. As in the case of the corporate income tax surcharge, and for the same reasons, Congress enacted a 10 percent surcharge on individual income taxes for the period April 1, 1968, through June 30, 1969. To illustrate the way the surtax works, assume a married couple had a taxable income of $12,000 for 1969. From Table 2–6 we find a tax of $2,260. Since the surtax was in effect for the first half of 1969, the effective annual surtax for this couple for 1969 was 5 percent. Therefore, their tax bill is calculated as:

$$\begin{aligned} \text{Tax} &= \$2{,}260 + (5\%)(\$2{,}260) \\ &= \$2{,}260 + \$113 \\ &= \$2{,}373 \end{aligned}$$

Capital Gains and Losses

As with corporations, the distinction between short-term and long-term gains and losses is the six-month holding period. Net short-term gains are taxed at regular rates; the tax on long-term gains may be computed in either of two ways. First, the taxpayer may pay a flat rate of 25 percent on net long-term gains. He may, instead, elect to pay the ordinary tax rate on *one half* the amount of the net long-term gains. The taxpayer should compute his tax under each of these methods and then select the one that results in the lower tax bill. For example, a married couple with an income of $32,000 from noncapital sources and a $10,000 long-term capital gain would compute their tax in two ways: (1) apply the normal tax rates on $32,000 plus ½ ($10,000) = $37,000 or (2) apply the normal tax on $32,000 plus 25 percent of $10,000. The first method would produce a tax of $10,790; the second, a tax of $11,160. The taxpayer would naturally elect the first method in this case. In general, for joint returns the 25 percent option is beneficial only if the taxable income exceeds $44,000, the point at which the marginal tax rate goes to 50 percent. Note that individual and corporate treatment differs in that corporations do not have the option of having only half of their capital gains taxed at normal rates.

Personal capital losses, short term or long term, can be carried forward without a time limit and deducted against either short-term or long-term capital gains. In addition, if the capital losses carried forward are not exhausted in the current year, a flat deduction of $1,000 per year against ordinary income with no time limit is permitted. In other words, an individual may deduct against ordinary income up to $1,000 of his net capital losses in any one year. If the net capital loss is in excess of $1,000, any amount above $1,000 may be carried forward until it is exhausted. Capital losses may not be carried back.

Moreover, Section 1244 of the Revenue Act of 1958 provides that individuals who invest in the stock of small corporations and suffer a loss on that stock may, for tax purposes, treat such a loss up to $25,000 a year ($50,000 on a joint return) as an ordinary loss rather than as a capital loss. A corporation is defined for this purpose as a small corporation, and the loss on its stock can be treated as an ordinary loss, if its common stock does not exceed $500,000 and if its total net worth—common stock plus retained earnings—does not exceed $1 million. This provision also encourages the formation of, and investment in, small corporations.

Dividend Income

The first $100 of dividend income received by an individual stockholder is excluded from taxable income. If stock is owned jointly by a husband and a wife, the exclusion is $200. However, if only one spouse owns stock, the total exclusion is generally only $100.

To illustrate, if a family's gross income consists of $12,000 of salary plus $500 of dividends on stock owned by the husband, the gross taxable income (before deductions) is $12,400. However, if the stock is jointly owned, the taxable gross income would be $12,300, because $200 of the dividend income would be excluded.

Personal Deductions

A $600 deduction is allowed for the taxpayer and each of his dependents; the deduction is doubled on any taxpayer who is over sixty-five years old or is blind. A family of four—husband, wife, and two dependent children, none blind or over sixty-five—would thus have personal deductions of 4 times $600, or $2,400.

Other Deductions

Certain other items are also deductible from income before computing taxes—medical expenses (subject to limitations), interest payments, state and local taxes, and contributions, among others. A taxpayer has the choice of either itemizing these deductions or taking the standard deduction, which is computed as the lower of $1,000 or 10 percent of gross taxable income.

> *Illustration.* A family of four filing a joint return has an income consisting of $11,000 salary and $500 dividends on stock owned jointly by the husband and the wife. They take the standard deduction. Their gross income is $11,500, but $200 dividends are excluded, leaving a gross taxable income of $11,300. Personal deductions are $2,400 and the standard deduction is $1,000, the lesser of $1,000 or 10 percent of $11,300; their taxable income is therefore $7,900. From Table 2–6 we find that the tax is $1,361, calculated as $620 plus 19 percent of $3,900.

Partnership or Proprietorship, or Corporation?

Subchapter S of the Internal Revenue Code provides that some incorporated businesses may elect to be taxed as proprietorships or partnerships. The main regulations governing permission to make this election include:

1. The firm must be a domestic corporation and must not be affiliated

with a group eligible to file consolidated tax returns. (Ordinarily 80 percent ownership of a subsidiary is required for filing consolidated returns.)

2. The firm may not have more than ten stockholders, all of whom must be individuals.

3. The firm may not derive over 20 percent of its gross receipts from royalties, rents, dividends, interest, annuities, and gains on sales of securities.

Although the foregoing tax factors make it difficult to generalize on whether the corporate or the noncorporate form is more advantageous from a tax standpoint, the essential variables for making an analysis are provided. In general, the advantage now seems to be on the side of the corporation, particularly since a firm may obtain the many benefits of its corporate status and yet elect to be taxed as a proprietorship or a partnership.

SUMMARY

This chapter provides some basic background on the tax environment within which business firms operate.

Corporate Taxes

The *corporate tax rate* structure is simple: The tax rate is 22 percent on income up to $25,000 and 48 percent on all income over $25,000. Estimated taxes are paid in quarterly installments during the year in which the income is earned; when the returns are filed, the actual tax liability will result either in additional payments or in a refund due. *Operating losses* may be carried back for three years and forward for five years. *Capital losses* may not be treated as a deduction from operating income, but they may be used to offset capital gains. Corporate capital losses may be carried forward for five years.

Eighty-five percent of the *dividends received* by a corporation owning stock in another firm is excluded from the receiving firm's taxable income, and the receiving firm must pay full taxes on the remaining 15 percent of the dividends. *Dividends paid* are not treated as a tax-deductible expense. Regardless of the size of its earnings a corporation does not have to pay dividends if it needs funds for expansion. If, however, the funds are not used for a legitimate purpose and if earnings are retained merely to enable stockholders to avoid paying personal income taxes on dividends received, the firm will be subject to an *improper accumulations tax. Interest received* is taxable as ordinary income; *interest paid* is a deductible expense.

Personal Income Tax

Unincorporated business income is taxed at the personal tax rates of the owners. Personal income tax rates for both individuals and married persons filing jointly are *progressive*—the higher one's income, the higher his tax rate. Personal income tax rates start at 14 percent of taxable income and rise to 70 percent of taxable income over $200,000. Corporate income tax rates range from 22 to 48 percent. Thus at lower incomes the personal income tax rate is lower, if a business is organized as a proprietorship or a partnership; at higher incomes the corporate tax rate is lower. This fact has a significant bearing on whether a business chooses to be taxed as a corporation or as a proprietorship or a partnership.

Short-term *capital gains* are taxed at ordinary rates; long-term gains, at 25 percent or one half the normal tax rate, whichever is lower. Capital losses can be used to offset capital gains. Net capital losses in any year can be deducted from ordinary income up to a limit of $1,000 a year. Capital losses in excess of $1,000 can be carried forward indefinitely until used up.

The foregoing material on the United States tax system is not designed to make a tax expert of the reader. It merely provides a few essentials for recognizing the tax aspects of business financial problems and for developing an awareness of the kinds of situations that should be taken to tax specialists for further guidance. These basics will, however, be referred to frequently in the remainder of the text, for income taxes are often an important factor in the making of business financial decisions.

QUESTIONS

2–1 Compare the marginal and the average tax rates of corporations with taxable incomes of $5,000, $50,000, $500,000, $5,000,000, and $50,000,000. Can you make such a comparison for sole proprietorships or for partnerships?

2–2 Which is the more relevant tax rate, the marginal or the average, in determining the form of organization for a new firm? Have recent changes in the tax laws made the form of organization more or less important than formerly?

2–3 For tax purposes, how does the treatment of interest expense compare with the treatment of common stock dividends from each of the following standpoints: a firm paying the interest or the dividends, an individual recipient, a corporate recipient?

2–4 Compare the treatment of capital gains and losses with ordinary gains and losses in income tax returns.

2–5 What is the present corporate carry-back and carry-forward tax provision for ordinary income? What is the purpose of this provision?

2–6 What is the purpose of the Internal Revenue Code provision dealing with improper accumulation of corporate surplus revenue?

2–7 Does the corporate tax rate structure give small firms the incentive to operate as multiple corporations?

2–8 Why is personal income tax information important for a study of business finance?

2–9 How do the tax rates for capital gains and losses affect an individual's investment policies and opportunities for financing a small business?

PROBLEMS

2–1 A corporation has a net income of $43,350 before interest charges. Assuming interest charges amount to $3,350:
a) How much income tax must the corporation pay?
b) What is the marginal tax rate?

2–2 Warren T. Lasser is a married man with one child. His gross income for 1968 is $12,000, which includes $1,250 of corporate dividends received by his wife. He files a joint return and takes the standard deduction. What is his personal income tax liability for 1968?

2–3 The taxable income (losses are shown in parentheses) of the Austin Corporation, formed in 1961, is shown below.

1962	$(300,000)
1963	150,000
1964	200,000
1965	300,000
1966	(150,000)

Corporate tax rates for these years are as follows:

1962 and 1963—first $25,000, 30%; excess, 52%
1964—first $25,000, 22%; excess, 50%
1965 and 1966—first $25,000, 22%; excess, 48%

What is the corporate tax liability for each year?

2–4 The Western Corporation income statement for 1965 is shown here.

Gross taxable income	$150,000
Tax payable (prepaid)	65,500
Net income after taxes	$ 84,500

PSR Manufacturing Corporation had a $75,000 loss in 1965. Western feels that its managerial talent can turn PSR into a profitable operation. If the two companies merged prior to January 1, 1966, what would be the merged corporation's income for 1965 after any refund of prepaid taxes? What is the difference in tax liability for Western before and after the merger?

2–5 In 1965, Alvin Manufacturing earned $150,000 before taxes on sales of $3 million. In 1963, it acquired working control of Markson Products, Inc. for $125,000 and disposed of the stock in 1965 for $350,000. (Alvin controlled less than 80 percent of Markson.) In addition, dividends paid by Markson to Alvin during 1965 amounted to $15,000.

a) What is Alvin's tax for 1965?

b) What would Alvin's tax have been if Markson had declared a further dividend of $50,000 in 1965 and if Alvin had sold the stock, purchased in 1963, for $300,000?

2–6 a) A corporation has an income of $100,000 after all expenses. What is the corporation's income tax liability?

b) Suppose the operations of the company are such that it could justify setting up five separate corporations (for example, a real estate company operating in five separate sections of a city). What tax is paid by each of the five corporations? and the total tax paid by all five? (Assume that each corporation had a net profit of $20,000.)

c) Now assume that a holding company, ABC, is formed and receives as its sole income the total after-tax income of the five corporations in the form of dividends. What is the total amount of tax paid by the six firms, assuming they file a consolidated tax return? unconsolidated tax returns? Assume no penalty rates.

Selected References

Butters, J. K., J. Lintner, and W. L. Cary, *Effects of Taxation, Corporate Mergers* (Boston: Harvard Business School, 1951).

Prentice-Hall Federal Taxes, (Englewood Cliffs, N.J.: Prentice-Hall, 1965).

Smith, D. T., *Effects of Taxation: Corporate Financial Policy* (Boston: Harvard Business School, 1952).

Tobolowsky, Sylvan, "New Cases Limit Changes in Ownership and Operations That Preserve Carryovers," *Journal of Taxation,* XXI (January 1961), pp. 26–42.

APPENDIX TO CHAPTER 2
Depreciation Methods

The four principal methods of depreciation—straight line, sum-of years-digits, double declining balance, and units of production—and their effects on a firm's taxes can be illustrated. We will begin by assuming that a machine is purchased for

$1,100 and has an estimated useful life of 10 years or 10,000 hours. It will have a scrap value of $100 after 10 years of use or after it has been used for 10,000 hours, whichever comes first. Table A2-1 illustrates each of the four depreciation methods and compares the depreciation charges of each method over the 10-year period.

Straight Line

With the straight-line methods, a uniform annual depreciation charge of $100 per year is provided. This figure is arrived at by simply dividing the functional life into the total cost of the machine minus the estimated salvage value:

$$\frac{(\$1{,}100 \text{ cost } - \$100 \text{ salvage value})}{10 \text{ years}} = \$100 \text{ per year depreciation charge.}$$

If the estimated salvage value is not in excess of 10 percent of the original cost, it can be ignored, but we are leaving it in.

Double Declining Balance

The double declining balance (DDB) method of accelerated depreciation requires the application of a constant rate of depreciation each year to the undepreciated value of the asset at the close of the previous year. In this case, since the annual straight-line rate is 10 percent per year ($1,000 ÷ $100), the double declining rate would be 20 percent (2 × 10 percent). When applied to the original $1,000 cost of the machine, this approach allows for a $200 depreciation charge in year 1 (20 percent × $1,000). Depreciation amounts to $160 in year 2 and is calculated by applying the 20 percent rate to the undepreciated value of the asset,

$$20\% \times (\$1000 - \$200) = \$160$$

and so on as the undepreciated balance declines.

A complication with the double declining balance method arises because it *never* fully depreciates an asset. As a consequence of this arithmetic feature of the method, the Internal Revenue Service permits a firm to switch from DDB to straight line at any time. In this example, the firm would switch in the seventh year. The total depreciation taken during the first six years is $738. Subtracting this figure from $1,000 leaves $262 to be depreciated over the remaining four years, or $65.50 per year. In actual practice, the depreciation charges taken for tax pur-

TABLE A2–1 COMPARISON OF DEPRECIATION METHODS FOR A 10-YEAR, $1,100 ASSET WITH A $100 SALVAGE VALUE

		DEPRECIATION METHODS			
Year		Straight line	Double declining balance	Sum-of-years-digits	Units of production*
1		$ 100	$200	$ 182	$ 200
2		100	160	164	180
3		100	128	145	150
4		100	102	127	130
5		100	82	109	100
6		100	66	91	80
7		100	52	73	60
8		100	42	55	50
9		100	34	36	30
10		100	28	18	20
	Total	$1,000	$894	$1,000	$1,000

* The assumption is that the machine is used the following hours: first year, 2000; second year, 1800; third year, 1500; fourth year, 1300; fifth year, 1000; sixth year, 800; seventh year, 600; eighth year, 500; ninth year, 300; tenth year, 200.

poses during the last four years would be $65.50, not the figures given in Table A2–1.[1]

Sum-of-Years-Digits

Under the sum-of-years-digits method, the yearly depreciation allowance is determined as follows:

1. Calculate the sum of the years' digits; in our example there are a total of 55 digits: $1 + 2 + 3 + 4 + 5 + 6 + 7 + 8 + 9 + 10 = 55$. This figure can also be arrived at by means of the sum of an algebraic progression equation where N is the life of the asset:

$$\text{Sum} = N\left(\frac{N+1}{2}\right)$$

$$= 10\left(\frac{10+1}{2}\right) = 55$$

[1] We should note that the switch from DDB to straight line is made in the seventh year, not before or after, because to switch in this year provides the maximum acceleration under the DDB method. If the switch was made in the sixth year, the straight-line depreciation would be less than that permitted under DDB; if the firm waited until the eighth year, straight-line depreciation during the seventh year would have been greater than that under DDB.

2. Divide the number of remaining years by the sum-of-years-digits and multiply this fraction by the depreciable value of the asset:

YEAR 1 $\frac{10}{55}$ (\$1,000) = \$182 depreciation

YEAR 2 $\frac{9}{55}$ (\$1,000) = \$164 depreciation

.
.
.

YEAR 10 $\frac{1}{55}$ (\$1,000) = \$18 depreciation

Units of Production

Under the units of production method, the expected useful life of 10,000 hours is divided into the depreciable cost (purchase price minus salvage value) to arrive at an hourly depreciation rate of \$.10. Since, in our example, the machine is run for 2,000 hours in the first year, the depreciation in that year is \$200; in the second year, \$180; and so on. With this method, depreciation charges cannot be estimated precisely ahead of time; the firm must wait until the end of the year to see what usage and, hence, depreciation turned out to be.

Effect of Depreciation on Taxes Paid

The effect of the accelerated methods upon a firm's income tax burden is easily demonstrated. In the first year, should the firm choose to use the straight-line method, only \$100 may be deducted from its earnings to arrive at earnings before taxes (the amount of earnings to which the tax rate applies). But using either of the other three methods, the firm would have a much greater deduction and, therefore, a lower tax liability.

Changing the Depreciable Life of an Asset

Depreciation charges may actually be accelerated without resorting to changing the depreciation method simply by shortening the useful life of an asset. The federal government establishes certain guidelines that set legal limits on the minimum life of classes of assets; by lowering these limits, the government can accomplish ends similar to permitting accelerated methods. Halving the minimum depreciable life of an asset, for example, would effectively double the annual rate of depreciation.

PART TWO

FINANCIAL ANALYSIS, PLANNING, AND CONTROL

3

Financial Analysis

Planning is the key to the financial manager's success. Financial plans may take many forms, but a good plan must be related to the firm's existing strengths and weaknesses. Its strengths must be understood if they are to be used to proper advantage, and its weaknesses must be recognized if corrective action is to be taken. For example, are inventories adequate to support the projected level of sales? Does the firm have too heavy an investment in accounts receivable, and does this condition reflect a lax collection policy? The financial manager can plan his future financial requirements in accordance with the forecasting and budgeting procedures developed in succeeding chapters, but his plan must begin with the type of financial analysis developed below.

BASIC TYPES OF FINANCIAL RATIOS

Each type of analysis has a purpose or use that determines the different types of relationships emphasized in the analysis. The analyst may, for example, be a banker considering whether or not to grant a short-term loan to a firm. He is primarily interested in the firm's liquid position and stresses ratios that measure liquidity. In contrast, long-term creditors place far more emphasis on earning power and on operating efficiency than on liquidity. They know that unprofitable operations will erode asset values, and a strong current position is no guarantee that funds will be available to repay a 20-year bond issue. Equity investors are similarly interested in long-term profitability and efficiency. Management is, of course, concerned with all these aspects of financial analysis—it seeks to repay its debts to the banker and to earn profits for the stockholder.

It is useful to classify ratios into four fundamental types:

1. *Liquidity ratios* measure the firm's ability to meet its maturing short-term obligations.
2. *Leverage ratios* measure the extent to which the firm has been financed by debt.
3. *Activity ratios* measure how effectively the firm is using its resources.
4. *Profitability ratios* measure management's over-all effectiveness as shown by the returns generated on sales and investment.

Specific examples of each ratio are given in the following sections with an actual case history used to illustrate their calculation and use. The company's name and the actual figures are disguised, of course, but the case is a good one to illustrate the process of financial analysis.

Walker-Wilson Manufacturing Company. The Walker-Wilson Manufacturing Company produces specialized machinery used in the automobile repair business. Formed in 1946, when Charles Walker and Ben Wilson set up a small plant to produce certain tools they had developed while in the Army, Walker-Wilson grew steadily and earned the reputation of being one of the best small firms in its line of business. In December 1966, both Walker and Wilson were killed in a crash of their private plane. For the next two years the firm was managed by Walker-Wilson's accountant. In 1968 the widows, who are the principal stockholders in Walker-Wilson, acting on the advice of the firm's bankers and attorneys, engaged David Thompson as president and general manager.

Thompson is experienced in this line of business, especially in production and sales; he does not, however, have a detailed knowledge of his new company. He has therefore decided to conduct a careful appraisal of the firm's position and, on the basis of this position, to draw up a plan for future operations. The most recent balance sheet and income statement—the starting points for any financial analysis—are presented in Tables 3–1 and 3–2.[1]

Liquidity Ratios

Generally, the first concern of the financial analyst is liquidity: Is the firm able to meet its maturing obligations? Walker-Wilson has debts totaling $300,000 that must be paid within the coming year. Can these obligations by satisfied? Although a full liquidity analysis requires the use of cash budgets (described in Chapter 5), ratio analysis, by relating the amount of cash and other current assets to the current obligations, provides some quick and easy-to-use measures of liquidity.

1. CURRENT RATIO. The current ratio is computed by dividing current liabilities into current assets. Current assets normally include cash, marketable securities, accounts receivable, and inventories; current liabilities consist of accounts payable, short-term notes payable, current maturities of long-term debt, accrued income taxes, and other accrued expenses (principally wages). The current ratio is the generally accepted measure of short-term solvency, since it indicates the extent to which the claims of short-term creditors are covered by assets that are expected to be converted to cash in a period roughly corresponding to the maturity of the claims.

The calculation of the current ratio for Walker-Wilson is shown below.

$$\text{current ratio} = \frac{\text{current assets}}{\text{current liabilities}} = \frac{\$700{,}000}{\$300{,}000} = 2.3 \text{ times}$$

$$\text{industry average} = 2.5 \text{ times}$$

The current ratio is slightly below the average for the industry, 2.5,

[1] There is no "standard form" for the balance sheet, income statement, or other financial statements. Moreover, certain words can be given more than one meaning, and a single concept can be called by several different titles. For example, "net income after taxes" is also called "net income," "net profit," "income," and "profit." Depreciation can refer to the accumulated reserve for depreciation or to the annual charge against operating income. The balance sheet is also called the "statement of condition" and the income statement, the "profit and loss statement." These and other ambiguities can cause confusion; if one is careful to determine the context within which the word is used, this confusion can be minimized.

TABLE 3–1 WALKER-WILSON COMPANY
ILLUSTRATIVE BALANCE SHEET
December 31, 1968

ASSETS		CLAIMS ON ASSETS	
Cash	$ 50,000	Accounts payable	$ 60,000
Marketable securities	150,000	Notes payable, 8%	100,000
Receivables, net	200,000	Accruals	10,000
Inventories	300,000	Provision for federal income taxes	130,000
Total current assets	$ 700,000	Total current liabilities	$ 300,000
Gross plant and equipment	$1,800,000	First mortgage bonds, 5%*	500,000
Less reserve for depreciation	500,000	Debentures, 6%	200,000
		Common stock	600,000
Net plant and equipment	$1,300,000	Retained earnings	400,000
		Total net worth	$1,000,000
Total assets	$2,000,000	Total claims on assets	$2,000,000

* The annual sinking fund requirement is $20,000.

but not low enough to cause concern. It appears that Walker-Wilson is about in line with most other firms in this particular line of business. Since current assets are near-maturing, it is highly probable that they could be liquidated at close to book value. With a current ratio of 2.3, Walker-Wilson could liquidate current assets at only 42.9 percent of book value and still pay off current creditors in full.

2. QUICK RATIO, OR ACID TEST. The quick ratio is calculated by deducting inventories from current assets and dividing the remainder by current liabilities. Inventories are typically the least liquid of a firm's current assets and the assets on which losses are most likely to occur in the event of liquidation. Therefore, this measure of ability to pay off short-term obligations without relying on the sale of inventories is important.

$$\text{quick, or acid test ratio} = \frac{(\text{current assets} - \text{inventory})}{\text{current liabilities}} = \frac{\$400{,}000}{\$300{,}000}$$
$$= 1.3 \text{ times}$$
$$\text{industry average} = 1.0 \text{ times}$$

The industry average quick ratio is 1, so Walker-Wilson's 1.3 ratio compares favorably with other firms in the industry. Thompson knows

TABLE 3–2 WALKER-WILSON COMPANY
ILLUSTRATIVE INCOME STATEMENT
For Year Ended December 31, 1968

Net sales		$3,000,000
Cost of goods sold		2,580,000
Gross profit		$ 420,000
Less: Operating expenses		
Selling	$22,000	
General and administrative	40,000	
Rent on office	28,000	90,000
Gross operating income		$ 330,000
Depreciation		100,000
Net operating income		$ 230,000
Add: Other income		
Royalties		15,000
Gross income		$ 245,000
Less: Other expenses		
Interest on notes payable	$ 8,000	
Interest on first mortgage	25,000	
Interest on debentures	12,000	45,000
Net before income tax		$ 200,000
Federal income tax (at 40 percent*)		80,000
Net income after income tax available to common stockholders		$ 120,000
Less: Common stock dividends		100,000
Increase in retained earnings		$ 20,000

* For most of the illustrations in the text a 50 percent corporate tax rate is used.

that if the marketable securities can be sold at par and if he can collect the accounts receivable, he can pay off his current liabilities without selling any inventory.

Leverage Ratios

Leverage ratios, which measure the contributions of owners as compared with the financing provided by the firm's creditors, have a number of implications. First, creditors look to the equity, or owner-supplied funds, to provide a margin of safety. If owners have provided only a small proportion of total financing, the risks of the enterprise are borne mainly by the creditors. Second, by raising funds through debt, the owners gain the benefits of maintaining control of the firm with a limited investment. Third, if the firm earns more on the borrowed funds than it pays in interest, the return to the owners is magnified. For example, if assets earn 6 percent and debt costs but 4 percent, there is a 2 percent differential, which accrues to the stockholders. Leverage cuts both ways, however; if the return on assets falls to 3 percent, the differential between that figure and the cost of debt must be made up from equity's share of total profits. In the first instance, where assets earn more than the cost of debt, leverage is favorable; in the second it is unfavorable.

Firms with low leverage ratios have less risk of loss when the economy is in a recession, but they also have lower expected returns when the economy booms. However, firms with high leverage ratios run the risk of large losses but also have a chance of gaining high profits. The prospects of high returns are desirable, but investors are averse to risk. Decisions about the use of leverage, then, must balance higher expected returns against increased risk.

In practice, leverage is approached in two ways. One approach involves examining balance sheet ratios and determining the extent to which borrowed funds have been used to finance the firm. The other approach measures the risks of debt by income statement ratios designed to determine the number of times fixed charges are covered by operating profits. These sets of ratios are complementary, and most analysts examine both types of leverage ratios.

3. DEBT TO TOTAL ASSETS. This ratio, generally called the debt ratio, measures the percentage of total funds that have been provided by creditors. Debt includes current liabilities and all bonds. Creditors prefer moderate debt ratios, since the lower the ratio, the greater the cushion against creditors' losses in the event of liquidation. In contrast to the creditors' preference for a low debt ratio, the owners may seek high leverage either (1) to magnify earnings or (2) because raising new equity means giving up some degree of control. If the debt ratio is too high, there is a danger of encouraging irresponsibility on the part of the owners. The stake of the owners can become so small that speculative activity, if it is successful, will yield a substantial percentage return to the owners. However, if the venture is unsuccessful, only a moderate loss is incurred by the owners, because their investment is small.

$$\text{debt ratio} = \frac{\text{total debt}}{\text{total assets}} = \frac{\$1{,}000{,}000}{\$2{,}000{,}000} = 50\%$$

$$\text{industry average} = 33\%$$

Walker-Wilson's debt ratio is 50 percent; this means that creditors have supplied half the firm's total financing. Since the average debt ratio for this industry—and for manufacturing generally—is about 33 percent, Walker-Wilson would find it difficult to borrow additional funds without first raising more equity capital. Creditors would be reluctant to lend the firm more money, and Thompson would probably be subjecting the stockholders to undue dangers if he sought to increase the debt ratio still more by borrowing.

4. TIMES INTEREST EARNED. The times-interest-earned ratio is determined by dividing earnings before interest and taxes (gross income in Table 3–2) by the interest charges. The times-interest-earned ratio measures the extent to which earnings can decline without resultant financial embarrassment to the firm because of inability to meet annual interest costs. Failure to meet this obligation can bring legal action by the creditors, possibly resulting in bankruptcy. Note that the before-tax profit figure is used in the numerator. Because income taxes are computed after deducing interest expense, the ability to pay current interest is not affected by income taxes.

$$\text{times interest earned} = \frac{\text{profit before taxes} + \text{interest charges}}{\text{interest charges}}$$

$$\frac{\$245{,}000}{\$45{,}000} = 5.4 \text{ times}$$

$$\text{industry average} = 8.0 \text{ times}$$

Walker-Wilson's interest charges consist of three payments totaling $45,000 (see Table 3–2). The firm's gross income available to service these charges is $245,000, so the interest is covered only 5.4 times. Since the industry average is 8 times, the company is covering its interest charges by a minimum margin of safety and deserves only a fair rating. This ratio reinforces the conclusion based on the debt ratio that the company is likely to face some difficulties in raising additional funds from debt sources.

5. FIXED CHARGE COVERAGE. The number of times fixed charges are covered is determined by dividing profit before fixed charges by the total fixed charges—interest, lease payments, sinking fund requirements, and the tax related to sinking fund payments.[2] This more inclusive ratio

[2] A sinking fund, discussed in detail in Chapter 19, is a required annual payment designed to amortize a bond issue. Sinking fund payments are not deductible for income tax purposes, so they must be paid with after-tax profits. This means, in effect, that the firm must earn sufficient profits before taxes to enable it to pay its tax bill and still have enough left to meet the sinking fund requirement. For this reason, the tax requirement must be included in the denominator of the fixed-charge-coverage ratio.

Since it is in the 40 percent tax bracket, Walker-Wilson must have a before-tax

provides an important supplement to the times-interest-earned figure, as it recognizes that financial problems may arise from the nonpayment of lease obligations or sinking fund charges as well as from the failure to meet interest payments.

$$\begin{aligned}\text{fixed charge coverage} &= \frac{\text{income available for meeting fixed charges}}{\text{fixed charges}}\\ &= \frac{\text{gross income} + \text{rent on office}}{\text{interest} + \text{rent} + \text{before-tax sinking fund}}\\ &= \frac{\$245{,}000 + \$28{,}000}{\$45{,}500 + \$28{,}000 + \$33{,}333}\\ &= \frac{\$273{,}000}{\$106{,}333} = 2.6 \text{ times}\\ \text{industry average} &= 4.0 \text{ times}\end{aligned}$$

Walker-Wilson's fixed charges are covered 2.6 times, as opposed to an industry average of 4 times. Again, this indicates that the firm is somewhat weaker than creditors would prefer it to be and further points up the difficulties Thompson would likely encounter if he should attempt additional borrowing.

Activity Ratios

Activity ratios measure how effectively the firm employs the resources at its command. These ratios all involve comparisons between the level of sales and the investment in various asset accounts. The activity ratios presume a proper balance between sales and the various asset accounts—inventories, accounts receivable, fixed assets, and others. As we shall see in the following chapter, this is indeed a good assumption.

6. INVENTORY TURNOVER. The inventory turnover we shall use is sales divided by inventories.

$$\begin{aligned}\text{inventory turnover} = \frac{\text{sales}}{\text{inventory}} = \frac{\$3{,}000{,}000}{\$300{,}000} &= 10 \text{ times}\\ \text{industry average} &= 9 \text{ times}\end{aligned}$$

---

income of \$33,333 to enable it to pay the tax and still have \$20,000 left after taxes. The general equation for finding the necessary before-tax income is:

$$\begin{aligned}\text{before-tax income required for sinking fund payment} &= \frac{\text{sinking fund payment}}{1.0 - \text{tax rate}}\\ &= \frac{\$20{,}000}{1.0 - 0.4} = \frac{\$20{,}000}{0.6}\\ &= \$33{,}333\end{aligned}$$

Walker-Wilson's turnover of 10 compares favorably with an industry average of 9 times. This suggests that the company does not hold excessive stocks of inventory; excess stocks are, of course, unproductive and represent an investment with a low or zero rate of return. This high inventory turnover also reinforces Thompson's faith in the current ratio. If the turnover had been low—perhaps 3 or 4 times—he would have wondered whether the firm was holding damaged or obsolete materials not actually worth their stated value.

Two problems arise in calculating and analyzing the inventory turnover ratio. First, sales are at market prices; if inventories are carried at cost, as they generally are, it would be more appropriate to use cost of goods sold in place of sales in the numerator of the formula. Established compilers of financial ratio statistics such as Dun & Bradstreet, however, use the ratio of sales to inventories carried at cost. To develop a figure that can be compared with those developed by Dun & Bradstreet, it is therefore necessary to measure inventory turnover with sales in the numerator, as we do here.

The second problem lies in the fact that sales occur over the entire year, whereas the inventory figure is for one point in time. This makes it better to use an average inventory, computed by adding beginning and ending inventories and dividing by 2. If it is determined that the firm's business is highly seasonal, or if there has been a strong upward or downward sales trend during the year, it becomes essential to make this relatively simple adjustment. Neither of these conditions holds for Walker-Wilson; to maintain comparability with industry averages, therefore, Thompson did not use the average inventory figure.

7. AVERAGE COLLECTION PERIOD. The average collection period, which is an alternative ratio for measuring the accounts receivable turnover, is computed as follows: First, the annual credit sales are divided by 360 to get the average daily sales.[3] Second, daily sales are divided into accounts receivable to find the number of days' sales tied up in receivables. This is defined as the average collection period, for it represents the average length of time that the firm must wait after making a sale before receiving cash.

$$\text{sales per day} = \frac{\$3{,}000{,}000}{360} = \$8{,}333$$

$$\text{average collection period} = \frac{\text{receivables}}{\text{sales per day}} = \frac{\$200{,}000}{\$8{,}333} = 24 \text{ days}$$

$$\text{industry average} = 20 \text{ days}$$

[3] For convenience, the financial community generally uses 360 rather than 365 as the number of days in the year for purposes such as the present one.

The calculations for Walker-Wilson show an average collection period of 24 days, slightly above the 20-day industry average. This ratio can also be evaluated by the terms on which the firm sells its goods. For example, Walker-Wilson's sales terms call for payment within 30 days, so the 24-day collection period is excellent. Even if the firm sold on a 20-day payment basis, the performance could be considered satisfactory, because some payment delays are customary. However, if the ratio's trend over the past few years has been rising while the credit policy has not changed, steps should be taken to expedite the collection of accounts receivable.

One nonratio financial tool should be mentioned in connection with accounts receivable analysis—the aging schedule, which breaks down accounts receivable according to how long they have been outstanding. This schedule for Walker-Wilson is given below.

AGE OF ACCOUNT (DAYS)	PERCENT OF TOTAL VALUE OF ACCOUNTS RECEIVABLE
0–10	50
11–30	20
31–45	15
46–60	3
over 60	12
Total	100

The 24-day collection period looked good by comparison with the 30-day terms, but the aging schedule shows that the firm is having serious collection problems with some of its accounts. Thirty percent are overdue, many for over a month. Others pay quite promptly, bringing the average down to only 24 days, but the aging schedule shows this average to be somewhat misleading.

8. FIXED ASSETS TURNOVER. The ratio of sales to fixed assets measures the turnover of capital assets.

$$\text{fixed asset turnover} = \frac{\text{sales}}{\text{fixed assets}} = \frac{\$3{,}000{,}000}{\$1{,}300{,}000} = 2.3 \text{ times}$$

$$\text{industry average} = 5.0 \text{ times}$$

Walker-Wilson's turnover of 2.3 times compares poorly with the industry average of 5 times, indicating that the firm is not using its fixed assets to as high a percentage of capacity as are the other firms in the industry. Thompson should bear this fact in mind when his production officers request funds for new capital investments.

9. TOTAL ASSETS TURNOVER. The final activity ratio measures the turnover of all the firm's assets—it is calculated by dividing sales by total assets.

$$\text{total assets turnover} = \frac{\text{sales}}{\text{total assets}} = \frac{\$3{,}000{,}000}{\$2{,}000{,}000} = 1.5 \text{ times}$$
$$\text{industry average} = 2.0 \text{ times}$$

Walker-Wilson's turnover of total assets is well below the industry average. The company is simply not generating a sufficient volume of business for the size of the asset investment. Sales should be increased or some assets should be disposed of or both steps should be taken.

Profitability Ratios

Profitability is the net result of a large number of policies and decisions. The ratios examined thus far reveal some interesting things about the way the firm is operating, but the profitability ratios give final answers as to how effectively the firm is being managed.

10. PROFIT MARGIN ON SALES. This ratio, computed by dividing net income after taxes by sales, gives the profit per dollar of sales.

$$\text{profit margin} = \frac{\text{net profit after taxes}}{\text{sales}} = \frac{\$120{,}000}{\$3{,}000{,}000} = 4\%$$
$$\text{industry average} = 5\%$$

Walker-Wilson's profit margin is somewhat below the industry average of 5 percent, indicating that the firm's sales prices are relatively low or that its costs are relatively high or both. With a 4 percent after-tax margin on sales and a 40 percent corporate tax rate, unit sales prices can decline by 6⅔ percent or costs rise by 6⅔ percent before the firm suffers an over-all loss. In general, profit margins indicate the magnitude of the margin of protection against losses resulting from falling prices or rising costs.

11. RETURN ON TOTAL ASSETS. The ratio of net profit to total assets measures the return on total investment in the firm.[4]

$$\text{return on total assets} = \frac{\text{net profit after taxes}}{\text{total assets}} = \frac{\$120{,}000}{\$2{,}000{,}000} = 6\%$$
$$\text{industry average} = 10\%$$

[4] In calculating the return on total assets, it is sometimes desirable to add interest to net profits after taxes to form the numerator of the ratio. The theory here

Walker-Wilson's 6 percent return is well below the 10 percent average for the industry. This low rate results from the low profit margin on sales and from the low turnover of total assets.

12. RETURN ON NET WORTH. The ratio of net profit after taxes to net worth measures the rate of return on the stockholders' investment.

$$\text{return on net worth} = \frac{\text{net profit after taxes}}{\text{net worth}} = \frac{\$120{,}000}{\$1{,}000{,}000} = 12\%$$

$$\text{industry average} = 15\%$$

Walker-Wilson's 12 percent return is below the 15 percent industry average.

Summary of the Ratios

The individual ratios, which are summarized in Table 3–3, can give Thompson a reasonably good idea of Walker-Wilson's main strengths and weaknesses. First, the company's liquidity position is reasonably good—its current and quick ratios appear to be satisfactory by comparison with the industry averages. Second, the leverage ratios suggest that the company is rather heavily indebted. With a debt ratio substantially higher than the industry average and with coverage ratios well below the industry averages, it is doubtful that Walker-Wilson could do much additional debt financing except on relatively unfavorable terms. Even if Thompson could borrow more, to do so would be subjecting the company to the danger of default and bankruptcy in the event of a business downturn.

Turning to the activity ratios, the inventory turnover and average collection period both indicate that the company's current assets are pretty well in balance, but the low fixed asset turnover suggests that there has been too heavy an investment in fixed assets. The low fixed asset turnover means, in effect, that the company probably could have operated with a smaller investment in fixed assets. Had the excessive

---

is that assets are "supplied" by both stockholders and creditors, and the ratio should measure the productivity of assets in providing returns to both classes of investors. We have not done so at this point for two reasons: (1) For manufacturing companies this addition is generally inconsequential. (2) The published averages we use for comparative purposes exclude interest. Later in the book, however, when we deal with public utilities, we do add back interest. This addition has a material bearing on the value of the ratio, and the revised ratio is the one normally used for utilities.

TABLE 3–3 SUMMARY OF FINANCIAL RATIO ANALYSIS

RATIO	FORMULA FOR CALCULATION	CALCULATION	INDUSTRY AVERAGE	EVALUATION
I. *Liquidity*				
1. Current	$\frac{\text{current assets}}{\text{current liab.}}$	$\frac{\$\ 700,000}{\$\ 300,000}$ = 2.3 times	2.5 times	Satisfactory
2. Quick, or acid test	$\frac{\text{(current assets} - \text{inventory)}}{\text{current liabilities}}$	$\frac{\$\ 400,000}{\$\ 300,000}$ = 1.3 times	1.0 times	Good
II. *Leverage*				
3. Debt to total assets	$\frac{\text{total debt}}{\text{total assets}}$	$\frac{\$1,000,000}{\$2,000,000}$ = 50%	33%	High
4. Times interest earned	$\frac{\text{profit before taxes plus interest charges}}{\text{interest charges}}$	$\frac{\$\ 245,000}{\$\ 45,000}$ = 5.4 times	8.0 times	Fair
5. Fixed charge coverage	$\frac{\text{income available for meeting fixed charges}}{\text{fixed charges}}$	$\frac{\$\ 273,000}{\$\ 106,333}$ = 2.6 times	4.0 times	Low
III. *Activity*				
6. Inventory turnover	$\frac{\text{sales}}{\text{inventory}}$	$\frac{\$3,000,000}{\$\ 300,000}$ = 10 times	9 times	Satisfactory
7. Average collection period	$\frac{\text{receivables}}{\text{sales per day}}$	$\frac{\$\ 200,000}{\$\ 8,333}$ = 24 days	20 days	Satisfactory
8. Fixed assets turnover	$\frac{\text{sales}}{\text{fixed assets}}$	$\frac{\$3,000,000}{\$1,300,000}$ = 2.3 times	5.0 times	Poor
9. Total assets turnover	$\frac{\text{sales}}{\text{total assets}}$	$\frac{\$3,000,000}{\$2,000,000}$ = 1.5 times	2 times	Low
IV. *Profitability*				
10. Profit margin on sales	$\frac{\text{net profit after taxes}}{\text{sales}}$	$\frac{\$\ 120,000}{\$3,000,000}$ = 4%	5%	Low
11. Return on total assets	$\frac{\text{net profit after taxes}}{\text{total assets}}$	$\frac{\$\ 120,000}{\$2,000,000}$ = 6.0%	10%	Low
12. Return on net worth	$\frac{\text{net profit after taxes}}{\text{net worth}}$	$\frac{\$\ 120,000}{\$1,000,000}$ = 12.0%	15%	Somewhat low

fixed asset investment not been made, the company could have avoided some of its debt financing and would now have lower interest payments. This, in turn, would have led to improved leverage and coverage ratios.

The profit margin on sales is low, indicating that costs are too high or that prices are too low or both. In this particular case, the sales prices are in line with other firms; high costs are, in fact, the cause of the low margin. Further, the high costs can be traced (1) to high depreciation charges and (2) to high interest expenses. These costs are, in turn, both attributable to the excessive investment in fixed assets.

Returns on both the total investment and net worth are also below the industry average. These relatively poor results are directly attributable to the low profit margin on sales, which lowers the numerator of the ratios, and to the excessive investment, which raises the denominator.

Trend Analysis

While the preceding ratio analysis gives a reasonably good picture of Walker-Wilson's operation, it is incomplete in one important respect—it ignores the time dimension. The ratios are snapshots of the picture at one point in time, but there may be trends in motion that are in the process of rapidly eroding a relatively good current position. Conversely, an analysis of the ratios over the past few years may suggest that a relatively weak current position is being improved at a rapid rate.

The method of trend analysis is illustrated in Figure 3–1, which shows a graph of Walker-Wilson's sales, current ratio, debt ratio, fixed asset turnover, and return on net worth. These figures are compared with industry averages. Industry sales have been rising steadily over the entire period, and the industry average ratios have been relatively stable throughout. Thus, any trends in the individual company's ratios are due to its own internal conditions, not to environmental influences affecting all firms. Second, Walker-Wilson's deterioration since the death of the two principal officers is also apparent. Prior to 1966, Walker-Wilson was growing more rapidly than the average firm in the industry; during the next two years, however, sales actually declined.

Walker-Wilson's liquidity position as measured by its current ratio has also gone downhill in the past two years. Although the ratio is only slightly below the industry average at the present time, the trend suggests that a real liquidity crisis may develop during the next year or two unless corrective action is taken immediately.

The debt ratio trend line shows that Walker-Wilson followed industry practices closely until 1966, when the ratio jumped a full 10 percentage points above the industry average. Similarly, the fixed asset turnover

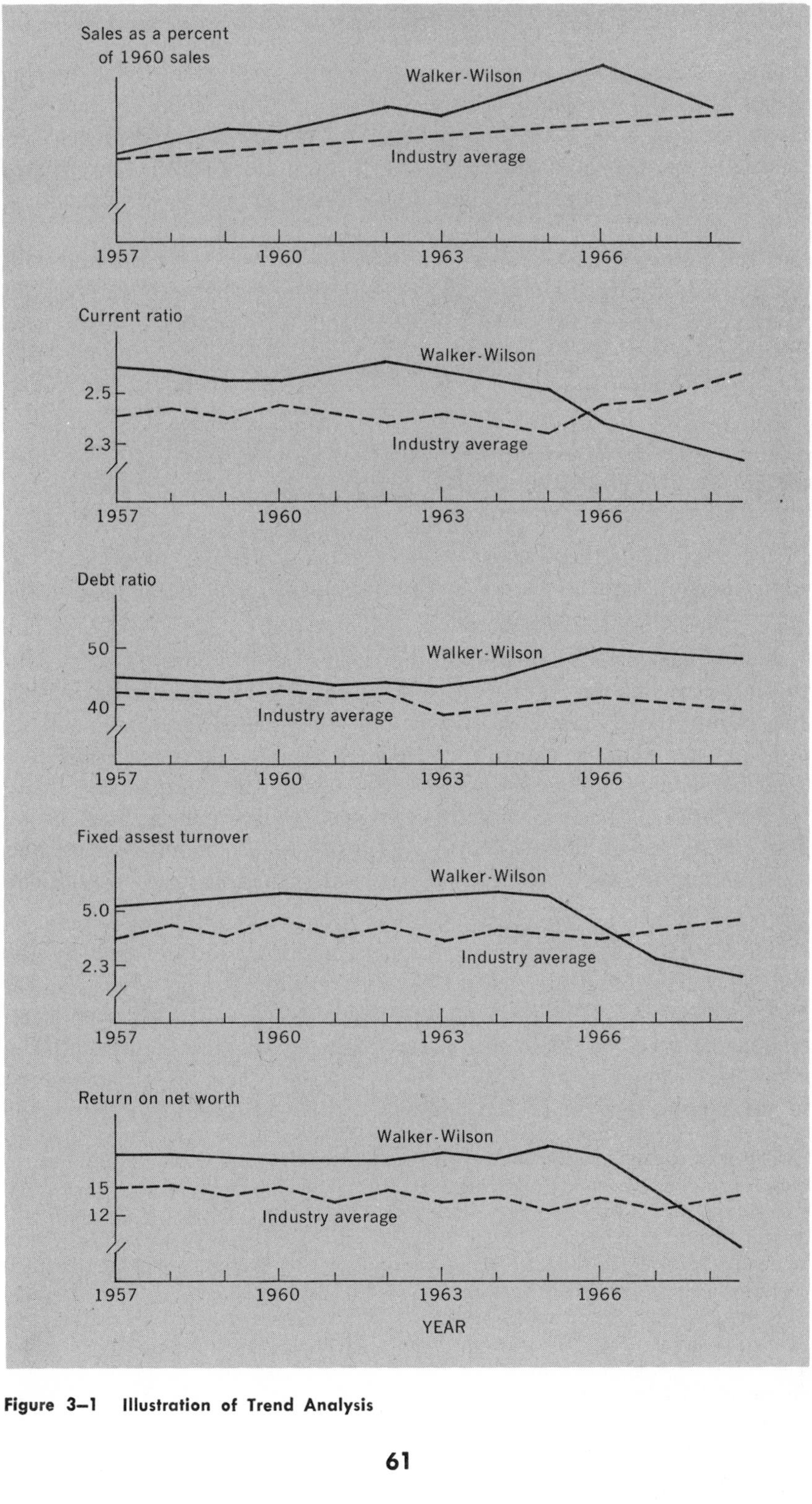

Figure 3–1 Illustration of Trend Analysis

declined during 1966, even though sales were still rising. The records reveal that the company borrowed heavily during 1966 to finance a major expansion of plant and equipment. Walker and Wilson had intended to use this additional capacity to generate a still higher volume of sales and to retire the debt out of expected high profits. Unfortunately, their untimely death led to a decrease in sales rather than an increase, and the expected high profits that were to be used to retire the debt did not materialize. The analysis suggests that the bankers were correct when they advised Mrs. Walker and Mrs. Wilson of the firm's need for a change in management.

SOURCES OF COMPARATIVE RATIOS

In the analysis of the Walker-Wilson Company, industry average ratios were frequently used. Where may one obtain such averages? Some important sources are listed below.

DUN & BRADSTREET. Probably the most widely known and used of the industry average ratios are those compiled by Dun & Bradstreet, Inc. "Dun & Brad" provides fourteen ratios calculated for a large number of industries. Sample ratios and explanations are shown in Table 3–4. The complete data give the fourteen ratios, with the interquartile ranges[5] for 125 lines of business activity based on their financial statements. The 125 types of business activity consist of 71 manufacturing and construction categories, 30 types of wholesalers, and 24 types of retailers.

ROBERT MORRIS ASSOCIATES. Another group of useful ratios can be found in the annual *Statement Studies* compiled and published by the Robert Morris Associates (RMA), which is the national association of bank loan officers. These are representative averages based on financial statements received by banks in connection with loans made. Eleven ratios are computed for 156 lines of business. The firms represented in the sample tend to be the larger and financially stronger firms; the

[5] The median and quartile ratios can be illustrated by an example. The median ratio of current assets to current debt of manufacturers of airplane parts and accessories, as shown in Table 3–4, is 1.78. To obtain this figure, the ratios of current assets to current debt for each of the 55 concerns were arranged in a graduated series, with the largest ratio at the top and the smallest at the bottom. The median ratio of 1.78 was the ratio halfway between the top and the bottom. The ratio of 2.26, representing the upper quartile, was one quarter of the way down the series from the top (or halfway between the top and the median). The ratio of 1.36, representing the lower quartile, was one quarter of the way up from the bottom (or halfway between the median and the bottom).

TABLE 3–4 DUN & BRADSTREET RATIOS FOR SELECTED INDUSTRIES, 1967

Line of Business (and number of concerns reporting)	Current assets to current debt (times)	Net profits on net sales (percent)	Net profits on tangible net worth (percent)	Net profits on net working capital (percent)	Net sales to tangible net worth (times)	Net sales to net working capital (times)	Collection period (days)	Net sales to inventory (times)	Fixed assets to tangible net worth (percent)	Current debt to tangible net worth (percent)	Total debt to tangible net worth (percent)	Inventory to net working capital (percent)	Current debt to inventory (percent)	Funded debts to net working capital (percent)
2871–72–79*	3.71	4.46	11.13	25.05	4.69	13.45	28	13.1	26.5	18.6	72.1	46.6	86.4	23.9
Agricultural Chemicals	1.88	2.17	6.90	10.43	3.08	5.98	56	6.9	53.2	56.8	115.9	74.4	150.4	51.1
(41)	1.34	0.79	1.45	3.95	1.67	3.91	107	4.3	68.5	110.4	244.5	153.8	258.4	185.9
3722–23–29	2.26	7.01	22.67	44.41	4.82	9.37	29	8.4	34.1	35.5	60.0	75.1	82.3	16.9
Airplane Parts &	1.78	4.44	16.67	26.26	3.23	5.22	39	5.9	55.1	61.8	93.5	103.7	98.1	44.3
Accessories (53)	1.36	2.92	8.10	14.98	2.35	4.35	55	4.2	77.0	88.7	127.1	176.9	159.8	74.7
2051–52	2.39	4.46	16.54	67.52	5.59	28.67	13	38.5	60.2	21.4	39.2	39.2	150.1	41.5
Bakery Products (92)	1.84	2.37	10.21	34.41	4.15	16.40	18	30.4	78.8	30.2	57.3	61.7	223.8	95.8
	1.39	0.94	3.79	12.75	2.98	10.32	24	22.5	103.9	48.5	103.6	99.5	315.2	214.8
3312–13–15–16–17 Blast	3.65	6.08	11.85	26.47	2.53	5.10	29	6.6	45.4	14.4	20.2	69.3	49.3	32.2
Furnaces, Steel Wks.	2.58	4.07	8.01	19.18	1.90	4.21	35	4.9	61.4	23.4	50.8	92.4	67.1	67.5
& Rolling Mills (63)	2.02	3.00	5.38	11.44	1.41	3.19	43	4.2	89.8	35.3	81.1	110.5	97.5	105.4
2331	2.64	2.01	17.21	22.70	13.18	15.24	27	20.6	3.5	51.3	75.9	56.0	104.7	5.7
Blouses & Waists,	1.73	0.69	7.86	9.28	8.58	9.80	36	13.0	7.2	130.7	175.3	86.0	152.0	23.6
Women's & Misses' (71)	1.41	0.19	1.33	1.47	6.32	8.00	50	8.8	14.8	217.2	359.5	123.4	254.1	53.4
2731–32	3.52	8.14	17.52	25.20	3.18	5.02	41	10.6	9.4	30.2	51.8	52.0	49.7	6.1
Books; Publ., Publ. &	2.63	5.20	10.44	16.13	2.32	2.86	58	4.1	28.8	45.7	77.2	71.4	85.4	28.1
Printing (43)	2.01	2.65	5.63	8.19	1.69	1.95	78	2.5	55.9	73.3	113.8	88.2	164.2	86.5
2211	4.32	5.67	10.90	22.49	2.11	5.35	26	6.8	45.1	12.1	22.0	57.5	49.5	9.7
Broad Woven Fabrics,	3.00	3.96	7.34	15.84	1.82	4.03	53	5.7	54.9	24.3	34.5	78.8	60.2	40.2
Cotton (38)	2.24	2.58	4.09	7.50	1.43	3.10	58	3.9	65.6	32.4	59.7	105.5	81.4	65.8
2031–32–33–34–35–36–37	2.40	6.16	17.28	43.40	4.91	13.41	15	7.6	39.3	30.7	51.7	82.9	59.9	24.6
Canned & Pres. Fruits,	1.63	2.80	11.25	20.02	3.13	7.45	24	5.1	51.9	63.5	121.7	148.5	86.3	55.2
Veg. & Sea Foods (75)	1.25	1.75	6.23	11.21	2.06	4.31	40	3.3	75.4	118.6	152.5	255.3	119.6	123.0

* Standard Industrial Classification (SIC) Categories.

SOURCE: *Key Business Ratios in* 125 *Lines*, 1967 (New York: Dun & Bradstreet, Inc.). Reprinted by permission of Dun & Bradstreet.

averages contained in the RMA studies, therefore, provide a relatively high-quality basis for comparison. However, for most industries the RMA studies now compute ratios for groups of firms based on total asset size to show how financial ratios vary with firm size.

QUARTERLY FINANCIAL REPORT FOR MANUFACTURING CORPORATIONS. The Federal Trade Commission (FTC) and the Securities and Exchange Commission (SEC) jointly publish quarterly data on manufacturing companies. Both balance sheet and income statement data are developed from a systematic sample of corporations. The reports are published within perhaps six months after the financial data have been made available by the companies. They include an analysis by industry groups and by asset size, as well as financial statements in ratio form (or common-size analysis). The FTC–SEC reports are a rich source of information and are frequently used for comparative purposes.

INDIVIDUAL FIRMS. Credit departments of individual firms compile financial ratios and averages (1) on their customers in order to judge their ability to meet obligations and (2) on their suppliers in order to evaluate their financial ability to fulfill contracts. The First National Bank of Chicago, for instance, compiles semiannual reports on the financial data for finance companies. The National Cash Register Company gathers data for a large number of business lines.

TRADE ASSOCIATIONS AND PUBLIC ACCOUNTANTS. Financial ratios for many industries are compiled by trade associations and constitute an important source to be checked by a financial manager seeking comparative data. In addition, accounting firms specializing in certain lines (for example, textiles or canning) will compile averages of financial ratios for the confidential use of their clients. These averages are usually the best obtainable. In addition to balance sheet data, they provide detailed information on operating expenses, which makes possible an informed analysis of the efficiency of the firms.

USE OF FINANCIAL RATIOS IN CREDIT ANALYSIS

Thus far in the chapter we have discussed a rather long list of ratios and have learned what each ratio is designed to measure. Sometimes it will be unnecessary to go beyond a few calculations to determine that a firm is in very good or very bad condition, but often the analysis is equivalent to a detective-story investigation—what one ratio will not indicate, another may. Also, a relation vaguely suggested by one ratio may be corroborated by another. For these reasons, it is often useful to calculate a number of different ratios.

In numerous situations, however, a few ratios will tell the story. For example, a credit manager who has a large number of invoices flowing across his desk each day may limit himself to three ratios as evidence of whether the prospective buyer of his goods will pay promptly: (1) The credit manager uses the current ratio to determine how burdened the prospective buyer is with current liabilities. (2) The credit manager uses the debt ratio to determine how much of the prospective buyer's own funds are invested in the business. If the funds of the prospective buyer are low, he is probably short of working capital and is likely to fall behind in his payments. (3) The credit manager uses one of the profitability ratios to see whether or not the firm has favorable prospects. If the profit margin is high enough, it may justify the risk of dealing with a slow-paying customer. Profitable companies are likely to grow and, thus, to become better customers in the future. However, if the profit margin is low relative to other firms in the industry, if the current ratio is low, and if the debt ratio is high, a credit manager probably will not approve a sale involving an extension of credit.[6]

Of necessity, the credit manager is more than a calculator and a reader of financial ratios. Qualitative factors may override quantitative analysis. Oil companies, for instance, in selling to truckers often find that the financial ratios are adverse and that if they based their decisions solely on financial ratios, they would not make sales. Or, to take another example, profits may have been low for a period, but if the customer understands why profits have been low and can remove the cause of the difficulty, a credit man may be willing to approve a sale to him. The credit man's decision is also influenced by his own firm's profit margin. If the selling firm is making a large profit on sales, then it is in a better position to take credit risks than if its margin is low. Ultimately, the credit manager must judge a customer with regard to his character and management ability, and intelligent credit decisions must be based on careful consideration of conditions in the selling as well as in the buying firm.

[6] Statistical techniques have been developed to improve the use of ratios in credit analysis. One such development is the discriminant analysis model reported recently by Edward I. Altman ("Financial Ratios, Discriminant Analysis, and the Prediction of Corporate Bankruptcy," *Journal of Finance,* XXIII, September 1968). In this model, Altman combines a number of liquidity, leverage, activity, and profitability ratios to form an index of a firm's probability of going bankrupt. His model predicted bankruptcy quite well one or two years in advance, but was not so satisfactory for longer periods. We can anticipate further work along these lines, and an increasing use of statistical techniques in credit and other types of financial analysis.

USE OF FINANCIAL RATIOS IN SECURITY ANALYSIS

We have emphasized the use of financial analysis internally—by the financial manager to seek ways of improving his firm's performance—and in extending credit. However, this type of analysis is also useful in security analysis, or the analysis of the investment merits of stocks and bonds. When the emphasis is on security analysis, the principal focus is on judging the long-run profit potential of the firm. Profitability is dependent in large part on the efficiency with which the firm is run; since financial analysis provides insights into this factor, financial analysis is useful to the security analyst.

REFERENCE GUIDES FOR RATIO ANALYSIS

Financial ratio analysis enables the financial manager to gauge the progress of his firm and to judge how it appears to others, especially stockholders and creditors. The number and the kinds of ratios he uses

TABLE 3–5 SUMMARY OF FINANCIAL RATIOS AND REFERENCE GUIDES FOR LARGE MANUFACTURING FIRMS

I. Liquidity	
1. Current ratio	2/1
2. Quick ratio	1/1
II. Leverage	
3. Debt to total assets	40 percent
4. Times interest earned	8 times
5. Fixed charge coverage	4 times
III. Activity	
6. Inventory turnover	9 times
7. Average collection period	varies with credit terms
8. Fixed assets turnover	varies
9. Total asset turnover	varies
IV. Profitability	
10. Gross profit on sales	4–6 percent
11. Return on total assets	10–12 percent
12. Return on net worth	13–15 percent

depend upon the nature of the industry and the size and age of the firm. The ratios discussed in this chapter are summarized with norms for large manufacturing firms, where such ratios are available, in Table 3–5. For most types of analyses the financial manager need not utilize all the ratios we have indicated. Usually, only a selected few are necessary. However, the financial manager will also find it useful to make trend comparisons or comparisons with other firms, or both.

It is also important to realize that for many types of decisions, financial ratios are only a beginning. They give the financial manager just a fraction of the information he needs for making a decision. Ultimately, the financial manager's success rests on his judgment of men and on his ability to judge future events.

SUMMARY

Ratio analysis, which relates balance sheet and income statement items to one another, permits the charting of the history of a firm and the evaluation of its present position. Thorough analysis also allows the financial manager to anticipate reactions of investors and creditors and, thus, gives him a good insight into how his request for funds is likely to be met.

Basic Types of Ratios

Ratios are classified into four basic types: (1) liquidity, (2) leverage, (3) activity, and (4) profitability. Data from the Walker-Wilson Manufacturing Company are used to compute each type of ratio and to show how a financial analysis is made in practice. An almost unlimited number of ratios may be calculated, but in practice a limited number of each type are sufficient. What are probably the twelve most common ratios are discussed in this chapter.

Use of Ratios

A ratio is not a meaningful number in and of itself—it must be compared with something before it becomes useful. The two basic kinds of comparative analysis are (1) trend analysis and (2) comparisons with other firms in the same industry. *Trend analysis* involves computing the ratios of a particular firm for several years and comparing the ratios over time to see if the firm is improving or deteriorating. *Comparative analysis,* as defined here, means comparing the key ratios of the firm under study with those of another firm in the same industry or, even better, with an industry average. These two types of comparisons are often combined in the kind of graphic analysis illustrated in Figure 3–1.

Some reference to ratios will be made in each remaining chapter in the text, so it is imperative that the student be thoroughly familiar with the nature of the key ratios. The following chapter will help in gaining this understanding, as it begins by showing how certain ratios are directly related to others.

QUESTIONS

3–1 "A uniform system of accounts, including identical forms for balance sheets and income statements, would be a most reasonable requirement for the SEC to impose on all publicly owned firms." Discuss.

3–2 There are four groups of financial ratios: liquidity, leverage, activity, and profitability. Financial analysis is conducted by four types of analysts: management, equity investors, long-term creditors, and short-term creditors.

a) Explain the nature of each type of ratio.

b) Explain the emphasis of each type of analyst.

c) Could the same basic approach to financial analysis be taken by each group of analysts?

3–3 How can a composite of industry averages be used as a norm for comparison with the financial ratios of an individual firm?

3–4 Why can norms with relatively well-defined limits be stated in advance for some financial ratios but not for others?

3–5 Why should financial ratio calculations be supplemented by trend analysis?

3–6 Why would the inventory turnover figure be more important to a grocery store than to a shoe repair store?

3–7 Can a firm have a high current ratio and still be unable to pay its bills?

3–8 Can the concept of financial ratio analysis be extended to the field of security analysis? Discuss.

PROBLEMS

3–1 The following data were taken from the financial statements of the Johnston Corporation for the calendar year 1969. The norms given below are from Dun & Bradstreet financial ratios for the metal stamping industry.

a) Fill in the ratios for Johnston.

b) Indicate by comparison with the industry norms the errors in management policies reflected in these financial statements.

JOHNSTON CORPORATION
BALANCE SHEET
December 31, 1969

Cash	$ 22,000	Accounts payable	$ 16,500
Receivables	27,500	Notes payable (5%)	22,000
Inventory	82,500	Other current liab.	11,000
Total current assets	132,000	Total current liab.	49,500
Net property	60,500	Long-term debt (6%)	22,000
		Net worth	121,000
Total assets	$192,500	Total claims on assets	$192,500

JOHNSTON CORPORATION
INCOME STATEMENT
For Year Ended December 31, 1969

Sales		$275,000
Cost of goods sold		
Materials	$104,500	
Labor	66,000	
Heat, light, and power	9,900	
Indirect labor	16,500	
Depreciation (10%)	6,050	202,950
Gross profit		$ 72,050
Selling expenses	$ 27,500	
General and administrative expenses	22,550	50,050
Operating profit		22,000
Less: Interest expense		1,320
Net profit before taxes		20,680
Less: Federal income taxes		10,340
Net profit		$ 10,340

RATIOS

Ratio	*Johnston*	*Norm*
$\frac{\text{current assets}}{\text{current liabilities}}$	______	2.5 times
$\frac{\text{sales}}{\text{inventories}}$	______	9.9 times
average collection period	______	33 days
$\frac{\text{sales}}{\text{total assets}}$	______	1.3 times (assumed)
$\frac{\text{net profit}}{\text{sales}}$	______	3.3%
$\frac{\text{net profit}}{\text{total assets}}$	______	3.8%
$\frac{\text{net profit}}{\text{net worth}}$	______	10.7%

3–2 For one set of the pairs of companies listed below, chart the following financial ratios over the past seven years (This problem requires library research. Data may be obtained from company reports or from an investment manual such as Moody's Industrials or Standard and Poor's Industrials). The data gathered for this problem should be kept, as it will be needed for problem 4-1.

Current ratio
Total debt to net worth
Sales to total assets
Average collection period
Sales to inventory (inventory turnover)
Profit after fixed charges and taxes to sales
Profit after fixed charges and taxes to net worth
Operating expenses to sales

General Motors and Chrysler
Boeing and Lockheed
Sperry Rand and International Business Machines
Standard Oil of New Jersey and Standard Oil of California
General Electric and Westinghouse

a) Compare the trends in the return on net worth for each of the two companies in the pair you are analyzing.
b) Indicate the reasons for any difference in trends in the rate of return on net worth suggested by your time-trend analysis.

3–3 After a 50-year history of prompt payments, the Greenwald Company, a small manufacturing firm, was unable to meet a scheduled payment on its bank loan. As a consequence, in January 1969, the president, Brooks Jones, and the financial vice president, Bob Avery, were preparing for a meeting with the bank. They planned to ask for an extension of the current note and an increase in the line of credit.

To finance its seasonal expansion of current assets, the company normally borrowed from the Merchants Bank and generally repaid the loans within two to three months. The current line of credit allowed unsecured borrowing up to $70,000, but it required full payment of the outstanding balance by February 1969.

During the second half of 1968, the market for Greenwald's products deteriorated, and competitive pressures narrowed profit margins. On the average, firms in the industry experienced sales declines of about 9 percent for the entire year. The Greenwald Company, however, achieved a small increase in sales during the last six months of 1968 because of an aggressive marketing program.

Jones and Avery knew that they could not continue the present sales level without an increase in the bank loan from $70,000 to

$100,000, as an additional $30,000 was required to liquidate overdue accounts payable. The company had been a good customer of the bank for many years, so Jones and Avery were confident that the funds would be made available.

The Federal Reserve had recently tightened credit considerably, and others of the bank's customers were also seeking additional credit. As a result, the current policy of the bank was to limit new loans, to review critically existing loans, and to grant credit increases only on an exception basis.

The chief loan officer of the bank, John Hill, was responsible for the Greenwald line of credit. The line of credit had been established in 1948, and it was Hill's policy to review all accounts whenever credit conditions changed markedly, as they had recently. This review had been under way even before Jones and Avery approached the bank for a loan extension.

Because the Greenwald Company had fallen behind on its payments to suppliers, Hill classified it as a "slow pay account." He figured the company had suffered from not being able to take advantage of the 2 percent trade discounts on $200,000 worth of purchases during 1968. In some cases, the company was even 60 days late in paying invoices carrying terms of 2/10, N/30.* He felt that if the situation continued, some suppliers might insist on cash on delivery.

In the loan officer's opinion, the working-capital problems of Greenwald Company were those related to rapid growth and overly ambitious expansion. Cash dividends by the company were nominal, but the bank had not been in favor of some of the large capital expenditures the company had made in recent years. In 1967, the company had an opportunity to purchase for $20,000 the lands and buildings that it had been renting for warehouse facilities. Jones thought this was a good buy because he felt the property was worth at least $30,000. In 1966, improvements were made in the equipment and machinery, costing $16,000. Both Hill and Avery, however, had expressed the opinion that these expenditures created an excessive cash drain on the firm.

In preparing for his meeting with Jones and Avery, the loan officer had reviewed the latest financial statements of Greenwald Company and compared them with a series of financial ratios for the industry.

a) If the loan from the bank was extended to June 30, 1969, would Greenwald Company be able to retire the loan?
b) From the analysis of the financial data, what action should Hill take concerning the extension of the loan and the request for an addition of $30,000 to the line of credit?

* The terms of purchase for Greenwald call for a 2 percent discount if payment is received within 10 days, and the full amount, due within 30 days, if the discount is not taken (that is, 2/10, net 30).

c) With the continued credit rationing policy of banks in general, what other techniques might Bob Avery and John Hill propose to Brooks Jones to get the company out of its current cash crisis?

GREENWALD COMPANY
COMPANY BALANCE SHEET
(as of December 31)

	1960	1966	1967	1968
Cash	$ 10,000	$ 15,000	$ 7,000	$ 5,000
Accounts receivable	40,000	60,000	68,000	95,000
Inventory	50,000	75,000	125,000	202,500
Total current assets	$100,000	$150,000	$200,000	$302,500
Land and building	$ 15,000	$ 12,000	$ 32,000	$ 30,000
Machinery	20,000	37,000	29,000	25,000
Other assets	12,000	7,000	2,000	1,500
Total assets	$147,000	$206,000	$263,000	$359,000
Notes payable, bank	—	—	$ 25,000	$ 70,000
Accounts and notes payable	$ 22,000	$ 24,000	38,000	75,000
Accruals	10,000	12,000	14,000	19,000
Total current liabilities	$ 32,000	$ 36,000	$ 77,000	$164,000
Mortgage	$ 15,000	$ 11,000	$ 10,000	$ 9,000
Common stock	50,000	50,000	50,000	50,000
Capital surplus	40,000	40,000	40,000	40,000
Earned surplus	10,000	69,000	86,000	96,000
Total liability and equity	$147,000	$206,000	$263,000	$359,000

GREENWALD COMPANY
INCOME STATEMENT

	1966	1967	1968
Net sales	$650,000	$675,000	$700,000
Cost of goods sold	520,000	540,000	560,000
Gross operating profit	$130,000	$135,000	$140,000
General admin. and selling	$ 50,000	$ 55,000	$ 60,000
Depreciation	20,000	25,000	30,000
Miscellaneous	10,000	21,000	30,000
Net income before taxes	$ 50,000	$ 34,000	$ 20,000
Taxes (50%)	25,000	17,000	10,000
Net income	$ 25,000	$ 17,000	$ 10,000

RATIOS

	Industry Average, 1968*
Current ratio	2.5
Inventory turnover	8x
Average collection period	30 days
Total asset turnover	2.5x
Return on net worth	14%

* Industry average ratios have been relatively constant over the past three years.

Selected References

Altman, E. I., "Financial Ratios, Discriminant Analysis, and the Prediction of Corporate Bankruptcy," *Journal of Finance,* XXIII, September 1968, pp. 589–609.

Bierman, Harold Jr., "Measuring Financial Liquidity," *Accounting Review,* XXXV (October 1960).

Davidson, Sidney, George H. Sorter, and Hemu Kalle, "Measuring the Defensive Position of a Firm," *Financial Analysts Journal,* XX (January–February 1964), 23–39.

Donaldson, Gordon, "New Framework for Corporate Debt Capacity," *Harvard Business Review,* XL (March–April 1962).

Foulke, Roy A., *Practical Financial Statement Analysis,* 5th ed. (New York: McGraw-Hill, 1961).

Graham, Benjamin. and George McGobrick, *The Interpretation of Financial Statements,* rev. ed. (New York: Harper & Row, 1964).

Helfert, Erich A., *Techniques of Financial Analysis,* rev. ed. (Homewood, Ill.: Irwin, 1967).

Horrigan, James O., "Some Empirical Bases of Financial Ratio Analysis," *Accounting Review,* XXXX, (July 1965).

Jaedicke, Robert K., and Robert T. Sprouse, *Accounting Flows: Income, Funds, and Cash.* (Englewood Cliffs, N.J.: Prentice-Hall, 1965).

McCloud, B. G., Jr., "Pitfalls in Statement Analysis," *Bulletin of the Robert Morris Associates,* 39 (January 1957), 143–148.

Meyer, John M., *Financial Statement Analysis,* 3d ed., (Englewood Cliffs, N.J.: Prentice-Hall, 1961).

Sanzo, R., *Ratio Analysis for Small Business,* Small Business Management Series, No. 20 (Washington, D.C.: U.S. Government Printing Office, 1957).

Sorter, George H., and George Benston, "Appraising the Defensive Position of a Firm: The Internal Measure," *Accounting Review,* XXXV (October 1960), 633–640.

4

Financial Control

The preceding chapter described certain ratios used in financial analysis. This chapter extends the analysis to show how the ratios relate to one another, and it then introduces two other tools of financial analysis—break-even charts and sources and uses of funds statements.

DU PONT SYSTEM OF FINANCIAL CONTROL[1]

The du Pont system of financial control has achieved wide recognition in American industry, and properly so. It brings

[1] Descriptions of the du Pont system are contained in T. C. Davis, *How the du Pont Organization Appraises Its Performance,* Financial Management Series, No. 94 (New York: American Management Association Treasurer's Department, 1950); C. A. Kline, Jr. and H. L. Hessler, "The du Pont Chart System for Appraising Operating Performance," *N.A.C.A. Bulletin* 33 (August 1952), 1595–1619; and *Executive Committee Control Charts,* prepared by E. I. du Pont de Nemours and Company (Wilmington, Delaware: E. I. du Pont de Nemours & Co., 1959).

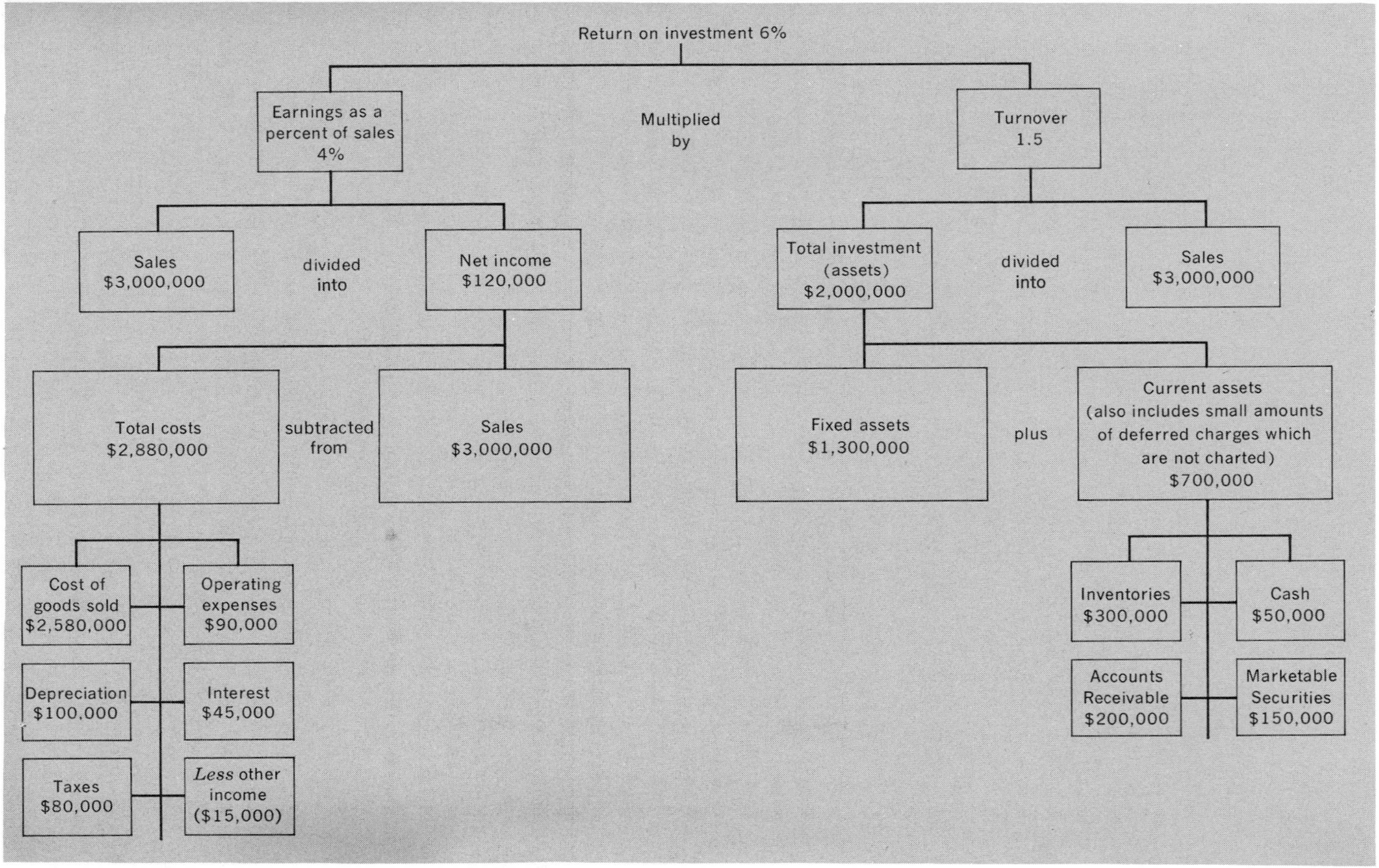

Return on investment 6%
Earnings as a percent of sales 4%
Multiplied by
Turnover 1.5
Sales $3,000,000
divided into
Net income $120,000
Total investment (assets) $2,000,000
divided into
Sales $3,000,000
Total costs $2,880,000
subtracted from
Sales $3,000,000
Fixed assets $1,300,000
plus
Current assets (also includes small amounts of deferred charges which are not charted) $700,000
Cost of goods sold $2,580,000
Operating expenses $90,000
Depreciation $100,000
Interest $45,000
Taxes $80,000
Less other income ($15,000)
Inventories $300,000
Cash $50,000
Accounts Receivable $200,000
Marketable Securities $150,000

Figure 4–1 Modified du Pont System of Financial Control

together the activity ratios and profit margin on sales and shows how these ratios interact to determine the profitability of assets. The nature of the system, modified somewhat, is set forth in Figure 4–1.

The right side of the figure develops the turnover ratio. This section shows how current assets (marketable securities, inventories, accounts receivable, and cash) added to fixed assets gives total investment. Total investment divided into sales gives the turnover of investment. The left side of the figure develops the profit margin on sales. The individual expense items plus income taxes are subtracted from sales to produce net profits after taxes. Net profits divided by sales gives the profit margin on sales. When the asset turnover ratio is multiplied by the profit margin on sales, the product is the return on total investment in the firm. This can be seen from the following formula.

$$\frac{\text{sales}}{\text{investment}} \times \frac{\text{profit}}{\text{sales}} = \frac{\text{profit}}{\text{investment}}$$

As analyzed in Chapter 3, Walker-Wilson's turnover was seen to be 1.5 times, as compared to an industry average of 2 times; its margin on sales was 4 percent, as compared to 5 percent for the industry. Multiplied together, turnover and profit margin produced a return on assets equal to 6 percent, a rate well below the 10 percent industry average. If Thompson is to bring Walker-Wilson back to the level of the rest of the industry, he should strive to boost both his profit margin and his total asset turnover. Tracing back through the du Pont system should help him in this task.

Extending the du Pont System to Include Leverage

Although Walker-Wilson's return on total investment is below the 10 percent industry average, the firm's 12 percent return on net worth is only slightly below the 15 percent industry average. How can the return on net worth end up so close to the industry average when the return on total assets is so far below the average? The answer is that Walker-Wilson uses more debt than the industry average.

Only one half of Walker-Wilson's assets are financed with net worth; the other half is financed with debt. This means that the entire 6 percent return on assets (which is computed after interest charges on debt) goes to the common and preferred stockholders, so their return is boosted substantially. The precise formula for measuring the effect of financial leverage on stockholder returns is shown below.

$$\text{percentage return on net worth} = \frac{\text{percentage return on assets}}{\text{percent of assets financed by net worth}}$$
$$= \frac{\text{percentage return on assets}}{1.0 - \text{debt ratio}}$$

Calculation for Walker-Wilson:

$$\text{return on net worth} = \frac{6\%}{1.0 - 0.50} = \frac{6\%}{0.5} = 12\%$$

Calculation for the industry average:

$$\text{return on net worth} = \frac{10\%}{1.0 - 0.33} = \frac{10\%}{0.67} = 15\%$$

This formula is useful for showing how financial leverage can be used to increase the rate of return on net worth.[2] But increasing returns on net worth by using more and more leverage causes the leverage ratios to rise higher and higher above the industry norms. Creditors resist this tendency, so there are limitations to the practice. Moreover, greater leverage increases the risk of bankruptcy and thus endangers the firm's stockholders. Since Mrs. Walker and Mrs. Wilson, the widows of the firm's founders, are entirely dependent on income from the firm for their support, they would be in a particularly bad position should the firm go into default. Consequently, Thompson would be ill-advised to attempt to use leverage to boost the return on net worth much further.

RATES OF RETURN IN DIFFERENT INDUSTRIES

Would it be better to have a 5 percent margin on sales and an assets turnover of 2 times, or a 2 percent sales margin and a turnover of 5 times? It makes no difference—in either case the firm has a 10 percent

[2] There are limitations on this statement—specifically, the return on net worth increases with leverage only if the return on assets exceeds the rate of interest on debt, after giving account to the tax deductibility of interest payments. This whole concept is explored in detail in Chapter 9, which is devoted entirely to financial leverage.

return on investment. Actually, most firms are not free to make the kind of choice posed in the above question. Depending on the nature of its industry, the firm *must* operate with more or fewer assets, and it will experience a turnover that depends on the characteristics of its particular line of business. In the case of a dealer in fresh fruits and vegetables, fish, or other perishable items, the turnover should be high—every day or two would be most desirable. In contrast, some lines of business require very heavy fixed investment or long production periods. A hydroelectric utility company, with its heavy investment in dams and transmission lines, for example, requires heavy fixed investment; a shipbuilder or an aircraft producer, for example, needs a long production period. Such companies necessarily have a low asset turnover rate but a correspondingly higher profit margin on sales.

If a grocery chain has a high turnover, and a chemical producer, with its heavy investment in fixed assets, a low turnover, would you expect to find differences in their profit margins on sales? In general, you would—the chemical producer should have a considerably higher profit margin to offset its lower turnover. Otherwise, the grocery business would be much more profitable than the chemical, investment would flow into the grocery industry, and profits in this industry would be eroded to the point where the rate of return was about equal to that in the chemical industry.

We know, however, that leverage must be taken into account when considering the rate of return on net worth. If the firms in one industry have a somewhat lower return on total assets but use slightly more financial leverage than do those in another industry, both sets of firms may end up with approximately the same rate of return on net worth.[3]

These points, which are all necessary to a complete understanding of ratio analysis, are illustrated in Table 4–1. Here we see how turnover and profit margins interact with each other to produce varying returns on assets and also how financial leverage affects the returns on net worth. Hercules, Inc., Safeway Stores, and the average of all manufacturing firms are compared. Hercules, with its very heavy fixed asset investment, is seen to have a relatively low turnover, while Safeway, a typical chain food store, has a very high sales-to-assets ratio. However, Hercules ends up with about the same rate of return on assets because its high profit margin on sales compensates for its low turnover. Both Safeway and Hercules use financial leverage to increase their return on net worth.

[3] The factors that make it possible for firms to use more leverage are taken up in Chapters 9, 10, and 11. It may be stated now, however, that the primary factor favoring leverage is sales stability.

TABLE 4–1 TURNOVER, PROFIT MARGINS, AND RETURNS ON NET WORTH, 1966

	SALES TO TOTAL ASSETS	PROFIT TO SALES	PROFIT TO TOTAL ASSETS	DEBT TO TOTAL ASSETS	PROFIT TO NET WORTH*
All manufacturing firms	1.60×	5.6%	8.9%	41%	15.1%
Hercules, Inc. (chemical producer)	1.15	8.5	9.8	32	14.4
Safeway Stores (food retailer)	5.23	1.8	9.4	40	15.7

* The figures in this column may be found as:

$$\text{profit to net worth} = \frac{\text{profit to total assets}}{1 - \text{debt to total assets}}$$

SOURCES: Moody's Investors Service, FTC-SEC Bulletins, Robert Morris Associates, and Annual Statement Studies.

BREAK-EVEN ANALYSIS

Break-even analysis, another important financial tool, is basically an analytical technique for studying the relations among fixed costs, variable costs, and profits. If a firm's costs were all variable, the problem of break-even volume would never arise. But by having some variable and some fixed costs, the firm must suffer losses up to a given volume.

Break-even analysis is a formal profit-planning approach based on established relations between costs and revenues. It is a device for determining the point at which sales will just cover total costs. If the firm is to avoid losses, its sales must cover all costs—those that vary directly with production and those that do not change as production levels change. Costs that fall into each of these categories are outlined below.

Fixed Costs[4]	*Direct or Variable Costs*
Depreciation on plant and equipment	Factory labor
Rentals	Materials
Interest charges on debt	Sales commissions
Salaries of research staff	
Salaries of executive staff	
General office expenses	

[4] Some of these costs—for example, salaries and office expenses—could be varied to some degree; however, firms are reluctant to reduce these expenditures in response to temporary fluctuations in sales.

The nature of break-even analysis is depicted in Figure 4–2, the basic break-even chart. The chart is on a unit basis, with volume produced shown on the horizontal axis and costs and income measured on the vertical axis. Fixed costs of $40,000 are represented by a horizontal line, that is, they are the same (fixed) regardless of the number of units produced. Variable costs are assumed to be $1.20 a unit. Total costs rise by $1.20, the amount of the variable costs, for each additional unit produced. Production is assumed to be sold at $2 a unit, so the total income is pictured as a straight line, which must also increase with production. The positive slope (or the rate of ascent) of the total-income line is steeper than that of the total-cost line. This must be true, because the firm is gaining $2 of revenue for every $1.20 paid out for labor and materials, the variable costs.

Up to the break-even point, found at the intersection of the total income and total-cost lines, the firm suffers losses. After that point, the

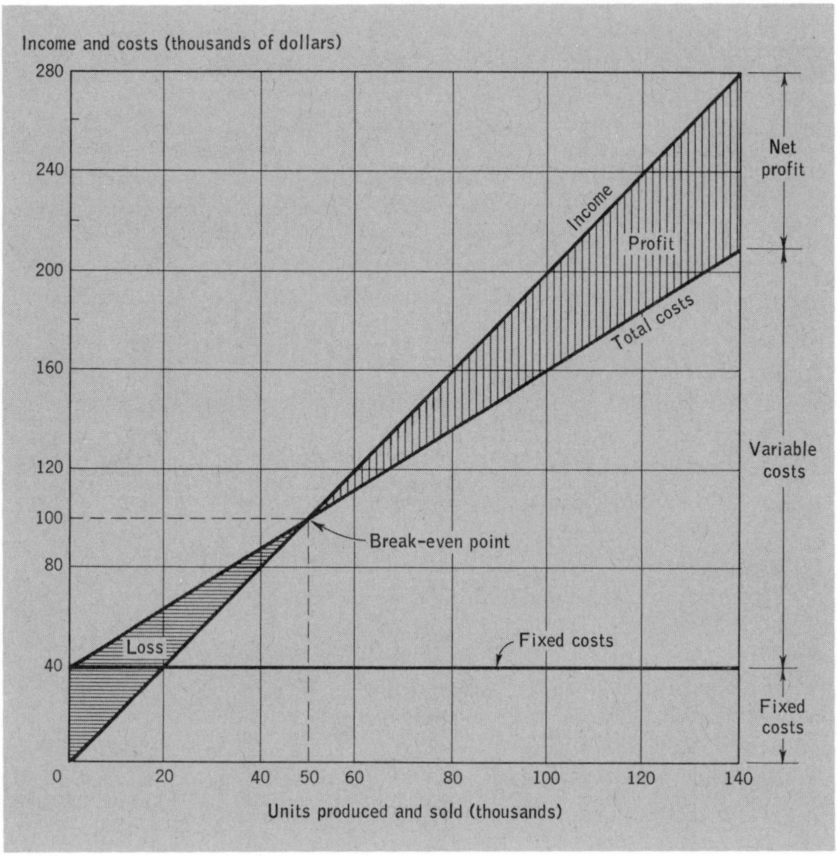

Figure 4–2 Break-Even Chart

TABLE 4–2 RELATIONS AMONG UNITS PRODUCED, TOTAL VARIABLE COSTS, FIXED COSTS, TOTAL COSTS, AND TOTAL INCOME

A. TRIAL-AND-ERROR CALCULATIONS

Units sold	Total variable costs	Fixed costs	Total costs	Sales	Net profit (loss)
20,000	$ 24,000	$40,000	$ 64,000	$ 40,000	$(24,000)
40,000	48,000	40,000	88,000	80,000	(8,000)
50,000	60,000	40,000	100,000	100,000	—
60,000	72,000	40,000	112,000	120,000	8,000
80,000	96,000	40,000	136,000	160,000	24,000
100,000	120,000	40,000	160,000	200,000	40,000
120,000	144,000	40,000	184,000	240,000	56,000
140,000	168,000	40,000	208,000	280,000	72,000

B. ALGEBRAIC SOLUTION TO BREAK-EVEN POINT

1. The break-even quantity is defined as that volume of output at which revenue is just equal to total costs (fixed costs plus variable costs).

2. Let:

P = sales price per unit
Q = quantity produced and sold
F = fixed costs
V = variable costs per unit

3. Then:

$$P \cdot Q = F + V \cdot Q$$
$$P \cdot Q - V \cdot Q = F$$
$$Q(P - V) = F$$
$$Q = \frac{F}{P - V} \text{ at break-even } Q$$

4. Illustration:

$$Q = \frac{\$40{,}000}{\$2.00 - \$1.20}$$
$$= 50{,}000 \text{ units}$$

firm begins to make profits. Figure 4–2 indicates a break-even point at a sales and costs level of $100,000 and a production level of 50,000 units.

More exact calculations of the break-even point can be carried out algebraically or by trial and error. In section A of Table 4–2, profit-and-loss relations are shown for various levels of sales; in section B the algebraic calculations are carried out.

Nonlinear Break-Even Analysis

In break-even analysis, linear (straight line) relationships are generally assumed. It complicates matters slightly, but it is easy enough to use nonlinear relationships. For example, it is reasonable to think that increased sales can be obtained if sales prices are reduced. Similarly, empirical studies suggest that the average variable cost per unit falls over some range of output, then begins to rise.

These assumptions are illustrated in Figure 4–3. Here we see a loss region when sales are low, a profit region (and a maximum profit), and another loss region at very high output levels.

Although nonlinear break-even analysis is intellectually appealing, linear analysis is probably more appropriate for the uses to which it

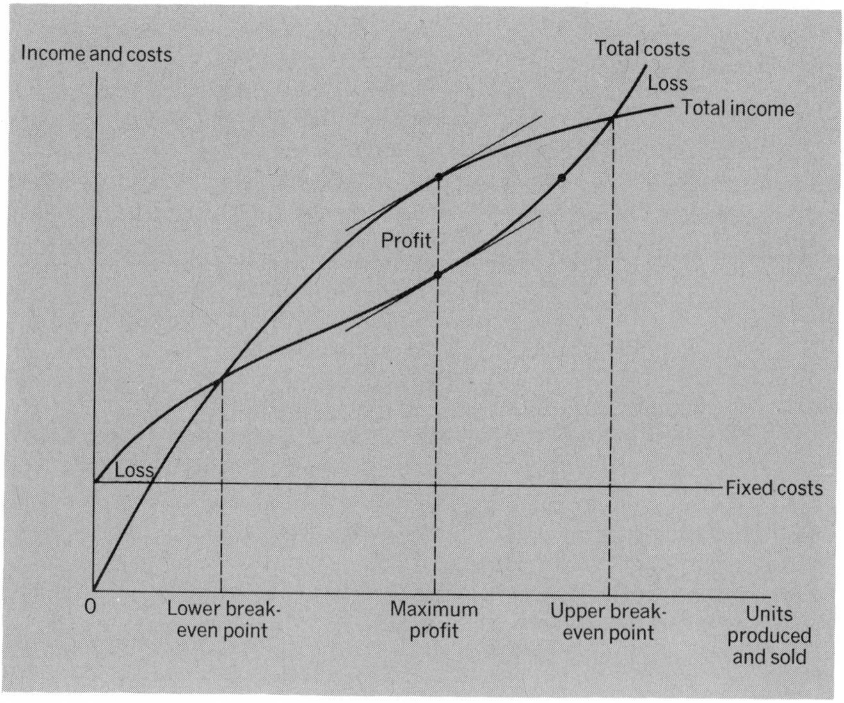

Figure 4–3 Nonlinear Break-Even Chart

NOTE: The angle of a line from the origin to a point on the total-income line measures price, that is, total income/units sold = price—and a line from the origin to the total-cost curve measures cost per unit. It can be seen that the angle of the line to the revenue curve declines as we move toward higher sales, which means the price is falling. Unit costs (Total Cost/Units Produced) declines to point X, the tangency point of a line from the origin to the total-cost curve, then begins to rise. The slopes of the total-cost and total-income lines measure marginal cost (MC) and marginal revenue (MR) respectively. At the point where the slopes of the two total curves are equal, $MR = MC$, and profits are at a maximum.

is put. Break-even charts allow focus to be placed on the key elements: sales, fixed costs, and variable costs. Even though linear break-even charts are drawn extending from *zero* output to very high output levels, no one who uses them would ordinarily be interested in or even consider the high and low extremes. In other words, users of break-even charts are really interested only in a "relevant range," and within this range linear functions are probably reasonably accurate.

An Example of Break-Even Analysis

The textbook publishing business is a good example of the effective use of break-even analysis. To illustrate, consider the following hypothetical example of the analysis for a college textbook. The costs and revenues are graphed in Figure 4–4.

FIXED COSTS	
Copy editing	$ 3,000
Art work	1,000
Type setting	36,000
Total fixed costs	$40,000
VARIABLE COSTS PER COPY	
Printing and binding	$ 1.10
Bookstore commissions	2.00
Salesman's commissions	.25
Author's royalties	1.00
General and administrative costs	.50
Total variable costs per copy	$ 4.85
Sales price per copy	$10.00

The fixed costs can be estimated quite accurately; the variable costs, which are set by contracts, can also be precisely estimated (and they are linear). The sales price is variable, but competition keeps prices within a sufficiently narrow range to make a linear total-revenue curve reasonable. Applying the formula, we find the break-even sales volume to be 7,767 copies.

Publishers know the size of the total market for a given book, "the competition," and so forth. With this data as a base, they can estimate the possibilities that a given book will reach or exceed the break-even point. If the estimate is that it will not, the publisher may consider cutting production costs by doing less art work and editing, using a lower grade of paper, negotiating with the author on royalty rates, and so on. In this particular business—and especially for new product deci-

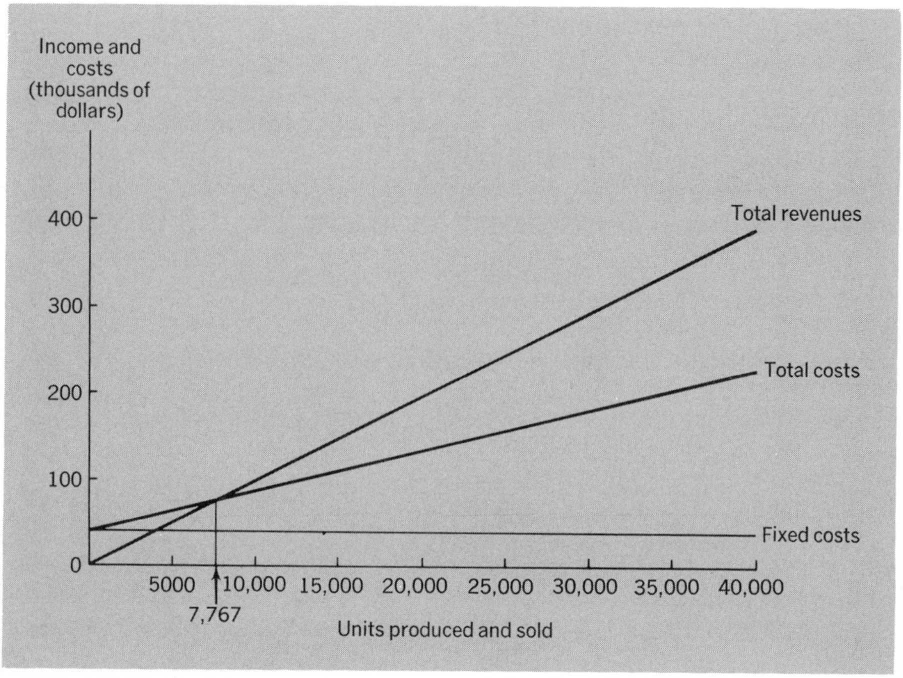

Figure 4–4 Break-Even Chart for a Hypothetical Textbook

sions in many others—linear break-even analysis has proved itself to be a useful tool.[5]

Break-Even Point Based on Totals

Calculating break-even points on the basis of dollar sales instead of on units of output is especially useful (see Table 4–3). The main advantage of this method is that it enables one to determine a general break-even point for a firm that sells several related products at varying

[5] Although it is not really relevant for pedagogic purposes, we ought to finish our analysis of the economics of textbook publishing. In terms that will be developed more fully in Chapter 8, textbook publishing is a "high variance" industry—most books do not come close to the break-even point, but a few are "real winners." Publishers can make an educated guess about how a book will do—and the better publishers are the better guessers—but there is still a great deal of uncertainty.

Because of the relatively low overhead and very high profit margin on sales, it pays publishers to gamble and to put out many books in the hope of getting a few that dominate the market. However, in our conversations with publishers, we get the impression that the industry is undergoing a change. Competition is forcing publishers to employ more costly production processes and techniques, and this is raising both fixed and variable costs and increasing the break-even point. This, of course, is making publishers be more careful in their selection process.

TABLE 4–3 CALCULATION OF BREAK-EVEN POINT BASED ON TOTALS

$$\text{Break-even point (sales volume)} = \frac{\text{total fixed costs}}{1 - \dfrac{\text{total variable costs}}{\text{total sales volume}}}$$

Procedure

Take any quantity and use the related data to determine the break-even point. For example, assume that 20,000 units are produced and use the data in Table 4–2.

$$\text{Break-even point} = \frac{\$40{,}000}{1 - \dfrac{\$24{,}000}{\$40{,}000}} = \frac{\$40{,}000}{0.4} = \$100{,}000$$

Rationale

1. At the break-even point, sales (S) are equal to fixed cost (FC) plus variable cost (VC):

$$S = FC + VC \qquad (1)$$

2. Because both the sales price and the variable cost per unit are assumed to be constant in break-even analysis, the ratio VC/S is also constant and may be found from the annual income statement.
3. Since variable cost is a constant percentage of sales, equation (1) can be rewritten as:

$$S = FC + \frac{VC}{S}(S)$$

$$S\left(1 - \frac{VC}{S}\right) = FC$$

$$S = \frac{FC}{1 - \dfrac{VC}{S}} \text{ at break-even } S$$

prices. Furthermore, the procedure requires a minimum of data. Only three values are needed: sales, fixed costs, and variable costs. Sales and total-cost data are readily available from annual reports of corporations and from investment manuals. Total costs can be determined by deducting net profits from sales. Total costs must then be segregated into fixed and variable components. The major fixed charges (rent, interest, depreciation, and general and administrative expenses) may be taken from the income statement. Finally, variable costs are calculated by deducting fixed costs from total costs.

Operating Leverage

Operating leverage is defined as the extent to which fixed costs are used in operations, and break-even analysis can be used to reflect the degree of operating leverage employed. The formal definition does not fully convey the meaning of leverage, but an example may help. If you were trying to lift the end of a large box in order to place a roller under it, you might insert an iron rod under the box with a sturdy object like a stone as the fulcrum to obtain leverage in lifting. With this lever system, a relatively small amount of pressure can lift a very heavy box. To complete the analogy, the fixed-cost element is the lever that allows a small change in sales to induce a relatively large change in profits.

The significance of the degree of operating leverage is further brought out by Figure 4–5. Three firms, A, B, and C, with differing degrees of leverage are contrasted. Firm A is considered to have a normal amount of fixed costs in its operations. It uses automated equipment (with which one operator can turn out a few or many units at the same labor cost) to about the same extent as the average firm in the industry. Firm B has lower fixed costs, but note the steeper rate of increase in variable costs of this firm over firm A. Firm B, however, breaks even at a lower level of operations than does firm A. At a production level of 40,000 units, firm A is losing $8,000 but firm B breaks even.

On the other hand, firm C has the highest fixed costs. It is highly automated, using expensive, high-speed machines that require very little labor per unit produced. With such an operation, its variable costs rise slowly. Because of the high overhead resulting from charges associated with the expensive machinery, firm C's break-even point is higher than that for either firm A or B. Once firm C reaches its break-even point, however, its profits rise faster than do those of the other firms.

High fixed costs and low variable costs provide the greatest percentage change in profits both upward and downward. The profit behavior follows from economic logic. High fixed costs arise from employing larger amounts of capital, which permit the firm to operate with reduced labor and, thereby, smaller variable costs.

The relative importance of fixed costs is likely to reflect both the technology of the industry and the stability of sales. The nature of the business influences how much equipment will be used in the production process. If sales are stable, the firm will acquire more specialized equipment. If sales fluctuate greatly, the firm will seek more flexibility by using less machinery relative to more purchased parts or labor.

Cash Break-Even Analysis

Another use of break-even analysis is in the analysis of the firm's situation on a cash basis. Some of the firm's fixed costs are noncash

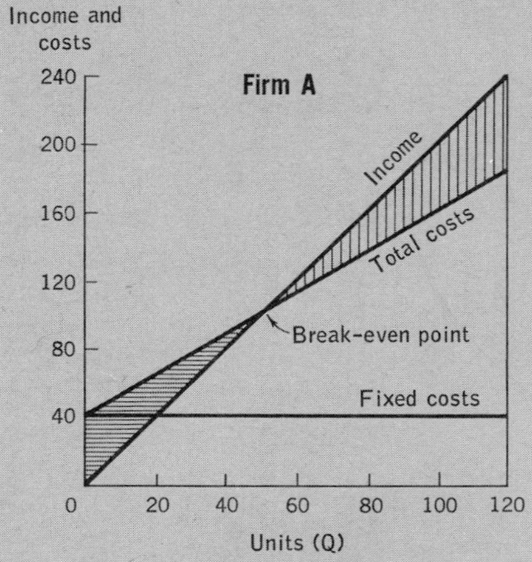

Selling price = $2.00
Fixed costs = $40,000
Variable costs = $1.20 Q

Units sold (Q)	Sales	Costs	Profit
20,000	$40,000	$64,000	−$24,000
40,000	80,000	88,000	−8,000
60,000	120,000	112,000	8,000
80,000	160,000	136,000	24,000
100,000	200,000	160,000	40,000
120,000	240,000	184,000	56,000

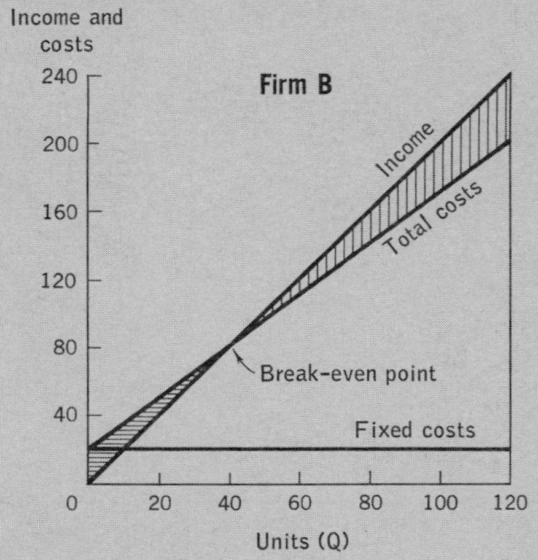

Selling price = $2.00
Fixed costs = $20,000
Variable costs = $1.50 Q

Units sold (Q)	Sales	Costs	Profit
20,000	$40,000	$50,000	−$10,000
40,000	80,000	80,000	0
60,000	120,000	110,000	10,000
80,000	160,000	140,000	20,000
100,000	200,000	170,000	30,000
120,000	240,000	200,000	40,000

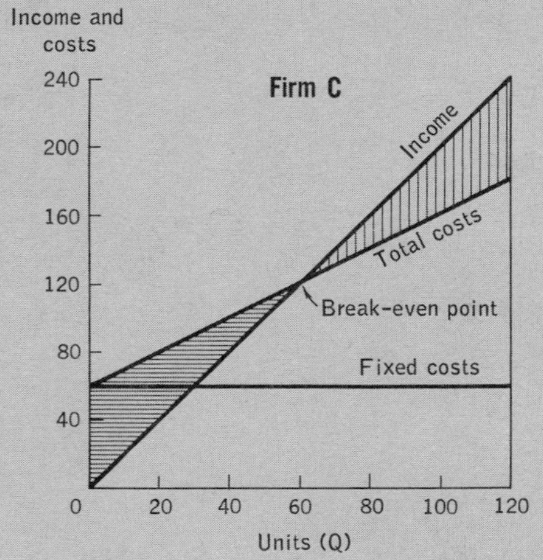

Selling price = $2.00
Fixed costs = $60,000
Variable costs = $1.00 Q

Units sold (Q)	Sales	Costs	Profit
20,000	$40,000	$80,000	−$40,000
40,000	80,000	100,000	−20,000
60,000	120,000	120,000	0
80,000	160,000	140,000	20,000
100,000	200,000	160,000	40,000
120,000	240,000	180,000	60,000

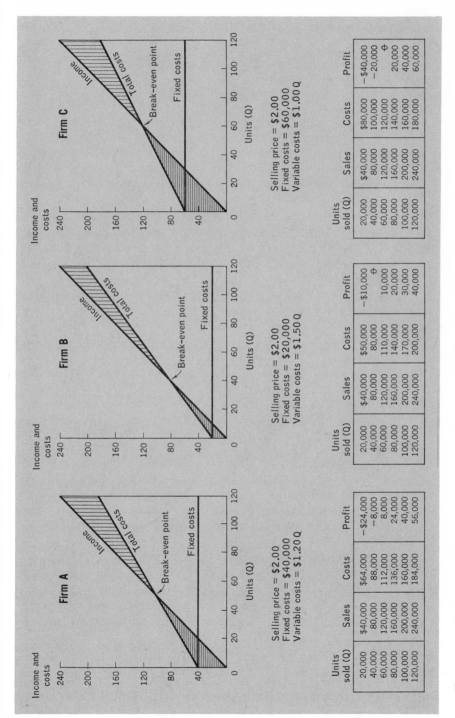

Figure 4–5 Operating Leverage

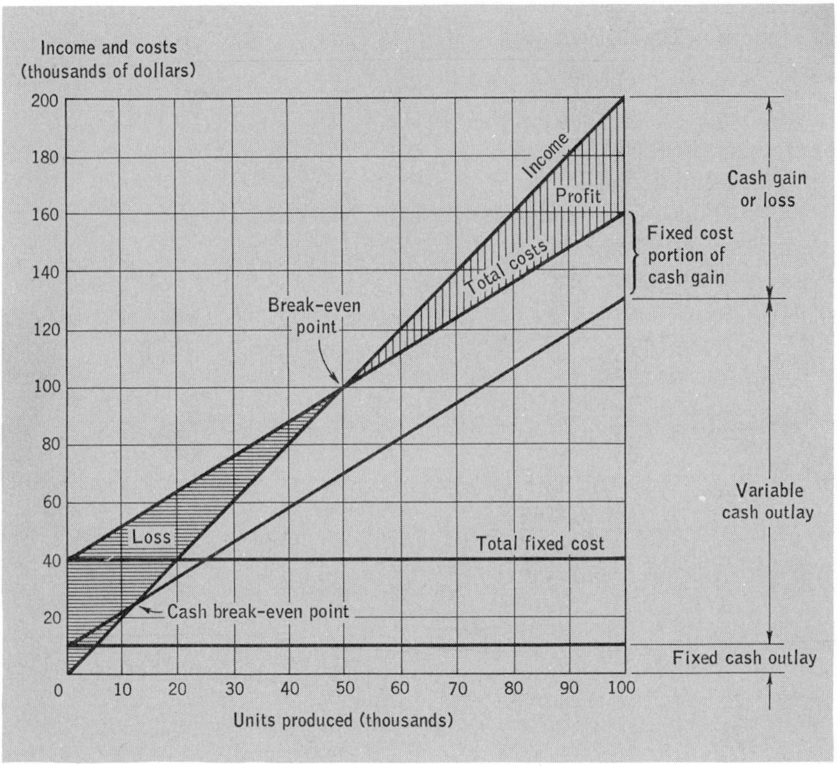

Figure 4–6 Cash Break-Even Analysis

outlays, and for a period some of its revenues may be in receivables. The cash break-even chart for firm D, constructed on the assumption that $30,000 of the fixed costs from the previous illustration are depreciation charges and, therefore, a noncash outlay, is shown in Figure 4–6. Because fixed-cash outlays are only $10,000, the cash break-even point is at 12,500 units rather than 50,000 units, which is the profit break-even point.

Cash break-even analysis does not fully represent cash flows—for this a cash budget is required. But cash break-even analysis is useful because it provides a picture of the flow of funds from operations. A firm could incur a level of fixed costs that would result in losses during periods of poor business but in large profits during upswings. If cash outlays are small, even during periods of losses, the firm might still be operating above the cash break-even point. Thus the risks of insolvency, in the sense of inability to meet cash obligations, would be small. This allows a firm to reach out for higher profits through automation and operating leverage.

Limitations of Break-Even Analysis

Break-even analysis is useful in studying the relations among volume, prices, and cost structure; it is thus helpful in pricing, cost control, and other financial decisions. It has limitations, however, as a guide to managerial actions.

Linear break-even analysis is especially weak in what it implies about the sales possibilities for the firm. Any given break-even chart is based on a constant selling price. Therefore, in order to study profit possibilities under different prices, a whole series of charts is necessary, one chart for each price.

With regard to costs, break-even analysis is also deficient—the relations indicated by the chart do not hold at all outputs. As sales increase, existing plant and equipment are worked to capacity, and both this situation and the use of additional workers and overtime pay cause variable costs to rise sharply. Additional equipment and plant are required, thus increasing fixed costs. Finally, over a period the products sold by the firm change in quality and quantity. Such changes in product mix influence the level and slope of the cost function. In short, break-even analysis is useful as a first step in developing the basic data required for pricing and making financial decisions. However, more detailed analysis is required before final judgments can be made.

SOURCES AND USES OF FUNDS STATEMENT

The sources and uses of funds statement is one of the most useful tools in the financial manager's analytical kit. The basic purpose of the funds statement is to indicate, on an historical basis, where cash came from and how it was used.

When a firm requests a loan, one of the first questions posed by the loan officer is, What has the firm done with the money it had? This question is answered by the sources and application statement. The information it provides may indicate that the firm is making progress or that problems are arising.

Rough-and-Ready Sources and Applications Analysis

To construct the sources and uses statement, one first tabulates the changes in balance sheet items from one year to the next. Each change in the balance sheet may be classified as either a source of funds or a use of funds, according to the following pattern:

Use of funds: (1) increase in asset item or (2) decrease in liability item

Source of funds: (1) decrease in asset item or (2) increase in liability item

An illustration of the financial manager's rough-and-ready analysis of sources and uses of funds is embodied in Tables 4–4 and 4–5.

TABLE 4–4 DALLAS FERTILIZER AND CHEMICAL COMPANY COMPARATIVE BALANCE SHEETS AND SOURCES AND USES OF FUNDS
(in millions of dollars)

	12/31/67	12/31/68	SOURCES	USES
Cash	$ 10	$ 5	$ 5	
Marketable securities	25	15	10	
Net receivables	15	20		$ 5
Inventories	25	30		5
Gross fixed assets	150	180		30
Less: Allowance for depreciation*	(40)	(50)	10	
Net fixed assets	110	130		
Total assets	$185	$200		
Accounts payable	$ 10	$ 6		4
Notes payable	15	10		5
Other current liabilities	10	14	4	
Long-term debt	60	70	10	
Preferred stock	10	10	—	—
Common stock	50	50	—	—
Retained earnings	30	40	10	
Total claims on assets	$185	$200	$49	$49

* The allowance for depreciation is actually a liability account, even though it appears on the left side of the balance sheet. Note that it is deducted, not added, when totaling the column.

Dallas obtained funds by drawing down cash balances, by selling marketable securities, by increasing other current liabilities, by incurring long-term debt, and by retaining earnings. Total funds from these sources were $39 million. An additional $10 million accrued from an increase in the reserve for depreciation. Depreciation expense itself does not produce cash, but it is a noncash outlay. Since it was deducted from revenues

TABLE 4–5 **DALLAS FERTILIZER AND CHEMICAL COMPANY STATEMENT OF SOURCES AND USES OF FUNDS, 1968**
(in millions of dollars)

	AMOUNT	PERCENT
Uses		
Gross fixed assets expansion	$30	61.2
Inventory investment	5	10.2
Increase in receivables	5	10.2
Reduction in notes payable	5	10.2
Reduction in accounts payable	4	8.2
Total use of funds	$49	100.0
Sources		
Increase in long-term debt	$10	20.4
Increase in retained earnings	10	20.4
Noncash depreciation outlay	10	20.4
Sale of marketable securities	10	20.4
Reduction in cash holdings	5	10.2
Increase in other liabilities	4	8.2
Total source of funds	$49	100.0

to arrive at the retained earnings figure, it must be added back as a source of funds in cash flow analysis.[6]

The total sources of funds, then, is $49 million. This amount was used to finance an increase in accounts receivable, to purchase inventories and fixed assets, and to reduce notes payable. Dallas Chemical had a net income of $12 million in 1968 and paid out $2 million in dividends,

[6] Treating depreciation as a source of funds is sufficiently worrisome to students to warrant elaboration. Consider Dallas's condensed 1968 income statement. Assume that sales are for cash and that all costs (except depreciation) and taxes are paid during the period.

Sales	$300,000,000
Costs excluding depreciation	270,000,000
Depreciation	10,000,000
Profit before taxes	20,000,000
Taxes	8,000,000
Profit after taxes	$ 12,000,000

Disregarding any possible changes in balance sheet accounts, how much cash was available from operations to finance new investment, to repay debt, and so on? The answer is $22 million, the sum of profits after taxes plus depreciation. In the actual case, of course, other events transpired and produced a different figure for total sources of funds. This example does show, however, the rationale behind the statement that depreciation is a source of funds.

so that the retained earnings of $10 million completely reconciles the surplus account.

What does this rough-and-ready statement of sources and uses of funds tell the financial manager? It tells him that plant size was expanded and that fixed assets amounting to $30 million were acquired. Inventories and net receivables also increased as sales increased. The firm needed funds to meet working capital and fixed assets demands.

Previously, Dallas had been financing its growth through bank credit (notes payable). In the present period of growth, management decided to obtain some of its financing from permanent sources (long-term debt). It obtained enough long-term debt not only to finance some of the asset growth but also to pay back some of its bank credit and reduce accounts payable. In addition to the long-term debt, funds were acquired from retained earnings and from depreciation charges of $10 million. Moreover, the firm had been accumulating marketable securities in anticipation of this expansion program, and these were sold to pay for new buildings and equipment. Finally, cash had been accumulated in excess of the firm's needs and was also worked down.

This example illustrates how the financial manager's rough-and-ready approach to sources and uses can give him a fairly complete picture of recent operations. Such an approach is not bogged down in details. Because refined adjustments usually amount to less than 4 or 5 percent of the total amounts involved, the financial manager can omit them and still obtain a good perspective on the flow of funds in his company.

SUMMARY

Chapter 3 described certain ratios commonly used in financial analysis. This chapter first extended the analysis to show how some of the ratios are related to one another and then presented two other tools of financial analysis—break-even charts and sources and uses of funds statements.

Du Pont System

The du Pont system shows how the return on investment is dependent upon turnover and the profit margin. The system is generally expressed in the form of the following equation:

$$\frac{\text{sales}}{\text{investment}} \times \frac{\text{profit}}{\text{sales}} = \frac{\text{profit}}{\text{investment}}$$

The first term, investment turnover, times the profit margin equals the rate of return on investment. The kinds of actions discussed in Chapter

3 can be used to effect needed changes in turnover and the profit margin and thus to improve the return on investment.

The du Pont system can be extended to encompass financial leverage and thus to examine the manner in which turnover, sales margins, and leverage all combine to determine the rate of return on net worth. The following equation is used to show this relationship:

$$\text{percent return on net worth} = \frac{\text{percent return on assets}}{1.0 - \text{debt ratio}}$$

The formula is useful for examining the way financial leverage can be used to increase the rate of return on net worth.

Rates of Return in Different Industries

The extended du Pont system shows why firms in different industries—even though they have widely different turnovers, profit margins, and debt ratios—may end up with very similar rates of return on net worth. In general, firms dealing with relatively perishable commodities would be expected to have high turnovers but low profit margins, and firms whose production processes require heavy investments in fixed assets would be expected to have low turnover ratios but high profit margins.

Break-Even Analysis

Break-even analysis is a method of relating fixed costs, variable costs, and total revenues to show the level of sales that must be attained if the firm is to operate at a profit. The analysis can be based on the number of units produced or on total dollar sales. It can also be used for the entire company or for a particular product or division. Further, with minor modifications, break-even analysis can be put on a cash basis instead of on a profit basis.

Sources and Uses of Funds Statement

The sources and uses of funds statement is used to indicate where cash came from and how it was used. When a firm wishes to borrow funds, one of the first questions posed by the loan officer is, What has the firm done with the money it had? This question is answered by the sources and uses statement. The information it provides may indicate that the firm is making progress or that problems are arising.

The du Pont system, break-even analysis, and sources and uses statements are all fundamental tools in the financial manager's kit, and they will be encountered time and time again throughout the remainder of this book.

QUESTIONS

4–1 "The higher the rate of return on investment, the better the firm's management." Is this statement true for all firms? Explain. If you disagree with the statement, give examples of businesses in which it might not be true.

4–2 What factors would you attempt to change if you wanted to increase a firm's rate of return (a) on assets or (b) on net worth?

4–3 Profit margins and turnover rates vary from industry to industry. What industry characteristics account for these variations? Give some contrasting examples to illustrate your answer.

4–4 Why is it particularly important for a rapidly growing young firm to concern itself with systems of control?

4–5 Are lower total costs *always* beneficial to a company? Why?

4–6 Which relation would you, as a financial manager, prefer: a profit margin of 10 percent with a capital turnover of 2 or a profit margin of 25 percent and a capital turnover of 1? Can you think of any firm with a relationship similar to the latter?

4–7 What benefits can be derived from break-even analysis?

4–8 What is operating leverage? Explain how profits or losses can be magnified in a firm with a great deal of operating leverage as opposed to a firm without this characteristic.

4–9 What portion of the selling price of a product goes toward covering fixed costs? Relate your answer to marginal analysis.

4–10 What data are necessary to construct a break-even chart?

4–11 What is the general effect of each of the following changes on a firm's break-even point?

a) An increase in selling price with no change in units sold.

b) A change from the leasing of a machine for $5,000 a year to the purchase of the machine for $100,000. The useful life of this machine will be 20 years, with no salvage value. Assume straight-line depreciation.

c) A reduction in variable labor costs.

4–12 What are the most important determinants of fixed asset and inventory requirements for a manufacturing firm?

4–13 Why do turnover ratios differ for firms in the same industry?

4–14 What effects would a price level increase have upon the level of investment in inventories and fixed assets, and what would be the net effect on the level of cash?

4–15 What are the similarities and differences between a source and uses analysis and a cash budget?

4–16 Are increases in a surplus account and in depreciation considered to be sources of funds?

PROBLEMS

4–1 Fill in the following outline of the du Pont pattern of analysis for one set of the pairs of companies listed below. (This problem requires library research. Data may be obtained from company annual reports or from an investment manual such as Moody's Industrials or Standard & Poor's Industrials. The data collected for problem 3–2 is applicable to this problem.)

General Motors and Chrysler
Boeing and Lockheed
Sperry Rand and International Business Machines
Standard Oil of New Jersey and Standard Oil of California
General Electric and Westinghouse

Sales to operating investment	______%	Cash to sales (percentage)	______
		Average collection period (days)	______
		Inventory turnover (times)	______
Return on investment	______%	Net fixed asset turnover (times)	______
		Total operating assets	$______
		Operating expenses to sales (percentage)	______
Profit to sales	______%	Net income before fixed charges and taxes to total assets (percentage)	______
		Net income after fixed charges and taxes	$______

a) Using data for the most recent year available, compare the return on investment for the two companies.
b) Indicate reasons for the observed differences in rates of return suggested by the du Pont analysis.

4–2 For the Moore Corporation the following relations exist: each unit of output is sold for $22; for output up to 20,000 units the fixed costs are $65,000; variable costs are $9 a unit.

a) What is the firm's gain or loss at sales of 4,000 units? of 6,000 units?
b) What is the break-even point? Illustrate by means of a chart.
c) What occurs to the break-even point if the selling price rises to $26? What is the significance of the change to financial management? Illustrate by means of a chart.

d) What occurs to the break-even point if the selling price rises to $26 but variable costs rise to $13 a unit? Illustrate by means of a chart.

4–3 The consolidated balance sheets for the Medfone Corporation at the beginning and end of 1969 are shown below.

MEDFONE CORPORATION
BALANCE SHEET
Beginning and End 1969
(in millions of dollars)

	(Jan. 2)	*(Dec. 31)*	*Sources*	*Use*
Cash	$ 30	$ 15		
Marketable securities	22	0		
Net receivables	45	60		
Inventories	105	150		
Total current assets	$202	$225		
Gross fixed assets	150	300		
Less: Reserves for depreciation	(52)	(82)		
Net fixed assets	98	218		
Total assets	$300	$443		
Accounts payable	$ 30	$ 37		
Notes payable	30	7		
Other current liabilities	15	30		
Long-term debt	15	52		
Common stock	75	127		
Retained earnings	135	190		
Total claims on assets	$300	$443		

The company bought $150 million worth of fixed assets. The charge for current depreciation was $30 million. Earnings after taxes were $75 million, and the company paid out $20 million in dividends.

a) Fill in the amount of source or use in the appropriate column.
b) Prepare a percentage statement of sources and uses of funds.
c) Briefly summarize your findings.

Selected References

Ansoff, H. Igor, "Planning As A Practical Management Tool," *Financial Executive,* XXXII (June 1964), 34–37.

Bierman, Harold Jr., "Measuring Financial Liquidity," *Accounting Review,* XXXV (October 1960).

Crowningshield, Gerald R. and George L. Battista, "Cost-Volume-Profit Analysis in Planning and Control," *N.A.A. Bulletin,* XLV (July 1963), 3–15.

Davidson, Sidney, George H. Sorter, and Hemu Kalle, "Measuring the

Defensive Position of a Firm," *Financial Analysts Journal,* XX (January-February 1964), 23–39.

Donaldson, Gordon, "New Framework for Corporate Debt Capacity," *Harvard Business Review,* XL (March-April 1962).

Foulke, Roy A., *Practical Financial Statement Analysis,* 5th ed. (New York: McGraw-Hill, 1961).

Graham, Benjamin, and George McGobrick, *The Interpretation of Financial Statements,* rev. ed. (New York: Harper & Row, 1964).

Helfert, Erich A., *Techniques of Financial Analysis,* rev. ed. (Homewood, Ill.: Irwin, 1967).

Horngren, Charles T., "The Funds Statement and Its Use by Analysts," *Journal of Accountancy,* XCIX (January 1956), 55–59.

Jaedicke, Robert K. and Robert T. Sprouse, *Accounting Flows: Income, Funds, and Cash* (Englewood Cliffs, N.J.: Prentice-Hall, 1965).

Jaedicke, Robert K. and Alexander A. Robichek, "Cost-Volume-Profit Analysis Under Conditions of Uncertainty," *Accounting Review,* XXXIX (October 1964).

McCloud, B. G., Jr., "Pitfalls in Statement Analysis, *Bulletin of the Robert Morris Associates,* 39 (January 1957), 143–148.

Meyer, John M., *Financial Statement Analysis,* 3d ed. (Englewood Cliffs, N.J.: Prentice-Hall, 1961).

Raun, D. L., "Limitations of Profit Graphs, Breakeven Analysis, and Budgets," *Accounting Review,* XXXIX (October 1964), 927–945.

Robbins, Sydney M., "Emphasizing the Marginal Factor in the Break-Even Analysis," *N.A.A. Bulletin,* XLI (June 1960), 53–60.

Soldofsky, R. M., "Accountant's vs. Economist's Concepts of Break-even Analysis," *N.A.A. Bulletin,* XLI (December 1959), 5–18.

Sorter, George H., and George Benston, "Appraising the Defensive Position of a Firm: The Internal Measure," *Accounting Review,* XXXV (October 1960), 633–640.

Trumbull, Wendell P., "Developing the Funds Statement as the Third Major Financial Statement," *N.A.A. Bulletin,* XLV (April 1963), 21–31.

Vatter, William J., "Fund Flows and Fund Statements," *Journal of Business,* XXVI (January 1953), 15–25.

Weiner, Julius, "To Better Results Through a More Accurate Break-Even Formula," *N.A.A. Bulletin,* XLI (July 1960), 5–18.

Willson, James D., "Practical Applications of Cost-Volume-Profit Analysis," *N.A.A. Bulletin,* XLI (March 1960), 5–18.

Henderson, Bruce D., and John Deardon, "New Systems for Divisional Control, *Harvard Business Review,* XLIV, (September-October 1966).

5

Financial Planning and Budgeting

The planning process is an integral part of the financial manager's job. As will be seen in subsequent chapters, long-term debt and equity funds are raised infrequently and in large amounts. Further, the cost per dollar raised by selling such securities decreases as the size of the issue increases, and this reduces the tendency to raise outside capital at frequent intervals. Because of these considerations, it is important that the firm have a working estimate of its total needs for funds for the next few years. It is therefore useful to examine methods of forecasting the firm's over-all needs for funds, and this is the subject of the first section of this chapter.

In addition to his long-range forecasts, the financial manager is also concerned with short-term needs for funds. It is embarrassing to a corporate treasurer to "run out of money." Even though he may be able to negotiate a bank loan on short notice, his plight may cause the banker to question the soundness of the firm's management and, accordingly, to reduce the company's line of credit with the bank. Therefore, attention must be given to short-term budgeting with special emphasis on cash forecasting, or *cash budgeting,* as it is commonly called. This is the subject of the second part of the chapter.

LONG-RANGE FINANCIAL FORECASTING

The most important variable that influences a firm's financing requirements is its projected dollar volume of sales. A good sales forecast is an essential foundation for forecasting financial requirements. The principal methods of forecasting financial requirements are described in the following sections. All use sales as the starting point for the forecast—the first method uses a fixed ratio relation between sales and asset components; the second, a variable ratio relationship; the third, a nonlinear relationship; and the fourth, a multiple variable relationship.

Percent-of-Sales Method

The simplest approach to forecasting financial requirements expresses the firm's needs in terms of the percentage of annual sales invested in each individual balance sheet item. As an example, consider the Moore Company, whose balance sheet as of December 31, 1968 is shown in Table 5–1. The company's sales are running at about $500,000 a year, which is its capacity limit; the profit margin after tax on sales is 4 percent. During 1968, the company earned $20,000 after taxes and paid

TABLE 5–1 THE MOORE COMPANY BALANCE SHEET December 31, 1968

ASSETS		LIABILITIES	
Cash	$ 10,000	Accounts payable	$ 50,000
Receivables	85,000	Accrued taxes and wages	25,000
Inventories	100,000	Mortgage bonds	70,000
Fixed assets (net)	150,000	Common stocks	100,000
		Retained earnings	100,000
Total assets	$345,000	Total liab. and net worth	$345,000

out $10,000 in dividends, and it plans to continue paying out half of net profits as dividends. How much additional financing will be needed if sales expand to $800,000 during 1969? The calculating procedure, using the percent-of-sales method, is explained below.[1]

First, isolate those balance sheet items that can be expected to vary directly with sales. In the case of the Moore Company, this step applies to *all* the assets—a higher level of sales would necessitate more cash for transactions, more receivables, higher inventory levels, and additional fixed plant capacity. On the liability side, accounts payable as well as accruals may be expected to increase with increases in sales. Retained earnings will go up as long as the company is profitable and does not pay out 100 percent of earnings, but the percentage increase is not constant. However, neither common stock nor mortgage bonds would increase spontaneously with an increase in sales.

Those items that can be expected to vary directly with sales are tabulated as a percentage of sales in Table 5–2. For every $100 increase in sales, assets must increase by $69; this $69 must be financed in some manner. Accounts payable will increase spontaneously with sales, as will accruals; these two items will supply $15 of new funds for each $100 increase in sales. Subtracting the 15 percent for spontaneously generated funds from the 69 percent funds requirement leaves 54 percent—thus, for each $100 increase in sales, the Moore Company must obtain $54 of financing either from retained earnings or from external sources.

In the case at hand, sales are scheduled to increase from $500,000 to $800,000, or by $300,000. Applying the 54 percent to the expected increase in sales leads to the conclusion that $162,000 will be needed.

Some of this need will be met by retained earnings. Total sales during 1969 will be $800,000; if the company earns 4 percent after taxes on this volume, profits will amount to $32,000. Assuming that the 50 percent dividend payout ratio is maintained, dividends will be $16,000 and $16,000 will be retained. Subtracting the retained earnings from the $162,000 that was needed leaves a figure of $146,000—this is the amount of funds that must be obtained through borrowing or by selling new common stock.

Notice what would have happened if the Moore Company's sales forecast for 1969 had been only $515,000—a not bad 3 percent gain. Applying the 54 percent net need for funds to the $15,000 sales increase gives

[1] We recognize, of course, that as a practical matter, business firms plan their needs in terms of specific items of equipment, square feet of floor space, and other factors, and not as a percentage of sales. However, the outside analyst does not have access to this information, and the manager, even though he has the information on specific items, needs to check his forecasts in aggregate terms. The percent-of-sales method serves both these needs surprisingly well.

an $8,100 funds requirement. Retained earnings ($10,300) would more than cover these requirements, so the firm would have no need of outside capital. The example shows not only that higher levels of sales bring about a need for funds, but also that while small percentage increases can be financed through retained earnings, larger increases cause the firm to go into the market for outside capital. In other words, a certain level of growth can be financed from internal sources, but higher levels of growth require external financing.

TABLE 5–2 THE MOORE COMPANY
BALANCE SHEET ITEMS EXPRESSED AS A PERCENT OF SALES
December 31, 1968

ASSETS		LIABILITIES	
Cash	2.0%	Accounts payable	10.0%
Receivables	17.0	Accrued taxes and wages	5.0
Inventories	20.0	Mortgage bonds	na
Fixed assets (net)	30.0	Common stock	na
		Retained earnings	na
Total assets	69.0%	Total liab. and net worth	15.0%

na = not applicable

Assets as a percent of sales	69.0%
Less: Spontaneous increase in liabilities	15.0
Percent of each additional dollar of sales that must be financed	54.0%

The percent-of-sales method of forecasting financial requirements is neither simple nor mechanical, although an explanation of the ideas requires simple illustrations. Experience in applying the technique in practice suggests the importance of understanding (1) the basic technology of the firm and (2) the logic of the relation between sales and assets for the particular firm in question. A substantial amount of experience and judgment is required to apply the technique in actual practice.

The percent-of-sales method is most appropriately used for forecasting relatively short-term changes in financing needs. It is less useful for longer term forecasting for reasons that are best described in connection with the analysis of the regression method of financial forecasting discussed in the next sections.

Scatter Diagram, or Simple Regression, Method

An alternative method used to forecast financial requirements is the scatter diagram, or simple regression, method. A scatter diagram is a graphic portrayal of joint relations. Proper use of the scatter diagram method requires practical but not necessarily statistical sophistication.

Table 5–3 and Figure 5–1 illustrate the use of the scatter diagram method and also demonstrate its superiority over the percent-of-sales method for long-range forecasting. As in all financial forecasting, the sales forecast is the starting point. The financial manager is given the sales forecast, or he may participate in formulating it. Suppose he has

TABLE 5–3 RELATIONS BETWEEN INVENTORY AND SALES

YEAR	SALES	INVENTORY	INVENTORY AS A PERCENT OF SALES
1963	$ 50,000	$22,000	44
1964	100,000	24,000	24
1965	150,000	26,000	17
1966	200,000	28,000	14
1967	250,000	30,000	12
1968	300,000	32,000	11
.	.	.	.
.	.	.	.
.	.	.	.
1973 (estimated)	500,000	40,000	8

data through 1968 and is making a forecast of inventories for 1973, as indicated in Table 5–3. If he is using the simple regression method, he draws a line through the points for 1963 through 1968, as shown in Figure 5–1. The line that fits the scatter of points in this example is a straight line. It is called the line of best fit, or the regression line. Of course, all points seldom fall exactly on the regression line, and the line itself may be curved as well as linear.[2]

[2] In these illustrations, inventories are used as the item to be forecast. Much theory suggests that inventories increase as a square root of sales; see, for example, the inventory control model developed in Chapter 14. This characteristic would tend to turn the line of regression between inventories and sales slightly downward. Also, improvements in inventory-control techniques would curve the line of relation downward. However, the increased diversity of types, models, and styles tends to increase inventories. Applications by the authors' students of the regressior method to hundreds of companies indicate that the linear straight line relations typically represent the line of best fit or, at worst, involve only small error. If the line were in fact curved over, a curved line could be fitted to the data and used for forecasting purposes.

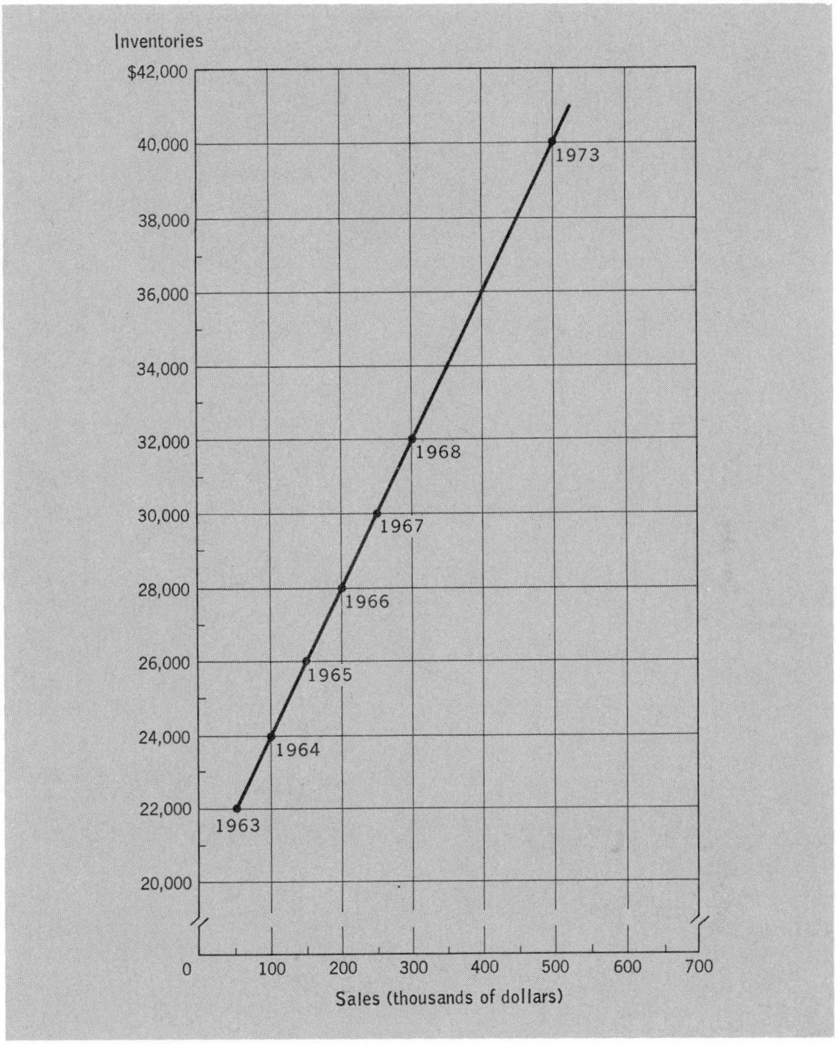

Figure 5–1 Illustrative Relation between Sales and Inventory

If the percent-of-sales method had been used, some difficulties would have arisen immediately. Table 5–3 gives percent of sales for 1963 through 1968. What relation could be used? the 44 percent for 1963? the 11 percent for 1968? some average of the relations? If the relation for 1968 had been used, a forecast of $55,000 for inventories in 1973 would have been made. This forecast represents a large error.

The regression method is thus seen to be superior for forecasting financial requirements, particularly for longer term forecasts. When a firm is likely to have a base stock of inventory or fixed assets, the ratio

TABLE 5–4 **GROSS NATIONAL PRODUCT AND STANDARD OIL COMPANY OF TEXAS DATA**
(in millions of dollars)

YEAR	GNP (BILLIONS OF DOLLARS)*	SALES	CASH, MARKET-ABLE SECURITIES	INVEN-TORIES	RECEIV-ABLES	TOTAL CURRENT ASSETS	NET FIXED ASSETS	MISC. ASSETS	ACCOUNTS PAYABLE	PROVISION FOR INCOME TAX
1962	440	$1,559	$193	$243	$250	$686	$1,629	$136	$164	$54
1963	480	1,565	189	238	253	675	1,759	143	165	48
1964	500	1,663	217	219	318	754	1,864	164	226	53
1965	520	2,046	219	252	347	820	2,105	191	286	56
1966	552	2,150	202	240	399	871	2,274	208	333	50
1967	586	2,203	204	267	446	917	2,397	230	344	50
1968	623	2,285	172	279	519	971	2,589	236	347	60

YEAR	OTHER CURRENT LIAB.	LONG-TERM DEBT	COMMON STOCK AND CAPITAL SURPLUS	RETAINED EARNINGS AND SURPLUS RESERVES	TOTAL ASSETS AND CLAIMS ON ASSETS	NET INCOME TO COMMON	CASH DIVIDENDS TO COMMON	PAYOUT PERCENTAGE DIVIDENDS ÷ EARNINGS	RETAINED EARNINGS
1962	$259	$179	$ 797	$1,215	$2,451	$258	$126	49%	$132
1963	259	175	797	1,347	2,578	254	126	50	128
1964	324	173	797	1,487	2,782	266	126	47	140
1965	394	172	962	1,569	3,117	286	126	44	160
1966	434	185	1,148	1,563	3,353	305	133	44	172
1967	451	183	1,148	1,741	3,545	314	139	44	175
1968	478	216	1,378	1,724	3,796	337	144	43	193

* In 1947 prices.

of the item to sales declines as sales increase. In such cases the ratio, or percent-of-sales method, results in large errors.[3]

ILLUSTRATION OF SIMPLE REGRESSION METHOD. In Table 5–4 the data for the Standard Oil Company of Texas are used to demonstrate the scatter diagram method for a complete financial forecast. In Figure 5–2, only selected variables are plotted. Chart (a) shows the relation between gross national product (GNP) and the Standard Oil Company's sales. A forecast of GNP, a good measure of the general level of business activity, is used to project company sales in chart (a) of Figure 5–2. Charts (b), (c), and (d) relate Standard Oil Company sales to net accounts receivable, inventories, and net fixed assets.

The procedure for carrying out a scatter diagram analysis is outlined below.

1. Forecast or project the sales of the firm by GNP, industry sales, or other logical business indicators.
2. Plot the scatter diagrams for major asset, liability, and net worth categories related to sales.
3. Fit the regression line by free hand (inspection) or by numerical calculations.
4. Project the regression lines and determine the level of each balance sheet category for the forecast value of sales (Projections for the Standard Oil Company of Texas are summarized in Table 5–5).
5. The difference between assets requirements and financing sources directly related to sales indicates financial requirements.

As is true of the ratio methods of forecasting financial requirements, the regression method can be used to forecast only the items of the balance sheet that are directly influenced by sales. Some items are directly tied to sales, while others are not.

BALANCE SHEET ITEMS DIRECTLY TIED TO INCREASES IN SALES		BALANCE SHEET ITEMS NOT DIRECTLY TIED TO INCREASES IN SALES	
Assets	Liabilities	Assets	Liabilities
Cash	Accounts payable	Investments	Notes payable
Receivables	Provision for income tax		Long-term debt
Inventories	Accruals		Preferred stock
Fixed assets	Retained earnings		Common stock

[3] The widespread use of the percentage method makes for lax control. It would be easy to improve on a $55,000 inventory level and still be inefficient because the correct target amount is closer to $40,000. A clear example of the use of correlation relations instead of ratios to set controls for travel expenses is set out in W. A. Wallis and H. V. Roberts, *Statistics* (New York: Free Press, 1956), pp. 549–555.

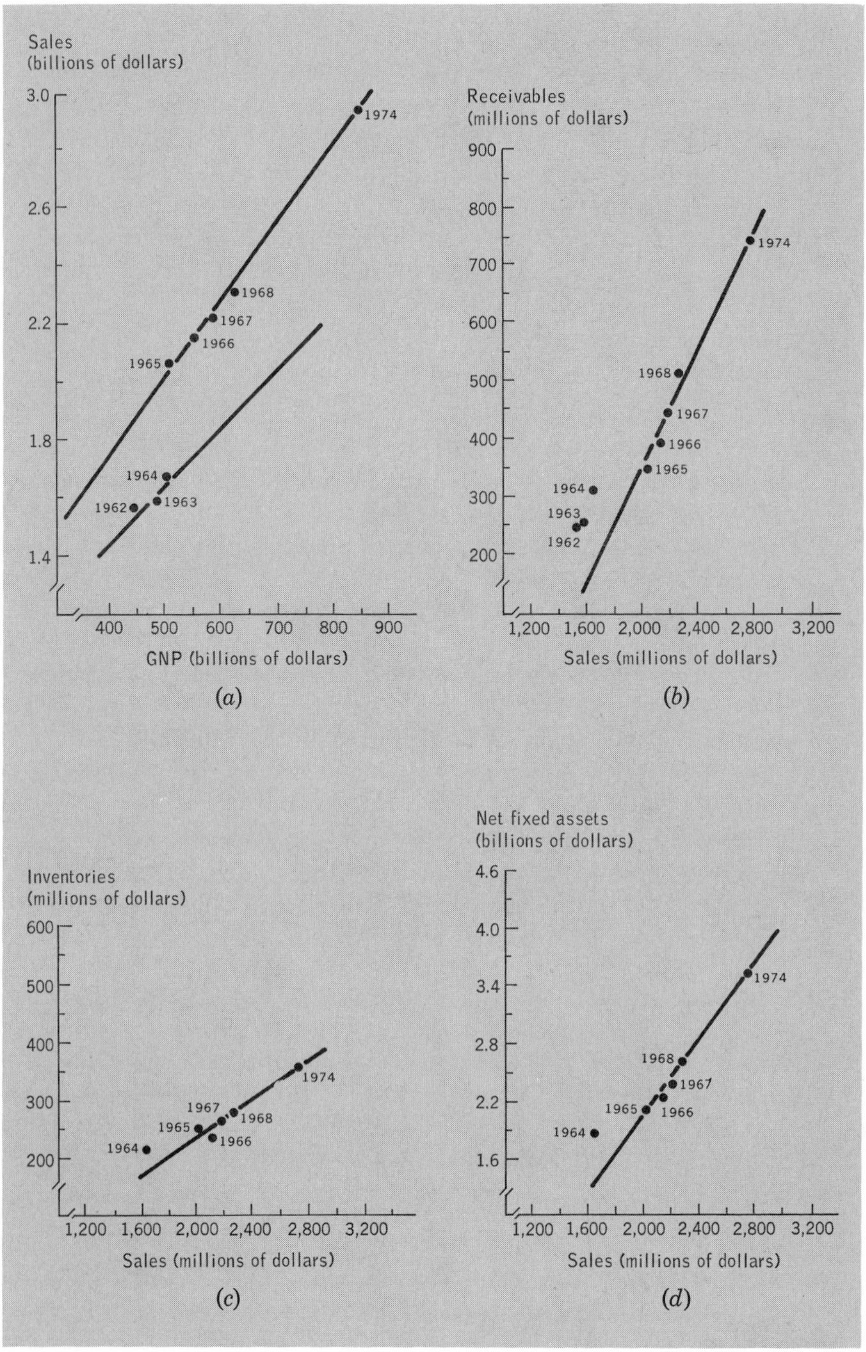

Figure 5–2 Scatter Diagrams: Standard Oil Company of Texas

As the above listing indicates, most of the asset items—the balance sheet items to be financed—vary with the increase in sales. When sales increase, these items are likely to increase in some predictable fashion. On the right-hand side of the balance sheet, some items similarly increase

TABLE 5–5 STANDARD OIL COMPANY OF TEXAS
PRO FORMA BALANCE SHEETS
1968 ESTIMATES COMPARED WITH 1968 ACTUAL
(in millions of dollars)

	1968 ACTUAL	1968 ESTIMATED	1974 ESTIMATED
GNP (in billions of dollars)	$ 623	$ 623	$ 850*
Company sales	2,285	2,285	2,780
Assets			
Cash and marketable securities	173	210	223
Receivables	519	480	750
Inventories	279	275	355
Total current assets	971	965	1,328
Miscellaneous assets	236	236	345
Net fixed assets	2,589	2,590	3,540
Total assets	$3,796	$3,791	$5,213
Liabilities			
Accounts payable	$ 348	$ 348	$ 455
Income taxes payable	60	60	74†
Other current liabilities	70	57	63
Total current liabilities	478	465	592
Long-term debt	216	216	216
Total liabilities	694	681	808
Capital			
Common stock	1,378	1,378	1,378
Retained earnings	1,724	1,724	2,904
Total capital	3,102	3,102	4,282
Subtotal	3,796	3,783	5,090
Additional financing needed	0	8	123
Total liab. and net worth	$3,796	$3,791	$5,213

* 5.5 percent growth rate.
† Assumed 20 percent of net income.

with incremental sales. Retained earnings, as indicated in the discussion of the ratio method, increase with total sales, not just incremental sales.

In the example provided in Table 5–5, the company's sales are projected to increase by some $495 million over the six-year period.

Total assets are expected to rise from $3,796 million to $5,213 million, an increase of $1,417 million. The increases in retained earnings and other selected current liability items can provide part of the additional funds required, but additional financing of some $123 million will be needed.

The difference between the financing required (increases in the asset items) and the financing provided (increases in certain liability and net worth items) is the additional financing required. This financing must come from one of four major sources: notes payable, long-term debt, preferred stock, or common stock.

Multiple Regression Method

A more sophisticated approach to forecasting a firm's sales calls for the use of *multiple regression analysis.* In simple regression, sales are assumed to be a function of only one variable; in multiple regression, sales are recognized to depend upon a number of variables. For example, in simple regression we might state that sales are strictly a function of GNP. With multiple regression, we might say that sales are dependent upon both GNP and a set of additional variables. For example, the sale of ski equipment depends upon (1) the general level of prosperity as measured by GNP, personal disposable income, or other indicators of aggregate economic activity; (2) population increases; (3) number of lifts operating; (4) weather conditions; (5) advertising, and so forth.

We shall not go into detail on the use of multiple regression analysis at this time. However, most computer installations have "canned" regression programs incorporated into their systems, making it extremely easy to use multiple regression techniques; multiple regression is widely used by at least the larger corporations. An illustration of the use of multiple regression analysis to measure the cost of capital to a firm is given in a later chapter (Chapter 12, Appendix A).[4]

A COMPARISON OF FORECASTING METHODS

Thus far we have considered four methods used in financial forecasting: (1) the percent-of-sales method, (2) the scatter diagram, or simple linear regression method, (3) curvilinear simple regression, and (4)

[4] Even more complex forecasting models involve the use of computer simulation and simultaneous equations, but we shall not discuss them.

multiple regression. This section summarizes and compares these four methods.

Percent-of-Sales Method

The percent-of-sales method of financial forecasting assumes that certain balance sheet items vary directly with sales. The postulated relationship is shown in Figure 5–3. Notice that the percent-of-sales method implicitly assumes a linear relationship that passes through the origin. The slope of the line representing the relationship may vary, but the line always passes through the origin. Implicitly, the relationship is established by finding one point, or ratio, such as that designated as X in Figure 5–3, and then connecting this point with the origin. Then, for any projected level of sales, the level of the particular balance sheet item can be determined.

Scatter Diagram, or Simple Linear Regression, Method

The scatter diagram method differs from the percent-of-sales method principally in that it does not assume that the line of relationship passes through the origin. In its simplest form, the scatter diagram method calls for calculating the ratio between sales and the relevant balance sheet item at two points in time, extending a line through these two points, and using the line to describe the relationship between sales and the balance sheet item. The accuracy of the regression is improved if more points are plotted, and the regression line can be fitted mathematically (by a technique known as the method of least squares) as well as drawn in by eye.

The scatter diagram method is illustrated in Figure 5–4, where the

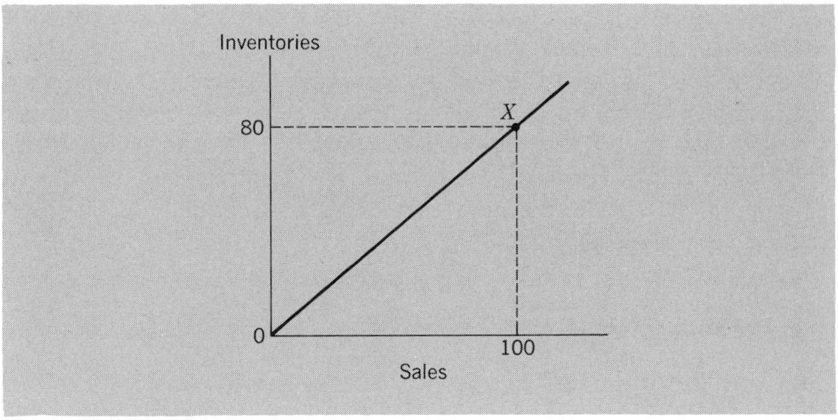

Figure 5–3 Illustration of the Percent-of-Sales Method

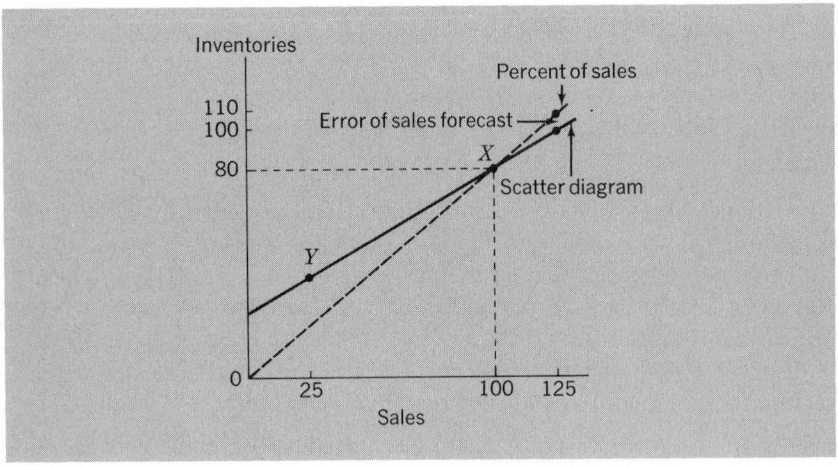

Figure 5–4 Scatter Diagram, or Simple Linear Regression

percent-of-sales relationship is also shown for comparison. The error induced by the use of the percent-of-sales method is represented by the gap between the two lines. At a sales level of 125, the percent-of-sales method would call for an inventory of 110 versus inventories of only 100 using a scatter diagram forecast. Notice that the error is very small if sales continue to run at approximately the current level, but the gap widens and the error increases as sales deviate in either direction from current levels, as they probably would if a long-run forecast was being made.

Simple Curvilinear Regression

Linear scatter diagrams, or linear regressions, assume that the slope of the regression line is constant. This condition does frequently exist, but this is not a universal rule. Figure 5–5 illustrates the application of curvilinear simple regression to forecasting financial relationships. We have drawn this hypothetical illustration to show a flattening curve, which implies a decreasing relationship between sales and inventory beyond point X, the current level of operations. In this case, the forecast of inventory requirements at a sales level of 125 would be too high if the linear regression method was used (but too low if sales declined from 100 to 50).

Multiple Regression

In our illustration to this point, we have been assuming that the observations fell exactly on the relationship line. This implies perfect correlation, something that, in fact, seldom occurs. In practice, the actual obser-

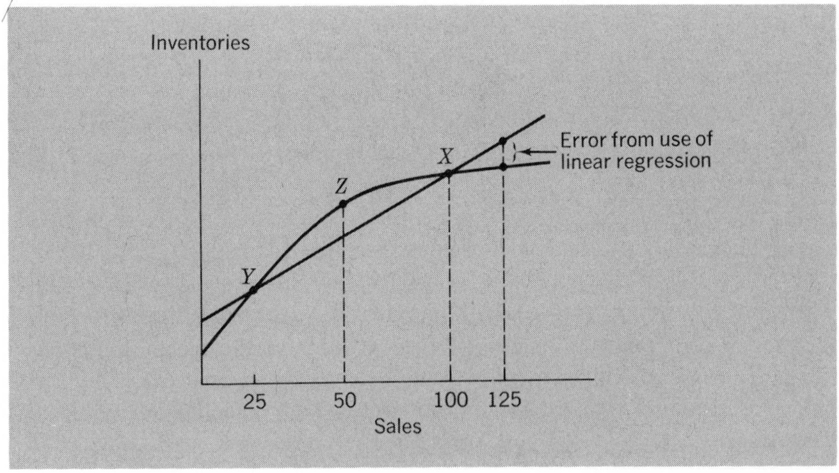

Figure 5–5 Curvilinear Simple Regression

vations would be scattered about the regression line as shown in Figure 5–6. What causes the deviations from the regression line? One obvious answer, if linear regression is used, is that the actual line of relationship might be curvilinear. But if curvilinear regression is used and deviations occur, we must seek other explanations for the scatter around the regression line. The most obvious answer is that balance sheet items, such as inventories, are determined by factors other than just sales. For example, inventory levels are certainly influenced by work stoppages at the plants of suppliers. If a steel fabricator anticipates a strike in the steel industry, he will stock up on steel products in anticipation of the strike. Such hedge buying would cause actual inventories to be above the level

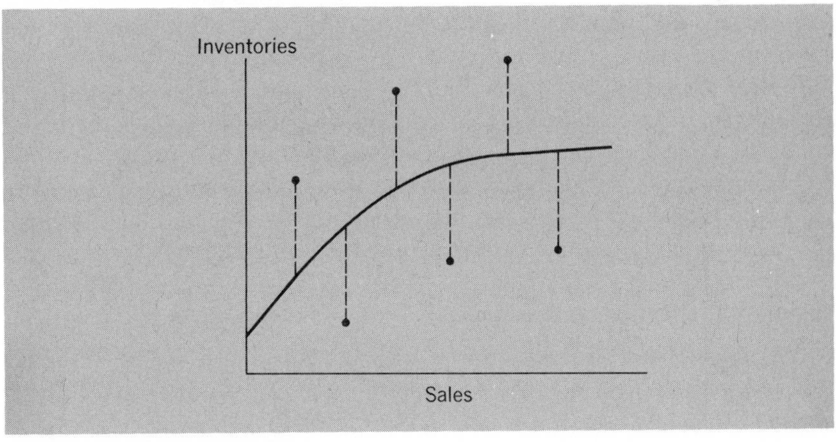

Figure 5–6 Multiple Regression

forecast on the basis of sales projections. Then, assuming a strike does occur and continues for many months, inventories will be drawn down and may end up well below the predicted level. Multiple regression techniques, which introduce additional variables (such as work stoppages) into the analysis, are employed to further improve financial forecasting.

The need to employ more complicated forecasting techniques varies from situation to situation. For example, the percent-of-sales method may be perfectly adequate for making short-run forecasts where conditions are relatively stable, while curvilinear multiple regression may be deemed essential for longer-run forecasts in more dynamic industries. As in all other applications of financial analysis, the cost of using more refined techniques must be balanced against the benefits of increased accuracy.

BUDGETING

The methods of financial forecasting covered thus far in this chapter are more effective for long-term planning than for short-term planning. The reason for this is that a firm's needs for inventories and plant equipment must, for large volume changes, conform to its level of sales. Assets are therefore closely related to sales in the long run. In the short run, however, the firm may have excess capacity that enables it to expand sales without proportional additions to inventories or plant and equipment. Or, in the short term, sales may contract; what happens to assets in this case depends on the expected duration and severity of the sales decline and upon the ability of management to adjust to a changed sales volume.

Budgeting is a management tool used for shorter term planning and control. In short, budgeting is a method of planning and control that emphasizes monthly and one- or two-year plans for the future. Historically, budgeting was treated as a device to limit expenditures. The more modern approach is to view the budgeting process as a tool for obtaining the most productive and profitable use of the company's resources.

Nature of the Budgeting Process

Fundamentally, the budgeting process is a method to improve operations; it is a continuous effort to get the job done in the best possible way. The budget requires a set of performance standards, or targets. Budgets are reviewed to compare plans and results, and this process has been called "controlling to plan." It is a continuous monitoring procedure, reviewing and evaluating performance with reference to the previously established standards.

Establishing standards requires a realistic understanding of the activities carried on by the firm. Arbitrary standards, set without a basic understanding of the minimum costs as determined by the nature of the firm's operations, can do more harm than good. Budgets imposed in an arbitrary fashion may represent impossible targets at the one extreme or standards that are too lax at the other. If standards are unrealistically high, frustrations and resentment will develop. If standards are unduly lax, costs will be out of control, profits will suffer, and morale will become flabby. However, a set of budgets based on a clear understanding and careful analysis of operations can play an important positive role for the firm.

Budgets, therefore, can provide valuable guides to both high-level executives and middle-management personnel. Well-formulated and effectively developed budgets make subordinates aware of the fact that top management has a realistic understanding of the nature of the operations in the business firm. Thus, the budget becomes an important communication link between top management and the divisional personnel whom they guide.

Budgets also represent planning and control devices that enable management to anticipate change and adapt to it. Business operations in today's economic environment are complex and subject to heavy competitive pressures. In such an environment many kinds of changes take place. The rate of growth of the economy as a whole fluctuates, and these fluctuations affect different industries in a number of different ways. If a firm plans ahead, the budget and control process can provide management with a better basis for understanding the firm's operations in relation to the general environment. This increased understanding leads to faster reactions to developing events, thus increasing the firm's ability to perform effectively.

The budgeting process, in summary, improves internal coordination. This element reflects the basic theme of this book: To show how financial decisions affect the profits and value of the firm and to show how these decisions may be improved. Decisions at every stage—for each product and at the research, engineering, production, marketing, personnel, and financial levels—all have an impact on the firm's profits. Planning and control is the essence of profit planning, and the budget system provides an integrated picture of the firm's operations as a whole. Therefore, the budget system enables each manager to see the relation of his part of the enterprise to the totality of the firm. For example, a production decision to alter the level of work-in-process inventories, or a marketing decision to change the terms under which a particular product is sold, can be traced through the entire budget system to show its effects on the firm's over-all profitability. The budgeting system is a most important financial tool.

The Budget System

The over-all nature of the budget process is outlined in Figure 5–7. Budgeting is a part of the total planning activity in the firm, so we

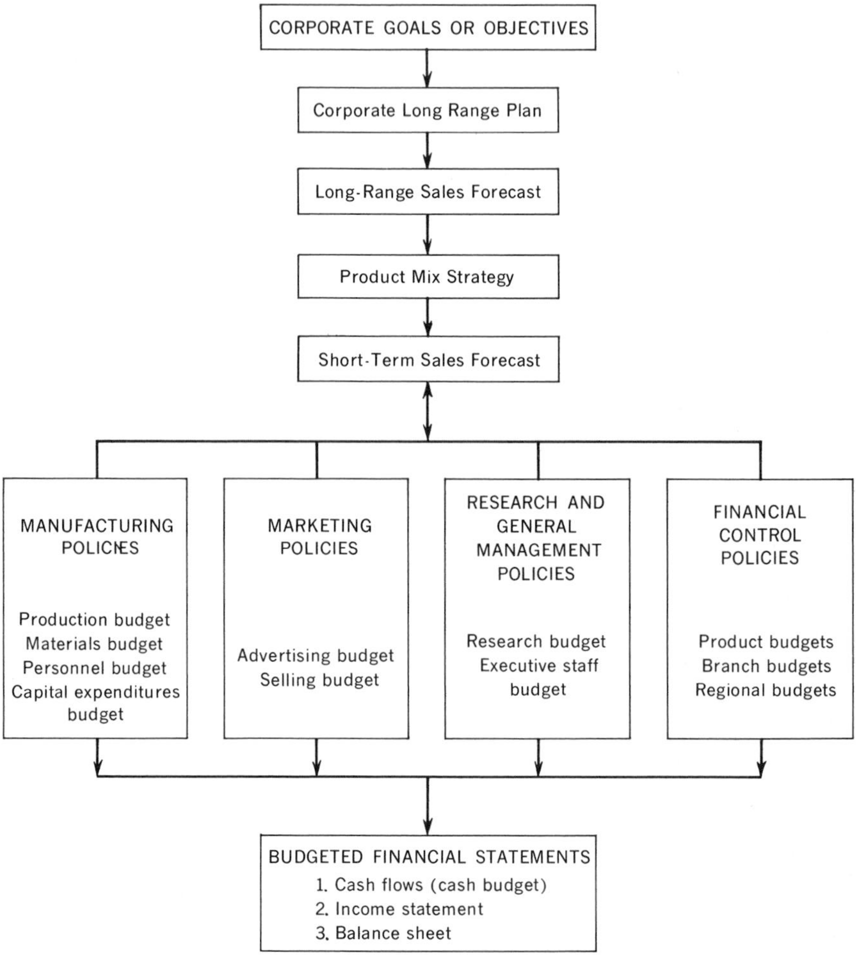

Figure 5–7 Over-All View of the Total Budgeting Process and Relations

must begin with a statement of corporate goals or objectives. The statement of goals (shown in the box at the top of the figure) determines the second part of the figure, the corporate long-range plan (shown in the second box). A segment of the corporate long-range plan includes a long-range sales forecast. This forecast requires a determination of the number and types of products that will be manufactured both at present and in the future years encompassed by the long-range plan. This is the *product mix strategy.*

Short term forecasts and budgets are formulated within the framework of the long-range plan. One might, for example, begin with a sales forecast covering six months or one year. The short-term sales forecast provides a basis for (and is dependent on) the broad range of policies indicated in the center of Figure 5–7. First, there are manufacturing policies covering the choice of types of equipment, plant layout, and production-line arrangements. In addition, the kind of durability built into the products and their associated costs will be considered. Second, a broad set of marketing policies must be formulated. These relate to such items as (1) the development of the firm's own sales organization versus the use of outside sales organizations; (2) the number of salesmen and the method by which they will be compensated; (3) the forms, types and amounts spent on advertising; and other factors. Third are the research and general management policies. Research policies relate to relative emphasis on basic versus applied research and the product areas emphasized by both types of research. Fourth are financial policies, discussed in the following section.

Financial Control Policies

Financial control policies include the organization and content of various types of financial control budgets. These include a budget for individual products and for every significant activity of the firm. In addition, budgets will be formulated to control operations at individual branch offices. These budgets, in turn, are grouped and modified to control regional operations.

In a similar manner, policies established at the manufacturing, marketing, research, and general management levels give rise to a series of budgets. For example, the production budget will reflect the use of materials, parts, labor, and facilities; each of the major elements in a production budget is likely to have its own individual budget program. There is likely to be a materials budget, a labor or personnel requirements budget, and a facilities or long-run capital expenditures budget. After the product is produced, the next step in the process will call for a marketing budget. Related to the over-all process are the general office and executive requirements, which will be reflected in the general and administrative budget system.

The results of projecting all these elements of cost are reflected in the budgeted, or projected, income statement. The anticipated sales give rise to the various types of investments needed to produce the products; these investments, plus the beginning balance sheet, provide the necessary data for developing the assets side of the balance sheet.

These assets must be financed; and a cash flow analysis—the cash budget—is required. The cash budget indicates the combined effects of the budgeted operations on the firm's cash flow. A positive net cash flow will indicate that the firm has ample financing. However, if an increase in the volume of operations leads to a negative cash flow, additional financing will be required. This leads directly to choices of financing, which is the subject of a considerable portion of the remainder of the book.

Since the structure of the income statement and balance sheet have already been covered in preceding chapters, the rest of this section will deal with the two remaining aspects of the budgeting process—the cash budget and the concept of variable, or flexible, budgets.

CASH BUDGETING

The cash budget, as indicated, determines not only the total amount of financing that will be required but its timing as well. The cash budget indicates the amount of funds that will be needed month by month or even week by week, and is one of the financial manager's most important tools. Because a clear understanding of the nature of cash budgeting is important, the process is described by means of an example that makes the elements of the cash budget explicit.

Marvel Toy is a medium-sized toy manufacturer. Sales are highly seasonal, with the peak occurring in September when retailers stock up for the Christmas season. All sales are made on terms that allow a cash discount on payments made within 30 days; if the discount is not taken, the full amount must be paid in 60 days. But Marvel, like most other companies, finds that some of its customers delay payment up to 90 days. Experience shows that on 20 percent of the sales, payment is made within 30 days; on 70 percent of the sales, payment is made during the second month after the sale; and on 10 percent of the sales, payment is made during the third month.

Production is geared to future sales. Purchased materials and parts amount to 70 percent of sales, and Marvel purchases materials and parts the month before the company expects to sell the finished product. Marvel's own purchase terms permit it to delay payment on its own purchases for one month. In other words, if August sales are forecast at $30,000, then purchases during July will amount to $21,000, and this amount will actually be paid in August.

Wages and salaries, rent, and other cash expenses are given in Table 5–6. The company also has a tax payment of $8,000 coming due in August. Its capital budgeting plans call for the purchase in July of a new machine tool costing $10,000, payment to be made in September. Assuming the company needs to keep a $5,000 cash balance at all times and it has $6,000 on July 1, what are Marvel's financial requirements for the period July–December?

The cash requirements are worked out in the cash budget shown as Table 5–6. The top half of the table provides a work sheet for calculating collections on sales and payments on purchases. The first line in the work sheet gives the sales forecast for the period May through December—May and June sales are necessary to determine collections for July and August. Next, cash collections are given. The first line of this section shows that 20 percent of the sales during any given month are collected that month. The second shows the collections on the prior month's sales—70 percent of sales in the preceding month. The third line gives collections from sales two months earlier—10 percent of sales in that month. The collections are summed to find the total cash receipts from sales during each month under consideration.

With the work sheet completed, the cash budget itself can be considered. Receipts from collections are given on the top line. Next, payments during each month are summarized. The difference between cash receipts and cash payments is the net cash gain or loss during the month; for July, there is a net cash loss of $4,200. The initial cash on hand at the beginning of the month is added to the net cash gain or loss during the month to yield the cumulative cash that will be on hand if no financing is done; at the end of July, Marvel Toy will have cumulative cash equal to $1,800. The desired cash balance, $5,000 is subtracted from the cumulative cash balance to determine the amount of financing that the firm needs if it is to maintain the desired level of cash. At the end of July we see that Marvel will need $3,200.

This same procedure is used in the following months. Sales will expand seasonally in August; with the increased sales will come increased payments for purchases, wages, and other items. Moreover, the $8,000 tax bill is due in August. Receipts from sales will go up too, but the firm will still be left with a $10,800 cash deficit during the month. The total

TABLE 5–6 MARVEL TOY COMPANY CASH BUDGET

	May	June	July	Aug.	Sept.	Oct.	Nov.	Dec.	Jan.
WORK SHEET									
Sales (net of cash discounts)	$10,000	$10,000	$20,000	$ 30,000	$ 40,000	$20,000	$20,000	$10,000	$10,000
Collections									
First month (20%)	$ 2,000	$ 2,000	$ 4,000	$ 6,000	$ 8,000	$ 4,000	$ 4,000	$ 2,000	$ 2,000
Second month (70%)		7,000	7,000	14,000	21,000	28,000	14,000	14,000	7,000
Third month (10%)			1,000	1,000	2,000	3,000	4,000	2,000	2,000
Total	$ 2,000	$ 9,000	$12,000	$ 21,000	$ 31,000	$35,000	$22,000	$18,000	$11,000
Purchases (70% of next month's sales)	$ 7,000	$14,000	$21,000	$ 28,000	$ 14,000	$14,000	$ 7,000	$ 7,000	
Payments (one month lag)		7,000	14,000	21,000	28,000	14,000	14,000	7,000	7,000
CASH BUDGET									
Receipts									
Collections			$12,000	$ 21,000	$ 31,000	$35,000	$22,000	$18,000	$11,000
Payments									
Purchases			14,000	21,000	28,000	14,000	14,000	7,000	
Wages and salaries			1,500	2,000	2,500	1,500	1,500	1,000	
Rent			500	500	500	500	500	500	
Other expenses			200	300	400	200	200	100	
Taxes			—	8,000	—	—	—	—	
Payment on machine			—	—	10,000	—	—	—	
Total payments			$16,200	$ 31,800	$ 41,400	$16,200	$16,200	$ 8,600	
Net cash gain (loss) during month			$(4,200)	$(10,800)	$(10,400)	$18,800	$ 5,800	$ 9,400	
Initial cash at start of month			6,000	1,800	(9,000)	(19,400)	(600)	5,200	
Cumulative cash (if no financing)			$ 1,800	$ (9,000)	$(19,400)	$ (600)	$ 5,200	$14,600	
Desired level of cash			5,000	5,000	5,000	5,000	5,000	5,000	
Cash above minimum needs (or financing needs)—cumulative minus desired			$(3,200)	$(14,000)	$(24,400)	$(5,600)	$ 200	$ 9,600	

financial requirements at the end of August will be $14,000—the $3,200 needed at the end of July plus the $10,800 cash deficit for August.

Sales peak in September, and the cash deficit during this month will amount to another $10,400. The total need for funds through September will increase to $24,400. Sales and, consequently, purchases and the payment for past purchases will fall markedly in October; the collections will be the highest of any month because they mainly reflect the high September sales. As a result, Marvel Toy will enjoy a healthy $18,800 cash surplus during October. This surplus can be used to pay off borrowings, so the need for financing will decline by $18,800 to $5,600.

Marvel will have another cash surplus in November, and this extra cash will permit the company to eliminate completely the need for financing. In fact, the company is expected to have $200 in extra cash by the month's end, and another cash surplus in December will swell the extra cash to $9,600. With such a large amount of unneeded funds, Marvel's treasurer will doubtless want to make investments in some type of interest-bearing securities or put the funds to use in some other way.

VARIABLE, OR FLEXIBLE, BUDGETS

Budgets are planned allocations of a firm's resources, based on forecasts for the future. Two important elements influence actual performance. One element is the impact of external influences—developments in the economy as a whole and competitive developments in the firm's own industry. The firm has essentially no control over these factors. The second element, which is controllable by the firm, is the level of efficiency at a given volume of sales. It is useful to separate the impact of these two elements, as this separation is necessary for evaluating individual performances.

The essence of the variable budget system is to introduce flexibility into budgets by recognizing that certain types of expenditures will vary at different levels of output. Thus, a firm might have an alternative level of outlay budgeted for different volumes of operation—high, low, medium. One of management's responsibilities is to determine which of these alternative budgets should be in effect for the planning period under consideration.

The scatter diagram method, described in the first part of this chapter in connection with financial forecasting, may also be utilized to establish the basis for flexible budgeting. The use of the concept can be illustrated by a specific example. Suppose that a retail store has had the experience

TABLE 5–7 HUBLER DEPARTMENT STORE
RELATIONSHIP BETWEEN SALES AND EMPLOYEES

MONTH	SALES (IN MILLIONS OF DOLLARS)	NUMBER OF EMPLOYEES
January	4	42
February	5	51
March	6	60
April	7	75
May	10	102
June	8	83
July	5	55
August	9	92

indicated by the historical data set forth in Table 5–7. It is apparent from the data that the number of employees the firm needs is dependent upon the dollar volume of sales that occurs during a month. This is seen more easily from a scatter diagram like that of Figure 5–8. The

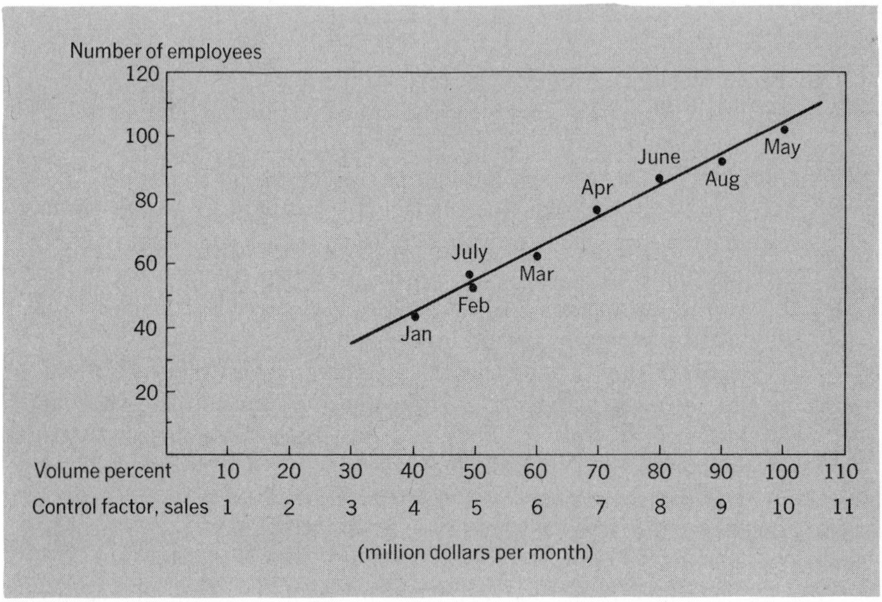

Figure 5–8 Scatter Diagram and Regression Line: Hubler Department Store

freehand regression line is sloped positively because the number of employees increases as the volume of sales increases. The independent variable, dollar volume of sales, is called the *control variable*. Variations in the control variable cause changes in total expenses. The volume of sales can be forecast, and the number of employees can be read from the regression chart. The relations can be expressed in tabular form (Table 5–8). Given the forecast of the volume of operations, standards

TABLE 5–8 HUBLER DEPARTMENT STORE BUDGET ALLOWANCE

VOLUME (IN PERCENTAGES)	EMPLOYEES	WEEKLY PAYROLL ESTIMATE (AVERAGE WAGE, $100)
60	62	$ 6,200
70	72	7,200
80	82	8,200
90	92	9,200
100	102	10,200
110	112	11,200

are provided for the expected number of employees and the weekly payroll.[5]

Problems of Budgeting

Four major problems are encountered when using budget systems. First, budgetary programs can grow to be so complete and so detailed that they become cumbersome, meaningless, and unduly expensive. Overbudgeting is dangerous.

Second, budgetary goals may come to supersede enterprise goals. Budgets are a tool, not an end in themselves. Enterprise goals by definition

[5] Note that regression analysis provides even more flexibility in budgeting than do the high, medium, and low levels mentioned earlier. Also, it is possible to include *confidence levels* when using the regression method. For example, Table 5–8 shows that when volume is at 80 percent, we expect to have 82 employees and a weekly payroll of $8,200. Although this relationship would probably not hold *exactly*, we might find that actual observations lie within 78 and 86 employees at this sales volume 95 percent of the time. Thus, 95 percent confidence levels would encompass the range 78–86. Similar ranges could be determined for other volumes; management might, as a matter of control policy, investigate whenever actual performances were outside this expected range.

supersede subsidiary plans of which budgets are a part. Also, budgets are based on future expectations that may not be realized. There is no acceptable reason for neglecting to alter budgets as circumstances change. This reasoning is the core of the argument in favor of more flexible budgets.

Third, budgets can tend to hide inefficiencies by continuing initial expenditures in succeeding periods without proper evaluation. Budgets growing from precedent usually contain undesirable expenditures. They should not be used as umbrellas under which slovenly, inefficient management can hide. Consequently, the budgetary process must contain provision for reexamination of standards and other bases of planning by which policies are translated into numerical terms.

Finally, case study evidence suggests that the use of budgets as a pressure device defeats their basic objectives. Budgets, if used as instruments of tyranny, cause resentment and frustrations, which in turn lead to inefficiency. In order to counteract this effect, it has been recommended that top management increase the participation of subordinates during the preparatory stages of the budgets.

USE OF FINANCIAL PLANS AND BUDGETS

Forecasts, or long-range plans, are necessary in all the firm's operations. The personnel department must have a good idea of the scale of future operations if it is to plan its hiring and training activities properly. The production department must be sure that the productive capacity is available to meet the projected product demand, while the finance department must be sure that funds are available to meet the firm's financial requirements.

The tools and techniques discussed in this chapter are actually used in several separate, but related, ways. First, the percent-of-sales method or, preferably, the regression method is used to make a long-range forecast of financial requirements over a projected three-to-five–year period. This forecast is then used to make the strategic financing plans during the planning period. The company might, for example, plan to meet its financial requirements with retained earnings and short-term bank debt during, say, 1969 and 1970, float a bond issue in 1971, use retained earnings in 1972, and finally sell an issue of common stock in 1973. Fairly long lead times are necessary when companies sell bonds or stocks; otherwise, they might be forced to go into the market during unfavorable periods.

In addition to this long-run strategic financial planning, the financial manager must also make accurate short-run forecasts to be sure that bank funds will be available to meet seasonal and other short-run requirements. He might, for example, have a meeting with his bank's loan officer to discuss his company's need for funds during the coming year. Prior to the meeting, he would have his accountants prepare a detailed cash budget showing the need for money during each of the coming 12 months. The cash budget would show the maximum amount that would be needed during the year, how much would be needed during each month, and how cash surpluses would be generated at some point to enable the firm to repay the bank loan.

The financial manager would also have his firm's most recent, as well as its projected, balance sheets and income statements. He would also have calculated the key financial ratios to show both its actual and its projected financial positions to the banker. If the firm's financial position is sound and if its cash budget appears reasonable, the bank will commit itself to make the required funds available. Even if the bank decides that the company's request is unreasonable and denies the loan request, the financial manager will have time to seek other sources of funds. While it might not be pleasant to have to look elsewhere for money, it is much better to know ahead of time that the loan request will be refused.

EXTERNAL USES OF FINANCIAL FORECASTS AND BUDGETS

We have stressed the use of planning and budgeting for internal purposes—increasing the efficiency of a firm's operations. These same tools and techniques can, with relatively minor modifications, be used in both credit analysis and security analysis. For example, outside security analysts can make a forecast of a given firm's sales and, through the income statement and balance sheet relationships, make *pro forma* (or projected) balance sheets and income statements. (Such *pro forma* statements are described in the appendix to this chapter.) Credit analysts can make similar projections to aid in estimating the likely need for funds by their customers and the likelihood that borrowers can make prompt repayment.

This type of analysis has actually been conducted on a large scale in recent years. Very complete financial data going back some 20 years on about 2,000 large, publicly owned corporations is now available on magnetic tapes (Standard and Poor's Compustat tapes). These tapes are being used by security analysts in highly sophisticated ways. From what we have seen, analyses conducted in such a manner offer large potential benefits. The same tapes, frequently supplemented with additional data, are being used by the major lending institutions—banks and insurance companies—to forecast their customers' needs for funds and, thus, to plan their own financial requirements.

SUMMARY

Financial forecasting is carried on at two levels—long-range forecasting and short-range forecasting, that is, forecasting requirements for several months. Generally, the shorter the period covered by the forecast, the higher the level of accuracy.

Long-Range Financial Forecasting

The most important causal variable in determining financial requirements is a firm's projected dollar volume of sales. Hence, a good sales forecast is an essential foundation for forecasting financial requirements. The two principal methods used to make financial forecasts are (1) the percent-of-sales method and (2) the regression method. The first has the virtue of simplicity—the forecaster computes past relationships between asset and liability items and sales, assumes these same relationships will continue, and then applies the new sales forecast to get an estimate of the financial requirements.

Since the percent-of-sales method assumes that the balance sheet/sales relationships will remain constant, it is only useful for relatively short-run forecasting. When longer forecasts are being made, the regression method is preferable because it allows for changing balance sheet/sales relationships.

Short-Range Financial Forecasting

The principal tool for making short-run financial forecasts is the cash budget. Cash budgets, if used properly, are highly accurate and can pinpoint the funds that will be needed, when they will be needed, and when cash flows will be sufficient to retire any loans that might be necessary.

Use of Financial Forecasts

The tools and techniques discussed in this chapter are used in several separate but related ways. First, one of the long-range forecasting techniques is used to make a long-run forecast of the firm's financial requirements over a three-to-five–year period following the short-run planning period. This forecast is then used to make the strategic financing plans during the planning period. Long lead times are necessary when companies sell bonds or stocks; otherwise, financial managers might be forced to go into the market for funds during unfavorable periods.

In addition to this long-run, strategic forecasting, the financial manager must also make accurate short-run forecasts to be sure that bank funds will be available to meet seasonal and other short-run requirements. If the firm's financial position is sound and if its cash budget appears reasonable, the bank will commit itself to make the required funds available. If the bank decides that the company's request is unreasonable and denies it, the financial manager will have time to seek other sources of funds.

QUESTIONS

5–1 What is the first step in forecasting financial requirements? Why is this the first step?

5–2 For what reasons does a firm hold cash?

5–3 Compare the relative advantages of holding cash as opposed to investing in short-term marketable securities.

5–4 If a firm's average collection period is 25 days and its daily credit sales are $1,000, what is the theoretical amount for accounts receivable on the balance sheet?

5–5 Describe the regression method for forecasting financial needs. What are the strengths and the weaknesses of this method?

5–6 What should be the approximate point of intersection between the sales/asset regression line and the vertical axis (Y-axis intercept) for the following: inventory, accounts receivable, fixed assets? State your answer in terms of positive, zero, or negative intercept. Can you think of any accounts that might have a negative intercept?

5–7 How does forecasting financial requirements in advance of needs assist the financial manager to perform his responsibilities more effectively?

5–8 Do you suppose the management of working capital would occupy more of the financial manager's time in a retailing concern or in an electric utility company? Why?

5–9 Explain how a downturn in the business cycle could either cause a cash shortage for a firm or have the opposite effect and generate excess cash.

5–10 Why do many "young" firms find it difficult to obtain working capital loans from commercial banks? Do you suppose that a given young firm would have an easier time getting a working capital loan than a loan to finance fixed assets?

5–11 What alternatives are available to a company when it finds it has excessive working capital in the form of cash?

5–12 Explain this statement: "Current assets to a considerable extent represent permanent assets."

5–13 If the United States lacked a highly developed banking system, making it difficult if not impossible for business to borrow to meet seasonal needs, what would be the effects on the cash balances maintained by business firms? What would be the effect on the general level of business and economic activity?

5–14 What advantages might multiple regression technique have over simple regression in forecasting sales? What might be some drawbacks in the actual use of this technique?

5–15 What use might a confidence interval scheme have in variable budgeting?

5–16 Why is a cash budget important even when there is plenty of cash in the bank?

5–17 How might individuals employ the techniques of financial planning and budgeting for their own use?

5–18 What is the difference between the long-range financial forecasting concept and the budgeting concept? How might they be used together?

PROBLEMS

5–1 The Townsend Supply Company is a wholesale steel distributor. It purchases steel in carload lots from more than twenty producing mills and sells to several thousand steel users. The items carried include shapes, plates, wire products, bolts, windows, pipe, and tubing.

The company owns two warehouses, each housing 10,000 square feet, and contemplates the erection of another warehouse of 15,000 square feet. The nature of the steel-supply business requires that the company maintain large inventories to take care of customer requirements in the event of mill strikes or other delays.

In examining patterns from 1963 through 1968 the company found a rather consistent relation between the following accounts as a percent of sales.

Current assets	50
Net fixed assets	20
Accounts payable	5
Other current liabilities, including accruals and provision for income taxes but not bank loans	5
Net profit after taxes	2

The company's sales for 1969 were $6 million, and its balance sheet on December 31, 1969, was as follows:

TOWNSEND SUPPLY COMPANY
BALANCE SHEET
December 31, 1969

Current assets	$3,000,000	Accounts payable	$ 300,000
Fixed assets	1,200,000	Notes payable	600,000
		Other current liabilities	300,000
		Total current liabilities	1,200,000
		Mortgage loan	200,000
		Common stock	500,000
		Earned surplus	2,300,000
Total assets	$4,200,000	Total liabilites and net worth	$4,200,000

The company expects its sales to grow by $400,000 each year. If this growth is achieved, what will its financial requirements be at the end of the five-year period? Assume that accounts not tied directly to sales (for example, notes payable) remain constant. Assume also that the company pays no dividends.

a) Construct a *pro forma* balance sheet for the end of 1974, using "additional financing needed" as the balancing item.
b) What are the crucial assumptions made in your projection method?

5–2 The annual sales of the Grossman Company are $2 million. Common stock and notes payable are constant. The percent of sales in each balance sheet item that varies directly with sales are as follows:

Cash	4
Receivables	12
Inventories	12
Net fixed assets	18
Accounts payable	10
Provision for income tax	4
Other current liabilities	5
Profit rate (after taxes) on sales	6

a) On the assumption that any excess funds will be invested in government securities complete the balance sheet below:

GROSSMAN COMPANY
BALANCE SHEET
December 31, 1969

Cash	______	Accounts payable	______
Receivables	______	Notes payable	$160,000
Inventory	______	Provision for income tax	______
Total current assets	______	Other current liabilities	______
Fixed assets	______	Total current liabilities	______
		Common stock	$260,000
		Retained earnings	______
Government securities	______	Total liabilities and net worth	
Total assets	______		______

b) Now suppose that in one year sales increase by $400,000, to $2.4 million. What will be the new balance sheet (no dividends paid)?

c) For any given increase in sales in one year, what will be the additional external financing requirements, expressed as a percentage of sales?

5–3 The current balance sheet of the Apex Corporation is shown here.

APEX CORPORATION
BALANCE SHEET
December 31, 1969

Cash	$ 55,000	Accounts payable	$ 49,500
Accounts receivable	264,000	Accruals	38,500
Inventories	198,000	Federal taxes payable*	44,000
Total current assets	517,000	Total current liabilities	$132,000
Fixed assets, net	132,000	Net worth	517,000
Total assets	$649,000	Total claims on assets	$649,000

* Payable $22,000 on March 15 and $22,000 on June 15, 1970.

The level of business activity is expected to rise 20 percent by the end of the six-month period January through June 1970. An expansion program requiring an additional investment of $66,000 in fixed assets is planned for this period. Assume that receivables, inventories, payables, and accruals increase by 20 percent. The estimated income statement for the six-month period is shown below.

APEX CORPORATION
INCOME STATEMENT
For Six Months Ended June 30, 1970

Net sales		$990,000
Cost of goods sold	$682,000	
Other operating expenses	231,000	
Depreciation expense	33,000	
Total cost of sales		946,000
Net income before federal income taxes		$ 44,000
Federal income taxes		21,120*
Net income after federal income taxes		$ 22,880

* Assume *these* taxes will not be paid until after the cash budgeting period.

a) Prepare a cash budget covering the six-month period as one unit of time.
b) Construct an estimated balance sheet for the end of the six-month period.
c) Calculate the current ratio and total-debt-to-net-worth ratio of the firm on June 30, 1970.
d) Assume that Apex raises $110,000 cash by selling long-term debt. What will be the effect on the two ratios obtained in c?
e) What is the financial significance of the problem of rapidly expanding sales?

5–4 Indicate the effects of the transactions listed below on each of the following: total current assets, working capital, current ratio, and net profit. Use + to indicate an increase, — to indicate a decrease, and 0 to indicate no effect. State necessary assumptions and assume an initial current ratio of more than 1 to 1.

	Total Current Assets	*Working Capital*	*Current Ratio*	*Effect on Net Profit*
1. Cash is acquired through issuance of additional common stock.	______	______	______	______
2. Merchandise is sold for cash.	______	______	______	______
3. Federal income tax due for the previous year is paid.	______	______	______	______
4. A fixed asset is sold for less than book value.	______	______	______	______
5. A fixed asset is sold for more than book value.	______	______	______	______
6. Merchandise is sold on credit.	______	______	______	______
7. Payment is made to trade creditors for previous purchases.	______	______	______	______
8. A cash dividend is declared and paid.	______	______	______	______
9. Cash is obtained through bank loans.	______	______	______	______

	Total Current Assets	*Working Capital*	*Current Ratio*	*Effect on Net Profit*
10. Short-term notes receivable are sold at a discount.	______	______	______	______
11. Previously issued stock rights are exercised by company stockholders.	______	______	______	______
12. A profitable firm increases its fixed asset depreciation allowance account.	______	______	______	______
13. Marketable securities are sold below cost.	______	______	______	______
14. Uncollectible accounts are written off against the allowance account.	______	______	______	______
15. Advances are made to employees.	______	______	______	______
16. Current operating expenses are paid.	______	______	______	______
17. Short-term promissory notes are issued to trade creditors for prior purchases.	______	______	______	______
18. Ten-year notes are issued to pay off accounts payable.	______	______	______	______
19. A wholly depreciated asset is retired.	______	______	______	______
20. A *cash* sinking fund for the retirement of bonds is created; a reserve for bond sinking fund is also created.	______	______	______	______
21. Bonds are retired by the use of the cash sinking fund.	______	______	______	______
22. Accounts receivable are collected.	______	______	______	______
23. A stock dividend is declared and paid.	______	______	______	______
24. Equipment is purchased with short-term notes.	______	______	______	______
25. The allowance for doubtful accounts is increased.	______	______	______	______
26. Merchandise is purchased on credit.	______	______	______	______
27. Controlling interest in another firm is acquired by the issuance of additional common stock.	______	______	______	______
28. Earnings are added to the reserve for bond sinking fund.	______	______	______	______
29. An unconsolidated subsidiary pays the firm a cash dividend from current earnings.	______	______	______	______
30. The estimated taxes payable are increased.	______	______	______	______

Selected References

Ansoff, H. Igor, "Planning As A Practical Management Tool," *Financial Executive,* XXXII (June 1964), 34–37.

Anton, Hector R., *Accounting for the Flow of Funds* (Boston: Houghton Mifflin, 1962).

Helfert, Erich H., *Techniques of Financial Analysis,* rev. ed. (Homewood, Ill.: Irwin, 1967).

Henning, Dale A., *Non-Financial Controls in Smaller Enterprises* (Seattle, Wash.: University of Washington, College of Business Administration, 1964).

Jaedicke, Robert K. and Robert T. Sprouse, *Accounting Flows: Income, Funds, and Cash* (Englewood Cliffs, N.J.: Prentice-Hall, 1965).

Jerrett, Robert, Jr., "Total Financial Planning," *Financial Planning for Greater Profits.* Management Report Number 44. (New York: American Management Association, 1960), 44–51.

Knight, W. D., and E. H. Weinwurn, *Managerial Budgeting* (New York: Macmillan, 1964).

Lewis, John P., "Short-Term General Business Conditions Forecasting—Some Comments on Method," *Journal of Business,* XXXII (October 1962), 343–356.

Weston, J. Fred, "Forecasting Financial Requirements," *Accounting Review,* XXXIII (July 1958), 427–440.

APPENDIX TO CHAPTER 5
An Illustrative Budget System

A complete system includes (1) a production budget, (2) a materials purchases budget, (3) a budgeted income statement, (4) a budgeted balance sheet, and (5) a capital expenditure budget. Since capital expenditures are related directly to problems of the firm's growth, they have been considered separately in Chapter 7.[1]

Tables A5–1 through A5–7 carry out a hypothetical budget system. In Tables A5–2 through A5–7 the lines are numbered consecutively from 1 to 54. This procedure has the advantage of making it easy to see the relations among the various budgets. Table A5–1 outlines the highly

[1] Outlays for capital equipment do, of course, affect the cash budget, the income statement, and the balance sheet. For consideration of the influence of capital expenditures on operating budgets, the reader is referred to A. Matz, O. J. Curry, and G. W. Frank, *Cost Accounting* (Cincinnati: South-Western, 1952), pp. 450–451.

TABLE A5–1 STANDARD COSTS BASED ON VOLUME OF 1,000 UNITS PER MONTH

	PER UNIT
Direct material: 2 pieces—$1 per piece	$2
Direct labor: 1 hour—$2 per hour	2
Variable manufacturing expense: $1 per unit	1
Fixed manufacturing expense: $1,000 per month*	1
Cost of goods produced per unit	$6

* Includes $200 depreciation charges.

TABLE A5–2 PRODUCTION BUDGET

Item	Monthly Average 1967	ESTIMATED 1968, FIRST QUARTER First Month	Second Month	Third Month	Source of Data
1. Sales at $10 per unit	$ 10,000	$ 10,000	$ 12,000	$ 12,000	Assumed
2. Unit sales	1,000	1,000	1,200	1,200	Line 1 divided by $10
3. Beginning inventory (units)	500	500	600	600	One half of current month's sales
4. Difference (units)	500	500	600	600	Line 2 minus line 3
5. Ending inventory (units)	500	600	600	600	One half of next month's sales
6. Production in units	1,000	1,100	1,200	1,200	Line 4 plus line 5
7. Estimated cost of goods produced	$ 6,000	$ 6,600	$ 7,200	$ 7,200	Line 6 times $6
8. Burden absorption, under or (over)	0	(100)	(200)	(200)	Line 6 times $1 less $1,000 fixed mfg. expense
9. Adjusted cost of goods produced	$ 6,000	$ 6,500	$ 7,000	$ 7,000	Line 7 less line 8
9a. Adjusted cost per unit	$ 6	$ 5.91	$ 5.83	$ 5.83	Line 9 divided by line 6
10. Value of ending inventory (finished goods)	$ 3,000	$ 3,545	$ 3,500	$ 3,500	Line 5 multiplied by line 9a (rounded)

summarized cost accounting system. It is based on the standard costs of goods sold per unit. Standard costs include direct material, direct labor, and variable and fixed manufacturing expense. Standard costs are the costs of goods produced when the firm is operating at a high level of efficiency and when operations are near a level that may be regarded as "normal."[2]

TABLE A5–3 MATERIALS PURCHASES BUDGET

		ESTIMATED 1968, FIRST QUARTER			
Item	Monthly Average 1967	First Month	Second Month	Third Month	Source of Data
11. Production in units	1,000	1,100	1,200	1,200	Line 6
12. Material used (units)	2,000	2,200	2,400	2,400	Line 11 times 2
13. Raw materials, ending inventory	2,200	2,400	2,400	2,400	Raw material requirements next month
14. Total	4,200	4,600	4,800	4,800	Line 12 plus line 13
15. Raw materials, beginning inventory	2,000	2,200	2,400	2,400	Raw material requirements this month
16. Raw materials purchases	$ 2,200	$ 2,400	$ 2,400	$ 2,400	(Line 14 less line 15) times $1

Production Budget

The illustrative production budget is based directly on the sales forecast and the estimated unit cost of production. It is assumed that the firm maintains its finished goods inventory at 50 percent of the following month's sales. In any month, the firm must produce the unit sales plus ending inventory less the beginning inventory level.

This example illustrates the financial consequences of a rise in sales from a $10,000-per-month level to a new plateau of $12,000. As production rises in response to increased sales, the (standard) cost of goods

[2] The terminology in this chapter follows accounting usage, but anyone familiar with economics can readily translate it into economic terms. For instance, "$6 per unit at standard output" is "average total (production) cost"; "marginal production cost" is "$5 per unit"; and so on.

TABLE A5–4 CASH BUDGET

Item	Monthly Average 1967	ESTIMATED 1968 First Month	Second Month	Third Month	Source of Data
Receipts					
17. Accounts receivable collected	$ 10,000	$ 10,000	$ 10,000	$ 12,000	Sales of previous month
Disbursements					
18. Accounts payable paid	$ 2,000	$ 2,200	$ 2,400	$ 2,400	Raw materials purchases of previous month
19. Direct labor	2,000	2,200	2,400	2,400	Line 6 times $2
20. Indirect labor	700	700	700	700	Assumed
21. Variable manufacturing expenses	1,000	1,100	1,200	1,200	Line 6 times $1
22. Insurance and taxes	100	100	100	100	Assumed
23. General and administrative expenses	2,500	2,500	2,500	2,500	Assumed
24. Selling expense	500	500	600	600	5% of line 1
25. Total disbursements	$ 8,800	$ 9,300	$ 9,900	$ 9,900	Sum of lines 18–24
26. Cash from operations	$ 1,200	$ 700	$ 100	$ 2,100	Line 17 less line 25
26a. Initial cash	5,000	6,200	6,900	7,000	Preceding month, line 26b
26b. Cumulative cash	6,200	6,900	7,000	9,100	Line 26 plus line 26a
27. Desired level of cash	5,000	5,000	6,000	6,000	50% of current month's sales; approx. 4.2% of annual sales
27a. Cash available (needed) cumulative	$ 1,200	$ 1,900	$ 1,000	$ 3,100	Line 26b less line 27

produced also rises. But the standard cost of goods produced increases faster than actual costs increase because the unit cost of $6 includes fixed charges of $1 per unit. An increase of one unit of production actually raises total costs by only $5. The estimated cost per unit, however, increases by $6. Estimates of the cost of goods produced are made and then adjusted by the amount of under or overabsorbed burden. Of course, the same result for calculating the adjusted cost of goods produced

(Table A5–2, line 9) is obtained by multiplying $5 by the number of units produced to get total variable costs, and adding $1,000 in fixed costs to reach total adjusted cost of goods produced.

The per unit adjusted costs of goods produced ($5.91 for the first month) is required to calculate the ending inventory. The first-in, first-out method of inventory costing is employed. The calculation of the

TABLE A5–5 BUDGETED INCOME STATEMENT

Item	Monthly Average 1967	ESTIMATED 1968, FIRST QUARTER: First Month	Second Month	Third Month	Source of Data
28. Sales	$ 10,000	$ 10,000	$ 12,000	$ 12,000	Line 1
29. Adjusted cost of sales	6,000	5,955	7,045	7,000	Line 54
30. Gross income	$ 4,000	$ 4,045	$ 4,955	$ 5,000	Line 28 less line 29
31a. General and administrative expenses	2,500	2,500	2,500	2,500	Assumed
31b. Selling	500	500	600	600	5% of line 1
32. Total expenses	$ 3,000	$ 3,000	$ 3,100	$ 3,100	Line 31a plus 31b
33. Net income before taxes	1,000	1,045	1,855	1,900	Line 30 less line 32
34. Federal taxes	500	522	927	950	50% of line 33
35. Net income after taxes	$ 500	$ 522	$ 927	$ 950	line 33 less line 34

ending inventory value is required for the work sheet (Table A5–6) used in developing the budgeted balance sheet (Table A5–7).

Materials Purchases Budget

The level of operations indicated by the production budget in Table A5–2 is based on sales forecast and inventory requirements. The materials purchases budget (Table A5–3) contains estimates of materials purchases that will be needed to carry out these production plans. Raw materials purchases depend in turn upon materials actually used in production, material costs (Table A5–1), size of beginning inventories, and requirements for ending inventory.

The example in Table A5–3 does not take into account economical ordering quantities (EOQs) as discussed in Chapter 14. EOQs are not integrated, primarily because they assume a uniform usage rate for raw materials, an assumption that is not met in the example. Also, the EOQ analysis assumes a constant minimum inventory, but the desired minimum inventory (Table A5–3, line 13) shifts with production levels. In a practical situation, these assumptions might be approximated,

TABLE A5–6 WORK SHEET

		ADJUSTED COST OF SALES			
		Estimated 1968, First Quarter			
Item	Monthly Average 1967	First Month	Second Month	Third Month	Source of Data
50. Adjusted cost of goods produced	$ 6,000	$ 6,500	$ 7,000	$ 7,000	Line 9
51. *Add:* Beginning inventory	3,000	3,000	3,545	3,500	Line 10 lagged one month
52. Sum	$ 9,000	$ 9,500	$ 10,545	$ 10,500	
53. *Less:* Ending inventory	3,000	3,545	3,500	3,500	Line 10
54. Adjusted cost of goods sold*	$ 6,000	$ 5,955	$ 7,045	$7,000	Line 52 less line 53

* Note difference from line 9, adjusted cost of goods produced.

and EOQs can then be used to determine optimum purchase quantities; or more sophisticated operations research techniques may be used.

Cash Budget

The cash budget—perhaps the most interesting of these statements to the financial officer—is generated from information developed in the production and materials purchases budgets. In addition, estimates for other expense categories are required.[3] In Table A5–4, only cash receipts from operations are considered in order to emphasize the logic of the budget system. No account is taken of receipts or expenditures for capital items. This is because of the emphasis in this illustration on budgeting consequences of short-term fluctuations in the sales volume of the firm, although in practical situations it is a simple matter to incorporate

[3] These are assumed to be paid in the months the expenses are incurred, in order to reduce the volume of explanatory information.

TABLE A5–7 BUDGETED BALANCE SHEET

Item	Monthly Average 1967	ESTIMATED 1968, FIRST QUARTER First Month	Second Month	Third Month	Source of Data
Assets					
36. Cash	$ 5,000	$ 5,000	$ 6,000	$ 6,000	Line 27
37. Govt. securities					Sales of current month
38. Net receivables	10,000	10,000	12,000	12,000	
39. Inventories					
Raw materials	2,200	2,400	2,400	2,400	Line 13
Finished goods	3,000	3,545	3,500	3,500	Line 10
40. Current assets	$ 20,200	$ 20,945	$ 23,900	$ 23,900	Total lines 36 through 39
41. Net fixed assets	80,000	79,800	79,600	79,400	$80,000 less $200 per month depreciation
42. Total assets	$100,200	$100,745	$103,500	$103,300	Total lines 40 and 41
Liabilities					
43. Accounts payable	$ 2,200	$ 2,400	$ 2,400	$ 2,400	Raw material purchases this month
44. Notes payable $3,200	2,000	1,300	2,200	100	$3,200 less line 27a
45. Provisions for federal income tax	500	1,022	1,950	2,900	Cumulation of line 34
46. Long-term debt	25,000	25,000	25,000	25,000	Assumed
47. Common stock, $50,000	50,000	50,000	50,000	50,000	Assumed
48. Surplus, $20,000	$ 20,500	$ 21,023	$ 21,950	$ 22,900	Cumulation line 35 plus $20,000
49. Total claims	$100,200	100,745	103,500	103,300	Sum of lines 43 through 48

capital expenditures into the cash budget. However, the fact that capital expenditures are ignored does not diminish their impact on cash flows. Capital expenditures occur sporadically and in amounts that sometimes overwhelm operating transactions.

Period. The three-month period used in the cash budget, Table A5–4, is not necessarily the length of time for which a firm will predict cash flows. Although this period does coincide with the length of traditional

90-day bank loans, the firm is more likely to utilize a six-month or one-year period. Normally, a six-month forecast is prepared on a monthly basis. Briefly, the cash budget period will vary with the line of business, credit needs, the ability to forecast the firm's cash flows for the distant future, and requirements of suppliers of funds.

Illustrative cash budget. The cash flow for a given period is the difference between receipts and expenditures for that period. In Table A5–4, for the 1967 monthly averages, cash from operations ($1,200) is the difference between accounts receivable collected ($10,000) and total disbursements ($8,800). Note that collections from accounts receivable and accounts payable paid depend upon sales and purchases from the preceding months rather than on current sales.

The significant figure for the manager is cash available (or needed). Cash from operations in the first month of 1968, plus the initial cash balance at the beginning of the month, total $6,900. The financial manager has previously determined that only $5,000 is needed to handle this level of sales. Consequently, the firm will have surplus cash of $1,900 by the end of the month, and $3,100 by the end of the third month. In the *pro forma* balance sheet (Table A5–7), it is assumed that these cash surpluses are used to pay off notes payable.

Use. As mentioned earlier in the chapter, the financial manager uses the cash budget to anticipate fluctuations in the level of cash. Normally, a growing firm will be faced with continuous cash drains. The cash budget tells the manager the magnitude of the outflow. If necessary, he can plan to arrange for additional funds. The cash budget is the primary document presented to a lender to indicate the need for funds and the feasibility of repayment.

In Table A5–4 the opposite situation is illustrated. The firm will have excess cash of at least $1,000 during each of the three months under consideration. The excess can be invested or it can be used to reduce outstanding liabilities. In this example, the firm retires notes payable (Table A5–7, line 44). Such a small amount as $1,000 might be held as cash or as a demand deposit, but the alert financial manager will not allow substantial amounts of cash to remain idle.

Budgeted Income Statement

After a cash budget has been developed, two additional financial statements can be formulated—the budgeted income statement (Table A5–5) and the budgeted balance sheet (Table A5–7). They are prepared on an accrual rather than a cash basis. For example, the income statement accounts for depreciation charges. Expenses recognized on an accrual basis are included in total expenses (Table A5–5, line 32); thus, calculated net income is lowered. The only accrual item assumed in this exhibit is depreciation, and this is assumed to be $200 monthly. The before-tax profit figure in the third month in the budgeted income statement (line 33) differs from line 26 in the cash budget only by the amount of depreciation.[4] This illustration makes clear the effect of noncash expenses on the income statement.

The preparation of the budgeted income statement follows standard accounting procedures. The major calculation involved is adjusted cost of sales, explained in Table A5–6.

The budgeted income statement shows the impact of future events on the firm's net income. Comparison of future income with that of past periods indicates the difficulties that will be encountered in maintaining or exceeding past performance. A forecast indicating low net income should cause management to increase sales efforts as well as to make efforts to reduce costs. Anticipation and prevention of difficulties can be achieved by a sound budgeting system.

Budgeted Balance Sheet

Lenders are interested in the projected balance sheet to see what the future financial position of the firm will be. Balance sheet projections discussed in the body of Chapter 5 were focused on year-to-year forecasts, and they assumed stable underlying relations. The budget technique deals with shorter term projections but is based on the same fundamental kinds of stable relations between the volume of sales and the associated asset requirements. Either method can be used, and each can operate as a check on the other. The budgeted balance sheet presented in Table A5–7, however, is the result of a more detailed and analytical forecast of future operations. It is the logical culmination of the budget system and provides a complete reconciliation between the initial balance sheet, the cash budget, and the income statement.

The required information is readily available from past balance sheets or is contained in other elements of the budget system. For example, the initial balance of notes payable is $3,200. An increase in cash available (Table A5–4, line 27a) is used to repay notes payable; a decrease is met by additional borrowing from a commercial bank. Other new items, such as long-term debt and common stock (Table A5–7, lines 46 and 47), are taken from previous balance sheets.

The foregoing exhibits present a simplified yet complete budget system. It contains all the elements found in a voluminous and complex actual budget system of a firm. If a person understands the logic and flow of this relatively simple budget system, he can approach an actual budget with perspective, looking for the fundamental relations involved. He can then apply the patterns to actual budget systems of any degree of complexity.

[4] This agreement holds only in a "steady state," that is, when inventories and receivables are not being raised or lowered. Prior to the third month this condition does not hold.

PART THREE

LONG-TERM INVESTMENT DECISIONS

6

The Interest Factor in Financial Decisions

The investment in fixed assets should, logically, be taken up at this point. However, the long-term nature of fixed investments makes it necessary to consider first the theory of compound interest—the "math of finance." Compound interest is essential to an understanding of capital budgeting, the topic of the following chapter. However, interest rate theory is also an integral part of several other topics taken up later in the text. Financial structure decisions, lease versus purchase decisions, bond refunding operations, security valuation techniques, and the whole question of the cost of capital are some other subjects that cannot be understood without a knowledge of compound interest.

Many people are afraid of the subject of compound interest and simply avoid it. It is certainly true that many successful businessmen—even some bankers—know essentially nothing of the subject. However, as technology advances, as more and more engineers become involved in general management, and as modern business administration programs turn out more and more highly qualified graduates, this "success in spite of himself" pattern will become more and more difficult to achieve. Furthermore, fear of compound interest relationships is quite unfounded—the subject matter is simply not that difficult. Practically all problems involving compound interest can be handled quite satisfactorily with only a few basic formulas.

COMPOUND VALUE

A person deposits $1,000 in a savings and loan association that pays 4 percent interest compounded annually. How much will he have at the end of one year? To treat the matter systematically, let us define the following terms:

P = principal, or beginning amount
i = interest rate
I = dollar amount of interest earned during a period
V = ending amount, or the sum of $P + I$

V may now be calculated as

$$\begin{aligned} V &= P + I \\ &= P + Pi \\ &= P(1 + i) \end{aligned} \tag{6–1}$$

This last equation shows that the ending amount is equal to the beginning amount times the factor $(1 + i)$. For the example, where $P = \$1{,}000$, V is

$$V = \$1{,}000(1.0 + .04) = \$1{,}000(1.04) = \$1{,}040$$

If the person leaves the $1,000 on deposit for five years, to what amount will it have grown at the end of that period? Equation 6–1 can be used to construct Table 6–1, which indicates the answer. Note that V_2, the balance at the end of the second year, is found as

$$V_2 = P_2(1 + i) = P_1(1 + i)(1 + i) = P_1(1 + i)^2$$

TABLE 6–1 COMPOUND INTEREST CALCULATIONS

YEAR	BEGINNING AMOUNT (P)	$\times$ $(1 + i)$ =	ENDING AMOUNT (V)
1	$1,000	1.04 =	$1,040
2	1,040	1.04 =	1,082
3	1,082	1.04 =	1,125
4	1,125	1.04 =	1,170
5	1,170	1.04 =	1,217

Similarly, V_3, the balance after three years, is found as

$$V_3 = P_3(1 + i) = P_1(1 + i)^3$$

In general, V_n, the compound amount at the end of any year n, is found as

$$V_n = P(1 + i)^n \qquad (6\text{–}2)$$

This is the fundamental equation of compound interest, and it can readily be seen that equation 6–1 is simply a special case of equation 6–2 where $n = 1$.

While it is necessary to understand the derivation of equation 6–2 in order to understand much of the material in the remainder of this chapter (as well as material to be covered in subsequent chapters), the concept can be applied quite readily in a mechanical sense. Tables have been constructed for values of $(1 + i)^n$ for wide ranges of i and n; Table 6–2 is illustrative. Table A–1, in Appendix A, is a more complete table.

Letting IF (interest factor) $= (1 + i)^n$, equation 6–2 may be written as $V = P(\text{IF})$. It is necessary only to go to an appropriate interest table to find the proper interest factor. The correct interest factor for the above illustration is found in Table 6–2. Look down the year column to 5 and across to the appropriate number in the 4 percent column to find the interest factor—1.217. Then, using this interest factor, we find the compound value of the $1,000 after five years as

$$V = P(\text{IF}) = \$1{,}000(1.217) = \$1{,}217$$

Notice that this is precisely the same figure that was obtained by the long method in Table 6–1.

TABLE 6–2 COMPOUND VALUE OF $1

YEAR	1%	2%	3%	4%	5%	6%	7%	8%	9%	10%
1	1.010	1.020	1.030	1.040	1.050	1.060	1.070	1.080	1.090	1.100
2	1.020	1.040	1.061	1.082	1.102	1.124	1.145	1.166	1.188	1.210
3	1.030	1.061	1.093	1.125	1.158	1.191	1.225	1.260	1.295	1.331
4	1.041	1.082	1.126	1.170	1.216	1.262	1.311	1.360	1.412	1.464
5	1.051	1.104	1.159	1.217	1.276	1.338	1.403	1.469	1.539	1.611
6	1.062	1.126	1.194	1.265	1.340	1.419	1.501	1.587	1.677	1.772
7	1.072	1.149	1.230	1.316	1.407	1.504	1.606	1.714	1.828	1.949
8	1.083	1.172	1.267	1.369	1.477	1.594	1.718	1.851	1.993	2.144
9	1.094	1.195	1.305	1.423	1.551	1.689	1.838	1.999	2.172	2.358
10	1.105	1.219	1.344	1.480	1.629	1.791	1.967	2.159	2.367	2.594
11	1.116	1.243	1.384	1.539	1.710	1.898	2.105	2.332	2.580	2.853
12	1.127	1.268	1.426	1.601	1.796	2.012	2.252	2.518	2.813	3.138
13	1.138	1.294	1.469	1.665	1.886	2.133	2.410	2.720	3.066	3.452
14	1.149	1.319	1.513	1.732	1.980	2.261	2.579	2.937	3.342	3.797
15	1.161	1.346	1.558	1.801	2.079	2.397	2.759	3.172	3.642	4.177

PRESENT VALUE

Suppose you were offered the alternative of either **$1,217** at the end of five years or X dollars today. There is no question but that the **$1,217** will be paid in full (perhaps the payer is the United States government) and, having no current need for the money, you would deposit it in a savings association paying a 4 percent dividend. (Four percent is defined to be your "opportunity cost.") How small must X be to induce you to accept the promise of $1,217 five years hence?

Referring to Table 6–2, it is seen that the initial amount of $1,000 growing at 4 percent a year yields **$1,217** at the end of five years. Hence, you should be indifferent in your choice between $1,000 today and $1,217 at the end of five years.

Finding present values (or discounting, as it is commonly called) is simply the reverse of compounding, and equation 6–2 can quite readily be transformed into a present value formula. Dividing both sides by $(1 + i)^n$ and dropping the subscript n from V_n, we have:

$$P = \frac{V}{(1 + i)^n} = V\left[\frac{1}{(1 + i)^n}\right] \qquad (6\text{–}3)$$

Tables have been constructed for the term in brackets for various values of i and n; Table 6–3 is an example. A more complete table,

TABLE 6–3 PRESENT VALUE OF $1

YEAR	1%	2%	3%	4%	5%	6%	7%	8%	9%	10%	12%	14%	15%
1	.990	.980	.971	.962	.952	.943	.935	.926	.917	.909	.893	.877	.870
2	.980	.961	.943	.925	.907	.890	.873	.857	.842	.826	.797	.769	.756
3	.971	.942	.915	.889	.864	.840	.816	.794	.772	.751	.712	.675	.658
4	.961	.924	.889	.855	.823	.792	.763	.835	.708	.683	.636	.592	.572
5	.951	.906	.863	.822	.784	.747	.713	.681	.650	.621	.567	.519	.497
6	.942	.888	.838	.790	.746	.705	.666	.630	.596	.564	.507	.456	.432
7	.933	.871	.813	.760	.711	.665	.623	.583	.547	.513	.452	.400	.376
8	.923	.853	.789	.731	.677	.627	.582	.540	.592	.467	.404	.351	.327
9	.914	.837	.766	.703	.645	.592	.544	.500	.460	.424	.361	.308	.284
10	.905	.820	.744	.676	.614	.558	.508	.463	.422	.386	.322	.270	.247

Table A–2, is found in Appendix A. For the illustrative case being considered, look down the 4 percent column to the fifth row. The figure shown there, 0.822, is the interest factor used to determine the present value of $1,217 payable in five years, discounted at 4 percent.

$$
\begin{aligned}
P &= V(\text{IF}) \\
&= \$1{,}217(0.822) \\
&= \$1{,}000
\end{aligned}
$$

'OMPOUND VALUE 'F AN ANNUITY

An annuity is defined as a series of payments of a fixed amount for a specified number of years. Each payment occurs at the end of the year.[1] For example, a promise to pay $1,000 a year for three years is a three-year annuity. If one were to receive such an annuity and were to deposit each annual payment in a savings account paying 4 percent interest, how much would he have at the end of three years? The answer is shown graphically in Figure 6–1. The first payment is

[1] Had the payment been made at the beginning of the period, each receipt would simply have been shifted back one year. The annuity would have been called an *annuity due;* the one in the present discussion, where payments are made at the end of each period, is called a *regular annuity* or, sometimes, a *deferred annuity.*

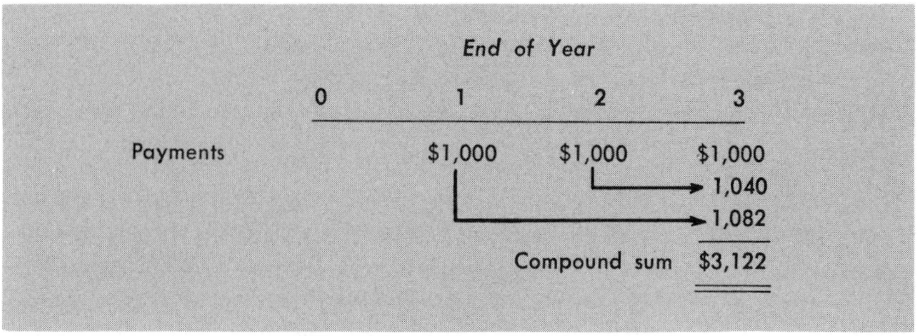

Figure 6–1 Graphic Illustration of an Annuity: Compound Sum

made at the end of year 1, the second at the end of year 2, and so on. The last payment is not compounded at all; the next to the last is compounded for one year; the second from the last for two years; and so on back to the first, which is compounded for $n - 1$ years. When the compound values of each of the payments are added, their total is the sum of the annuity. For the example, this total is $3,122.

Expressed algebraically, with S_n defined as the compound sum, R as the periodic receipt, and n as the length of the annuity, the formula for S_n is:

$$\begin{aligned} S_n &= R(1+i)^{n-1} + R(1+i)^{n-2} + \cdots + R(1+i)^1 + R(1+i)^0 \\ &= R[(1+i)^{n-1} + (1+i)^{n-2} + \cdots + (1+i)^1 + 1] \\ &= R[\text{IF}] \end{aligned}$$

The expression in brackets has been given values for various combinations of n and i. An illustrative set of these annuity interest factors is given in Table 6–4; a more complete set may be found in Table

TABLE 6–4 SUM OF AN ANNUITY OF $1 FOR N YEARS

YEAR	1%	2%	3%	4%	5%	6%	7%	8%
1	1.000	1.000	1.000	1.000	1.000	1.000	1.000	1.000
2	2.010	2.020	2.030	2.040	2.050	2.060	2.070	2.080
3	2.030	3.060	3.091	3.122	3.152	3.184	3.215	3.246
4	4.060	4.122	4.184	4.246	4.310	4.375	4.440	4.506
5	5.101	5.204	5.309	5.416	5.526	5.637	5.751	5.867
6	6.152	6.308	6.468	6.633	6.802	6.975	7.153	7.336
7	7.214	7.434	7.662	7.898	8.142	8.394	8.654	8.923
8	8.286	8.583	8.892	9.214	9.549	9.897	10.260	10.637
9	9.369	9.755	10.159	10.583	11.027	11.491	11.978	12.488
10	10.462	10.950	11.464	12.006	12.578	13.181	13.816	14.487

A–3 in Appendix A. To find the answer to the three-year \$1,000 annuity problem, simply refer to Table 6–4, look down the 4 percent column to the row for the third year, and multiply the factor 3.122 by \$1,000. The answer is the same as the one derived by the long method illustrated in Figure 6–1.

$$\begin{aligned} S_n &= R \times \text{IF} \\ &= \$1{,}000 \times 3.122 = \$3{,}122 \end{aligned} \tag{6–4}$$

RESENT VALUE OF AN ANNUITY

Suppose you were offered the following alternatives: a three-year annuity of \$1,000 a year or a lump-sum payment today. You have no need for the money during the next three years, so if you accept the annuity you would simply deposit the receipts in a savings account paying 4 percent interest. How large must the lump-sum payment be to make it equivalent to the annuity? Again, a graphic illustration (Figure 6–2) will help to explain the problem.

The present value of the first receipt is $R[1/(1+i)]$; the second is $R[1/(1+i)]^2$; and so on. Defining the present value of an annuity of n years as A_n, we may write the following equation:

$$\begin{aligned} A_n &= R\left[\frac{1}{1+i}\right]^1 + R\left[\frac{1}{1+i}\right]^2 + \cdots + R\left[\frac{1}{1+i}\right]^n \\ &= R\left[\frac{1}{(1+i)} + \frac{1}{(1+i)^2} + \cdots + \frac{1}{(1+i)^n}\right] \\ &= R[\text{IF}] \end{aligned} \tag{6–5}$$

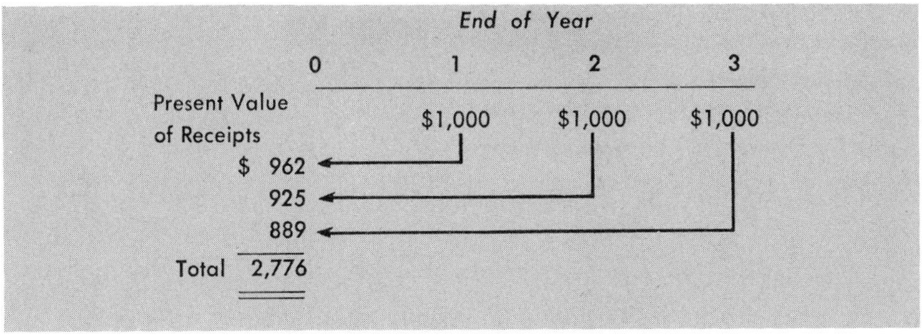

Figure 6–2 Graphic Illustration of an Annuity: Present Value

Again, tables have been worked out for the interest factor, the term in the brackets. Table 6–5 is illustrative, and a more complete table

TABLE 6–5 PRESENT VALUES OF AN ANNUITY OF $1

YEAR	1%	2%	3%	4%	5%	6%	7%	8%	9%	10%
1	0.990	0.980	0.971	0.962	0.952	0.943	0.935	0.926	0.917	0.909
2	1.970	1.942	1.913	1.886	1.859	1.833	1.808	1.783	1.759	1.736
3	2.941	2.884	2.829	2.775	2.723	2.673	2.624	2.577	2.531	2.487
4	3.902	3.808	3.717	3.630	3.546	3.465	3.387	3.312	3.240	3.170
5	4.853	4.713	4.580	4.452	4.329	4.212	4.100	3.993	3.890	3.791
6	5.795	5.601	5.417	5.242	5.076	4.917	4.766	4.623	4.486	4.355
7	6.728	6.472	6.230	6.002	5.786	5.582	5.389	5.206	5.033	4.868
8	7.652	7.325	7.020	6.733	6.463	6.210	6.971	5.747	5.535	5.335
9	8.566	8.162	7.786	7.435	7.108	6.802	6.515	6.247	5.985	5.759
10	9.471	8.983	8.530	8.111	7.722	7.360	7.024	6.710	6.418	6.145

is found in Table A–4 in Appendix A. From this table, the IF for a three-year 4 percent annuity is found to be **2.775**. Multiplying this factor by the **$1,000** annual receipt gives **$2,775**, the present value of the annuity. This figure departs from the long-method answer shown in Figure 6–2 only by a rounding difference.

$$\begin{aligned} A_n &= R \times \text{IF} \\ &= \$1{,}000 \times 2.775 \\ &= \$2{,}775 \end{aligned} \qquad (6\text{–}6)$$

ANNUAL PAYMENTS FOR ACCUMULATION OF A FUTURE SUM

Suppose we want to know the amount of money that must be deposited at 5 percent for each of the next five years, in order to have $10,000 available to pay off a debt at the end of the fifth year. Dividing both sides of equation 6–4 by IF, we obtain

$$R = \frac{S_n}{\text{IF}}$$

Looking up the interest factor for five years at 5 percent in Table 6–4 and dividing this figure into $10,000, we find

$$R = \frac{\$10{,}000}{5.526} = \$1{,}810$$

Thus, if $1,810 is deposited each year in an account paying 5 percent interest, at the end of five years the account will have accumulated $10,000.

ANNUAL RECEIPTS FROM AN ANNUITY

Suppose that on September 1, 1969, you receive an inheritance of $7,000. The money is to be used for your education and is to be spent during the academic years beginning September 1970, 1971, and 1972. If you place the money in a bank account paying 4 percent annual interest and make three equal withdrawals at each of the specified dates, how large can each withdrawal be to leave you with exactly a zero balance after the last one has been made?

The solution requires application of the present value of an annuity formula, equation 6–6. Here, however, we know that the present value of the annuity is $7,000, and the problem is to find the three equal annual payments when the interest rate is 4 percent. This calls for dividing both sides of equation 6–6 by IF to make equation 6–7.

$$A_n = R(\text{IF}) \qquad (6\text{–}6)$$

$$R = \frac{A_n}{\text{IF}} \qquad (6\text{–}7)$$

The interest factor (IF) is found in Table 6–5 to be 2.775, and substituting this value into equation 6–7 we find the three equal annual withdrawals to be $2,523 a year:

$$R = \frac{\$7{,}000}{2.775} = \$2{,}523$$

This particular type of calculation is used frequently in setting up insurance and pension plan benefit schedules, and it is also used to find the periodic payments necessary to retire a loan within a specified period.

For example, if you wanted to retire a $7,000 bank loan drawing interest at 4 percent on the unpaid balance in three equal installments, each payment would be $2,523. In this case, you would be the borrower and the bank would be "buying" an annuity with a present value of $7,000.

PRESENT VALUE OF AN UNEVEN SERIES OF RECEIPTS

Recall that the definition of an annuity includes the words *fixed amount*—in other words, annuities deal with constant, or level, payments or receipts. Although many financial decisions do involve constant payments, many important decisions are concerned with uneven flows of cash. In particular, the kinds of fixed asset investments dealt with in the following chapter very frequently involve uneven flows. Consequently, it is necessary to expand the present analysis to deal with varying payment streams. Since most of the applications call for present values, not compound sums or other figures, this section is restricted to the present value (PV).

To illustrate the calculating procedure, suppose someone offered to sell you a series of payments consisting of $300 after one year, $100 after two years, and $200 after three years. How much would you be willing to pay for the series, assuming the appropriate discount rate (interest rate) is 4 percent? To determine the purchase price, simply compute the present value of the series; the calculations are worked out in Table 6–6 below.

TABLE 6–6 CALCULATING THE PRESENT VALUE OF AN UNEVEN SERIES OF PAYMENTS

YEAR	RECEIPT	×	INTEREST FACTOR (IF)	=	PRESENT VALUE (PV)
1	$300		.962		$288.60
2	100		.925		92.50
3	200		.889		177.80
			PV of investment		$558.90

The receipts for each year are shown in the second column; the discount factors (from Table 6–3) are given in the third column; and the product of these two columns, the present value of each individual receipt, is given in the last column. When the individual present values in the last column are added, the sum is the present value of the investment, \$558.90. Under the assumptions of the example, you should be willing to pay this amount for the investment.

Had the series of payments been somewhat different—say \$300 at the end of the first year, then nine annual payments of \$100 each—we would probably want to use a different procedure for finding the investment's present value. We could, of course, set up a calculating table, such as Table 6–6, but the fact that most of the payments are part of an annuity permits us to use a short cut. The calculating procedure is shown in Table 6–7, and the logic of the table is diagrammed in Figure 6–3.

TABLE 6–7 CALCULATING PROCEDURE FOR AN UNEVEN SERIES OF PAYMENTS THAT INCLUDES AN ANNUITY

1. PV of \$300 due in 1 year \$300(0.962)	\$ 288.60
2. PV of nine-year annuity with \$100 receipts	
a. PV at beginning of next year \$100(7.435) = \$743.50	
b. PV of \$743.50 \$743.50(0.962)	715.25
3. PV of total series	\$1,003.85

Section 1 of the table deals with the \$300 received at the end of the first year; its present value is found to be \$288.60. Section 2 deals

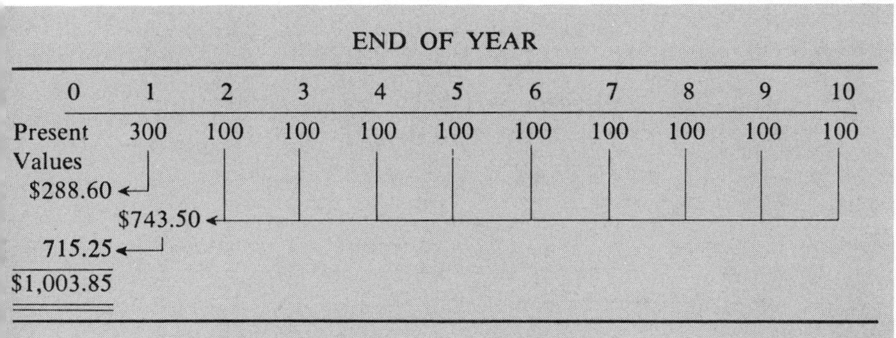

Figure 6–3 Graphic Illustration of Present Value Calculations

with the nine $100 payments. In part a, the value of a $100, 9-year, 4 percent annuity is found to be $743.50. However, the annuity does not start until *next* year, so it is worth less than $743.50 today. Specifically, it is worth the present value of $743.50, discounted back one year at 4 percent, or $715.25; this calculation is shown in part b of section 2. When the present value of the initial payment is added to the present value of the annuity component, the sum is the present value of the entire investment, or $1,003.85.

SEMIANNUAL AND OTHER COMPOUNDING PERIODS

In all the examples used thus far, it has been assumed that returns were received once a year, or annually. For example, in the first section of the chapter, dealing with compound values, it was assumed that funds were placed on deposit in a savings and loan association and grew by 4 percent a year. However, suppose the advertised rate had been 4 percent compounded *semiannually*. What would this have meant? Consider the following example.

A person deposits $1,000 in a bank savings account and receives a return of 4 percent compounded semiannually. How much will he have at the end of one year? Semiannual compounding means that interest is actually paid each six months, a fact taken into account in the tabular calculations in Table 6–8. Here the annual interest rate is divided by

TABLE 6–8 COMPOUND INTEREST CALCULATIONS WITH SEMIANNUAL COMPOUNDING

PERIOD	BEGINNING AMOUNT (P)	×	$(1 + i)$	=	ENDING AMOUNT (V)
1	$1,000.00		(1.02)		$1,020.00
2	1,020.00		(1.02)		1,040.40

2, but twice as many compounding periods are used because interest is paid twice a year. Comparing the amount on hand at the end of the second six-month period, $1,040.40, with what would have been on hand under annual compounding, $1,040, shows that semiannual compounding is better from the standpoint of the saver. This result occurs, of course, because he earns interest on interest more frequently.

General formulas can be developed for use when compounding periods are more frequent than once a year. To demonstrate this, equation 6–2 is modified as follows:

$$V_n = P(1 + i)^n \tag{6–2}$$

$$V_n = P\left(1 + \frac{i}{m}\right)^{mn} \tag{6–8}$$

Here m is the number of times per year compounding occurs. When banks compute daily interest, the value of m is set at 365 and equation 6–8 is applied.

The tables can be used when compounding occurs more than once a year. Simply divide the nominal, or stated, interest rate by the number of times compounding occurs, and multiply the years by the number of compounding periods per year. For example, to find the amount to which $1,000 will grow after five years if semiannual compounding is applied to a stated 4 percent interest rate, divide 4 percent by 2 and multiply the five years by 2. Then look in Table 6–2 (or Appendix Table A–1) under the 2 percent column and the row for the tenth year. You find an interest factor of 1.219. Multiplying this by the initial $1,000 gives a value of $1,219, the amount to which $1,000 will grow in five years at 4 percent compounded semiannually. This compares with $1,217 for annual compounding.

The same procedure is applied in all the cases covered—compounding, discounting, single payments, and annuities. To illustrate semiannual compounding in finding the present value of an annuity, for example, consider the case described in the section on the present value of an annuity above—$1,000 a year for three years, discounted at 4 percent. With annual compounding (or discounting) the interest factor is 2.775, and the present value of the annuity is $2,775. For semiannual compounding look under the 2 percent column and year 6 row of Table 6–5, to find an interest factor of 5.601. This is now multiplied by half of $1,000, or the $500 deposited each six months, to get the present value of the annuity—$2,800. The payments come a little more rapidly—the first $500 is paid after only six months (similarly with other payments) so the annuity is a little more valuable if payments are received semiannually rather than annually.

By letting m approach infinity, equation 6–8 can be modified to the special case of *continuous compounding*. Continuous compounding, while extremely useful in theoretical finance, has not been used frequently in practical applications. Further, its development is highly technical and requires the use of integral calculus. We have, therefore, elected to treat it in an appendix to this chapter rather than in the body of the chapter itself.

APPROPRIATE INTEREST RATE

Throughout the chapter an assumed interest rate has been used in the examples. Before closing, however, it is necessary to give some idea of what the appropriate interest rate for a particular investment might be.

The starting point is, of course, the general level of interest rates in the economy as a whole. This level is set by the interaction of supply-and-demand forces, with demand for funds coming largely from businesses, individual borrowers, and, when it is running a deficit, the federal government. Funds are supplied by individual and corporate savers and, under the control of the Federal Reserve System, by the creation of money by banks. Depending on the relative levels of supply and demand, the basic pattern of interest rates is determined.

There is no one rate of interest in the economy—rather, there is, at any given time, an array of different rates. The lowest rates are found on the safest investments, the highest rates on the most risky ones. Usually, there is less risk on investments that mature in the near future than on longer term investments, so generally higher rates are associated with long-term investments. There are other factors that affect interest rate differentials (also called "yield" differentials), but a discussion of these factors is best deferred until later in the book.

A person faced with the kinds of decisions considered in this chapter must accept the existing set of interest rates found in the economy. If he has money to invest, he can invest in short-term United States government securities and incur no risk whatever. However, he will generally have to accept a relatively low yield on his investment. If he is willing to accept a little more risk, he can invest in high-grade corporate bonds and get a higher fixed rate of return. If he is willing to accept still more risk, he can move into common stocks to obtain variable (and hopefully higher) returns (dividends plus capital gains) on his investment. Other alternatives include bank and savings and loan deposits, long-term governments, mortgages, apartment houses, and so on.

Risk Premiums

With only a limited amount of money to invest, one must pick and choose among investments, and the final selection will involve a choice between risk and returns. Suppose, for example, that you are indifferent between a five-year government bond yielding 4 percent a year, a five-year corporate bond yielding 5 percent, and a share of stock on which you can expect to receive a 6 percent return. Given this situation, you can take the government bond as a riskless security, and you attach a 1 percent risk premium to the corporate bond and a 2 percent risk premium to the share of stock. Risk premiums, then, are the added returns that risky investments must command over less risky ones if there is to be a demand for risky assets. The concept of the risk premium is discussed in more detail in Chapter 8 and also in the chapters dealing with the cost of capital.

Opportunity Costs

Although there are many potential investments available in the economy at any given time, a particular individual actively considers only a limited number of them. After making adjustments for risk differentials, he ranks the various alternatives from the most attractive to the least. Then, presumably, our investor puts his available funds in the most attractive investment. If he is offered a new investment, he must compare it with the best of the existing alternatives. If he takes the new investment, he must give up the opportunity of investing in the best of his old alternatives. *The yield on the best of the alternatives is defined as the opportunity cost of investing in the new alternative.* The interest rates used in the preceding examples were all determined as opportunity costs available to the person in the example. This concept is also used in the following chapter, where we consider business decisions on investments in fixed assets, or the *capital budgeting decision.*

SUMMARY

A knowledge of compound interest and present value techniques is essential to an understanding of many important aspects of finance: capital budgeting, financial structure, security valuation, and many other topics. The basic principles of compound interest, together with the most important formulas used in practice, were described in this chapter.

Compound Value

Compound value (V_n), or compound amount, is defined as the sum to which a beginning amount of principal (P) will grow over n years when interest is earned at the rate of i percent a year. The equation for finding compound values is:

$$V_n = P(1 + i)^n$$

Tables giving the present value of \$1 for a large number of different years and interest rates have been prepared. The present value of \$1 is called the interest factor (IF); illustrative values are given in Table 6–2, and a more complete set of interest factors is given in Appendix Table A–1.

Present Value (PV)

The present value of a future payment (P) is the amount which, if we had it now and invested it at the specified interest rate (i), would equal the future payment (V) on the date the future payment is due. For example, if one is to receive \$1,217 after five years and decides that 4 percent is the appropriate interest rate (it is called "discount" rate when computing present values), then he could find the present value of the \$1,217 to be \$1,000 by applying the following equation:

$$P = V\left[\frac{1}{(1 + i)^n}\right] = \$1{,}217[0.822] = \$1{,}000$$

The term in brackets is called the present value interest factor (IF), and values for it have been worked out in Table 6–3 and Appendix Table A–2.

Compound Value of an Annuity

An annuity is defined as a series of payments of a fixed amount (R) for a specified number of years. The compound value of an annuity is the total amount one would have at the end of the annuity period if each payment was invested at a certain interest rate and held to the end of the annuity period. For example, suppose we have a three-year \$1,000 annuity invested at 4 percent. There are formulas for annuities, but tables are available for the relevant interest factors. The IF for the compound value of a three-year annuity at 4 percent is 3.122, and it can be used to find the present value of the illustrative annuity:

$$\text{compound value} = \text{IF} \times \text{annual receipt} = 3.122 \times \$1{,}000 = \$3{,}122$$

Thus, \$3,122 is the compound value of the annuity.

Present Value of an Annuity

The present value of an annuity is the lump sum one would need to have on hand today in order to be able to withdraw equal amounts (R) each year and end up with a balance exactly equal to zero at the end of the annuity period. For example, if one wanted to withdraw \$1,000 a year for three years, he could deposit \$2,775 today in a bank account paying 4 percent interest, withdraw the \$1,000 in each of the next three years, and end up with a zero balance. Thus, \$2,775 is the present value of an annuity of \$1,000 per year for three years when the appropriate discount rate is 4 percent. Again, tables are available for finding the present value of annuities. To use them, one simply looks up the interest factor (IF) for the appropriate number of years and interest rate, then multiplies the IF by the annual receipt.

$$\text{PV of annuity} = \text{IF} \times \text{annual receipt} = 2.775 \times \$1{,}000 = \$2{,}775$$

Relation of Interest Factors to One Another

All interest factors (IF) given in the tables are for \$1; for example, 2.775 is the IF for finding the present value of a three-year annuity. It must be multiplied by the annual receipt, \$1,000 in the example, to find the actual value of the annuity. Students—and even financial managers—sometimes make careless mistakes when looking up interest factors, using the wrong table for the purpose. This can be avoided if one recognizes the following sets of relations.

Compound value, single payment. The IF for the compound value of a single payment, with the normal interest rates and holding periods generally found, is *always* greater than 1.0 but seldom larger than about 3.0.

Present value, single payment. The IF for the present value of a single payment is *always* smaller than 1.0; for example, 0.822 is the present value IF for 4 percent held for five years. The *compound* value IF is larger than 1.0; the *present* value IF is smaller than 1.0.

Compound value of an annuity. The IF for the compound value of an annuity is *always* larger than the number of years the annuity has to run. For example, the IF for a three-year annuity will be larger than 3.0, while the IF for a 10-year annuity will be larger than 10.0. Just how much larger depends on the interest rate—at low rates the interest factor is slightly larger than n; at high rates it is very much larger.

Present value of an annuity. The IF for the present value of an annuity is smaller than the number of years it has to run. For example, the IF for the present value of a three-year annuity is less than 3.0.

Other Uses of the Basic Equations

The four basic interest formulas can be used in combination to find such things as the present value of an uneven series of receipts. The formulas can also be transformed to find (1) the annual payments necessary to accumulate a future sum, (2) the annual receipts from a specified annuity, and (3) the periodic payments necessary to amortize a loan.

Appropriate Interest Rate

The appropriate interest rate to use is critical when working with compound interest problems. The true nature of the interest rates to be used when working with business problems can be understood only after the chapters dealing with the cost of capital have been examined; this chapter concluded with a brief discussion of some of the factors that determine the appropriate rate of interest for a particular problem—the risk of the investment and the investor's opportunity cost of money.

QUESTIONS

6–1 What types of financial decisions require explicit consideration of the interest factor?

6–2 Compound interest relations are important for decisions other than financial ones. Why are they important to marketing managers?

6–3 Would you rather have an account in a savings and loan association that pays 5 percent interest compounded semiannually or 5 percent interest compounded daily? Why?

6–4 For a given interest rate and a given number of years, is the interest factor for the sum of an annuity larger or smaller than the interest factor for the present value of the annuity?

6–5 Suppose you are examining two investments, A and B. Both have the same maturity, but A pays a 6 percent return and B yields 5 percent. Which investment is probably riskier? How do you know it is riskier?

PROBLEMS

6–1 At a growth rate of 8 percent, how long does it take a sum to double?

6–2 Which amount is worth more at 5 percent: $1,000 today or $1,400 after 7 years?

6–3 On December 30, Philip P. Potter buys a building for $20,000, payable 10 percent down and the balance in twenty-five equal annual installments that are to include principal plus 6 percent compound interest on the declining balance. What are the equal installments?

6–4 a) What amount would be paid for a $1,000, 10-year bond that pays $25 interest semiannually ($50 a year) and is sold to yield 6 percent, compounded semiannually?

b) What would be paid if the bond is sold to yield 4 percent?

c) What would be paid if semiannual interest payments are $30 and the bond is sold to yield 10 percent?

6–5 The Westwood Company is establishing a sinking fund to retire a $200,000 mortgage that matures on December 31, 1978. The company plans to put a fixed amount into the fund each year for 10 years. The first payment will be made on December 31, 1969, the last on December 31, 1978. The company anticipates that the fund will earn 5 percent a year. What annual contributions must be made to accumulate the $200,000 as of December 31, 1978?

6–6 You are considering two investment opportunities, A and B. A is expected to pay $100 a year for the first 10 years, $200 a year for the next 20 years, and nothing thereafter. B is expected to pay $400 a year for 11 years, and nothing thereafter. You find that alternative investments of similar risk yield 3 percent and 7 percent for A and B respectively.

a) Find the present value of each investment. Show calculations.

b) Which is the more risky investment? Why?

c) Assume that your rich uncle will give you your choice of investments without cost to you, and that (i) you must hold the investment for its entire life (cannot sell it) or (ii) you are free to sell it at its going market price. Which investment would you prefer under each of the two conditions?

Selected References

Allen, R. G. D., *Mathematical Analysis for Economists* (London: Macmillan & Co., 1956), Chaps. IX and X.

Hodgman, C. D. (ed.), *Mathematical Tables* (Cleveland: Chemical Rubber Publishing Company, 1954).

APPENDIX TO CHAPTER 6
Continuous Compounding

In Chapter 6 we implicitly assumed that growth occurs at discrete intervals—annually, semiannually, and so forth. For some purposes it is better to assume instantaneous, or *continuous,* growth. The relationship between discrete and continuous compounding is illustrated in Figure A6–1. Figure A6–1(a) shows the annual compounding case, where interest is added once a year; in Figure A6–1(b) compounding occurs twice a year; in Figure A6–1(c) interest is earned continuously.

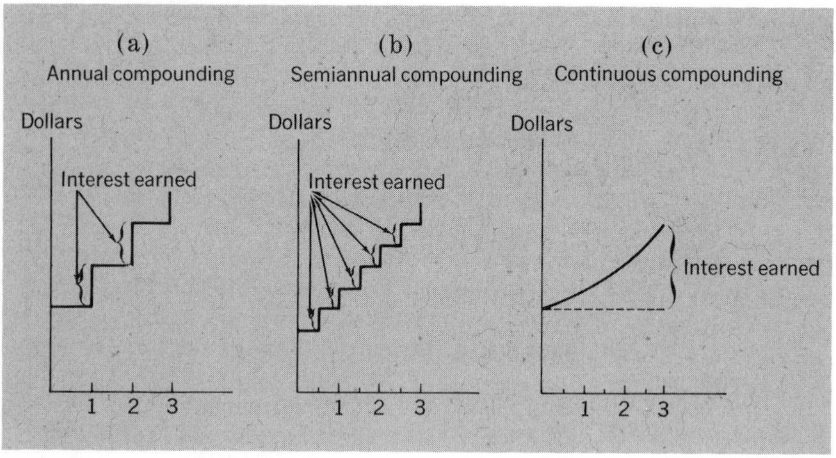

Figure A6–1 Annual, Semiannual, and Continuous Compounding

In Chapter 6, equation 6–8 was developed to allow for any number of compounding periods per year:

$$V_n = P\left(1 + \frac{i}{m}\right)^{mn} \qquad (6\text{–}8)$$

Equation 6–8, in turn, can be modified to allow for continuous compounding. The steps in this modification are developed below. In this development, the notation is slightly modified to make it consistent with the majority of the literature. In discrete compounding n is generally used to denote years, and i to denote the interest rate. In the literature of finance, where continuous compounding is employed, t is used for years (time) and g for the rate of interest (growth).

Step 1

First, assume that g, the interest or growth rate, is 100 percent ($g = 100\% = 1.0$); that is, assume that with annual compounding the initial principal (P) will double each year:

$$\begin{aligned} V_t &= P(1 + g)^t \\ &= P(1 + 1)^t \\ &= P(2)^t \end{aligned}$$

Step 2

Now suppose that $P = 1$ and that g remains at 100 percent, but compounding occurs m times per year. The value after one year will be

$$V_1 = \left(1 + \frac{1}{m}\right)^m \qquad (A6\text{–}1)$$

As m is increased, V_1 increases (but at a decreasing rate), and equation A6–1 approaches the value 2.718 as m approaches infinity. The value e is defined as this limiting case:

$$e = \lim_{m \to \infty} \left(1 + \frac{1}{m}\right)^m = 2.718 \cdots \tag{A6–2}$$

Step 3

Returning to equation 6–8, the general case of compound growth (but using the new notation), we can develop an equation for the special case of continuous compounding. Starting with

$$V_t = P\left(1 + \frac{g}{m}\right)^{mt} \tag{6–8}$$

and noting that, since we can multiply mt by g/g, we can set $mt = (m/g)(gt)$ and rewrite equation 6–8 as

$$V_t = P\left[\left(1 + \frac{g}{m}\right)^{m/g}\right]^{gt} \tag{A6–3}$$

Step 4

Defining $k = m/g$ and noting that $g/m = 1/(m/g) = 1/k$, we can rewrite equation A6–3 as

$$V_t = P\left[\left(1 + \frac{1}{k}\right)^{k}\right]^{gt} \tag{A6–4}$$

As the number of compounding periods, m, approaches infinity (that is, compounding occurs continuously), k also approaches infinity. Since the term in brackets is essentially the same as equation A6–1, this term must approach the value $e \approx 2.718$ as m approaches ∞. Thus, we may substitute e for the bracketed term, rewriting equation A6–4 as

$$V_t = Pe^{gt} \tag{A6–5}$$

for the case of continuous compounding (or continuous growth).

Step 5

Interest factors (IF) can be developed for continuous compounding; developing the factors requires the use of natural, or Naperian, logarithms.[1] First, letting $P = 1$, we can rewrite equation A6–5 as

$$V_t = e^{gt} \tag{A6–6}$$

Setting equation A6–6 in log form and noting that ln denotes the log to the base e, we obtain

$$\ln V_t = gt \ln e \tag{A6–7}$$

Since e is defined as the base of the system of natural logarithms, ln e must equal 1.0 (that is, $e^1 = e$, so $\ln e = 1.0$). Therefore,

$$\ln V_t = gt \tag{A6–8}$$

One simply looks up the product gt in a table of natural logarithms and obtains the value V_t as the antilog. For example, if t = five years and g = 10 percent, the product is .50. Looking up this value in Table A6–1, a table of natural logs, we find .5 to lie between .49470 and .50078, whose antilogs are 1.64 and 1.65 respectively. Interpolating, we find the antilog of .5 to be 1.648. Thus, 1.648 is the interest factor for a 10-percent growth rate compounded continuously for five years; $1 growing continuously at this compound rate would equal $1.648 after five years.

Since continuous compounding is seldom applied in practice, we have not provided a table of continuous interest factors. It should be noted, however, that the $1.648 obtained for five years of *continuous* compounding compares closely with $1.629, the figure for semiannual compounding, and with the $1.611 obtained with annual compounding. Thus, continuous compounding does not produce values materially different from semiannual or annual compounding. As was pointed out earlier, the importance of continuous compounding is its convenience in theoretical work where calculus must be employed.

Continuous Discounting

Equation A6–5 can be transformed into equation A6–9 and used to determine present values under continuous compounding. Using k as the discount rate (again, this is the standard notation), we obtain

$$PV = \frac{V_t}{e^{kt}} = V_t e^{-kt} \tag{A6–9}$$

[1] Recall that the logarithm of a number is the power, or exponent, to which a specified base must be raised to equal the number; that is, the log (base 10) of 100 is 2 because $(10)^2 = 100$. In the system of natural logs the base is $e \approx 2.718$.

TABLE A6–1 NATURAL LOGARITMS OF NUMBERS BETWEEN 1.0 AND 4.99

N	0	1	2	3	4	5	6	7	8	9
1.0	0.00000	.00995	.01980	.02956	.03922	.04879	.05827	.06766	.07696	.08618
.1	.09531	.10436	.11333	.12222	.13103	.13976	.14842	.15700	.16551	.17395
.2	.18232	.19062	.19885	.20701	.21511	.22314	.23111	.23902	.24686	.25464
.3	.26236	.27003	.27763	.28518	.29267	.30010	.30748	.31481	.32208	.32930
.4	.33647	.34359	.35066	.35767	.36464	.37156	.37844	.38526	.39204	.39878
.5	.40547	.41211	.41871	.42527	.43178	.43825	.44469	.45108	.45742	.46373
.6	.47000	.47623	.48243	.48858	.49470	.50078	.50682	.51282	.51879	.52473
.7	.53063	.53649	.54232	.54812	.55389	.55962	.56531	.57098	.57661	.58222
.8	.58779	.59333	.59884	.60432	.60977	.61519	.62058	.62594	.63127	.63658
.9	.64185	.64710	.65233	.65752	.66269	.66783	.67294	.67803	.68310	.68813
2.0	0.69315	.69813	.70310	.70804	.71295	.71784	.72271	.72755	.73237	.73716
.1	.74194	.74669	.75142	.75612	.76081	.76547	.77011	.77473	.77932	.78390
.2	.78846	.79299	.79751	.80200	.80648	.81093	.81536	.81978	.82418	.82855
.3	.83291	.83725	.84157	.84587	.85015	.85442	.85866	.86289	.86710	.87129
.4	.87547	.87963	.88377	.88789	.89200	.89609	.90016	.90422	.90826	.91228
.5	.91629	.92028	.92426	.92822	.93216	.93609	.94001	.94391	.94779	.95166
.6	.95551	.95935	.96317	.96698	.97078	.97456	.97833	.98208	.98582	.98954
.7	.99325	.99695	*.00063	*.00430	*.00796	*.01160	*.01523	*.01885	*.02245	*.02604
.8	1.02962	.03318	.03674	.04028	.04380	.04732	.05082	.05431	.05779	.06126
.9	.06471	.06815	.07158	.07500	.07841	.08181	.08519	.08856	.09192	.09527
3.0	1.09861	.10194	.10526	.10856	.11186	.11514	.11841	.12168	.12493	.12817
.1	.13140	.13462	.13783	.14103	.14422	.14740	.15057	.15373	.15688	.16002
.2	.16315	.16627	.16938	.17248	.17557	.17865	.18173	.18479	.18784	.19089
.3	.19392	.19695	.19996	.20297	.20597	.20896	.21194	.21491	.21788	.22083
.4	.22378	.22671	.22964	.23256	.23547	.23837	.24127	.24415	.24703	.24990
.5	.25276	.25562	.25846	.26130	.26413	.26695	.26976	.27257	.27536	.27815
.6	.28093	.28371	.28647	.28923	.29198	.29473	.29746	.30019	.30291	.30563
.7	.30833	.31103	.31372	.31641	.31909	.32176	.32442	.32708	.32972	.33237
.8	.33500	.33763	.34025	.34286	.34547	.34807	.35067	.35325	.35584	.35841
.9	.36098	.36354	.36609	.36864	.37118	.37372	.37624	.37877	.38128	.38379
4.0	1.38629	.38879	.39128	.39377	.39624	.39872	.40118	.40364	.40610	.40854
.1	.41099	.41342	.41585	.41828	.42070	.42311	.42552	.42792	.43031	.43270
.2	.43508	.43746	.43984	.44220	.44456	.44692	.44927	.45161	.45395	.45629
.3	.45862	.46094	.46326	.46557	.46787	.47018	.47247	.47476	.47705	.47933
.4	.48160	.48387	.48614	.48840	.49065	.49290	.49515	.49739	.49962	.50185
.5	.50408	.50630	.50851	.51072	.51293	.51513	.51732	.51951	.52170	.52388
.6	.52606	.52823	.53039	.53256	.53471	.53687	.53902	.54116	.54330	.54543
.7	.54756	.54969	.55181	.55393	.55604	.55814	.56025	.56235	.56444	.56653
.8	.56862	.57070	.57277	.57485	.57691	.57898	.58104	.58309	.58515	.58719
.9	.58924	.59127	.59331	.59534	.59737	.59939	.60141	.60342	.60543	.60744

* Add 1.0 to indicated figure.

Thus, if \$1.648 is due in five years and if the appropriate *continuous* discount rate k is 10 percent, the present value of this future payment is

$$PV = \frac{\$1,648}{1.648} = \$1,000$$

Continuous Compounding and Discounting for Annuities

The treatment of continuous compounding for single values is more complex than that for discrete compounding, but it still involves nothing more than algebra. For continuously compounding and discounting *streams* of payments ("annuities"), however, elementary integral calculus must be employed. The procedures involved are outlined below.

Step 1

First, observe Figure A6–2(a). An amount R is received at the end of each year. It is left on deposit and grows at the rate g; thus the accumulated sum at the end of any year N is

$$\begin{aligned} S_n &= R(1+g)^0 + R(1+g)^1 + R(1+g)^2 + \cdots R(1+g)^{t-1} \\ &= R + R(1+g)^1 + R(1+g)^2 + \cdots R(1+g)^{t-1} \\ &= \sum_{t=1}^{N} R(1+g)^{t-1} \end{aligned}$$

The accumulated sum of the payments, S_n, is equal to the sum of the rectangles in Figure A6–2(a); this is the area under the discontinuous curve formed by the tops of the rectangles.

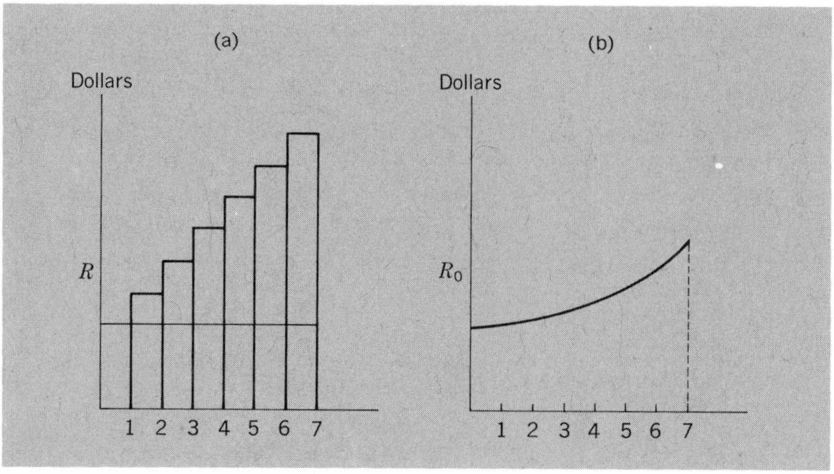

Figure A6–2 Sum of an "Annuity" under Discrete and Continuous Compounding

Step 2

Exactly the same principle is involved in finding the accumulated sum of the continuous equivalent of an annuity, or a stream of receipts received continuously. The accumulated sum is again represented by the area under a curve, but now the curve is continuous as in the Figure A6–2(b). In the discrete case, the area under the curve was obtained by adding the rectangles; in the continuous case, the area must be found by the process of integration.

Note that the stream of receipts, or the value of R_t, is found by taking the initial receipt, R_0 (*not* R_1), and letting it grow at the continuous rate g:

$$R_t = R_0 e^{gt} \qquad \text{(A6–10)}$$

Equation A6–10 defines the curve, and the area under the curve (S_n) is represented by the integral

$$S_n = \int_{t=0}^{N} R_0 e^{gt}\, dt = R_0 \int_{t=0}^{N} e^{gt}\, dt \qquad \text{(A6–11)}$$

Step 3

Given a discrete series of receipts such as those shown in Figure A6–2(a) and a discount rate, k, we find their PV as

$$PV = \sum_{t=1}^{N} R_t(1 + k)^{-t}$$

If the receipts accrue continuously, as do those in Figure A6–2(b), we must find the present value of the stream of payments by calculus. First, note that by equation A6–9 we find the PV of the instantaneous receipt for period t as

$$PV = R_t e^{-kt} \qquad \text{(A6–9)}$$

The present value of the entire stream of receipts is given as the integral

$$PV = \int_{t=0}^{N} R_t e^{-kt}\, dt \qquad \text{(A6–12)}$$

Step 4

Although the primary equations (A6–11 and A6–12) developed thus far in this section are seldom used individually, one of the most important theoretical formulations in the field of finance—the Gordon model—is developed by combining them. The Gordon model is discussed at some length in the Appendix to Chapter 12, but we can facilitate that discussion by showing, at this point, how these equations can be combined.

First, note that $R_t = R_0 e^{gt}$ from equation A6–10. Next substitute this value into equation A6–12, obtaining

$$PV = \int_{t=0}^{N} R_0 e^{gt} e^{-kt}\, dt \tag{A6–13}$$

Now remove the constant term, R_0, from within the integral and combine the exponents of the e term, obtaining

$$\begin{aligned} PV &= R_0 \int_{t=0}^{N} e^{gt-kt}\, dt \\ &= R_0 \int_{t=0}^{N} e^{-(k-g)t}\, dt \end{aligned} \tag{A6–14}$$

Equation A6–14 is of the form $\int e^{ax}dx$ where $a = k - g$ and $x = -t$. When integrated, the solution is:

$$\int e^{ax}\, dx = \frac{e^{ax}}{a}$$

Therefore, the integration of equation A6–14 yields an indefinite integral of the form:

$$PV = \frac{R_0 e^{-(k-g)t}}{k - g}$$

that, when evaluated at $t = \infty$, is equal to 0 and when evaluated at $t = 0$, is equal to

$$-\frac{R_0}{k - g}$$

Subtracting the lower bound from the upper (which is 0) yields:

$$\begin{aligned} PV &= 0 - \left[-\frac{R_0}{k - g}\right] \\ &= \frac{R_0}{k - g} \end{aligned} \tag{A6–15}$$

Equation A6–15 is, thus, the present value of a continuous stream of receipts growing at a rate g and discounted at a rate k. The basic Gordon model, which is essentially equation A6–15, is extremely important in both theoretical and empirical finance, but its further development is deferred to Chapter 12.

7

Capital Budgeting Techniques

Capital budgeting involves the entire process of planning expenditures whose returns are expected to extend beyond one year. The choice of one year is arbitrary, of course, but it is a convenient cutoff time for distinguishing between types of expenditures. Obvious examples of capital outlays are expenditures for land, buildings, and equipment and for permanent additions to working capital (especially inventories) associated with plant expansion. Also, an advertising or promotion campaign, or a program of research and development, is likely to have an impact beyond one year and, hence, come within the classification of a capital budgeting expenditure.[1]

[1] Though this discussion is focused on capital budgeting related to expenditures on fixed assets, the theory and techniques are equally applicable to all kinds of asset investments by business. Therefore, while the authors follow traditional practices of relating capital budgeting to investment in fixed assets, it should be remembered that the techniques discussed

Capital budgeting is not only important for the future well-being of the firm, but it is also a complex, conceptually difficult topic. As we shall see later in this chapter, the optimum capital budget—the level of investment that maximizes the present value of the firm—is simultaneously determined by the interaction of supply and demand forces under conditions of uncertainty. Supply forces refer to the supply of capital to the firm, or its *cost of capital schedule.* Demand forces relate to the investment opportunities open to the firm, as measured by the *stream of revenues* that will result from an investment decision. *Uncertainty* enters the decision because it is impossible to know exactly either the cost of capital or the stream of revenues that will be derived from a project.

To facilitate the exposition of the investment decision process, we have broken the topic down into its major components. In this chapter, we consider the capital budgeting process and the techniques generally employed by reasonably sophisticated business firms. We abstract from a refined treatment of uncertainty by assuming single point estimates for both project costs and the revenues from projects. We abstract from the problem of the cost of capital by assuming that it is given and constant—that is, that the cost of each dollar raised to finance capital expansion is the same, regardless of how much capital is raised. Some of these assumptions are relaxed in Appendix A to this chapter and others in later chapters. Uncertainty is explicitly and formally considered in Chapter 8, and the cost of capital concept is developed and related to capital budgeting in Chapters 9 through 12.

SIGNIFICANCE OF CAPITAL BUDGETING

A number of factors combine to make capital budgeting one of the most important areas of strategic decision-making with which financial management is involved. First and foremost, the fact that the results continue over an extended period means that the decision-maker loses some of his flexibility. He must make a commitment into the future. For example, the purchase of an asset with an economic life of 10 years requires a long period of waiting before the final results of the action

---

are applicable to all types of management decisions. In concept, investments in cash, receivables, or inventory must be justified by earning a satisfactory return on these asset items.

can be known. The decision-maker must commit funds for this period and, thus, become a hostage of future events.

Asset expansion is fundamentally related to expected future sales. A decision to buy or to construct a fixed asset that is going to last five years involves an implicit five-year sales forecast. Indeed, the economic life of an asset purchased represents an implicit forecast for the duration of the economic life of the asset. Hence, failure to forecast accurately will result in overinvestment or underinvestment in fixed assets.

An erroneous forecast of asset needs can result in serious consequences for a firm. If the firm has invested too much in assets, it will be incurring unnecessarily heavy expenses. If it has not spent enough on fixed assets, two serious consequences may arise. First, its equipment may not be sufficiently modern to enable it to produce competitively. Second, if it has inadequate capacity, it may lose a portion of its share of the market to rival firms. To regain lost customers typically requires heavy selling expenses or price reductions or both.

Another problem is to properly phase the availability of capital assets in order to have them come "on stream" at the proper time. For example, the executive vice-president of a decorative tile company recently gave the authors an illustration of the importance of capital budgeting. His firm tried to operate near capacity most of the time. For about four years there had been intermittent spurts in the demand for its product; when these spurts occurred, the firm had to turn away orders. After a sharp increase in demand, the firm would add capacity by renting an additional building, then purchasing and installing the appropriate equipment. It would take six to eight months to have the additional capacity ready. At this point the company would find that there was no demand for its increased output—other firms had already expanded their operations and had taken an increased share of the market, with the result that demand for this firm had leveled off. If the firm had properly forecast demand and had planned its increase in capacity six months or one year in advance, it would have been able to maintain its market—indeed, to obtain a larger share of the market.

Good capital budgeting will also improve the timing of asset acquisitions and the quality of assets purchased. This situation follows from the nature of capital goods and of their producers. Capital goods are not ordered by firms until they see that sales are going to press on capacity. Such occasions occur simultaneously for many firms. When the heavy orders come in, the producers of capital goods go from a situation of idle capacity to one where they cannot meet all the orders that have been placed. Consequently, large backlogs of orders accumulate. Since the production of capital goods involves a relatively long work-in-process period, a year or more of waiting may be involved before the additional capital goods are available. This factor has obvious implications for purchasing agents and plant managers.

Another reason for the importance of capital budgeting is that asset expansion typically involves substantial expenditures. When a firm is going to spend a considerable amount of money, it must make the proper plans—large amounts of funds are not available automatically. A firm contemplating a major capital expenditure program may need to arrange its financing several years in advance to be sure of having the funds required for the expansion.

Finally, it has been said with a great deal of truth that many firms fail not because they have too much capital equipment but because they have too little. While the conservative approach of having a small amount of capital equipment may be appropriate at times, such an approach may also be fatal if a firm's competitors install modern, automated equipment that permits them to produce a better product and sell it at a lower price.

A SIMPLIFIED VIEW OF CAPITAL BUDGETING

Capital budgeting is, in essence, an application of a classic proposition from the economic theory of the firm: namely, a firm should operate at the point where its marginal revenue is just equal to its marginal cost. When this rule is applied to the capital budgeting decision, marginal revenue is taken to be the percentage rate of return on investments, while marginal cost is the firm's cost of capital.

A simplified version of the concept is depicted in Figure 7–1(a). Here the horizontal axis measures the dollars of investment during a year, while the vertical axis shows both the percentage cost of capital and the rate of return on projects. The projects are denoted by the boxes—project A, for example, calls for an outlay of $3 million and promises a 17 percent rate of return; project B requires $1 million and yields about 16 percent; and so on. The last investment. project G, simply involves buying 4 percent government bonds, which may be purchased in unlimited quantities. In Figure 7–1(b) the concept is generalized to show smoothed investment opportunity schedules (IRR)[2], and three alternative schedules are presented.

[2] The investment opportunity schedules measure the rate of return on each project. The rate of return on a project is generally called the *internal rate of return*

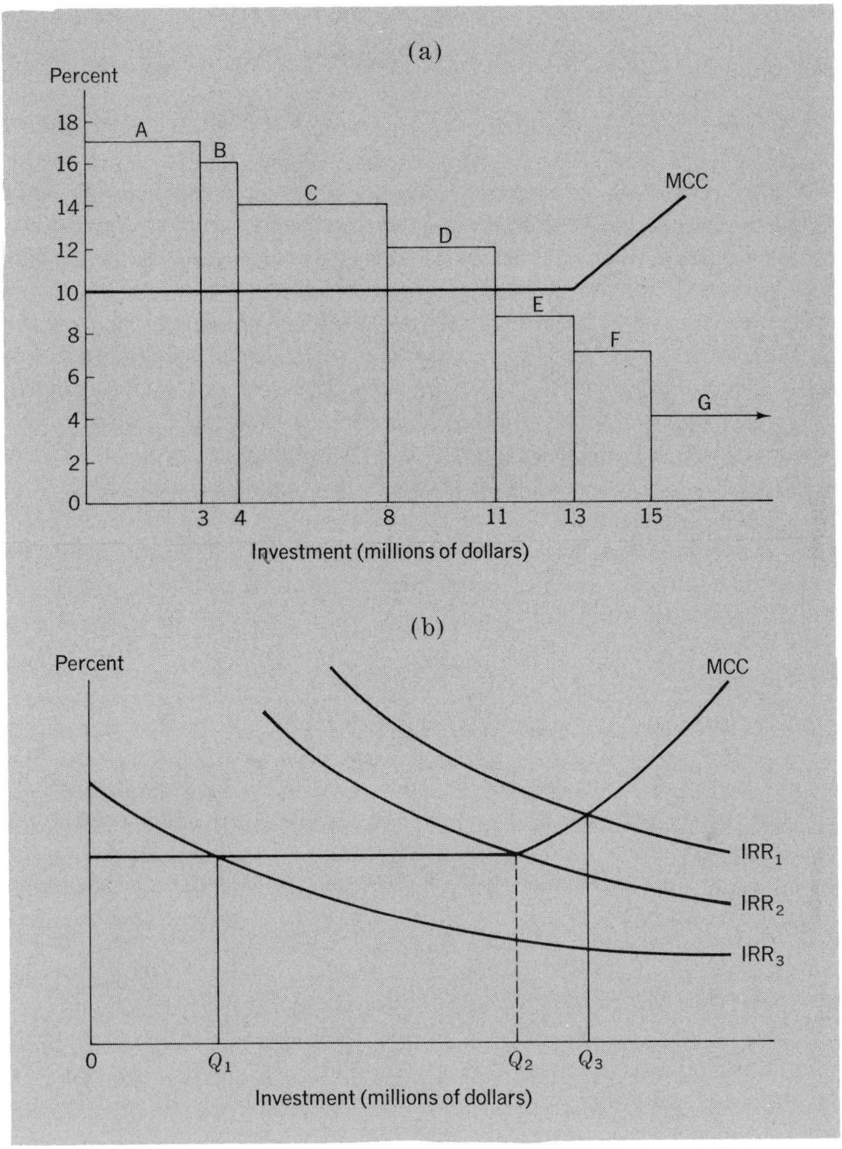

Figure 7–1 Illustrative Capital Budgeting Decision Process (a) Discrete investment projects (b) A smoothed investment opportunity schedule

The curve MCC designates the marginal cost of capital, or the cost of each additional dollar acquired for purposes of making capital ex-

---

(IRR). This is why we label the investment opportunity schedules IRR. The process of calculating the IRR is explained later in this chapter.

penditures. As it is drawn in 7–1(a), the marginal cost of capital is constant at 10 percent until the firm has raised $13 million, after which the cost of capital turns up. To maximize profits, the firm should accept projects A through D, obtaining and investing $11 million, and reject E, F, and G.

Notice that three alternative investment opportunity schedules are shown in 7–1(b). IRR_1 designates relatively many good investment opportunities, while IRR_3 designates relatively few good projects. The three different curves could be interpreted as applying either to three different firms or to one firm at three different times. As long as the IRR curve cuts the MCC curve to the left of Q_2—for example, at Q_1—the marginal cost of capital is constant. To the right of Q_2—for example, at Q_3—the cost of capital is rising. Therefore, if investment opportunities are such that the IRR cuts the MCC curve to the right of Q_2, the *actual* marginal cost of capital (a single point) is not constant; rather, it depends upon the IRR curve. In this chapter we *assume* that the IRR curve cuts the MCC curve to the left of Q_2, thus permitting us to assume that the cost of capital is constant. We might mention at this time that, while the assumption of a constant cost of capital certainly does not hold for all firms, and especially not for small, new, and rapidly growing ones, our investigations suggest that it generally is approximately correct for most large, mature corporations.

APPLICATION OF THE CONCEPT

At the applied level, the capital budgeting process is considerably more complex than the preceding example would suggest. Projects do not just appear; a continuing stream of good investment opportunities results from hard thinking, careful planning, and, often, large outlays for research and development. In addition, some very difficult measurement problems are involved; the sales and costs associated with particular projects must be estimated, frequently for many years into the future, in the face of great uncertainty. Last, some difficult conceptual and empirical problems arise over the methods of calculating rates of return and the cost of capital.

Businessmen are required to take action, however, even in the face of the kinds of problems described; this requirement has led to the development of procedures that assist in making optimal investment decisions. One of these procedures, forecasting, was discussed in Chapter

5; uncertainty will be discussed in formal terms in the next chapter; and the important subject of the cost of capital is deferred to Chapter 11. The essentials of the other elements of capital budgeting are taken up in the remainder of this chapter.

Investment Proposals

Aside from the actual generation of ideas, the first step in the capital budgeting process is to assemble the proposed new investments, together with the data necessary to appraise them. Although practices vary from firm to firm, proposals dealing with asset acquisitions are frequently grouped according to the following categories:

1. Replacements
2. Expansion: additional capacity in existing product lines
3. Expansion: new product lines
4. Other

These groupings are somewhat arbitrary, and it is frequently difficult to decide the appropriate category for a particular investment. In spite of such problems, the scheme is used quite widely and, as shall be seen, with good reason.

Ordinarily, replacement decisions are the simplest to make. Assets wear out and become obsolete, and they must be replaced if production is to continue. The firm has a very good idea of the cost savings to be obtained by replacing an old asset, and it knows the consequences of nonreplacement. All in all, the outcomes of most replacement decisions can be predicted with a high degree of confidence.

An example of the second investment classification is a proposal for adding more machines of the type already in use or the opening of another branch in a city-wide chain of food stores. Expansion investments are frequently incorporated in replacement decisions. To illustrate, an old, inefficient machine may be replaced by a larger and more efficient one.

A degree of uncertainty—sometimes extremely high—is clearly involved in expansion, but the firm at least has the advantage of examining past production and sales experience with similar machines or stores. When it considers an investment of the third kind, expansion into new product lines, little if any experience data are available on which to base decisions. To illustrate, when General Motors decided to develop the diesel engine for commercial application, it had very little idea of either the development costs or the specific applications to which the engine could be put. Under such circumstances, any estimates must at best be treated as very crude approximations.

The "other" category is a catchall and includes intangibles; an example is a proposal to boost employee morale by installing a music system. Pollution control devices are another example of the "other" category. Major strategic decisions such as plans for overseas expansion or mergers might also be included here, but more frequently they are treated separately from the regular capital budget.

Administrative Details

The remaining aspects of capital budgeting involve administrative matters. Approvals are typically required at higher levels within the organization as we move away from replacement decisions and as the sums involved increase. One of the most important functions of the board of directors is to approve the major outlays in a capital budgeting program. Such decisions are crucial for the future well-being of the firm.

The planning horizon for capital budgeting programs varies with the nature of the industry. When sales can be forecast with a high degree of reliability for 10 to 20 years, the planning period is likely to be correspondingly long; electric utilities are an example of such an industry. Also, when the product-technology developments in the industry require an 8-to-10-year cycle to develop a new major product, as in certain segments of the aerospace or the electronics industries, a correspondingly long planning period is necessary.

After a capital budget has been adopted, payments must be scheduled. Characteristically, the finance department is responsible for scheduling payments and for acquiring funds to meet payment schedule requirements. In addition, the finance department will be primarily responsible for cooperating with the members of operating divisions to compile systematic records on the uses of funds and the uses of equipment purchased in capital budgeting programs. Effective capital budgeting programs require such information as the basis for periodic review and evaluation of capital expenditure decisions—the feedback and control phase of capital budgeting.

The foregoing represents a brief overview of the administrative aspects of capital budgeting; the analytical problems involved are considered next.

CHOOSING AMONG ALTERNATIVE PROPOSALS

In most firms there are more proposals for projects than the firm is able or willing to finance. Some proposals are good, others are poor, and methods must be developed for distinguishing between them. Essentially, the end product is a ranking of the proposals and a cutoff point for determining how far down the ranked list to go.

In part, proposals are eliminated because they are *mutually exclusive.* Mutually exclusive proposals are alternative methods of doing the same job. If one piece of equipment is chosen to do the job, the others will not be required. Thus, if there is a need to improve the materials handling system in a chemical plant, the job may be done either by conveyer belts or by fork trucks. The selection of one method of doing the job makes it unnecessary to use the others. They are mutually exclusive items.

Independent items are pieces of capital equipment that are being considered for different kinds of projects or tasks that need to be accomplished.[3] For example, in addition to the materials handling system, the chemical firm may need equipment to package the end items. The work would require a packaging machine, and the purchase of equipment for this purpose would be independent of the equipment purchased for materials handling.

To distinguish among the many items that compete for the allocation of the firm's capital funds, a ranking procedure must be developed. This procedure involves, first, calculating the estimated benefits from the use of equipment and, second, translating the estimated benefits into a measure of the advantage of the purchase of the equipment. Thus, an estimate of benefits is required, and a conversion of the benefits into a ranking measure must be developed.

IMPORTANCE OF GOOD DATA

Most discussions of measuring benefits are relatively brief, but it is important to emphasize *that in the entire capital budgeting procedure, probably nothing is of greater importance than a reliable estimate of the cost savings or revenue increases that will be achieved from the prospective outlay of capital funds.* But these estimates are likely to be more closely related to the facts of particular situations than they are subject to generalizations.

[3] We should at this point distinguish between *statistical* independence and *economic* independence. Two projects are statistically independent if their returns, over time, are uncorrelated. This concept is discussed at length in Chapter 8 when portfolio theory is considered. Economic independence, which means that the returns of one project are not affected by the existence of another project *in a cause and effect* manner, is the concept we have in mind here.

The nature of the task of calculating savings from a proposed investment is indicated by a brief consideration of the items that may affect benefits: examples are changes in quality and quantity of direct labor, in amount and cost of scrap and rework time, and in maintenance expenses, down time, safety, flexibility, and so on. So many variables are involved that it is obviously impossible to make neat generalizations. However, this should not minimize the crucial importance of the required analysis of the benefits derived from capital expenditures. Each capital equipment expenditure must be examined in detail for possible additional costs and additional savings.

All the subsequent procedures for ranking projects are no better than the data input. Above all, the data formulation requires good judgment in expressing the amount of the benefits. This is not a routine clerical task to be performed on a mechanical basis. It requires continuous monitoring and evaluation of estimates by individuals competent to make such evaluations—engineers, accountants, economists, cost analysts, and other qualified persons.

After the estimates of costs and benefits have been made, they are utilized for ranking alternative investment proposals. How this grading is accomplished is the next topic.

RANKING INVESTMENT PROPOSALS

The point of capital budgeting—indeed, the point of all financial analysis—is to make decisions that will maximize the value of the firm's common stock. The capital budgeting process is designed to answer two questions: (1) which of several mutually exclusive investments should be selected; (2) how many projects, in total, should be accepted, if the value of the stock is to be maximized?

Among the many methods for ranking investment proposals, four are discussed here. The first, payback, is included because it is so widely used; it is not, however, a conceptually sound method. The other three procedures are included because they are conceptually sound.[4] The name and a brief description of each are set forth below. *Future returns are,*

[4] There are also a number of "average rate of return" methods that are encountered in practice. We consider them all to be fundamentally unsound and have elected not to discuss them here. We should also note that there are basic differences between the different discounted cash flow methods—NPV, IRR, and PI—having to do with the assumed rate of return at which future cash flows are reinvested. These differences will be taken up later; depending on the circumstances, one or another of these methods may not be "conceptually sound" for practical decisions on capital budgeting.

in all cases, defined as the net proceeds before depreciation but after taxes that result from a project. In other words, returns are synonymous with cash flows from investments.

1. Payback method: number of years required to return the original investment
2. Net present value (NPV) method: present value of future returns discounted at the appropriate cost of capital minus the cost of the investment
3. Internal rate of return (IRR) method: interest rate which equates the present value of future returns to the investment outlay
4. Benefit/Cost Ratio, or profitability index (PI): present value of future returns divided by present value of the investment outlay

The nature and characteristics of the four methods are illustrated and explained. To make the explanations more meaningful, the same data are used to illustrate each method.

Assume that two projects are being considered by a firm. Each requires an investment of $1,000. The firm's cost of capital is 10 percent.[5] The net cash flows from investments A and B are shown in Table 7–1.

TABLE 7–1 NET CASH FLOWS
(profit after taxes plus depreciation)

YEAR	A	B
1	$500	$100
2	400	200
3	300	300
4	100	400
5		500
6		600

Payback Period

The *payback period* is the number of years it takes a firm to recover its original investment from net returns before depreciation but after taxes. The payback period is two and one third years for project A and four years for project B. If the firm were employing a three-year pay-

[5] A discussion of how the cost of capital is calculated is presented in Chapter 11. At this point, cost of capital should be considered as the firm's opportunity cost of making a particular investment.

back period, project A would be accepted but project B would be rejected.

Although the payback period is very easy to calculate, it can lead to the wrong decisions. As the illustration demonstrates, it ignores income beyond the payback period. If the project is one maturing in later years, the use of the payback period can lead to the selection of less desirable investments. Projects with longer payback periods are characteristically those involved in long-range planning—developing a new product or tapping a new market. These are just the strategic decisions which determine a firm's fundamental position, but they also involve investments which do not yield their highest returns for a number of years. This means that the payback method may be biased against the very investments that are most important to a firm's long-run success.

In spite of its shortcomings, the payback method has been widely used by American industry. A survey made by the Machinery and Allied Products Institute indicated that 60 percent of the surveyed firms use the payback period. On equipment with a service life of 10 years or more, 28 percent of those using the method set a three-year payback, and 34 percent set a five-year payback. Only 16 percent use a payoff period of more than five years. Thus, the relatively belated initiation of effective long-range planning by American firms is probably related to the widespread use of the payback period in analyzing alternative investments. Since its emphasis is on the very short run, the payback method simply does not require inquiry into the far-distant future.

Recognition of the longer period over which an investment is likely to yield savings points up another weakness in the use of the payback method for ranking investment proposals: its failure to take into account the interest factor. To illustrate, consider two assets, X and Y. each costing $300 and each having the following cash flows:

YEAR	X	Y
1	200	100
2	100	200
3	100	100

Each project has a two-year payback; hence, each would appear equally desirable. However, we know that a dollar today is worth more than a dollar next year, so project X, with its faster cash flow, is certainly more desirable.

The use of the payback period is sometimes defended on the ground that returns beyond three or four years are fraught with such great uncertainty that it is best to disregard them altogether in a planning decision. However, this is clearly an unsound procedure. Some of the investments with highest returns are those which may not come to fruition for 8, 9, or 10 years. The new product cycle in industries involving advanced technologies may not have a payoff for eight or nine years. Furthermore, even though returns that occur after three or four or five years are most uncertain, it is important to make a judgment about the likelihood of their occurring. To ignore them is to assign a zero probability to these distant receipts. This can hardly produce the best results.

A final defense of the payback method is that a firm which is short of cash must necessarily give great emphasis to a quick return of its funds so that they may be put to use in other places or in meeting other needs. It can only be said that this does not relieve the payback method of its many shortcomings, and that there are better methods for handling the cash shortage situation.[6]

Net Present Value Method

As the flaws in the payback method were recognized, people began to search for methods of evaluating projects that would recognize that a dollar received immediately is preferable to a dollar received at some future date. This recognition led to the development of *discounted cash flow techniques* to take account of the time value of money. One such discounted cash flow technique is called the "net present value method," or sometimes simply the "present value method." *To implement this approach, simply find the present value of the expected net cash flow of an investment, discounted at the cost of capital, and subtract from it the initial cost outlay of the project.*[7] If the net present value is positive, the project should be accepted; if negative, it should be rejected. If the two projects are mutually exclusive, the one with the higher net present value should be chosen.

The equation for the net present value (NPV) is:

$$NPV = \left[\frac{R_1}{(1+k)^1} + \frac{R_2}{(1+k)^2} + \cdots + \frac{R_N}{(1+k)^N}\right] - C$$
$$= \sum_{t=1}^{N} \frac{R_t}{(1+k)^t} - C \qquad (7\text{–}1)$$

[6] We interpret a cash shortage to mean that the firm has a high opportunity cost for its funds and a high cost of capital. We would consider this high cost of capital in the following ranking procedures: the internal rate of return, the profitability index, or the net present value method. We would thus take account of the cash shortage.

[7] If costs are spread over several years, this must be taken into account. Suppose, for example, that a firm bought land in 1965, erected a building in 1966, installed equipment in 1967, and started production in 1968. One could treat 1965 as the base year, comparing the present value of the costs as of 1965 to the present value of the benefit stream as of that same date.

Here R_t is the net cash flow in year t; k is the cost of capital; C is the cost of the investment project; and N is the project's expected life.

The net present values of projects A and B are calculated in Table 7–2. Project A has a NPV of \$80, while B's NPV is \$400. On this basis, both should be accepted if they are independent, but B should be the one chosen if they are mutually exclusive.

TABLE 7–2 CALCULATING THE NET PRESENT VALUE (NPV) OF PROJECTS WITH \$1,000 COST

	PROJECT A			PROJECT B		
Year	Net Cash Flow	IF (10%)	PV of Cash Flow	Net Cash Flow	IF (10%)	PV of Cash Flow
1	\$500	.91	\$ 455	\$100	.91	\$ 91
2	400	.83	332	200	.83	166
3	300	.75	225	300	.75	225
4	100	.68	68	400	.68	272
5				500	.62	310
6				600	.56	336
	PV of Inflows		\$1,080			\$1,400
	Less Cost		−1,000			−1,000
	NPV		\$ 80			\$ 400

Internal Rate of Return Method

The internal rate of return (IRR) is defined as the *interest rate that equates the present value of the expected future receipts to the cost of the investment outlay.* The equation for calculating the internal rate of return is:

$$C = \frac{R_1}{(1+r)^1} + \frac{R_2}{(1+r)^2} + \cdots + \frac{R_N}{(1+r)^N} = \sum_{t=1}^{N} \frac{R_t}{(1+r)^t} \qquad (7\text{–}2)$$

Some value of r will cause the sum of the discounted receipts to equal the initial cost of the project, and that value of r is defined to be the internal rate of return.

Notice that the internal rate of return formula, equation 7–2, is simply the NPV formula, equation 7–1, solved for that particular value of k that causes the NPV to equal zero. In other words, the same basic equation is used for both methods, but (1) in the NPV method the discount rate is specified and the NPV is found, while (2) in the IRR method the NPV is specified to equal zero and the value of r that forces the NPV to equal zero is found.

The internal rate of return must be found by trial and error. First, compute the present value of the cash flows from an investment, using an arbitrarily selected interest rate. Then compare the present value so obtained with the investment's cost. If the present value is higher than the cost figure, try a higher interest rate and go through the procedure again. Conversely, if the present value is lower than the cost, lower the interest rate and repeat the process. Continue until the present value of the flows from the investment are approximately equal to its cost. *The interest rate that brings about this equality is defined as the internal rate of return.*[8]

This calculation process is illustrated in Table 7–3 for projects A and B. First, the 4 percent interest factors are obtained from Appendix Table A–2. These factors are then multiplied by the cash flows for the corresponding years, and the present values of the annual cash flows are placed in the appropriate columns. For example, the IF (interest factor) 0.96 is multiplied by $500, and the product, $480, is placed in the first row of column A.

The present values of the yearly cash flows are then summed to get the investment's total present value. Subtracting the cost of the project from this figure gives the net present value. As the net present values of both investments are positive at the 4 percent rate, increase the rate to 10 percent and try again. Once again the net present values are positive, so the rate is stepped up to 15 percent. *At this point the net present value of investment A is approximately zero, which indicates that its internal rate of return is approximately 15 percent. Continuing, B is found to have an internal rate of return of approximately 20 percent.*

What is so special about the particular interest rate that equates the cost of a project with the present value of its receipts? Suppose that a firm obtains all of its capital by borrowing from a bank and

[8] In order to reduce the number of trials required to find the internal rate of return, it is important to minimize the error at each iteration. One reasonable approach is to make as good a first approximation as possible, then to "straddle" the internal rate of return by making fairly large changes in the interest rate early in the iterative process. In practice, if many projects are to be evaluated or if many years are involved, one would not work out the calculations by hand but would use a computer. Computer programs using differential calculus to minimize the number of iterations are readily available (the typical program uses "Newton's Method" for finding the roots of polynomials).

TABLE 7–3 PRESENT VALUE CALCULATIONS

		CASH FLOW	
	Year	A	B
Investment = $1,000	1	$500	$100
	2	400	200
	3	300	300
	4	100	400
	5		500
	6		600

	4 PERCENT			10 PERCENT			15 PERCENT		
		Present Value			Present Value			Present Value	
Year	*IF*	*A*	*B*	*IF*	*A*	*B*	*IF*	*A*	*B*
1	0.96	480	96	0.91	455	91	0.87	435	87
2	0.92	368	184	0.83	332	166	0.76	304	152
3	0.89	267	267	0.75	225	225	0.66	198	198
4	0.86	86	344	0.68	68	272	0.57	57	228
5	0.82		410	0.62		310	0.50		250
6	0.79		474	0.56		336	0.43		258
Present value		1,201	1,775		1,080	1,400		994	1,173
Net *PV*		201	775		80	400		(6)	173

	20 PERCENT			24 PERCENT			32 PERCENT		
		Present Value			Present Value			Present Value	
Year	*IF*	*A*	*B*	*IF*	*A*	*B*	*IF*	*A*	*B*
1	0.83	415	83	0.81	405	81	0.76	380	76
2	0.69	276	138	0.65	260	130	0.57	228	114
3	0.58	174	174	0.52	156	156	0.43	129	129
4	0.48	48	192	0.42	42	168	0.33	33	132
5	0.40		200	0.34		170	0.25		125
6	0.33		198	0.28		168	0.19		114
Present value		913	985		863	873		770	690
Net *PV*		(87)	(15)		(137)	(127)		(230)	(310)

that the interest cost of this debt is 6 percent. If the internal rate of return on a particular project is calculated to be 6 percent, the same as the cost of capital, then the firm would be able to invest in the project, use the cash flow generated by the investment to pay off the principal and interest on the bank loan, and come out exactly even on the transaction. If the internal rate of return exceeded 6 percent, the project would be profitable, while if the internal rate of return was

TABLE 7–4 THE PROSPECTIVE-PROJECTS SCHEDULE

NATURE OF PROPOSAL	AMOUNTS OF FUNDS REQUIRED	CUMULATIVE TOTAL	IRR
1. Purchase of leased space	$2,000,000	$ 2,000,000	23%
2. Mechanization of accounting system	1,200,000	3,200,000	19
3. Modernization of office building	1,500,000	4,700,000	17
4. Addition of power facilities	900,000	5,600,000	16
5. Purchase of affiliate	3,600,000	9,200,000	13
6. Purchase of loading docks	300,000	9,500,000	12
7. Purchase of tank trucks	500,000	10,000,000	11
			10% cutoff
8. Installation of conveyor system	200,000	10,200,000	9
9. Construction of new plant	2,300,000	12,500,000	8
10. Purchase of executive aircraft	200,000	12,700,000	7

less than 6 percent, taking on the project would result in losses. It is this characteristic that makes us interested in the internal rate of return.

Assuming that the firm uses a cost of capital of 10 percent, the internal rate of return criterion states that, if the two projects are independent, both should be accepted. If they are mutually exclusive, B ranks higher and should be accepted, while A should be rejected.[9] A more complete illustration of how the internal rate of return would be used in practice is given in Table 7–4. Assuming a 10 percent cost of capital, the firm

[9] The validity of this statement must be qualified. As will be discussed later, it is possible that the NPV and IRR (and also PI) methods will give different rankings for mutually exclusive projects. In such cases the IRR method's ranking will not necessarily be the correct one.

should accept projects 1 through 7, reject projects 8 through 10, and have a total capital budget of $10 million.

The Benefit/Cost Ratio, or Profitability Index

The *benefit/cost ratio,* or *profitability index* (PI), is calculated by dividing the present value of future returns (discounted at the cost of capital) by the required investment outlay.[10]

$$\text{PI} = \frac{\displaystyle\sum_{t=1}^{N} \frac{R_t}{(1+k)^t}}{\text{Cost}} \qquad (7\text{–}3)$$

Projects A and B each cost $1,000 and have a present value of returns (discounted at 10 percent, the cost of capital) equal to $1,080 and $1,400 respectively. Therefore, the PIs are 1.08 for A and 1.40 for B.

Independent projects should be accepted whenever the PI is greater than 1.0. Therefore, both A and B should be accepted if they are independent. The one with the larger index should be selected if they are mutually exclusive; accordingly, B should be accepted and A rejected if they are mutually exclusive.

Which Discounted Cash Flow Technique Should Be Used?

Under ordinary circumstances, all three of the discounted cash flow methods—the net present value, the internal rate of return, and the profitability index—will give identical rankings to mutually exclusive projects. Therefore, using any of the methods will result in the same selection when choosing among competing projects. Further, the three methods ordinarily make identical (and "correct") statements about how far down the list of capital projects to go; that is, they give identical answers to the question of how large the total capital budget should be. However, if any of the conditions listed in Table 7–5 exist, the three methods may give different rankings to two competing projects.

We are deliberately vague about "significant differences" in project lives, about what is meant by one project being "substantially larger" than another, and the like. To specify precisely when such differences are "significant" would require a sensitivity analysis in which a theo-

[10] If costs are incurred over more than one year, the present value of costs is used in the denominator of the ratio.

$$\text{PI} = \frac{\text{PV of Returns}}{\text{PV of Cost}}$$

retically correct value is determined; deviations from this value could then be observed as differences in asset sizes, length of lives, and so on, increased. When a difference is "significant" is a matter of judgment. In practice, sophisticated firms use sensitivity analysis to determine just how large an error is involved in using a rule-of-thumb procedure. If "too large" an error is involved, the method of analysis will be refined. Both the increased costs of added precision and the value of

TABLE 7–5 CONDITIONS UNDER WHICH NPV, IRR, AND PI MAY RANK CONFLICTING PROJECTS DIFFERENTLY

A. PROJECT CHARACTERISTICS

1. The cash flow of one project increases over time, while that of the other decreases.
2. The projects have significantly different expected lives.
3. The cost of one project is substantially larger than that of the other.

B. FIRM CHARACTERISTICS

4. Investment opportunities in the future are expected to be substantially different than they are this year, and the direction of change (better or worse) is known.
5. The firm is making investments at such a high rate that the marginal cost of capital curve is sharply upward sloping; that is, in terms of Figure 7–1(b), the firm is operating to the right of Q_2.
6. Capital rationing (discussed later in this chapter) is being imposed upon the firm.

NOTE: When we consider capital budgeting under uncertainty in the next chapter, we will see that the present list must be expanded to include the effects of diversification, or "portfolio effects."

improved decisions will enter the decision to upgrade the decision process.

Fortunately, most competing projects do not exhibit the first three characteristics listed in Table 7–5, and most firms are not subject to the last three. Therefore, it ordinarily does not matter which method is used. If these conditions are not met, and if the different selection criteria make conflicting choices, it is not possible to generalize about the relative merits of one over another. The theoretical differences between the methods, and the implications of choosing one over another, are discussed in Appendix A to this chapter.

DETERMINING CASH FLOWS

Thus far the problem of measuring cash flows—the benefits used in the present value calculations above—has not been dealt with directly. This matter will now be discussed and a few simple examples given.

Simplified Model for Determining Cash Flows

One way of considering the cash flows attributable to a particular investment is to think of them in terms of comparative income statements. This is illustrated in the following example.

The Widget Division of the Culver Company, a profitable, diversified manufacturing firm, purchased a machine five years ago at a cost of $7,500. The machine had an expected life of 15 years at time of purchase and a zero estimated salvage value at the end of the 15 years. It is being depreciated on a straight-line basis and has a book value of $5,000 at present. The division manager reports that he can buy a new machine for $10,000 (including installation) which, over its 10-year life, will expand sales from $10,000 to $11,000. Further, it will reduce labor and raw materials usage sufficiently to cut operating costs from $7,000 to $5,000. The old machine's current market value is $1,000. Taxes are at a 50 percent rate and are paid quarterly, and the firm's cost of capital is 10 percent. Should Culver buy the new machine?

The decision calls for three steps: (1) estimating the actual cash outlay attributable to the new investment, (2) determining the present value of the incremental cash flows, and (3) seeing if the IRR exceeds the cost of capital, if the NPV is positive, or if the PI is greater than 1.0. These steps are explained further in the following discussion.

1. ESTIMATED CASH OUTLAY. Culver must make a $10,000 payment to the manufacturer of the machine, but its next quarterly tax bill will be reduced by $2,000. The tax reduction occurs because the old machine, which is carried at $5,000, will be written down by $4,000 ($5,000 less $1,000 salvage value) immediately if the new one is purchased. To illustrate, suppose the Culver Company's taxable income in the quarter in which the new machine is purchased would be $100,000 without the purchase of the new machine and the consequent write-off of the old machine. With a 50 percent tax rate, Culver would have to write a check for $50,000 to pay its tax bill. However, if it buys the new machine and sells the old one, it takes an operating loss of $4,000—the $5,000 book value on the old machine less the salvage value. (The loss is an

operating loss, not a capital loss, because it is in reality simply recognizing that depreciation charges, an operating cost, were too low during the old machine's five-year life.) With this $4,000 additional operating cost, taxable income is reduced from $100,000 to $96,000, and the tax bill from $50,000 to $48,000. This means, of course, that the firm's cash outflow for taxes is $2,000 less *because* it purchased the new machine. In addition, there is a cash inflow of $1,000 from the sale of the old machine. The result is that the purchase of the new machine involves a net cash outlay of $7,000; this is its cost for capital budgeting purposes.[11]

Invoice price of new machine	$10,000
Less: Tax savings	−2,000
Salvage of old machine	−1,000
Net cash outflow	$ 7,000

2. PRESENT VALUE OF BENEFITS. The first column in Table 7–6 shows the Widget Division's estimated income statement as it would be without the new machine; the second column shows the statement as it will look if the new investment is made. (It is assumed that these figures are applicable for each of the next 10 years; if this is not the case, then cash flow estimates must be made for each year.) The difference between the new and the old cash flows, $1,750, is the incremental cash flow produced by the new machine; this is the benefit stream to be discounted at the cost of capital.

The interest factor for a 10-year 10 percent annuity is found to be 6.145 from Appendix Table A–4. This factor, multiplied by the $1,750 incremental cash flow, shows the investment to have a present value of $10,754.

3. NET PRESENT VALUE. Subtracting the $7,000 cost figure from the $10,754 gives the investment a net present value of $3,754. Since the net present value is positive, the new machine should be purchased.[12]

[11] It is also useful to point out at this time that when the investment tax credit is allowed, the outlay cost of new investments in machinery and equipment is reduced by the amount of the investment tax credit. In other words, if the asset has a cost of $1,000 and a depreciable life of at least eight years, the outlay cost will be reduced by a 7 percent tax credit, or by $70. This obviously raises the net present value over what it would otherwise be and thus stimulates investment. It is for this reason, of course, that Congress created the investment tax credit. When Congress feels the economy needs to be stimulated, the tax credit is put into force. When Congress feels that the economy is "overheated" and should be restrained, the credit is suspended. The tax credit has therefore been used as an instrument of fiscal policy.

[12] Alternatively, the internal rate of return on the project could have been com-

TABLE 7–6 COMPARATIVE INCOME STATEMENT FRAMEWORK FOR CONSIDERING CASH FLOWS

	WITHOUT NEW INVESTMENT	WITH NEW INVESTMENT
Sales	$10,000	$11,000
Operating costs	−7,000	−5,000
Depreciation (D)	−500	−1,000
Taxable income	$ 2,500	$ 5,000
Income taxes	−1,250	−2,500
Profit after taxes (P)	$ 1,250	$ 2,500
Cash flow ($P + D$)	$ 1,750	$ 3,500

Change in cash flow: $3,500 − $1,750 = $1,750

NOTE: The effects of the sale of the old machine on the income statement are not considered here. These effects are accounted for in the estimate of the cash outlay for the new machine.

Work Sheet for Replacement Decisions

Table 7–7 shows a work sheet for making replacement decision calculations. The top section of the table sets forth the cash outflows at the time the investment is made. All these flows occur immediately, so no discounting is required, and the present value factor is 1.0. No tax adjustment is necessary on the invoice price of the new machine, but, as we saw above, the $4,000 loss on the old machine gives rise to a $2,000 tax reduction, which is deducted from the price of the new machine. Also, the $1,000 salvage value on the old machine is treated as a reduction in cash outflows necessary to acquire the new machine. Notice that since the $1,000 is a recovery of capital investment it is not considered to be taxable income; hence, no tax adjustment is made for the salvage value.

In the lower section of the table we see that revenues increase by $3,000 a year—a sales increase of $1,000 plus a cost reduction of $2,000. However, this amount is taxable, so with a 50 percent tax, the after-tax benefits are reduced to $1,500. This $1,500 is received each year for 10 years, so it is an annuity. The present value of the annuity, discounted at the 10 percent cost of capital, is $9,217.

Cash inflows also come from the depreciation on the new machine—

puted and found to be 21 percent. Since this is substantially in excess of the 10 percent cost of capital, the internal rate of return method also indicates that the investment should be undertaken. Also, the PI exceeds 1.0.

$1,000 before, or $500 after, taxes. Again, this is a 10-year annuity, and its present value is $3,073. Observe that the depreciation on the old machine is *subtracted* from the inflows section. The logic here is that, had the replacement *not* been made, the company would have had the benefit of the $500 depreciation each year for the next 10 years.

TABLE 7–7 CALCULATIONS FOR REPLACEMENT DECISIONS

	AMOUNT BEFORE TAX	AMOUNT AFTER TAX	YEAR EVENT OCCURS	PV FACTOR AT 10%	PV
Outflows at time investment is made:					
Investment in new equipment	10,000	10,000	0	1.00	$10,000
Salvage value of old	(1,000)	(1,000)	0	1.00	(1,000)
Tax loss on sale	(4,000)	(2,000)	0	1.00	(2,000)
Total outflows (present value of costs)					$ 7,000
Inflows, or annual returns:					
Benefits*	3,000	1,500	1–10	6.145	9,217
Depreciation on new (annual)	1,000	500	1–10	6.145	3,073
Depreciation on old (annual)†	(500)	(250)	1–10	6.145	(1,536)
Salvage value on new‡	—	—	—	—	—
Total inflows (present value of benefits)					$10,754
PV of inflows less present value oi outflows = $3,754					

* $1,000 sales increase + $2,000 cost saving = $3,000 benefit.
† Had the replacement not been made, Culver would have had $500 depreciation a year on the old machine—$5,000 book value divided by 10 years. But since they made the replacement, this depreciation is no longer available. The $5,000 has been recovered as $1,000 salvage plus $4,000 deductible loss. The depreciation of $500 a year must, therefore, be subtracted from inflows. It would be possible, of course, for Culver not to sell the old machine, not to take the immediate loss, and to continue getting the $500 yearly depreciation. If Culver chose to do this, however, the PV would be only $1,536 as against $3,000 ($2,000 + $1,000) for the sale and tax loss.
‡ The new machine has a zero estimated salvage value at the time it is purchased. However, the table is structured to show how salvage value would be handled in cases where it is applicable.

With the replacement, however, all this depreciation is taken as an operating loss immediately and is shown as the tax loss on sale in the upper section of the table.

Table 7–7 gives the same net present value, $3,754, as was derived under the comparative income statement approach. In general, the tabular approach is somewhat more convenient for use in the management decisions illustrated in the end-of-chapter problems.

CAPITAL RATIONING

Ordinarily, firms operate as illustrated in Figure 7–1; that is, they take on investments to the point where the marginal returns from investment are just equal to their (constant) marginal cost of capital. For firms operating in this way the decision process is as described above—they make those investments having positive net present values, reject those whose net present values are negative, and choose between mutually exclusive investments on the basis of the higher net present value. However, a firm will occasionally set an absolute limit on the size of its capital budget in any one year that is less than the level of investment it would undertake on the basis of the criteria described above. The rationale behind such a decision is discussed in the following section.

Limiting the Total Capital Budget

It is sometimes a fallacy to consider that what is true of the individual parts will be true of the whole. Although individual projects appear to promise a relatively attractive yield, when they are taken together difficulties might be involved in achieving all the favorable results simultaneously. One problem is that other firms in the same industry may be engaging in similar capital expenditure programs in an attempt to increase their capacity or, by cost reductions, to obtain a larger share of the product market. For a given growth rate in the industry, it is obviously impossible for every firm to obtain increases in sales that would fully utilize all the capital expenditure projects being undertaken.

Another problem is that while individual projects promise favorable yields, to undertake a large number of projects simultaneously might involve a very high rate of expansion by the individual firm. Such substantial additional personnel requirements and organizational problems may be involved that over-all rates of return will be diminished. Top management, at some point in the capital budgeting process, must therefore make a decision regarding the total volume of favorable projects that may be successfully undertaken without causing a significant reduction in the prospective returns from individual projects.

Reluctance to Obtain Outside Financing

The situation just described—that is, placing a ceiling on the total capital budget in order to keep the over-all rate of expansion within reasonable limits—is one reason for capital rationing. Another reason for limiting the capital budget, and one that perhaps better meets the strict definition of "capital rationing," is the reluctance of some managements to engage in external financing (borrowing or selling stock).

One management, recalling the plight of firms with substantial amounts of debt in the 1930s, may simply refuse to use debt. Other managements, which have no objection to selling debt, may not want to sell equity capital for fear of losing some measure of voting control. Still others may refuse to use any form of outside financing, considering safety and control to be more important than additional profits. These are all cases of capital rationing, and they result in limiting the rate of expansion to a slower pace than would be dictated by "purely rational profit-maximizing behavior."[13]

Project Selection under Capital Rationing

Under conditions of capital rationing, the net present value criterion may not give that ranking of projects which maximizes the value of the firm. For reasons discussed in Appendix A to this chapter, the authors recommend that investments be ranked by the profitability index whenever capital rationing is imposed. The firm should start at the top of its list of projects, taking investments of successively lower rank until the available funds have been exhausted. However, no investment with a PI of less than 1.0 should be undertaken.

[13] We should make two points here. First, we *do not* necessarily consider a decision to hold back on expansion irrational. If the owner of a firm has what *he* considers to be plenty of income and wealth, then it might be quite rational for him to "trim his sails," relax, and concentrate on enjoying what he has already earned rather than on earning still more. Such behavior would not, however, be appropriate for a publicly owned firm. More will be said on this subject in subsequent chapters.

The second point is that it is not correct to interpret as capital rationing a situation where the firm is willing to sell additional securities at the going market price but finds that it cannot because the market will simply not absorb more of its issues. Rather, such a situation indicates that the cost-of-capital curve is rising. If more acceptable investments are indicated than can be financed, then the cost of capital being used is too low and should be raised. This matter will be discussed further in Chapter 12.

A firm might, for example, have the investment opportunities shown in Table 7–8 and only $6 million available for investment. In this situation, the firm would probably accept projects 1 through 4 and project 6, ending with a total capital budget of $5.9 million. Under no circumstances should it accept projects 8, 9, or 10, as they all have profitability indexes of less than 1.0 (and also net present values less than zero).

TABLE 7–8 THE PROSPECTIVE-PROJECTS SCHEDULE

Nature of Proposal	PROJECT'S COST (1)	PV OF BENEFITS (2)	PI (2)/(1)	CUMULATIVE TOTAL OF COSTS Sum of (1)
1. Purchase of leased space	$2,000,000	$3,200,000	1.60	$ 2,000,000
2. Mechanization of accounting system	1,200,000	1,740,000	1.45	3,200,000
3. Modernization of office building	1,500,000	2,070,000	1.38	4,700,000
4. Addition of power facilities	900,000	1,125,000	1.25	5,600,000
5. Purchase of affiliate	3,600,000	4,248,000	1.18	9,200,000
6. Purchase of loading docks	300,000	342,000	1.14	9,500,000
7. Purchase of tank trucks	500,000	540,000	1.08	10,000,000
——1.00 Cutoff——				
8. Installation of conveyer system	200,000	186,000	.93	10,200,000
9. Construction of new plant	2,300,000	2,093,000	.91	12,500,000
10. Purchase of executive aircraft	200,000	128,000	.64	12,700,000

Before closing this section, we should emphasize two points. First, as we explain in Appendix A to this chapter, none of the selection criteria discussed in this chapter will *necessarily* give optimal decisions if capital rationing (or any other point listed in Table 7–5) is imposed on the firm. Under capital rationing, only a mathematical programming solution will yield optimal budgets in the sense of maximizing the value of the firm.

The second point is that, based on our experience, we doubt that many firms are truly subject to capital rationing or exhibit the other characteristics listed in Table 7–5. Accordingly, we believe that in the great majority of cases the net present value approach provides a completely satisfactory selection criterion for capital investment decisions.

SUMMARY

Capital budgeting, which involves commitments for large outlays whose benefits (or drawbacks) extend well into the future, is of the greatest significance to a firm. Decisions in these areas will, therefore, have a major impact on the future well-being of the firm. This chapter focused on how capital budgeting decisions can be made more effective in contributing to the health and growth of a firm. The discussion stressed the development of systematic procedures and rules for preparing a list of investment proposals, for evaluating them, and for selecting a cutoff point.

The chapter emphasized that one of the most crucial phases of the process of evaluating capital budget proposals is obtaining a dependable estimate of the benefits that will be obtained from undertaking the project. It cannot be overemphasized that the firm must allocate to competent and experienced personnel the making of these judgments.

Ranking Investment Proposals

Four commonly used procedures for ranking investment proposals were discussed in the chapter.

Payback, which is defined as the number of years required to return the original investment. Although the payback method is used frequently, it has serious conceptual weaknesses, because it ignores the facts (a) that some receipts come in beyond the payback period and (b) that a dollar received today is more valuable than a dollar received in the future.

Net present value, which is defined as the present value of future returns discounted at the cost of capital minus the cost of the investment.

$$\text{NPV} = \sum_{t=1}^{N} \frac{R_t}{(1 + k)^t} - C$$

The NPV method overcomes the conceptual flaws noted in the use of the payback method.

Internal rate of return, which is defined as the interest rate that equates the present value of future returns to the investment outlay.

$$C = \sum_{t=1}^{N} \frac{R_t}{(1 + r)^t}$$

The internal rate of return method, like the NPV method, meet the objections to the payback approach.

Benefit/cost ratio, or profitability index, which is defined as the present value of future benefits divided by the present value of the investment outlay. This method also meets the objections to payback.

$$\text{PI} = \frac{\displaystyle\sum_{t=1}^{N} \frac{R_t}{(1+k)^t}}{\text{Cost}}$$

Under ordinary circumstances, the three discounted cash flow methods give identical answers to these questions: Which of two mutually exclusive projects should be selected? How large should the total capital budget be? However, whenever any of the conditions listed in Table 7–5 hold, conflicts arise. In general, the NPV method is preferred in the absence of capital rationing, but the profitability index method is the better choice if capital rationing is imposed. The reasons for these preferences are described in Appendix A7.

Determining Cash Flows

The cash inflows from an investment consist of the incremental profit after taxes plus the incremental depreciation; the cash outflow is the cost of the investment less the sum of the salvage value received on an old machine plus any tax loss when the machine is sold.

Capital Rationing

Although individual projects appear to promise a relatively attractive yield, when they are taken together difficulties might arise in achieving all the favorable projects simultaneously. Several factors must be considered in this connection: expansion plans of other firms in the industry, capital limitations, personnel problems if expansion rates are too high, and so on. Top management, at some point in the capital budgeting process, must make a decision regarding the total volume of favorable projects that can be successfully undertaken without causing a significant reduction in the returns from individual projects. Ordinarily, however, this is not a problem for larger firms—they plan for expansion and are able to take advantage of good investment opportunities as they arise.

QUESTIONS

7–1 Why will a firm often continue to use obsolete equipment instead of installing new replacements? How does the use of this obsolete equipment affect the company and the economy?

7–2 Are there conditions under which a firm might be better off if it chooses a machine with a rapid payback rather than one with the largest rate of return?

7–3 Company X uses the payback method in evaluating investment proposals and is considering new equipment whose additional earnings will be $150 a year. The equipment costs $500 and its expected life is 10 years (straight-line depreciation). The company uses a three-year payback as its criterion. Should the equipment be purchased under the above assumptions? Cash flow 600 yes

7–4 What are the most critical problems that arise in calculating a rate of return for a prospective investment?

7–5 What other factors in addition to rate of return analysis should be considered in determining capital expenditures?

7–6 Would it be beneficial for a firm to review its past capital expenditures and capital budgeting procedures? Why?

7–7 Fiscal and monetary policies are tools used by the government to stimulate the economy. Explain, using the analytical devices developed in this chapter, how each of the following might be expected to stimulate the economy by stimulating investment.

a) The investment tax credit
b) A speed-up of tax-allowable depreciation (for example, the accelerated methods permitted in 1954 or the guideline depreciable life revisions of 1962)
c) An easing of interest rates
d) Passage of the War on Poverty Program

7–8 The only "correct" solution to capital budgeting decisions in the general case calls for a programming formulation through which the firm maximizes the present value of its future cash flows; the capital budgeting criteria described in the chapter all represent "rules of thumb" designed to approximate this correct (but difficult if not impossible to implement) solution. Under certain conditions, one rule of thumb will work best; under other conditions, another rule of thumb will be superior. What are the fundamental differences between the following rule of thumb criteria, and under what conditions should each of them be used?

a) PV
b) IRR
c) PI

PROBLEMS

7–1 The Jordan Company is using a machine whose original cost was $15,000. The machine is five years old and has a current market (salvage) value of $2,000. The asset is being depreciated over a

15-year original life toward a zero estimated salvage value. Depreciation is on a straight-line basis and the tax rate is 50 percent.

Management is contemplating the purchase of a replacement which costs \$10,000 and whose estimated salvage value is \$2,000. The expected savings with the new machine are \$3,000 a year. Depreciation is on a straight-line basis over a 10-year life, the cost of capital is 10 percent, and a 50 percent tax rate is applicable.

a) Should the firm replace the asset? Set up your solution as shown in Table 7–7.
b) How would your decision be affected if the expected savings from the investment in the new machine increase to \$4,400 a year but the expected life of the new machine decreases to five years?
c) Disregarding the changes in b (that is, assuming again that expected savings are \$3,000 a year and that the expected life is 10 years), how would your decision be affected if a second new machine is available that costs \$20,000, has a \$4,000 estimated salvage value, and is expected to provide \$6,000 in annual savings over its 10-year life? Depreciation is still on a straight-line basis.
d) Disregarding the changes in b and c (that is, under the original assumption), how would your decision be affected if a new generation of equipment is expected to be on the market in about two years that will provide increased annual savings and have the same cost, asset life, and salvage value?
e) Disregarding all preceeding changes, what factors in addition to the quantitative factors listed above are likely to require consideration in a practical situation?

7–2 The Denver Company is considering the purchase of a new machine tool to replace an obsolete one. The machine being used for the operation has both a tax book value and a salvage value of zero; it is in good working order and will last, physically, for at least an additional 10 years. The proposed machine will perform the operation so much more efficiently the Denver Company engineers estimate that labor, material, and other direct costs of the operation will be reduced \$3,000 a year if it is installed. The proposed machine costs \$12,000 delivered and installed, and its economic life is estimated to be 10 years with zero salvage value. The company expects to earn 14 percent on its investment after taxes (14 percent is the firm's cost of capital). The tax rate is 50 percent, and the firm uses straight-line depreciation.

a) Should Denver buy the new machine?
b) Assume that the tax book value of the old machine had been \$4,000, that the annual depreciation charge would have been \$400, and that it had no sale value. How do these assumptions affect your answer?

c) Change b to give effect also to the sale of the old machine for $2,000.
d) Change b to assume that the annual savings would be $4,000. (The change in c is not made; the machine is *not* sold for $2,000.)
e) Rework part a assuming the relevant cost of capital is now 5 percent. What is the significance of this? What can be said about parts b, c, and d under this assumption?
f) In general, how would each of the following factors affect the investment decision, and how should each be treated?
   (1) The expected life of the existing machine decreases.
   (2) Capital rationing is imposed upon the firm.
   (3) The cost of capital is not constant but is rising.
   (4) Improvements in the equipment to be purchased are expected to occur each year, and the result will be to increase the returns or expected savings from new machines over the saving expected with this year's model for every year in the foreseeable future.

7–3 Each of two mutually exclusive projects involves an investment of $1,000. Cash flows (after-tax profits plus depreciation) are $660 a year for two years for project S and $265 a year for six years for project L.

a) Compute the present value of each project if the firm's cost of capital is 6 percent, 10 percent, 20 percent.
b) Compute the internal rate of return for each project.
c) Which project is better?
d) Graph the present values of the two projects, putting *PV* on the *Y* axis and the cost of capital on the *X* axis.
e) What is the significance of your results?
f) How would your analysis be affected if the cost of the second project, L, was $11,000 and cash flows (after-tax profits plus depreciation) were $2,650 a year for six years?

Selected References

Bailey, Martin J., "Formal Criteria for Investment Decisions," *Journal of Political Economy*, LXVII (October 1959).

Baumol, William J., and Richard E. Quandt, "Investment and Discount Rates Under Capital Rationing—A Programming Approach," *The Economic Journal*, LXXV (June 1965), 317–329.

Ben-Shahar, Haim, and Marshall Sarnat, "Reinvestment and the Rate of Return on Common Stocks," *Journal of Finance*, XXI (December 1966), 737–742.

Bierman, Harold, Jr., and Seymour Smidt, *The Capital Budgeting Decision*. (New York: Macmillan 1966.)

Bodenhorn, Diran, "On the Problem of Capital Budgeting," *Journal of Finance,* XIV (December 1959), 473–492.

Cheng, Pao L., and John P. Shelton, "A Contribution to the Theory of Capital Budgeting—The Multi-Investment Case," *Journal of Finance,* XIIX (December 1963), 622–636.

Dean, Joel, *Capital Budgeting.* (New York: Columbia University Press, 1951.)

Dougall, Herbert E., "Payback as an Aid in Capital Budgeting," *Controller,* XXIX (February 1961), 67–72.

Edson, Harvey O., "Setting a Standard for Your Company's Return on Investment," *Controller,* XXVI (September 1958), 411–415.

Haynes, W. Warren and Martin B. Solomon, Jr., "A Misplaced Emphasis in Capital Budgeting," *Quarterly Review of Economics and Business* (February 1962).

Heebink, David V., "Postcompletion Audits of Capital Investment Decisions," *California Management Review,* VI (Spring 1964), 47–52.

Hunt, Pearson, *Financial Analysis in Capital Budgeting.* (Boston: Graduate School of Business Administration, Harvard University, 1964.)

Jean, William H., "On Multiple Rates of Return," *Journal of Finance,* XXIII, 1 (March 1968), 187–192.

Jeynes, Paul H., "The Significance of Reinvestment Rate," *Engineering Economist,* XI (Fall 1965), 1–9.

Krainer, Robert E., "A Neglected Issue in Capital Rationing—The Asset Demand for Money," *Journal of Finance,* XXI (December 1966), 731–736.

Lerner, Eugene M., "Capital Budgeting and Financial Management," in Alexander A. Robichek, ed., *Financial Research and Managerial Decisions.* (New York: Wiley, 1967), pp. 72–89.

———, and Willard T. Carleton, *A Theory of Financial Analysis* (New York: Harcourt 1966).

———, "The Integration of Capital Budgeting and Stock Valuation," *American Economic Review,* LIV (September 1964), 682–702

Lindsay, J. R., and A. W. Sametz, *Financial Management: An Analytical Approach* (Homewood, Ill.: Irwin, 1967).

Lorie, James H. and Leonard J. Savage, "Three Problems in Rationing Capital," *Journal of Business,* XXVIII (October 1955).

Mao, James C. T., "The Internal Rate of Return as a Ranking Criterion," *Engineering Economist,* XI (Winter 1966), 1–13.

Merrett, A. J. and Allen Sykes, *Capital Budgeting and Company Finance.* (London: Longmans, Green & Company, Ltd., 1966).

Quirin, G. David, *The Capital Expenditure Decision* (Homewood, Ill.: Irwin, 1967).

Robichek, Alexander A., and James C. Van Horne, "Abandonment Value and Capital Budgeting," *Journal of Finance,* XXII (December 1967), 577–590.

Sarnat, M., and H. Ben-Shahar, "Reinvestment and the Rate of Return on Common Stocks," *Journal of Finance,* XXIII, 1 (December 1966), 737–742.

Solomon, Ezra, "The Arithmetic of Capital-Budgeting Decisions," *Journal of Business,* XXIX (April 1956).

Solomon, Ezra, and J. C. Laya, *Measuring Profitability* (Englewood Cliffs, N.J.: Prentice-Hall, 1969).

———, *The Management of Corporate Capital* (New York: The Free Press of Glencoe, Inc., 1959).

———, *The Theory of Financial Management* (New York: Columbia University Press, 1963).

Teichroew, Daniel, "Mathematical Analysis of Rates of Return Under Certainty," *Management Science,* XI (January 1965), 395–403.

Weingartner, H. Martin, "Capital Budgeting of Interrelated Projects: Survey and Synthesis," *Management Science,* XII (March 1966), 485–516.

———, "The Generalized Rate of Return," *Journal of Financial and Quantitative Analysis,* I (September 1966), 1–29.

———, *Mathematical Programming and the Analysis of Capital Budgeting Problems* (Englewood Cliffs, N.J.: Prentice-Hall, 1963).

APPENDIX A TO CHAPTER 7

Some Differences between Discounted Cash Flow Selection Criteria

As we indicated in Chapter 7, the NPV, IRR, and PI generally give the same "answers" to the important questions in capital budgeting: (1) which of two mutually exclusive projects is "better" and (2) how many projects should be accepted, that is, how large should the total capital budget be? However, if any of the conditions listed in Table 7–5 hold, the different selection criteria could reach conflicting conclusions. This appendix considers some fundamental differences between the methods and shows why they sometimes give conflicting answers.

NPV Versus IRR

Reinvestment Rate Assumption. In Chapter 7, the net present value was defined as the difference between the present value of a project's receipts, discounted at the cost of capital, and the initial outlay

$$\begin{aligned} \text{NPV} &= \left[\frac{R_1}{(1+k)^1} + \frac{R_2}{(1+k)^2} + \cdots + \frac{R_N}{(1+k)^N}\right] - C \\ &= \sum_{t=1}^{N} \frac{R_t}{(1+k)^t} - C \end{aligned} \tag{A7–1}$$

The internal rate of return method, on the other hand, found the value of r that equates the two sides of the following equation:

$$\begin{aligned} C &= \frac{R_1}{(1+r)^1} + \frac{R_2}{(1+r)^2} + \cdots + \frac{R_N}{(1+r)^N} \\ &= \sum_{t=1}^{N} \frac{R_t}{(1+r)^t} \end{aligned} \tag{A7–2}$$

Referring back to Table 6–1, it will be recalled that the entire concept of present value as it was developed hinged on the assumption of reinvestment. In the example used in Table 6–1, we started with $1,000, added the interest received during the first year, reinvested the total sum at the same 4 percent, and so on. Exactly the same concept is involved in the capital budgeting equations, and herein lies the difference between the NPV and IRR methods. *The IRR calculation assumes that the cash flows from the projects—the Rs—can be reinvested in other projects that will yield* r, *the internal rate of return. The NPV calculation, by contrast, assumes that cash flows are reinvested at k, the cost of capital.*

Which is the better assumption? In general, if (1) the firm is not subject to capital rationing and (2) the marginal cost of capital is constant, the NPV method is more nearly correct in the sense that, if the firm uses the NPV method, the present value of *the firm* (or, alternatively, the value of the firm at some future date) will be maximized. The reason for this is that, conceptually, a firm should invest to the point where its marginal rate of return on new investment (the internal rate of return on the last acceptable project) is just equal to its marginal cost of capital. As cash flows come in, they simply replace other sources of investment capital; hence, they merely save the firm the cost of the replaced capital. From this it is concluded that the rate of return at which incremental cash flows are invested is equal to the marginal cost of capital. Therefore, under the no-capital-rationing, constant-marginal-

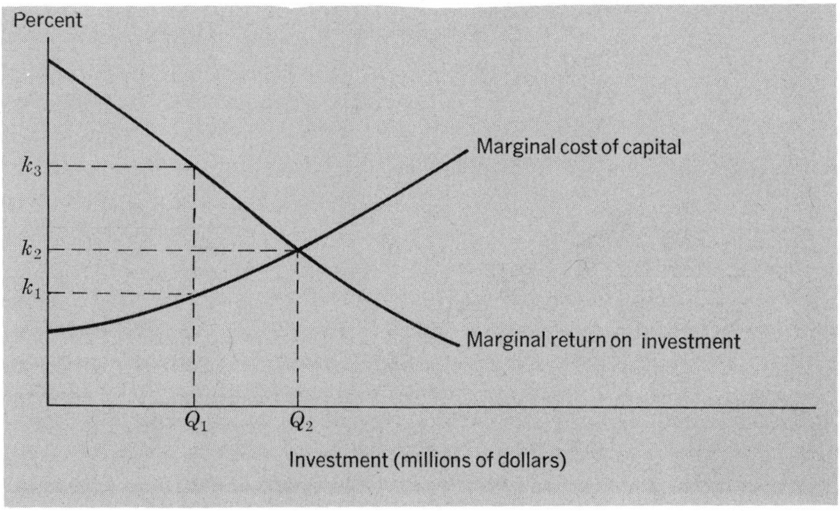

Figure A7–1 Hypothetical Investment and Cost of Capital Schedules

cost-of-capital conditions, the assumption of the net present value method—that funds are reinvested at the cost of capital—is the correct one.

If the firm is subject to capital rationing or if its MCC curve is rising rapidly, then it may be more nearly correct to assume that cash flows from a project are reinvested at the project's IRR than at the cost of capital. This situation is illustrated in Figure A7–1. A capital rationing edict might set the maximum that could be spent on capital assets at Q_1, while, without capital rationing, investment would be taken on to Q_2. At a level of investment Q_1, the marginal cost of capital, k_1, is well below k_3, the minimum rate of return earned on new investment. Under such circumstances it might well be that cash flows can be invested at an average rate of return equal to the internal rate of return, and it certainly appears that assuming reinvestment at the cost of capital involves an understatement. This lends appeal to the IRR method.

Time Pattern of Returns. If two projects are being appraised by the IRR and NPV methods, their ranking will ordinarily be the same under either method unless (1) their estimated lives are materially different or (2) the annual cash flows of one project increase over the project's life (for example, a new store is opened and returns increase as the market grows) while those of the other decline (for example, a mine is opened and returns fall as the ore body is depleted). The first case listed above—different estimated lives—is really a special case of the second, so it need not be considered separately.

Consider two projects, A and B. A's cash flows are higher in the early years; B's cash flows increase over time. In the example given below, A has cash flows of \$1,000 in year 1, \$500 in year 2, \$100 in year 3; B has cash flows of \$100 in year 1, \$600 in year 2, and \$1,100 in year 3. Each project costs \$1,200, and their NPV's, discounted at the specified rates, are shown below.

	NPV	
Discount Rate	A	B
0	\$400	\$600
5	300	400
10	200	200
15	100	50
20	50	(85)
25	(25)	(175)
30	(100)	(250)

At the zero discount rate, the NPV of each project is simply the sum of its receipts less its cost. Thus the NPV of project A at O percent is \$1,000 + \$500 + \$100 — \$1,200 = \$400; that of project B is \$100 + \$600 + \$1,100 — \$1,200 = \$600. As the discount rate rises from zero, the NPV's of the two projects fall from these values. The NPVs are plotted against the appropriate discount rates in Figure A7–2, a graph defined as a *present value profile*. Because its largest cash flows come late in its life, when the compounding effects of time are most significant, B's NPV falls rapidly as the interest rate rises. A's cash flows come early, when the impact of higher rates is not so severe, so its NPV falls less rapidly as interest rates increase.

The definition of the internal rate of return is that point where NPV is zero; therefore, A's IRR is 22 percent while B's is 17 percent. Notice that, at a cost of capital of 5 percent, B has the higher NPV but the lower IRR. At a higher cost of capital, say 12 percent, A has both the higher NPV and the higher IRR. We can generalize these results: *Whenever the profit profiles of two projects cross one another, the NPV of the one with the lower IRR will exceed that of the one with the higher IRR to the left of the crossover point. Therefore, if the cost of capital is less than the crossover discount rate, the IRR and the NPV methods will yield conflicting results.*

When such conflicts arise, they can only be reconciled by asking which reinvestment rate assumption is more nearly correct—the cost of capital or the IRR. If cash flows will be reinvested at the cost of capital—and we think this is the usual case—then the conflict should be resolved in favor of the project with the higher NPV.

Multiple Solutions to IRR. Another problem with the IRR is that, under certain circumstances, several different values of r can be used to solve

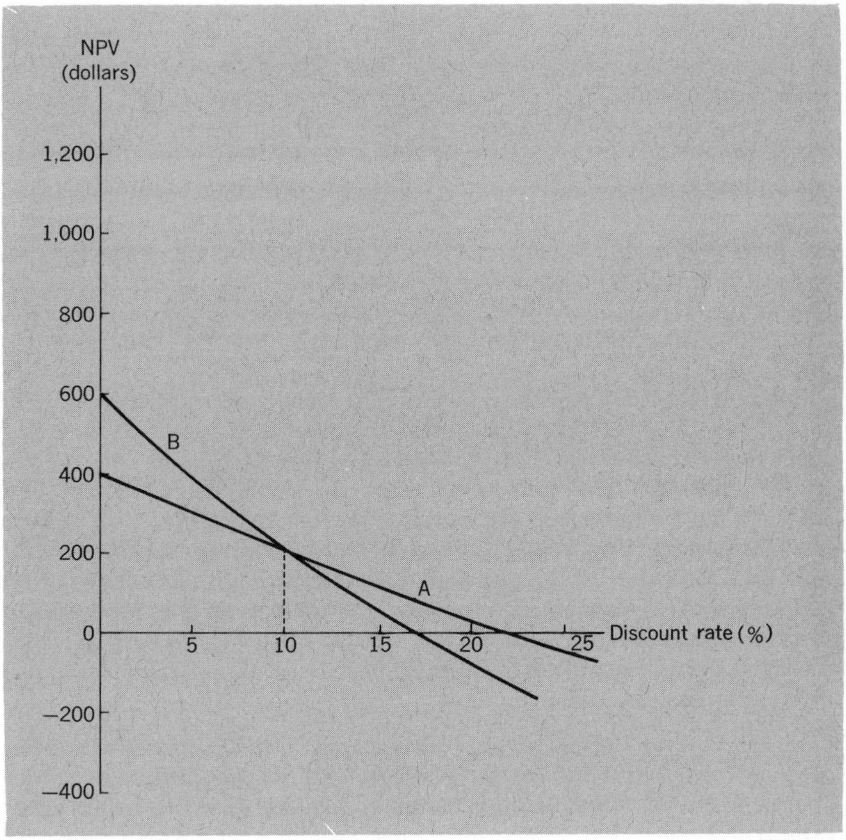

Figure A7–2 Present Value Profiles

equation A7–2. Notice that this equation is a polynominal of degree N. Therefore, there are N different roots, or solutions, to the equation. All except one of the roots are imaginary numbers when investments are "normal"—a normal investment is one that has one or more outflows (costs) followed by a series of inflows (receipts)—so in the normal case only one value of r appears. If, however, a project calls for a large outflow sometime during the life of the project or at the end of the project's life, it is a "nonnormal" project and the possibility of multiple real roots arises. Examples of nonnormal projects where negative flows might occur would be (1) an oil field where water flooding is required at some point to complete recovery of the oil or (2) a strip coal mine where the excavation must be filled and planted when the coal has been removed.

Whenever nonnormal investments are encountered, one must worry about obtaining multiple roots and, if more than one IRR is found, about how to interpret the two rates of return. Generally, the rates are simply examined, one is judged to be "unreasonable," and the other is selected as being the appropriate one. "Unreasonable" means that cash flows from the project cannot be reinvested at so high a rate.

NPV Versus Profitability Index

Since both the NPV and PI methods use equation A7–1 to calculate the present value of benefits, they both assume reinvestment at the cost of capital. How, then, could they give conflicting rankings to two alternative projects? If the projects to be compared are of about the same size, then conflicts will not arise. However, if the projects differ markedly, conflicts can arise.

Suppose, for example, that we are comparing project A, which calls for an investment of $1 million in a conveyor belt system for handling goods in a storage warehouse, with project B, which calls for an expenditure of $300,000 to do the same thing by employing a fleet of fork trucks. The conveyor-belt system has lower operating costs, so its cash flows are larger; the net present values are found to be $200,000 for A and $100,000 for B. Using this as the criterion, we would select project A. However, if we compute the ratios of the present value of their returns to their cost, we find A's ratio to be 1.20 and B's ratio to be 1.33. Using the PI for ranking, we would select project B because it produces higher net returns for each dollar invested.

Constant Cost of Capital. Given this conflict, which project should be accepted? Alternatively stated, is it better to use the net present value approach on an absolute basis or on a relative basis? Barring either capital rationing or a sharply rising cost of capital schedule, the authors recommend the absolute value (NPV method) for the following reason. First, the differential between the initial outlays of the two projects ($700,000) can be looked upon as an investment itself, project C. This differential investment produces a net present value equal to the differential between the NPV of the first two projects, or $100,000. Since the hypothetical project has a positive net present value, it should be accepted. The result is to accept project A.

	A	−	B	=	C
Cost	$1,000,000		$300,000		$700,000
Net present value	200,000		100,000		100,000

Put another way, project A can be split into two components, one costing $300,000 and having a net present value of $100,000, the other costing $700,000 and having a net present value of $100,000. As each of the two components has a positive net present value, both should be accepted. But if project B is accepted, in effect the second component of project A is being rejected. Hence the conclusion that, since the PI method selects project B while the NPV method selects project A, the absolute value method is the better one.

Under certain circumstances, the ratio method obviously gives the better answer. If one project cost $1 million and had a net present value of $100,000, while another cost $100,000, and had a net present value of $99,000, the latter would certainly be selected. The benefits are almost as great but the amount of funds invested is much smaller. We are abstracting from risk in this chapter, but it should be noted that if approximately the same return is expected from a project that requires less funds to be invested at risk, then the smaller project will probably be less risky and will be the preferred investment. However, such an example is not very realistic. Mutually exclusive investments represent alternative ways of doing essentially the same thing, and it is unlikely that they will involve such substantial cost differentials. But if they did, this would simply be one more among many examples demonstrating that no mechanical rule can be substituted for judgment.

Rising Cost of Capital. If the cost of capital is rising sharply at the approximate cutoff point of the total capital budget, or if capital rationing is imposed, then the profitability index may well make "better" choices between competing projects.

The reasoning here is similar to that used when the IRR and NPV methods were compared. Recall that the differences between the IRR and the NPV lies in the assumptions made about reinvestment rates. Similarly, as can be seen from the conveyor-belt-versus-fork-truck example above, the difference between the NPV and PI method lies in the assumption made about the return that will be earned on the funds not spent if the lower cost project is accepted. If the cost of capital is constant, then this is the rate of return that will be earned. If, however, the cost of capital is rising, we cannot specify the appropriate reinvestment rate. We are faced with the same type of dilemma we faced in comparing the NPV and IRR methods. The solution to the dilemma—if it can in fact be solved—lies in one of the mathematical programming approaches outlined below.

Programming Approaches to Capital Rationing

If none of the problems listed in Table 7–5 apply, the NPV method always provides the "best" answers to the critical capital budgeting questions: (1) How large should the capital budget be? (2) How should mutually exclusive projects be ranked? (3) Which independent projects should be accepted? If any one of the conditions listed in the table does hold, however, the NPV method as it was described in Chapter 7 will not necessarily give the right answers. In any of these cases it will be necessary to expand the NPV approach to encompass varying

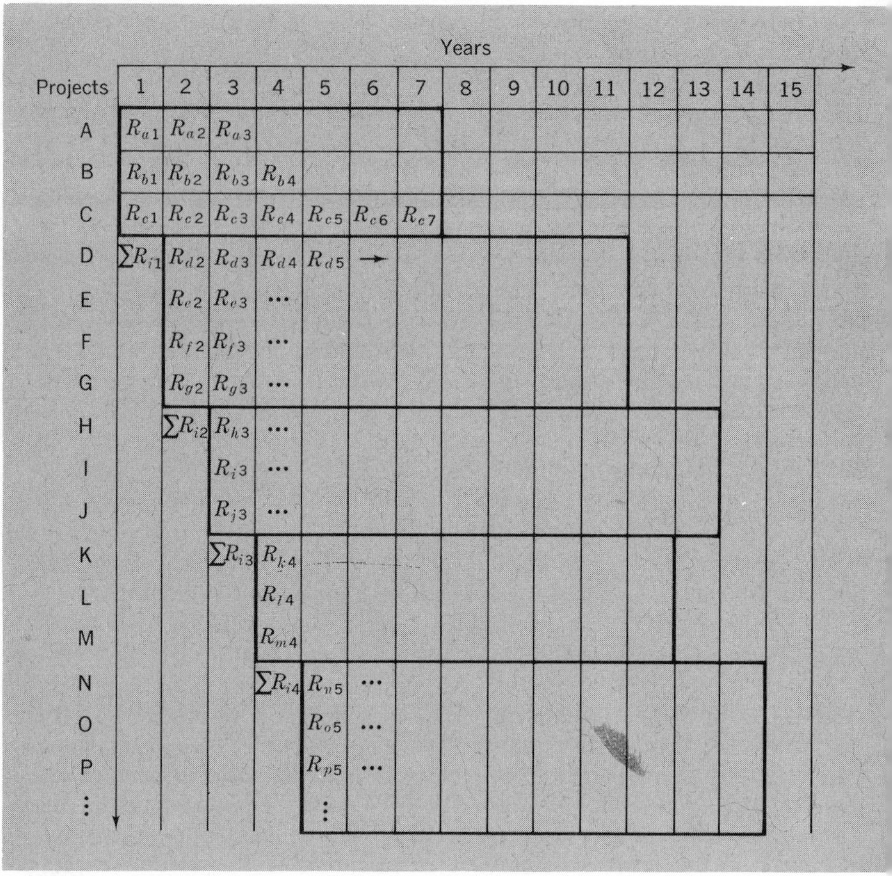
Years
Projects
1 2 3 4 5 6 7 8 9 10 11 12 13 14 15
A R_{a1} R_{a2} R_{a3}
B R_{b1} R_{b2} R_{b3} R_{b4}
C R_{c1} R_{c2} R_{c3} R_{c4} R_{c5} R_{c6} R_{c7}
D $\sum R_{i1}$ R_{d2} R_{d3} R_{d4} R_{d5}
E R_{e2} R_{e3} ...
F R_{f2} R_{f3} ...
G R_{g2} R_{g3} ...
H $\sum R_{i2}$ R_{h3} ...
I R_{i3} ...
J R_{j3} ...
K $\sum R_{i3}$ R_{k4}
L R_{l4}
M R_{m4}
N $\sum R_{i4}$ R_{n5} ...
O R_{o5} ...
P R_{p5} ...

Figure A7–3 Matrix of Future Investment Opportunities

NOTES: 1. The firm's time horizon is 15 years.
2. Projects A, B, and C are available in year 1; D, E, F, and G in year 2; and so on.
3. The cash flows—the R_{ij}, where i designates project number and j designates year in which the cash flow occurs—are generally negative in the first year of the project's life and positive thereafter, but this condition is not necessary.
4. $\sum_{i=1}^{m} R_{ij}$ = the net cash flow during year j.

discount (reinvestment) rates by the programming approach outlined below.

Capital Rationing. As a first step, consider a procedure that can at least conceptually improve on our decision in the capital rationing case. Figure A7–3, gives a matrix of investments in and cash flows from alternative projects. The values in the cells of the matrix are the net cash flows attributable to projects A, B, . . . m over years 1, 2, . . . , n.

The rows of the matrix thus represent the investment opportunities available during the forecast period, while the columns of the matrix represent the net cash flows from all projects during a given year. The cash flows in a particular cell can be either positive or negative. A negative cash flow represents an investment, while a positive cash flow represents the benefits resulting from the investment. The columns, when summed, show the firm's net cash flow during a particular year.

If the firm is not subject to capital rationing, then it can make its capital budgeting decision in any year without explicit consideration of investment opportunities in future years.[1] The present value of the firm will be maximized by accepting all investment opportunities whose net present value is greater than zero.

However, if the firm is subject to capital rationing, then it should pay close attention to the effects of investment decisions in one year on the ability to take advantage of investment opportunities in future years. Suppose, for example, that our firm has an initial amount of money available for investment at the beginning of year 1. It can invest this amount but no more. Further, assume that the funds available for investment in future years must come from cash generated from investments in the past. Therefore, the funds available for investment in year 2 will depend upon the set of investments chosen in year 1; investment funds available in year 3 will depend upon cash throw-off from investments in years 1 and 2, and so forth.

If the projects available for investment in year 2 are highly profitable—that is, have high internal rates of return—then the firm should select investments in year 1 that will have fast paybacks. This will make funds available for the profitable investment opportunities in year 2.

Conceptually, the firm should select its investments in each year (subject to the capital rationing constraint) so as to maximize the net present value of future cash flows. Future cash flows should, of course, be discounted at the firm's cost of capital; if the cost of capital is not constant, further problems arise. If the investment opportunities were infinitely divisible—for example, if the investment opportunities were securities such as stocks or bonds that could be purchased in larger or smaller quantities—then the firm could use a technique known as *linear programming* to determine the optimal set of investment opportunities. If investment opportunities are not infinitely divisible—and in capital budgeting they typically are not—then a more complex procedure known as *integer programming* must be used to find the optimum investment strategy.[2]

[1] Provided, of course, that the cost of capital is constant.

[2] H. Martin Weingartner, *Mathematical Programming and the Analysis of Capital Budgeting Problems* (Englewood Cliffs, N.J.: Prentice-Hall, 1963), has shown how integer programming can be used in capital budgeting decisions. To this point, however, information and computer processing requirements have ruled out the use of the approach on real-world problems.

Rising Cost of Capital. Assuming that the cost of capital is constant, or at least rising rather slowly, linear or integer programming offers a conceptual solution to the capital budgeting problem under capital rationing. This is not, however, a solution to the rising cost of capital problem. If the cost of capital is rising at the point where the IRR curve cuts the MCC curve, the wealth-maximizing set of projects—with regard both to the total budget and to the choices among competing projects—can only be determined by an iterative, or "trial-and-error," process. With linear (or integer) programming, the cost of capital must be given as an input. If, however, the cost of capital *depends* upon the size of the capital budget, then the cost of capital obviously cannot be *assumed* when determining the capital budget. What is required is a programming model that, through an iterative process, *simultaneously* determines the capital budget and the marginal cost of capital.

We shall return to this topic—the simultaneous determination of the capital budget and the cost of capital—after the determinants of the cost of capital schedule have been dealt with in detail. To close out this appendix, we can anticipate our results by stating that, at present, this simultaneous approach is practical only on illustrative and hypothetical problems. However, in the great majority of cases this is not a serious problem because (1) the net present value approach gives the theoretically correct solution when the cost of capital is approximately constant and (2) the profitability index generally gives satisfactory solutions when capital is rationed or when the MCC curve is rapidly rising.

APPENDIX B TO CHAPTER 7 Accelerated Depreciation

In the illustrations of capital budgeting given in Chapter 7, it was assumed that straight-line depreciation was used, thus enabling us to derive uniform cash flows over the life of the investment. Realistically, however, firms usually employ accelerated depreciation methods; when such is the case, it is necessary to modify the procedures outlined thus far. In terms of the framework given in Table 7–6, accelerated depreciation makes it necessary to recompute the differential cash flow for each year during the life of the investment. In terms of the approach given in Table 7–7, the depreciation figures are modified simply by applying another PV factor.

Table B7–1 contains present value factors for accelerated depreciation. The table is constructed as follows:

1. Assume that an asset with a \$2 cost, a five-year depreciable life, and zero salvage value is to be depreciated by the sum-of-years-digits method (see Appendix to Chapter 2 for an explanation of the

method). The firm is taxed at a 50 percent rate. Therefore, the $2 of depreciation will save $1 of income taxes.

2. Assume that the firm's cost of capital is 10 percent, and discount the depreciation tax savings at this rate. This produces the present value of the depreciation flows.
3. Calculations:

YEAR	DEPRECIATION FRACTION APPLIED TO ASSET COST	TAX SAVING EQUALS ½ OF AMOUNT OF DEPRECIATION	10% DISCOUNT FACTOR	SUM-OF-YEARS-DIGITS DEPRECIATION FACTOR
1	5/15	$0.33333	0.909	$0.303
2	4/15	0.26667	0.826	0.220
3	3/15	0.20000	0.751	0.150
4	2/15	0.13333	0.683	0.091
5	1/15	0.06667	0.621	0.042
Totals	1.00	$1.00000		$0.806

4. The present value of the tax savings on the depreciation from a $2 investment, discounted at 10 percent when sum-of-years-digits and a five-year life are used, is $0.806. The factor 0.806 can be found in Table B7–1. All the other factors in the table were constructed in a similar manner.

To modify the results given in Table 7–7 to allow for accelerated depreciation, it is necessary to change only that section of the table headed "Depreciation on new (annual)." In place of the annual depreciation, use the total depreciation and apply a factor taken from Table B7–1. In Table B7–2, assume that the new investment is depreciated by the DDB method over a 10-year period; hence the factor 0.685 is applied to the after-tax depreciation figure of $5,000, obtaining a present value of $3,425 for the depreciation tax shelter.[3]

No modification is necessary for the old machine's depreciation—its tax shelter is still a straight-line annuity. Thus, the present value of the shield is still found to be $1,536. Had we desired to modify the example still further—to have the old machine being depreciated by an accelerated method—the procedure would have been handled exactly the same as for the new machine. Naturally, the present value of the old machine's tax shield would be larger if the deductions came sooner because of accelerated depreciation.

Note that the modifications incorporated in Table B7–2 make the

[3] The term "tax shelter" or "tax shield" is frequently used to denote the value of depreciation and other items which "shelter" or "shield" income from taxes.

TABLE B7–1 TABLES FOR PRESENT VALUE OF DEPRECIATION FOR SUM-OF-YEARS-DIGITS AND DOUBLE DECLINING BALANCE METHODS

SUM-OF-YEARS-DIGITS

Period	6%	8%	10%	12%	14%	15%	16%
1	—	—	—	—	—	—	—
2	—	—	—	—	—	—	—
3	0.908	0.881	0.855	0.831	0.808	0.796	0.786
4	0.891	0.860	0.830	0.802	0.776	0.763	0.751
5	0.875	0.839	0.806	0.775	0.746	0.732	0.719
6	0.859	0.820	0.783	0.749	0.718	0.703	0.689
7	0.844	0.801	0.761	0.725	0.692	0.676	0.661
8	0.829	0.782	0.740	0.702	0.667	0.650	0.635
9	0.814	0.765	0.720	0.680	0.643	0.626	0.610
10	0.800	0.748	0.701	0.659	0.621	0.604	0.587
11	0.786	0.731	0.683	0.639	0.600	0.582	0.565
12	0.773	0.715	0.665	0.620	0.581	0.562	0.545
13	0.760	0.700	0.648	0.602	0.562	0.543	0.526
14	0.747	0.685	0.632	0.585	0.544	0.525	0.508
15	0.734	0.671	0.616	0.569	0.527	0.508	0.491
16	0.722	0.657	0.601	0.553	0.511	0.492	0.475
17	0.711	0.644	0.587	0.538	0.496	0.477	0.460
18	0.699	0.631	0.573	0.524	0.482	0.463	0.445
19	0.688	0.618	0.560	0.510	0.468	0.449	0.432
20	0.677	0.606	0.547	0.497	0.455	0.436	0.419

DOUBLE DECLINING BALANCE

Period	6%	8%	10%	12%	14%	15%	16%
1	—	—	—	—	—	—	—
2	—	—	—	—	—	—	—
3	0.920	0.896	0.873	0.851	0.831	0.821	0.811
4	0.898	0.868	0.840	0.814	0.789	0.777	0.766
5	0.878	0.843	0.811	0.781	0.753	0.739	0.727
6	0.858	0.819	0.783	0.749	0.718	0.704	0.689
7	0.840	0.796	0.756	0.720	0.687	0.671	0.656
8	0.821	0.774	0.731	0.692	0.657	0.641	0.625
9	0.804	0.753	0.708	0.667	0.630	0.614	0.597
10	0.787	0.733	0.685	0.643	0.605	0.588	0.571
11	0.771	0.714	0.664	0.620	0.582	0.564	0.547
12	0.755	0.696	0.644	0.599	0.559	0.541	0.524
13	0.740	0.678	0.625	0.579	0.539	0.521	0.504
14	0.725	0.661	0.607	0.560	0.520	0.501	0.484
15	0.711	0.645	0.590	0.542	0.502	0.483	0.466
16	0.697	0.630	0.573	0.526	0.485	0.466	0.450
17	0.684	0.615	0.558	0.510	0.469	0.451	0.434
18	0.671	0.601	0.543	0.495	0.454	0.436	0.419
19	0.659	0.587	0.529	0.480	0.440	0.422	0.405
20	0.647	0.574	0.515	0.467	0.427	0.409	0.392

TABLE B7–2 CALCULATIONS FOR REPLACEMENT DECISION: ACCELERATED DEPRECIATION

	AMOUNT BEFORE TAX	AMOUNT AFTER TAX	YEAR EVENT OCCURS	PRESENT VALUE FACTOR AT 10%	PRESENT VALUE
Outflows at time investment is made					
Investment in new equipment	10,000	10,000	—	1.00	$10,000
Salvage value of old*	(1,000)	(1,000)	0	1.00	(1,000)
Tax loss on sale	(4,000)	(2,000)	0	1.00	(2,000)
Total outflows (present value of costs)					$ 7,000
Inflows, or annual returns					
Benefits	3,000	1,500	1–10	6.145	$ 9,217
Depreciation on new (total)	10,000	5,000	1–10	0.685	3,425
Depreciation on old (annual)	(500)	(250)	1–10	6.145	(1,536)
Salvage value on new*	—	—	—	—	—
Total inflows (present value of benefits)					$11,106
Present value of inflows less present value of outflows = 4,106					

* Salvage value is not an issue in this example. However, the table is structured to show how salvage values would be handled in cases where they are applicable.

new machine an even more advantageous investment. The reason for this, of course, is that with accelerated depreciation the cash flows accrue faster. If the comparison was made by the method outlined in Table 7–6, computing a different cash flow for each year, this would be seen quite clearly.

8

Capital Budgeting Under Uncertainty

In order to focus on capital budgeting procedures and techniques as they are most commonly employed in industry, the "riskiness" of alternative projects was not treated explicitly in the preceding chapter. However, since investors and financial managers are risk averters, if two projects are not equally risky this fact should be taken into account when choosing between the projects. Several approaches to risk analysis are discussed in this chapter.

We should point out at the outset that in the literature of finance, risk analysis is frequently treated in either of two distinctly different ways—it is either ignored, as we did for the most part in the preceding chapter, or it is treated in a highly formalistic, mathematical manner. The first approach, ignoring risk, is dangerous at best and downright misleading at worst. The second, the mathematical approach, is frequently not feasible in business situations because (1) vital statistical information is unavailable and (2) all the theoretical concepts, and especially those associated with utility analysis, have not yet been completely worked out. We are unwilling to ignore risk, but we are reluctant to take a formal, mathematical approach to the subject in an introductory textbook. Accordingly, we attempt to chart a middle course by presenting the essential elements of risk analysis at an intuitive level in the body of this chapter, and then, in the appendixes to Chapter 8, by providing enough formalism to show the reader the directions in which the finance field is moving.

OME BASIC EFINITIONS

Definition of Risk

The riskiness of a project is defined in terms of the likely variability of returns on the project. For example, if the "project" is an investment of $1,000 in short-term government bonds expected to yield 5½ percent, then the expected return, 5½ percent, can be estimated quite precisely, and the project is defined to be relatively risk free. However, if the $1,000 is invested in the stock of a company just being organized to prospect for uranium in central Africa, then the probable return cannot be estimated precisely. The rate of return on the $1,000 investment could range from minus 100 percent to some extremely large figure, and because of this high variability the project is defined to be relatively risky.

Risk Versus Uncertainty

Sometimes a distinction is made between *risk* and *uncertainty*. When the distinction is made, risk is defined as those situations in which a probability distribution of the returns to a given project can be estimated; uncertainty is defined as those situations in which insufficient evidence is available even to estimate a probability distribution.[1] We do not make this distinction; risk and uncertainty are used synonymously in this chapter.

We do, however, recognize that probability distributions of expected returns can themselves be estimated with greater or lesser precision. In some instances, the probability distribution can be estimated *objec-*

[1] The concept of a probability distribution is discussed later in this section and is illustrated in Figure 8-1.

tively with statistical techniques. For example, a large oil company may be able to estimate the probability distribution of recoverable oil reserves in a given field from past recovery data. When statistical procedures can be used, risk is said to be measured by *objective probability distributions*. There are, however, many situations in which statistical data cannot be used. For example, a firm considering the idea of producing a totally new product will have some idea about the required investment outlay, the demand for the product, the production costs, and so forth. These estimates will not, however, be determined by statistics; they will be determined subjectively and are defined as *subjective probability distributions*.

Variation of Returns as a Measure of Risk

If the probability distributions of rates of returns on a set of projects are normally distributed, then the mean (μ) and the standard deviation (σ) can be used to represent the entire probability distribution. The mean return (μ) is frequently defined as *the expected return;* all other things the same, the higher the expected return, the more attractive the project. The higher the standard deviation, the greater the variability of returns and, by definition, the greater the riskiness of the project.

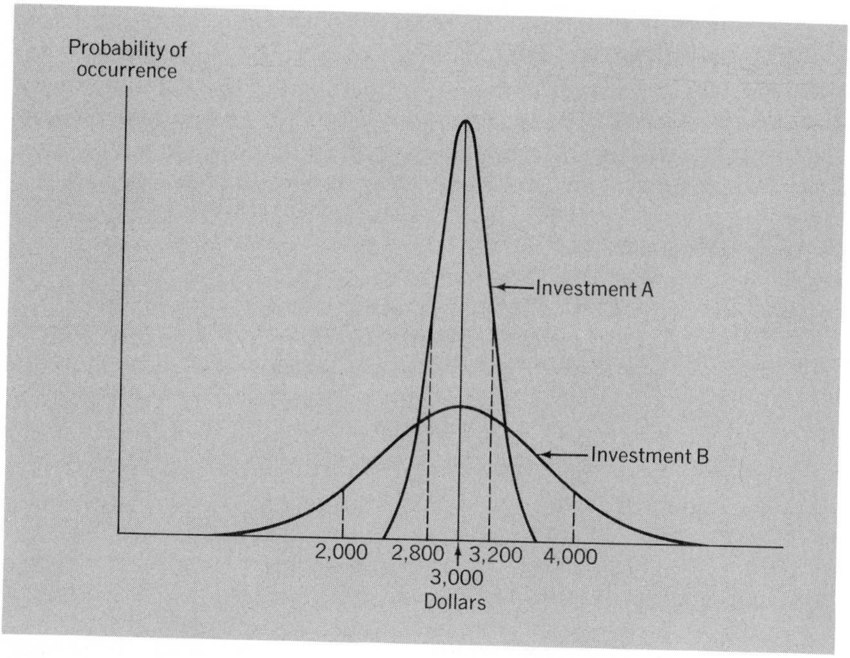

Figure 8–1 Probability Distributions of Two Investments with the Same Expected Dollar Return

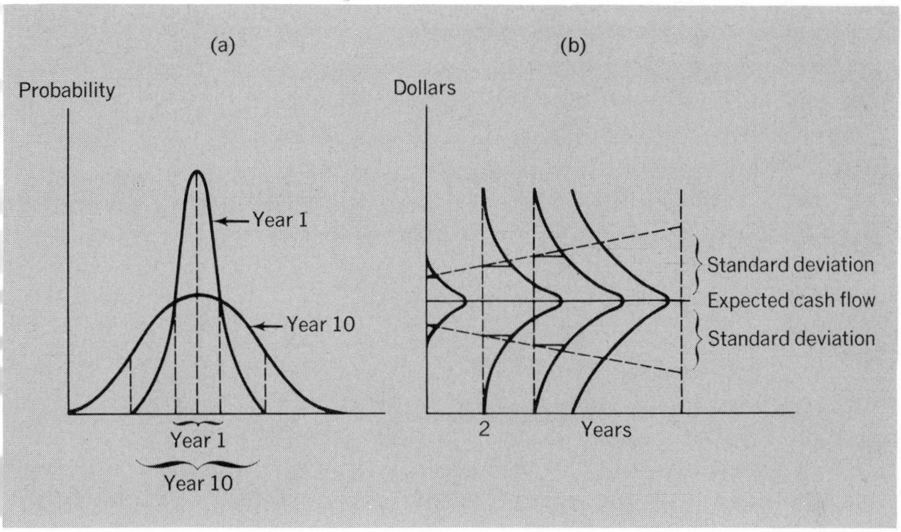

Figure 8–2 Risk as a Function of Time

To illustrate, consider Figure 8–1, which gives probability distributions of the returns from two investments. Both of the investments have expected returns of \$3,000, but project A has a standard deviation of \$200 and project B has a standard deviation of \$1,000. Since we measure risk by the standard deviation, investment A is defined to be less risky than investment B.

Riskiness of Time

We can also use Figure 8–1 to consider the riskiness of a stream of receipts over time. Visualize, for example, investment A as being the expected cash flow from a particular project during year 1 and investment B as being the expected cash flow from the *same* project in the tenth year. The expected return is the same for each of the two years, but the subjectively estimated standard deviation is larger for the more distant return. In this case, riskiness is *increasing over time.*

Figure 8–2 may help to clarify the concept of increasing riskiness over time. Figure 8–2(a) simply shows the probability distribution of expected cash flows in two years—years 1 and 10. Figure 8–2(b) represents a three-dimensional plot of the expected cash flows over time and their probability distributions. The probability distributions should be visualized as extending out from the page. The dashed lines show the standard deviations attached to the cash flows of each year, and the fact that these lines diverge from the expected cash flow line indicates

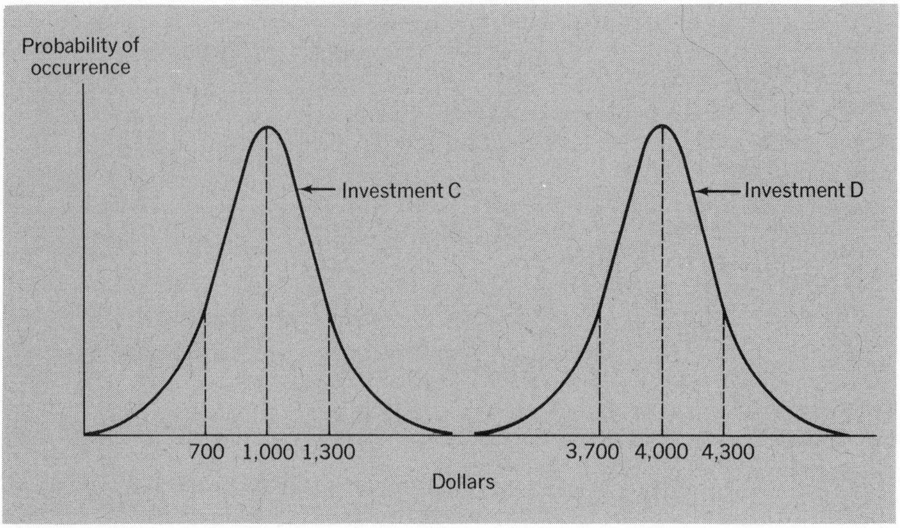

Figure 8–3 Probability Distributions of Two Investments with Different Expected Returns

that riskiness is increasing over time.[2] If risk was thought of as being constant over time—that is, if the cash flow in a distant year could be estimated equally as well as the cash flow of a close year—then the standard deviation would be constant and the boundary lines would not diverge from the expected cash flow line.

Coefficient of Variation

Certain problems can arise when the standard deviation is used as a measure of risk. To illustrate, consider Figure 8–3, which shows the probability distributions for investments C and D. Investment C has an expected return of $1,000 and a standard deviation of $300. Investment D also has a standard deviation of $300, but its expected return is $4,000. The likely percentage deviation from the mean of investment C is considerably higher than that from the mean of investment D. On this basis, it is reasonable to assign a higher degree of risk to investment C than to investment D in spite of the fact that they have identical standard deviations.

One way of eliminating this problem is to divide the standard devia-

[2] The standard deviation lines are sometimes called *confidence level boundaries*. With a 1 standard deviation confidence level, the cash flow for a given year will lie within the boundary, that is, within ± 1 standard deviation, 67 percent of the time, provided we have normal distributions. Normality is, incidentally, generally a good approximation in the real world. Higher degrees of confidence could be placed in the actual cash flows lying within 2σ, 3σ, and other boundaries.

tion by the mean expectation to obtain the *coefficient of variation* (v). For investment C, we divide the $300 standard deviation by the $1,000 mean expectation, obtaining .30 as the coefficient of variation; investment D's coefficient of variation is calculated to be .075. Henceforth, we shall use the coefficient of variation to compare the riskiness of alternative investments whenever the standard deviation would be misleading. In general, the standard deviation is appropriate when percentage *rates of return* are considered, while the coefficient of variation is appropriate if *dollar* returns are considered. The reason for this distinction is that rates of return are already "standardized" for size of investment, but some form of standardization is necessary when dollar returns are considered.

Covariance of Returns, or Portfolio Risk

When considering the riskiness of a particular investment, it is frequently useful to consider the relationship between the investment in question and other existing assets or potential investment opportunities. To illustrate, a steel company may decide to diversify into residential construction materials. It knows that when the economy is booming, the demand for steel is high and the returns from the steel mill are large. Residential construction, on the other hand, tends to be countercyclical; when the economy as a whole is in a recession, the demand for construction materials is high.[3] Because of these divergent cyclical patterns, a diversified firm with investments in both steel and construction could expect to have a more stable pattern of revenues than would a firm engaged exclusively in either steel or residential construction. In other words, the variance of the returns on the *portfolio of assets*, σ^2, may be less than the sum of the variances of the returns from the individual assets.[4]

This point is illustrated in Figure 8–4: 8–4(a) shows the cyclical cash flow variations for the steel plant, 8–4(b) shows the cash flow fluctuations for the residential construction material division, and 8–4(c)

[3] The reason for the countercyclical behavior of the residential construction industry has to do with the availability of credit. When the economy is booming, interest rates are high. High interest rates seem to discourage potential home buyers more than they do other demanders of credit. As a result, the residential construction industry shows marked countercyclical tendencies.

[4] These conclusions obviously hold also for portfolios of financial assets—stocks and bonds. In fact, the basic concepts of portfolio theory were developed specifically for common stocks by Harry Markowitz and first presented in his article, "Portfolio Selection," *Journal of Finance,* VII, No. 1 (March 1952), 77–91. The logical extension of portfolio theory to capital budgeting calls for considering firms as having "portfolios of tangible assets."

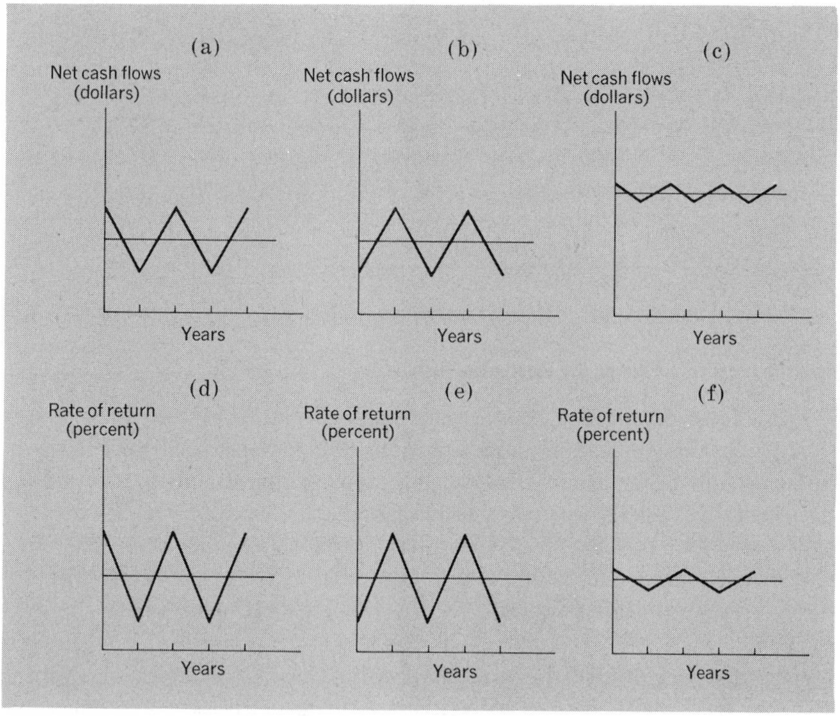

Figure 8–4 Relationship of Returns on Two Hypothetical Investments

NOTE: *upper* (a) Steel (b) Residential construction (c) Combined
lower (d) Steel (e) Residential construction (f) Combined

shows the cash flows for the combined company. When the cash flows from steel are large, those from residential construction are small, and vice versa. As a consequence, the combined cash flows are relatively stable.

Assuming that the funds invested in the projects remain relatively constant over time, then annual rates of return on steel and on residential construction fluctuate in the same manner as do the net cash flows; the computed annual rate of return on the combined projects is more stable than is that on either plant considered separately. These relationships are shown in Figure 8–4(d), 8–4(e), and 8–4(f).

If we calculated the correlation between rates of return on the steel and construction divisions, we would find the correlation coefficient to be negative—whenever rates of return on the steel plant are high, those on the construction material plant are low. If any two projects have a high degree of negative correlation, then taking on the two investments reduces the firm's over-all risk, and this risk reduction is defined as a *portfolio effect*. The example presented in Figure 8–4 illustrates *favorable portfolio effects*.

On the other hand, had there been a high *positive* correlation between projects A and B—that is, if returns on A were high at the same time those on B were high—over-all risk could not have been reduced significantly by diversification. If the correlation between A and B had been +1.0, the risk reduction would have been zero.

If the returns from the two projects were completely uncorrelated, that is, if the correlation coefficient between them was zero, the diversification would benefit the firm to at least some extent. The larger the number of uncorrelated, or independent, projects the firm takes on, the smaller will be the variation in its over-all rate of return.[5] Uncorrelated projects are not as useful for reducing risk as are negatively correlated ones, but they are better than positively correlated projects.

We can summarize the arguments on portfolio risk that have been presented thus far:

1. If *perfectly negatively correlated* projects are available in sufficient number, then diversification can completely eliminate risk. Perfect negative correlation is, however, almost never found in the real world.
2. If *uncorrelated* projects are available in sufficient number, then diversification can reduce risk significantly—to zero at the limit.
3. If all alternative projects are *perfectly positively correlated,* then diversification does not reduce risk at all.

In fact, most projects are positively correlated, but not perfectly correlated. The degree of intercorrelation among projects depends upon economic factors, and these factors are usually amenable to analysis. Returns on investments in projects closely related to the firm's basic products and markets will ordinarily be highly correlated with returns on the remainder of the firm's assets, and such investments will not generally reduce the firm's risk. However, investments in other product lines and in other geographic markets may have a low degree of correlation with other components of the firm and may, therefore, reduce over-all risk. Accordingly, if an asset's returns are not too closely related

[5] The principle involved here is the so-called law of large numbers. As the number of independent projects is increased, then the standard deviation of the returns on the portfolio of projects will decrease with the square root of the number of projects taken on. This statement assumes, of course, that the means and standard deviations of the individual projects are approximately equal.

to the firm's other major assets (or, better yet, are negatively correlated with other investments), this asset is more valuable to a risk-averting firm than is a similar asset whose returns are positively correlated with the bulk of the assets. The recognition of this fact was one of the driving forces behind the trend toward conglomerate mergers during the 1950s and 1960s.

Portfolio effects are discussed at greater length in a later section of this chapter. In addition, Appendix A to the chapter sets forth some formal relationships between project variability, project size, correlations between projects, and the resultant portfolio effects of diversification. These formal relationships are interesting, but we have elected not to incorporate them into the body of the text because, given the state of the art and the availability of data on correlations, it is not generally possible to use these formal processes in capital budgeting decisions. Covariations among projects are, however, considered on an informal, subjective basis by most business executives.

ALTERNATIVE METHODS OF TREATING RISK

Investors and managers are risk averters, so if two propects have different degrees of riskiness, this fact should be taken into account. The definition of risk should, of course, include either the standard deviation or coefficient of variation of returns on a project; it should also contain the covariance between the returns on a particular project and on the firm's other existing or potential assets (the "portfolio effect" of the project). For simplification, in this section we shall assume that all projects are perfectly correlated with one another, permitting us to disregard portfolio effects and to define a project's risk simply in terms of its variability.

Several different approaches may be taken to risk analysis. The most common—(1) the *informal treatment* method, (2) the *risk-adjusted discount rate* method, and (3) the *certainty equivalent* method—are examined in the following discussion.

Informal Treatment

The most common method of dealing with risk is on a strictly informal basis. For example, the net present values based on single-valued estimates of annual returns (using the firm's cost of capital) might be calculated. The decision-maker would recognize that some projects are "riskier" than others. If the net present values on two mutually exclusive projects are "reasonably" close to one another, the "less risky" one is chosen. The extent by which the net PV of the riskier project must exceed that of the less risky project before the riskier project will be selected is not specified—the decision rules are strictly internal to the decision-maker.

This approach may be formalized slightly by presenting the decision-maker with both the mean expectation and the standard deviation (or coefficient of variation) of the net PVs. These provide the decision-maker with an objective estimate of risk, but he still chooses among risky projects in an unspecified manner.

Risk-Adjusted Discount Rate

The process of choosing among risky assets can be formalized by using higher discount rates for more risky projects. Suppose, for example, that a firm has determined its cost of capital (k) to be 10 percent. It could use this figure as the discount rate for computing the net present value of projects that are estimated to be of "average" risk. It could use progressively lower discount rates for less risky projects, and higher rates for riskier projects.

To illustrate, an integrated oil company might compute its over-all average cost of capital to be 10 percent and use this figure for evaluating "standard" investments—refinery additions, development wells for proven reserves, and so on. For evaluating service stations on toll roads, where competition is limited and demand is highly predictable, a discount rate of only 8 percent might be deemed appropriate. However, 20 percent might be used to evaluate investments in off-shore exploratory drilling operations.

When the risk-adjusted discount rate approach is employed—and it is by far the most widely used formal method of recognizing differing degrees of project riskiness—different discount rates are prescribed for the various divisions. In the oil company example, the refining division might be told by corporate headquarters to use 10 percent as its cost of capital; the service station division might be directed to use 8 percent; and the exploratory drilling division might be given a 20 percent discount rate.

These divisional figures would, of course, be averages, and the various divisions would differentiate among types of investments by the investments' individual riskiness. Within the refining division, for example, cost-reducing replacement decisions with rather precisely estimated savings might be evaluated with an 8 percent cost of capital, while projects

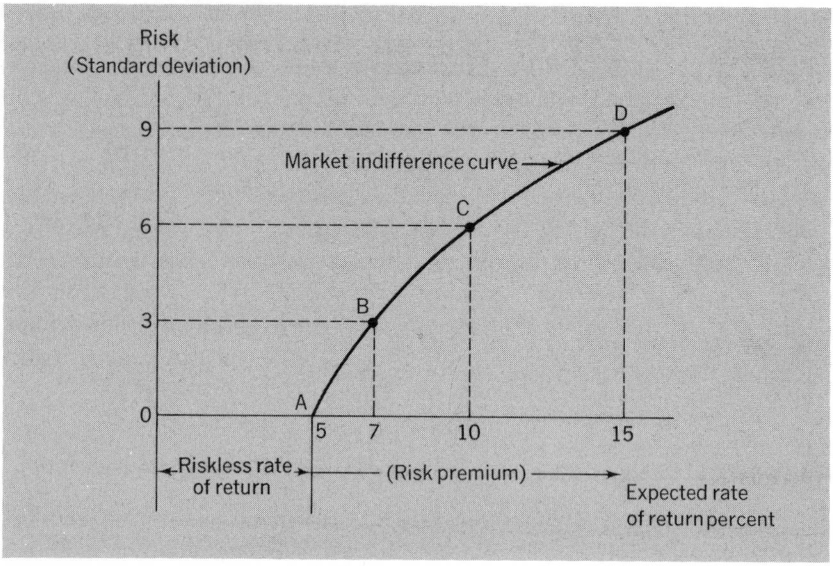

Figure 8–5 Hypothetical Market Relationships between Risk and Return

calling for expansion into such new product lines as petrochemicals might call for a 15 percent discount rate.

These discount rate differentials, or *risk adjustments,* should reflect both the estimated standard deviation (or coefficient of variation) of expected returns and investors' attitudes toward risk.[6] Suppose, for example, a firm determines that its stockholders are willing to trade between risk and returns as shown in Figure 8–5. The curve is defined as a *market indifference curve.* The average investor is indifferent to a riskless asset with a "sure" 5 percent rate of return, a "moderately" risky asset with a 7 percent expected return, and a "very" risky asset with a 15 percent expected return. As risk increases, higher and higher expected returns on investment are required to compensate investors for the additional risk.

The difference between the expected rate of return on a particular risky asset and the rate of return on a riskless asset is defined as the *risk premium* on the risky asset. In the hypothetical situation depicted in Figure 8–5, the riskless rate is assumed to be 5 percent; a 2 percent risk premium is required for a standard deviation of 3 percent, and a 5 percent risk premium is attached to an investment with a standard deviation as high as 6 percent. The "average investor" is indifferent to risky investments B, C, and D, and the riskless asset A; the rate of re-

[6] In addition, if favorable portfolio effects would result from the investment, this fact should be considered. Note also that investor attitudes toward risk are discussed in more detail in Appendix D to this chapter.

turn on the riskless asset is the *riskless rate of return,* or the *risk-free yield.*

If a particular firm's stock is located at point C on the risk indifference curve—that is, investors' expect the rate of return on the stock to be 10 percent, but the standard deviation of returns is 6 percent—then it should use a 10 percent discount rate for "average" projects, higher rates for more risky projects (15 percent at point D where $\sigma = 9$ percent), and lower rates for less risky projects (7 percent for point B where $\sigma = 3$ percent).[7]

Certainty Equivalents

Under the risk-adjusted discount rate approach to allowing for uncertainty, we find the PV of a project as

$$\text{PV} = \sum_{t=1}^{N} \frac{R_t}{(1+k)^t} \tag{8-1}$$

R_t, the expected value of the net receipts from the project in each year t, is discounted back to the present by the risk-adjusted discount rate k.

An alternative approach is to adjust for risk in the numerator, replacing the risk-adjusted discount factor k with the riskless rate i in the denominator and multiplying R_t by a risk adjustment factor α_t, which is defined as a *certainty equivalent factor* for reasons that will be made clear below. Here $0 \leq \alpha_t \leq 1$, and its value is determined as that value that makes investors indifferent between R_t and C_t, where C_t is a certain payment due in t years (as is a U.S. government savings bond). Thus, $\alpha_t R_t = C_t$ in the eyes of investors, and α_t is calculated as

$$\alpha_t = \frac{C_t}{R_t} \tag{8-2}$$

In this case, C_t is the *certainty equivalent* of the risky return R_t; the average investor is indifferent between $\alpha_t R_t$ and C_t.

Conceptually, α_t could be determined from a market risk indifference curve similar to that shown in Figure 8–5, but with dollars instead of rates of return on the horizontal axis. Here α_t for any year t would be found as

$$\alpha_t = \frac{\text{certain cash flow}}{\text{risky cash flow}} = \frac{C_t}{R_t}$$

[7] For simplification, we assume at this point that the firm is financed with only equity capital. This assumption is relaxed when the cost of capital is considered in detail in Chapter 11.

The equation used in the capital budgeting process would be:

$$PV = \sum_{t=1}^{N} \frac{\alpha_t R_t}{(1 + i)^t} \tag{8-3}$$

where i = riskless discount rate. To illustrate, suppose investors are indifferent between a risky return of $100 to be received after five years and a certain $50 to be received after five years. In this case, α_5 is calculated as

$$\alpha_5 = \frac{\$50}{\$100} = .5$$

The present value of the risky return is

$$PV = \frac{.5(\$100)}{(1.05)^5} = \$39.20$$

if the riskless rate of interest is 5 percent.

Certainty Equivalents versus Risk-Adjusted Discount Rates

Project risk can be handled by making adjustments to the numerator of the present value equation (the certainty equivalent method) or to the denominator of the equation (the risk-adjusted discount rate method). The risk-adjusted discount rate method is the one most frequently used, probably because it is easier to estimate suitable discount rates than it is to derive certainty equivalent factors. However, Robichek and Myers[8] recently advocated the certainty equivalent approach as being theoretically superior to the risk-adjusted discount rate method. However, they, as well as H. Y. Chen,[9] showed that if risk is perceived to be an increasing function of time, then using a risk-adjusted discount rate is a theoretically valid procedure.

They showed that risk-adjusted rates tend to lump together the pure rate of interest (a risk premium) and time (through the compounding process), while the certainty equivalent approach keeps risk and the pure rate of interest separate. This separation gives an advantage to certainty equivalents.[10] However, financial managers are more familiar with the concept of risk-adjusted discounts, and it is easier to use market

[8] A. A. Robichek and S. C. Myers, "Conceptual Problems in the Use of Risk-Adjusted Discount Rates," *Journal of Finance,* XXI (December 1966), 727–730.

[9] H. Y. Chen, "Valuation Under Uncertainty," *Journal of Financial and Quantitative Analysis,* II (September 1967), 313–326.

[10] The implications of the timing of receipts when using risk-adjusted discount rates is considered in Appendix B to this chapter.

data to develop adjusted discount rates, which are clear advantages to risk-adjusted discount rates. We do feel, however, that the certainty equivalent method deserves further study and that it may eventually turn out to be the generally accepted method of taking risk into account in the capital budgeting process.

COVARIANCE, OR PORTFOLIO EFFECTS

It was shown earlier that when the correlation between two investment opportunities is less than 1.0, the risk inherent in a portfolio of investments is less than the risk attached to the individual assets. A method has been developed by Harry Markowitz to select a portfolio of risky assets such that the rate of return is maximized for a given degree of risk or, conversely, such that the risk is minimized for a given rate of return.[11] Stated another way, if the maximum risk that a particular investor is willing to accept is equal to σ, then the Markowitz technique selects the particular portfolio that provides the maximum possible return without exceeding this specified risk limit.

Markowitz's portfolio selection technique generates what is known as an *efficient set of portfolios*. Each portfolio has (1) some degree of risk that can be measured by its standard deviation[12] and (2) an expected rate of return. The set of all possible portfolios is defined as the *attainable set*. This concept is illustrated in Figure 8–6, where the shaded area is the attainable set of portfolios.[13]

As we noted earlier, investors are averse to risk—they prefer less risk to more risk, other things held constant. In Figure 8–6, point B on the efficient set represents the portfolio with the least possible risk. Point E represents the portfolio with the highest possible rate of return.

[11] The procedure was developed largely by Harry Markowitz and first reported in his article, "Portfolio Selection," *Journal of Finance,* VII, No. 1 (March 1952), 77–91. The Markowitz technique measures risk by the variance (σ^2) of the rate of return.

[12] Markowitz actually uses the *variance,* which is the square of the standard deviation.

[13] We are herein considering only risky assets. It is possible to include riskless assets (cash, government bonds) in the portfolio, but this extension is excluded here. Cf. W. F. Sharpe, "Capital Asset Prices: A Theory of Market Equilibrium under Conditions of Risk," *Journal of Finance,* XIX (September 1964).

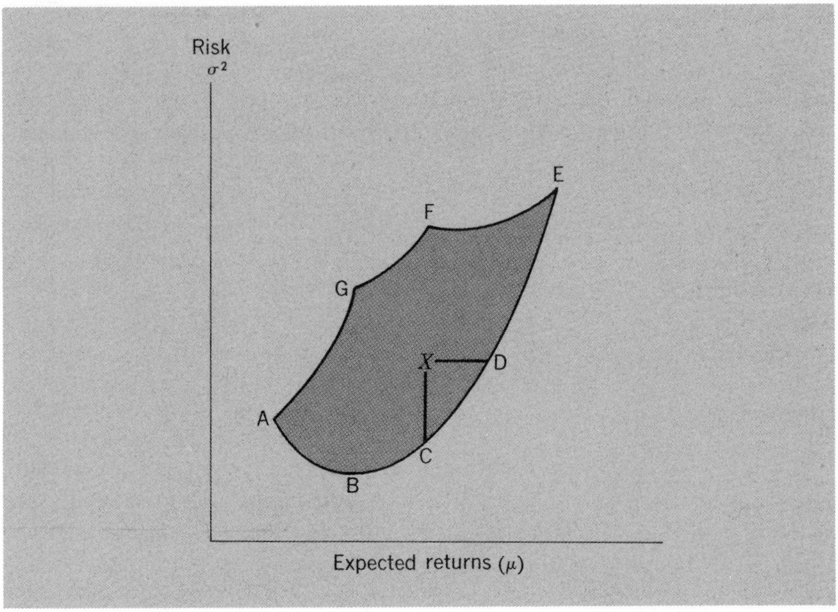

Figure 8–6 The Efficient Set of Investments

(Actually, at point E the "portfolio" contains only one asset—the one with the highest expected return.) The boundary BCDE defines the *efficient set.* Portfolios to the right of the efficient set are not possible because they lie outside the attainable set. Portfolios to the left of the efficient set are inefficient because some other portfolio could provide either a higher return with the same degree of risk or a lower risk for the same rate of return. To illustrate, consider point X. Portfolio C provides the same rate of return as does portfolio X, but C is less risky. At the same time, portfolio D is as risky as portfolio X, but D provides a higher expected rate of return. Points C and D (and other points on the boundary of the efficient set between C and D) are said to *dominate* point X.

Markowitz's portfolio selection technique was developed for securities, especially common stocks, in the early 1950s. However, because of complexities involved in using the technique and difficulties encountered in obtaining reliable estimates of expected returns and covariances, it has not, to our knowledge, been employed in portfolio selection except in experimental cases.

Conceptually, the Markowitz approach could be employed in capital budgeting decisions. However, the problems in this application are even more severe than those encountered with common stocks. In the first place, it is probably easier to estimate the rates of return and covariances for common stocks than it is for capital assets. A second and even more serious problem is that the Markowitz solution can be employed only when assets are divisible. This presents no trouble in the case of common stocks, but it is a very serious problem in the case of capital assets, as partial projects are not generally feasible.

Management versus Stockholders

One additional question should be raised in connection with portfolio analysis: Whose risk preferences, managements' or stockholders', are relevant in the capital budgeting decision? Put another way, if stockholders are able to diversify their own investment portfolios, why should individual firms be concerned with diversification?

If capital markets were perfect, if management personnel were concerned only with maximizing stockholders' wealth, if bankruptcy costs (both money costs and the intangible stigma attached to bankruptcy and reorganization) were minimal, if income taxes were zero, and if no frictions were involved in contracting and expanding business organizations, then perhaps diversification at the investor level would be sufficient. However, bankruptcy is extremely inefficient and costly; lenders (and to a lesser extent stockholders) are very much averse to the prospects of taking losses and of having to explain why they incurred losses; good managements would be hard to obtain and retain if they faced strong probabilities of losing their jobs through the failure of their firms; the tax laws make it preferable for losses to be sustained by a division of a profitable firm rather than by a separate firm; and so forth.

In consequence, we doubt that investors' diversification can completely replace corporate diversification. Accordingly, we believe that firms must and should be concerned about risk and that portfolio theory is an important element in the capital budgeting decision.[14] The question of how stockholder diversification and corporate diversification should

[14] An analogy with the theory of financial leverage is, perhaps, relevant here. As will be noted in Chapters 11 and 12, a theory has been put forth by two distinguished economists, Franco Modigliani and Merton Miller, that corporate leverage is irrelevant because individuals, by lending or borrowing on their own personal account, can alter the effects of corporate leverage. In other words, if a company has no debt (is unleveraged), an individual can create "home made" leverage by buying the company's stock on margin (borrowing to buy the stock). Modigliani and Miller's theoretical arguments are impeccable; on the grounds that their assumptions are incorrect—individuals are reluctant to borrow on personal account because they do not have limited liability (as do corporations), individuals pay higher interest rates than corporations, and so on—their theory has been criticized as not being relevant in the real world. The same kind of argument could be made against replacing corporate diversification by investor diversification.

be balanced, however, is still an open one, a question that could certainly use further research.

PUBLIC EXPENDITURE DECISIONS

Before concluding this chapter, we should point out that capital budgeting under uncertainty faces governmental agencies as well as individuals and firms. A series of hearings before Congress on methods and procedures of capital budgeting at the federal level revealed (1) that congressional leaders and the heads of the major governmental agencies agreed that governmental capital budgeting should be conducted under a method equivalent to our risk-adjusted discount rate procedure, but (2) that federal agencies are having a difficult time determining appropriate discount rates.[15] In other words, the federal government is (or soon will be) following the same capital budgeting procedures as do the more sophisticated business firms, and the procedures described in this and the preceding chapter are applicable to both.

SUMMARY

Risk lies at the heart of all capital budgeting decisions—indeed, it is of paramount importance throughout the realm of finance. This chapter presents the nature of risk analysis at an intuitive level, then goes on to show how the problem of risk analysis can be formalized.

We define risk in terms of the likely variability of returns on a project or of the *probability distribution of expected returns*. Specifically, we measure risk by the *standard deviation* (or *coefficient of variation*) of the probability distribution. The probability distribution itself can be measured statistically, in which case we have an *objective probability distribution*, or subjectively, in which case we have a *subjective probability distribution*.

Provided the returns from two projects are not perfectly correlated through time, diversification can be employed to reduce investment risk. Such diversification-induced risk reduction is defined as *portfolio effects*, or *covariance effects*. Portfolio effects are minimal if returns from different assets are highly correlated; they can provide important benefits, however, if correlations are low or, better yet, negative. To date, no

[15] U.S. Congress, Subcommittee on Economy in Government of the Joint Economic Committee, *Economic Analysis of Public Investment Decisions: Interest Rate Policy and Discounting Analysis* (Washington, D.C.: U.S. Government Printing Office, 1968).

practical method of taking portfolio effects into the capital budgeting decision has been developed, but work along these lines is being undertaken. Corporate executives do, however, consider portfolio effects at an informal level when making capital budgeting decisions.

Most aspects of risk—variability of project returns, covariance effects, and riskiness over time—are all dealt with on an informal rather than a formal basis by most firms. The more sophisticated corporations are beginning to make use of formal risk analysis. When formal methods are employed, by all odds the most common procedure is to use *risk-adjusted discount rates*—different discount rates for projects with different degrees of risk, higher risk calling for higher discount rates (or a higher cost of capital). An alternative approach, the *certainty equivalent method,* has been recommended as theoretically superior to the use of risk-adjusted discount rates. It seems to us that certainty equivalents are theoretically better, but that it is easier to use market data to obtain reasonable estimates of appropriate risk-adjusted discount rates. Accordingly, we expect the latter method to be the most commonly used formal method in the foreseeable future.

QUESTIONS

8–1 Define the following terms:
a) Risk
b) Uncertainty
c) Objective probability
d) Subjective probability
e) Coefficient of variation
f) Portfolio effects
g) Risk-adjusted discount rate
h) Certainty equivalent factor

8–2 The probability distribution of a less risky expected return is more peaked than that of a risky return. What shape would the probability distribution have for (1) completely certain returns and (2) completely uncertain returns?

8–3 In this chapter we have defined risk in terms of the variability of expected returns, where the expectations may be derived either subjectively or objectively. In constructing this measure of risk, we have implicitly given equal weight to variations on both sides of the expected return—higher returns or lower returns. Can you see any problems resulting from this treatment?

8–4 One frequently encounters the term "utility theory," which deals with the marginal utility of money, in economics courses. What is the relationship between utility theory and the type of risk analysis discussed in this chapter. (See pages 270–274.)

8–5 "On reflection, the use of the market indifference curve concept illustrated in Figure 8–5 as a basis for determining risk-adjusted discount rates is all right in theory, but it cannot be applied in practice. Market estimates of investor's reaction to risk cannot be measured precisely, so it is impossible to actually construct a set of risk-adjusted discount rates for different classes of investment." Comment on this statement.

8–6 Assume that residential construction and industries related to it are countercyclical to the general economy and are countercyclical to steel in particular. Does this negative correlation between steel and construction-related industries necessarily mean that a savings and loan association, whose profitability tends to vary with construction levels, would be less risky if it diversified by acquiring a steel distributor?

PROBLEMS

8–1 The Gertz Products Co., Inc., is considering replacing a 10-year-old machine that has a book value of $2,000 and a current salvage value of $7,000. It is looking at two mutually exclusive alternatives:

1) Replacement with a similar new machine with a $20,000 cost and net cash flows (after-tax profits plus depreciation) of $2,500 a year.
2) Replacement with a new type of machine, previously untried by either the company or its competitors, for sale by its inventor for $30,000. The expected net cash flows with the new type machine are $7,000 a year.

The first machine has an expected salvage value of $7,000 at the end of its 10-year life, and the new type machine has no expected salvage value at the end of its 10-year life. Net depreciation benefits for both machines are included in the calculations of net cash flows above. The firm's cost of capital is 10 percent.

a) Should the firm replace the existing machine, and if so, should replacement be with a similar new machine or with the new type of machine?
b) How would your results be affected if a risk-adjusted discount rate of 24 percent were used for the new type machine?
c) What factors and issues in addition to those treated above are likely to require consideration in a practical situation?

8–2 Traditions, Inc.'s marketing division is reviewing its annual advertising plans in conjunction with the firm's annual capital budget. Due to management's desire to retain a controlling equity position, each division has been given a budget limitation—$300,000 has been allocated to the marketing division. This department is considering two mutually exclusive investments for promotion of new business for the firm's plastic products. The first is the continuation of the firm's direct mail advertising program. Its costs are $.10 a mailing, enabling the firm to mail 3,000,000 pieces a year. Over many years, responses have averaged 1 percent of pieces mailed—ranging from 0.8 to 1.2 percent in 95 percent of the years for which experience is available. One-third of these responses are converted to sales that average $250 with a $100 pretax profit margin after all costs except advertising. There are no substantial lagged effects for direct mail returns, but there may be additional lagged benefits from newspaper advertising.

The local sales representative of a five-city national newspaper chain has proposed the following contract to the director of marketing: A four-column, 4-inch ad (usual cost $448 a day) running 365 days in five major newspapers with an average circulation of 800,000 each (4,000,000 guaranteed minimum average circulation) for a total cost of $300,000. This represents an average daily cost of $824 versus a $2,240 normal daily rate for the five papers. The newspaper chain also agrees to provide 100 hours of free copywriting consulting time. Depending upon the effectiveness of the advertising copy, responses per day could be expected to range from 400 to only four. The following subjective probabilities have been assigned to responses by the marketing director:

Daily Responses	*Probability*
400	.4
100	.2
40	.2
4	.2

The division has been assigned a 12 percent discount rate by corporate headquarters division due to the stability of its past return on investment. The applicable tax rate is 50 percent.

a) Calculate the expected return for each project. Which project should the division adopt?
b) What other factors not specified in the problem should be considered?

8–3 Serve-U Vending, Inc., is considering an investment in one of two mutually exclusive proposals: project A, which involves an initial outlay of $1,700; project B, which has an outlay of $1,500. The certainty equivalent approach is employed in evaluating risky investments. The current yield on Treasury bills is 5 percent; the company uses this as the riskless rate.

EXPECTED VALUES OF NET CASH FLOWS

Year	Project A	Project B
1	$ 900	$ 900
2	1,000	900
3	1,100	1,000

The certainty equivalents determined by the company to be appropriate for risk analysis in this specific instance are:

Year	Project A	Project B
1	.8	.9
2	.7	.8
3	.5	.6

a. Calculate the NPV, risk-adjusted by the certainty equivalent method, for each project.
b. Which project is riskier? How do you know?
c. Does the firm's management have a linear utility for money schedule? How do you know? (Consult first section of Appendix 8D.)
d. If the company was to use the risk-adjusted discount rate method, which project would be analyzed with the *higher* rate? How do you know?
e. Show how to find a set of risk-adjusted discount rates which, if used, would give an identical solution to this problem as was obtained by the certainty equivalent method.

8–4 The Alves Company is analyzing the prospective returns from two mutually exclusive one-year projects. For the period under consideration, the probable net cash flows are as follows:

PROJECT I		PROJECT II	
Probability	*Net Cash Flow*	*Probability*	*Net Cash Flow*
.15	$200	.05	$200
.35	400	.45	400
.30	500	.45	500
.20	700	.10	700

If the decision-maker is averse to risk, which project should be preferred, all other circumstances being the same? Support your answer by setting forth your calculation of the mean, standard deviation, and coefficient of variation for each project.

8–5 For project II above, assume the cash flows change to those shown below. How do these changes affect your recommendation?

PROJECT II

Probability	*Net Cash Flow*
.05	$300
.45	600
.40	800
.10	900

8–6 The Davis Company is considering investment in two mutually exclusive proposals: project A involves initial outlays of $2,500, project B, outlays of $2,800. If the certainty-equivalent approach is employed in evaluating risky investments, which project should be selected? The current yield on Treasury bills is 5 percent. Project A has a cost of $2,500; B, a cost of $2,800.

EXPECTED VALUES OF NET CASH FLOWS

Year	*Project A*	*Project B*
1	$1,050	$2,100
2	2,204	1,102
3	1,158	1,158

The certainty equivalents determined by the company for the projects are:

Year	*Project A*	*Project B*
1	.8	.9
2	.7	.8
3	.5	.6

Selected References

Adelson, R. M., "Criteria for Capital Investment: An Approach Through Decision Theory," *Operational Research Quarterly,* XVI (March 1965), 19–50.

Bauman, W. Scott, "Evaluation of Prospective Investment Performance," *Journal of Finance,* XXIII, No. 2 (May 1968), 276–295.

Baxter, Nevins D., "Marketability, Default Risk, and Yields on Money Market Instruments," *Journal of Financial and Quantitative Analysis,* IV (March 1968), 75–86.

Cohen, Kalman J., and Edwin J. Elton, "Inter-temporal Portfolio Analysis Based on Simulation of Joint Returns," *Management Science,* XIV (September 1967), 5–18.

Cord, Joel, "A Method for Allocating Funds to Investment Projects When Returns are Subject to Uncertainty," *Management Science,* X (January 1964), 335–341.

Dietz, Peter O., "Measurement of Performance of Security Portfolios Components of a Measurement Model: Rate of Return, Risk and Timing," *The Journal of Finance,* XXIII, No. 2 (May 1968), 267–275.

English, J. M., "Economic Comparison of Projects Incorporating a Utility Criterion in the Rate of Return," *Engineering Economist,* X (Winter 1965), 1–14.

Farrar, Donald F., *The Investment Decision Under Uncertainty* (Englewood Cliffs, N.J.: Prentice-Hall, 1962).

Freund, Rudolf J., "The Introduction of Risk in a Programming Model," *Econometrica,* XXIV (July 1956), 253–263.

Grayson, C. Jackson, Jr., *Decisions under Uncertainty: Drilling Decisions by Oil and Gas Operators* (Boston, Mass.: Division of Research, Harvard Business School, 1960).

———, "Introduction of Uncertainty into Capital Budgeting Decisions," *N.A.A. Bulletin,* XLIII (January 1962), 79–80.

Hertz, David B., "Risk Analysis in Capital Investment," *Harvard Business Review,* XLII (January–February 1964), 95–106.

Hespos, Richard F., and Paul A. Strassmann, "Stochastic Decision Trees for the Analysis of Investment Decisions," *Management Science,* XI (August 1965), 244–259.

Hillier, Frederick S., "The Derivation of Probabalistic Information for the Evaluation of Risky Investments," *Management Science,* IX (April 1963).

———, and David V. Heebink, "Evaluation of Risky Capital Investments," *California Management Review,* VIII (Winter 1965), 71–80.

Hirshleifer, Jack, "Efficient Allocation of Capital in an Uncertain World," *American Economic Review,* LIV (May 1964), 77–85.

———, "On the Theory of Optimal Investment Decision," *Journal of Political Economy,* LXVI (August 1958), 329–352.

———, "Risk, the Discount Rate and Investment Decisions," *American Economic Review,* LI (May 1961), 112–120.

Latane, H. A., "Criteria for Choice Among Risky Ventures," *Journal of Political Economy,* LXVII (April 1959), 144–155.

———, and Donald L. Tuttle, "Decision Theory and Financial Management," *Journal of Finance,* XXI, No. 2 (May 1966), 228–244.

Lintner, John, "Security Prices, Risk and Maximal Gains from Diversification," *Journal of Finance,* XX (December 1965), 587–616.

———, "The Evaluation of Risk Assets and the Selection of Risky Investments in Stock Portfolios and Capital Budgets," *Review of Economics and Statistics,* XLVII, (February 1965), 13–37.

Magee, J. F., "How to Use Decision Trees in Capital Investment," *Harvard Business Review,* XLII (September–October 1964), 79–96.

Myers, Stewart C., "Procedures for Capital Budgeting under Uncertainty," Working Paper. (Cambridge, Mass.: Sloan School of Management, Massachusetts Institute of Technology, 1967).

Naslund, Bertil, and Andrew Whinston, "A Model of Multi-period Investment Under Uncertainty," *Management Science,* IX (January 1962), 184–200.

Paine, Neil R., "Uncertainty and Capital Budgeting," *Accounting Review,* XXXIX (April 1964), 330–332.

Quirin, G. David, *The Capital Expenditure Decision* (Homewood, Ill.: Irwin, 1967).

Robichek, A., and S. Myers, "Risk Adjusted Discount Rates," *Journal of Finance,* XXI No. 4 (December 1966), 727–730.

———, and James C. Van Horne, "Abandonment Value and Capital Budgeting," *Journal of Finance,* XXII, No. 4 (December 1967), 577–590.

———, *Optimal Financing Decisions* (Englewood Cliffs, N.J.: Prentice-Hall, 1965), Chapter 5.

Sharpe, W. F., "Security Prices, Risk, and Maximal Gains from Diversification," *Journal of Finance,* XXI, No. 4 (December 1966), 743–744.

———, "Capital Asset Prices: A Theory of Market Equilibrium," *Journal of Finance,* XIX (September 1964), 425–442.

Swalm, Ralph O., "Utility Theory—Insights into Risk Taking," *Harvard Business Review,* XLIV (November–December 1966), 123–136.

Teichroew, Daniel, Alexander A. Robichek, and Michael Montalbano, "An Analysis of Criteria for Investment and Financing Decisions Under Certainty," *Management Science,* XII (November 1965), 151–179.

Tuttle, Donald L., and Robert H. Litzenberger, "Leverage, Diversification and Capital Market Effects on a Risk-Adjusted Capital Budgeting Framework," *Journal of Finance,* XXIII (June 1968), 427–444.

U.S. Congress, Subcommittee on Economy in Government of the Joint Economic Committee, *Economic Analysis of Public Investment Decisions: Interest Rate Policy and Discounting Analysis* (Washington, D.C.: U.S. Government Printing Office, 1968).

Van Horne, James, "Capital Budgeting Decisions Involving Combinations of Risky Investments," *Management Science,* XIII (October 1966), 84–92.

———, "Capital Budgeting for the Liquid Company," *Financial Executive,* XXXIV (April 1966), 50–52, 60.

Wallingford, B. A., "A Survey and Comparison of Portfolio Selection Models," *Journal of Financial and Quantitative Analysis,* III (June 1967), 85–106.

Woods, Donald H., "Improving Estimates That Involve Uncertainty," *Harvard Business Review,* XLV (July–August 1966), 91–98.

Woodworth, G. Walter, and Alden C. Olson, "Discussion," *Journal of Finance,* XXIII, No. 2 (May 1968), 296–302.

APPENDIX A TO CHAPTER 8
Formal Treatment of Portfolio Risk

In the text we dealt on an informal and intuitive basis with the use of diversification to reduce risk. There is, however, a well-developed body of formal theory, *portfolio theory,* dealing with the subject. This appendix describes the essential elements of this theory.

Recall that in the text we illustrated the portfolio effects of diversification with an example of a steel company diversifying into the residential construction industry. In this case, *negative correlation* was assumed to exist between steel and construction; we could see visually that diversification reduced the variance of overall corporate returns. We went on to indicate that portfolio effects were greatest when strong negative correlation exists, but that some favorable portfolio effects could be gained from diversification as long as different investments were not *perfectly positively correlated.*

The correlation coefficient between projects A and B, P_{AB}, can range between +1.0 and —1.0. If returns on the two projects are perfectly correlated with one another, the correlation coefficient will be +1.0, and *perfect positive correlation* is said to exist. If the correlation coefficient between two projects is —1.0, then a *perfect negative correlation* exists. If the correlation coefficient between returns on the two projects is zero, then the returns on the two projects are *independent* of one another.

The covariance (Cov) between two projects depends upon (1) the correlation between the two projects and (2) the standard deviation of each project, and it is calculated as follows:

$$\text{Cov}_{AB} = P_{AB}\sigma_A\sigma_B \tag{A8–1}$$

where Cov_{AB} = covariance between projects A and B, P_{AB} = correlation coefficient between A and B, and σ_A and σ_B are the standard deviations of the two projects' returns.

The necessity of introducing the standard deviations of the two projects can be seen intuitively by realizing that, even though two projects were perfectly negatively correlated, cyclical variations in their combined returns could not be completely eliminated (assuming equal investments in each) if one fluctuated widely and the other hardly at all. Complete dampening of the combined fluctuations could occur only if (1) they are perfectly negatively correlated and (2) they have identical standard deviations.

It is, of course, possible to make unequal investments in two projects that have unequal standard deviations, with the larger investment going into the project with the smaller standard deviation. With perfect negative correlation, an appropriate balancing of the two projects can offset the fact that they do not have identical standard deviations and can permit diversification to completely dampen fluctuations in rates of return.

Generalization of the Two Asset Case

We can combine the various threads of the problem of using diversification to reduce portfolio risk. We define the risk of a portfolio as the standard deviation of the portfolio, σ_P, and calculate it as follows:

$$\sigma_P = \sqrt{x^2\sigma_A^2 + (1 - x)^2\sigma_B^2 + 2x(1 - x)\,\text{Cov}_{AB}} \tag{A8–2}$$

or, substituting equation A8–1 for Cov_{AB},

$$\sigma_P = \sqrt{x^2\sigma_A{}^2 + (1-x)^2\sigma_B{}^2 + 2x(1-x)P_{AB}\sigma_A\sigma_B} \qquad \text{(A8–3)}$$

Here x is the percentage of the total portfolio value invested in project A; $(1 - x)$ is the percent of the portfolio invested in project B; σ_A is the standard deviation of project A; σ_B is the standard deviation of project B; Cov_{AB} is the covariance between projects A and B; and P_{AB} is the correlation coefficient between the projects.

Several points can be seen by an inspection of equation A8–3. First, observe that if projects A and B are independent of one another, the correlation coefficient is zero ($P_{AB} = 0$). In this case, the last term in the equation is also zero. Second, if $P_{AB} > 0$, the standard deviation of the portfolio, σ_P, is greater than it would be if $P_{AB} = 0$. Third, if $P_{AB} < 0$, the covariance term is negative and σ_P is less than it would be if $P_{AB} \geqslant 0$. Finally, a close inspection of equation A8–3 reveals that risk can be totally eliminated ($\sigma_P = 0$) only if the third term is equal to the sum of the first two terms. This can occur only if (1) $P_{AB} = -1$ and (2) the percentage of the portfolio invested in project A, x, is set equal to equation A8–4:[1]

$$x = \frac{\sigma_B}{\sigma_A + \sigma_B} \qquad \text{(A8–4)}$$

Some examples will perhaps clarify these statements.

Example 1 Assume the following: 1. $\sigma_A = \sigma_B = 5$
2. $P_{AB} = -1.0$
3. $x = (1 - x) = .5$

Substituting these values into equation A8–3, we obtain:

$$\begin{aligned}\sigma_P &= \sqrt{(.5)^2(5)^2 + (.5)^2(5)^2 + 2(.5)(.5)(-1.0)(5)(5)} \\ &= \sqrt{(.25)(25) + (.25)(25) - 2(.25)(25)} \\ &= 0\end{aligned}$$

Therefore, with perfect negative correlation and equal project standard deviations, diversification can completely eliminate risk.

Example 2 Assume the same situation as existed in Example 1 except that $x = .4$ and $(1 - x) = .6$. In other words, the projects are perfectly negatively correlated and have equal standard deviations. However, equal percentages of the portfolio

[1] Equation A8–4 is found by differentiating equation A8–3 with respect to x and setting this derivative equal to zero.

are not invested in the two projects. Making the necessary substitutions in equation A8–3, we obtain:

$$\begin{aligned}\sigma_P &= \sqrt{(.4)^2(5)^2 + (.6)^2(5)^2 + 2(.4)(.6)(-1)(5)(5)} \\ &= \sqrt{(.16)(25) + (.36)(25) - 2(.24)(25)} \\ &= \sqrt{4 + 9 - 12} \\ &= \sqrt{1} = 1\end{aligned}$$

Here the portfolio has a standard deviation greater than zero, and diversification has not completely eliminated portfolio risk. The reason for this result is that the proportion of the portfolio invested in each of the two projects was not determined in accordance with equation A8–4. We could show that as the proportion of the portfolio invested in the two projects deviates further and further from the equation A8–4 value, portfolio risk increases more and more from zero.

Example 3 Assume the following:

1. $\sigma_A = 3$
2. $\sigma_B = 9$
3. $P_{AB} = -1.0$
4. $x = .75$
5. $(1 - x) = .25$

Making the necessary substitutions in equation A8–3, we obtain:

$$\begin{aligned}\sigma_P &= \sqrt{(.75)^2(3)^2 + (.25)^2(9)^2 + 2(.75)(.25)(-1.0)(3)(9)} \\ &= \sqrt{(.5625)(9) + (.0625)(81) - 2(.1875)(27)} \\ &= \sqrt{5.0625 + 5.0625 - 2(5.0625)} \\ &= 0\end{aligned}$$

This example demonstrates that if perfect negative correlation exists between two projects, risk can be completely eliminated by a proper balancing of the portfolio even though the standard deviations of the individual assets are unequal. In the present example, it could be shown that equal proportions of the two projects would not eliminate risk because the standard deviations of the projects are unequal.

Example 4 Assume the same conditions as in Example 3, but let the correlation coefficient between the projects equal the following values:

Case A: $P_{AB} = -0.5$
Case B: $P_{AB} = 0.0$
Case C: $P_{AB} = +0.5$
Case D: $P_{AB} = +1.0$

Notice that the first two terms in equation A8–3 continue to equal 5.0625 in each of these cases. Also, notice that only P_{AB} in the third term changes, and the effect of this alteration is to change the -2 by which the 5.0625 is multiplied to -1.0, 0.0, $+1.0$ and $+2.0$, in Cases A through D, respectively. As a result of these changes, the following portfolio standard deviations are obtained:

Case A: $P_{AB} = -.5$

$$\begin{aligned}\sigma_P &= \sqrt{5.0625 + 5.0625 - 2.2501(5.0625)} \\ &= \sqrt{5.0625} \\ &= 2.250\end{aligned}$$

Case B: $P_{AB} = 0$

$$\begin{aligned}\sigma_P &= \sqrt{5.0625 + 5.0625 - 2.2500(5.0625)} \\ &= \sqrt{10.125} \\ &= 3.173\end{aligned}$$

Case C: $P_{AB} = +.5$

$$\begin{aligned}\sigma_P &= \sqrt{5.0625 + 5.0625 + 1(5.0625)} \\ &= \sqrt{15.1875} \\ &= 3.895\end{aligned}$$

Case D: $P_{AB} = +1.0$

$$\begin{aligned}\sigma_P &= \sqrt{5.0625 + 5.0625 + 2(5.0625)} \\ &= \sqrt{20.2500} \\ &= 4.5\end{aligned}$$

If no diversification had occurred, then the total risk of the two projects would be the weighted sum of their individual standard deviations:

$$\begin{aligned}\text{Total undiversified risk} &= x(\sqrt{\sigma_A^2}) + (1 - x)(\sqrt{\sigma_B^2}) \\ &= .75(\sqrt{3^2}) + .25(\sqrt{9^2}) \\ &= .75(3) + .25(9) \\ &= 4.5\end{aligned}$$

Since the undiversified risk is equal to the portfolio risk of perfectly positively correlated projects, this demonstrates that favorable portfolio effects occur *only* when projects are *not* perfectly positively correlated. The example also demonstrates that portfolio risk is less than the sum of the risks of the individual projects taken separately whenever the returns of the individual projects are not perfectly correlated; also, the smaller the correlation between the projects, the greater the benefits of diversification.

Graphic Illustration of Portfolio Effects

The various cases just described are graphically illustrated in Figure A8–1. Risk is measured on the vertical axis, and the percentage of the portfolio invested in assets A and B is shown on the horizontal axis. Point A on the left vertical axis shows that if 100 percent of the portfolio is invested in asset A, then the portfolio risk is equal to 3, the standard deviation of asset A. Point B on the right axis denotes a risk of $\sigma_P = 9$ when 100 percent of the portfolio is invested in asset B.

If the assets are perfectly positively correlated ($P_{AB} = 1.0$), the portfolio risk is a linear function, or weighted average, of the assets' standard deviations. This is shown by the line labeled $P_{AB} = 1$. The other curves show that portfolio risk deviates further and further from the linear weighted average as the correlation between assets A and B declines.

Note that, if assets A and B each had the same expected rate of return, only asset A would be chosen (the portfolio would be 100 percent invested in A) unless $P_{AB} < 0$. In terms of the possibilities shown in Figure A8–1, diversification would be practical if $P_{AB} = -.5$ or -1.0,

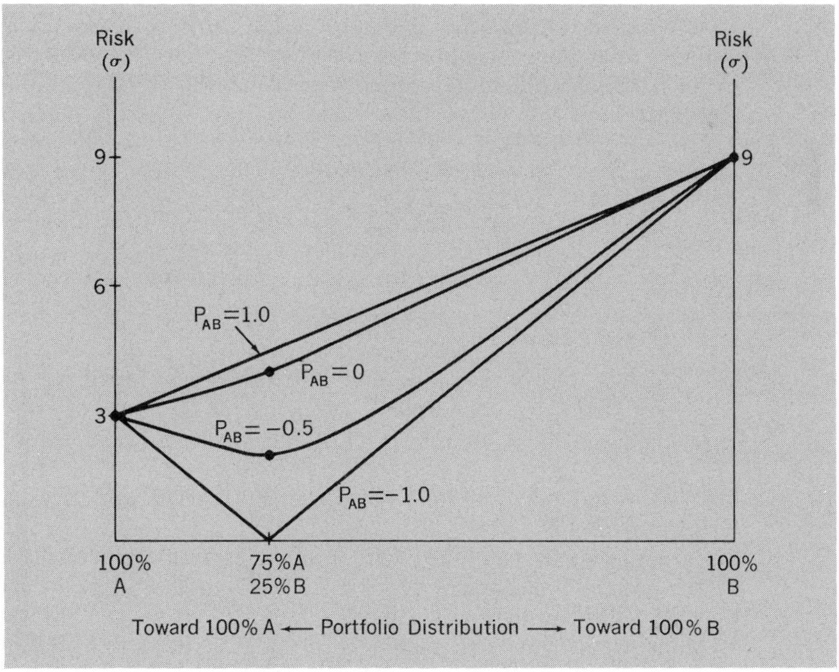

Figure A8–1 Relationship beween Asset Risk and Portfolio Risk

but it would not make sense if $P_{AB} = 0$ or $+1.0$. In general, we would expect the rate of return of B to be greater than the rate of return of A and the portfolio rate of return to be a weighted average of these two rates of return. The Markowitz portfolio selection process, mentioned briefly at the conclusion of Chapter 8, selects portfolios (that is, assigns values to x in the N-asset version of equation A8–3) so as to minimize the portfolio variance for any given expected rate of return. In terms of Figure 8–6, but in a two-asset context, point B in that figure would represent a 100 percent investment in asset A (the less risky, lower yielding asset) while point E would represent a 100 percent investment in asset B. Points C and D, and other points on the efficient set, would represent various combinations of assets A and B.

This appendix has dealt only with the special case of a two-asset portfolio. Portfolio theory has, however, been developed for the generalized N-asset case. The interested reader is referred to Harry Markowitz, *Portfolio Selection* (New York: Wiley, 1959). We should note that the conclusions reached in the two-asset case are equally applicable in the N-asset case. Computationally, of course, the N-asset case is considerably more difficult than the simple two-asset situation.

PROBLEM

A8–1 The Whalen Corporation plans to invest in *two* independent projects to reduce total risk to the firm through diversification of its portfolio. Assume the following about the three available proposals:

PROJECT 1	PROJECT 2	PROJECT 3
$\sigma_1 = 6\%$	$\sigma_2 = 4\%$	$\sigma_3 = 5\%$
rate of return = 12%	rate of return = 9%	rate of return = 10%

a) Calculate σ_p, the portfolio standard deviation that gives the lowest risk if the correlation coefficients for the projects are: $r_{12} = .7$, $r_{23} = .5$, and $r_{13} = .4$. (Investment in each project will be 50 percent of the total portfolio).
b) What would the portfolio risk be if 100 percent was invested in project 1?
c) If project 2 is combined with project 1, with 25 percent of the portfolio invested in project 1 and 75 percent in project 2, what will your decision be now?
d) What would your investment be if the expected rate of return of project 2 increased to equal that of project 1?

APPENDIX B TO CHAPTER 8
Risk and the Timing of Returns

In our discussion of risk-adjusted discount rates in Chapter 8, we discussed the concept of a market risk indifference curve and illustrated it in Figure 8–5. Four projects were discussed: Project A, which promises to yield a riskless 5 percent; project B, with an expected return (μ_B) of 7 percent but a standard deviation (σ_B) of 3 percent; project C with $\mu_C = 10$ percent and $\sigma_C = 6$ percent; and project D with $\mu_D = 15$ percent and $\sigma_D = 9$ percent.

Under the risk-adjusted discount rate method, the discount rates used for projects B, C, and D are constant over time at 7 percent, 10 percent, and 15 percent, respectively. Therefore, with a riskless rate of 5 percent, the risk premiums of the three projects are also constant and equal to 2 percent, 5 percent, and 10 percent, respectively. Does the constant risk premium imply that the relative riskiness of the projects' cash flows in the various years is also perceived to be constant? The answer is "No"; but to see why, let us first define the riskiness of the expected cash flows from any project in any year t in terms of a "risk index" (RI) calculated as a function of the present value interest factor for a riskless cash flow divided by the present value interest factor for the risky asset:[1]

$$RI_t = \frac{IF_{\text{riskless asset}}}{IF_{\text{risky asset}}} = \frac{(1 + \text{riskless rate})^{-t}}{(1 + \text{risky rate})^{-t}} \qquad \text{(B8–1)}$$

To illustrate, suppose we are calculating the risk index for a cash flow expected after 10 years when the riskless rate is 5 percent and the risky rate is 10 percent. The interest factors are found from Appendix Table A–2 to be .614 and .386 for the riskless and risky assets, respectively, so the risk index is:

$$RI_{10} = \frac{.614}{.386} = 1.59$$

Equation B8–1 has some interesting implications that can be seen in Table B8–1, which works out the risk index for a pair of interest rates over time, and from Figure B8–1, where these values (and others) are plotted. Risk, as measured by equation B8–1, is an increasing function of both *time* and the *differential between the riskless and risky discount rates*. In other words, a given risk premium has a larger and larger impact on the risk index as the time horizon is lengthened. This phenomenon occurs, of course, because of the compounding effect.

[1] This discussion parallels that of Robichek and Myers, "Risk Adjusted Discount Rates," *Journal of Finance*, XXI, No. 4 (December 1966), 727–730. Our risk index is the reciprocal of their α_t.

TABLE B8–1 CALCULATION OF RELATIVE RISK INDEX

	RISKLESS PROJECT	RISKY PROJECT	RI
Discount Rate—Years	5%	10%	
0	1.000	1.000	1.00
1	.952	.909	1.04
10	.614	.386	1.59
20	.377	.149	2.53
30	.231	.057	4.15

NOTE: The RI = 1.0 when $t = 0$ because:

$$\frac{IF_{riskless}}{IF_{risky}} = \frac{(1+i)^0}{(1+k)^0} = 1$$

where i = riskless rate and k = risky rate.

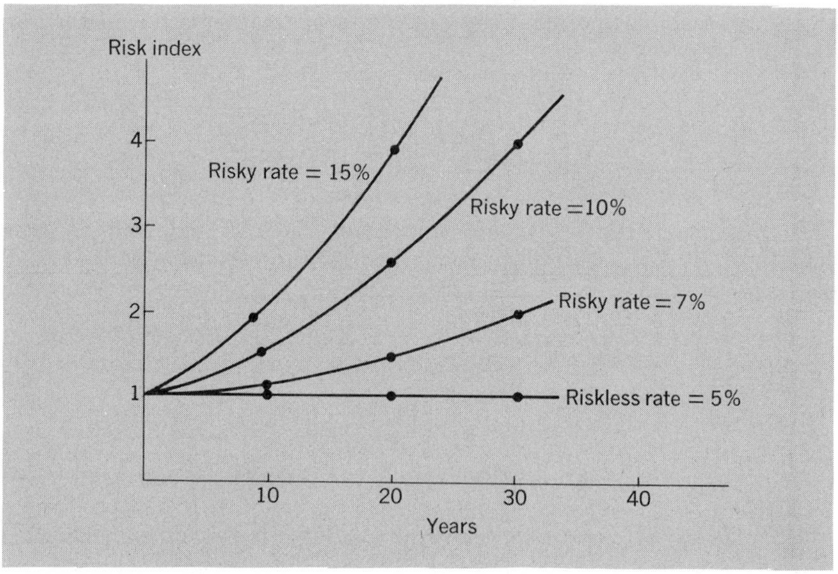

Figure B8–1 Index of Perceived Risk (riskless rate, 5 percent)

NOTE: 1. For a given riskless rate (for example, 5 percent) and risky rate (for example, 10 percent), the index of perceived risk rises over time; that is, for a constant risk premium, the rising curve indicates that perceived risk increases with time. Therefore, a constant risk premium (and risk-adjusted discount rate) implies that risk of an individual cash flow is perceived to be higher and higher the further into the future the cash flow is due.

2. At any given future point in time (other than $t = 0$), the index of perceived risk is higher the higher the risk premium. At the point 10 years, for example, the risk index is 1.21 for the 2 percent risk premium attached to the 7 percent risky rate, 1.59 for the 5 percent risk premium, and 2.48 for the 10 percent risk premium.

This concept can be expressed analytically. Let the risk index for any year t, RI_t, be designated as:

$$RI_t = \frac{(1 + i)^{-t}}{(1 + i + P)^{-t}} = \frac{(1 + i + P)^t}{(1 + i)^t}$$

where $i =$ the riskless rate and $P =$ the risk premium. For a longer period of $t + 1$ years, and holding constant P and i,

$$\begin{aligned} RI_{t+1} &= \frac{(1 + i + P)^{t+1}}{(1 + i)^{t+1}} \\ &= \frac{(1 + i + P)^t}{(1 + i)^t} \cdot \frac{(1 + i + P)}{(1 + i)} \\ &= RI_t \left(\frac{1 + i + P}{1 + i}\right) \end{aligned}$$

Therefore, $RI_{t+1} > RI_t$ provided $P > 0$. Since the risk index is an increasing function of time, risk must be perceived to be *increasing* over time whenever the risk premium, P, is a constant. Further, note that the risk-adjusted discount rate, k, is equal to $i + P$. If i and P are both constants, then k is also a constant and

$$RI_{t+1} = RI_t \left(\frac{1 + k}{1 + i}\right)$$

Therefore, a constant k implies that risk (RI_t) is increasing over time.

The relationship between k, risk, and time is graphed in Figure B8–2. If risk is thought to increase over time (in terms of Figure 8–2, the estimated standard deviation of returns is increasing), then the risk index should also increase over time. A constant value of k implies increasing risk; this condition is shown in Figure B8–2(a). However, if the riskiness of returns is no higher for distant than for close-at-hand returns, then distant returns should be discounted at a *lower* k than close returns; this condition is shown in Figure B8–2(b). Note again that the reason behind this result is the fact that the risk premium component of k is being compounded.

Implications

As we pointed out in Chapter 8, firms tend to use risk-adjusted discount rates when making capital budgeting decisions. A firm taking this approach will have an over-all rate that generally reflects its over-all, market-determined riskiness. This rate will be used for "average" projects. Lower rates will be used for less risky projects, and higher rates will be used for riskier projects.

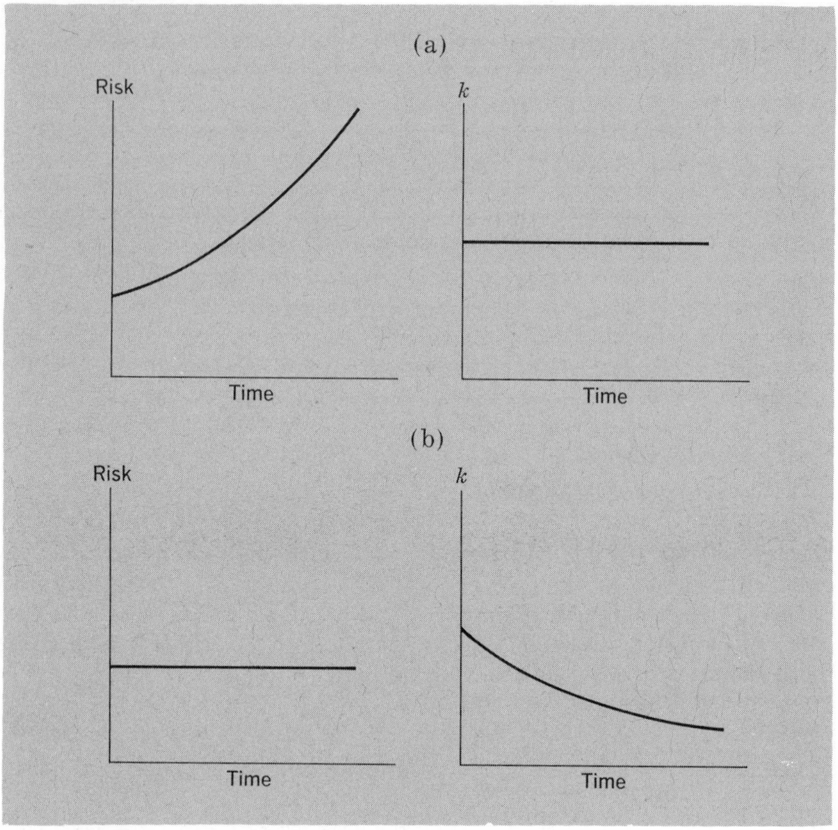

Figure B8–2 Relationship between Risk and Time

NOTE: (a) Riskiness of distant returns greater than riskiness of early returns
(b) Riskiness of returns constant over time

To facilitate the decision process, corporate headquarters prescribes rates for different divisions and for different classes of investments (for example, replacement, expansion of existing lines, expansion into new lines). Then, investments of a given class within a given division are analyzed in terms of the prescribed rate. For example, replacement decisions in the retailing division of an oil company might all be evaluated with an 8 percent cost of capital.

Notice what such a procedure implies about risk: risk increases with time, and it imposes a relatively severe burden on long-term projects. This means that short-payoff alternatives will be selected over those with longer payoffs when, for example, there are alternative ways of performing a given task, and that less capital-intensive methods of performing given tasks will be employed.

There probably are a substantial number of projects for which distant returns are *not* more difficult to estimate than near-term returns. For example, the estimated returns on a water pipeline serving a developing community may be quite uncertain in the short run because the rate of growth of the community is uncertain. However, the water company may be quite sure that in time the community will be fully developed and will utilize the full capacity of the pipeline. Similar situations could exist in many public projects—water projects, highway programs, schools, and so forth; in public utility investment decisions; and when industrial firms are building plants to serve specified geographic markets.

To the extent that this implicit assumption of rising risk over time reflects the facts, then a constant discount rate, k, is quite appropriate. In the vast majority of business situations, risk actually is an increasing function of time; a constant risk-adjusted discount rate is appropriate. There are, however, situations for which this is not true; one should be aware of the relationships described in this appendix and avoid the pitfall of unwittingly penalizing long-term projects when they are not, in fact, more risky than shorter-term projects.

APPENDIX C TO CHAPTER 8 Procedures for Evaluation of Risky Investments

In the first sections of Chapter 8 some intuitive ideas for the analysis of investments with uncertain returns were set forth and illustrated by Figures 8–1 and 8–2. These concepts are now made more precise and clarified by some numerical examples. The basic theory is expressed in the following equations:

Expected return for one year

$$\bar{R}_t = \sum_{j=1}^{m} (R_{jt}P_{jt}) \tag{C8–1}$$

Variation of expected return for one year

$$\sigma_t = \left[\sum_{j=1}^{m} (R_{jt} - \bar{R}_t)^2 P_{jt}\right]^{1/2} \tag{C8–2}$$

Expected present value of investment

$$\text{PV} = \sum_{t=0}^{m} \left[\frac{\bar{R}_t}{(1+k)^t}\right] \tag{C8–3}$$

Variation of expected present value of the investment

$$\sigma_{\text{PV}} = \left[\sum_{t=0}^{m} \frac{\sigma_t^2}{(1+k)^{2t}}\right]^{1/2} \tag{C8–4}$$

where:

R_{jt} = return associated with the jth probability in year t
P_{jt} = probability of the jth return in year t
$\bar{R}_t$ = expected return from the investment in the tth year, a weighted average weighted by probabilities
σ_t = standard deviation of the expected returns in the tth year
PV = present value of all expected returns over the n-year life of the investment
k = appropriate rate of discount for the future returns
σ_{PV} = standard deviation of the present value of expected returns

Equation C8–1 calculates the expected returns of an investment for a given year, t, as a weighted average, the items to be averaged being the possible outcomes and the weights being the probability distribution of returns for the year. Equation C8–2 calculates the standard deviation of the expected return in year t. Equation C8–3 discounts the expected returns over each year of the project's life to find the present value of the project, and Equation C8–4 calculates the standard deviation of the expected PV of the project. The first two equations deal with the returns and risk for individual years, while the last two equations deal with returns and risk of the project as a whole. The use of these formulas is illustrated below.

Comparison of Two Investments with Uncertain Returns over Future Time Periods

The application and significance of the basic formulas can best be conveyed by illustrative examples. The relevant data and calculations are set forth in Tables C8–1 and C8–2. For project A, the cash investment is $100. Returns are expected over three periods. There are five possible "states of the world"; that is, $j = 1, 5$, and the outcomes for each of these states are given in the columns headed R_{j1}, R_{j2}, R_{j3}. Note that the range of possible returns widens in the later periods.

The associated probabilities are in the third column. It should be noted that in period 2 the probability distribution is somewhat flatter, and that in period 3 the probability distribution is even more flat and skewed somewhat to the left, or toward the possibility of lower returns. Thus, the combination of a wider range of outcomes and flatter probability distribution for period 2 and for period 3 indicates that greater uncertainty is associated with returns expected in the more distant future. This is the type of situation shown in Figure 8–2 in the body of this chapter.

Given this data, the expected returns for project A for each period are calculated and found to be $70, $60, and $50, respectively. The standard deviation of each of these returns is then calculated as shown in the next section of Table C8–1. Finally, using formulas C8–3 and C8–4,

TABLE C8–1 PROBABLE RETURNS FROM RISKY INVESTMENT A

INVESTMENT A $100 (CASH OUTFLOW IN PERIOD 0)

Calculation of Expected Returns

State (j)	Period 1 R_{j1}	P_{j1}	$R_{j1}P_{j1}$	Period 2 R_{j2}	P_{j2}	$R_{j2}P_{j2}$	Period 3 R_{j3}	P_{j3}	$R_{j3}P_{j3}$
1	50	.10	5	20	.10	2	−40	.10	−4
2	60	.20	12	40	.25	10	30	.30	9
3	70	.40	28	60	.30	18	50	.30	15
3	80	.20	16	80	.25	20	80	.20	16
5	90	.10	9	100	.10	10	140	.10	14

$$\sum_{j=1}^{5}(R_{j1}P_{j1}) = \bar{R}_1 = 70 \qquad \bar{R}_2 = 60 \qquad \bar{R}_3 = 50$$

Calculation of Standard Deviation

State (j)	$(R_{j1}-\bar{R}_1)^2$	P_{j1}	$(R_{j1}-\bar{R}_1)^2P_{j1}$	$(R_{j2}-\bar{R}_1)^2$	P_{j2}	$(R_{j2}-\bar{R}_2)P_{j2}$	$(R_{j3}-\bar{R}_3)^2$	P_{j3}	$(R_{j3}-\bar{R}_3)P_{j3}$
1	400	.10	40	1600	.10	160	8100	.10	810
2	100	.20	20	400	.25	100	400	.30	120
3	0	.40	0	0	.30	0	0	.30	0
4	100	.20	20	400	.25	100	900	.20	180
5	400	.10	40	1600	.10	160	8100	.10	810

$$\sum_{j=1}^{5}(R_{j1}-\bar{R}_1)^2P_{j1} = 120 = \sigma_1^2 \qquad \sigma_2^2 = 520 \qquad \sigma_3^2 = 1920$$

$$\sigma_1 = \sqrt{120} = 10.95 \qquad \sigma_2 = \sqrt{520} = 22.80 \qquad \sigma_3 = \sqrt{1920} = 43.82$$

$$(3)\ \text{PV} = \frac{70}{1.06} + \frac{60}{(1.06)^2} + \frac{50}{(1.06)^3} = \frac{70}{1.060} + \frac{60}{1.124} + \frac{50}{1.191} = \$161.40$$

$$(4)\ \sigma_{\text{PV}} = \left[\frac{120}{(1.06)^2} + \frac{520}{(1.06)^4} + \frac{1920}{(1.06)^6}\right]^{1/2} = \left[\frac{120}{1.124} + \frac{520}{1.262} + \frac{1920}{1.419}\right]^{1/2}$$

$$= [106.76 + 412.04 + 1{,}353.07]^{1/2} = [1{,}871.87]^{1/2} = 43.25$$

project A's present value is calculated as \$161.40, and the standard deviation of that present value is calculated to be \$43.25.

In Table C8–2, similar calculations are performed for project B, which also involves an outlay of \$100. To simplify the calculations, it is assumed that the indicated probabilities are the same for each of the three periods, but note that the expected returns drop with each successive year. The standard deviation of expected returns for each year, \$10.95, is the same for each of the three periods. Note, however, that the coefficient of variation, which is the standard deviation divided by the mean return, is lower for the earlier returns because expected returns are declining. Thus, the riskiness of project B is also increasing over time. Equations C8–3 and C8–4 are again used to calculate the present value of the expected returns, \$134.66, and the standard deviation of that expected value, \$16.91.

TABLE C8–2 PROBABLE RETURNS FROM RISKY INVESTMENT B

INVESTMENT B = \$100

Cash Inflows

P_{jt}	R_{j1}	R_{j2}	R_{j3}
.10	40	30	20
.20	50	40	30
.40	60	50	40
.20	70	60	50
.10	80	70	60
$\bar{R}_t$	60	50	40

(2) $\sigma_t = [.10(20)^2 + .20(10)^2 + .20(10)^2 + .10(20)^2]^{1/2} = [120]^{1/2} = \$10.95$

(3) $PV = \dfrac{60}{1.060} + \dfrac{50}{1.124} + \dfrac{40}{1.191} = 56.60 + 44.48 + 33.58 = \$134.66$

(4) $\sigma_P = \left[\dfrac{120}{1.124} + \dfrac{120}{1.262} + \dfrac{120}{1.419}\right]^{1/2} = [106.76 + 95.08 + 84.57] = [286.40]^{1/2} = \$16.91$

These results are further developed in Figure C8–1, which presents a graph of the probability distributions of the present values of investments A and B. Assuming that the present values are normally distributed, then, knowing the expected present value and its standard deviation for each project, we can plot the probability distributions of present values. Table C8–3 gives the ordinates (points on the vertical axis) and areas under the normal curve for different confidence levels (t values). The expected present value of each investment has an ordinate of .3989. At $t = \pm 1$, the ordinate is .2420, and the associated present

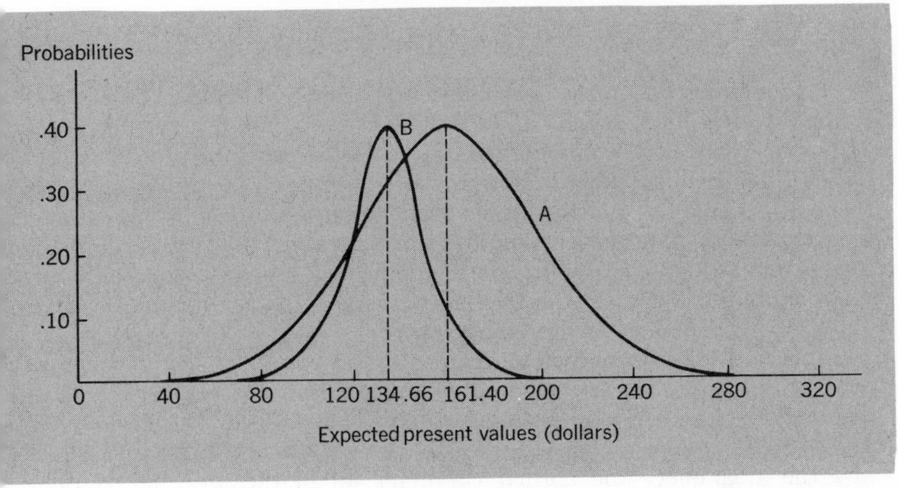

Figure C8–1 Probability Distributions of Expected Present Values of Projects A and B

value is equal to the expected present value plus or minus one standard deviation. For example, for investment A at $t = -1$, the ordinate is .2420 and the present value is \$161.40 — \$43.25 = \$118.15; at $t = -2$ the ordinate is .0540 and the present value is \$161.40 — \$86.50 = \$74.90. Other points are calculated similarly, and they are then used to plot Figure C8–1.

TABLE C8–3 ORDINATE AND AREA UNDER THE NORMAL CURVE OF ERROR

t	ORDINATE	AREA	2 × AREA
0.0	.3989	.0000	.0000
0.5	.3521	.1915	.3830
1.0	.2420	.3413	.6826
1.5	.1295	.4332	.8664
2.0	.0540	.4773	.9546
2.5	.0175	.4938	.9876
3.0	.0044	.4987	.9974

t = number of standard deviations from the mean.

The area under the curve between any two points on the X axis represents the probability that the present value will actually fall within the specified interval. Thus, the probability that the actual realized present value of investment A will lie within $\pm 1\sigma$ of the expected present value, or within the range \$118.50 to \$204.65, is 68.26 percent. (From the $t = 1.0$ row and the $2 \times$ area column of Table C8–3, find .6826 = 68.26 percent.)

This information on the probabilities associated with indicated returns from investments A and B can be expressed best, from a practical standpoint, in terms of the probabilities of achieving expected present values of *at least* some specified target amounts. These relationships are represented in Table C8–4. Since the investment outlay for each of the investments is $100, it is quite simple to go from present value to net present value by deducting $100 from each indicated expected present value. A profitability index (PI) is also calculated by simply dividing the $100 into the indicated expected present values.

By using the information in Table C8–3 on areas under the normal curve, one can find the cumulative probabilities for expected returns from investments A and B set forth in Table C8–4. The probability of a present value of at least $31.65 for investment A is represented by the area under the normal curve for all of the area to the right of the midpoint of the curve and all of the area to the left up through $t = -3$. This represents $.5 + .4987$, or a probability of 99.9 percent. The probability of achieving a return of each indicated amount is shown for other probability levels. Note that the probability of achieving at least the mean or expected value of the net present expected values of investments A and B is exactly 50 percent. Finally, note that the last two rows of the table indicate that the probability of at least breaking even on the projects is 92.2 percent for investment A and 98.0 percent for investment B.

A comparison between the two investments can also be facilitated by another form of analysis. Table C8–5 presents a comparison of profitability indexes for investments A and B for a range of probability distributions, and this data is graphed in Figure C8–2. The data are developed by the same procedures that were described for the probabilities shown in Table C8–4 earlier. However, Table C8–4 presented probabilities and associated values for multiples of the standard deviations around the expected mean and for break-even returns, while Table C8–5 and Figure C8–2 set forth the profitability indexes for a full range of probabilities. This facilitates a comparison between the two investments.

It is clear that investment A has a higher expected return than investment B. However, disregarding covariance, investment B is less risky than A. A selection between A and B would depend upon the decision-maker's attitude toward risk, as well as upon how the two investments might fit in with the firm's other assets.

Hillier and Hertz Approaches

The foregoing presentation represents a general method for dealing with *independent* expected returns between periods, that is, when the returns of one period do not depend upon outcomes in other years. We also assumed that the variations in the expected returns for a given year followed the normal curve of error. When these conditions of inde-

TABLE C8–4 CUMULATIVE PROBABILITIES OF EXPECTED PRESENT VALUES OF INVESTMENTS A AND B

EXPECTED PV OF AT LEAST		EXPECTED NPV OF AT LEAST		EXPECTED PI OF AT LEAST			CUMULATIVE PROBABILITY
A	B	A	B	A	B	t Value[a]	
\$ 31.65	\$ 83.93	(68.35)	(16.07)	.32	.84	$-3t$	99.9%[b]
74.90	100.84	(25.10)	.84	.75	1.01	$-2t$	97.7
118.15	117.75	18.15	17.75	1.18	1.18	$-1t$	84.1
161.40	134.66	61.40	34.66	1.61	1.35	—	50.0
204.65	151.57	104.65	51.57	2.05	1.52	$+1t$	15.9[c]
247.90	168.48	147.90	68.48	2.48	1.68	$2t$	2.3
291.15	185.39	191.15	85.39	2.91	1.85	$3t$	.1
\$100.0		0.0		1.00		1.42	92.2%[d]
	\$100.0		0.0		1.00	2.05	98.0[e]

[a] t = number of standard deviations from mean PV.
[b] .5000 *plus* areas under *left* tail of normal curve; for example, .5000 + .4987 = 99.9 percent for $t = -3$.
[c] .5000 *less* areas under *right* tail of normal curve; for example, .500 = .4773 = 2.3 percent for $t = 2$.
[d] NPV = PV − Cost

$$t = \frac{\text{NPV}}{\sigma_{\text{NPV}}} \text{ where NPV} = 0$$

Since the PV differs from the NPV by a constant, $\sigma_{\text{NPV}} = \sigma_{\text{PV}}$, so

$$t = \frac{61.40}{43.25} = 1.42$$

The area under the right tail of the normal curve associated with $t = 1.42$ is .4222, so

$$.5000 + .4222 = .9222$$

and the probability of at least PV = \$100 is 92.2 percent.

$$t = \frac{34.66}{16.91} = 2.05 \text{ where NPV} = 0$$

Associated area = .5000 + .4798 = .9798, so probability of at least PV = \$100 is 98 percent.

TABLE C8–5 CUMULATIVE PROBABILITY DISTRIBUTIONS OF PROFITABILITY INDEXES

CUMULATIVE PROBABILITY	PROFITABILITY INDEX OF AT LEAST A	B
10%	2.17	1.56
20	1.98	1.49
30	1.84	1.43
40	1.72	1.39
50	1.61	1.35
60	1.50	1.30
70	1.39	1.26
80	1.25	1.20
90	1.06	1.13
95	.75	1.01
99	.32	.84

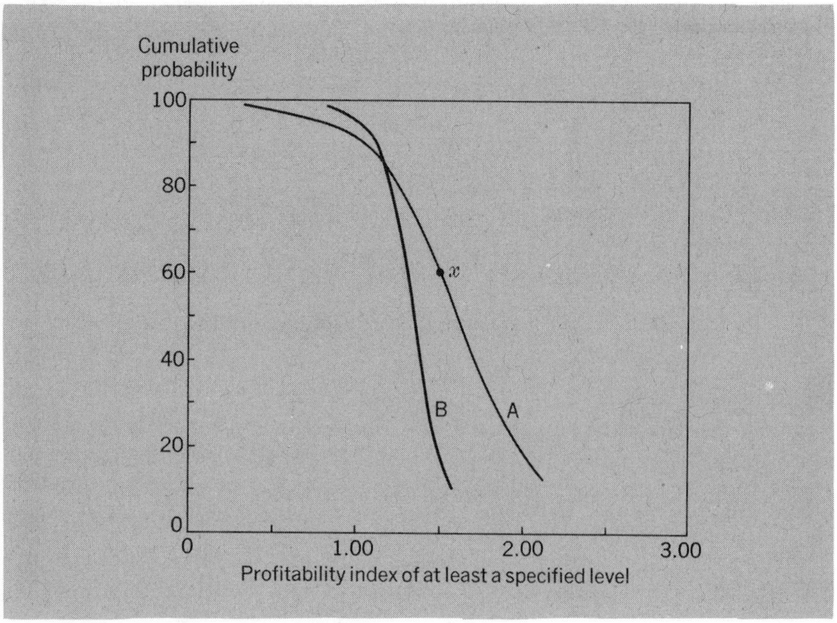

Figure C8–2 Cumulative Probability Analysis of Profitability Index Levels of Investments A and B

NOTE: Point x on the curve for investment A indicates that there is a 60 percent probability of receiving a profitability index of at least 1.5. Other points on the curves may be interpreted similarly.

pendence and normality do not hold, the calculations become more complicated. The models for which expected net cash flows between periods are correlated (the expected returns between time periods are dependent), and for which some of the returns of an investment are correlated and some are independent, have been treated by Frederick S. Hillier.[1] Mathematical techniques are also available for dealing with nonnormal probability distributions. We shall not go into the technical methodology involved, but Hillier's approach has proved to be a useful way of dealing with uncertainty in practical situations.

A similar approach to capital budgeting under uncertainty is presented in an article by David B. Hertz.[2] He is particularly persuasive in indicating that, taking probabilities into account, the expected rate of return may be quite different from the conventional best single estimate approach. Hertz illustrates the use of the probability information in an approach that requires only a range of high and low values around expected values of such key variables as sales, profit margins, and so forth. Under his method, the decision-maker is not required to assign probabilities to the variables; he must choose only (1) the expected value, (2) an upper estimate, and (3) a lower estimate. The Monte Carlo[3] method, which involves using a table of random numbers to generate the possible probabilities, is used to generate the required probability distributions.

The Monte Carlo method also permits assignment of values that reflect differing degrees of dependence between some events and some subsequent events. For example, the expected sales for the firm, as well as its selling prices, might be determined by the intensity of competition in conjunction with the total size of market demand and its growth rate. A further advantage of the Hertz technique is that, by separating the individual factors that determine profitability, the separate effects of each factor can be estimated and the sensitivity of profitability to each factor can be determined. If the effects of a particular factor on the final results are negligible, it is not necessary for management to analyze that particular factor in any great detail.

Abandonment Value

Preliminary to the discussion of decision trees in investment choices, the methodology required for handling decisions with respect to aban-

[1] See Frederick S. Hillier, "The Derivation of Probabilistic Information for the Evaluation of Risk Investments," *Management Science,* IX (April 1963), 443–57, and Frederick S. Hillier and David V. Heebink, "Evaluating Risky Capital Investments," *California Management Review,* VIII (Winter 1965), 71–80.

[2] David B. Hertz, "Risk Analysis in Capital Investment," *Harvard Business Review,* XLII (January-February 1964), 95–106.

[3] For a discussion of the nature of the Monte Carlo method and some applications, see C. McMillan and R. F. Gonzalez, *Systems Analysis* (Homewood, Ill.: Irwin, 1965), 76–121.

donment value in evaluating projects is now set forth. Consideration of abandonment before the economic life of a project ends may increase the expected net present value of the project and reduce its standard deviation of returns; this aspect of the abandonment project is considered first.[4] The next consideration is whether a project should be abandoned or continued.

The analysis required for taking abandonment value into account in evaluating an investment project involves no principles beyond those already set forth. But it does represent an important aspect of decision-making with respect to evaluating projects. Hence it is useful to have a decision model which takes into account judgments about abandonment value in the framework for evaluating individual projects.

The principles involved may best be conveyed through a specific example illustrating the role of abandonment value in evaluating projects under uncertainty.

The Palmer Corporation has invested $300 in new machinery with expected cash flows over two years as follows:

TABLE C8–6

YEAR 1		YEAR 2	
Cash Flow	*Initial Probability* P (1)	*Cash Flow*	*Conditional Probability* P (2/1)
$200	(.3)	$100	(.3)
		200	(.5)
		300	(.2)
300	(.4)	200	(.3)
		300	(.5)
		400	(.2)
400	(.3)	300	(.3)
		400	(.4)
		500	(.3)

The project is not expected to have any returns after the second year. The firm's cost of capital is 12 percent. To indicate the role of abandonment value, we first calculate the expected net present value of the investment and its expected standard deviation without considering abandonment value.

[4] Alexander A. Robichek and James C. Van Horne, "Abandonment Value and Capital Budgeting," *Journal of Finance,* XXII, No. 4 (December 1967), 577–590.

TABLE C8–7 CALCULATION OF EXPECTED NET PRESENT VALUE

YEAR 1			YEAR 2			JOINT PROBABILITY ANALYSIS		
Cash Flow	PV Factor	Present Value	Cash Flow	PV Factor	Present Value	Present Value of Total Cash Flow	Joint Probability	Expected Value
(1)	(2)	(3) = (1×2)	(4)	(5)	(6) = (4×5)	(7) = (3+6)	(8)	(9) = (7×8)
			$100	.797	80	$259	.09	$ 23
$200	.893	179	200	.797	159	338	.15	51
			300	.797	239	418	.06	25
			200	.797	159	427	.12	51
300	.893	268	300	.797	239	507	.20	101
			400	.797	319	587	.08	47
			300	.797	239	596	.09	54
400	.893	357	400	.797	319	676	.12	81
			500	.797	398	755	.09	68
							1.00	501

Expected present value = $501
Expected net present value = $201

Next we calculate the standard deviation of the future cash flows.

TABLE C8–8 CALCULATION OF STANDARD DEVIATION

NPV* − NPV	= DEVIATIONS	DEVIATIONS²	× JOINT PROBABILITY	= AMOUNT
(41) − 201 =	(242)	58,564	× .09	= 5,271
38 − 201 =	(163)	26,569	× .15	= 3,985
118 − 201 =	(83)	6,889	× .06	= 413
127 − 201 =	(74)	5,476	× .12	= 657
207 − 201 =	6	36	× .20	= 7
286 − 201 =	85	7,225	× .08	= 578
296 − 201 =	95	9,025	× .09	= 812
375 − 201 =	174	30,276	× .12	= 3,633
455 − 201 =	254	64,516	× .09	= 5,806
			1.00	21,162

Expected standard deviation $= \sigma = (21{,}162)^{1/2} = \$145$

* Value from column 7, Table C8–7, minus $300 cost.

We now expand the analysis to have the decision-maker take abandonment value into account. It is estimated that the abandonment value of the project at the end of the first year would be $250. The present value of this estimated $250 abandonment value is compared with the expected present values of the cash flows occurring during the second year which would be experienced if abandonment did not take place at the end of the second year. We must therefore calculate the second-year expected cash flows based on the conditional probabilities rather than the joint probabilities applied in the preceding analysis. This calculation is shown below.

TABLE C8–9 EXPECTED PRESENT VALUES OF CASH FLOWS DURING THE SECOND YEAR

Cash Flow	Present Value Factor	Present Value	Conditional Probability		Expected Present Value
$100	.797	80	.3		$ 24
200	.797	159	.5		80
300	.797	239	.2		48
				Branch total	$152
200	.797	159	.3		$ 48
300	.797	239	.5		120
400	.797	319	.2		64
				Branch total	$232
300	.797	239	.3		$ 72
400	.797	319	.4		128
500	.797	398	.3		119
				Branch total	$319

We next compare the present value of the $250 abandonment value, $250 times .893 = $223, with the branch expected present values for each of the three possible cash flow patterns (branches) depicted above. If the $223 present value of abandonment exceeds one or more of the expected present values of the possible branches of cash flows, taking abandonment value into account will improve the indicated returns from the project. In general, we would make a recalculation, substituting abandonment value for the present value of cash flows wherever abandonment value exceeds the present value of cash flows. This alternative calculation is presented in the following tabulation of expected present values with abandonment taken into consideration.

We may now compare the results when abandonment value is taken into account with the results when abandonment value is not taken into account. Taking abandonment value into account increases the expected net present value from $201 to $223, and it reduces the expected standard deviation of returns from $145 to $118. Thus, taking abandonment value into account improves the attractiveness of the investment for the set of facts given in the problem.

TABLE C8–10 EXPECTED NET PRESENT VALUE WITH ABANDONMENT VALUE INCLUDED

YEAR 1 Cash Flow	PV Factor		YEAR 2 Cash Flow	PV Factor		PRESENT VALUE OF TOTAL CASH FLOW		JOINT PROBABILITY		EXPECTED VALUE
$450 ×	.893	= 402				$402	×	.30	=	$121
			200 ×	.797	= $159	427	×	.12	=	51
300 ×	.893	= 268	300 ×	.797	= 239	507	×	.20	=	101
			400 ×	.797	= 319	587	×	.08	=	47
			300 ×	.797	= 239	596	×	.09	=	54
400 ×	.893	= 357	400 ×	.797	= 319	676	×	.12	=	81
			500 ×	.797	= 398	755	×	.09	=	68
								1.00		
						Expected present value			=	$523
						Expected net present value			=	223

TABLE C8–11 CALCULATION OF STANDARD DEVIATION FOR NET CASH FLOW WITH ABANDONMENT VALUE INCLUDED

NPV_s − NPV =	DEVIATION	DEVIATION²	×	JOINT PROBABILITY	=	AMOUNT
102 − 223 =	(121)	14,641	×	.30	=	4,392
127 − 223 =	(96)	9,216	×	.12	=	1,106
207 − 223 =	(16)	256	×	.20	=	51
287 − 223 =	64	4,096	×	.08	=	328
296 − 223 =	73	5,329	×	.09	=	480
376 − 223 =	153	23,409	×	.12	=	2,809
455 − 223 =	232	53,824	×	.09	=	4,844
						14,010

Expected standard deviation = $(14{,}010)^{1/2}$ = $118

Taking abandonment value into account has another effect on the decision process. The decision whether to continue the project or to abandon it sometime during its life depends upon which branch of possibilities occurs during each time period. For example, suppose that during year 1 the cash flow actually obtained was $200. Then the three possibilities associated with year 2 are the three that were conditionally dependent upon the events of the first year. At the end of the first year, therefore, the abandonment decision is influenced by which of the three probable branches of possibilities was actually experienced. A calculation is then made of the second-year net cash flow series, discounted one year.

TABLE C8–12 CALCULATION OF EXPECTED NET CASH FLOWS FOR SECOND PERIOD WHEN $200 WAS EARNED DURING THE FIRST YEAR

CASH FLOW		PRESENT VALUE FACTOR		PRESENT VALUE		PROBABILITY FACTOR		DISCOUNTED EXPECTED CASH FLOW
$100	×	.893	=	$ 89	×	.3	=	$ 27
200	×	.893	=	179	×	.5	=	90
300	×	.893	=	268	×	.2	=	54
				Expected present value			=	$171

At the end of the first year the abandonment value is $250. This is compared with the expected present value of the second-year net cash flow series, discounted one year. This value is determined to be $171, so the abandonment value of $250 exceeds the net present value of returns for the second year. Therefore, the project should be abandoned at the end of the first year. Note that it is not necessary to compare the standard deviations, because with abandonment the standard deviation of returns is zero. This is therefore certain to be lower than the standard deviation of returns for the second-year net cash flow series related to the branch of cash flows actually experienced during the first year.

As indicated at the beginning of the discussion, abandonment value involves no new fundamental principles. However, it does represent an important aspect of the decision-making process that should be incorporated into decision models for evaluating risky investments. The formulation of the problem involves branches of possible returns and conditional and joint probability concepts. The method of solution is essentially that used in a decision tree analysis of investment choices. The foundation for this topic thus having been developed, we now turn to a formal development of the use of decision trees in investment choices.

Use of Decision Trees in Investment Choices

Investment decisions under uncertainty involve a number of variables, and probability judgments must be made about a large number of factors that influence the net cash flows from alternative investments. These factors include the prospective size of the market, its growth rate, the number of competitors, the firm's market share, the expected volume of sales, selling prices, fixed and variable costs, size of investment required, and possible competitive reactions in the future. Thus, at a minimum, we must simultaneously consider the size of investment, future cash flows, probabilities associated with the future cash flows, choice of discount rate, opportunities for modifying the original investment, and scale economies.

To aid in systematically evaluating the alternatives, the device of a tree diagram, or decision tree diagram, has been developed. The decision tree is a device for setting forth graphically the pattern of relationships among decisions and chance events. It is especially useful for displaying the nature of dependence between investments and returns involving conditional probabilities, that is, where the probability of one event is dependent upon the outcome of another event.

Figure C8–3 illustrates a relatively general type of decision process, where the choice is between a large investment and a series of smaller investments made sequentially as more information becomes available. The initial large investment is more efficient if full capacity can be used because of economies of scale in plant construction. The decision

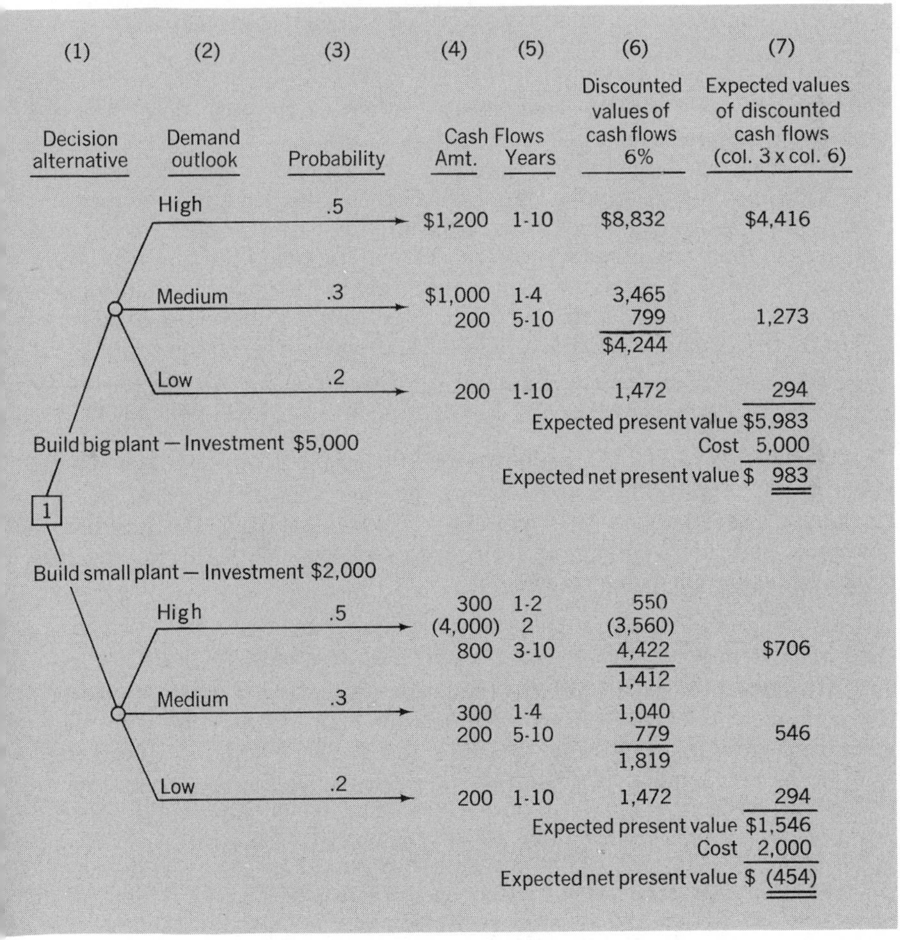

Figure C8–3 Decision Tree Analysis of Alternative Investment Choices

is to build a plant costing $5,000 or one costing $2,000. The capacity of the $5,000 plant would support a sales volume that provides a net cash flow of $1,200, whereas the smaller plant would support a sales capacity of only $300 a year. However, at the end of two years the capacity of the small plant could be increased to $800 a year at a cost of $4,000. If the small plant is built, sales beyond its capacity of $300 would not be possible until capacity is added.

In comparing the two investments, the outlook for the potential volume of sales must receive careful analysis. The decision tree indicates that the probability of a high level of demand is .5, the probability of medium demand is .3, and the probability of low demand is .2. With the indicated future cash flow prospects and the associated probabilities, a quantitative assessment of the mutually exclusive alternatives can be made. First, the discounted values of the cash flows are calculated for the appropriate period. The indicated cash flows, by both amount and years, are shown in column 5 of Figure C8–3. Next, the discounted cash values are calculated and listed in column 6. Finally, the associated probabilities are applied to yield the expected present values of the cash flows that are given in column 7.

Building the larger plant is clearly the superior alternative—a gain of $983 in comparison to a loss of $454 on the smaller initial investment. This follows from the particular facts of this case. First, the economies of scale that are assumed are substantial. Second, the probability of a high demand is as large as are the probabilities of a medium or low demand combined. Third, a considerable amount of potential sales is lost if the demand levels are high with the capacity of the small plant limited to sales of $300 a year. Fourth, the additional expenses required to add capacity are quite large relative to the cost of building the capacity at the outset.

We do not mean to imply that the decision is always in favor of the larger plant. The result depends on the facts of the case; but the value of the decision tree method is that it sets out the alternative choices and their consequences, then proceeds systematically to a quantitative evaluation of the choices.

A Complex Illustration[4]

We have presented a relatively simple example of decision trees thus far. For complicated decisions, the decision tree becomes one with many branches and many possible decisions and chance events. An illustration of a more complex decision tree analysis, where two decision points are involved, is given in Figure C8–4. The new figure builds on the material presented in Figure C8–3. Instead of a decision concerning

[4] For additional examples of decision trees, see John F. Magee, "Decision Trees for Decision Making," *Harvard Business Review,* XLII (July-August 1964), 126–138; and his "How to Use Decision Trees in Capital Investment," *Harvard Business Review,* XLII (September-October 1964), 79–96.

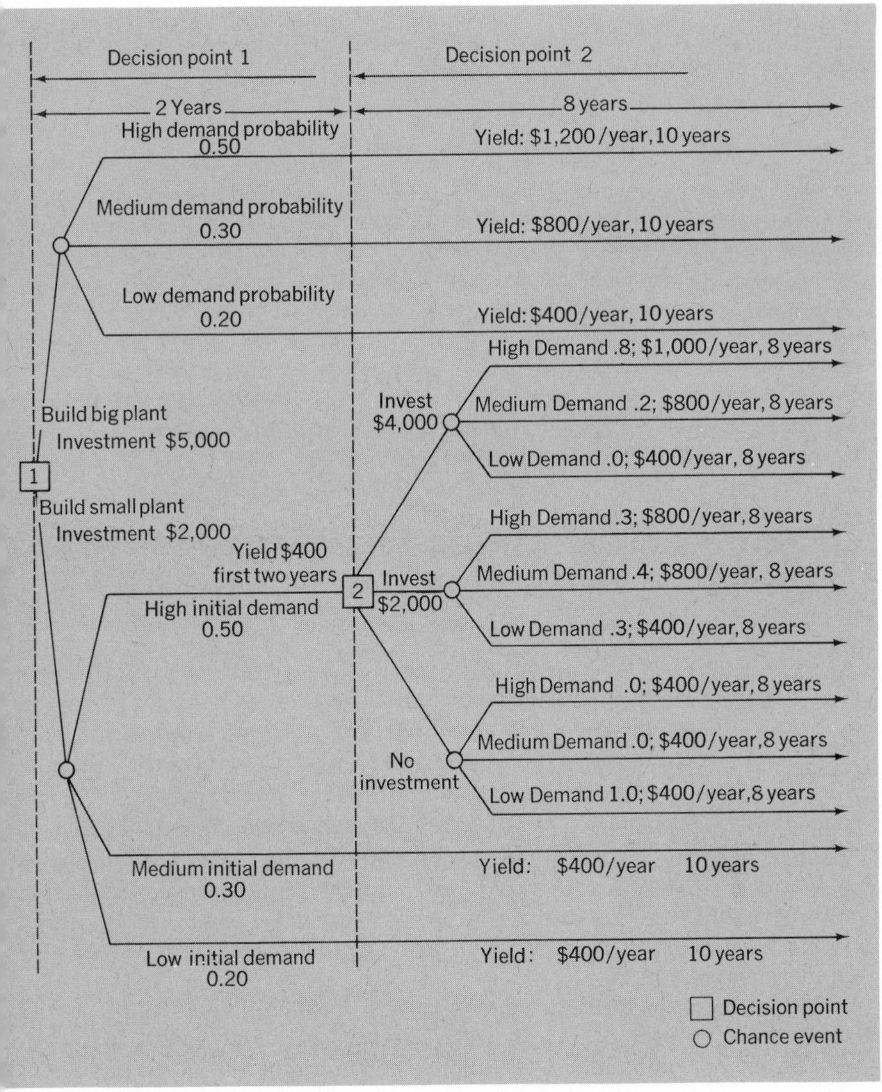

Figure C8–4 Decison Tree Analysis of Investment Choices

whether to build a plant with additional capacity at the end of the second year if demand is strong, the decision-maker contemplates three alternatives: (1) to build capacity for sales of $1,000 a year by investing $4,000, (2) to invest $2,000 to obtain capacity of $800, or (3) to make no change in the present plant capacity.

The alternative decision choices at decision point 2 and the possible levels of demand with their associated probabilities, having experienced a high initial demand during the first two years, are given in Figure

C8–4. The solution process first involves an analysis of decision point 2 to determine its position value. This is carried out in Table C8–13,

TABLE C8–13 ANALYSIS OF DECISION AT POINT 2

CHOICE	CHANCE EVENT	YIELD	PV FACTOR	PRESENT VALUE	PROBABILITY	EXPECTED VALUE
Expansion ($4,000)	High demand	$1,000, 8 yrs.	6.210	$6,210	0.80	$4,968
	Medium demand	$ 600, 8 yrs.	6.210	3,726	0.20	745
	Low demand	$ 700, 8 yrs.	6.210	4,347	0.00	0
				Total PV		$5,713
				Less cost		4,000
				NPV		$1,713
Expansion ($2,000)	High demand	$ 700, 8 yrs.	6.210	$4,347	0.80	$3,478
	Medium demand	$ 700, 8 yrs.	6.210	4,347	0.20	869
	Low demand	$ 400, 8 yrs.	6.210	2,484	0.00	0
				Total PV		$4,347
				Less cost		2,000
				NPV		$2,347
No expansion	High demand	$ 400, 8 yrs.	6.210	$2,484	0.80	$1,987
	Medium demand	$ 400, 8 yrs.	6.210	2,484	0.20	497
	Low demand	$ 400, 8 yrs.	6.210	2,484	0.00	0
				Total PV		$2,484
				Less cost		0
				NPV		$2,484

where the expected present value of each alternative decision is calculated. Under the assumptions of the analysis, the No-expansion choice yields the greatest net expected present value. Since the No-expansion alternative has the greatest net expected present value, this is a position value from decision point 2 that can be "rolled back" into an analysis of decision point 1.

The analysis of decision point 1 is performed in Table C8–14. Again, the present values of the indicated returns are first calculated; then the associated probabilities are applied to determine the expected present values set forth in the final column of the table. Note that the decision point 2 position value of $2,484 for the choice of No expansion at the end of two years under conditions of high initial demand when the small plant was built is carried into the analysis under the choice to build a small plant. The yield under high initial demand when the small plant is built has added to it the position value of $2,484 discounted by the present value factor for two years to give an expected present value of $1,106 for the position value.

Under the facts assumed in the illustration, the net expected present value of building a large plant is $1,771. The net expected value of building the small plant and then reviewing the decision if initial demand

TABLE C8–14 ANALYSIS OF DECISION AT POINT 1

CHOICE	CHANCE EVENT	YIELD	PV FACTOR	PRESENT VALUE	PROBABILITY	EXPECTED VALUE
Large plant	High demand	$1,200, 10 yrs.	7.360	$8.832	0.50	$4,416
	Medium demand	800, 10 yrs.	7.360	5,888	0.30	1,766
	Low demand	400, 10 yrs.	7.360	2,944	0.20	589
				Total PV		$6,771
				Less cost		5,000
				NPV		$1,771
Small plant	High initial demand	$400, 2 yrs.	1.833	$ 733	0.50	$ 366
		Decision 2 $2,484 at end of 2 years	.890	2,211	0.50	1,106
	Medium initial demand	$400, 10 yrs.	7.360	2,944	0.30	883
	Low initial demand	$400, 10 yrs.	7.360	2,944	0.20	589
				Total PV		$2,944
				Less cost		2,000
				NPV		$ 944

is high is a net $944. Thus, the indicated net present value of building the large plant is almost double that of building the small plant. The analysis, accordingly, suggests building the larger plant.

PROBLEMS

C8–1 The financial vice-president for the Lewy Manufacturing Company is analyzing the potential of a $1,500 investment in a new machine. His estimate of the cash-flow distribution for the three-year life of the machine is shown below.

PERIOD 1		PERIOD 2		PERIOD 3	
Probability	Cash Flow	Probability	Cash Flow	Probability	Cash Flow
.10	$800	.10	$800	.20	$1,200
.20	600	.30	700	.50	900
.40	400	.40	600	.20	600
.30	200	.20	500	.10	300

Probability distributions are assumed to be independent. Treasury bills are yielding 5 percent. To evaluate the investment, the vice-president has asked you to make the following calculations.

a. The expected net present value of the project.
b. The standard deviation about the expected value.
c. The probability that the net present value will be zero or less (assume the distribution is normal and continuous).
d. The probability that the net present value will be greater than zero.
e. The probability that the net present value will equal the mean.
f. The profitability index of the expected value.
g. The probability that the profitability index will be (1) less than 1 or (2) greater than 2.

C8–2 The Redford Machine Tool Company is considering an investment in a project that requires an initial outlay of $3,000 with an expected net cash flow generated over three periods as follows:

PERIOD 1		PERIOD 2		PERIOD 3	
Probability	Cash Flow	Probability	Cash Flow	Probability	Cash Flow
.10	800	.100	800	.20	800
.20	1,000	.30	1,000	.50	1,000
.40	1,500	.40	1,500	.20	1,500
.30	2,000	.20	2,000	.10	2,000

a. What is the expected net present value of this project? (Assume that the probability distributions are independent and that Treasury bills are yielding 5 percent).
b. Calculate the standard deviation about the expected value.
c. Find the probability that the net present value will be zero or less. (Assume that the distribution is normal and continuous.) What is the probability that the NPV will be greater than zero?
d. Calculate the profitability index of the expected value. What is the probability that the index will be less than 1.00? Of being greater than 2.00?

C8–3 The Ajax Company has the following probability distributions for net cash flows during the first year for a potential project.

PROBABILITY	CASH FLOW
.50	$100
.30	200
.20	300

Performance of similar projects in the past has indicated that the net cash flow distributions are not independent. The level of demand and the related net cash flow returns experienced in period 1 influence the achievements in period 2 in the following way:

If year 1 = $100, the distribution for year 2 is:

.70	$100
.20	200
.10	300

If year 1 = $200, the distribution for year 2 is:

.10	$100
.60	200
.30	300

If year 1 = $300, the distribution for year 2 is:

.10	$100
.20	200
.50	300
.20	400

a. If $200 is earned in year 1, what is the probability that the second year's earnings will be $200 or less?
b. What is the probability that earnings for year 1 will be $100 and for year 2 $200?
c. What is the probability that the Ajax Company will earn more than $300 on this project in the second year?
d. If earnings for the first year are $300, what is the probability that $200 or more will be earned the second year?
e. What is the probability that Ajax will earn more than $600 over the life of the project?

C8–4 In its first year of operation at Special Steel Corporation, a new electric furnace produced a savings of $400 a month over the basic oxygen furnace.

The scrap steel division at Special Steel is quite old and inefficient. Before the new electric furnace was installed, management estimated that the company could save $4,980 a year if the scrap-melting division is eliminated. Management must decide what action to take for the second year. The new furnace has no scrap value. The required rate of return for the firm is 6 percent.

a. If the savings in the second year are equal to those obtained in the first year, should the melting division be abandoned?
b. What decision would be reached if the cost analysis of savings per month with the electric furnace for the second year is:

PROBABILITY	AMOUNT
.05	$200
.15	300
.50	400
.20	500
.10	600

C8–5 A firm has invested $4,000 in automated machinery with the expected probable net cash flows over two years as follows:

YEAR 1		YEAR 2	
Net Cash Flow	Initial Probability P (1)	Net Cash Flow	Conditional Probability P (2/1)
		$2,500	(.3)
$3,000	(.3)	3,000	(.5)
		3,500	(.2)
		3,000	(.3)
4,000	(.4)	4,000	(.5)
		5,000	(.2)
		4,000	(.3)
5,000	(.2)	5,000	(.4)
		6,000	(.3)

The firm's cost of capital is 12 percent.

a. Calculate the expected value of the net present value of the investment and standard deviation without considering abandonment value.
b. If the abandonment value at the end of year 1 is $2,800, calculate the new expected net present value and standard deviation of the project.
c. During period 1, the cash flow actually experienced was $3,000. Should the project now be abandoned or should it be continued through period 2?

APPENDIX D TO CHAPTER 8 Risk and Utility Theory

Risk and utility theory are integrally connected, and it is appropriate to set forth this relationship. That is the purpose of this last appendix to Chapter 8.

In Chapter 8, we *assumed* that investors were averse to risk, that is, that they prefer less risk to more, all other things being the same. This statement involves an implicit assumption about the *utility of money* (either income or wealth), namely, that the marginal utility of money declines as the level of income or wealth increases. Other possibilities, of course, are that the marginal utility of money is an increasing function of income or wealth, or that the marginal utility of income or wealth is constant.

These alternatives are graphed in Figure D8–1, where dollars of income or wealth are shown on the horizontal axis and "utiles" are shown on the vertical axis. If an individual has a constant utility for money, his utility rises linearly with wealth (Curve *B*). If he has an increasing utility of money, his utility rises more than proportionately as wealth increases (Curve *A*). If his marginal utility of money is declining,

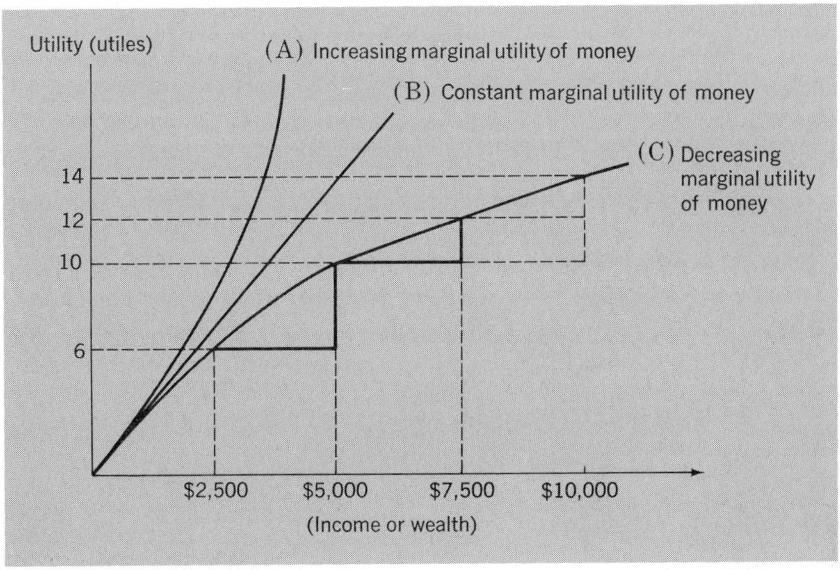

Figure D8–1 Relation between Utility and Money

each additional dollar brings less satisfaction than the previous one (Curve *C*). For example, we can see, along Curve *C*, that a $2,500 increase in wealth from $2,500 to $5,000 brings with it a 4 utile increase, from 6 to 10 utiles; a $2,500 wealth increase from $5,000 to $7,500 provides only 2 additional utiles.

Most *investors* (as opposed to people who go to Las Vegas for the fun of it or because of pathological problems) appear to have a declining marginal utility for money, and this directly affects their attitude toward risk. Risk means, in essence, the likelihood that a given return will turn out to be lower than was expected. If it comes out on the high side, fine; if it is low, it is bad. Someone who has a constant marginal utility for money will value each dollar of "extra" returns just as highly as each dollar of expected returns not earned in the event of the "bad" outcome. On the other hand, someone with a diminishing marginal utility for money will get more "pain" from a dollar lost than "pleasure" from a dollar gained. Because of his utility of money function, the second individual will be very much opposed to risk, and he will require a very high return on an investment that is subject to much risk. In curve *C* of Figure D8–1, for example, a gain of $2,500 from a base of $5,000 would bring 2 utiles of additional satisfaction, but a $2,500 loss would cause a 4 utile satisfaction loss. Therefore, a person with this utility function and $5,000 would be unwilling to make a fair bet with a 50-50 chance of winning or losing $2,500.

Based on these utility relationships, the relationships between risk and required rates of return for those with increasing marginal utility

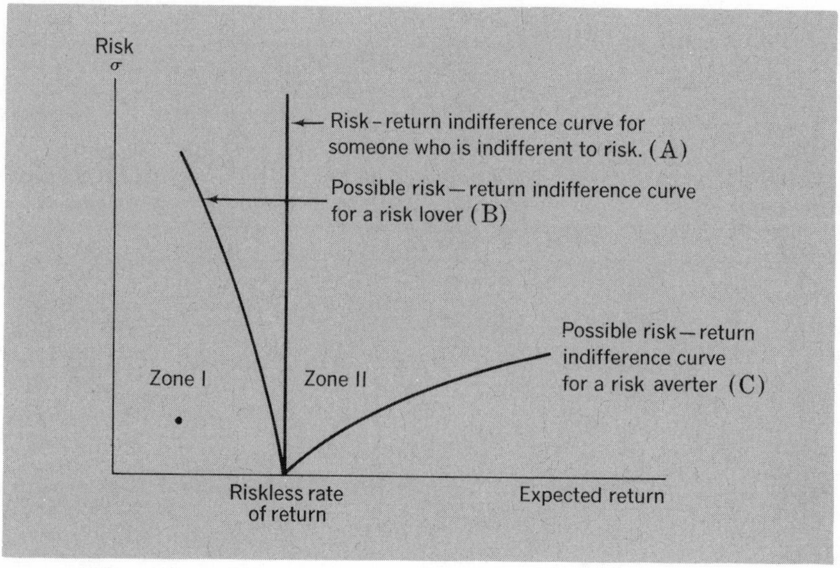

Figure D8–2 Relation between Risk and Expected Returns

of money (risk lovers), those with constant marginal utility for money (indifferent to risk), and those with declining marginal utility for money (risk averters), are shown in Figure D8–2.[1] The vertical line is the indifference curve for a person with a linear utility of money function (curve *B* in Figure D8–1). If a particular investment had an expected return of 5 percent (or \$500 on a \$10,000 investment), it would not matter to him if the 5 percent was a "sure thing" like a U.S. Treasury bill or a very risky venture whose actual potential returns ranged from a 100 percent loss (−\$10,000) to a 100 percent gain (+\$10,000), but which averaged out to an expected 5 percent (+\$500) gain.

A person who *preferred* more risk to less would be willing to accept a lower expected return on a more risky project (if he had to in order to get a risky project). Zone I, which contains all points to the left of the vertical line (curve *A*) is the region in which risk-lovers' indifference curves would lie, and curve *B* is one possible risk-return indifference curve for a risk lover. Risk averters would have indifference curves that fall in zone II, to the right of the vertical line. One such possible risk-averter indifference curve is shown as *C* in Figure D8–2.

If the majority of investors are risk averters, as in fact they are, then the actual risk-return market opportunity curve will lie in zone

[1] For a further analysis of the interrelation between these factors and their implications, see, Henry A. Latane, "Criteria for Choice Among Risky Ventures," *The Journal of Political Economy,* LXVII (April 1959), 144–155; and Henry A. Latane and Donald L. Tuttle, "Decision Theory and Financial Management," *Journal of Finance,* XXI (May 1966), 228–244.

II; curve C in Figure D8–2 could represent the market risk-return opportunity line. The strongest risk averters would buy the least risky investments, while the risk lovers would move out the risk-return curve, getting their desired higher risk plus a higher expected rate of return as a bonus. The point emphasized, though, is that the market opportunity line is an aggregate of individual risk-preference functions, and these preference functions, in turn, are fundamentally dependent upon marginal utility of money functions.

Since utility is a psychological attitude or preference, its measurement involves the same kind of problems as does the measurement of temperature. An arbitrary choice of origin and unit of measurement is made. Then useful comparisons can be made and utility functions developed. A procedure associating utility with various levels of income has been suggested by Friedman and Savage:

> Select any two incomes, say \$500 and \$1,000. Assign any arbitrary utilities to these incomes, say 0 utiles and 1 utile, respectively. This corresponds to an arbitrary choice of origin and unit of measure. Select any intermediate income, say \$600. Offer the consumer unit the choice between (1) a chance α of \$500 and $(1 - \alpha)$ of \$1,000 or (2) a certainty of \$600, varying α until the consumer unit is indifferent between the two. . . . Suppose this indifference value of α is $\frac{2}{5}$. If the hypothesis is correct, it follows that,
>
> $$U(600) = \tfrac{2}{5}U(500) + \tfrac{3}{5}U(1000) = \tfrac{2}{5} \cdot 0 + \tfrac{3}{5} \cdot 1 = \tfrac{3}{5} = .60.$$
>
> In this way, the utility attached to every income between \$500 and \$1,000 can be determined.[2]

TABLE D8–1 ILLUSTRATION OF DECISION MAKER'S UTILITY FOR RANGE OF RETURNS

DOLLAR PAYOFF	UTILITY
\$1,000	1.000
900	.975
800	.925
700	.800
650	.720
600	.600
500	.000

[2] M. Friedman and L. J. Savage, "The Utility Analysis of Choices Involving

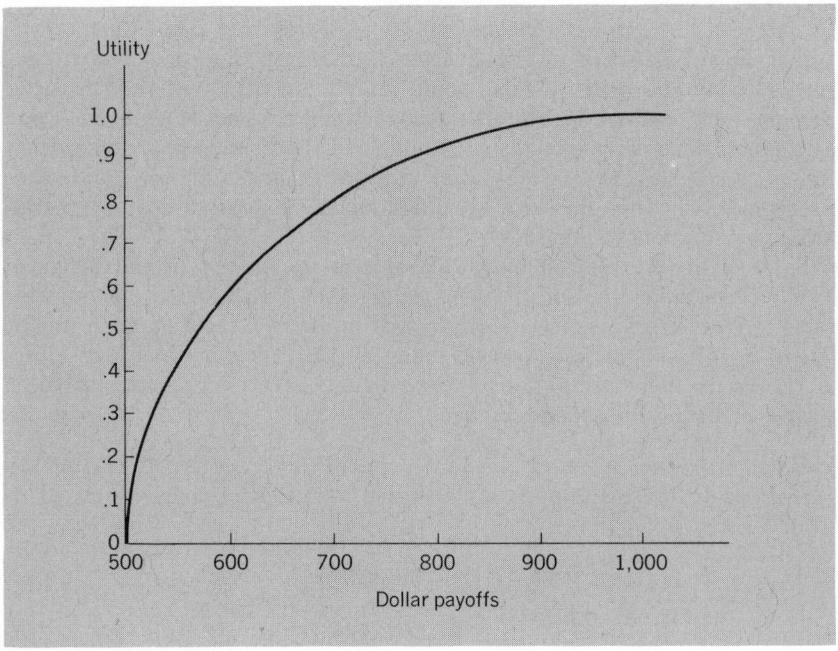

Figure D8–3 Relation between Utility and Dollar Payoffs

While the nature or quantity of utility (utiles) is arbitrary, its measurement is possible. By measurement is meant an effort to formulate explicitly the shape and position of the utility preference function so that the decision maker's utility function can be established. By the procedure described in the quotation from Friedman and Savage, relationships between utility and monetary value may be established. Illustrative relationships are set forth in Table D8–1 and Figure D8–3.

Consistent Behavior

These relationships can now be employed to illustrate the principles of consistent choices in decisions involving uncertainty. The judgments can be set forth in the framework of a payoff table or decision tree for working through systematically to a consistent course of action. The use of a payoff table is illustrated by Table D8–2.

The first column in Table D8–2 indicates possible states of the world

---

Risk," *Journal of Political Economy,* LVI (August 1948), 279–304. See also R. Duncan Luce and Howard Raiffa, *Games and Decisions* (N.Y.: Wiley, 1957), Chapter 2; Ralph O. Swalm, "Utility Theory—Insights into Risk Taking," *Harvard Business Review* XLIV (November-December 1966), 123–136. A comprehensive coverage of the subject is now provided in a book of readings by Alfred N. Page, *Utility Theory* (N.Y.: Wiley, 1968).

TABLE D8–2 PAYOFF TABLE OF MONETARY VALUES

State of the World	Probability of State	OUTCOME IF MAKE	
		Investment 1	Investment 2
S	.60	$1,000	$700
W	.40	500	600
Expected monetary value		$ 800	660

or of the economy. For the relevant time horizon, the decision-maker formulates a judgment of a 60 percent probability of strong demand (for example, the total market for the product increases by 6 percent over the period) and a 40 percent probability of a weak demand (the total market for the product increases by only 2 percent during the period.) If the market increases strongly as indicated by S, investment 1 would yield a net present value of $1,000, while investment 2 would yield $700. If the market increase is only moderate, investment 1 will yield $500 while investment 2 will yield $600. By applying the indicated probabilities of .6 and .4, it is found that the net expected monetary value of investment 1 is $800 and that of investment 2 is $660.

It is not sufficient to stop at this point, however, as the choice between the two risky investments depends upon the shape of the decision-maker's utility function. To illustrate this point, we now substitute utility values (from Table D8–1) for the monetary values, then calculate the results of the payoff table in terms of expected utility, shown in Table D8–3.

TABLE D8–3 PAYOFF TABLE OF EXPECTED UTILITIES

State of the World	Probability of State	UTILITY OF OUTCOME	
		Investment 1	Investment 2
S	.60	1.00	.80
W	.40	.00	.60
Expected Utility		.60	.72

The decision-maker would have selected investment 1 on the basis of expected net discounted monetary values. But to be consistent with his utility preference function, the decision-maker should select investment 2, as it maximizes his expected utility. It should be recognized that these results follow from the shape of the decision-maker's utility preference function. If the shape of the function were different, representing different degrees of risk aversion or risk preference, the calculations of expected utility would reflect these different utility functions.

The expected utility from each of the two investments has a cash equivalent or certainty equivalent indicated by reference, again, to Table D8–1. The certainty equivalent of investment 1 is $600, the dollar payoff corresponding to a utility level of .6; the certainty equivalent of investment 2 is $650, the dollar payoff corresponding to .72 expected utility.

We have not, to this point, indicated how much the initial cash outlays would have to be for each of the two investments except to indicate that the amounts were the same so that the returns could be compared. But, regardless of the cost of each of the investments, we know what their selling prices would be if all investors have the same expectations and utility functions. These are indicated by the certainty equivalent values of the two expected utility outcomes. Thus, the decision-maker would be unwilling to sell investment 1 for less than $600 or investment 2 for less than $650. But the expected monetary value of investment 1 is $800 and of investment 2 is $660, as indicated by Table D8–2.

If other investors have different utility-risk functions, or different probability expectations, they might have different expected utilities for the two investment opportunities. In this case, the market value might be higher or lower than the "reservation price" of the initial investor, in which case he would sell the investment or continue to hold it.

Decision Trees for Utility Analysis

A decision tree can also be used to analyze choices among uncertain outcomes as shown in Appendix C to Chapter 8. For the example we have been discussing, a decision tree analysis is shown in Figure D8–4. The results of the comparison between the two investments will, of course,

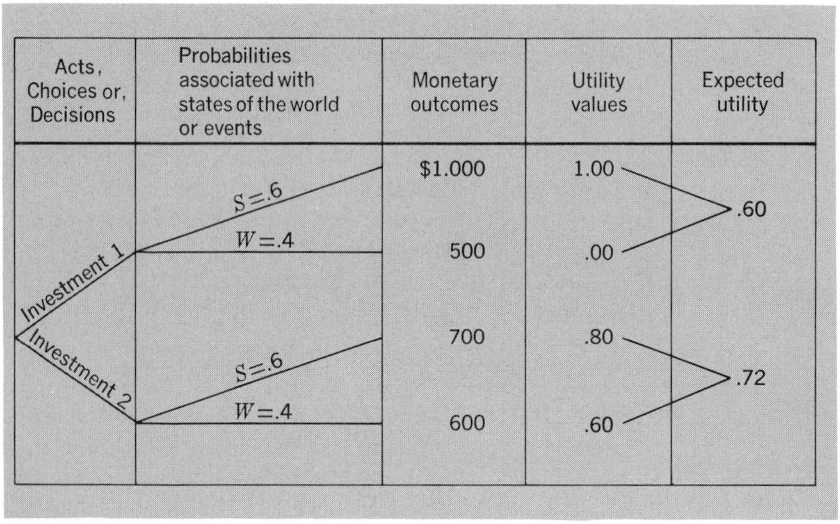

Figure D8–4 Decision Tree Analysis of Uncertain Outcomes

be the same when analyzed through the decision tree structure or the payoff table. The value of the decision tree framework is to permit a clear visualization of the alternatives.

Sensitivity Analysis

Another valuable tool for the appraisal of alternatives is to perform a sensitivity analysis of the uncertain outcomes. The probability judgments expressed about the states of the world or the events that may transpire contain elements of subjectivity. These judgments are, of course, subject to error. Therefore it is useful to analyze the range of possible variation in these judgments of the alternative states of the world *before* the choice between the two alternative investments described in Table D8–3 would be changed.

Let P represent the probability that the demand outlook for the market is strong and $(1 - P)$ the probability that the demand outlook for the market is weak. We seek to determine a value of P that would make the expected utility of the two investments equal. This is expressed in the following equation:

$$1.00(P) + .00(1 - P) = .80(P) + .60(1 - P)$$
$$P = .75$$

If the probability of a strong market rose to .75 and the complementary probability of a weak market fell to .25, the expected utility of investment 1 would rise and the expected utility of investment 2 would fall, making the expected utilities of the two investments equal. If the probability of a strong market rose to exceed .75, then investment 1 would have an expected utility greater than investment 2.

The decision-maker can now review his judgment. Is the probability of a strong market very strong (almost certain, that is, greater than 75 percent)? Is the probability of a strong market just somewhat greater than the probability of a weak market? Note that under the facts of the example set forth, it would take a relatively high probability of a strong market to make investment 1 dominate investment 2. But if the probability of a strong market is from zero to 80 percent, investment 2 dominates investment 1. With this kind of visibility and assessment of the possible states of the world, we are confident that whatever the inherent abilities of the decision-maker, his choices will be better than they otherwise would have been without the help of the tools of systematic analysis presented in Chapter 8 and the associated appendixes.

PROBLEMS

D8–1 Serve-U Vending, Inc., is considering an investment in one of two mutually exclusive proposals: project A, which involves an initial outlay of $1,700, and project B, which has an outlay of $1,500.

The certainty equivalent approach is employed in evaluating risky investments. The current yield on Treasury bills is 5 percent; the company uses this as the riskless rate.

EXPECTED VALUES OF NET CASH FLOWS

YEAR	PROJECT A	PROJECT B
1	900	900
2	1,000	900
3	1,100	1,000

The certainty equivalents the company has determined to be appropriate for risk analysis in this specific instance are:

YEAR	PROJECT A	PROJECT B
1	.8	.9
2	.7	.8
3	.5	.6

a. For each project, calculate the NPV, risk-adjusted by the certainty equivalent method.
b. Which project is riskier? How do you know?
c. Does the firm's management have a linear utility for money schedule? How do you know?
d. If the company was to use the risk-adjusted discount rate method, which project would be analyzed with the *higher* rate? How do you know?
e. Show how to find a set of risk-adjusted discount rates which, if used, would give an identical solution to this problem, as was obtained by the certainty equivalent method.

D8–2 James Walters seeks to maximize his utility on one of two mutually exclusive alternatives. Investment A is a piece of real estate. Investment B is in a joint venture with an established firm.

Walters estimates that the probabilities of the net cash flow will be distributed as follows:

INVESTMENT A		INVESTMENT B	
.25	−200	.10	−50
.20	−100	.20	100
.10	300	.40	300
.20	600	.20	500
.25	900	.10	700

a. Calculate the mean and the coefficient of variation. Using this approach, which investment should be selected?
b. As a risk averter, Walters has the following diminishing marginal utility for money. What investment should he choose to maximize expected utility?

DOLLAR PAYOFF	UTILITY
−400	−90
−350	−55
−200	−28
−100	−13
−50	−5
0	0
100	9
300	26
400	29
500	31
600	33
700	34
900	35

D8–3 Assume the same facts as in problem D8–2 except that the probabilities of the expected net cash flow are distributed as follows:

INVESTMENT A		INVESTMENT B	
.10	−50	.10	−50
.20	100	.20	100
.40	400	.40	300
.20	500	.20	500
.10	700	.10	700

Answer the same questions as those asked in problem D8–2.

PART FOUR

VALUATION AND FINANCIAL STRUCTURE

9

Financial Structure and the Use of Leverage

Once the financial manager has determined his firm's approximate financial requirements, his next task is to see to it that these funds are on hand.[1] Assuming that the company has a history of sound management and is not trying to expand too rapidly, there should be no problem in raising the necessary capital. However, capital comes in many forms—long- and short-term debt, secured and unsecured debt, preferred stock, common stock, retained earnings, and such hybrid instruments as convertibles and long-term leases. What are the character-

[1] The financial manager cannot, of course, detemine his financial requirements *precisely* until he knows the firm's cost of capital schedule. In the two preceding chapters we *assumed* that the cost of capital was given and examined the investment opportunities schedule. Now we shall assume the investment schedule to be given and examine the cost of capital schedule. In Chapter 12, these two schedules will be combined.

istics of these different securities? Which particular form is the best one to use in a given situation? Or should a package consisting of some of each kind be tried? These are the questions to which we now turn. Our first task, and the one considered in this chapter, is to examine the firm's financial structure and the effects of using financial leverage.

BASIC DEFINITIONS

To avoid ambiguity in the use of key concepts, the meanings of frequently used expressions are given here. *Financial structure* refers to the right-hand side of the balance sheet—the financing of the resources acquired by the firm. *Capital structure* is the permanent financing of the firm, represented by long-term debt, preferred stock, and *net worth*. Net worth is the *common* stockholders' equity and includes common stock, capital surplus, earned surplus (retained earnings), and net worth reserves.[2]

Our key concept for this chapter is *financial leverage*, or the *leverage factor*, defined as the ratio of total debt to total assets. For example, a firm having assets of $100 million and a total debt of $50 million would have a leverage factor of 50 percent. Some writers use only long-term debt in the numerator of the ratio, but this is not a generally accurate measure of financial leverage. While long-term debt might be more or less appropriate in an industry such as electric utilities, where little short-term debt is employed, it would be clearly inappropriate in other industries, such as aerospace, where firms rely on current debt as an important source of financing. Further, the smaller firms in most industries tend to make extensive use of short-term liabilities, particularly trade accounts payable. Therefore, to ignore current debt in measuring the risk incurred by using financial leverage would be to ignore the major (sometimes the only) form of debt employed.

Long & short-term debt

Finally, we should distinguish at the outset between *business risk*

[2] Note that preferred stock is excluded from net worth here. Preferred stock is a hybrid security with some of the characteristics of common stock and some of the characteristics of bonds. When viewed from the point of view of the firm's creditors, preferred is very much like common. From the viewpoint of common stockholders, preferred shares are similar to debt. Consequently, preferred stock can be classified either as a part of net worth or as debt, depending on the purpose of the analysis. If we look at leverage from the creditor's point of view, preferred is included with equity. If we look at leverage from the position of the common stockholder, it is excluded from net worth. This seemingly ambiguous point is discussed in more detail in Chapter 19.

and *financial risk*. By business risk we mean the inherent uncertainty, or variability of expected returns, on the firm's "portfolio" of assets. By financial risk we mean the additional riskiness to the common stock that is induced by the use of financial leverage.

THEORY OF FINANCIAL LEVERAGE

Perhaps the best way to understand the proper use of financial leverage is to analyze its impact on profitability under varying conditions. Suppose there are three firms in a particular industry, and these firms are identical except for their financial policies. Firm A has used no debt and consequently has a leverage factor of zero; firm B, financed half by debt and half by equity, has a leverage factor of 50 percent; firm C has a leverage factor of 75 percent. Their balance sheets are shown below.

FIRM A

		Total debt	$ 0
		Net worth	200
Total assets	$200	Total claims	$200

FIRM B

		Total debt (6%)	$100
		Net worth	100
Total assets	$200	Total claims	$200

FIRM C

		Total debt (6%)	$150
		Net worth	50
Total assets	$200	Total claims	200

How do these different financial patterns affect stockholder returns? As can be seen from Table 9–1, the answer depends upon the state of the industry's economy. When the economy is depressed, sales and profit margins are low; the firms earn only 2 percent on assets. When

TABLE 9–1 STOCKHOLDER RETURNS UNDER VARIOUS LEVERAGE AND ECONOMIC CONDITIONS

	ECONOMIC CONDITIONS					
	Very Poor	Poor	Indiffer-ence	Nor-mal	Good	Very Good
Rate of return on total assets before interest	2%	5%	6%	8%	11%	14%
Dollar returns on total assets before interest	$4	$10	$12	$16	$22	$28
	Firm A: Leverage Factor 0%					
Earnings in dollars	$4	$10	$12	$16	$22	$28
Less: Interest expense	0	0	0	0	0	0
Gross income	4	10	12	16	22	28
Taxes (50%)*	2	5	6	8	11	14
Available to common stock	2	5	6	8	11	14
Percent return on common stock	1%	2.5%	3%	4%	5.5%	7%
	Firm B: Leverage Factor 50%					
Earnings in dollars	$4	$10	$12	$16	$22	$28
Less: Interest expense	6	6	6	6	6	6
Gross income	(2)	4	6	10	16	22
Taxes (50%)*	(1)	2	3	5	8	11
Available to common stock	(1)	2	3	5	8	11
Percent return on common stock	−1%	2%	3%	5%	8%	11%
	Firm C: Leverage Factor 75%					
Earnings in dollars	$4	$10	$12	$16	$22	$28
Less: Interest expense	9	9	9	9	9	9
Gross income	(5)	1	3	7	13	19
Taxes (50%)*	(2.5)	.5	1.5	3.5	6.5	9.5
Available to common stock	(2.5)	.5	1.5	3.5	6.5	9.5
Percent return on common stock	−5%	1%	3%	7%	13%	19%

* The tax calculation assumes that losses are carried back and result in tax credits.

conditions become somewhat better, the return on assets is 5 percent. Under normal conditions, the returns rise to 8 percent, while in a moderate boom the figure goes to 11 percent. Finally, under extremely favorable circumstances, the companies have a 14 percent return on assets. These percentages, multiplied by the $200 of assets, give the earnings before interest and taxes for the three companies under the various states of the economy.

Table 9–1 demonstrates how the use of financial leverage magnifies the impact on the stockholders of changes in the rate of return on assets. When economic conditions go from normal to good, for example, returns on assets go up 37.5 percent. Firm A uses no leverage, gets no magnification, and consequently experiences the same 37.5 percent jump in the rate of return to stockholders. Firm B, on the other hand, enjoys a 60 percent increase in stockholder returns as a result of the 37.5 percent rise in returns on assets. Firm C, which uses still more leverage, has an 86 percent increase. Just the reverse holds in economic downturns, of course: the 37.5 percent drop in returns on assets when the economy goes from normal to poor results in return-on-net-worth declines of 37.5 percent, 60 percent, and 86 percent for firms A, B, and C, respectively.

Using the same illustrative numbers, Figure 9–1 gives a graphic presentation of the interaction between the rates of return on assets and net worth, given the three different leverage factors. The interesting point to note here is the intersection of the three lines at the point where assets are returning 6 percent, the interest cost of debt. At this point,

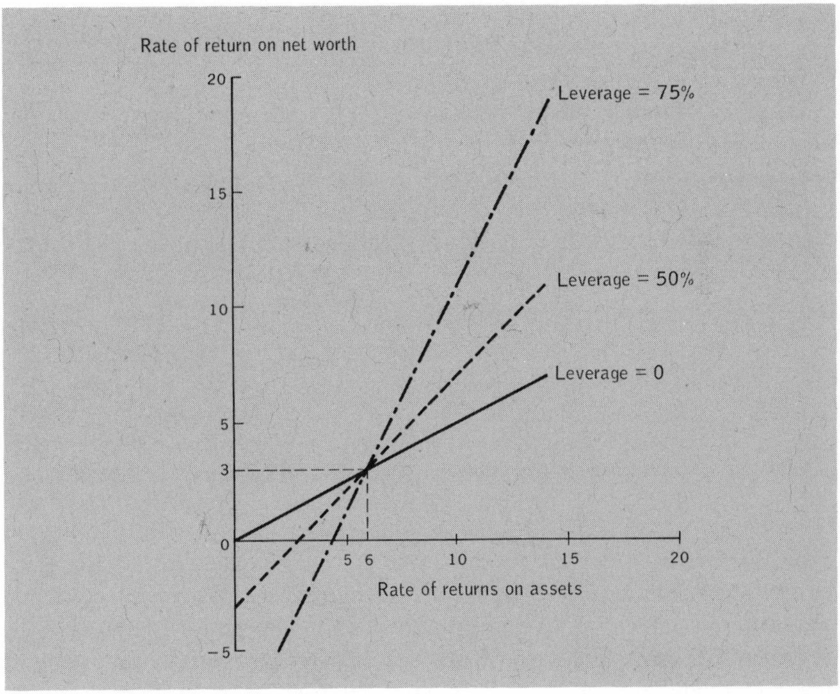

Figure 9–1 Relation between Rates of Return on Assets and Rates of Return on Net Worth under Different Leverage Conditions

the return on net worth is 3 percent. The assumed 50 percent tax rate reduces the 6 percent return on total assets to a return of 3 percent on net worth, regardless of the degree of leverage. When returns on assets are higher, leverage improves stockholder returns and is said to be *favorable;* when assets earn less than 6 percent, returns to stockholders are reduced and the leverage is defined as *unfavorable. In general, whenever the return on assets exceeds the cost of debt, leverage is favorable, and the higher the leverage factor the higher the rate of return on common equity.*

EFFECTS OF FINANCIAL LEVERAGE

To show that the results of alternative financial decisions are useful in judging the relative merits and demerits of various plans, a specific example is given. This example illustrates how future earnings prospects affect financing decisions.

The Universal Machine Company, whose latest balance sheet is shown in Table 9–2, manufactures equipment used by steel producers. As is

TABLE 9–2 UNIVERSAL MACHINE COMPANY
BALANCE SHEET*
December 31, 1968

Cash	$ 200,000	Accounts payable	$1,200,000
Receivables (net)	1,100,000	Other current liabilities	800,000
Inventories	1,600,000	Total liabilities	$2,000,000
Plant (net)	2,500,000	Common stock ($10 par)	2,500,000
Equipment (net)	2,800,000	Surplus	3,700,000
Total assets	$8,200,000	Total claims on assets	$8,200,000

* Figures are rounded for convenience.

typically the case for the producers of durable capital assets, the company's sales fluctuate widely, far more than does the over-all economy. For example, during 9 of the last 25 years, sales have been below the break-even point, so losses have been relatively frequent. In the past few years, however, machinery demand has been heavy and has actually been rising; if Universal is to continue sharing in this expansion, it will have to increase capacity. For this increase, $3 million is required.

James Walter, the financial vice-president, learns that he can net $3 million by selling bonds with a 5 percent coupon. Alternatively, he can raise the money by selling 75,000 shares of common stock.

During the past five years, Universal's sales have fluctuated between $500,000 and $4,000,000; at the higher volume, the firm is operating at full capacity and has to turn down orders. With the additional plant expansion, sales capacity will increase to $6 million. Fixed costs, after the planned expansion, will be $500,000 a year, and variable costs (excluding interest on the debt) will be 40 percent of sales.

Although Walter's recommendation will be given much weight, the final decision for the method of financing rests with the company's board of directors. Procedurally, the financial vice-president will analyze the situation, evaluate all reasonable alternatives, come to a conclusion, and then present the alternatives with his recommendations to the board. For his own analysis, as well as for presentation to the board, Walter prepares the materials shown in Table 9–3.

In the top third of the table, earnings before interest and taxes are calculated for different levels of sales ranging from $0 to $6 million. The firm suffers an operating loss up to a little under $1 million of sales, but beyond that point it shows a rapid rise in gross profit.

The middle third of the table shows the financial results that will occur with bond financing at the various sales levels. First, the $150,000 annual interest charges are deducted from the earnings before interest and taxes calculated above. Next, taxes are taken out. Notice that if the sales level is so low that losses are incurred, the firm receives a tax credit. Finally, net profits after taxes are divided by the 250,000 shares outstanding to obtain earnings per share of common stock.[3]

In the bottom third of the table, the financial results that will occur with stock financing are calculated. No interest payments are involved, so the earnings-before-tax figure is the same as the one computed at the top of the table. Net profit after taxes is divided by 325,000 shares—the original 250,000 plus the new 75,000—to find earnings per share.

Walter next plots the earnings for each share under the two methods of financing, as shown in Figure 9–2. If sales were depressed to zero, the debt financing line would cut the *Y* axis at —$1.30, below the —$0.78 intercept of the common stock financing line. The debt line has a steeper slope and rises faster, however, showing that earnings per share will go up faster with increases in sales if debt is used. The two lines cross at sales of about $2 million. Below that volume of sales the firm would be better off issuing common stock; above that level, debt financing would produce higher earnings per share.

[3] The shares outstanding can be calculated by dividing the $2,500,000 common stock figure given on the balance sheet by the $10 par value.

TABLE 9–3 UNIVERSAL MACHINE COMPANY
PROFIT CALCULATIONS AT VARIOUS SALES LEVELS

Sales	$ 0	$ 500,000	$1,000,000	$2,000,000	$4,000,000	$6,000,000
Fixed costs	$ 500,000	$ 500,000	$ 500,000	$ 500,000	$ 500,000	$ 500,000
Variable costs (40% of sales)	–0–	200,000	400,000	800,000	1,600,000	2,400,000
Total costs (except interest)	$ 500,000	$ 700,000	$ 900,000	$1,300,000	$2,100,000	$2,900,000
Earnings before interest and taxes	$(500,000)	$(200,000)	$ 100,000	$ 700,000	$1,900,000	$3,100,000
	FINANCING WITH BONDS					
Less: Interest (5% × $3,000,000)	$ 150,000	$ 150,000	$ 150,000	$ 150,000	$ 150,000	$ 150,000
Earnings before taxes	$(650,000)	$(350,000)	$ (50,000)	$ 550,000	$1,750,000	$2,950,000
Less: Income taxes (50%)*	(325,000)	(175,000)	$ (25,000)	275,000	875,000	1,475,000
Net profit after taxes	$(325,000)	$(175,000)	$ (25,000)	$ 275,000	$ 875,000	$1,475,000
Earnings per share on 250,000 shares of common	$–1.30	$–0.70	$–0.10	$1.10	$3.50	$5.90
	FINANCING WITH STOCK					
Earnings before taxes†	$(500,000)	$(200,000)	$ 100,000	$ 700,000	$1,900,000	$3,100,000
Less: Income taxes (50%)*	$(250,000)	(100,000)	50,000	350,000	950,000	1,550,000
Net profit after taxes	$(250,000)	$(100,000)	$ 50,000	$ 350,000	$ 950,000	$1,550,000
Earnings per share on 325,000 shares of common	$–0.77	$–0.31	$+0.15	$1.08	$2.92	$4.77

* Assumes tax credit on losses.
† Earnings before tax is the same as earnings before interest and tax because interest is zero with stock financing.

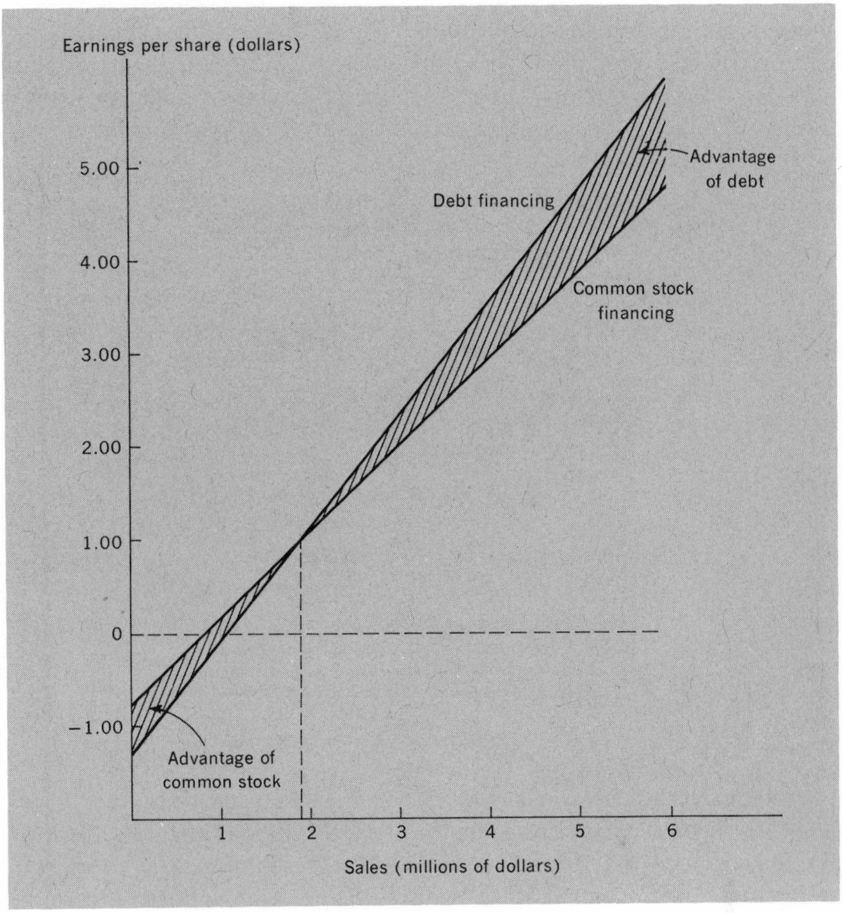

Figure 9–2 Earnings per Share for Stock and Debt Financing

If Walter and his board of directors *knew for sure* that sales would never again fall below $2 million, bonds would be the preferred method of financing the asset increase. But they cannot know this for certain; in fact, they probably have good reason to expect future business cycles to drive sales down to, and even below, this critical level. They know that during the past five years sales have been as low as $500,000. If sales fall to this level again, the company would not be earning enough to cover its interest charges. Such a situation, if it continues for several years, could jeopardize the very existence of the firm. However, if sales continue to expand, there would be higher earnings per share from using bonds; no officer or director would want to forgo these substantial advantages.

When industry standards for leverage are applied, we see that the firm's debt ratio, after financing, will be 45 percent as compared to a norm for manufacturing firms of only 37 percent (see Table 9–4). Since Universal Machine is a capital goods producer and is thus subject to wider fluctuations than the average manufacturer, it might be argued that a 45 percent debt ratio is too high for Universal Machine.

TABLE 9–4 VARIATION IN FINANCIAL LEVERAGE IN INDUSTRY GROUPS, 1963–1964

NAME OF INDUSTRY	DEBT TO TOTAL ASSETS (IN PERCENTAGES)
Service	65
Public utilities	61
Wholesale trade	54
Agriculture	54
Retail trade	51
Mining	38
Manufacturing	37

SOURCE: United States Treasury Department, Internal Revenue Service, *Statistics of Income, U.S. Business Tax Returns, 1963* (Washington, D.C.: U.S. Government Printing Office, 1967).

Walter's recommendations and the decision of each director will depend (1) upon each person's appraisal of the future and (2) upon his psychological attitude toward risk. The pessimists, or risk averters, will prefer to employ common stock, while the optimists, or those less sensitive to risk, will favor bonds. This example, which is typical of many real-world situations, suggests that the major disagreements over the choice of forms of financing are likely to reflect uncertainty about the future levels of the firm's sales. Such uncertainty, in turn, reflects the characteristics of the firm's environment—general business conditions, industry trends, and quality and aggressiveness of management.[4]

[4] Investors' appraisal of uncertainty is embodied in the capitalization rate applied to earnings to determine the value of the firm. Maximizing expected earnings will not be the best policy for stockholders if, by so doing, risk is increased to the point where the rising risk-adjusted discount rate more than off-sets the higher expected earnings. This point is discussed in more detail in the next three chapters.

It would, of course, be possible to appraise financial risk through the same types of probability analysis discussed in Chapter 8 and its appendices. This is not generally done in practical decision making, and we see no pedagogic advantages in formalizing leverage risk analysis. Therefore, we have elected not to take a formal subjective probability approach to leverage decisions in this book.

ARIATIONS IN FINANCIAL TRUCTURE

As might be expected, wide variations in the use of financial leverage may be observed among industries and among the individual firms in each industry. Illustrative of these differences is the range of ratios of total debt to total assets, shown in Table 9–4, for certain broad groups of industries. Service industries use the most leverage, reflecting (1) that services include certain financial institutions that typically have high liabilities and (2) that there are many smaller firms in the service industries, and small firms as a group are heavy users of debt. Public utility use of debt stems from a heavy fixed asset investment, coupled with extremely stable sales. Mining and manufacturing firms use relatively little debt because of their exposure to fluctuating sales.

Within the broad category "manufacturing," wide variations are observed for individual industries. Table 9–5 presents an array of total-

TABLE 9–5 TOTAL-DEBT-TO-ASSETS RATIOS FOR SELECTED MANUFACTURING INDUSTRIES (1965)

MANUFACTURING INDUSTRIES	PERCENT
Fabrics: Cotton, silk, wool, synthetic	27
Household furniture except upholstered	32
Automotive parts and accessories	35
Flour and other grain mill products	35
Iron and steel forgings	35
Iron and steel foundries	39
Drugs and medicines	40
Machine tools and metalworking equipment	40
Canned and dried fruits and vegetables	41
Industrial chemicals	42
Electronic components and accessories	42
Precision instruments	44
Books	45
Bread and other bakery products	46
Ready mixed concrete	47
Sporting and athletic goods	48
Meat packing	49
Dairy products	53
Veneer and plywood	55
Distilled liquor, wines, and liqueurs	59

SOURCE: *Annual Statement Studies* (Philadelphia: Robert Morris Association, 1966).

debt-to-total-assets ratios for selected manufacturing industries. The lowest ratios are found among textile companies, in which competitive pressures continue to be great. Low debt ratios are also found among the durable goods industries. The highest debt ratios are found in consumer nondurable goods, where demand is relatively insensitive to fluctuations and general business activity.

Even within a given industry there are wide variations in the use of financial leverage, as illustrated for the electric utility industry in Table 9–6. These variations reflect a number of different considerations,

TABLE 9–6 DEBT-TO-TOTAL-ASSETS RATIO (SELECTED ELECTRIC UTILITY COMPANIES, 1966)

Montana Power	46
Consolidated Edison of New York	55
Central Illinois Public Service	59
Detroit Edison	60
Tampa Electric	65
Missouri Public Service	66

SOURCE: *Moody's Public Utility Manual*, 1967.

including the volatility of business in the companies' operating areas, the extent to which they use preferred stock, and their managements' willingness to assume risk. Montana Power, for example, sells a large proportion of its electricity to copper producers, whose volume of business, hence demand for power, is quite cyclical. This largely explains its low debt ratio. Missouri Public Service, by contrast, has a stable demand pattern, which permits its relatively high leverage factor.

FACTORS INFLUENCING FINANCIAL STRUCTURE

Thus far the discussion has touched on the factors that are generally considered when a firm formulates basic policies relating to its financial structure. The more important of these capital structure determinants are now listed and briefly discussed.

1. Growth rate of future sales
2. Stability of future sales
3. Competitive structure of the industry
4. Asset structure of the industry
5. Control position and attitudes toward risk of owners and management
6. Lender attitudes toward firm and industry

Growth Rate of Sales

The future growth rate of sales is a measure of the extent to which the earnings per share of a firm are likely to be magnified by leverage. If sales and earnings grow at an 8-to-10 percent rate a year, for example, financing by debt with limited fixed charges should magnify the returns to owners of the stock.[5] This can be seen from Figure 9–2 above.

However, the common stock of a firm whose sales and earnings are growing at a favorable rate commands a high price; thus, it sometimes appears that equity financing is desirable. The firm must weigh the benefits of using leverage against the opportunity of broadening its equity base when it chooses between future financing alternatives. Such firms may be expected to have a moderate-to-high rate of debt financing. For example, at the end of 1960, International Business Machines had a debt ratio of 37 percent. Litton Industries, another growth company, had a debt ratio of 60 percent.[6]

Sales Stability

Sales stability and debt ratios are directly related. With greater stability in sales and earnings, a firm can incur the fixed charges of debt with less risk than it can when its sales and earnings are subject to periodic declines; in the latter instance it will have difficulty in meeting its obligations. The stability of the utility industry, combined with relatively favorable growth prospects, has resulted in high leverage ratios in that industry.

[5] Such a growth rate is also often associated with a high profit rate.

[6] There is, however, another factor at work in the case of profitable, growing firms. The fact that they are profitable means that relatively large amounts of funds are being generated, and these are equity funds that can be used to finance further expansion. But rapidly growing companies have needs for asset expansion that typically exceed the retained earnings available from high profit rates. Others have emphasized the same point; for example, Gordon Donaldson, *Corporate Debt Capacity* (Boston: Harvard University, 1961). In general, it appears that growing firms are the ones that employ debt to the greatest extent.

Entry Conditions

Debt servicing ability is dependent upon the profitability as well as the volume of sales. Hence, the stability of profit margins is as important as the stability of sales. The ease with which new firms may enter the industry and the ability of competing firms to expand capacity will influence profit margins. A growth industry promises higher profit margins, but such margins are likely to narrow if the industry is one in which the number of firms can be easily increased through additional entry. For example, pleasure-boat manufacturing and neighborhood bowling alleys were highly profitable industries in the later 1950s, and it was relatively easy for new firms to enter these industries and go into competition with the older firms. As these industries matured during the early 1960s, the capacity of the old and the new firms grew at an increased rate. As a consequence, profit margins declined.

Other firms in other industries are better able to resist competitive pressures. For example, to duplicate the unique technical, service, and distribution facilities of the International Business Machines Corporation would be very difficult, a fact suggesting that profit margins for this firm are less subject to erosion.

Asset Structure

Asset structure influences the sources of financing in several ways. Firms with long-lived fixed assets, especially when demand for their output is relatively assured—for example, utilities—use long-term mortgage debt extensively. Firms whose assets are mostly receivables and inventory whose value is dependent on the continued profitability of the individual firm—for example, those in wholesale and retail trade—rely less on long-term debt financing and more on short term.

Management Attitudes

The management attitudes that most directly influence the choice of financing are those concerning (1) control of the enterprise and (2) risk. Large corporations whose stock is widely owned may choose additional sales of common stock because they will have little influence on the control of the company. Also, because management represents a stewardship for the owners, it is often less willing to take the risk of heavy fixed charges.[7]

[7] It would be inappropriate to delve too far into motivational theory in an introductory finance textbook, but it is interesting to note that the managers of many larger, publicly owned corporations have a relatively small ownership position and derive most of their income from salaries. Some writers assert that

In contrast, the owners of small firms may prefer to avoid issuing common stock in order to be assured of continued control. Because they generally have confidence in the prospects of their companies and because they can see the large potential gains to themselves resulting from leverage, managers of such firms are often willing to incur high debt ratios.

The converse can, of course, also hold—the owner-manager of a small firm may be *more* conservative than the manager of a large company. If the net worth of the small firm is, say, $1 million, and if it all belongs to the owner-manager, he may well decide that he is already pretty well off and elect not to risk using leverage in an effort to become still more wealthy. In the terms of Appendix D to Chapter 8, he may have a diminishing marginal utility of money.

Lender Attitudes

Regardless of managements' analysis of the proper leverage factors for their firms, there is no question but that lenders' attitudes are frequently an important—sometimes the most important—determinant of financial structures. In the majority of cases, the corporation discusses its capital structure with lenders and gives much weight to their advice. But when management is so confident of the future that it seeks to use leverage beyond norms for the industry, lenders may be unwilling to accept such debt increases. They will emphasize that excessive debt reduces the credit standing of the borrower and the credit rating of the securities previously issued. The lenders' point of view has been expressed by a borrower, a financial vice-president, who stated that his policy is "to determine how much debt we can carry and still maintain an AA bond rating, then use that amount less a small margin for safety."[8]

---

in such cases managements do not strive for profits, especially if this effort involves using leverage with its inherent risk. Presumably, these managers feel that the risks of leverage for them, the ones who actually decide to use debt or equity, outweigh the potential gains from successful leverage. If sales are low, there is a chance of failure and the loss of their jobs, whereas if sales and profits are high, it is the stockholders, not management, who receive the benefits. Another way of looking at the situation is to say that most stockholders are more diversified than most managers—if the firm fails, a stockholder only loses that percentage of his net worth invested in the firm, but the manager loses 100 percent of his job. While there is undoubtedly some merit to this argument, it should be pointed out that companies are increasingly using profit-based compensation schemes—bonus systems and stock-option plans—to motivate management to seek profitability, and low leverage companies are subject to takeover bids. (See Chapter 21.)

[8] Bond ratings, which are discussed in detail in Chapter 19, are basically indices of the risk that lenders incur when buying particular bonds. A rating of AAA is the best, denoting the lowest risk, and AA is just below it.

GUIDELINES FOR FINANCIAL STRUCTURES

On the basis of the foregoing considerations, broad guidelines or reference levels for the financial structures of wide industrial segments are presented in Table 9–7. In examining these figures, keep in mind all that has been said about the importance of carefully appraising the individual situation and the dangers of relying on industry norms. The guidelines do, however, have a rational basis, and it would be wise to evaluate critically the reasons behind any given company's decision to step outside the reference boundaries.

Manufacturing Industries

Detailed studies of financial ratios among manufacturing firms reveal wide variations among industries and, to a lesser degree, among firms in the same industry. Within a given industry, firms tend to cluster about a certain financial structure, as the major factors influencing financial structure tend to operate in the same direction.

Table 9–7 suggests that the percentage of the financial structure in current liabilities should be smallest for utilities, next for manufacturing, and highest for firms engaged in wholesale and retail trade. As a group, manufacturing firms tend to operate with relatively small percentages

TABLE 9–7 REFERENCE LEVELS FOR FINANCIAL STRUCTURES

	PERCENTAGE OF TOTAL ASSETS					
	Current Liabilities	Long-term Debt	Preferred Stock	Common Equity or Net Worth	Current Ratio	Times Interest Earned
Large, established firms						
Manufacturing	20–25%	15–20%	0–4%	55–65%	2×	8×
Utilities	5–10	45–50	10–15	30–35	1	4
Trade	30–35	16–18	0–2	50–55	2.5	7
Small, rapidly growing, profitable firms						
Manufacturing	40–45%	0–5%	0–10%	40–60%	1×	9×
Trade	50–60	0–5	0–5	30–40	1.5	10

of long-term debt in their financial structures. They incur long-term debt during periods of rapid expansion and follow the policy of paying off debt as rapidly as permitted by earnings retention or flotation of new shares of common stock. Preferred stock is used mainly as a substitute for debt where firms seek to gain the benefits of trading on the equity but are unwilling to bear the risks of fixed charges. The reference ranges suggested for manufacturing indicate that total-debt-to-total-assets ratios should approximate 40 percent.

Utility Industries

Current debt is a much smaller percentage of total assets for utilities than it is for any other industry. Cash is a small portion of total assets because of the synchronization of inflows and outflows of cash. The average collection period is short and receivables are low, because terms of sales are on presentation of invoice, and service may be cut off if bills are not paid. By the nature of the business, inventories are small. Because of heavy fixed plant and stability of earnings, long-term debt is large. Preferred stock is used to a greater extent by utilities than by any other category of firms. The tax disadvantage of preferred stock is somewhat mitigated, because taxes are considered to be a cost of service, and utility rates (charges made for service) are adjusted upward to offset additional taxes incurred if preferred stock is substituted for debt.

For utilities, the ratio of preferred stock and debt to total assets runs about 60 to 65 percent. Greater clustering occurs in debt ratios of utility companies than of other industrial categories, although even here, as was seen in Table 9–6, variations can occur. It is interesting to speculate on what the impact of the rapid substitution of nuclear energy plants for plants operated on fossil fuel, such as coal, will be over the next 10 to 15 or 20 years. The long life of the use of the specific durable assets which led to high debt ratios for utilities in past years may no longer be justified. With the rapid increase in the pace of technological change, particularly in the telephone and communications business, appropriate debt ratios may move downward.

Wholesale and Retail Trade

Firms engaged in wholesale and retail trade utilize current debt to the highest degree, but their use of long-term debt and preferred stock is smallest. Net worth percentages are moderately smaller for wholesale and retail trade than for manufacturing firms, with the ratio of debt to total assets rising to between 46 and 54 percent.

Current Ratio

The levels of current ratios reflect the characteristic asset structures in the three categories of industrial activity. The traditional 2-to-1 rule-of-thumb ratio fits most categories in the industrial field; because of relatively small amounts of current assets, the 1-to-1 ratio for utilities is appropriate. Since trade firms have heavier inventories and receivables, a ratio of 2.5 or 3 to 1 is desirable here.

Times Interest Earned

Times interest earned is one of the tests widely applied by investors. The coverage suggested here reflects characteristic recommendations found in works on investments and security analysis.[9] Because these are the coverages expected by investors, the determination of the appropriate levels must reflect investor preferences as well as financial structure considerations. The logic involved here is to protect creditors by having expected earnings adequately cover interest requirements. The earnings level to be used should reflect the best judgment of future earnings levels, taking into account past experience and prospective changes in the economic environment that may affect earnings both in the industry and in the company under study, with allowance for possible declines.

Modification of Standards for Small Firms

In formulating broad reference guides for evaluating the financial structures of business firms, a number of factors in addition to the industry of the firm are important. Among these are the age, size, growth rate, and profitability of the firm. To reflect these factors and yet avoid unduly proliferating the categories, the second section of Table 9–7 indicates suitable modifications in the basic reference ranges for small, rapidly growing, profitable firms. A new, small firm starts from such a limited base that success, measured by profitability, is likely to be accompanied by rapid growth. Since they are likely to occur together, the influence of age, size, growth rate, and profitability may be conveniently grouped.

The small, successful firm is likely to employ leverage to a much greater degree than its older, larger counterpart. Current ratios will be lower, and the firm may actually be slow in meeting its bills. Because of this, the required coverage of fixed charges should be somewhat greater

[9] See, for example, B. Graham, D. L. Dodd, and S. Cottle, *Security Analysis* (New York: McGraw-Hill, 1961), pp. 343–352.

for protection to creditors. Debt-to-total-assets ratios may run as high as 60 percent for manufacturing firms and 70 to 75 percent for trade firms. As the firm grows and begins to present a record of success, its access to the equity markets is likely to improve. It will then probably have a common stock flotation that will help bring its financial structure into better balance.

The guidelines presented to this point have been very broad. They have been developed for the purpose of providing a framework for critical evaluation of the financial structures of firms. Finer distinctions must be made, however, and the following section describes how financial structures can be developed to reflect the characteristics of individual industries.

USE OF FINANCIAL RATIO COMPOSITES IN DETERMINING THE FINANCIAL PLAN

Chapter 3 described how financial data summarized by industry averages can be used to evaluate the financial ratios for individual firms in these industries. Such industry composites can also be used to provide a basis for formulating the financial plan of an individual firm. Financial structures so developed conform to general industry practice. While simply conforming to the structure of other firms in a particular line of business is not necessarily desirable, such a standard can be a useful starting point. This is especially true if the capital structure of a new enterprise is being planned; here the use of such guidelines can be helpful in suggesting what the financial requirements are likely to be.[10]

Developing a *pro forma* balance sheet,[11] based on the average of financial ratios of firms in a given line of business, is the first step. To use the method of financial ratio composites to construct the *pro forma* financial plan, it is necessary to know only two things: (1) the industry of the firm and (2) its size, measured by estimated annual sales. An illustration of the technique is given for an industrial machinery firm with estimated annual sales of $120,000. The Dun & Bradstreet median

[10] Provisions must also be made for organization expenses and various start-up costs, such as losses incurred. The losses incurred may result from relatively heavy fixed costs that will cause losses until the sales volume grows to the point where initial fixed capacity is effectively utilized.

[11] A *pro forma* financial statement is one that is *projected*. It is an estimate of how a future statement will appear.

financial ratio composites for that industry for the most recent year are:

Sales to net worth	3 times
Current debt to net worth	40%
Total debt to net worth	60%
Current ratio	3 times
Net sales to inventory	4 times
Average collection period	42 days
Fixed assets to net worth	40%

On the basis of this information, the following *pro forma* balance sheet can be constructed:

PRO FORMA BALANCE SHEET

Cash	$ 4,000		Current debt	$16,000
Accounts receivable	14,000		Long-term debt	8,000
Inventory	30,000		Total debt	24,000
Current assets		$48,000	Net worth	40,000
Fixed assets		16,000		
			Total liab.	
Total assets		$64,000	and net worth	$64,000

Calculations:

1. Net worth = sales ÷ net worth turnover

$$\frac{\$120{,}000}{3} = \$40{,}000$$

2. Total debt = 60% of net worth

$$\$40{,}000 \times 60\% = \$24{,}000$$

3. Current debt = 40% of net worth

$$\$40{,}000 \times 40\% = \$16{,}000$$

4. Long-term debt = total debt — current debt

$$\$24{,}000 - \$16{,}000 = \$8{,}000$$

5. Total claims on assets = net worth + total debt

$$\$40{,}000 + \$24{,}000 = \$64{,}000$$

6. Current assets = current debt × current ratio

$$\$16{,}000 \times 3 = \$48{,}000$$

7. Inventory = sales ÷ inventory turnover

$$\frac{\$120{,}000}{4} = \$30{,}000$$

8. Accounts receivable = average collection period × sales per day

$$\frac{\$120{,}000}{360} \times \frac{42}{1} = \$14{,}000$$

9. Cash = current assets — (receivables + inventory)

$$\$48{,}000 - (\$14{,}000 + \$30{,}000) = \$4{,}000$$

10. Fixed assets = net worth × 40%

$$\$40{,}000 \times 40\% = \$16{,}000$$

11. Total assets = current assets + fixed assets

$$\$48{,}000 + \$16{,}000 = \$64{,}000$$

Profitability and income statement relations can also be developed by reference to industry data, with the data being based on any of the wide variety of sources of financial ratio compilations described in Chapter 3. Alternatively, a financial manager may develop his own guidelines by constructing averages based on a selected number of firms most similar (in his judgment) to his own business—for example, firms of comparable age and size operating in his same geographic market area.

The use of financial ratio composites as a guideline to financial structures may be questioned on theoretical grounds. Because these composites are computed averages, some firms must be above the average and some below. But it is of interest to know on which side of the average an individual firm stands. Further, a strong practical consideration reinforces the value of such comparisons—bank lending officers and other credit and financial analysts place heavy reliance on such comparisons between individual firms and industry norms. Thus the financial structure of the firm will, in practice, be checked against industry data.

Of course, neither financial managers nor lenders need be held in a strait jacket by an industry average. The average is primarily a standard for reference, and many factors may cause an individual firm to depart from the industry pattern. For example, it has already been noted that age, size, growth rate, control position of owners, and management attitudes toward risk may all strongly influence the financial policies of a firm.

Financial structures suggested by industry practices actually represent only a starting point. Sound reasons may exist to cause an individual firm's financial structure to depart from the reference levels provided by industry data. But it is important that the financial manager understand the reasons for these differences and be able to explain them effectively to potential creditors. Sometimes the differences may represent elements of strength or the almost unavoidable growing pains of a rapidly developing company. However, departures from industry norms may also signal weaknesses requiring correction.

SUMMARY

Financial leverage, which means using debt to boost rates of return on net worth over the returns available on assets, is the primary topic covered in this chapter. Whenever the return on assets exceeds the cost of debt, leverage is favorable and the return on equity is raised by using it. However, leverage is a two-edged sword, and if the returns on assets are less than the cost of debt, then leverage reduces the returns on equity. This reduction is greater the more leverage a firm employs. As a net result, leverage may be used to boost stockholder returns, but using it is done at the risk of increasing losses if the firm's economic fortunes decline.

Financial structure, defined as the method of financing a firm's assets, represents another way of looking at the leverage question. In part, financial structures are determined by management. But firms are constrained by the amount of debt lenders are willing to advance, and this willingness is partially conditioned by the characteristics of the industry and by the financial structures of other firms in the industry.

For this reason, the authors have analyzed the factors causing capital structures to differ among industries.

Thus far, the analysis has been more intuitive than rigorous. In the following two chapters, the concepts developed to this point will be extended to the formal theory of the cost of capital and the theory of security valuation. The way investors appraise the relative desirability of increased returns versus higher risks is seen to be a most important consideration, one that, in general, invalidates the theory that firms should strive for maximum earnings per share regardless of the risks involved.

QUESTIONS

9–1 How will each of the following be changed by the occurrences listed below: financial structure, capital structure, and net worth?
- a) The firm has retained earnings of $100 for the year.
- b) A preferred stock issue is refinanced with bonds.
- c) Bonds are sold for cash.
- d) The firm repurchases 10 percent of its outstanding common stock with excess cash.
- e) An issue of convertible bonds is converted.

9–2 From an economic and social standpoint, is the use of financial leverage justifiable? Explain by listing some advantages and disadvantages.

9–3 Financial leverage and operating leverage are similar in one very important respect. What is this similarity and why is it important?

9–4 What are some reasons for variations of debt ratios among the firms in a given industry?

9–5 Why is the following statement true? "Other things being the same, firms with relatively stable sales are able to incur relatively high debt ratios."

9–6 Why do public utility companies usually pursue a different financial policy from that of trade firms?

9–7 The use of financial ratios and industry averages in the financial planning and analysis of a firm should be approached with caution. Why?

9–8 Some economists believe that the swings in the business cycles have not been as wide in recent years as they have been in the past. Assuming that they are correct in their analysis, what effect can this added stability have on the types of financing used by firms in the United States? Would your answer be true for all firms?

PROBLEMS

9–1 One useful test or guide for evaluating a firm's financial structure in relation to its industry is by comparison with financial ratio composites for its industry. A new firm or one contemplating entering a new industry may use such industry composites as a guide to what its financial position is likely to approximate after the initial settling-down period.

The following data represent the ratios for the furniture manufacturing industry for 1968:

Estimated annual sales	$400,000
Sales to net worth	4 times
Current debt to net worth	50%
Total debt to net worth	80%
Current ratio	2.2 times
Net sales to inventory	8 times
Average collection period	40 days
Fixed assets to net worth	70%

EXCELSIOR FURNITURE DESIGNS
Pro Forma BALANCE SHEET
1968

Cash	$______	Current debt	$______
Accounts receivable	______	Long-term debt	______
Inventory	______	Total debt	______
Current assets	______	Net worth	______
Fixed assets	______		
Total assets	$______	Total liab. and net worth	$______

a) Complete the above *pro forma* balance sheet. (Round to nearest thousands.)
b) What does the use of the financial ratio composites accomplish?
c) What other factors will influence the financial structure of the firm?

9–2 In early 1967, the Gusher Company was thinking of raising $300 million additional funds to finance growth. About the same time the Streamer Company was thinking of raising $100 million to finance growth in sales.
From data given below, which firm should sell 4.5 percent debentures and which should sell common stock? (In your answer, *do not* try to determine the effects of stock or bond financing on earnings per share. Rather, look at such things as debt ratios, interest costs, and so on, and make a subjective evaluation of the situation.)

GUSHER AND STREAMER OIL COMPANIES
BALANCE SHEETS
(in millions of dollars)

	Gusher	Streamer
Current assets	$3,000	$ 650
Investments	400	100
Net fixed assets	4,600	1,750
Total assets	$8,000	$2,500
Current liabilities	$1,400	$ 300
Long-term debt	1,600	200
Total debt	$3,000	$ 500
Common stock outstanding		
Gusher (200 million shares), $10 par	$2,000	
Streamer (40 million shares), $25 par		$1,000
Surplus (earned and paid in)	3,000	1,000
Net worth	$5,000	$2,000
Total claims	$8,000	$2,500
Sales (in billions of dollars)		
1962	5.4	1.7
1963	5.6	1.7
1964	5.8	1.8
1965	6.4	1.9
1966	7.1	2.0
Net income (in millions of dollars)	Gusher	Streamer
1962	540	136
1963	560	136
1964	580	144
1965	640	152
1966	700	152

GUSHER AND STREAMER OIL COMPANIES
INCOME STATEMENTS
For Period Ended June 30, 1966
(in millions of dollars)

	Gusher	Streamer
Sales	$7,100	$2,000
Total costs	6,128	1,820
Net income before taxes	$ 972	$ 180
Interest on debt (4.5% for Gusher, 4% for Streamer)	72	8
	$ 900	$ 172
Federal income taxes	200	20
Net income after taxes	$ 700	$ 152
	Gusher	Streamer
Sales to total assets	0.89	0.80
Earnings per share	$3.50	$3.80
Dividends per share	1.85	1.25
Price/earnings ratio*	20×	15×
Market price	$ 70	$ 57

* The price/earnings ratio is the market price per share divided by earnings per share. It represents the amount of money an investor is willing to pay for $1 of current earnings.

9–3 The Beaumont Company plans to expand assets by 50 percent; to finance the expansion, it is choosing between a straight 6 percent debt issue and common stock. Its current balance sheet and income statement are shown below.

BEAUMONT COMPANY
BALANCE SHEET
December 31, 1967

		Debt, 5%	$ 40,000
		Common stock, $10 par	100,000
		Earned surplus	60,000
Total assets	$200,000	Total claims	$200,000

BEAUMONT COMPANY
INCOME STATEMENT
For Year Ended December 31, 1967

Sales	$600,000
Total costs (excluding interest)	538,000
Net income before taxes	$ 62,000
Debt interest	2,000
Income before taxes	$ 60,000
Taxes at 50%	30,000
Net income	$ 30,000

Earnings per share: $\frac{30,000}{10,000} = \$3$

Market price: $12 \times 3 = \$36$

If the Beaumont Company finances the $100,000 expansion with debt, the rate on the incremental debt will be 6 percent and the price/earnings ratio of the common stock will be 10 times. If the expansion is financed by equity, the new stock can be sold at $33⅓, the rate on debt will be 5 percent, and the price/earnings ratio of all the outstanding common stock will remain at 12 times earnings.

a) Assuming that net income before interest on debt and before taxes is 10 percent of sales, calculate earnings per share at sales assumptions of $0, $50,000, $200,000, $280,000, $400,000, $600,000, $800,000 and $1,000,000, when financing is with common stock in contrast to debt. Assume no fixed costs.
b) Make a break-even chart for the earnings under *a*.
c) Using the price earnings ratio indicated, calculate the market value per share of common stock for each sales level for both the debt and the equity methods of financing.
d) Make a break-even chart of market value per share for the company with data found in *c*.
e) If the firm follows the policy of seeking to maximize the market price of its stock, which form of financing should be employed?

f) What other factors should be taken into account in choosing between the two forms of financing?

g) Would it matter if the presently outstanding stock was all owned by Mr. Beaumont and that this represented his entire net worth? Would it matter if the final decision maker, the president, was compensated entirely by a fixed salary? that he had a substantial number of stock options?

Selected References

Ghandhi, J. K. S., "On the Measurement of Leverage," *Journal of Finance,* XXI (December 1966), 715–726.

Guzzardi, Walter Jr., "The Optimistic World of Henry Kaiser," *Fortune* (April 1963).

Lerner, Eugene M., and Willard T. Carleton, "Financing Decisions of the Firm," *Journal of Finance,* XXI (May 1966), 202–214.

10

Valuation and Rates of Return

In the discussion of the capital budgeting process in Chapter 7, it was seen that the discount rate used in the calculations is of vital importance. Relatively small changes in the discount rate produce significant changes in computed net present values and sometimes cause a reversal in the decision to accept or to reject a particular project. In the discussion of capital budgeting, it was *assumed* that the cost of capital—the discount rate used in the present value process—was known, and this rate was used in the calculations. We did indicate in both Chapters 7 and 8, however, that the cost of capital was related (1) to the firm's riskiness and (2) to the amount of funds raised during a given period. Then, in Chapter 9, we showed how risk is magnified through the use of financial leverage. Now we devote specific attention to the problem of deriving the cost of capital for individual firms.

Since the cost of capital to the firm is integrally connected with investors' returns on capital, the basic principles underlying valuation theory are discussed in the present chapter. The following chapter, building on valuation theory, considers the costs of various types of capital and shows how they may be combined to produce the firm's over-all cost of capital.

DEFINITIONS OF VALUE

Value determined by supply + demand

While it may be difficult to ascribe monetary returns to certain types of assets—works of art, for instance—the fundamental characteristic of business assets is that they give rise to income flows. Sometimes this flow is easy to determine and measure—the interest return on a bond is an example. At other times, the cash flows attributable to the asset must be estimated, as was done in Chapter 7 in the evaluation of projects. Regardless of the difficulties of measuring income flows, it is the prospective revenues from assets that give them value.

Liquidating versus Going Concern Value

Several different definitions of "value" exist in the literature and are used in practice, with different ones being appropriate at different times. The first distinction that must be made is that between *liquidating value* and *going concern value*. Liquidating value is defined as the amount that could be realized if an asset or a group of assets (the assets of an entire firm, for example) are sold separately from the organization that has been using them. If the owner of a machine shop decides to retire, he might auction off his inventory and equipment, collect his accounts receivable, then sell his land and buildings to a grocery wholesaler for use as a warehouse. The sum of the proceeds from each category of assets that he receives would be the liquidating value of the assets. If his debts are subtracted from this amount, the difference would represent the liquidating value of his ownership in the business.

On the other hand, if the firm is sold as an operating business to a corporation or another individual, the purchaser would pay an amount equal to the going concern value of the company. If the going concern value exceeds the liquidating value, the difference represents the value of the organization as distinct from the value of the assets.

Book Value versus Market Value

Another distinction must be made between *book value,* or the accounting value at which an asset is carried, and *market value,* the price at which an asset can be sold. If the asset in question is a firm, it actually has two market values—a liquidating value and a going concern value. Only the higher of the two is generally referred to as *the* market value.

Market Value versus Intrinsic Value

The distinction between *intrinsic value* and *market value* has been stated clearly and succinctly by Graham, Dodd, and Cottle:

> A general definition of intrinsic value would be "that value which is justified by the facts, e.g., assets, earnings, dividends, definite prospects, including the factor of management." The primary objective in using the adjective "intrinsic" is to emphasize the distinction between value and *current market price,* but not to invest this "value" with an aura of permanence. In truth, the computed intrinsic value is likely to change at least from year to year, as the various factors governing that value are modified. But in most cases intrinsic value changes less rapidly and drastically than market price, and the investor usually has an opportunity to profit from any wide discrepancy between the current price and the intrinsic value as determined at the same time.[1]

Although the authors cited develop this concept for security (that is, stocks and bonds) valuation, the idea is applicable to all business assets. What it involves, basically, is estimating the future net cash flows attributable to an asset; determining an appropriate capitalization, or discount rate; and then finding the present value of the cash flows. This, of course, is exactly what was done in Chapters 6 and 7, where the concept of intrinsic value was developed for application in finding the present value of investment opportunities.

CAPITALIZATION OF INCOME

The procedure for determining an asset's intrinsic value is known as the *capitalization-of-income method of valuation.* This is simply a fancy name for an old friend, the present value of a stream of earnings,

[1] B. Graham, D. L. Dodd, and S. Cottle, *Security Analysis* (New York, McGraw-Hill, 1961), p. 28.

discussed at length in Chapter 6. The following example illustrates the technique for valuing a bond. Following this, the technique is illustrated with preferred and common stocks. From this point on, whenever the word "value" is used, we mean the intrinsic value found by capitalizing future cash flows. Further, for purposes of exposition, we shall assume that the current market prices of stocks or bonds are equal to their intrinsic values. This assumption is relaxed in future chapters, where we see that *differences* between management estimates of intrinsic values and market prices have a significant bearing on the type of security—stock or bond—used to raise funds at a given time.

Bond Valuation

Bond values are relatively easy to determine. As long as the bond is not expected to go into default, the expected cash flows are the annual interest payments plus the principal amount to be paid when the bond matures. Capitalization rates applied to bonds differ among bonds depending primarily upon differences in risk of default on interest or principal. A U.S. Treasury security, for example, would have less risk than one issued by the Westbrig Corporation; consequently, a lower discount (or capitalization) rate would be applied to its interest payments.

The actual calculating procedures employed in bond valuation are illustrated by the following examples.

EXAMPLE 1. After the Napoleonic Wars (1814), England sold a huge bond issue that was used to pay off many smaller issues that had been floated in prior years to pay for the war. Since the purpose of the new issue was to consolidate past debts, the individual bonds were called Consols. Suppose the bonds had a par value of $1,000 (actually, they were stated in pounds) and paid $50 interest annually into perpetuity. What would the bonds be worth under current market conditions?

First, note that the value (V) of any perpetuity[2] is computed as

[2] A perpetuity is a bond that never matures; it pays interest indefinitely. Equation 10–1 is simply the present value of an infinite series and is proved in any college algebra textbook. Its proof is also demonstrated in a round-about way in Appendix A to Chapter 12. Here we show that (using the notation of this chapter):

$$V = \frac{R}{i - g}$$

where g = the growth rate of R. But here R is constant, so $g = 0$ and

$$V = \frac{R}{i}$$

follows:

$$V = \frac{\text{constant annual receipts}}{\text{capitalization rate}} = \frac{R}{i} \tag{10–1}$$

We know that the Consol's annual interest payment is $50; therefore, the only other thing we need in order to find its value is the appropriate capitalization rate. This is commonly taken as the going interest rate, or yield, on bonds of similar risk. Suppose we find such bonds to be paying 4 percent under current market conditions. Then the Consol's value is determined as

$$V = \frac{R}{i} = \frac{\$50}{0.04} = \$1{,}250$$

If the going rate of interest rises to 5 percent, the value of the bond falls to $1,000 ($50/0.05 = $1,000). If interest rates continue rising, when the rate goes as high as 6 percent the value of the Consol will be only $833.33. Values of this perpetual bond at a range of interest rates are given in the following tabulation.

CURRENT MARKET INTEREST RATE	CURRENT MARKET VALUE
0.02	$2,500.00
0.03	1,666.67
0.04	1,250.00
0.05	1,000.00
0.06	833.33
0.07	714.29

EXAMPLE 2. Now suppose the British government issues bonds with the same risk of default as the Consols, but with a three-year maturity. The new bonds also pay $50 interest and have a $1,000 par value. What will be the value of these new bonds at the time of issue if the going rate of interest is 4 percent? The solution requires the calculations, which are given in the following tabulation.[3]

[3] If the bond has a longer maturity, 20 years for example, we would certainly want to calculate its present value by finding the present value of a 20-year annuity and then adding to that the present value of the $1,000 principal amount received at maturity. Special bond tables have been devised to simplify the calculation procedure.

YEAR	RECEIPT	4 PERCENT DISCOUNT FACTORS	PRESENT VALUE
1	$50	0.962	$ 48.10
2	$50	0.925	46.25
3	$50 + $1,000	0.889	933.45
		bond value	$1,027.80

At the various rates of interest used in the preceding example, this three-year bond would have the following values.

INTEREST RATE	CAPITAL VALUE
0.02	$1,086.15
0.03	1,056.45
0.04	1,027.80
0.05	1,000.00
0.06	973.65
0.07	947.20

Figure 10–1 shows how the values of the long-term bond (the consol) and the short-term bond change in response to changes in the going market rate of interest. Note how much less the bond value changes with given changes in interest rates when the term to maturity is only three years. At a going rate of interest equal to 5 percent, both the perpetuity and the short-term bonds are valued at $1,000. When rates fall to 2 percent, the long-term bond rises to $2,500, while the short-term security goes to only $1,086. A similar situation occurs when rates rise above 5 percent. *This differential responsiveness to changes in interest rates always holds true—the longer the maturity of a security, the greater its price change relative to a given change in capitalization rates.* Thus, even if the risk of default on two bonds is exactly the same, the value of the one with the longer maturity is exposed to more risk from a rise in interest rates. This greater risk explains why short-term bonds usually have lower yields, or rates of return, than long-term bonds. It also explains why corporate treasurers are reluctant to hold their near-cash reserves in the form of long-term debt instruments—these near-cash reserves are held for precautionary purposes; a treasurer would be unwilling to sacrifice safety for a little higher yield on a long-term bond.

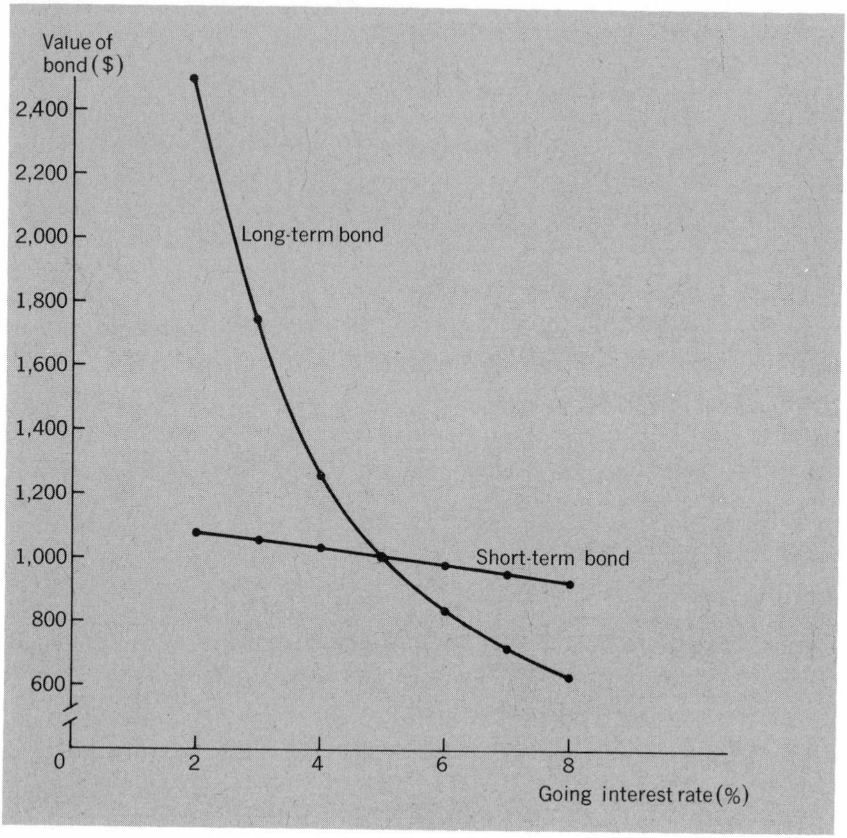

Figure 10–1 Values of Long-Term and Short-Term Bonds at Different Interest Rates

Preferred Stock Valuation

Most preferred stocks entitle their owners to regular, fixed dividend payments similar to bond interest. Although some preferred issues are retired, this is unusual; for the most part, they are perpetuities, whose value is found as follows:

$$V = \frac{R}{i}$$

In this case, R is simply the dividend on the preferred stock. For example, General Motors has a preferred stock outstanding that pays a \$3.75 annual dividend. The appropriate capitalization rate at the time the stock was issued (1925) was 7.5 percent, so it sold at \$50 at the time of issue. Today, however, GM is a much stronger company and its preferred stock is much less risky. Also, interest rates are lower today than in the late 1920s. The combined result is that the yield on GM's preferred issue has fallen to 5¼ percent and the value of the stock has climbed to $71 a share.

$$V = \frac{\$3.75}{0.0525} = \$71$$

Common Stock Valuation[4]

While the same principles apply to the valuation of common stocks as to bonds, preferred stocks, or other assets, two features make their analysis much more difficult. First is the degree of certainty with which receipts can be forecast. For bonds and preferred stocks, this forecast presents very little difficulty, as the interest payments or preferred dividends are known with relative certainty. But in the case of common stocks, the forecasting of future earnings, dividends, and stock prices is exceedingly difficult, to say the least. The second complicating feature is that, unlike interest and preferred dividends, common stock earnings and dividends are generally expected to grow, not remain constant. Hence, standard annuity formulas cannot be applied, and more difficult conceptual schemes must be used.

The investment value of a share of common stock depends upon the dollar returns an investor will receive if he buys the stock. Now what are the returns? They are, of course, the dividends the investor receives while he holds the stock plus the price he receives when he sells it; the ending price is equal to the beginning price plus capital gains or minus capital losses.

To illustrate, suppose you are thinking of buying a share of American Rubber common stock. If you buy the stock, you will hold it for one year. The current market price is $40 a share. You note that American Rubber is earning $3.60 a share and paying $2 a year in dividends and that dividends, earnings, and the price of the company's stock have been rising at about 4 percent a year over the past 10 to 15 years. This 4 percent growth rate, incidentally, is about the same as the rate of growth in GNP and in stock prices generally (in real terms, that is, after deducting increases in the general level of prices).

[4] The concepts involved in the theory of common stock valuation are, unfortunately, relatively difficult. In an effort to convey them, we cover the basics in this section, expand on the idea of growth in the Appendix to this chapter, and then return to the basic concept in Appendix A to Chapter 12, where the theoretical model underlying much of this book, the Gordon model, is described.

Using this information and the investment evaluation techniques described in Chapters 6 and 7, you could calculate the expected rate of return, k, on American Rubber's stock as follows:

$$\text{present price} = \frac{\text{dividend}}{(1+k)} + \frac{\text{price in 1 year}}{(1+k)}$$

$$\text{present price} = \frac{\text{dividend}}{(1+k)} + \frac{\text{present price} \times (1 + \text{growth rate})}{(1+k)}$$

$$\$40 = \frac{\$2.00}{(1+k)} + \frac{\$40(1.04)}{(1+k)}$$

$$\$40 = \frac{\$2.00}{(1+k)} + \frac{\$41.60}{(1+k)} = \frac{\$43.60}{(1+k)}$$

$$1 + k = \frac{\$43.60}{\$40.00} = 1.090$$

$$k = 1.090 - 1.00 = 0.090, \text{ or } 9\%$$

Let us examine the steps here and the assumptions involved. First, note that the first equation sets up the purchase of the share of stock as an investment (1) with a cost equal to the present price and (2) with returns equal to the dividend plus the ending price one year from now. The second equation shows that the ending price is equal to the present price plus the 4 percent expected price increase. The remainder of the equations simply substitute in the appropriate values and solve the basic equation for k, the rate of return on the stock, which turns out to be 9 percent.

The expected rate of return, k, can be split into two components, one from capital gains and one from dividends. This is done below:

$$\text{dividend yield} = \frac{\text{dividends}}{\text{current price}} = \frac{\$2}{\$40} = 0.05, \text{ or } 5\%$$

$$\text{capital gains yield} = \frac{\text{price increase}}{\text{current price}} = \frac{\$1.60}{\$40.00} = 0.04, \text{ or } 4\%$$

In this instance, the expected dividend yield turns out to be 5 percent, and the capital gains yield, 4 percent.

The total return, or yield, is equal to the dividend yield plus the capital gains yield.

$$\begin{aligned}\text{total return} &= \text{dividend yield} + \text{capital gains yield}\\ &= \frac{\text{expected dividend}}{\text{current price}} + \frac{\text{expected increase in price}}{\text{current price}}\end{aligned}$$

Dividends are abbreviated to D, the current price to P, and the second term in the equation—the increase in price divided by the current price, or the growth rate—to G. The following fundamental equation is thus produced.

$$k = \text{rate of return} = \frac{D}{P} + G \qquad (10\text{–}2)$$

To repeat, the rate of return on a share of common stock is equal to its dividend yield plus the expected growth in the price of the stock, or the capital gains yield.[5]

Two critical assumptions are involved in the calculations: (1) that the dividend will be paid and (2) that the stock price will continue to grow at a 4 percent rate.[6] For a stable, solid company like American Rubber the dividend assumption is probably a good one, but the growth assumption will almost surely not hold exactly. Depending on a great many factors—but most importantly the performance of the entire stock market—the ending price will turn out to be more or less than $41.60. And, depending on whether the final price is higher or lower than the one forecast, the rate of return will turn out to be more or less than anticipated. If, for example, the stock market soars and American Rubber goes up to $50 a share, the $10 capital gain plus the $2 dividend will provide a 30 percent rate of return. If, however, the market slumps badly and American Rubber falls to $30, the return will be *minus* 20 percent.

One other point should be observed in connection with these calculations for American Rubber. Notice that the company is expected to earn $3.60 a share and to pay out $2 in dividends. This means that $1.60 will be retained. Suppose the company reinvests these retained earnings in projects that yield 9 percent. Future earnings will increase by $0.14 ($1.60 × 0.09). Capitalized at 9 percent, the additional earnings add $1.60 to the value of the stock ($0.14/0.09). This $1.60 is exactly equal to the expected capital gain found above. The company *has* been retaining about 45 percent of its earnings, and it *has* been earning about

[5] Strictly speaking, this equation holds only if the growth rate is expected to remain constant in the future. Both the Appendix to this chapter and the Appendix to Chapter 12 discuss this point at length.

[6] We are only using a one-year holding period. In the general case, where the holding period is of any length, the equation is still used, but another assumption must be added: namely, the dividend must grow at the same rate as the stock price. Again, for a stable company such as American Rubber this is a good assumption—dividends and stock prices *do* move more or less together. Both the Appendix to this chapter and Appendix A to chapter 12 discuss this point at length.

9 percent on new equity. The fact that earnings have been retained and reinvested in profitable projects explains why American Rubber has enjoyed a record of rising stock prices.

This exposition has been based on only a one-year holding period, but it can be expanded to any holding period with exactly the same results. The procedures are much more complicated, however, as one can see by examining some of the technical materials cited in the end of Chapter references and in the Appendix to this Chapter.[7]

We next look at the factors that cause differentials in the expected rates of returns among securities and then examine historical patterns of returns on stocks and bonds.

FACTORS LEADING TO VARIATIONS IN RETURNS AMONG SECURITIES

Risk and Rates of Return

The most important factor leading to differential expected rates of return among different securities is differences in risk. Here *risk* is defined as uncertainty about the return that will actually be realized. For example, if the asset in question is a 60-day Treasury bill, the expected returns can be estimated quite accurately—there is little risk of not realizing in full the promised yield. If the security is a corporate bond, there is always some danger that the firm will default; thus, there is some uncertainty about the final return.

Uncertainty is greater yet when we move to common stocks. Dividends are not always predictable, and the capital gains component is quite uncertain. Within common stocks, different companies' stocks are more uncertain than others. Such well-established firms as AT&T, General Motors, and du Pont have long histories of earnings, dividends, and management performance. On the other hand, there is more uncertainty

[7] While most authorities would agree with our beliefs that stock prices are determined by such fundamentals as earnings, dividends, and rates of return on retained earnings, some argue that securities, especially common stocks, are valued by an essentially irrational process which involves psychology, stockbroker recommendations, and several other factors. Such essentially random phenomena do have a profound influence on short-run price movements. Nevertheless, we argue that the long-run value of a stock is determined by investors capitalizing expected future returns.

in the case of new companies and those developing new and essentially untried products—in these cases, risk is high relative to the AT&Ts, GMs, and other blue chips.

Would you expect returns to be higher or lower on risky investments? Although some individuals are gamblers by nature and seem to prefer more to less risk, investors as a group dislike risk, or are "risk averters." Given risk aversion, securities with higher risk must sell on the basis of higher expected yields. For example, a 9 percent expected return might be acceptable for American Rubber's stock, but a more stable and predictable electric utility common stock might sell on an 8 percent return basis. On the other hand, investors might be unwilling to buy stock in a wildcat oil drilling concern unless they can expect to make 50 percent. This is, of course, an informal application of the risk-adjusted discount rate concept discussed in Chapter 8.[8]

For a given firm, its bonds are less risky to investors than its common stocks, so expected yields are higher on stocks than on bonds. Risks on preferred stocks lie between those on bonds and common stocks, so returns on these securities should also fall in the middle.[9]

One might also observe that different degrees of risk are incurred by individual firms within particular industries. If, for example, one firm has a strong research and development (R&D) program, excellent recruitment and management training programs, and broad geographic and product diversification, while another has none of these features, the first will be regarded as less risky than the second and will sell on a lower yield basis. If small firms, because of less product or geographic diversification, lower R&D expenditures, greater management succession problems, or any other reasons are considered to be more risky than large firms, investors will require a higher rate of return on small firms' securities.

Marketability and Rates of Return

Investors also value flexibility, or maneuverability. If one becomes disenchanted with a particular investment, or if he needs funds for consumption or other investments, it is highly desirable for him to be able to liquidate his holdings. Other things the same, the higher the liquidity,

[8] If a particular company's earnings are *negatively correlated* with most other stocks, then holding this stock may reduce the risk of a *portfolio* of stocks. One should therefore consider covariances among stocks when appraising their riskiness in a portfolio holding.

[9] As will be pointed out in Chapter 19, much of the dividend yield on a preferred stock is tax free if it is held by a corporate investor. Because of this fact, *before tax* yields on preferreds are frequently lower than before tax bond yields.

or marketability, the lower an investment's required rate of return. Accordingly, one would expect to find listed stocks selling on a lower yield basis than over-the-counter stocks, and publicly owned stocks selling at lower yields than stocks with no established market. Since investments in small firms are generally less liquid than those in large companies, we have another reason for expecting to find higher required yields among smaller companies.

Changes in Stock Price Levels

Equity yields differ among firms because of differences in inherent risks and marketability, but they also differ for an individual stock over time. If the demand for funds is relatively heavy and, at the same time, the supply is restricted, the law of supply and demand requires that the price of funds—the interest rate on debt or the required rate of return on equity—be higher than when supply and demand conditions are reversed. In the late 1940s, for example, many corporations were expanding and seeking equity funds to finance this expansion, while many investors were expecting a serious postwar depression and were not interested in purchasing stocks. The result was a very high required rate of return on equity issues and low common stock prices.

As it became clear that the booming economy was not headed for a depression, investors began putting more money into the equity markets. Simultaneously, productive capacity began to catch up with demand, lowering corporate demands for funds. The net result was a pronounced decline in required rates of return and a much higher level of stock prices. These changes are illustrated in Figure 10–2.

Stock prices change for either of two reasons—changes in required rates of return or changes in growth expectations. For example, the 1949–1968 increase in stock prices may have been caused by either declining required equity yields, higher growth expectations, or a combination of the two.

This idea can be illustrated by reference to American Rubber. Recall that when the stock is selling for $40, is paying a $2 dividend, and is expected to grow at about 4 percent during the next year, the expected rate of return is calculated to be 9 percent.

Now suppose supply and demand conditions in the capital markets change so that the equilibrium rate of return—the point where supply equals demand—on American Rubber's stock declines to 8 percent. Assuming that dividend and growth expectations remain constant, this decline in the capitalization rate causes the current price to jump from

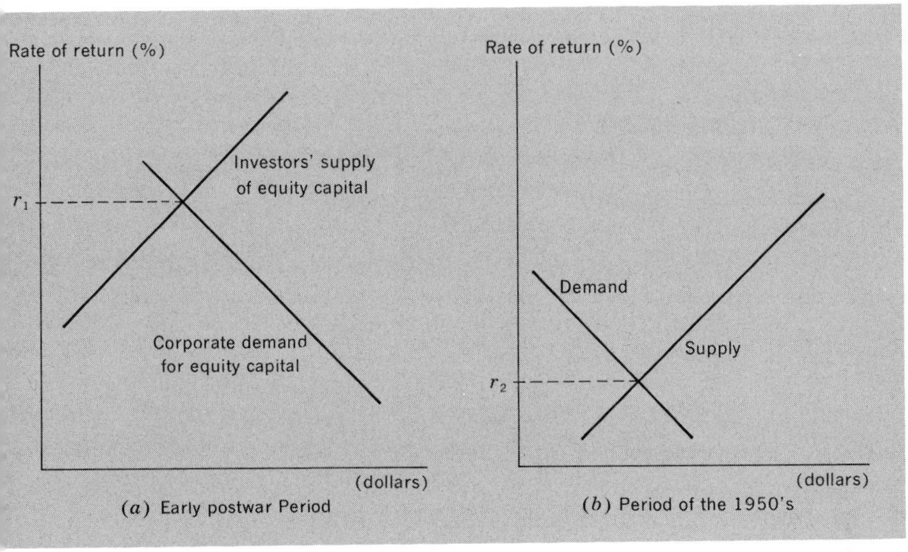

Figure 10–2 Hypothetical Supply and Demand for Equity Securities

\$40 to \$50. The reasons are explained below. First, note that the current price is determined as:

$$\text{current price or value} = \frac{\text{dividend}}{1 + \text{capitalization rate}} + \frac{\text{current price} \times (1 + \text{growth rate})}{1 + \text{capitalization rate}}$$

Substituting in the known quantities—the \$2 dividend, the 8 percent capitalization rate, and the 4 percent growth rate—we find the current price of the stock.

$$\begin{aligned}
\text{current price} &= \frac{\$2.00}{1.08} + \frac{\text{current price } (1.04)}{1.08} \\
&= \frac{\$2.00 + 1.04 \text{ current price}}{1.08} \\
1.08 \text{ current price} &= \$2.00 + 1.04 \text{ current price} \\
1.08 \text{ current price} &- 1.04 \text{ current price} = \$2 \\
0.04 \text{ current price} &= \$2.00 \\
\text{current price} &= \frac{\$2.00}{0.04} = \$50 \text{ a share}
\end{aligned}$$

Therefore, if the average investor expects American Rubber to pay a

$2 dividend and to experience a 4 percent stock price appreciation from the reinvestment of retained earnings, and if he is to receive an 8 percent return on his investment, then the initial investment—the current price—must be $50.[10]

A change in growth expectations could produce a similar change. With the capitalization rate 9 percent and the growth rate 4 percent, the current price is $40. Now suppose the company announces a development that leads investors to expect a higher rate of growth—say 5 percent a year. Substituting this new growth rate into the price equation and solving for the current price, we find a new price of $50 per share.

$$\text{current price} = \frac{\$2.00}{1.09} + \frac{\text{current price } (1.05)}{1.09} = \$50$$

For American Rubber, then, we see that a sharp stock price increase (or decrease) can arise from changes in market capitalization rates or growth expectations, or from a combination of the two. These ideas can be generalized for the stock market as a whole, and they can be used to explain changes in the level of stock prices.

Historical Rates of Return

EQUITY YIELDS. Various financial researchers investigating returns on publicly-owned stocks over long periods have found them to average about 9 percent. When measured from stock market lows, returns are relatively high; conversely, when the market is high in the base period, stockholder yields are relatively low. For example, had one bought a portfolio of stocks at the average price prevailing in the depressed year 1949 and held them until 1965, his return would have been about 15 percent. The same group of stocks, bought during the high market in 1961, would have yielded a little over 6 percent by 1965.

Some rough averages of estimated stock yields under different market

[10] For those interested in generalized formulas, one applicable to a perpetual growth situation is:

$$P = \frac{D}{k - g}$$

where P = current price, D = current dividend, k = required rate of return, and g = the growth rate.

$$P = \frac{\$2.00}{0.08 - 0.04} = \frac{\$2.00}{0.04} = \$50 \text{ in the example}$$

The basic Gordon model, developed in Appendix A to Chapter 12, generalizes the concepts involved here. See also footnote 3, page 334.

conditions are shown in Table 10–1. To the extent (1) that the future approximates the past and (2) that investors base expected future returns on those realized in the past, the figures in the table should give some idea of stockholders' required rates of return under different market, risk, and liquidity conditions.[11]

TABLE 10–1 ESTIMATED RATES OF RETURN ON COMMON STOCKS

	STOCK MARKET CONDITION		
Company Characteristics	High	Normal	Low
Low risk, high marketability	6½	7	9½
Average risk and marketability	7–8	8–10	12–15
High risk, low marketability	9	12	20

TABLE 10–2 BANK RATES ON BUSINESS LOANS IN 19 LARGE CITIES

	SIZE OF LOAN (IN THOUSANDS OF DOLLARS)			
	1–10	10–100	100–200	200 and over
1958	5.5%	5.0%	4.6%	4.1%
1962	5.9	5.5	5.2	4.8
1966 (December)	6.8	6.7	6.5	6.2

SOURCE: *Federal Reserve Bulletin* (January 1967), 112.

DEBT YIELDS. Debt yields, or rates of return, also vary over time and with the characteristics of the individual loan. Many different statistics could be presented to support this assertion, but Table 10–2 illustrates it sufficiently. The year 1958 was a period of monetary ease, 1962 might be characterized as "normal" for recent years, and 1966 was a period of extremely tight money. A glance down any of the columns will show how bank interest rates varied between periods.

[11] We should note, however, that the Table 10–1 figures are based on a period when interest rates were much lower than they are today (Winter 1969). Because of the interrelationship between bond interest rates and stock prices, it may be necessary to raise the Table 10–1 figures by about 2 percentage points unless bond yields fall back to their earlier levels.

Variations across the rows of the table are somewhat more difficult to explain. In part, interest rates on loans decline as the size of the loan increases because of the fixed costs of making and servicing loans. In addition, part of the decline occurs because small firms borrow small amounts, and small firms are inherently more risky than large ones. At any rate, it is clear that returns on debt, like those on stock, vary over time and with the characteristics of the borrower.

The concepts of valuation and rates of return on debt and equity securities developed in this chapter are fundamentally related to the cost of capital concept. This is the subject of the following chapter.

SUMMARY

In the discussion of the capital budgeting process in Chapter 7, the discount rate used in the calculations was seen to be of vital importance. At that time, we simply assumed that the cost of capital—the discount rate used in the present value process—was known; we used this assumed rate in the calculations. In this chapter, however, we turned our attention to the theory of the cost of capital.

Since the cost of capital is integrally related to investors' returns on capital, the basic principles underlying valuation theory were discussed and a number of definitions of value were presented: (1) liquidating versus going concern value, (2) book versus market value, and (3) market versus "intrinsic" value. This last concept, intrinsic value, is fundamentally dependent upon discounted cash flow concepts and procedures; it involves estimating future cash flows and discounting them back to the present at an appropriate rate of interest. This rate of interest, defined as the "required rate of return," is a function of the investment's risk and the investor's opportunity costs.

Rates of return on bonds and preferred stocks are simple to understand and to calculate, but common stock returns are more difficult. First, common stock returns consist of (1) dividends and (2) capital gains, not a single type of payment as occurs with bonds and preferred stocks. This fact necessitates the development of a rate of return formula that considers both dividends and capital gains; the rate of return formula for common stock is, therefore, a two-part equation:

$$\text{rate of return} = \text{dividend yield} + \text{capital gains yield}$$

The second complicating feature of common stock is the degree of uncertainty involved. Bond and preferred stock payments are relatively predictable, but forecasting common stock dividends and, even more, capital gains, is a highly uncertain business.

Note also that risk is of two types: (1) a basic business risk having to do with the nature of the industry and the firm and (2) a financial risk dependent upon the extent to which financial leverage is employed. A firm that manufactures producers' durables—for example, railroad locomotives—is inherently more risky than an electric utility or chain of grocery stores. However, firms can and do alter their basic risks by using more or less financial (and also operating) leverage. As a result, a firm in a relatively stable industry may, because of excessive financial leverage, end up in a more risky position than one in an unstable industry.

As investors generally dislike risk, the required rate of return is higher on more risky securities. Bonds, as a class, are less risky than preferred stocks, and preferred stocks, in turn, are less risky than common stocks. As a result, the required rate of return is lowest for bonds, next for preferred stocks, and highest for common stocks. Within each of these security classes, there are variations among the issuing firms' risks; hence, required rates of return vary among firms. Also, supply and demand conditions in the capital markets change over time, so a given firm's securities will have different required rates of return at different points in time. Tables were presented to give some idea of the levels of the required rates of return on different types of securities and during different periods.

QUESTIONS

10–1 Most inheritance tax laws state that for estate tax purposes, property shall be valued on the basis of "fair market value." Describe how an inheritance tax appraiser might use the valuation principles discussed in this chapter to establish the value (1) of shares of a stock listed on the New York Stock Exchange and (2) of shares representing 20 percent of a stock that is not publicly traded.

10–2 How does the level of interest rates influence stock and bond prices?

10–3 Using the theoretical concepts developed in this chapter and certain preceding ones, develop an argument to support the frequently encountered statement that a rising level of interest rates depresses the stock market. (It is true that higher interest rates tend to deflate the economy, hence corporate profits and stock prices, but this is not the desired answer to this question.)

10–4 Explain why bonds with longer maturities experience wider price movements from a given change in interest rates than do shorter maturity bonds. Preferably, give your answer (1) in words (intuitively) and (2) mathematically.

10–5 Describe the factors that determine the market rate of return on a particular stock at a given point in time.

10–6 Table 10–1 gives some estimates of rates of return on common stocks. Using this or similar tables, would you expect ten "experts" to reach the same conclusion about expected market yields on a given firm's common stock? Why or why not?

PROBLEMS

10–1 a) The Bay State Company is earning $4 million a year after taxes. Its common stock has a $10 par value; 3 million shares are authorized; and 1 million shares are outstanding. What are the company's earnings per share?

b) Common stocks of electronic companies in the same risk class as Bay State sell to yield 5 percent on earnings. What would be the expected price of Bay State's stock? Why? (Note: Earnings yield is the earnings/price ratio.)

c) At what price/earnings ratio does Bay State common sell?

d) If Bay State common sold on an 8 percent earnings yield basis, what would be its price? its price/earnings ratio?

e) Bay State pays a yearly dividend of $2 a share. If Bay State sells to yield 5 percent on earnings, what is the dividend yield basis on which it sells? (Note: Dividend yield is dividend/price.)

10–2 a) The bonds of the Carolina Corporation are perpetuities bearing a 5 percent coupon and rated AAA. Bonds of this type yield 4 percent. What is the price of Carolina's bonds? Their par value is $1,000.

b) Interest rate levels rise to the point where such bonds now yield 6 percent. What will be the price of the Carolina bonds now?

c) Interest rate levels drop to 5 percent. At what price will the Carolina bonds sell?

d) How would your answer to parts *a*, *b*, and *c* change if the bonds had a definite maturity date of 20 years?

10–3 Mike Dunn contemplates the purchase of a small electronic firm. Expected sales of the company are $2 million a year. For this line of business, firms earn 5.5 percent on sales after taxes.

Dunn feels that his money should earn a 20 percent return on investment in an area as risky as electronics. What is the largest amount he would pay for the electronics firm?

10–4 Because of ill health and old age Robert McKenzie contemplates the sale of his hardware store. His corporation has the following balance sheet:

Assets		*Liabilities and Net Worth*	
Cash	$ 8,000	Notes payable—bank	$ 3,500
Receivables, net	3,000	Accounts payable	5,000
Inventories	19,000	Accruals	1,500
Fixtures and equipment less $10,000 reserve for depreciation	20,000	Common stock plus surplus	40,000
Total assets	$50,000	Total liabilities and net worth	$50,000

Annual before-tax earnings (after rent, interest, and salaries) for the preceding three years have averaged $12,000.

McKenzie has set a price of $60,000, which includes all the assets of the business except cash; the buyer assumes all debts. The assets include a five-year lease and the goodwill associated with the name of McKenzie Hardware. Assume both McKenzie and the potential purchaser are in the 50 percent tax bracket.

a) Is the price of $60,000 a reasonable one? Explain?

b) What other factors should be taken into account in arriving at a selling price?

c) What is the significance, if any, of the rental option?

10–5 The Doyle Company is a small machine-tool manufacturer. It has been successful and has grown. Doyle is planning to sell an issue of common stock to the public for the first time. It faces the problem of setting an appropriate price on its common stock. The company feels that the proper procedure is to select firms similar to Doyle with publicly traded common stock and to make relevant comparisons.

The company finds several machine-tool manufacturers similar to it with respect to product mix, size, asset composition, and debt/equity proportions. Of these, Western and Olympic are most similar.

Relation	*Western*	*Olympic*	*Doyle Totals*
Earnings per share, 1966	$ 3.00	$ 5.00	$ 800,000
Average, 1960–1966	2.00	4.00	600,000
Price per share, 1966	24.00	50.00	—
Dividends per share, 1966	1.50	2.50	400,000
Average, 1960–1966	1.20	2.50	300,000
Book value per share	20.00	50.00	6,000,000
Market-book ratio	120%	100%	—

a) How would these relations be used in guiding Doyle in arriving at a market value for its stock?
b) What price would you recommend if Doyle sells 200,000 shares?

Selected References

Arditti, Fred D., "Risk and the Required Return on Equity," *Journal of Finance,* XXII (March 1967), 19–36.

Baxter, Nevins D., "Leverage, Risk of Ruin, and the Cost of Capital," *Journal of Finance,* XXII (September 1967), 395–404.

Ben-Shahar, Haim, and Abraham Ascher, "Capital Budgeting and Stock Valuation: Comment," *American Economic Review,* LVII (March 1967), 209–214.

Beranek, William, *The Effects of Leverage on the Market Value of Common Stocks* (Madison, Wisc.: Bureau of Business Research and Service, University of Wisconsin, 1964).

Bosland, Chelcie C., "The Valuation of Public Utility Enterprises by the Securities and Exchange Commission," *Journal of Finance,* XVI (March 1961), 52–64.

Brigham, Eugene F., and James L. Pappas, "Duration of Growth, Changes in Growth Rates, and Corporate Share Prices," *Financial Analysts Journal,* XXIV, (May-June 1966), 157–162.

Crockett, Jean and Irwin Friend, "Capital Budgeting and Stock Valuation: Comment," *American Economic Review,* LVII (March 1967), 214–220.

Edwards, Charles E. and James G. Hilton, "High-Low Averages as an Estimator of Annual Average Stock Prices," *Journal of Finance,* XXI (March 1966), 112–115.

Helwing, R. C., *The Valuation of Small Bank Stocks* (East Lansing, Mich.: Bureau of Business and Economic Research, Michigan State University, 1966).

Herzog, John P., "Investor Experience in Corporate Securities: A New Technique for Measurement," *Journal of Finance,* XIX (March 1964), 46–62.

Holt, Charles C., "The Influence of Growth Duration on Share Prices," *Journal of Finance,* XVII (September 1962), 465–475.

Malkiel, Burton G., "Equity Yields, Growth, and the Structure of Share Prices," *American Economic Review,* LIII (December 1963), 467–494.

Mao, James C. T., "The Valuation of Growth Stocks: The Investment Opportunities Approach," *Journal of Finance,* XXI (March 1966), 95–102.

Myers, Stewart, C., "A Time-State-Preference Model of Security Valuation," *Journal of Financial and Quantitative Analysis,* III, (March 1968), 1–34.

Ortner, Robert, "The Concept of Yield on Common Stock," *Journal of Finance,* XIX (May 1964), 186–198.

Soldofsky, Robert M. and Roger Biderman, "Yield-Risk Measurement of the Performance of Common Stocks," *Journal of Financial and Quantitative Analysis,* III, (March 1968), 59–74.

Soldofsky, Robert M., "The History of Bond Tables and Stock Valuation Models," *Journal of Finance,* XXI (March 1966), 103–111.

——— and James T. Murphy, *Growth Yields on Common Stock—Theory and Tables* (Iowa City, Iowa: State University of Iowa, 1963).

———, "The Return on Common Stock: Growth Yield or Current Yield" *Quarterly Review of Economics and Business,* II (May 1962), 21–30.

Solomon, Ezra, "Leverage and the Cost of Capital," *Journal of Finance,* XVIII (May 1963), 273–279.

Wendt, Paul F., "Current Growth Stock Valuation Methods," *Financial Analysts Journal,* XXXIII (March-April 1965), 3–15.

Wippern, Ronald F., "Financial Structure and the Value of the Firm," *Journal of Finance,* XXI (December 1966), 615–634.

APPENDIX TO CHAPTER 10
A Note on the Theory of Valuing Common Stocks[1]

When the future receipts of an asset are expected to be constant and to continue indefinitely, its value is found as:

$$V = \frac{R}{k} \qquad \text{(A10–1)}$$

where V = value, R = the constant annual return, and k = the capitalization rate.

Although this is an appropriate procedure for valuing many types of assets, the fact that it assumes constant receipts makes it inappro-

[1] The material in this appendix is developed and extended in E. F. Brigham and J. L. Pappas, "Duration of Growth, Changes in Growth Rates, and Corporate Share Prices," *Financial Analysts Journal* (May 1966).

priate for evaluating most common stocks. Corporate earnings and dividends, on the average, have had a history of growth, with some firms growing more rapidly than others. To allow for such growth, a valuation scheme that considers growth is needed.

Dividends and Stock Values

Before the actual valuation techniques are discussed, it is necessary to pause briefly to consider the nature of the revenue stream that is being discounted. It will be shown that dividends, and only dividends, go into the calculation of the intrinsic value of common stocks held as investments.[2] This fact can be demonstrated as follows:

1) Suppose an average investor buys a stock, planning to hold it for one year. What is the value of the stock to him? It is the value of the expected dividend, discounted back one year, plus the discounted value of the price that he expects to receive on selling the stock. (Taxes are ignored, although we could adjust for them.)

$$P_o = \frac{D_1}{1+k} + \frac{P_1}{1+k} \qquad \text{(A10–2)}$$

where:

P_o = price of the stock today
D_1 = dividend to be received at the end of the first year
P_1 = price of the stock at the end of the first year
k = appropriate capitalization rate

2) Some other "typical" investor will buy the share at the end of the year, paying P_1. If this investor also expects to hold the stock for only one year, he establishes the value as:

$$P_1 = \frac{D_2}{1+k} + \frac{P_2}{1+k} \qquad \text{(A10–3)}$$

3) P_2, the price at the end of the second year, and all future prices are determined in the same manner, so equation (A10–2) may be expressed as:

$$P_o = \frac{D_1}{(1+k)^1} + \frac{D_2}{(1+k)^2} + \frac{D_3}{(1+k)^3} + \cdots \qquad \text{(A10–4)}$$

If the initial stockholder plans to hold the stock for some period longer

[2] If stock is held to enable its owner to control a corporation, then its value is not necessarily dependent upon expected dividends. Control may bring with it employment on favorable terms, a sense of power, income from ancillary activities, and other nondividend benefits.

than a year, say two years, then equation (A10–2) would simply be written as follows:

$$P_o = \frac{D_1}{(1+k)^1} + \frac{D_2}{(1+k)^2} + \frac{P_2}{(1+k)^2} \qquad \text{(A10–5)}$$

and we would continue as before. In similar fashion, any time period may be accommodated. Thus, the present intrinsic value of a share of stock is dependent upon its future dividends.

But is this statement really true? What about a person who buys a stock, such as Litton Industries, that has never paid a cash dividend? Can it be said that dividends determine this stock's value? Again, the answer is yes, it can. Litton pays no dividend today; by retaining earnings, it is building up to its earning power base and will, some time in the future, be able to pay quite large dividends. In terms of equation (A10–4) the first few D_t values are zero, but at some point investors expect the firm to begin to pay dividends.

The alternative theory of stock valuation might be called the "bigger fool" theory. Under this theory, the purchaser of a stock might pay a price above what he thinks the stock is worth in an intrinsic sense (the discounted dividends approach) because he thinks he can find a "bigger fool" who will pay still more for the stock. Such behavior has undoubtedly dominated the stock market in the past, as in the late 1920s, and it may dominate again. We maintain, however, that, ordinarily, stocks are bought for their investment value. Therefore, in this Appendix, we shall concentrate on the discounted cash flow approach to security valuation.

Stock Values with Zero Growth

Returning now to the valuation technique, suppose the rate of growth is measured by the rate at which dividends are expected to increase. If future growth is expected to be zero, the value of the stock is simply:

$$\text{price} = \frac{\text{dividends}}{\text{capitalization rate}}$$

$$P = \frac{D}{k} \qquad \text{(A10–6)}$$

"Normal" Growth

Year after year, the earnings and dividends of most companies have been increasing. In general, this growth is expected to continue in the foreseeable future at about the same rate as GNP. On this basis, it is expected that an average, normal company will grow at a rate of from 3 to 5 percent a year. Thus, if such a company's most recent dividend is D_o, its dividend in any future year may be forecast as $D_t = D_o(1+g)^t$ where g = the expected rate of growth. For example, if the ABC Company's last dividend was $1 and a 3 percent growth rate is expected, the estimated dividend five years hence will be:

$$\begin{aligned} D_t &= D_o(1+g)^t \\ &= \$1.00(1.03)^5 \\ &= \$1.00(1.159) \\ &= \$1.16 \end{aligned}$$

Using this method of estimating future dividends, equation (A10–4) may be rewritten as:

$$\begin{aligned} P_o &= \frac{D_1}{(1+k)^1} + \frac{D_2}{(1+k)^2} + \frac{D_3}{(1+k)^3} + \cdots \\ &= \frac{D_o(1+g)^1}{(1+k)^1} + \frac{D_o(1+g)^2}{(1+k)^2} + \frac{D_o(1+g)^3}{(1+k)^3} + \cdots \\ &= \sum_{t=1}^{\infty} \frac{D_o(1+g)^t}{(1+k)^t} \end{aligned} \qquad \text{(A10–7)}$$

It can be shown that equation (A10–7) may be rewritten as:[3]

$$P_o = \frac{D_1}{k-g} \qquad \text{(A10–8)}$$

[3] The proof of equation (A10-8) is as follows. Rewrite equation A10-7 as:

$$P_o = D_o\left[\frac{(1+g)}{(1+k)} + \frac{(1+g)^2}{(1+k)^2} + \frac{(1+g)^3}{(1+k)^3} + \cdots\right] \qquad (1)$$

Multiply both sides of equation (1) by $(1+k)/(1+g)$:

$$\left[\frac{(1+k)}{(1+g)}\right] P_o = D_o\left[1 + \frac{(1+g)}{(1+k)} + \frac{(1+g)^2}{(1+k)^2} + \cdots\right] \qquad (2)$$

Assuming $k > g$, we can subtract equation (1) from equation (2) to obtain:

$$\left[\frac{(1+k)}{(1+g)} - 1\right] P_o = D_o$$

$$\left[\frac{(1+k)-(1+g)}{(1+g)}\right] P_o = D_o$$

$$(k-g)\,P_o = D_o(1+g) = D_1$$

$$P_o = \frac{D_1}{k-g} \qquad \text{Q.E.D.}$$

To illustrate, suppose company G is growing at a rate of 3 percent per year; the next expected dividend is \$1.03, and the risk on investments of this type calls for an 8 percent capitalization rate. The estimated value of the firm's stock is:

$$P_o = \frac{\$1.03}{0.08 - 0.03} = \frac{\$1.03}{0.05} = \$20.60$$

If the stock is bought at this price, it provides a 5 percent initial dividend yield (\$1.03/\$20.60 = 5%), but the dividend rises at the rate of 3 percent a year. And as the dividend rises, the price of the stock rises proportionately, so the investor has a 3 percent capital gain a year. The 3 percent capital gain plus the 5 percent dividend yield totals to the 8 percent required rate of return.[4]

Note that equation A10–8 is sufficiently general to encompass the no-growth case described above. If growth is zero, this is simply a special case, and equation A10–8 is equal to equation A10–6.

"Supernormal" Growth

As will be seen in Chapter 24, firms typically go through "life cycles," during part of which their growth is much faster than that of the economy as a whole. Automobile manufacturers in the 1920s and television makers in the 1950s are examples. Figure A10–1 illustrates such supernormal growth and compares it with normal growth, zero growth, and declining situations.[5]

The illustrative supernormal growth firm is expected to grow at a 10 percent rate for ten years, then to have its growth rate fall to 3 percent, the norm expected for the economy. The value of a firm with such a growth pattern is determined by the following equation:

$$P_o = \sum_{t=1}^{N} \frac{D_o(1+g_s)^t}{(1+k)^t} + \sum_{t=N+1}^{\infty} \frac{D_N(1+g_n)^{t-N}}{(1+k)^t} \qquad \text{(A10–9)}$$

[4] This can also be seen by solving equation A10–8 for k:

$$k = \frac{D_1}{P_o} + g$$

In this form, it is easy to see that for normal growth companies—those whose growth is expected to continue indefinitely—the required rate of return is equal to the current dividend yield plus the expected growth rate.

One technical point should at least be mentioned here. The logic underlying the analysis implicitly assumes that investors are indifferent to dividend yield or capital gains. Empirical work has not conclusively established whether this is true or not, but the question is discussed at length in the Appendix to Chapter 12.

[5] A declining company is simply one with a negative growth rate.

where g_s = the supernormal growth rate and g_n the normal growth rate. The first summation is the present value of the dividends received during the early, rapid-growth period, while the second is the present value of the remainder of the expected dividends.[6]

Working through an example will help make this clear. It was seen that the supernormal growth company pays a $1 dividend at present and is expected to grow by 10 percent a year for 10 years and thereafter at 3 percent a year indefinitely. If stockholders' required rate of return is 8 percent on an investment with this degree of risk, what is the value of the stock? Based on the calculations in Table A10–1, the value is found to be $35.84, the present value of the dividends during the first 10 years plus the present value of the stock at the end of the tenth year.

If desired, equation A10–9 could be expanded to include as many different growth periods as seem desirable. For example, it might be desired to evaluate a firm expected to grow at 15 percent for the next five years; at 10 percent for the following five years; then at 5 percent indefinitely. To handle this situation additional terms could simply be added to equation A10–9.[7]

Comparing Companies with Different Expected Growth Rates

It is useful to summarize this section of the Appendix by making certain comparisons of the four illustrative firms whose dividend trends are shown in Figure A10–1. Using the valuation equations developed above, the conditions assumed in the preceding examples, and the additional assumption that each of the firms pays out 75 percent of its reported earnings (therefore earnings per share currently are $1.33 for each company), we show prices, dividend yields, and price-earnings ratios (hereafter written P/E) in Table A10–2.

Investors expect a return of 8 percent on each of the stocks. For the declining firm, this return consists of a relatively high current dividend yield combined with a capital loss amounting to 4 percent a year. For the no-growth firm, there is neither a capital gain nor a capital loss expectation, so the 8 percent return must be obtained entirely from the dividend yield. The normal growth firm provides a relatively low current dividend yield, but a 3 percent a year capital gain expectation. Finally, the supernormal growth firm has the lowest current yield but the highest capital gain expectation.

[6] Note that the summation of the second term in equation A10–9 is from $N + 1$ to ∞. Having the summation originate at $t = N + 1$, rather than at $t = 1$, discounts the second term back to the present. We point this out because it caused some confusion to readers of the second edition of *Managerial Finance*.

[7] A generalized model for varying growth rates is presented in Brigham and Pappas, "Duration of Growth, Changes in Growth Rates, and Corporate Share Prices," *Financial Analysts Journal* (May 1966).

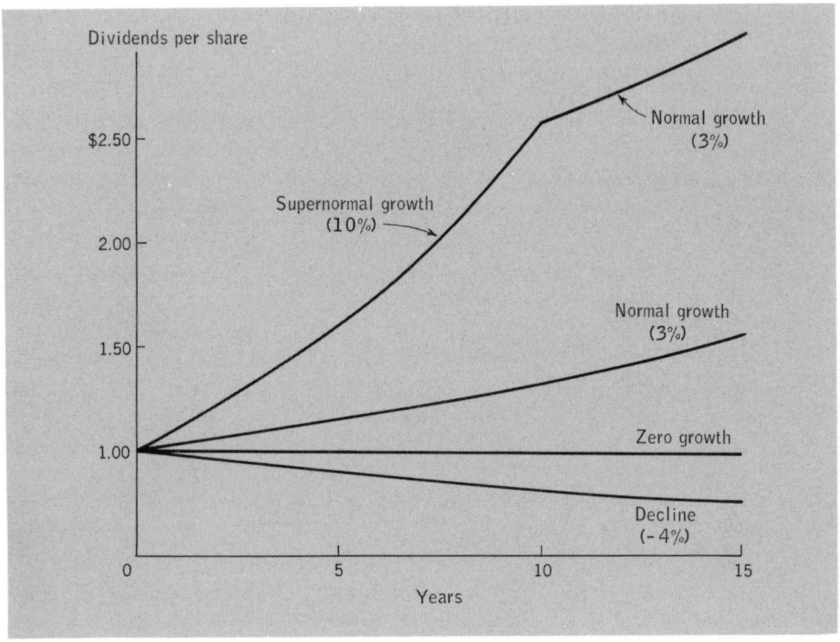

Figure A10–1 Illustrative Dividend Growth Rate

The relationships among the P/E ratios are also similar to what one would intuitively expect—the higher the expected growth, the higher the P/E ratio.[8]

Changes in Required Rate of Return

Up to this point, 8 percent has been used as k, the rate of return stockholders require on investments in common stocks as risky as the ones in the examples. If the risk is higher, investors will require a larger return; on less risky securities, they will accept a lower expected return. For example, the 8 percent return considered thus far might be the one applicable to the automobile-parts manufacturing industry, one with about average risk as compared with other industrial sectors. For the electric utility industry, with its more stable sales and more predictable prices, risks are lower; a 6 percent expected return might be appropriate. Using 6 percent in the valuation formulas and assuming the same earnings, dividends, and expected growth rates, the stock prices, dividend yields, and P/E ratios are found as given in Table A10–3. Here stock

[8] Although the fact has not been demonstrated, the longer the supernormal growth rate is expected to continue, the higher the current price, the lower the current dividend yield, and the higher the current P/E ratio.

TABLE A10–1 METHOD OF CALCULATING THE VALUE OF A STOCK WITH SUPERNORMAL GROWTH

1) *Assumptions*
   a) Stockholders' capitalization rate (k) is 8 percent.
   b) Growth rate is 10 percent for 10 years, 3 percent thereafter.
   c) The initial dividend is \$1.

2) *Present value of dividends during rapid growth period*

Year	Dividend $\$1\,(1.10)^t$	DISCOUNT FACTOR $\frac{1}{(1.08)^t}$	Present Value
1	1.100	0.926	\$ 1.02
2	1.210	0.857	1.04
3	1.331	0.794	1.06
4	1.464	0.735	1.08
5	1.611	0.681	1.10
6	1.772	0.630	1.12
7	1.949	0.583	1.14
8	2.144	0.540	1.16
9	2.358	0.500	1.18
10	2.594	0.463	1.20
			\$11.10

3) *Value of stock at end of year 10*

$$P_{10} = \frac{D_{11}}{k - g} = \frac{\$2.594(1.03)}{.05} = \$53.43$$

4) *Value today of price in year 10*

$$P_{10}\left(\frac{1}{1+k}\right)^{10} = \$53.43(0.463) = \$24.74$$

5) *Value of stock today*

$$P_o = \$11.10 + \$24.74 = \$35.84$$

TABLE A10–2 PRICES, DIVIDEND YIELDS, AND PRICE-EARNINGS RATIOS FOR 8 PERCENT RETURNS UNDER DIFFERENT GROWTH ASSUMPTIONS

		PRICE	CURRENT DIVIDEND YIELD	P/E RATIO*
Declining firm	$P_o = \dfrac{D_1}{k - g} = \dfrac{\$0.96}{0.08 - (-0.04)} = \dfrac{\$0.96}{0.12}$	\$ 8.00	12%	6.0
No-growth firm	$P_o = \dfrac{D_1}{k} = \dfrac{\$1}{0.08}$	\$12.50	8%	9.4
Normal growth firm	$P_o = \dfrac{D_1}{k - g} = \dfrac{\$1.03}{0.08 - 0.03} = \dfrac{\$1.03}{.05}$	\$20.60	5%	15.5
Supernormal growth firm	$P_o =$ (See Table A10–1)	\$35.84	3%	26.9

* It was assumed at the beginning of this example that each of the companies is earning \$1.33 initially. This \$1.33, divided into the various prices, gives the current P/E ratios.

prices and P/E ratios are very much higher for the various growth rates than they were at the higher required rate of return, while the dividend yields are considerably lower. This is seen by a comparison of Tables A10–2 and A10–3.

TABLE A10–3 PRICES, DIVIDEND YIELDS, AND PRICE-EARNINGS RATIOS FOR 6 PERCENT RETURNS UNDER DIFFERENT GROWTH ASSUMPTIONS

	PRICE	CURRENT DIVIDEND YIELD	P/E RATIO
Declining firm ($g = -4\%$)	\$10.00	10%	7.5
No-growth firm ($g = 0$)	\$16.67	6%	12.5
Normal growth firm ($g = 3\%$)	\$33.33	3%	25.1
Supernormal growth firm ($g = 10\%, 3\%$)	\$67.49	1.5%	50.7

11

The Cost of Capital

In the preceding chapter, the nature of the valuation process and the concept of expected rates of return were considered in some detail. In the discussion of the cost of capital, the subject of this chapter, extensive use will be made of these valuation concepts. First, the costs of the individual components of the capital structure—debt, preferred stock, and equity—are considered; because the riskiness of different classes of securities varies (to the investor), there are variations in the costs of different securities. Second, the individual component costs are brought together to form a weighted cost of capital. Third, the conceptual ideas developed in the first two sections are illustrated with an example of the cost of capital calculation for an actual company. Finally, the interrelationships between the cost of capital and the investment opportunity scheduled is developed, and the simultaneous determination of the marginal cost of capital and the marginal return on investment is discussed.

DEBT CAPITAL

If a firm borrows $100,000 for one year at 6 percent interest, its before-tax dollar cost is $6,000 and its before-tax percentage cost is 6 percent. *As a first approximation, the cost of debt is defined as the rate of return that must be earned on debt-financed investments in order to keep unchanged the earnings available to common shareholders.*[1] Hence, the cost of debt turns out to be the interest rate on debt, for if the firm borrows and invests the borrowed funds to earn a before-tax return just equal to the interest rate, then the earnings available to common stock remain unchanged. This is demonstrated below.

EXAMPLE. The ABC Company has sales of $1 million, operating costs of $900,000, and no debt, and is taxed at the rate of 50 percent. Its income statement is shown in the Before column below. Then it borrows $100,000 at 6 percent and invests the funds in assets whose use causes sales to rise by $7,000 and operating costs to rise by $1,000. Hence, profits before interest rise by $6,000. The new situation is shown in the After column. Earnings after taxes are unchanged, as the investment just earns its cost of capital.

	INCOME STATEMENTS	
	Before	After
Sales	$1,000,000	$1,007,000
Operating costs	900,000	901,000
Earnings before interest and taxes (EBIT)	$ 100,000	$ 106,000
Interest (I)	—	6,000
Earnings before taxes (EBT)	$ 100,000	$ 100,000
Taxes (T)	50,000	50,000
Earnings after taxes (EAT)	$ 50,000	$ 50,000

Note that the cost of debt is applicable to *new* debt, not to the interest on old, previously outstanding debt. In other words, we are

[1] Note that this definition is a *first approximation;* it will be modified to take account of the deductibility of interest payments for income tax purposes. Note also that here the cost of debt is considered in isolation. The impact of the debt on the cost of equity, as well as on future increments of debt (in a sense, the true marginal cost of debt), will be treated when the weighted cost of a combination of debt and equity is derived.

interested in the cost of incremental debt, or the *marginal* cost of debt. The primary concern with the cost of capital is to use it in a decision-making process—the decision whether to obtain capital to make new investments; the fact that the firm borrowed at high or low rates in the past is irrelevant.

PREFERRED STOCK

Preferred stock, described in detail in Chapter 19, is a hybrid between debt and common stock. Like debt, preferred stock carries a fixed commitment on the part of the corporation to make periodic payments; in liquidation, the claims of the preferred stockholders take precedence over those of the common stockholders. Unlike debt, however, failure to make the preferred dividend payments does not result in bankruptcy. Preferred stock is thus somewhat more risky *to the firm* than common stock, but it is less risky than bonds. Just the reverse holds for investors. To the investor, preferred is less risky than common but more risky than debt.

The definition of the cost of preferred stock is similar to that of the cost of debt—it is that rate of return that must be earned on preferred stock-financed investments in order to keep unchanged the earnings available to common shareholders. This required rate of return turns out to be the preferred dividend per share (D_p) divided by the net price that the firm could realize from the sale of one share of a new issue of preferred stock (P_n).

$$\text{cost of preferred stock} = \frac{D_p}{P_n}$$

For example, if a firm sells an issue of $100 par value preferred stock with a $6 dividend and nets $95 a share after underwriting commissions, then its cost of preferred stock is 6.3 percent ($6/$95).

TAX ADJUSTMENT

As they stand, the definitions of the cost of debt and preferred stock capital are incompatible because, for tax purposes, interest payments are deductible and preferred dividends are not. The following example is an illustration.

EXAMPLE. The ABC Company can borrow $100,000 at 6 percent, or it can sell 1,000 shares of $6 preferred stock to net $100 a share. Its before-investment situation is given in the Before column below. At what rate of return must it invest the proceeds from the new financing to keep the earnings available to common shareholders from changing?

		INVEST IN ASSETS YIELDING		
		6%		12%
	Before	*Debt*	*Preferred*	*Preferred*
EBIT	$100,000	$106,000	$106,000	$112,000
I	—	6,000	—	—
EBT	100,000	100,000	106,000	112,000
T (50%)	50,000	50,000	53,000	56,000
Preferred dividends	—	—	6,000	6,000
Available for common dividends	$ 50,000	$ 50,000	$ 47,000	$ 50,000

As can be seen from the tabulations, if the funds are invested to yield 6 percent before taxes, earnings available to common stockholders are constant if debt is used but they fall if the financing is with preferred stock. To maintain the $50,000 net earnings requires that funds generated from the sale of preferred stock be invested to yield 12 percent before taxes or 6 percent after taxes.

Cost-of-capital calculations may be made either on a before-tax or an after-tax basis. Ultimately, however, business decision-makers must consider after-tax effects. Therefore, just as in Chapter 9 in the discussion of the rates of return on investments, only the cost of capital *after* corporate taxes will be dealt with. The cost of preferred stock is already on an after-tax basis as defined, but a simple adjustment is needed to arrive at the after-tax cost of debt. It is recognized that interest payments are tax deductible, and the cost of debt capital is reduced as follows:

$$\text{after-tax cost of debt} = (\text{before-tax cost}) \times (1.0 - \text{tax rate})$$

EXAMPLE:

before-tax cost of debt = 6 percent; tax rate = 48 percent
after-tax cost = (0.06) (1 − 0.48) = (0.06)(0.52) = 3.12 percent

Had the tax rate been 50 percent, as is usually assumed for ease of calculations, the after-tax cost of debt would have been one half the interest rate. Also, we should note that for a firm with losses the tax rate is zero; therefore, for a loss corporation the cost of debt is not reduced.

COST OF EQUITY

The cost of equity capital is defined as the minimum rate of return that must be earned on equity-financed investments to keep unchanged the value of the existing common equity. In other words, if 10 percent is a corporation's cost of equity capital, then the value of the equity used to finance an investment will exceed its cost if—and only if—the internal rate of return on the investment exceeds 10 percent. This is an opportunity cost concept. If investors can find investments of similar risk outside the firm that yield at least 10 percent—that is, if their opportunity cost of funds tied up in the business is 10 percent—then they do not want the firm to invest equity capital to yield less than 10 percent.

In general, there is a different cost of capital applicable to equity capital raised by retaining earnings than to that raised by selling new common stock. These points are covered below.

Retained Earnings[2]

The cost of retained earnings, or the return that might be earned on investments financed by retained earnings, is equal to the rate of return that investors expect to receive on the stock. To illustrate, consider Aubey Rents, a firm currently earning \$2 a share, paying a \$1 dividend, and selling at \$20 a share. The company's earnings, dividends, and stock price have all been growing at about 5 percent a year; this growth rate is expected to continue indefinitely. Using this information and the procedures developed in Chapter 10, we compute the expected rate of return on the stock, k, as follows:

$$\text{expected, or required, rate of return} = \frac{\text{dividend}}{\text{price}} + \text{expected growth}$$

$$k = \frac{\$1}{\$20} + 5\% = 10\%$$

[2] Our treatment of the cost of retained earnings abstracts from certain complications caused by personal income taxes on dividend income and by brokerage costs incurred in reinvesting dividend income. Similarly, we do not explicitly treat the cost of depreciation-generated funds in the chapter. The problems are, however, discussed at length in the Appendix to this chapter.

The expected growth rate in the price of the shares is 5 percent; on the \$20 initial price, this leads to a \$1 increase in the value of the stock. This price increase will be attained (barring changes in the general level of stock prices) if the company retains \$1 and invests this amount to yield 10 percent. However, if the \$1 of retained earnings is invested to yield only 5 percent, then earnings will grow by only \$0.05 during the year, not by the expected \$0.10 a share. The new earnings will be \$2.05, not the expected \$2.10. This represents a growth of only 2½ percent, not 5 percent. If investors believe that the firm will earn only 5 percent on retained earnings in the future and thus attain only a 2½ percent growth rate, they will reappraise the value of the stock downward as follows:

$$\text{current price} = \frac{\text{dividend}}{(1+k)} + \frac{\text{current price} \times (1 + \text{expected growth})}{(1+k)}$$

$$P = \frac{\$1.00}{1.10} + \frac{P \times (1.025)}{1.10}$$

$$= \frac{\$1.00 + 1.025P}{1.10}$$

$$1.10P = \$1.00 + 1.025P$$

$$1.100P - 1.025P = \$1.00$$

$$0.075P = \$1.00$$

$$P = \$13.33.$$

Note, however, that Aubey Rents suffered this price decline because it invested equity funds—retained earnings—at less than its cost of capital. Had it refrained from making this investment and paid all its earnings out in dividends, it would have cut its growth rate to zero. However, the price of the stock would not have fallen because investors would still have been getting the required 10 percent rate of return on their investments.

$$k = \frac{D}{P} + G = \frac{\$2}{\$20} + 0 = 10 \text{ percent}$$

All the return would have been coming in the form of dividends, but the rate of return would have been the required 10 percent.[3]

[3] Notice that we are implicitly assuming that investors are indifferent as to whether the return on their investment is in the form of dividends or capital gains. The validity of this assumption is discussed in Chapter 12, and the results of an empirical test of the indifference assumption are reported in Appendix A to that chapter.

New Common Stock

The cost of new common stock, or *external* equity capital, k_e, is higher than the cost of retained earnings, k, because of the flotation costs involved in selling new common stock. To demonstrate, let us continue with the example of Aubey Rents. The company has 10,000 shares of stock outstanding, no debt, and is expected to earn \$20,000, or \$2 a share during the coming year. Investors anticipate that the company will continue its policy of paying out 50 percent of earnings as dividends, so \$1 is the dividend expectation for the coming year. The firm has also been growing at 5 percent a year, and this growth rate is expected to be maintained. Investors require a 10 percent rate of return on the stock, so it is selling for \$20 a share.

Now suppose Aubey Rents sells 5,000 shares of stock to the public at \$20 a share, incurs a selling cost of \$2 a share, and thus nets \$18 a share, or a total of \$90,000. If this \$90,000 is invested to yield 10 percent, will the earnings, dividend, and price expectations be met? First, we calculate the new earnings per share, giving effect to the stock sale and to the new investment.

$$\begin{aligned}
\text{incremental profits} &= \$90{,}000 \times 0.10 = \$9{,}000 \\
\text{total profits} &= \$20{,}000 + \$9{,}000 = \$29{,}000 \\
\text{incremental shares} &= 5{,}000 \\
\text{total shares} &= 10{,}000 + 5{,}000 = 15{,}000 \\
\text{new earnings per share} &= \frac{\$29{,}000}{15{,}000} = \$1.93
\end{aligned}$$

The \$1.93 is below the expected \$2 a share. The sale of the new shares has diluted earnings, and the price of the stock will fall below \$20 a share. Thus, the investment has not met the definition of cost of capital—the return on the investment financed by new stock did not earn the cost of capital because the incremental profits were not sufficient to keep the price of the stock from falling.

What rate of return must be earned on funds raised by selling stock to make this action worthwhile or, to put it another way, what is the cost of new common stock? The answer is found by applying the following formula.

$$\text{cost of new common stock, } k_e, = \frac{\text{required rate of return on common stock}}{1 - \text{percentage cost of floating new common stock}}$$

In our example, the flotation cost on new equity issues is 10 percent

(\$2/\$20), so applying the formula we find the cost of new common stock to be 11.1 percent.

$$k_e = \frac{10\%}{1.0 - 0.10} = \frac{10\%}{0.9} = 11.1\%$$

If Aubey earns 11.1 percent on investments financed by new common stock issues, earnings per share will not fall below previous expectations, the price of the stock will not fall, and the investments will have covered their cost of capital.

Finding the Basic Required Rate of Return on Common Stock

It is obvious by now that the basic rate of return required by investors on a firm's common stock, k, is a most important quantity. This required rate of return is the cost of retained earnings and, used with the cost of floating common stock, it forms the basis for the cost of capital obtained from new stock issues. How is this all-important quantity estimated?

Although one *can* use very involved, highly complicated procedures for making this estimation, satisfactory estimates may, in general, be obtained in either of two ways.[4]

1. Simply look at the average rate of return that investors have obtained in the past, assume that in the future stocks will continue to have about the same rates of return as in the past, and use these historical averages as estimates of the current cost of equity capital.

   For this, we recommend the figures given in Table 10–1. To use the table for this purpose, one must first make judgment decisions (a) about the risk/liquidity position of the stock in question and (b) about the state of the stock market. Suppose, for example, we decide that our particular company is of about average risk and liquidity and that the stock market is about normal—the market is not, in our judgment, either abnormally high or abnormally low. In this case we would simply assign 9 percent as the basic cost of equity capital. Later on, if the market dropped sharply, we might re-evaluate the cost of equity upward to 10 or, perhaps, even to 12 percent.

   Notice that some very fine judgments are required in this process. It would be nice to pretend that these judgments are unnecessary and to specify a precise way of determining the exact cost of equity capital. Unfortunately, this is not possible. Finance is in large part a matter of judgment, and one simply must face this fact.

[4] An illustration of a relatively elaborate cost of capital study is given in the Appendix to Chapter 12.

2. An alternative procedure, the use of which is recommended in conjunction with the one described above, is to estimate the basic required rate of return as

$$\text{rate of return} = \frac{\text{dividends}}{\text{price}} + \text{average growth rate}$$

$$k = \frac{D}{P} + g$$

The rationale for this equation, which was discussed in Chapter 10 and is developed in detail in Appendix A to Chapter 12, is that stockholder returns are derived from dividends and capital gains. The total of the dividend yield plus the average growth rate over the past 5 to 10 years gives an estimate of the total returns that stockholders probably expect in the future from a particular share of stock.

For normal companies—those that are growing at a rate approximately equal to that of the entire economy—the two procedures generally give similar results. If recent growth has been extremely high, so high that it is doubtful the rate can be maintained, then the first procedure is the better one.

WEIGHTED COST OF CAPITAL

Suppose a particular firm's cost of debt is estimated to be 2½ percent (the interest rate on new debt issues is 5 percent), its cost of equity is estimated to be 8 percent, and the decision has been made to finance next year's projects by selling debt. The argument is frequently advanced that the cost of these projects is 2½ percent because debt will be used to finance them.

This position contains a basic fallacy. To finance a particular set of projects with debt implies that the firm is also using up some of its potential for obtaining new low-cost debt. As expansion takes place in subsequent years, at some point the firm will find it necessary to use additional equity financing or else the debt ratio will become too large.

To illustrate this point, suppose the firm has a 2½ percent cost of debt and a 10 percent cost of equity. In the first year it borrows heavily, using up its debt capacity in the process, to finance projects yielding 3 percent. In the second year it has projects available that yield 9 percent, three times the return on first-year projects, but it cannot accept them because they would have to be financed with 10 percent equity money. To avoid this problem, the firm should be viewed as an on-going concern and its cost of capital should be calculated as a weighted average of the various types of funds it uses: debt, preferred stock, and equity.

Calculating Procedure

Before discussing the proper set of weights to be employed in computing the weighted average, it is useful to look briefly at the calculating procedure. The method is demonstrated in the following example.

Example. The right-hand-side of the Simple Company's balance sheet is shown in column 2 of Table 11–1, and the dollars are converted to percentages of the total in column 3. Column 4 gives the after-tax costs of the different types of capital: debt, preferred stock, and equity. Column 5 shows the product of column 3 and column 4. Summing column 5 gives the weighted average cost of the firm's capital—0.0775, or 7.75 percent.

TABLE 11–1 SIMPLE COMPANY

(1) CAPITAL COMPONENTS	(2) BALANCE SHEET FIGURES	(3) PER-CENT OF TOTAL	(4) COMPO-NENT COST (AFTER TAXES)	(5) COLUMN 3 TIMES COLUMN 4	(6) COLUMN 2 TIMES COLUMN 4
Debt	$ 30,000,000	30%	3%	0.0090	$ 900,000
Preferred stock	5,000,000	5	7	0.0035	350,000
Net worth	65,000,000	65	10	0.0650	6,500,000
Total	$100,000,000	100%		0.0775	$7,750,000

An alternative method that gives identical results is to multiply the dollar figures in column 2 by the component costs in column 4 to get the figures in column 6, then add column 6 and divide the sum by the total amount of capital. Thus, the total dollar cost of $7.750 million divided by the $100 million of capital is 7.75 percent. We use whichever method provides the easiest calculations for the specific application.

Weighting System

Although both financial theorists and corporate financial managers disagree over particular aspects of debt policy, there is general agreement that firms do seek optimum capital structures. "Optimum" is defined

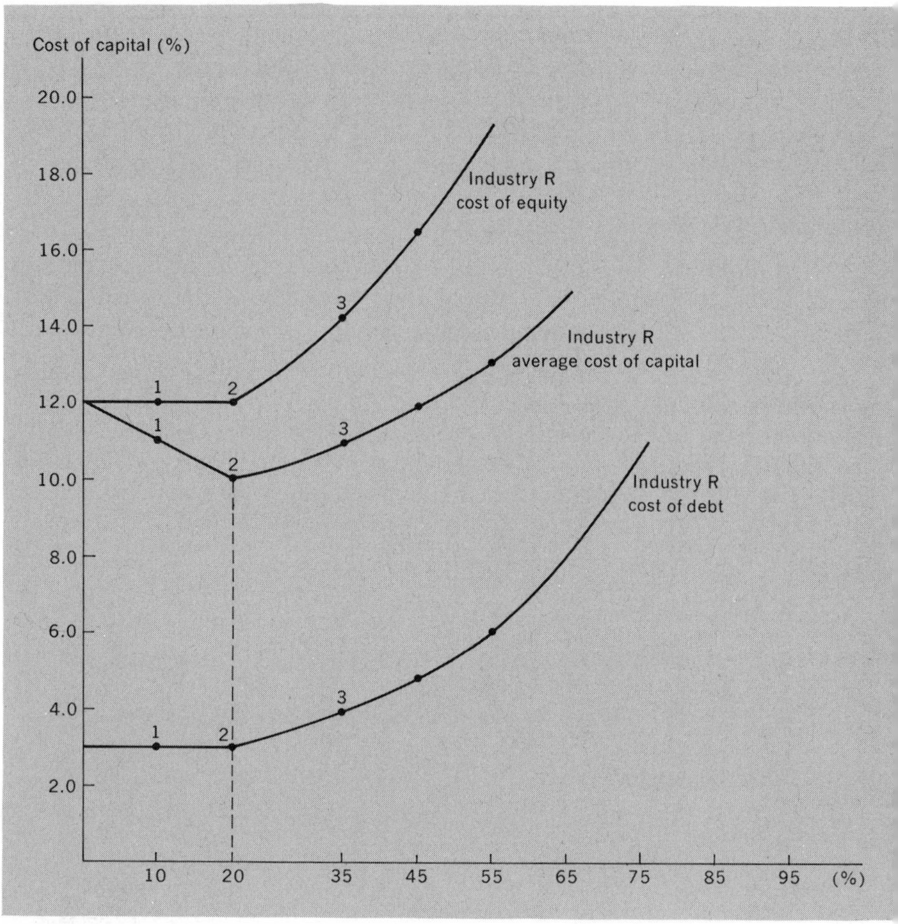

Figure 11–1 Hypothetical Cost of Capital Schedules for an Industry

as the capital structure that minimizes the weighted cost of capital, and the concept is illustrated below. To minimize confusion, it is assumed that firms have no preferred stock.

Figure 11–1 shows a scatter diagram of the cost of debt and the cost of equity capital plotted against the debt ratio for a hypothetical industry R. Each dot represents one of the firms in the industry. For example, the dots labeled "1" represent firm 1, a company with only 10 percent debt. Firm 1's after-tax cost of debt is 3 percent, while its cost of equity is 12 percent. Firm 2 uses 20 percent debt and also has a 3 percent cost of debt and a 12 percent cost of equity. Firm 3 has a 14 percent cost of equity and a 4 percent cost of debt. It uses 35 percent debt, and investors consider this to be a sufficiently high debt level to require higher yields on the firm's securities. In this particular industry, the threshold debt ratio that begins to worry investors is 20 percent. Below 20 percent debt, investors are totally unconcerned about any risk induced by debt; above 20 percent, they are aware of the higher risk and require compensation in the form of higher rates of return.

The debt and the equity costs may be averaged on the basis of their respective weights of debt and equity capital. Firm 1 has a weighted average cost equal to 11.1 percent, firm 2 has a weighted average cost of 10.2 percent, and firm 3 has a weighted cost of 10.5 percent. These weighted costs, together with those of the other firms in the industry, are also plotted in Figure 11–1. We can see that firm 2 has the lowest weighted cost of capital—*20 percent debt is the debt ratio that minimizes the average cost of capital, so the optimal capital structure requires that firms use 20 percent debt.* According to the theory, the other firms in the industry should move toward a 20 percent debt ratio.

Shown in Figure 11–2 are the cost-of-capital schedules for firms in a risky industry (R) and a stable industry (S). Industry R, the one on which Figure 11–1 was based, might consist of diesel locomotive manufacturers and industry S of electric utilities. The highest line on the graph shows the relationship between the cost of equity and the debt ratio for firms in industry R. With no debt, their cost of equity is 12 percent. It remains at this level until debt reaches 20 percent, but beyond this point costs rise because of the increasing risk of greater amounts of debt. The second curve from the bottom shows the relationship between the cost of debt and the debt ratio for the R firms. This curve starts at 3 percent after taxes, is constant for a while, and then rises as a larger percentage of assets is financed with debt. The average cost of capital for R firms, the second line from the top, is 12 percent where all financing is with relatively expensive equity capital. After declining for a while as additional low-cost debt is averaged in with equity, the average cost of capital for R industry begins to rise when debt has reached 20 percent of total capital. Beyond this point, the fact that both debt and equity are becoming more expensive offsets the fact that debt costs less than common equity.

While the same principles apply to firms in the less risky industry S, its cost functions are quite different from those of industry R. In the first place, S's over-all risk is lower, giving rise to lower debt and equity costs at all debt levels. Further, its relative stability means that less risk is attached to any given percentage of debt; therefore, its cost of both debt and equity—and, consequently, its average cost of capital, turn up further to the right than do those for R firms. Its optimum debt ratio (Q_2) is at 35 percent as compared to only 20 percent for industry R firms.

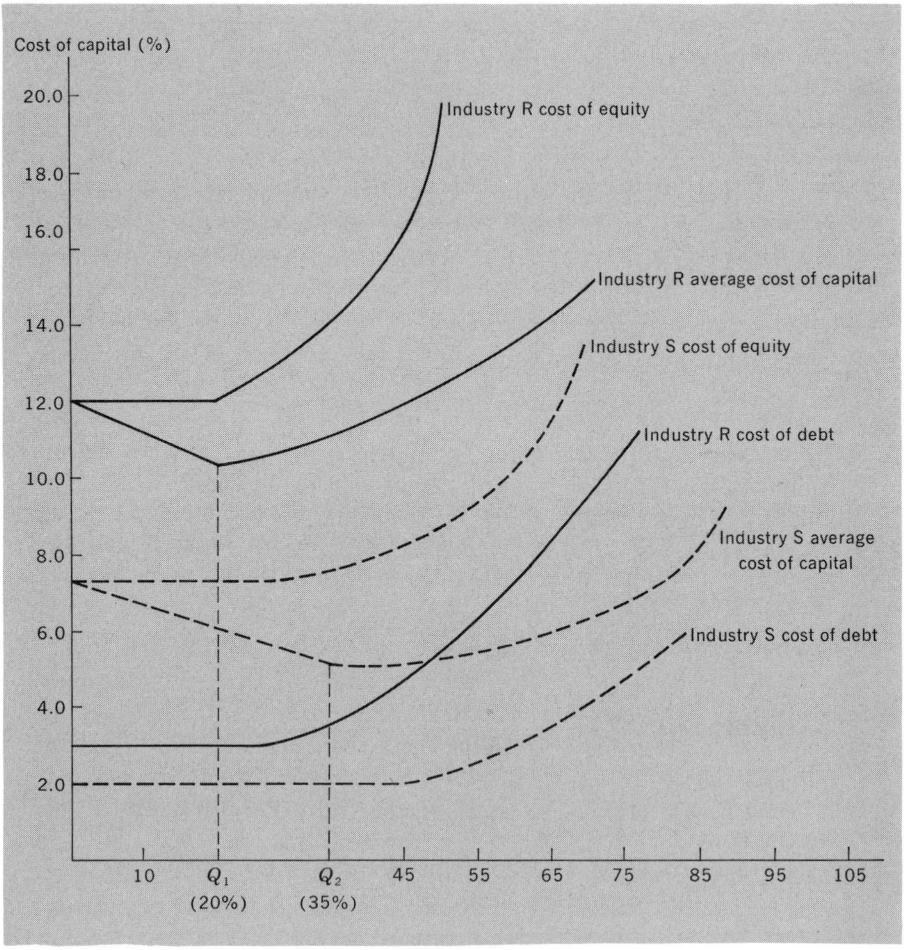

Figure 11–2 Hypothetical Cost of Capital Schedules for High-Risk and Low-Risk Industries

Determining the actual optimum capital structure for a specific firm requires both analysis and judgment, and it is up to a firm's financial management to decide on the best capital structure for its company. Once this decision has been reached, the weighting system for the average cost of capital calculation is also determined. Unless otherwise noted, we will assume that management deems its present capital structure to be optimal, and we shall use this set of weights in our calculations.[5]

[5] If the book value of a firm's capital differs from its market value, it is possible to define two alternative sets of capital weights. In strict accordance with theoretical concepts, it is preferable to use market value weights. If a firm's equity sells for more than its book value—the typical situation for most healthy firms—

ALCULATING COST OF CAPITAL OR AN ACTUAL COMPANY

The procedures discussed above are now applied to an actual company, the Continental Can Company, to illustrate the cost-of-capital calculation. Continental Can is a large firm, with assets of over $950 million and sales of over $1 billion. Sales and earnings are relatively stable, as food and beverage companies make up the bulk of the firm's customers. Dividends have been paid since 1923, even during the depression of the 1930s. Based on an indicated dividend rate of $2 and a current price of $50 per share, the dividend yield is 4 percent. Over the past 10 years, earnings, dividends, and the price of the stock have grown at a rate of about 6 percent; all indications suggest that this same rate of growth will be maintained in the foreseeable future. Since internally generated funds provide sufficient equity, only the costs of internal equity, taken in accordance with the preceding discussion of retained earnings to be 10 percent, need be considered.

The average interest rate on Continental Can's outstanding long-term debt is 4.5 percent, but much of this debt was issued in earlier years when interest rates were much lower than they are now. Current market yields (Winter 1969) are about 7 percent, and approximately this cost will be associated with new debt issues. After a 48 percent income tax, the cost of debt is estimated to be 3.6 percent. The preferred stock is stated to be 3.75 percent preferred, but it was also issued when rates were low. Based on current market yields, the estimated cost of preferred stock is 7½ percent.

---

then using book value weights produces a weighted *average* cost of capital that is too low. However, the weighted *marginal* cost of capital is not generally influenced to any significant degree by the choice of weights used to calculate it. The reason for this is that the *market* values of *marginal* debt and equity are approximately equal to their *book* values.

Two additional points are also worth mentioning here. First, when book and market values differ, it is *impossible* to maintain capital structures constant in terms of both book and market values. That is, if debt constitutes 50 percent of capital when book values are used but only 30 percent when market values are used, then raising additional capital *necessarily* causes one or the other of these ratios to change. Raising new debt and equity on a 50–50 basis will maintain the 50 percent book value debt ratio, but it will cause the 30 percent debt ratio at market values to increase. The second point is that in practice most firms seem to consider their book value capital structures when making decisions about new financing. These two reasons, combined with the fact that weights do not particularly matter when considering the *marginal* cost of capital, lead us to use book weights in spite of the theoretical superiority of market value weights.

The right-hand side of Continental Can's balance sheet is given in Table 11–2. A large portion (24 percent) of the firm's funds are "free" in the sense that no interest is charged for them—accounts payable, accruals, and reserves are in this class. Some would argue that in the calculation of the over-all cost of capital, this "free" capital, plus short-term debt, should be included. Under certain circumstances this procedure is valid; usually, however, only permanent, long-term capital need be considered. The principal reason for ignoring short-term capital and "free" capital is a practical one: the cost of capital is used primarily in capital budgeting for long-term assets, which are generally financed with long-term, permanent funds.[6] Of the target, or chosen long-term

TABLE 11–2 CONTINENTAL CAN COMPANY RIGHT-HAND SIDE OF BALANCE SHEET
(millions of dollars)

			LONG-TERM FUNDS ONLY	
Payables and accruals	$120	12.5%		
Tax accruals	33	3.5		
Total current liabilities	$153	16.0%		
Reserve for deferred taxes	$ 66	6.9%		
Other reserves (primarily pension fund)	11	1.1		
Total reserves	$ 77	8.0%		
Long-term debt	$160	16.7%	$160	22%
Preferred stock	7	0.8	7	1
Common equity	560	58.5	560	77
Long-term funds	727	76.0%	$727	100%
Total Financing	$957	100.0%		

[6] Another justification for ignoring "free" capital is that, in the capital budgeting process, these spontaneously generated funds are netted out against the required investment outlay, then ignored in the cost-of-capital calculation. To illustrate, consider a retail firm thinking of opening a new store. According to customary practices, the firm should (1) estimate the required outlay, (2) estimate the net receipts (additions to profits) from the new store, (3) discount the estimated receipts at the cost of capital, and (4) accept the decision to open the new store only if the net present value of the expected revenue stream exceeds the investment outlay. The estimated accruals, trade payables, and other costless forms of credit are deducted from the investment before making the calculation.

capital structure, 22 percent is debt, 1 percent is preferred stock, and 77 percent is common equity.

If management believed that some other capital structure was optimal, then other weights would be used; for purposes of illustration it is assumed that the existing structure has been determined to be the optimum. On the basis of these weights and the previously determined costs of debt, equity, and preferred stock, the calculations shown in Table 11–3

TABLE 11–3 CONTINENTAL CAN ILLUSTRATIVE CALCULATION OF COST OF CAPITAL
(dollars in millions)

USING DOLLAR AMOUNTS OF CAPITAL FOR WEIGHTS

	Amount of Capital (1)	Component Cost (2)	Amount of Cost (Column 1 times Column 2) (3)
Long-term debt	$160	3.6%	$ 5.76
Preferred stock	7	7.5	.53
Common equity	560	10.0	56.00
	$727		$62.29

$$\frac{\$62.29}{\$727} = 8.57\%$$

USING CAPITAL PROPORTIONS FOR WEIGHTS

Long-term debt	22.0%	3.6%	.0079
Preferred stock	1.0	7.5	.0008
Common equity	77.0	10.0	.0770
	100.0%		.0857 = 8.57%

indicate that Continental Can's weighted cost of capital is 8.6 percent.[7] As long as Continental Can finances in the indicated manner, its new funds should cost this amount.[8]

[7] Using market instead of book value weights, the weighted cost of capital is 9.0 percent.

[8] In this situation, the average and marginal costs of new capital are constant and equal to one another. Its average cost of capital in a *historical* sense is, of course, different because of the lower costs of the old debt and preferred stock. But historical costs are irrelevant for decision-making purposes.

MARGINAL COST OF CAPITAL

In the preceding example of Continental Can, we assumed that the company would finance only with debt and internally generated equity. On this basis, we found their over-all weighted cost of capital to be 8.6 percent. What would have occurred had the firm's need for funds been so great that it was forced to sell new common stock? The answer is that its marginal cost of capital would have increased significantly. To show why this is so, we shall extend the Continental Can example.

First, suppose that during 1968 Continental Can had total earnings of \$59 million available for common stockholders, paid \$27 million in dividends, and retained \$32 million. We know that to keep the capital structure in balance and the average cost of capital at 8.6 percent, the retained earnings should equal 77 percent of the net addition to capital, the other 23 percent being debt and preferred stock. Therefore, the total new capital that can be obtained on the basis of the retained earnings is:

$$\text{retained earnings} = 0.77 \times \text{new capital}$$

$$\text{new capital} = \frac{\text{retained earnings}}{0.77}$$

$$= \frac{\$32 \text{ million}}{0.77} = \$41.6 \text{ million}$$

Next, we note that 1 percent of the new capital, or about \$400,000 should be preferred stock and that 22 percent, or \$9.2 million, should be debt. In other words, Continental Can can raise a total of \$41.6 million—\$32 million from retained earnings, \$9.2 million in the form of debt, and \$400,000 in the form of preferred stock—and still maintain its target capital structure in exact balance.

If all financing up to \$41.6 million is in the prescribed proportions, the cost of each dollar of new capital up to that point is still 8.6 percent, the previously computed weighted cost of capital. As soon as the total of the required funds exceeds \$41.6 million, however, Continental Can must begin relying on more expensive new common stock. Therefore, beyond \$41.6 million we must compute a new weighted cost of capital. Assuming Continental Can would incur a flotation cost on new equity issues equal to 10 percent, we could compute the cost of capital for funds over \$41.6 million as follows:

1. Find the cost of new equity:

$$\text{cost of new common stock} = \frac{\text{required rate of return}}{1 - \text{flotation costs}}$$

$$= \frac{10 \text{ percent}}{0.9} = 11.1\%$$

2. Get a new weighted cost of capital (marginal cost of capital), using new common stock:

	Proportion ×	Component Cost	= Product
Debt	22%	3.6	.0079
Preferred stock	1	7.5	.0008
Equity (new)	77	11.1	.0855
	100.0%		.0942 or 9.4%

Figure 11–3 gives another view of this concept. The relationships obtained are shown in Figure 11–3(*a*). Here we see that up to $41.6 million—the total of retained earnings, incremental debt, and incremental preferred stock—the cost of capital is constant at 8.6 percent. Immediately beyond $41.6 million, however, the cost of capital jumps to 9.4 percent.[9]

Figure 11–3(*a*) is, of course, highly idealized; in fact, the actual cost of capital curve looks much more like that shown in Figure 11–3(*b*). Here we see that the curve is flat until it reaches the vicinity of $41.6 million; then it turns up gradually and continues rising. It will go up gradually rather than suddenly because the firm will probably make small adjustments in its target debt ratio, in the actual types of securities it uses, and so on. And the curve will continue to rise because, as more and more of its securities are put on the market during a fairly short period, it will experience more and more difficulty in getting the market to absorb the new securities. These two topics—the wide assortment

[9] It should be noted that we are ignoring depreciation in this illustration—the illustration is concerned with *new* capital raised, not the total. However, as is pointed out in the appendix to this chapter, the cost of depreciation-generated capital is equal to the average cost of capital over that segment of the curve before the firm must sell new common stock. Therefore, to bring depreciation into the analysis one need only extend the first section of the curve to the right by the amount of depreciation. This is of no concern to us here, but it is important later on when the cost of capital schedule is combined with the investment opportunity schedule to determine the optimum capital budget.

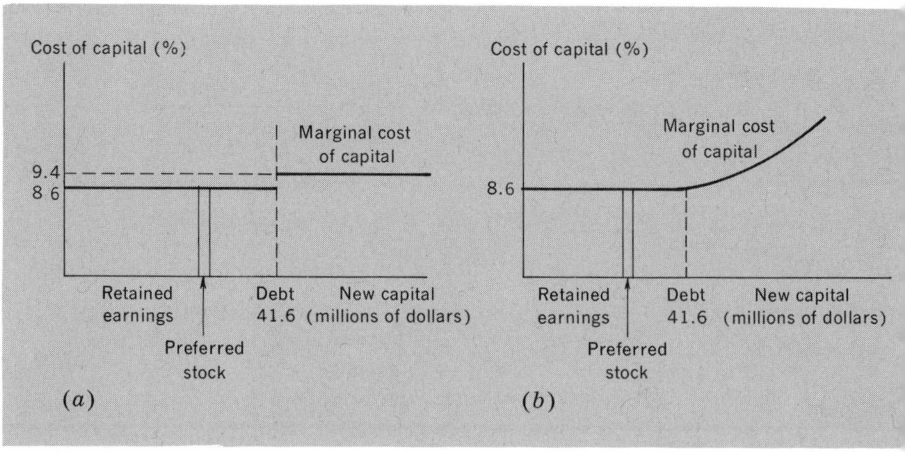

Figure 11–3 Relation between the Marginal Cost of Capital and the Amount of Funds Raised

of securities available to the financial manager and the ability of the securities markets to absorb the firm's debt and equity instruments—are considered in the following sections of the book. Note also that we cannot specify the exact cost of capital until we know how much capital will be raised. But the amount of capital that we raise depends on investment opportunities as determined in the capital budgeting decision. Capital budgeting and cost of capital operate jointly on one another, and both must be determined simultaneously. This simultaneous determination is considered in Chapter 12, where dividend policy and internal financing decisions are discussed.

SUMMARY

In Chapter 10, the nature of the valuation process and the concept of expected rates of return were considered in some detail. The present chapter used these valuation concepts to develop a weighted cost of capital for the firm. First, the cost of the individual components of the capital structure—debt, preferred stock, and equity—were analyzed. Next, these individual component costs were brought together to form a weighted cost of capital. Finally, the conceptual ideas developed in the first two sections were illustrated with an example of the cost of capital for an actual company—Continental Can Co.

Cost of Individual Capital Components

The cost of debt is defined to be the interest rate that must be paid on new increments of debt capital. Preferred stock's cost to the company is the effective yield and is found as the annual preferred dividend divided by the net price the company receives when it sells new preferred stock. In equation form, the cost of preferred stock is

$$\text{cost of preferred stock} = \frac{\text{preferred dividend}}{\text{net price of preferred}}$$

Since interest payments on debt are deductible for tax purposes but preferred dividends are not, it is necessary to make an adjustment to reconcile the cost of debt and that of preferred stock. Our procedure is to put both costs on an after-tax basis. The cost of preferred as calculated above is already on an after-tax basis; debt cost can be adjusted for taxes by multiplying the effective interest rate by a tax factor.

$$\text{after-tax cost of debt} = \text{interest rate} \times (1.0 - \text{tax rate})$$

The cost of equity is defined as the minimum rate of return that must be earned on equity-financed investments to keep the value of the existing common equity unchanged. This required rate of return is the rate of return that investors expect to receive on the company's common stock—the dividend yield plus the capital gains yield. Generally, we assume that investors expect to receive about the same rates of return in the future that they have received in the past; therefore, we estimate the required rate of return on the basis of actual historical returns.

Equity capital comes from two sources, retained earnings and sale of new issues of common stock. The basic required rate of return is used for the cost of retained earnings. However, new stock has a higher cost, because of the presence of flotation costs associated with the sale of stock. The cost of new common stock issues is computed as follows.

$$\text{cost of new stock} = \frac{\text{required rate of return on common stock}}{1.0 - \text{percentage cost of floating new common stock}}$$

New common stock is, therefore, more expensive than retained earnings.

Weighted Cost of Capital

The first step in calculating the weighted cost of capital is to determine the cost of the individual capital components as described above. The next step is to establish the proper set of weights to be used in the averaging process. Unless we have reason to think otherwise, we generally assume that the present capital structure of the firm is at an optimum, where optimum is defined as the capital structure that will produce the minimum average cost of capital for raising a given amount of funds. The optimum capital structure varies from industry to industry, with more stable industries having optimum capital structures that call for the use of more debt than in the case of unstable industries.

Relation between Cost of Capital and Amount of Funds Raised

Generally, the marginal cost of capital of a firm is constant until it has raised an amount of new capital equal to its retained earnings plus the amount of incremental debt and preferred stock that can be supported by retained earnings. Beyond this point, the firm must sell new common stock. Since new common stock has a higher cost than retained earnings, the marginal cost of capital rises when new common stock must be sold. Actually, the cost of capital rises gradually, not abruptly; firms make small adjustments in their target debt ratios, begin to use an assortment of securities, retain more of their earnings, and so on, as they reach the limit of internally generated equity funds. These important topics—the wide assortment of securities available to the financial manager, changing debt ratios, and the decision to retain earnings or pay them out in dividends—are covered in the following sections of the book.

QUESTIONS

11–1 Suppose the basic business risks to all firms in a given industry are similar.
a) Would you expect all firms in each industry to have approximately the same cost of capital?
b) How would the averages differ among industries?

11–2 Why are internally generated retained earnings less expensive than equity raised by selling stock?

11–3 Prior to the 1930s the corporate income tax was not very important, as rates were fairly low. Also prior to the 1930s preferred stock was much more important than it has been since that period. Is there a relation between the rise of corporate income taxes and the decline in importance of preferred stock?

11–4 Describe how each of the following would affect the cost of capital to corporations in general.
a) The federal government solves the problem of business cycles (that is, cyclical stability is increased).
b) The Federal Reserve Board takes action to lower interest rates.
c) The cost of floating new stock issues rises.

11–5 The formula $k = (D/P) + g$, where D = current dividend, P = the current price of a stock, and g = the past rate of growth in dividends, is sometimes used to estimate k, the cost of equity capital. Explain the reasoning behind the formula and this use of it.

PROBLEMS

11–1 On January 1, 1968, the total assets of XYZ Company were $100 million. By the end of the year total assets are expected to be $150 million. The firm's capital structure, shown below, is considered to be optimal. Assume there is no short-term debt.

Debt (3% coupon bonds)	$ 35,000,000
Preferred stock (4%)	15,000,000
Net worth	50,000,000
	$100,000,000

New bonds will have a 4 percent coupon rate and will be sold at par. Preferred will have a 5 percent rate and will also be sold at par. Common stock, currently selling at $50 a share, can be sold to net the company $45 a share. Stockholders' required rate of return is estimated to be 8 percent. Retained earnings are estimated to be $5 million (ignore depreciation). The marginal corporate tax rate is 50 percent.

a) Assuming all asset expansion (gross expenditures for fixed assets plus related working capital) is included in the capital budget, what is the dollar amount of the capital budget? (Ignore depreciation.)
b) To maintain the present capital structure, how much of the capital budget must be financed by equity?
c) How much of the new equity funds needed must be generated internally? externally?
d) Calculate the cost of each of the equity components.
e) Compute the weighted cost of equity.
f) Compute an average cost of capital for XYZ.
g) According to the information given, would the average cost of capital have been higher or lower if the firm's rate of expansion had been lower? Why?

11–2 The ABC Manufacturing Company has the following capital structure as of April 15, 1968; the board of directors has decided that these same proportions of *debt, preferred, and equity* capital are to be maintained.

Short-term debt	Trivial
Long-term debt (4½%)	$60,000,000
Preferred stock (5½%)	30,000,000
Net worth	90,000,000

Earnings per share have grown steadily from \$1.25 in 1961 to \$2.50 estimated for 1968. The investment community, expecting this growth to continue, capitalizes current earnings per share at about 3½ percent, giving a current market price of \$71.43. ABC is paying a current annual dividend of \$.80, and it expects the dividend to grow at the same rate as earnings.

New securities can be sold as follows: bonds to yield investors 4½ percent; preferred to yield 5½ percent; and common stock at the current market price less \$2 a share selling commission. These figures all assume that the capital relations set out above are maintained and that \$20 million or less is raised during the year. If more than \$20 million is obtained, the figures must be revised as follows: bonds, 5 percent; preferred, 6 percent; common stock selling cost, \$4 a share. These latter figures apply to the entire amount of funds raised, if an excess of \$20 million is acquired.

Compute the cost of capital (a) for less than \$20 million and (b) for more than \$20 million.

Selected References

Archer, Stephen H., and LeRoy G. Faerber, "Firm Size and the Cost of Equity Capital," *Journal of Finance,* XXI (March 1966), 69–84.

Arditti, Fred D., "Risk and the Required Return on Equity," *Journal of Finance,* XXII (March 1967), 19–36.

Barges, Alexander, *The Effect of Capital Structure on the Cost of Capital* (Englewood Cliffs, N.J.: Prentice-Hall, 1963).

Baxter, Nevins D., "Leverage, Risk of Ruin, and the Cost of Capital," *Journal of Finance,* XXII (September 1967), 395–404.

Ben-Shahar, Haim, and Abraham Ascher, "Capital Budgeting and Stock Valuation: Comment," *American Economic Review,* LVII (March 1967), 209–214.

Bodenhorn, Diran, "A Cash Flow Concept of Profit," *Journal of Finance,* XIX (March 1964), 16–31.

Boness, A. James, "A Pedagogic Note on the Cost of Capital," *Journal of Finance,* XIX (March 1964), 99–106.

Brewer, D. E., and J. Michaelson, "The Cost of Capital, Corporation Finance, and the Theory of Investment: Comment," *American Economic Review,* LV (June 1965), 516–524.

Brigham, Eugene F., and Keith V. Smith, "The Cost of Capital to the Small Firm," *The Engineering Economist,* XIII, Fall 1967, 1–26.

Crockett, Jean and Irwin Friend, "Capital Budgeting and Stock Valuation: Comment," *American Economic Review,* LVII (March 1967), 214–220.

Durand, David, "Costs of Debt and Equity Funds for Business: Trends and Problems of Measurement," reprinted in Ezra Solomon, ed., *The Management of Corporate Capital* (New York: Free Press, 1959), pp. 91–116.

Farrar, Donald E., and Lee L. Selwyn, "Note on Taxes, Corporate Financial Policy and the Cost of Capital to the Firm." Working Paper (Cambridge, Mass.: Sloan School of Management: Massachusetts Institute of Technology, 1967).

Friedland, Seymour, *The Economics of Corporate Capital,* Part II (Englewood Cliffs, N.J.: Prentice-Hall, 1966).

Haley, Charles, W., "A Note on the Cost of Debt," *Journal of Financial and Quantitative Analysis,* I (December 1966), 72–93.

Lerner, Eugene M., and Willard T. Carleton, "Financing Decisions of the Firm," *Journal of Finance,* XXI (May 1966), 202–214.

———, "The Integration of Capital Budgeting and Stock Valuation," *American Economic Review,* LIV (September 1964), 683–702. "Reply," *American Economic Review,* LVII (March 1967), 220–222.

———, *A Theory of Financial Analysis,* (New York: Harcourt, 1966).

Lindsay, J. R., and H. W. Sametz, *Financial Management: An Analytical Approach* (Homewood, Ill., Irwin, 1967).

Lintner, John, "The Cost of Capital and Optimal Financing of Corporate Growth," *Journal of Finance,* XVIII (May, 1963), 292–310.

———, "Dividends, Earnings, Leverage, Stock Prices and the Supply of Capital to Corporations," *Review of Economics and Statistics,* XLIV (August 1962), 243–269.

———, "Security Prices, Risk, and Maximal Gains from Diversification," *Journal of Finance,* XX (December 1965), 587–616.

Miller, M. H., and Franco Modigliani, "Cost of Capital to Electric Utility Industry," *American Economic Review,* LVI (June 1966), 333–391.

Modigliani, Franco and M. H. Miller, "The Cost of Capital, Corporation Finance and the Theory of Investment." *American Economic Review,* XLVIII (June 1958), 261–297.

———, "The Cost of Capital, Corporation Finance and the Theory of Investment: Reply," *American Economic Review,* IL (September 1958), 655–669. "Taxes and the Cost of Capital: A Correction,"

American Economic Review, LIII (June 1963), 433–443. "Reply," *American Economic Review,* LV (June 1965), 524–527.

Robichek, A. A., J. G. McDonald, and R. C. Higgins, "Some Estimates of the Cost of Capital to Electric Utilities, 1954–1957: Comment," *American Economic Review,* LVII (December 1967), 1278–1288.

———, and John G. McDonald, "The Cost of Capital Concept: Potential Use and Misuse," *Financial Executive,* 33 (June, 1965), 2–8.

———, and Stewart C. Myers, *Optimal Financial Decisions* (Englewood Cliffs, N.J.: Prentice-Hall, 1965).

———, "Problems in the Theory of Optimal Capital Structure," *Journal of Financial and Quantitative Analysis,* I (June 1966), 1–35.

Schwartz, Eli, "Theory of the Capital Structure of the Firm," *Journal of Finance,* XIV (March 1959), 18–39.

———, and J. Richard Aronson, "Some Surrogate Evidence in Support of the Concept of Optimal Capital Structure," *Journal of Finance,* XXII (March 1967), 10–18.

Solomon, Ezra, "Measuring a Company's Cost of Capital," *Journal of Business,* XXVIII (October 1955), 240–252.

———, *The Theory of Financial Management.* (New York: Columbia University Press, 1963).

———, *The Management of Corporate Capital.* (New York: Free Press, 1959.)

Vickers, Douglas, "Elasticity of Capital Supply, Monopsonistic Discrimination, and Optimum Capital Structure," *Journal of Finance,* XXIII (March 1967), 1–9.

Weston, J. Fred, "A Test of Cost of Capital Propositions," *Southern Economic Journal,* XXX (October 1963), 105–212.

Wippern, Ronald, F., "Financial Structure and the Value of the Firm," *Journal of Finance,* XXI (December 1966), 615–634.

APPENDIX TO CHAPTER 11
Some Unresolved Issues on the Cost of Capital

In this Appendix it will be shown how some of the issues glossed over earlier can affect the cost of capital calculation. The purpose here is as much to raise questions as to answer them, and the material is more theoretical than practical. However, anyone engaged in financial management must understand all the implications underlying the practical, rule-of-thumb procedures that the financial manager will necessarily be forced to follow.

Cost of Retained Earnings[1]

Whenever a firm retains a portion of its net income rather than paying it out in dividends, there is an "opportunity cost" to the stockholders. If the firm in question has a required rate of return (k) equal to 8 percent, then presumably its shareholders could have invested the retained earnings in other firms of similar risk and received an 8 percent return. This 8 percent is, under certain assumptions, the opportunity cost of retained earnings. The two assumptions are (1) that the stockholder pays no income tax on dividends and (2) that he incurs no brokerage costs when reinvesting dividend receipts. To the extent that these assumptions are not met, the opportunity cost of retained earnings, hence the cost of capital from retained earnings, is lower than the cost of new common stock. The following example is an illustration.

The ABC Company has net earnings of \$1 million, and all of its stockholders are in the 30 percent marginal tax bracket. Management estimates that under present conditions stockholders' required rate of return is 8 percent. If the earnings are paid out as dividends, the recipients will pay income taxes, then reinvest the proceeds in the stock of similar firms and obtain an 8 percent return. The brokerage costs to the stockholders will average 3 percent of the new investments. What rate of return must be earned internally to provide the stockholders with incremental earnings equal to what they would receive externally?

1. After-tax proceeds of dividend payment = \$1,000,000 — taxes
   = \$1,000,000 — \$300,000
   = \$ 700,000
2. Net investment after brokerage costs = \$ 700,000 — brokerage
   = \$ 700,000 — \$21,000
   = \$ 679,000
3. Earnings on new investment = (679,000) (0.08) = \$54,320
4. Internal rate of return (k_r) necessary to provide stockholders with incremental income of \$54,320:

$$\$54{,}320 = (\$1{,}000{,}000)(k_r)$$
$$(k_f) = 5.432\%$$

5. Therefore, if the firm is able to earn 5.432 percent on retained earnings, the stockholders will be as well off as they would be if all earnings were paid out and then reinvested to yield 8 percent.

[1] There is a question of whether investors prefer to receive their rewards from stock investments in the form of dividends or capital gains. The question is considered in some detail in Chapter 12, but here it is assumed that investors are indifferent between dividends and capital gains.

6. In general, the internal opportunity cost, or the required rate of return on retention-financed investments, is less than stockholders' required rate of return and may be calculated as follows:

$$k_r = k(1 - T)(1 - B)$$

where k_r = the required return on retention-financed investments, k = stockholders' required rate of return, T = the stockholders' marginal tax rate, and B = the percentage brokerage cost. In the example being considered,

$$k_r = 0.08(0.7)(0.97) = 0.054, \text{ or } 5.4\%$$

This procedure actually involves an overstatement. The retained earnings will give rise to an increase in the price of the stock; if the investor sells it, he will be subject to a capital gains tax. The capital gains tax rate is lower than the rate applicable to dividends (generally); as it is deferred, it has a lower present value.

Two limiting cases can be applied. First, it can be assumed that the stockholder never sells the stock, passing it on to his heirs, who do the same, *ad infinitum*. In this case, the procedures in the example are correct. At the other limit, it can be assumed that the investor holds the stock for the minimum holding period (six months) to receive capital gains tax treatment, then sells the stock and pays a tax at one half his normal tax rate (or 25 percent, if this is lower). In this case, the value of T for the example should be 15 percent, and the resultant cost of retained earnings is computed to be:

$$k_r = 0.08(0.85)(0.97) = 0.066, \text{ or } 6.6\%$$

The correct figure probably lies somewhere between these two extremes, but there is no way of knowing exactly where.

The example shows that, in general, the required rate of return on retention-financed investment (k_r) is less than the regular required rate of return (k) by the amount of brokerage costs on reinvested dividends receipts and by stockholders' marginal tax rates. But suppose there are many stockholders, and their marginal tax rates range from zero to 70 percent. Now what should be done? There simply is no one correct answer. One could use one half the average marginal tax rate of individual stockholders in general—it has averaged about 40 percent in recent years[2]—the 25 percent maximum capital gains tax, the tax rate of the controlling stockholder, or one could try to estimate the average tax rate of all the firm's stockholders and use one half that number.

[2] Vincent Jolivet, "The Weighted Average Marginal Tax Rate on Dividends Received by Individuals in the U.S.," *American Economic Review,* (June 1966).

Stock Purchases

Under certain circumstances, the procedure discussed in the preceding section is invalid or, at least, unnecessary. If k, the market-determined rate of return on the stock of the firm in question or of firms in the same risk class, is 8 percent, and if the firm can buy its own or similar stocks to yield 8 percent, then this sets a lower limit on project returns. The firm would never invest in assets yielding less than 8 percent, the value of k, because it can obtain this yield on market securities.

Several points make this line of reasoning questionable. First, a company whose stock is not publicly traded cannot buy its own stock on the open market. Second, privately held firms could not buy large amounts of the stock of publicly owned firms without the Internal Revenue Service stepping in and imposing penalties under the improper accumulation of retained earnings tax (see Chapter 2). Third, publicly owned companies that can legally buy their own stock on the open market under certain conditions are generally averse to doing so, thereby admitting that they are unable to generate acceptable projects in a bouyant, growing economic setting. Also, if a firm engages in large-scale purchases of its own stock, it will probably run the price up and the yield down during the period in which it is making the acquisition.

The question of open-market purchases has never been investigated in a satisfactory manner. We are convinced that many firms, especially privately owned companies, cannot use open-market purchases (or mergers either) to avoid the effects of personal taxes on dividends; at least, for these companies, the cost of retained earnings is somewhat lower than the basic required rate of return. In our own experience, we have seen situations in which the stockholders of closely held firms were in high tax brackets and, therefore, directed the firms to make internal investments at rates of return less than the expected market returns on common stock for precisely the reasons outlined here. Further, we find it difficult to question their logic and their judgment that their cost of retained earnings is less than their external required rate of return. For publicly owned firms, we ourselves have questions. In our own work with public companies, we use the basic required rate of return as the cost of retained earnings but not without a feeling of uneasiness. There are many areas of finance that need further research, and this is certainly one of them.[3]

Cost of Depreciation-generated Funds

The very first increment of equity funds used to finance any year's capital budget is depreciation-generated funds. In their statements of sources and uses of funds, corporations generally show depreciation charges to be one of the most important sources of funds, if not the

[3] H. Bierman and R. West discuss some of the theoretical issues in "The Acquisition of Stock by the Corporate Issuer." *Journal of Finance,* XXI (December 1966), 687–696, as do the prior papers cited in their article. To our knowledge, the important empirical questions are unresolved at this time.

most important. For capital budgeting purposes, should depreciation be considered "free" capital; should it be ignored completely; or should a charge be assessed against it? The answer is that a charge should indeed be assessed against these funds, and that their cost is approximately equal to the average cost of capital before outside equity is used.

The reasoning here is that the firm could, if it so desired, distribute the depreciation-generated funds to its stockholders and creditors, the parties who financed the assets in the first place. For example, if $10 million of depreciation-generated funds were available, the firm could either reinvest them or distribute them. If they are to be distributed, the distribution must be to both bondholders and stockholders in proportion to their shares of the capital structure; otherwise the captial structure will change. Obviously, this distribution should take place if the funds cannot be invested to yield the cost of capital, but retention should occur if the internal rate of return exceeds the cost of capital. Since the cost of depreciation-generated funds is equal to the average cost of capital, depreciation does not enter the calculation of the average cost of capital.

Net-monetary–debtor-creditor Theory[4]

The net-monetary-debtor-creditor theory, developed by A. A. Alchian and Rubin Kessel, asserts that the value of the common stock of a firm will be greatly influenced by its capital structure. The Alchian-Kessel theory suggests that the relative cost of debt versus equity financing is influenced by expected price level movements. It makes the following assertions:

Net-monetary debtors gain during inflation.
Net-monetary creditors lose during inflation.
Net-monetary debtors lose during deflation.
Net-monetary creditors gain during deflation.

Balance sheet items are classified as *monetary* assets or liabilities (M), or *real* assets or liabilities (R), as set forth below.

CLASSIFICATION OF BALANCE SHEET ITEMS

(M)	Cash	(M)	Accounts payable
(M)	Marketable securities	(M)	Notes payable
(M)	Receivables	(M)	Provisions for income tax
		(M)	Accruals
(R)	Inventories	(M)	Bonds and long-term notes
(R)	Investments	(M)	Preferred stock
(R)	Fixed plant		
		(R)	Common stock
		(R)	Surplus

[4] The theory and its empirical tests are set forth in R. A. Kessel, "Inflation-caused Wealth Redistribution: A Test of a Hypothesis," *American Economic Review,* XLVI (March 1956), 128–141. Other writings by Kessel and A. A. Alchian suggest use of the expression "the Alchian-Kessel theory."

A net-monetary debtor is one whose monetary liabilities exceed his monetary assets. A net-monetary creditor is one whose monetary assets exceed his monetary liabilities. A firm may have either high leverage or low leverage from a debt standpoint and be either a monetary debtor or a monetary creditor. The following tables of balance sheets show the distinction between monetary-debtor status and the degree of trading on the equity.

Table A11–1 shows the balance sheet for a firm that has a heavy debt-to-equity ratio of 150 percent. It is a net-monetary debtor because monetary assets are 40 and monetary debts are 60. In the balance sheet in Table A11–3, the firm has the same debt-to-equity ratio but becomes a net-monetary creditor because the composition of assets shifted as shown. Similarly, in the other two balance sheets, a small amount of trading on the equity is associated with both types of debtor-creditor relations.

TABLE A11–1 HIGH-LEVERAGE MONETARY DEBTOR

(M)	Cash and receivables	$ 40	(M)	Accounts, notes, and bonds payable	$ 60
(R)	Inventories and fixed assets	60	(R)	Equity accounts	40
		$100			$100

TABLE A11–2 LOW-LEVERAGE MONETARY DEBTOR

(M)	Cash and receivables	$ 10	(M)	Accounts, notes, and bonds payable	$ 20
(R)	Inventories and fixed assets	90	(R)	Equity accounts	80
		$100			$100

TABLE A11–3 HIGH-LEVERAGE MONETARY CREDITOR

(M)	Cash and receivables	$ 80	(M)	Accounts, notes, and bonds payable	$ 60
(R)	Inventories and fixed assets	20	(R)	Equity accounts	40
		$100			$100

The influence of a firm's net-monetary position on equity values is shown by the following illustration. We start with a firm's balance sheet at a price level of 100 (Table A11–4).

TABLE A11–4 LOW-LEVERAGE MONETARY CREDITOR

(M)	Cash and receivables	$ 80	(M)	Accounts, notes, and bonds payable	$ 20
(R)	Inventories and fixed assets	20	(R)	Equity accounts	80
		$100			$100

The price level and all nonmonetary asset values are now assumed to double. Cash and payables, however, do not change in value because they are fixed dollar claims. However, fixed assets would double in value. The value of equity is a residual. Since total assets are now 100 (20

TABLE A11–5 BALANCE SHEET PRICE LEVEL, 100

Cash	$20	Accounts payable	$40
Fixed assets	40	Equity	20
Total	$60	Total	$60

cash and 80 fixed assets) and accounts payable are 40, equity must be 60. Equity tripled in value as the price level doubled because the firm had been a net-monetary debtor of 200 percent.

The Alchian-Kessel studies of the experience of companies during both inflationary and deflationary periods confirm that in fact the common stocks of net-monetary–debtor companies gained during inflation. Furthermore, the relative advantage of net-monetary–debtor companies during inflations was in proportion to the ratio of monetary debts to monetary assets. During deflations, net-monetary creditors gained in proportion to their net-monetary–creditor status.

The theory and empirical findings that support the debtor-creditor theory suggest that prospective price level changes may be another important variable influencing choice of financial structure. If financial managers correctly anticipate the direction of changes and lenders erroneously expect smaller than actual price changes, the choice of an appropriate financial structure will increase the value of a firm's common stock. The cost of capital to the firm will thereby be affected by its net-monetary–debtor or –creditor position.

The crucial assumption of the net-monetary–debtor-creditor theory is that lenders on the average underestimate future price level changes. If lenders on the average overestimated the extent of future price changes, debtors would lose in inflation and creditors would gain. If expectations about future price level changes were correct, prices would reflect these judgments; neither gains nor losses would result from price level changes. Expected price level changes would have been correctly taken into account both by investor-lenders and by firms in their planning.[5]

[5] Barthold W. Sorge has described how the net-monetary–debtor position may be used in international business finance as an inflation hedge. He recommends that a firm with monetary claims in the currency of a country with a record of inflation should hedge these claims. Among the methods of hedging he describes is that of incurring monetary obligations in the currency of the same country to offset, in a debtor position, the firm's position as a creditor in monetary claims of a depreciating currency. See Barthold W. Sorge, *The Prevention of Financial Losses in Foreign Operations* (PhD Dissertation, Graduate School of Business, University of California at Los Angeles, 1965), Chapter 9.

We should also note that in a recent article Donald Nichols extended the effects of inflation on corporate values to include a consideration of a firm's depreciation position. (Donald Nichols, "A Note on Inflation and Common Stock Prices," *Journal of Finance,* XXIII (September 1968), 655–658.

12

Dividend Policy and Internal Financing

Dividend policy determines the division of earnings between payments to stockholders and retained earnings. Retained earnings are one of the most significant sources of funds for the financing of corporate growth, but dividends constitute the cash flows that accrue to equity investors. Although both growth and dividends are desirable, these two goals are in conflict—a higher dividend rate means less retained earnings and, consequently, a slower rate of growth in earnings and stock prices. One of the financial manager's most important functions is to determine the allocation of profits after taxes between dividends and retained earnings, as this decision may have a critical influence on the value of the firm. The factors that influence the allocation of earnings to dividends or retained earnings are the subject of this chapter.

IMPORTANCE OF DIVIDEND POLICY

Table 12–1 sets forth the relationship between corporate internal sources of funds and total uses of funds since 1954. For the 12-year period between 1955 and 1966, the total uses of funds by corporations was $705 billion. Internal sources financed over two-thirds of the total uses—depreciation accounted for 45 percent and retained earnings for some 24 percent. If depreciation charges are deducted from gross total funds, net total funds in the amount of $390 billion is obtained. Retained earnings financed 43 percent of the net total increase in corporate funds—the firm's growth—during the 12-year period.

Significance of Internal Financing

Comprehensive studies in capital formation and financing underscore the important role of internal financing. In commenting on the progress report of a National Bureau of Economic Research project on "Long-term Trends in Capital Formation and Financing,"[1] Eli Shapiro has called attention to the significance of internal financing.

> Indeed, it may be stated categorically that one of the most important features of all three papers is the stress placed on internal financing of capital formation over the first half of the twentieth century. The presence of the dominance of internal financing of capital formation is hard to rationalize in the light of the disproportionate space devoted to the role of financial institutions in the so-called business or corporate finance textbooks published as recently as the late forties or early fifties.

Because of the great importance of internal financing, dividend policy, which determines the division of corporate earnings between outflows and retained earnings, must be recognized as one of the central decision areas for financial managers.

Patterns in Dividend Payouts

Studies of dividend patterns over extended periods beginning in 1870 indicate that, over all, corporations have paid in dividends two-thirds of their earnings after taxes. However, this percentage has varied considerably from year to year. Table 12–2 shows that immediately following World War II dividend payout dropped to about 36 percent. This de-

[1] *Journal of Finance,* X (May 1955), 281.

TABLE 12–1 CORPORATE INTERNAL SOURCES AS PERCENT OF TOTAL FUNDS, 1955–1966
(in billions of dollars)

YEAR	TOTAL FUNDS	RETAINED EARNINGS	PERCENTAGE OF RETAINED EARNINGS TO TOTAL FUNDS	DEPRECIATION	PERCENTAGE OF DEPRECIATION TO TOTAL SOURCES	TOTAL INTERNAL SOURCES	PERCENTAGE OF TOTAL INTERNAL SOURCES TO TOTAL SOURCES
(1)	(2)	(3)	(4)	(5)	(6)	(7)	(8)
1955	$ 51.4	$ 13.9	27.0%	$ 17.0	33.1%	$ 30.9	60.1%
1956	43.1	13.2	30.6	18.4	42.7	31.6	73.3
1957	40.0	11.8	29.5	20.3	50.8	32.1	80.3
1958	42.1	8.3	19.7	21.4	50.8	29.7	70.5
1959	54.3	12.6	23.2	22.9	42.2	35.5	65.4
1960	45.3	10.0	22.0	24.2	53.4	34.2	75.5
1961	55.0	10.2	18.5	25.4	46.2	35.6	64.7
1962	61.6	12.4	20.1	29.2	47.4	41.6	67.5
1963	65.8	13.6	20.7	30.8	46.8	44.4	67.5
1964	67.1	18.5	27.6	32.8	48.9	51.3	76.5
1965	87.3	21.7	24.8	35.1	40.2	56.8	65.1
1966	92.0	23.0	25.0	37.6	40.9	60.6	65.9
1955–1960	276.2	69.8	25.3	124.2	44.9	194.0	70.2
1961–1966	428.8	99.4	23.2	190.9	44.5	290.3	67.7
1955–1966	$705.0	$169.2	24.3%	$315.1	44.7%	$484.3	68.9%

SOURCE: *Economic Report of the President* (Washington, D.C., U.S. Government Printing Office, 1967), p. 294.

TABLE 12–2 CORPORATE PROFITS AND DIVIDENDS, 1929–1966
(dollar amounts in billions)

YEAR	CORPORATE PROFITS AFTER TAX	DIVIDENDS	PAYOUT PERCENTAGE
1929	$ 8.6	$ 5.8	6%
1930	2.9	5.5	190
1931	−0.9	4.1	0
1932	−2.7	2.5	0
1933	0.4	2.0	500
1934	1.6	2.6	163
1935	2.6	2.8	108
1936	4.9	4.5	92
1937	5.3	4.7	89
1938	2.9	3.2	110
1939	5.6	3.8	68
1940	7.2	4.0	56
1941	10.1	4.4	44
1942	10.1	4.3	43
1943	11.1	4.4	40
1944	11.2	4.6	41
1945	9.0	4.6	51
1946	15.5	5.6	36
1947	20.2	6.3	31
1948	22.7	7.0	31
1949	18.5	7.2	39
1950	24.9	8.8	35
1951	12.6	8.6	40
1952	19.6	8.6	44
1953	20.4	8.9	44
1954	20.6	9.3	45
1955	27.0	10.5	39
1956	27.2	11.3	42
1957	26.0	11.7	45
1958	22.3	11.6	52
1959	28.5	12.6	44
1960	26.7	13.4	50
1961	27.2	13.8	51
1962	31.2	15.2	49
1963	33.1	16.5	49
1964	38.7	17.3	45
1965	44.5	19.2	43
1966	48.1	20.9	43

(*Continued*)

TABLE 12–2 (*Continued*)

YEAR	CORPORATE PROFITS AFTER TAX	DIVIDENDS	PAYOUT PERCENTAGE
1929–1939	31.2	41.5	133
1940–1945	58.7	26.3	45
1945–1950	110.8	39.5	36
1950–1955	134.1	54.7	41
1955–1960	157.7	71.1	45
1960–1966	249.5	116.3	47

SOURCE: *Economic Report of the President,* (Washington, D.C.: U.S. Government Printing Office, 1967), p. 290.

crease was due partly to the "overstatement" of earnings because of the use of historical methods of costing during a period of rising price levels. More importantly, it was due to the rapid growth of firms and their need for funds to finance inventories and fixed assets at higher price levels.

In the period 1950–1955, dividend payouts averaged about 41 percent of earnings. Writers in the mid-fifties observed that, of corporate earnings before taxes, one half was paid to the government. Of the remainder, 40 to 45 percent was distributed to the stockholders. Thus, if a corporation earned $20 million, the corporate income tax would take $10 million, corporate dividends would be about $4 million, and retained earnings would be about $6 million.

It is interesting to note the payout pattern during the 1960s (1960–1966). In the early part of the period, payouts were high, averaging about 50 percent. This was a period of relatively slack economic activity—investment opportunities were not particularly strong, and debt funds were available at low rates of interest. Without an especially pressing need for funds and with plenty of low-cost debt money available, dividend payouts were high. In 1964, 1965, and 1966, however, investment demand was booming and debt funds were scarce and expensive. This caused firms to reduce dividend payouts and to rely more heavily on retained earnings.

Cash Flows as Determinant of Payouts

Cash flows are earnings plus depreciation and depletion charges. When dividends are related to cash flows rather than to earnings, the payout patterns show two changes. First, the payout percentages drop to lower levels. For all manufacturing corporations, the payout appears to drop from the two-thirds ratio to a one-third ratio.

The second change is that the payout ratio appears to be more stable when dividends are related to cash flows rather than to earnings. If dividends were tied more directly to cash flows than to earnings, this would suggest that cash flows rather than earnings may be the primary determinant of dividends. However, the apparent increased stability in the dividend-to-cash-flow ratio may be an arithmetical accident instead of a cause-and-effect relation. For example, consider the following data:

YEAR	EARNINGS	DIVIDENDS	PAYOUT PERCENTAGE	DEPRE-CIATION	CASH FLOWS	PAYOUT PERCENTAGE
1	20	10	50	20	40	25
2	15	10	67	20	35	29
3	10	10	100	20	30	33
4	30	10	33	20	50	20

The payout percentage based on cash flows is clearly more stable than the payout based on earnings. But this result flows from adding a constant figure to the earnings. The greater stability may simply come about because a relatively fixed amount of depreciation is added to earnings.

FACTORS INFLUENCING DIVIDEND POLICY

The economic patterns described above indicate the great significance of retained earnings in financing the growth of firms. This poses the fundamental question: What determines the extent to which a firm will pay out dividends instead of retain earnings? This question may be answered by a consideration of the factors influencing dividend policy. First, the major influences on dividend policy will be described. Second, this check list will be used to attempt to explain differences in dividend patterns observed among different industries and among firms in the same industry.

Legal Rules

The state statutes and court decisions governing dividend policy are complicated, but their essential nature may be stated briefly. The legal rules provide that dividends be paid from earnings, either from the current year's earnings or from past years' earnings as reflected in earned surplus. State laws emphasize three rules: (1) the net profits rule, (2) the capital impairment rule, and (3) the insolvency rule.

The *net profits* rule provides that dividends may be paid from past and present earnings. The *capital impairment* rule protects shareholders and creditors by forbidding the payment of dividends from capital. Paying dividends from capital would be distributing the investment in the company rather than its earnings.[2] The *insolvency* rule provides that corporations may not pay dividends while insolvent. Insolvency is here defined in the bankruptcy sense that liabilities exceed assets.

Legal aspects are significant. They provide the framework within which dividend policies can be formulated. However, within these boundaries important financial and economic factors will have a major influence on policy.

Cash Position

Profits held as retained earnings (which show up in the right-hand side of the balance sheet in the surplus or retained earnings account) may be invested in assets required for the conduct of the business. Thus, although a firm has had a record of earnings, it may not be able to pay cash dividends because of its liquidity position. Indeed, a growing firm, even a very profitable one, typically has a pressing need for funds. In such a situation the firm may elect not to pay cash dividends.

Need to Repay Debt

When a firm has sold debt to finance expansion or to substitute for other forms of financing, it is faced with two alternatives: It can refund the debt at maturity by replacing it with another form of security, or it can make provision for paying off the debt. Since the retained earnings of a growing firm are likely to be tied up in operating assets, it will not be able to liquidate assets. Therefore, a debt obligation implies that the firm is planning either retention of earnings to pay off the debt or new external financing in the future.

Restrictions in Debt Contracts

Debt contracts, particularly when long-term debt is involved, frequently restrict a firm's ability to pay cash dividends. Such restrictions, which are designed to protect the position of the lender, usually state (1) that future dividends can be paid out of earnings generated only

[2] It is possible, of course, to return stockholders' capital; however, when this is done, it must be clearly stated as such. A dividend paid out of capital is called a *liquidating* dividend.

after the signing of the loan agreement (that is, future dividends cannot be paid out of past earned surplus) and (2) that dividends cannot be paid when net working capital (current assets minus current liabilities) is below a specified amount. Similarly, preferred stock agreements generally state that no cash dividends can be paid on the common stock until all accrued preferred dividends have been paid. Such restrictions are discussed in Chapter 19.

Rate of Asset Expansion

The more rapid the rate at which the firm is growing, the greater will be its needs for financing asset expansion. A fast-growing firm will anticipate a substantial need for funds in the future. The greater the future need for funds, the more likely the firm is to retain earnings rather than to pay them out.

Profit Rate

The profit rate of a firm is a highly important variable. The profitability with which the firm employs funds will determine the relative attractiveness of paying out earnings in the form of dividends to stockholders who will use them elsewhere, compared with the productivity of their use in the present enterprise. The internal profitability rate of the firm provides a basis for comparing the productivity of retained earnings to the alternative return that could be earned elsewhere.

Stability of Earnings

If earnings are relatively stable, a firm is better able to predict what its future earnings will be. It is therefore more likely to pay out a higher percentage of its earnings in dividends than is a firm with fluctuating earnings. The latter firm is not certain that in subsequent years the hoped-for earnings will be realized, and it is more likely to retain a high proportion of earnings in order to maintain dividends should earnings fall off in the future.

Access to the Capital Markets

A large, well-established firm with a record of profitability and some stability of earnings will have easy access to capital markets and other forms of external financing. The small, new, or venturesome firm, however, has a greater amount of risk for potential investors. Its ability to raise equity or debt funds from capital markets is restricted, and it must retain more earnings to finance its operations. A well-established firm is likely to have a higher dividend payout rate than is a new or small firm.

Control

Another important variable is the effect of alternative sources of financing on the control situation in the firm. Some corporations, as a matter of policy, will expand only to the extent of their internal earnings. This policy is defended on the grounds that raising funds by selling additional common stock dilutes the control of the dominant group in the company. At the same time, selling debt increases the risks of fluctuating earnings to the present owners of the company. Reliance on internal financing in order to maintain control reduces the dividend payout.

Tax Position of Stockholders

The tax position of the owners of the corporation will greatly influence the desire for dividends. For example, a corporation closely held by a few taxpayers in high income tax brackets is likely to pay out a relatively low dividend. The owners of the corporation are interested in taking their income in the form of capital gains rather than in ordinary dividends, which are subject to higher personal income tax rates. However, the stockholders in a large, widely held corporation may be interested in a high dividend payout.

At times there is a conflict of interest in large corporations between stockholders in high income tax brackets and those in low income tax brackets. The former will prefer to see a low dividend payout and a high rate of earnings retention in the hope of an appreciation of the capital stock of the company. The lower income stockholder will prefer a relatively high dividend payout rate. The dividend policy of such a firm may be a compromise between a low and a high payout, that is, an intermediate payout ratio. If, however, one group dominates and sets, let us say, a low payout policy, those stockholders who seek income are likely to sell their shares over time and shift into higher yielding stocks. Thus, to at least some extent, a firm's payout policy determines its stockholder types, as well as vice versa.

Corporate Tax Liabilities

In order to prevent wealthy stockholders from using the corporation as an "incorporated pocketbook" by which they can avoid the high rates of personal income tax, tax regulations applicable to corporations provide for a special surtax on improperly accumulated income. This was the subject of the famous Section 102 of the Internal Revenue Code, which is now Section 531 of the Revenue Act of 1954 law. The 1954 law placed the burden of proof on the Internal Revenue Service to justify penalty rates for accumulation of earnings. That is, earnings retention is justified unless the Internal Revenue Service can prove otherwise.

The eleven factors outlined above influence corporations to different degrees, depending upon the particular situation. The effects of these factors result in different dividend patterns from industry to industry and from company to company. How these forces influence dividend policy will be indicated in the following section.

TABILITY OF IVIDEND POLICY

A fundamental relation observed in dividend policy is the widespread tendency of corporations to pursue a relatively stable dividend policy. Profits of firms fluctuate considerably with changes in the level of business activity. Figure 12–1 shows that dividends are more stable.

As John Lintner[3] has observed, most corporations seek to maintain

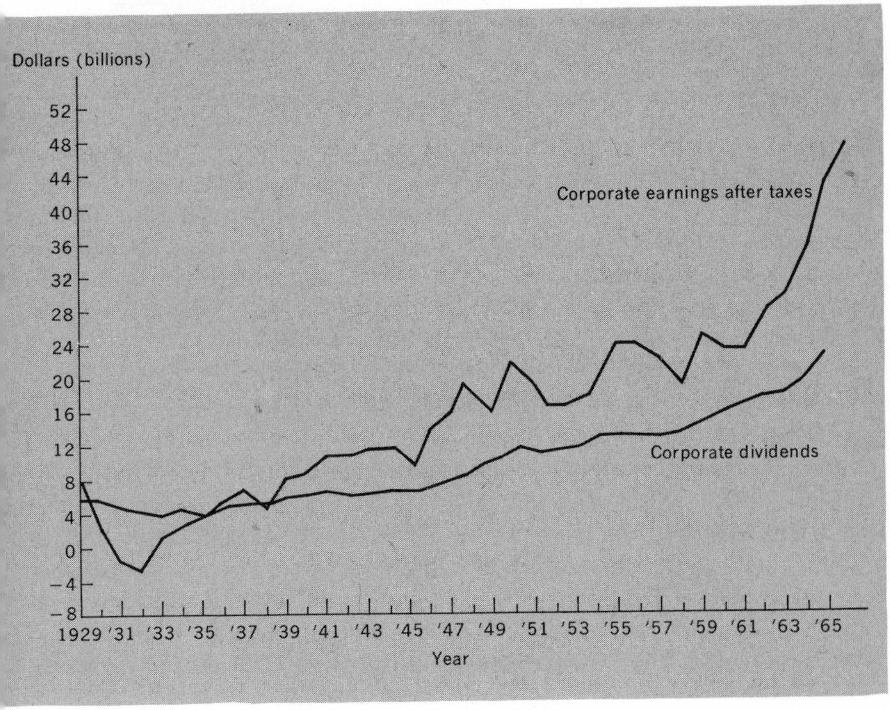

Figure 12–1 Corporate Earnings after Taxes and Dividends (billions of dollars)

[3] For an excellent discussion providing a foundation for understanding dividend policy, see John Lintner, "Distribution of Incomes of Corporations among Divi-

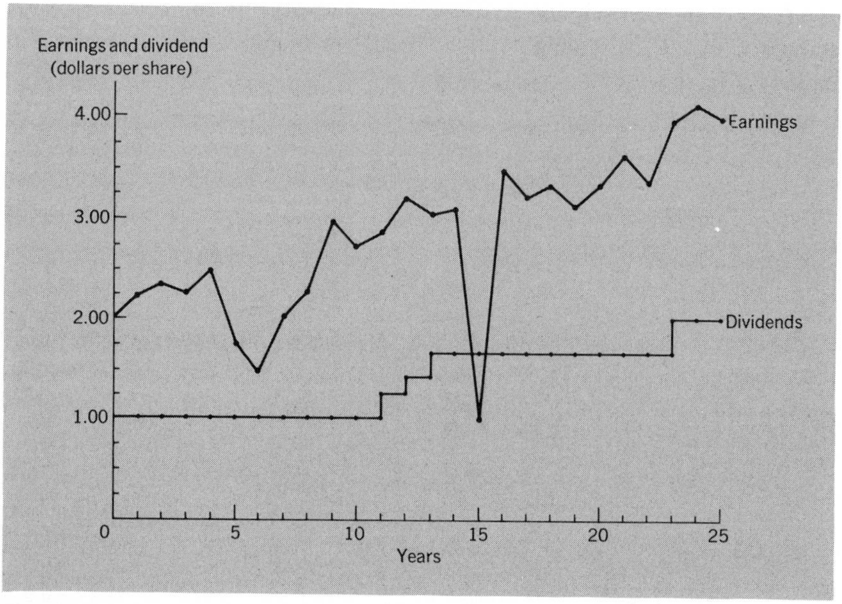

Figure 12–2 Dividend and Earnings Pattern of a Typical Corporation

a target dividend payout ratio. However, dividends increase with a lag after earnings rise. Only after an increase in earnings appears clearly sustainable and relatively permanent are dividends increased. When dividends have been increased, strenuous efforts are made to maintain them at the new level. If earnings decline, until it is clear that an earnings recovery will not take place, dividends will be maintained.

Figure 12–2 illustrates these ideas for a typical firm for a 25-year period. Initially, earnings are $2 and dividends $1 per share, providing a 50 percent payout ratio. Earnings rise for four years while dividends remain constant; thus, the payout falls during this period. During the fifth and sixth years, earnings fall substantially; however, the dividend is maintained and the payout rises above the 50 percent target. During the period between the seventh and fourteenth years, earnings experience a sustained rise. Dividends are held constant for a time, while management seeks to determine whether the earnings increase is permanent. At the eleventh year, the earnings gain seems permanent, and dividends

---

dends, Retained Earnings and Taxes," *American Economic Review,* XLVI (May 1956), 97–113. See also J. A. Brittain, *Corporate Dividend Policy* (Washington, D.C.: Brookings Institute, 1966).

are raised in three steps to re-establish the 50 percent payout. During the fifteenth year, a strike causes earnings to fall below the regular dividend; assuming the earnings decline to be temporary, management maintains the dividend. Earnings fluctuate on a fairly high plateau from the sixteenth year through the twenty-second, during which time dividends remain constant. A new increase in earnings induces management to raise the dividend in the twenty-third year to re-establish the 50 percent payout ratio. This explains why, in Figure 12–1, the amount of dividends will rise moderately in years when earnings increase sharply.

This company kept its dividend at a steady dollar amount but allowed its payout ratio to fluctuate. An alternative policy would have been to maintain a stable payout ratio and let the dividend fluctuate. Still a third alternative—one favored by such firms as General Motors—is to set a relatively low "regular" dividend and then supplement it with year-end "extras" in years when earnings are high.

As earnings of the firm increase, at first the customary quarterly dividend will not be altered. Year-end "extras," however, will be declared. Only after it is clear that earnings have risen to a new plateau will the "customary" amount of dividends be increased.

We may now evaluate this practice of following a stable dividend payout policy. First, consider the stable dividend policy from the standpoint of the stockholders as owners of a company. Their acquiescence with the general practice must imply that stable dividend policies lead to higher stock prices on the average than do alternative dividend policies. Is this a fact? Does a stable dividend policy maximize security values for a corporation? As there has been no truly conclusive empirical study of this question, on a factual basis there is really no answer to the question.[4]

On a priori grounds, however, it would be expected that a stable dividend policy would lead to higher stock prices. First, a stable dividend policy is likely to lead to higher stock prices because investors will value more highly dividends they are more certain to receive. If dividends fluctuate, investors may discount, with some percentage probability factor, the likelihood of receiving any particular amount of dividends. That is, the same average amounts of dividends received under a fluctuating dividend policy are likely to have a higher discount factor applied to them than to dividends under a stable dividend policy. In the terms used in Chapter 10, this means that a firm with a stable dividend would have a lower required rate of return—or cost of capital—than one whose dividends fluctuated.

Second, many stockholders live on income received in the form of dividends. Such stockholders would be greatly inconvenienced by fluc-

[4] An empirical study that does cast some light on the question is reported in Appendix A to this chapter.

tuating dividends, and they would likely pay a premium for a stock with a relatively assured minimum dollar dividend.

A third advantage of a stable dividend from the standpoint of a corporation and its stockowners is the requirement of legal listing. Legal lists are lists of securities in which mutual savings banks, pension funds, insurance companies, and other fiduciary institutions are permitted to invest. One of the criteria for placing a stock on the legal list is an uninterrupted payment of dividends. Thus, legal listing encourages pursuance of a stable dividend policy.

On the other hand, if a firm's investment opportunities fluctuate from year to year, should it not retain more earnings during some years in order to take advantage of these opportunities when they appear, then increase dividends when good internal investment opportunities are scarce? This line of reasoning would lead to the recommendation of a fluctuating payout for companies whose investment opportunities are unstable. However, the logic of the argument is diminished by recognizing that it is possible to maintain a reasonably stable dividend by using outside financing, especially debt, to smooth out the differences between the funds needed for investment and the amount of money provided by retained earnings.

GRAPHIC THEORY OF DIVIDEND POLICY

In the preceding chapters on capital budgeting and the cost of capital, we indicated that, generally, the cost of capital schedule and the investment schedule must be combined before the cost of capital can be established. In other words, the optimum capital budget, the marginal cost of capital, and the marginal rate of return on investment are *simultaneously* determined. In this section we examine this simultaneous solution in the framework of what might be called *the residual theory of dividend policy*.[5] The theory draws on materials developed earlier in the book—capital budgeting and the cost of capital—and serves to provide a bridge between these key concepts.

The starting point in the theory is that investors prefer to have the firm retain and reinvest earnings rather than pay them out in dividends *if the returns on reinvested earnings exceed the rate of return the investor could, himself, obtain on other investments*. In other words, if the corporation can reinvest retained earnings and get a 20 percent rate of

[5] "Residual" implies "left over." The residual theory of dividend policy implies that dividends are paid after internal investment opportunities have been exhausted.

return, while the best rate the stockholder can obtain if the earnings are passed on to him in the form of dividends is 10 percent, then the stockholder would prefer to have the firm retain the profits.

We have seen in Chapter 11 that the cost of equity capital obtained from retained earnings is an *opportunity cost* that reflects rates of return open to equity investors. If a firm's stockholders could buy other stocks of equal risk and obtain a 10 percent dividends-plus-capital-gains yield, then 10 percent is the firm's cost of retained earnings. The cost of new outside equity raised by selling common stock is higher because of the costs of floating the issue.

Most firms have an optimum debt ratio that calls for at least some debt, so new financing is done partly with debt and partly with equity. Debt has a different, and generally lower, cost than equity, so the two forms of capital must be combined to find the *weighted cost of capital.* As long as the firm finances at the optimum point, using an optimum amount of debt and equity, its marginal cost of capital is equal to the weighted average cost of capital.[6]

Internally generated equity (retained earnings) is available for financing a certain amount of new investment; beyond this amount, the firm must turn to more expensive new common stock. At the point where new stock must be sold, the cost of equity and, consequently, the weighted cost of capital, begins to rise. In other words, the minimum point on the weighted cost of capital curve—and this minimum point is the marginal cost of capital—rises when the firm uses up its retained earnings and must sell common stock.

These concepts, which were developed in Chapter 11, are illustrated in Figure 12–3. Figure 12–3(*a*) shows the construction of the weighted cost of capital (1) for internal equity (retained earnings) and (2) after the firm has exhausted its retained earnings and must sell new common stock. The optimum debt ratio is seen to be 50 percent in this hypothetical case, and the minimum points on the weighted cost of capital curves are designated points X and Y for retained earnings and for new common stock, respectively. Point X, which has a value of 10 percent, is the marginal cost of capital as long as equity comes only from retained earnings. Point Y, which has a value of 13 percent, is the marginal cost of all capital raised after the firm begins selling new common stock. We assume that the firm uses no preferred stock.

Our hypothetical firm has $50 million of retained earnings and a 50 percent optimum debt ratio. Therefore, it can make net investments

[6] It is demonstrated in elementary economics textbooks that the marginal cost curve cuts the average cost curve where the average curve is at a minimum—that is, the marginal and the average curves are *equal* where the average curve is at a *minimum*.

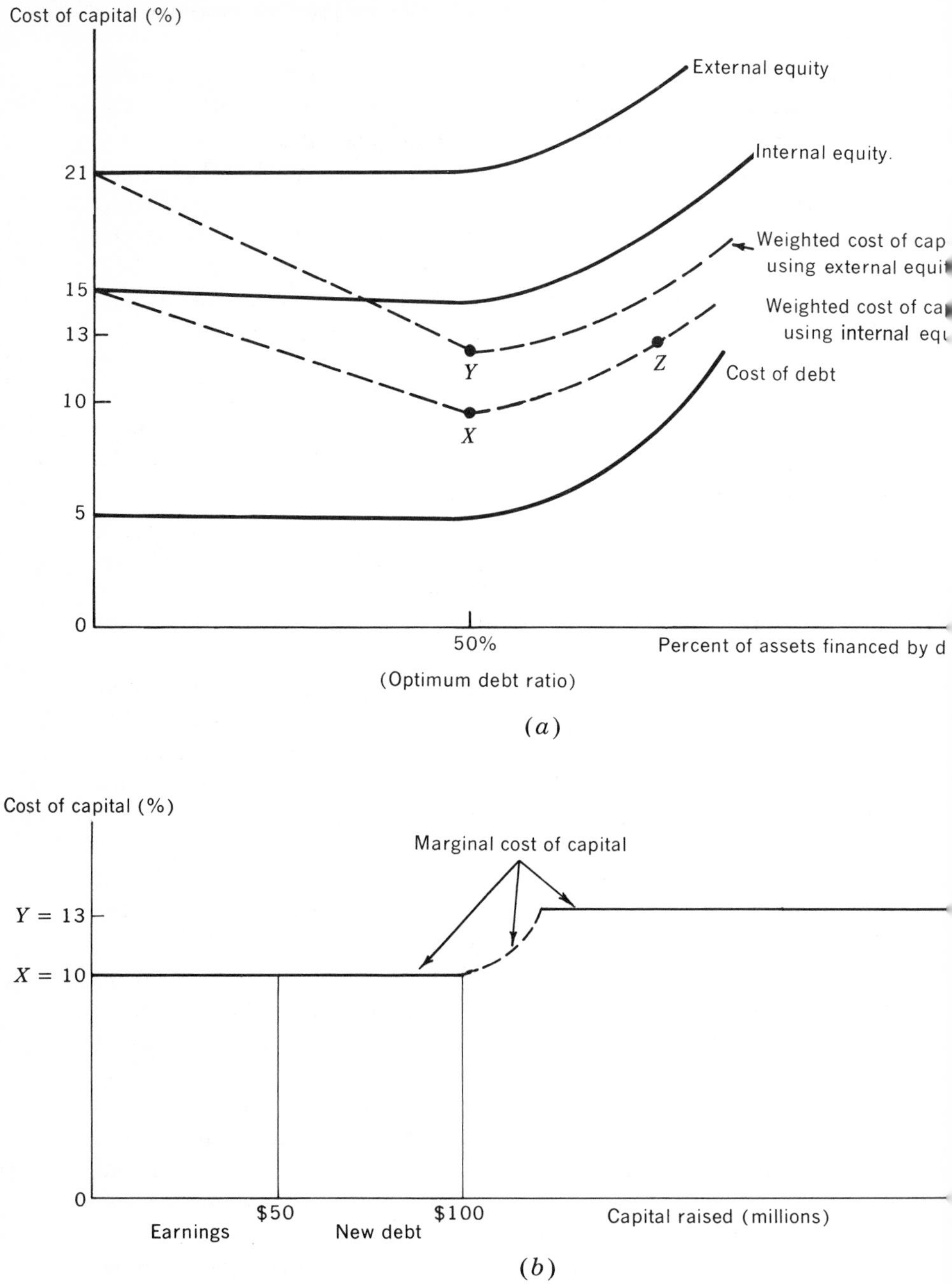

Figure 12–3 The Cost of Capital

(investments in addition to asset replacements financed from depreciation) up to \$100 million—\$50 million retained earnings plus \$50 million new debt supported by the retained earnings. Therefore, its marginal cost of capital is constant at 10 percent for up to \$100 million of capital.

Beyond \$100 million, the firm would employ more debt, and its marginal cost of capital would be represented by points between X and Z on the "weighted cost of capital using internal equity." Beyond point Z, where the marginal cost of capital is 13 percent, the firm should use external equity, return to the optimum capital structure, and have a constant 13 percent marginal cost of capital. This is shown in Figure 12–3, panel (b).

Next, suppose the firm's capital budgeting department draws up a list of investment opportunities, ranked in the order of their IRR, and plots them on a graph. The investment opportunity curves of three different years—one for a "good" year (IRR_1), one for a "normal" year (IRR_2), and one for a "bad" year (IRR_3)—are shown in Figure 12–4. IRR_1 shows that the firm can invest more money at higher rates of return than it can when the investment opportunities are those given in IRR_2 and IRR_3.

Now we combine the investment opportunities schedules with the cost of capital; this is done in Figure 12–5. The point where the investment opportunity curve cuts the cost of capital curve defines the proper level of new investment. When investment opportunities are relatively poor, the optimum level of investment is \$25 million; when opportunities are about normal, \$75 million should be invested; and when opportunities are relatively good, the firm should make new investments in the amount of \$125 million.

Consider the situation where IRR_1 is the appropriate schedule The firm has \$50 million in earnings and a 50 percent target debt ratio,

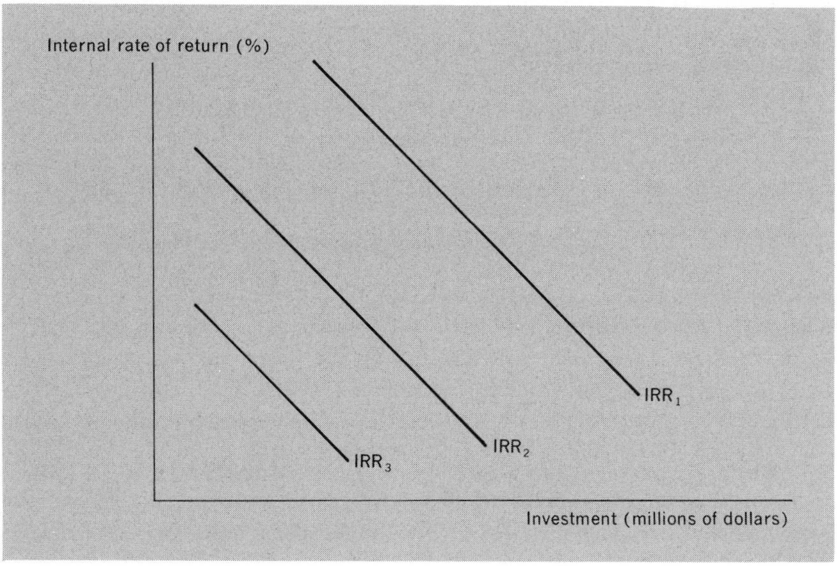

Figure 12–4 Investment Opportunities

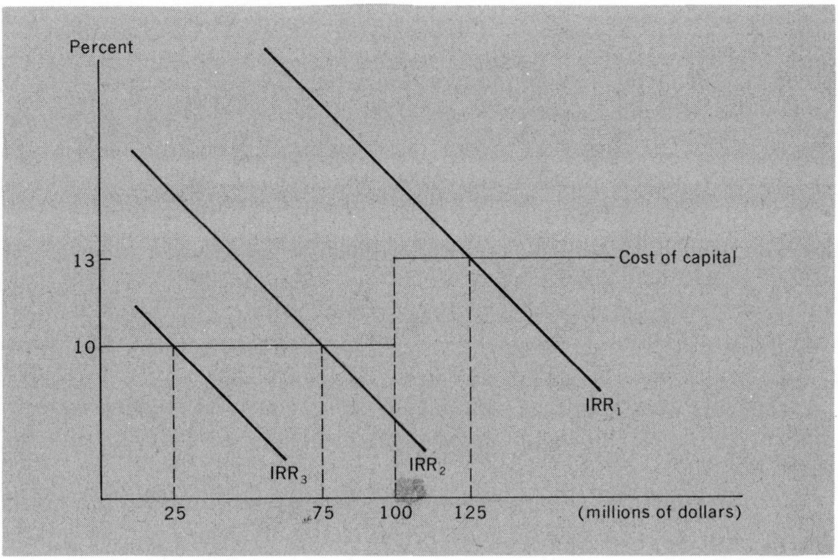

Figure 12–5 Interrelation among Cost of Capital, Investment Opportunities, and New Investment

so it can finance \$100 million, \$50 million earnings plus \$50 million debt, from retained earnings plu. new debt *if it retains all its earnings.* If it pays part of the earnings in dividends, then it will have to begin using expensive new common stock sooner, so the cost of capital curve will jump sooner. This suggests that under the conditions of IRR_1 the firm should retain all its earnings and actually sell some new common stock in order to take advantage of its investment opportunities. Its payout ratio is thus zero percent.

Under the conditions of IRR_2, however, the firm should invest only \$75 million. How should this investment be financed? First, notice that if it retains the full amount of its earnings, \$50 million, it will need to sell only \$25 million of new debt. But retaining \$50 million and selling only \$25 million of new debt will cause the company to move away from its target capital structure. To stay on target, the required \$75 million must be financed half by equity—retained earnings—and half by debt, or \$37.5 million of retained earnings and \$37.5 million of debt. Now if the firm has \$50 million in total earnings and decides to retain and reinvest \$37.5 million, it must pay \$12.5 million in dividends.[7] In this case, the payout ratio is 25 percent (\$12.5 divided by \$50).

[7] Actually it could buy back its common stock instead of paying dividends. Also, the firm might prefer to engage in merger activities rather than raise its payout ratio, using retained earnings to acquire other firms. This possibility is discussed in Chapter 21.

Finally, under the "bad" conditions of IRR_3 the firm should invest only \$25 million. Because it has \$50 million in earnings, it could finance the entire \$25 million out of retained earnings and still have \$25 million available for dividends. Should this be done? Under the assumptions, this would not be a good decision because it would move the firm away from its target debt ratio. To stay in the 50–50 debt/equity position, the firm must retain \$12.5 million and sell \$12.5 million of debt. When the \$12.5 million of retained earnings is subtracted from the \$50 million of earnings, we are left with a residual of \$37.5, the amount that should be paid out in dividends. In this case the payout ratio is 75 percent.

ONG-RUN VIEWPOINT

There seems to be a conflict between the theory and the statement made in the preceding section that firms should and do maintain reasonably stable cash dividends. How can this conflict be reconciled?

Actually, this reconciliation is quite simple if we recognize that the theory is not meant to be applied *exactly*. In other words, we would not recommend that a firm adjust its dividend each and every year—indeed, this is not necessary. Firms do have target debt ratios, but they also have a certain amount of flexibility—they can be moderately above or below the target debt position in any one year with no adverse consequences. This means that if an unusually large number of good investments are available in a particular year, the firm does not necessarily have to cut its dividend to take advantage of them—it can borrow somewhat more heavily than usual in that particular year without getting its debt ratio too far out of line. Obviously, however, this excessive reliance on debt could not continue for too many years without getting the debt ratio seriously out of line, necessitating either a sale of new stock or a cut in dividends and an attendant increase in the level of retained earnings.

IIGH AND LOW DIVIDEND PAYOUT INDUSTRIES

Some industries are experiencing rapid growth in the demand for their products, providing the firms in these industries with many good investment opportunities. Electronics, office equipment, and color television are examples of such industries in recent years. Other industries, however, have experienced much slower growth, or perhaps even declines. Examples of such slow-growth industries are cigarette manufacturing, textiles, and coal mining. Still other industries are growing at about the same rate as the general economy—oil, steel, and banking are representative.

The theory suggests that firms in rapidly growing industries should generally have IRR curves that are relatively far out to the right on graphs such as Figure 12–5; for example, Xerox, Fairchild Camera, and IBM might have investment opportunities similar to IRR_1. The tobacco companies, on the other hand, could be expected to have investment schedules similar to IRR_3, while IRR_2 might be appropriate for Standard Oil of New Jersey or U.S. Steel.

Each of these firms would, of course, experience shifts in investment opportunities from year to year, but the curves would *tend* to be in about the same part of the graph. In other words, firms like Xerox would *tend* to have more investment opportunities than money, so they would *tend* to have a zero (or very low) payout ratio. Reynolds Tobacco, on the other hand, would *tend* to have more money than good investments, so we would expect to find Reynolds paying out a relatively high percentage of earnings in dividends. These companies do, in fact, conform with our expectations.

CONFLICTING THEORIES ON DIVIDENDS

Two basic schools of thought on dividend policy have been expressed in the theoretical literature of finance. One school, associated with Myron Gordon and John Lintner, among others, holds that the capital gains expected to result from earnings retention are more risky than are dividend expectations. Accordingly, this school suggests that the earnings of a firm with a low payout ratio will typically be capitalized at higher rates than will the earnings of a high payout firm.

The other school, associated with Merton Miller and Franco Modigliani, holds that investors are basically indifferent between returns coming in the form of dividends or as capital gains. Miller and Modigliani believe that any effect that a change in dividends has on the price of a firm's stock is related primarily to *information about expected future earnings conveyed by a change in dividends*. Recalling that corporate managements dislike cutting dividends, Miller and Modigliani assert that increases in cash dividends raise expectations about the level of future earnings—dividend increases have favorable *information content.* In terms of Figure 12-2 above, Miller and Modigliani would say that the dividend increases in the 11th, 12th, 13th, and 23d years had information content about future earnings—these dividend increases signaled to stockholders that management expected the recent earnings increases to be permanent.

Dividends are probably less uncertain than capital gains, but dividends are taxed at a higher rate than capital gains. How do these two forces balance out? Some argue that the uncertainty factor dominates, others feel that the differential tax rate is the stronger force and causes investors to favor corporate retention of earnings. Still others—and we put ourselves in this group—argue that it is difficult to generalize. Depending on the tax status and current income needs of its set of stockholders (and both brokerage costs and capital gains taxes make it difficult for stockholders to shift companies), as well as the firm's internal investment opportunities, the optimum dividend policy will vary from firm to firm.

Some of these questions are considered in more detail—at both a theoretical and empirical level—in Appendix A to this chapter.

IVIDEND AYMENTS

Dividends are normally paid quarterly. For example, Union Carbide paid dividends of $2.00 during 1968, 50 cents each quarter. In common financial language, we say that Union Carbide's *regular quarterly dividend* is 50 cents, or that its *regular annual dividend* is $2.00. Management, sometimes by an explicit statement in the annual report and sometimes by implication, conveys to stockholders an expectation that the regular dividend will be maintained if at all possible. Further, management conveys its belief that earnings will be sufficient to maintain the dividend.

Under other conditions, a firm's cash flows and investment needs may be too volatile for it to set a very high regular dividend; on the average, however, it needs a high dividend payout to dispose of funds not necessary for reinvestment. In such a case, the directors can set a relatively low regular dividend—low enough that it can be maintained even in low profit years or in years when a considerable amount of reinvestment is needed—and supplement it with an *extra dividend* in years when excess funds are available. As was pointed out earlier, General Motors, whose earnings fluctuate widely from year to year, has long followed the practice of supplementing its regular dividend with an *extra dividend* paid at the end of the year, when its profits and investment requirements are known.

PAYMENT PROCEDURE

The actual payment procedure is of some importance, and the following is an outline of the payment sequence.

1. The directors meet, say on November 15, and declare the regular dividend. The directors would, on this date, issue a statement similar to the following: "On November 15, 1967, the directors of the XYZ Company met and declared the regular quarterly dividend of $0.50 per share, plus an extra dividend of $0.75 per share, to holders of record on December 15, payment to be made on January 1, 1968."
2. On December 15, the *holder of record date,* the company closes its stock transfer books and makes up a list of the shareholders as of that date. If XYZ Company is notified of the sale and transfer of some stock before December 16, the new owner receives the dividend. If notification is received on or after December 16, the old stockholder gets the dividend.
3. Suppose Edward Johns buys 100 shares of stock from Robert Noble on December 13; will the company be notified of the transfer in time to list Noble as the new owner and, thus, pay the dividend to him? To avoid conflict, the stock brokerage business has set up a convention of declaring that the right to the dividend remains with the stock until four days prior to the holder of record date; on the fourth day before the record date, the right to the dividend no longer goes with the shares. The date when the right to the dividend leaves the stock is called the *ex-dividend date.*

   In this case, the ex-dividend date is four days prior to December 15, or December 11. Therefore, if Johns is to receive the dividend, he must buy the stock by December 10. If he buys it on December 11 or later, Noble will receive the dividend.

   The total dividend, regular plus extra, amounts to $1.25, so the ex-dividend date is important. Barring fluctuations in the stock market, we would normally expect the price of a stock to drop by approximately the amount of the dividend on the ex-dividend date.
4. The company actually mails the checks to the holders of record on January 1, the payment date.

TOCK DIVIDENDS AND STOCK SPLITS

One of the significant issues of dividend policy in which the financial manager plays an important policy formulation role is that of *stock dividends* and *stock splits*. A stock dividend is paid in additional shares of stock instead of cash, and simply involves the transfer of surplus to the capital stock account.[8]

An interesting example of the use of stock dividends is the case of the Commonwealth Edison Company. In October 1958, it announced that almost all the annual earnings would be distributed each year in the form of cash and stock dividends. The company would continue to pay the regular 50 cents a share quarterly cash dividend, plus one annual dividend in stock, equivalent to the difference between the amount earned on common stock in that year and the $2 cash dividend paid. This device gives investors a combination of both cash and stock dividends.

In a *stock split* there is no change in the total capital account or surplus. A larger number of shares of common stock are issued. In a two-for-one split, each stockholder would have two shares for each one previously held. Book value per share would be cut in half. The par, or stated, value per share of common stock is similarly changed.

From a practical standpoint there is little difference between a stock dividend and a stock split. The New York Stock Exchange considers any distribution of stock totaling 24 percent or less of outstanding stock to be a stock dividend. Any distribution of stock of 25 percent or more is regarded as a stock split. Since the two are similar, the issues outlined below are discussed in connection with both stock dividends and stock splits.

PRICE EFFECTS. The results of a careful empirical study of the effects of stock dividends are available and can be used as a basis for observa-

[8] One point that should be made in connection with stock dividends is that the transfer from earned surplus to the capital stock account must be based on market value. In other words, if a firm's shares are selling for $100 and it has 1 million shares outstanding, a 10 percent stock dividend requires the transfer of $10 million (100,000 × $100) from earned surplus to capital stock. Quite obviously, stock dividends are thus limited by the size of earned surplus. The rule was put into effect to prevent the declaration of stock dividends unless the firm has had earnings. This is another in a long series of rulings designed to prevent investors from being fooled by the practices of unscrupulous firms.

tions on the price effects of stock dividends.[9] The findings of the study are presented in Table 12–3. When stock dividends were associated with a cash dividend increase, the value of the company's stock six months after the ex-dividend date had risen by 8 percent. On the other hand, where stock dividends were not accompanied by cash dividend increases, stock values fell by 12 percent during the subsequent six-month period.

TABLE 12–3 PRICE EFFECTS OF STOCK DIVIDENDS

	PRICE AT SELECTED DATES (IN PERCENTAGES)		
	Six Months Prior to Ex-dividend Date	At Ex-dividend Date	Six Months after Ex-dividend Date
Cash Dividend Variable			
Cash dividend increase	100	109	108
No cash dividend increase	100	99	88

These data seem to suggest that stock dividends are seen for what they are—simply additional pieces of paper—and that they do not represent true income. When they are accompanied by higher earnings and cash dividend increases, investors bid up the value of the stock. However, when stock dividends are not accompanied by increases in earnings and cash dividends, the dilution of earnings and dividends per share causes the price of the stock to drop. The fundamental determinant is underlying earnings and dividend trends.

EFFECTS ON EXTENT OF OWNERSHIP. Table 12–4 shows the effect of stock dividends on common stock ownership. Large stock dividends resulted in the largest percentage increases in stock ownership. The use of stock dividends increased ownership by 25 percent on the average. For companies and industries that did not offer stock splits or stock dividends, the increase in ownership was only 5 percent. Furthermore, the degree of increase in ownership increased with the size of the stock dividend.

This evidence suggests that stock dividends increase share ownership. Regardless of the effect on market price, the use of stock dividends

[9] C. A. Barker, "Evaluation of Stock Dividends," *Harvard Business Review*, XXXVI (July-August 1958), 99–114.

TABLE 12–4 EFFECTS OF STOCK DIVIDENDS ON STOCK OWNERSHIP

	PERCENTAGE INCREASE IN STOCKHOLDERS, 1950–1953
Stock dividend, 25% and over	30
Stock dividend, 5–25%	17
All stock dividends	25
No stock dividends or splits	5

SOURCE: C. Austin Barker, "Evaluation of Stock Dividends," *Harvard Business Review,* XXXVI (July-August 1958), 99–114.

effectively increases stock ownership by lowering the price at which shares are traded to a more popular range.

UMMARY

Dividend policy determines the extent of internal financing by a firm. The financial manager decides whether to release corporate earnings from the control of the enterprise. Because dividend policy affects the financial structure, the flow of funds, corporate liquidity, stock prices, and investor satisfaction—to list a few ramifications—the manager exercises a high degree of judgment in establishing a dividend pattern.

In theory, once the firm's debt policy and cost of capital have been determined, dividend policy should automatically follow. Under our theoretical model, dividends are simply a residual after investment needs have been met; if this policy is followed, and if investors are indifferent between receiving their investment returns in the form of dividends or capital gains, stockholders are better off than under any other possible dividend policy. However, the financial manager simply does not have all the information assumed in the theory, and rule-of-thumb guidelines are needed.

As a guide to boards of directors responsible for dividend policy, the following check list summarizes the major economic and financial factors influencing dividend policy and the direction of the influence.

1. *Rate of Growth and Profit Level.* Economic theory suggests that high growth rates are associated with higher profit opportunities and lower growth rates with smaller profit margins. The higher the growth

rate and the larger the prospective margins, the lower the dividend payout is likely to be.

2. *Stability of Earnings.* If earnings are relatively stable from the standpoint of both long-term growth and cyclical fluctuations, the dividend payout is likely to be higher.

3. *Age and Size of Firm.* A well-established, large firm has better access to the capital markets than has a new and small firm. Hence, the dividend payout, other things being equal, will be higher for the larger and older firm.

4. *Cash Position.* The stronger a firm's cash or liquidity position in relation to its prospective future need for funds, the higher the probable dividend payout.

5. *Need to Repay Debt.* A firm that has incurred heavy indebtedness has implicitly committed itself to a relatively high rate of earnings retention unless it seeks to prepare the markets for a common stock or debt-refunding issue. This factor may be reinforced by provisions in the debt contract that prevent the payment of cash dividends unless certain conditions are met.

6. *Control.* If maintenance of existing control is an important consideration, the dividend payout may be lower to permit financing from retained earnings. The procedure avoids issuance of additional securities, which would involve dilution of ownership or the increased risks of debt. However, if a struggle for control of the firm with opposition groups is in progress or is threatened, the dividend payout may be higher to appeal to stockholder goodwill.

7. *Maintenance of a Target Dividend.* The objective of a stable dividend policy will make for low payouts when profits are temporarily high and high payouts when profits are temporarily depressed; and it will cause dividends to lag behind profit growth until the establishment of new earnings levels is strongly assured.

8. *Tax Position of Stockholders.* Corporations closely held by a few taxpayers in high income brackets are likely to have a lower dividend payout. Corporations widely held by small investors will tend to have higher dividend payouts.

9. *Tax Position of the Corporation.* Potential penalties for excessive accumulation of retained earnings may cause dividend payouts to be higher than economic and financial considerations alone would indicate.

Of the factors listed, some make for higher dividend payouts, some for lower. It is not possible to provide a formula that can be used to establish the proper dividend payout for a given situation. This is a task requiring the exercise of judgment. The considerations summarized above provide a check list for guiding dividend decisions.

Empirical studies indicate a wide diversity of dividend payout ratios not only among industries but also among firms in the same industry. Studies also show that dividends are more stable than earnings. Firms are reluctant to raise dividends in years of good earnings, and they resist dividend cuts as earnings decline. In view of investors' observed preference for stable dividends and of the probability that a cut in dividends is likely to be interpreted as forecasting a decline in earnings, stable dividends make good sense.

Stock Dividends and Splits

Neither stock splits nor stock dividends alone exert a fundamental influence on prices. The fundamental determinant of the price of the company's stock is the company's earning power compared with the earning power of other companies. However, both stock splits and stock dividends can be used as an effective instrument of financial policy. They are useful devices for reducing the price at which stocks are traded, and studies indicate that stock dividends and stock splits tend to broaden the ownership of a firm's shares.

QUESTIONS

12–1 Discuss the advantages and disadvantages of each of the following dividend policies:
- a) Constant payout ratio.
- b) Constant dollar dividend per share.
- c) Constant regular quarterly dividend plus a year-end extra when earnings are sufficiently high or corporate investment needs are sufficiently low.

12–2 How would each of the following changes probably affect aggregate payout ratios? Explain your answer.
- a) An increase in the personal income tax rate.
- b) A liberalization in depreciation policies for federal income tax purposes.
- c) A rise in interest rates.
- d) An increase in corporate profits.
- e) A decline in investment opportunities.

12–3 Aggregate dividend payout ratios have been increasing since the end of World War II. Why?

12–4 Discuss the pros and cons of having the directors formally announce what a firm's dividend policy will be in the future.

12–5 What purpose do stock dividends and stock splits accomplish?

12–6 What is the difference between a stock dividend and a stock split? As a stockholder, would you prefer to see your company declare a 100 percent stock dividend or a two-for-one split?

12–7 "The cost of retained earnings is less than the cost of new outside equity capital. Consequently, it is totally irrational for a firm to sell a new issue of stock and, during the same year, pay dividends." Discuss this statement.

PROBLEMS

12–1 Listed below are pertinent financial data for the common stocks of Cerro Corp., Polaroid, and National Fuel Gas. Cerro is a leading producer of copper, zinc, and lead, whose product demand is quite cyclical. Polaroid manufactures cameras and film. National Fuel Gas is an integrated gas system serving the Northeastern United States.

CERRO CORPORATION

Year	*Earnings*	*Dividends*	*Price Range*	*Payout*	*Price/ Earnings* Ratio*
1964	$4.59	$1.14	46–19	25%	10–4
1963	2.25	0.73	21–12	32	9–5
1962	0.99	0.69	21–11	70	18–10
1961	0.87	0.66	27–18	76	25–17
1960	2.01	0.58	24–15	29	11–7
1959	1.73	0.54	27–19	31	14–9
1958	0.95	0.46	25–13	48	20–10
1957	1.11	0.79	29–12	71	22–9
1956	2.19	0.75	37–26	34	12–8
1955	2.78	0.64	28–16	23	7–4
			POLAROID		
1964	$1.16	$0.06	46–32	5%	40–28
1963	0.71	0.05	53–30	7	88–32
1962	0.63	0.05	55–20	8	115–85
1961	0.52	0.05	60–44	10	116–72
1960	0.56	0.05	65–41	9	68–35
1959	0.69	0.05	47–24	7	59–23
1958	0.47	0.05	27–11	11	37–18
1957	0.36	0.04	13–6	11	30–13
1956	0.22	0.03	7–3	14	21–11
1955	0.13	0.02	3–2	15	23–15
			NATIONAL FUEL GAS		
1964	$2.17	$1.36	34–31	63%	16–14
1963	2.29	1.30	37–29	57	16–13
1962	2.15	1.23	31–23	57	14–11
1961	1.84	1.20	33–24	65	18–13
1960	1.86	1.20	24–22	64	13–12
1959	1.74	1.15	25–21	66	14–12
1958	1.78	1.10	24–17	62	13–10
1957	1.30	1.10	20–16	85	15–13
1956	1.58	1.03	22–19	65	14–12
1955	1.57	1.00	23–20	64	15–12

* Price/earnings ratios are the high and the low for the year according to *Standard & Poor's Reports*.

a) What differences are revealed by the data on the dividend policy of the three firms? What explanations can be given for these differences?

b) What is the relationship of dividend policy to the market price of the stock?

12–2 In the following table, earnings and dividend data are shown for American Telephone and Telegraph and Sun Oil Company, a closely held, growing firm.

Explain the difference in the percentage of dividends paid out by each.

AMERICAN TELEPHONE AND TELEGRAPH

Year	*Earnings*	*Dividend*	*Payout*	*Average Price*
1964	$3.24	$1.95	60%	70
1963	3.03	1.80	59	64
1962	2.90	1.80	62	59
1961	2.76	1.73	63	60
1960	2.77	1.65	60	47
1959	2.61	1.58	60	40
1958	2.34	1.50	64	33
1957	2.17	1.50	69	28
1956	2.20	1.50	68	30
1955	2.19	1.50	68	30
		SUN OIL COMPANY		
1964	$4.30	$0.95	22%	59
1963	3.85	0.90	23	46
1962	3.29	0.85	26	41
1961	3.09	0.81	26	43
1960	3.05	0.75	25	37
1959	2.64	0.73	28	44
1958	1.98	0.70	35	46
1957	2.93	0.67	23	50
1956	3.48	0.63	18	49
1955	2.95	0.58	20	44

12–3 Union spokesmen have presented arguments similar to the following: "Corporations such as General Foods retain about one half their profits—that is, they do not pay them out in dividends. Therefore, their profits are too high, because if they financed by selling common stock instead of by retained earnings, their prices or profits would not need to be so high." Evaluate the statement.

12–4 Select a pair of companies in problems 1 and 2 and calculate dividend payout based on cash flows. Would your previous explanation of dividend policies be affected by the cash flow pay-out patterns? The following financial data are appropriately scaled.

CERRO CORPORATION

Year	*Net Income**	*Depreciation and Depletion**
1964	$26.00	$8.78
1963	12.69	8.83
1962	5.53	8.98
1961	4.94	8.18
1960	9.38	7.56
1959	8.00	6.95
1958	3.98	6.27

POLAROID CORPORATION

1964	$18.32	$5.24
1963	11.22	4.39
1962	9.96	3.41
1961	8.11	3.75
1960	8.81	2.87
1959	10.74	2.18
1958	7.21	1.58

NATIONAL FUEL GAS

1964	$11.05	$4.64
1963	11.66	4.65
1962	10.96	4.60
1961	9.35	4.20
1960	9.16	3.96
1959	8.56	3.95
1958	8.78	3.90

* After taxes, in millions of dollars.

AMERICAN TELEPHONE AND TELEGRAPH

Year	*Net Income**	*Depreciation and Depletion**
1964	$1,658.6	$1,469.4
1963	1,479.5	1,332.1
1962	1,388.2	1,219.0
1961	1,284.6	1,099.9
1960	1,213.0	1,007.8
1959	1,113.2	930.0
1958	952.3	834.0

SUN OIL COMPANY

1964	$68.51	$57.71
1963	61.22	62.19
1962	53.19	57.12
1961	49.79	65.60
1960	49.27	63.33
1959	42.84	52.81
1958	32.06	56.42

Selected References

Barker, C. A., "Price Effects of Stock Dividend Shares, at Ex-Dividend Dates," *Journal of Finance,* XIV (September 1959), 373–378.

——— "Evaluation of Stock Dividends," *Harvard Business Review,* XXXVI (July-August, 1958), 99–114.

———, "Stock Splits in a Bull Market," *Harvard Business Review,* XXXV (May-June 1957), 72–79.

———, "Effective Stock Splits," *Harvard Business Review,* XXXIV (January-February 1956), 101–106.

Baumol, William J., "On Dividend Policy and Market Imperfection," *Journal of Business,* XXXVI (January 1963), 112–115.

Bierman, Harold Jr., and Richard West, "The Acquisition of Common Stock by the Corporate Issuer," *Journal of Finance,* XXI (December 1966), 687–696.

Benishay, Haskel, "Variability in Earnings-Price Ratios of Corporate Equities, *American Economics Review,* LI (March 1961), 81–94.

Boness, A. James, "Elements of a Theory of Stock-Option Value," *Journal of Political Economy,* LXXII (April 1964), 163–175.

Boorstin, Robert L., "A Rational Dividend Policy for Savings and Loan Companies," *Financial Analysts Journal,* XIX (July-August 1963), 33–46.

Brewer, D. E., and J. Michaelson, "The Cost of Capital, Corporation Finance, and the Theory of Investment: Comment," *American Economic Review,* LV (June 1965), 516–524.

Brigham, Eugene, "The Profitability of a Firm's Repurchase of Its Own Common Stock," *California Management Review,* VII (Winter 1964), 69–75.

———, and Myron J. Gordon, "Leverage, Dividend Policy, and the Cost of Capital," *Journal of Finance,* XXIII (March 1968), 85–104.

———, and James L. Pappas, "Rates of Return on Common Stocks," *Journal of Business,* XLII (July 1969).

Brittain, J. A., *Corporate Dividend Policy.* (Washington, D.C.: The Brookings Institute, 1966.)

Darling, Paul G., "The Influence of Expectations and Liquidity on Dividend Policy," *Journal of Political Economy,* LXV (June 1957), 209–224.

Dobrovolsky, S. P., "Economics of Corporate Internal and External Financing," *Journal of Finance,* XIII (March 1958), 35–47.

Ellis, Charles D., "Repurchase Stock to Revitalize Equity," *Harvard Business Review,* XLIII (July-August 1965), 119–128.

Elton, Edwin J., and Martin J. Gruber, "The Effect of Share Repurchases on the Value of the Firm," *Journal of Finance,* XXIII (March 1968), 135–150.

Friend, Irwin, and Marshall Puckett, "Dividends and Stock Prices," *American Economic Review,* LIV (September 1964), 656–682.

Gordon, Myron, J., "Optimal Investment and Financing Policy," *Journal of Finance,* XVIII (May 1963), 264–272.

———, "The Savings Investment and Valuation of a Corporation," *Review of Economics and Statistics,* XLIV (February 1962).

———, *The Investment, Financing, and Valuation of the Corporation* (Homewood, Ill.: Irwin, 1962).

———, "Dividends, Earnings and Stock Prices," *Review of Economics and Statistics,* XLI (May 1959), 99–105.

———, and Eli Shapiro, "Capital Equipment Analysis: The Required Rate of Profit," *Management Science,* III (October 1956), 102–110.

Guthart, Leo A., "Why Companies Are Buying Back Their Own Stock," *Financial Analysts Journal,* XXIII (April-May 1967), 105–110.

———, "More Companies Are Buying Back Their Stock," *Harvard Business Review,* XLIII (March-April 1965), 40–45.

Harkavy, Oscar, "The Relation Between Retained Earnings and Common Stock Prices for Large Listed Corporations," *Journal of Finance,* VIII (September 1953), 283–297.

Holland, Daniel M., *Dividends Under the Income Tax* (New York: National Bureau of Economic Reearch, 1962).

Johnson, Keith B., "Stock Splits and Price Changes," *Journal of Finance,* XXI (December 1966), 675–686.

Lerner, Eugene, M., "Capital Budgeting and Financial Management," in Alexander A. Robichek, ed., *Financial Research and Managerial Decisions.* (New York: Wiley, 1967), pp. 72–89.

———, "The Integration of Capital Budgeting and Stock Valuation," *American Economic Review,* LIV (September 1964), 683–702.

——— and Willard T. Carleton, *A Theory of Financial Analysis* (New York: Harcourt, Brace, 1966).

———, and Willard T. Carleton, "Financing Decisions of the Firm," *Journal of Finance,* XXI (May 1966), 202–214.

Lintner, John, "Optimal Dividends and Corporate Growth Under Uncertainty," *Quarterly Journal of Economics,* LXXXVIII (February 1964), 49–95.

———, "Distribution of Incomes of Corporations Among Dividends, Retained Earnings, and Taxes," *American Economic Review,* XLVI (May 1956), 97–113.

———, "Dividend Policy and Market Valuation: A Reply," *Journal of Business,* XXXVI (January 1963), 116–119.

———, "Dividends, Earnings, Leverage, Stock Prices and the Supply of Capital to Corporations," *Review of Economics and Statistics,* XLIV (August 1962), 243–269.

Miller, Merton H., and Franco Modigliani, "Dividend Policy, Growth, and the Valuation of Shares," *Journal of Business,* XXXIV (October 1961), 411–433.

Porterfield, James T. S., "Dividends, Dilution, and Delusion," *Harvard Business Review,* XXXVII (November-December 1959), 156–161.

Quirin, G. David, *The Capital Expenditure Decision* (Homewood, Ill.: Irwin, 1967).

Robichek, Alexander A. and Stewart C. Myers, "Conceptual Problems in the Use of Risk-Adjusted Discount Rates," *Journal of Finance,* XXI (December 1966), 727–730.

———, *Optimal Financing Decisions,* (Englewood Cliffs, N.J.: Prentice-Hall, 1965).

Solomon, Ezra, *The Theory of Financial Management* (New York: Columbia University Press, 1963).

———, *The Management of Corporate Capital* (New York: Free Press, 1959).

Stevenson, Richard, "Corporate Stock Reacquisitions," *Accounting Review,* XLI (April 1966), 312–317.

Sussman, M. R., *The Stock Dividend* (Ann Arbor, Mich.: Bureau of Business Research, University of Michigan, 1962).

Vickers, Douglas, "Profitability and Reinvestment Rates: A Note on the Gordon Paradox," *Journal of Business,* XXXIX (July 1966), 366–370.

Walter, James E., *Dividend Policy and Enterprise Valuation* (Belmont, California: Wadsworth Publishing Company, 1967).

———, "Dividend Policy: Its Influence on the Value of the Enterprise," *Journal of Finance,* XVIII (May 1963), 280–291.

———, "Dividend Policies and Common Stock Prices," *Journal of Finance,* XI (March 1956), 29–41.

APPENDIX A TO CHAPTER 12
The Gordon Model[1]

Myron J. Gordon's theoretical model has probably been used as the basis of more recent theoretical and empirical work on stock prices and the cost of capital than has

[1] See M. J. Gordon, *The Investment, Financing, and Valuation of the Corporation,* (Homewood, Illinois: Irwin, 1962) for a detailed development of the Gordon model.

any other formulation.[2] Since most of the literature on the theory of finance assumes a knowledge of Gordon's basic model, it is appropriate to outline its essential features. Following Gordon, the definitions given below are used throughout the appendix.

P = The current price of a share of stock.
D_t = The dividend per share paid by the corporation during period t.
Y_t = Income per share earned during t.
r = The average rate of return investors expect the firm to earn on past and future investments.
b = The fraction of income the corporation is expected to retain in every future period. The dividend payout rate is $(1 - b)$.
k = Return that stockholders require on the corporation's stock.

The future values of subscripted variables represent investors' mean, or average, expectations. These expectations are, of course, subject to uncertainty and have associated probability distributions. The unsubscripted variables are assumed to remain constant in the future; that is, although they are subject to variation and will doubtless move within a range of values, investors are unable to forecast the direction of changes so they are *assumed* to remain constant.

Gordon uses continuous compounding to develop his model. This enables him to use continuous functions in certain advanced applications and to employ differential calculus to reach optional financing and investment decisions. The model can, however, be developed with discrete compounding; for people whose knowledge of calculus is hazy, this approach may be clearer. We shall, therefore, show first the discrete development, then the continuous case.

We should note at the outset that while Gordon's basic model assumes that all financing is done through retained earnings, the model can easily be extended to encompass the use of debt, provided the debt ratio is assumed to remain constant. In this case, one need simply interpret the rate of return variable given below, r, as the rate of return on *equity* instead of the rate of return on *assets*.

Discrete Compounding

The retention rate, b, is assumed to be a constant, so the dividend in any future period is given by the following equation:

$$D_t = (1 - b)Y_t \tag{A12–1}$$

[2] The articles listed in the end-of-chapter references by Brigham and Gordon, Gordon, Lerner and Carlton, Lintner, and Malkiel are examples.

Defining the initial earnings per share as Y_0, the earnings per share at any future period t can be found as:

$$Y_t = Y_0(1 + g)^t \qquad \text{(A12–2)}$$

where g is the expected growth rate in earnings.

Under Gordon's initial assumptions, all financing is done from retained earnings, and assets (both incremental and those previously held) earn an average rate of return, r. If no earnings were retained, growth in earnings would be zero. If all earnings were retained, expected growth would be at the rate r. With the percentage of earnings retained equal to b, the expected growth rate in earnings is equal to b times r. To illustrate, if a firm retained *all* of its earnings ($b = 100\%$, or 1.0), and if it earned 10 percent on the retained earnings ($r = 10$ percent), the growth rate would be calculated as:

$$g = br = 1.0 \times 10\% = 10\%$$

If the firm paid out 60 percent of its earnings in dividends ($b = 1 - .6 = .4$, or 40 percent), then

$$g = br = .4 \times 10\% = 4\%$$

while, if it paid out *all* of its earnings as dividends ($b = 1 - 1 = 0$), then

$$g = br = 0 \times 10\% = 0\%$$

Note that in Chapter 6, when we developed the compound interest equations, we implicitly assumed that all interest earned was reinvested; that is, that $b = 100$ percent. This enabled us to treat the interest rate as a growth rate.

We can use the fact that the growth rate in earnings is equal to b times r to rewrite equation A12–2 as:

$$Y_t = Y_0(1 + br)^t \qquad \text{(A12–3)}$$

If b is the percentage of earnings retained, $(1 - b)$ must be the percent of earnings paid out in dividends; that is, if $b = 60$ percent, then 40 percent must be the dividend payout ratio. We can, therefore, calculate dividends in any year as:

$$D_t = (1 - b)Y_t \qquad \text{(A12–4)}$$

Substituting equation A12–3 into equation A12–4, we find

$$D_t = (1 - b)Y_0(1 + br)^t \tag{A12–5}$$

Gordon defines the value of a share of the firm's stock, P, as the present value of the future dividends, discounted at the rate k:

$$P = \frac{D_1}{(1 + k)^1} + \frac{D_2}{(1 + k)^2} + \cdots \tag{A12–6}$$

Substituting equation A12–5 for dividends (D_t) in equation A12–6, we obtain

$$\begin{aligned} P &= \frac{(1 - b)Y_0(1 + br)^1}{(1 + k)^1} + \frac{(1 - b)Y_0(1 + br)^2}{(1 + k)^2} + \cdots \\ &= \sum_{t=1}^{\infty} \frac{(1 - b)Y_0(1 + br)^t}{(1 + k)^t} \end{aligned} \tag{A12–7}$$

Equation A12–7 is an infinite geometric progression with a first term equal to

$$\frac{(1 - b)Y_0(1 + br)}{(1 + k)}$$

and a ratio equal to $(1 + br)/(1 + k)$.[3] The sum of an infinite series, S, is found as

$$S = \frac{a}{1 - r} \tag{A12–8}$$

[3] If the ratio is greater than 1, there is no finite solution to the series—the price of the stock is infinite. Since infinitely large stock prices cannot and do not exist, we can assume that the constant ratio is less than 1. This, in turn, requires that $k > br$. Note that the growth rate, br, is constant from now to *eternity*. If br as measured by recent data for a given firm is high relative to the growth rate of GNP, then it cannot be assumed that this same high growth will continue *forever*. IBM, if it continues to grow at 20 percent per year, will have sales that *exceed* national income by the early 1990s, assuming national income continues to grow at a 4 percent rate. This is patently absurd and demonstrates the fallacy of projecting high growth rates for long periods.

where a = the first term and r = the constant ratio.[4]

Substituting for S, a, and r in equation A12–8 yields:

$$P = S = \frac{\dfrac{(1 - b)Y_0(1 + br)}{1 + k}}{1 - \dfrac{(1 + br)}{(1 + k)}}$$

$$= \frac{(1 - b)Y_0(1 + br)}{1 + k} \cdot \frac{1 + k}{(1 + k) - (1 + br)}$$

$$= \frac{(1 - b)Y_0(1 + br)}{1 + k - 1 - br}$$

$$= \frac{(1 - b)Y_0(1 + br)}{k - br} \qquad \text{(A12–9)}$$

Recognizing that $(1 - b)Y_0 = D_0$ and that br = growth rate, we can rewrite equation A12–9 as

$$P = \frac{D_0(1 + g)}{k - g} = \frac{D_1}{k - g} \qquad \text{(A12–10)}$$

or

$$k = \frac{D_1}{P} + g \qquad \text{(A12–11)}$$

The Gordon model as expressed in equations A12–9 and A12–10 states that the current price of a share of stock is equal to the dividend expected at the end of the current period divided by the discount rate minus the growth rate. Equation A12–11 states that the cost of equity capital is equal to the dividend yield plus the growth rate. The model is of fundamental importance, but we shall defer a discussion until after developing it under the assumption of continuous compounding.

The Continuous Compounding Model

Gordon actually developed his model for continuous compounding; for many purposes, the continuous form is more convenient than the discrete form. One can, however, omit this section without loss of continuity and skip immediately to the section dealing with implications of the model.

In the continuous development we make use of an equation developed

[4] See any college algebra text book for a proof of equation (A12–8). See footnote 3 on page 334 for an alternative proof of equation (A12–10).

in the Appendix to Chapter 6, 6–12, and the fact that $g = br$ to rewrite equation A12–3 as:

$$Y_t = Y_0e^{gt} = Y_0e^{brt} \tag{A12–12}$$

Gordon defines the value of the firm's stock, P, as the present value of the future stream of dividends, discounted at the rate k:

$$P = \int_0^\infty D_te^{-kt}\,dt \tag{A12–13}$$

Substituting equation A12–1 into equation A12–13 yields

$$P = \int_0^\infty (1 - b)Y_te^{-kt}\,dt \tag{A12–14}$$

and further substituting equation A12–12 into equation A12–14 gives

$$P = \int_0^\infty (1 - b)Y_0e^{brt}e^{-kt}\,dt \tag{A12–15}$$

Removing the constant from the integral, we obtain

$$P = (1 - b)Y_0 \int_0^\infty e^{brt}e^{-kt}\,dt$$

and consolidating the exponents of e leaves

$$P = (1 - b)Y_0 \int_0^\infty e^{-(k-br)t}\,dt \tag{A12–16}$$

Assuming that $k > br$ (otherwise the function cannot be integrated because the integral is infinitely large), we integrate equation A12–16 to obtain a fundamentally important equation:[5]

$$P = \frac{(1 - b)Y_0}{k - br} \tag{A12–17}$$

Recognizing that $(1 - b)Y_0 = D_0$, the current dividend, and that $br = g$, the growth rate, we can express equation A12–17 as:

$$P = \frac{D_0}{k - g} \tag{A12–18}$$

[5] This integration was performed in Chapter 6.

or, solving equation A12–18 for k,

$$k = \frac{D_0}{P} + g \tag{A12–19}$$

It should be noted that equations similar to A12–18 and A12–19 were developed in the preceding section for the discrete case, the only difference being that the discrete solution has D_1 in the numerator, while the continuous solution has D_0.

Implication of the Gordon Model

The assumptions in Gordon's model may at first appear severely restrictive. However, they do not depart greatly from important aspects of the behavior of large, mature industrial and utility corporations during much of the early post-World War II period. This fact has been pointed out in theoretical and empirical research testing and extending Gordon's basic model.[6] In this section, we describe the theoretical and empirical implications of the model. The theoretical material focuses mainly on the interrelationships between the fundamental variables in the model, while the empirical material provides a test of the model by comparing measurements with values predicted by the theory. In our discussion, we shall refer to the set of equations developed in the continuous case. Note, however, that all the statements would hold for the discrete equations except that it would not be possible to use calculus.

THEORETICAL STUDIES. Equation A12–17, which is repeated below, states that the price of a share of stock is equal to its current dividend divided by the total of the stockholders' required rate of return minus the growth rate:

$$P = \frac{(1 - b)Y_0}{k - br} \tag{A12–17}$$

The required rate of return, k, is determined by market forces. If, however, management can lower the value of k by such actions as improving public relations, broadening the market for the firm's shares, and so on, these actions will simultaneously induce a proportionate increase in the price of the stock. Similarly, any action that increases the firm's expected rate of return on investment, r, also raises the price of the stock.

Naturally, any event that changes the level of k or r for firms in general will also change the prices of individual stocks. To illustrate, the required rate of return on a stock, k, is partly determined by the opportunity cost of not investing in bonds. This opportunity cost is,

[6] See the references cited in footnote 2 of this appendix.

of course, influenced directly by the general level of interest rates. Thus, if Federal Reserve action drastically raises interest rates, one would expect a rise in k and a subsequent decline in stock prices, other things held constant.

Changes in b, the retention rate, might either raise or lower the price of the shares. Increasing b lowers the dividend, and this reduces the stock's price. Simultaneously, the increase in b serves to increase the growth rate, and this raises the price of the shares. If k, r, and b are all independent of one another, then equation A12–17 can be differentiated with respect to b to determine the optimum, or price-maximizing retention rate (and, of course, the optimum dividend policy).

$$P = \frac{(1 - b)Y_0}{k - br} \qquad \text{(A12–17)}$$

$$\frac{\partial P}{\partial b} = \left[\frac{Y_0}{(k - br)^2}\right](r - k) \qquad \text{(A12–20)}$$

To maximize P, set equation A12–20 equal to zero:

$$\left[\frac{Y_0}{(k - br)^2}\right](r - k) = 0 \qquad \text{(A12–21)}$$

Assuming, as we have been thus far, that Y_0, k, and r are all greater than zero and that $0 \leq b \leq 1$, equation A12–21 can be equal to zero if, and only if, $r = k$. If $k < r$, then equation A12–21 is positive, meaning that an increase in b will raise the price of the stock. If $k > r$, the reverse holds, and the firm should reduce b and increase dividends. So long as $k < r$, the Gordon model indicates that b, the retention rate, should be increased. This means that income should be retained rather than paid out as dividends. Conversely, if $k > r$, earnings should be paid out in dividends.[7]

A problem is immediately apparent: we have thus far assumed that k, r, and b are all constants that are independent of one another. This being the case, three possible alternatives exist:

1. $k > r$
2. $k < r$
3. $k = r$

If the first, $k > r$, holds, the firm should retain no earnings, paying them all out in dividends, and eventually liquidate. The rates of return available for this firm are less than opportunities elsewhere. If the second case, $k < r$, holds, the firm should retain all of its earnings. Finally,

[7] This conclusion is precisely the same as that reached by Walter in an earlier article; thus, in their basic forms, Gordon's and Walter's formulas are equivalent.

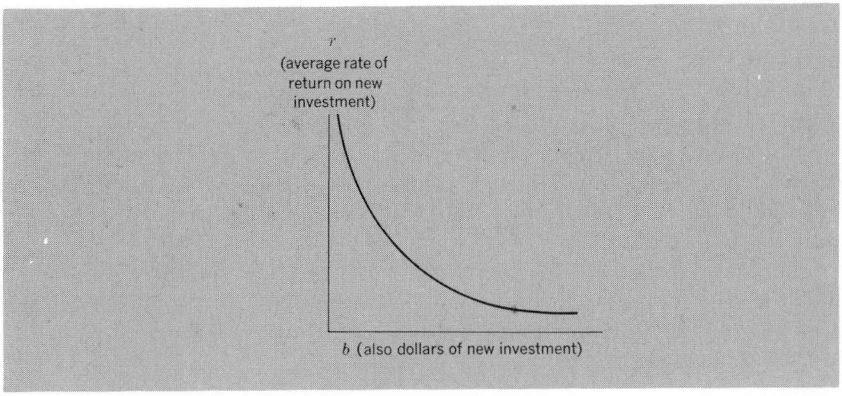

Figure A12–1 General Relationship between r and b

if $k = r$, it does not matter if the firm pays dividends or retains earnings—neither action will affect the price of the stock. Both k and r are assumed to be constant (and independent of b), so dividend policy cannot affect the price of the stock.

These conclusions, which follow from the strict Gordon model, are not very interesting—k may well be related to b, and r is almost certainly a function of the level of investment (represented by b). The general relationship one would expect to find between r and b is shown in Figure A12–1. As b—and with it the level of investment—rises, the average rate of return on investment declines.[8]

The general relationship between k and b is more questionable, but three possible relationships are graphed in Figure A12–2. If investors

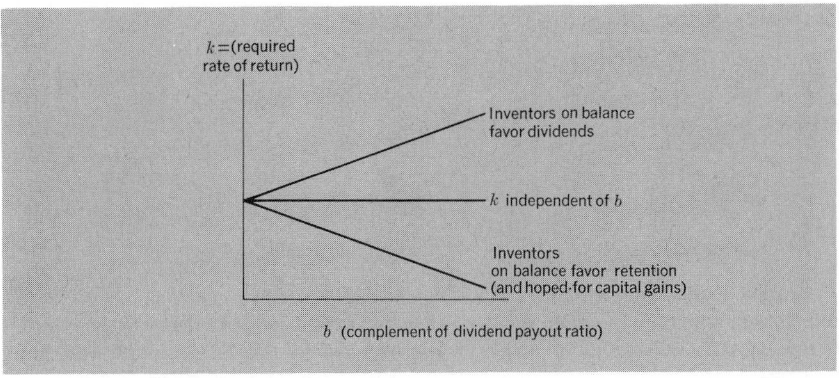

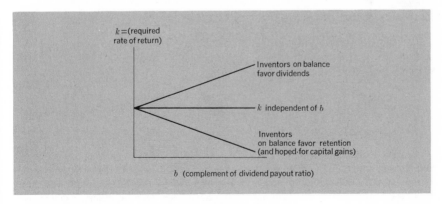

Figure A12–2 Some Possible Relationships between k and b

[8] This relation does not hold in the case of regulated utilities, whose average rates of return on investment are prescribed by utility commissions. This fact is important in developing the empirical results reported in the following section.

feel that dividends in the hand are better than capital gains in the bush—that is, dividends are less risky than capital gains—then k will rise with b. If, however, because of the differential tax on dividends and capital gains (or anything else), investors prefer retention-generated capital gains, then k will decline with increases in b. The actual form of the relationship has not been resolved to this point, although in our own judgment the theoretical and empirical studies suggesting that k is an increasing function of b are the more persuasive.

The basic Gordon model can be extended to allow for the dependency between b and r, as well as for that between k and b, simply by letting r and k be functions of b and substituting these functions, $r^* = f_r(b)$ and $k^* = f_k(b)$ for r and k in equation A12–17;

$$P = \frac{(1 - b)Y_0}{k^* - br^*} \tag{A12–22}$$

The functional relationships for r^* and k^* could be developed and substituted into equation A12–22, and the equation could then be differentiated to find the optimal (that is, price maximizing) value of b. To do this, however, requires precise knowledge about the actual shape of the functions r^* and k^*. Work has been done along these lines, but it has not been conclusive. This being the case, it would not be appropriate for us to report these extensions. Rather, we simply want to indicate the direction in which the theory of finance is moving and to point out that practical use of the theoretical developments are not far behind. One example of a practical use of the theory is given below.

Empirical Studies of the Cost of Capital

The Gordon model has been used as the basis for obtaining an approximation to k, the cost of equity capital.[9] To illustrate, equation A12–19, which is repeated below,

$$k = \frac{D}{P} + g \tag{A12–19}$$

[9] Gordon made some estimates in his book. These were extended in the Brigham and Gordon paper, and Gordon did further work along these lines that was introduced as evidence in an important series of hearings before the FCC on the structure of AT&T's rates. Many other similar studies have been done by other academicians, by corporations, and by the security analysis sections of financial institutions. Very complete financial data going back over 20 years is now available on magnetic tapes for most important corporations (Standard and Poor's Compustat Tapes); this data, together with high speed computers, has greatly accelerated the pace of empirical research.

can be written as:

$$\frac{D}{P} = k - g \qquad \text{(A12–23)}$$

Values of D and P can be observed, and past data can be used to obtain an estimate of the value of g expected by investors. Given these inputs, k can be estimated by running a linear regression of the dividend yield, D/P, on an estimate of the rate of growth expected by investors, g. The regression will be of the form $Y = a_0 + a_1X$, where Y is the dependent variable, in this case D/P; a_0 is the intercept; a_1 is the regression coefficient, which specifies the slope of the line; and X is the growth rate, g:

$$\frac{D}{P} = a_0 + a_1g \qquad \text{(A12–24)}$$

In equation A12–24 the intercept term a_0 is an estimate of k, the basic cost of equity capital, and a_1 should equal —1. The logic of this statement can be seen by comparing equations A12–23 and A12–24 and noting that these two equations are identical if and only if $a_0 = k$ and $a_1 = -1$. It might also help to give an illustration. Suppose the firm in question is judged to be risky enough to warrant, given opportunity costs in the present stock market, a 10 percent rate of return; that is, $k = 10$ percent. This rate of return could come from dividend yield, D/P, or from capital gains, g; for example, D/P might equal 4 percent and capital gains 6 percent, or any other combination of D/P and g that adds up to 10 percent. *The important point to note, however, is that this trade-off holds only if investors are indifferent between dividend yield and capital gains, and this indifference implies, first, the equivalence of equations* A12–23 *and* A12–24 *and, second, that* $a_0 = k$ *and* $a_1 = -1$.

Of course, other factors such as the risk inherent in a firm's industry, its own risk from financial leverage, the marketability of its stock, and so on, will influence stock prices and dividend yields. However, these factors can be incorporated into the estimating equation by adding variables. To illustrate, one could use the past variance in earnings before interest and taxes as a measure of inherent business risk, u; the risk of financial leverage could be approximated by the debt (or leverage) ratio, L; and marketability could be proxied by a size of firm variable, S. Adding these terms to equation A12–24, we obtain:

$$\frac{D}{P} = a_0 + a_1g + a_2u + a_3L + a_4S \qquad \text{(A12–25)}$$

This equation (together with several variants) was fitted with data from the electric utility industry and used to estimate the cost of equity capital for each year during the period 1958 to 1962.[10] The cost of equity capital estimates obtained averaged about 7 percent.

Influence of Leverage and Dividend Policy on the Cost of Capital

DIVIDEND POLICY. An examination of the regression coefficients of equation A12–25 can provide clues to the influence of leverage and dividend policy on the cost of equity capital. First, if $a_1 = -1$, this suggests that investors are indifferent between dividends and capital gains; this point was explained above. Second, if $a_1 > -1$ (for example $-.5$), investors prefer dividends to growth through retained earnings; for example, 4 percent of dividend yield is valued as highly as is 8 percent of the more risky capital gains. And, third, if $a_1 < -1$ (for example, -2.0), investors prefer growth through retained earnings to dividends; for example, 4 percent of capital gains yield is as desirable as is 8 percent of dividend yield.

This can be seen from Figure A12–3, where hypothetical market relationships as they might be obtained from a regression analysis are plotted. The X-axis intercept shows the maximum obtainable growth rate (yield from capital gains), $g = br = r$ when all earnings are retained; the three possible Y-axis intercepts show the maximum obtainable dividend yields if $b = 0$ and all earnings are paid out. The three alternative lines represent, in effect, price lines, or market opportunity lines, and show the market-determined substitutability between dividend yield and growth (capital gains). If $a_1 = -1$, this indicates that "the market" is indifferent between returns from dividends (dividend yield) or from capital gains (growth yield). If $a_1 = -2.0$, this indicates that investors must be given 2.0 percent of additional dividend yield to compensate them for the loss of one percent of capital gains—that is, investors prefer earnings retention and capital gains to dividend yield. If $a_1 = -.5$, investors prefer dividend yield to earnings retention.

When the curves were estimated by regression analysis, the coefficients obtained averaged about $-.49$. Thus, the regression analysis suggests that investors view dividends in the electric utility industry as being

[10] See Brigham and Gordon. Several more complicated models were also tested (and found to give better results in terms of the statistical measures of how well they fit). The electric utility industry was chosen for the study because (1) consistent data is readily available; (2) the industry's stability permits investors to make relatively good estimates of growth, and so on; and (3) r is relatively constant and independent of b.

While the influence of regulation may limit the generality of the results, there is no reason to presume that investors' reactions to dividends versus capital gains will be different for a utility than for a nonutility. Also, while their reaction to a *given* percentage debt ratio would be different for a utility than for a less stable industrial company, investors can be presumed to react similarly to departures from industry averages for utility and nonutility companies.

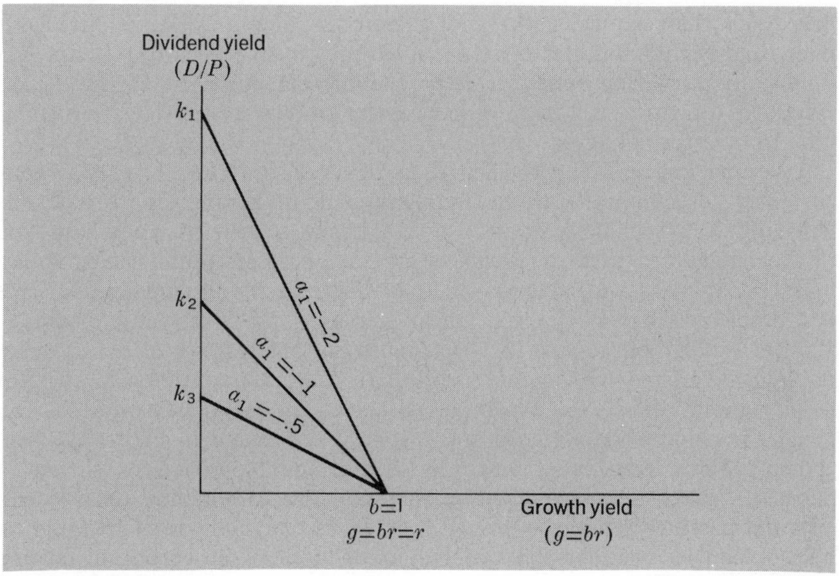

Figure A12–3 Possible Relationships between D/P and Growth

Notes:

(1) Basic equations:

$$k = \frac{D}{P} + g \tag{A12–19}$$

or

$$\frac{D}{p} = k - g \tag{A12–23}$$

Fitted as:

$$\frac{D}{P} = a_0 + a_1 g \tag{A12–24}$$

The graph gives alternative possible relationships as defined by the values of a_1 and a_2.

(2) Since r is assumed to be a constant, the maximum dollar dividend obtainable (when $b = 0$) is also a constant, and the Y-axis intercepts (k_1, k_2, and k_3) must vary because of changes in P. Let P_{k1}, P_{k2}, and P_{k3} be the resulting stock prices if $a_1 = -.5, -1.0$, and -2.0 respectively. At $b = 0$, $P_{k3} > P_{k2} > P_{k1}$; these price differentials cause the dividend yield differentials. In other words, if all earnings were paid out as dividends ($b = 1$), then $P_{k3} = P_{k2} = P_{k1}$, and $k_3 = k_2 = k_1 = g = r$. If $a_1 = -1$, then P would be constant even though b was increased and dividends were substituted for capital gains. If $a_1 = -2$, then P would *decline* as dividends were substituted for capital gains; this decline causes

$$k_1 = \frac{D}{P_{k1}} > \frac{D}{P_{k2}} = k_2.$$

Conversely, if $a_1 = -.5$, P would *rise* as b is reduced and dividends are substituted for capital gains.

less risky than capital gains and, therefore, value a dollar of dividends more highly than a dollar of retained earnings.[11] In other words, k appears to be an increasing function of b; the bottom curve in Figure A12–3 (and the top curve in Figure A12–2) seems to be a reasonable approximation to investor behavior.

Leverage Policy. The coefficient for leverage in A12-25, a_3, was consistently positive and statistically significant, indicating that k is an increasing function of leverage. In their famous article, Modigliani and Miller concluded that the weighted average cost of capital curve is flat, not U-shaped as we have drawn it in this text. Modigliani and Miller's reasoning is that, as the debt ratio increases, the rising cost of equity capital exactly offsets the fact that more and more low cost debt capital is being averaged with equity capital. In other words, the rising cost of equity capital offsets the larger percentage of low cost debt capital.[12]

The position of Modigliani and Miller is illustrated in Figure A12–4b. Their view is contrasted with the "traditional" position as shown in Figure A12–4a. The solid lines in A12–4b show Modigliani and Miller's original position, while the dashed lines represent their views after giving recognition to the fact that interest is deductible for corporate income tax purposes.

If the "traditional" view of the relationship between the cost of capital and the debt ratio is correct, then we would expect to find a_3 constant over some range of values and then rising relatively steeply. If Modigliani and Miller are correct, we would expect to find a_3 to be a constant whose value is determined by the corporate income tax rate.[13]

When the regressions were actually run, a nonlinear relationship such as that shown in Figure A12–4c was found between the cost of equity capital and the debt ratio. Thus, the empirical results suggest that neither the traditional view nor the view of Modigliani and Miller is totally correct—the actual state of affairs lies somewhere between these two extreme positions. Note, however, that while the results of Brigham and Gordon confirm the existence of an optimum capital structure, the U-shaped average cost curve seems to be relatively flat over a wider

[11] This finding is consistent with the earlier theoretical work of Gordon and with the conclusions of Lintner, Lerner and Carlton, and Malkiel. It is contrary to the conclusions of Miller and Modigliani.

[12] Modigliani and Miller define the relationship between k and debt as follows:

$$k = k^* + (k^* - i)\frac{D}{E}$$

where k is the cost of equity capital; k^* is the cost of equity capital the firm would have if it had no debt; i is the interest cost of debt; and D/E is the debt/equity ratio. This is a linear equation with intercept k^* and constant slope $(k^* - i)$.

[13] The value of a_3 that should be expected, if the hypothesis of Modigliani and Miller is correct, given the existence of corporate taxes, is described in the Brigham and Gordon article.

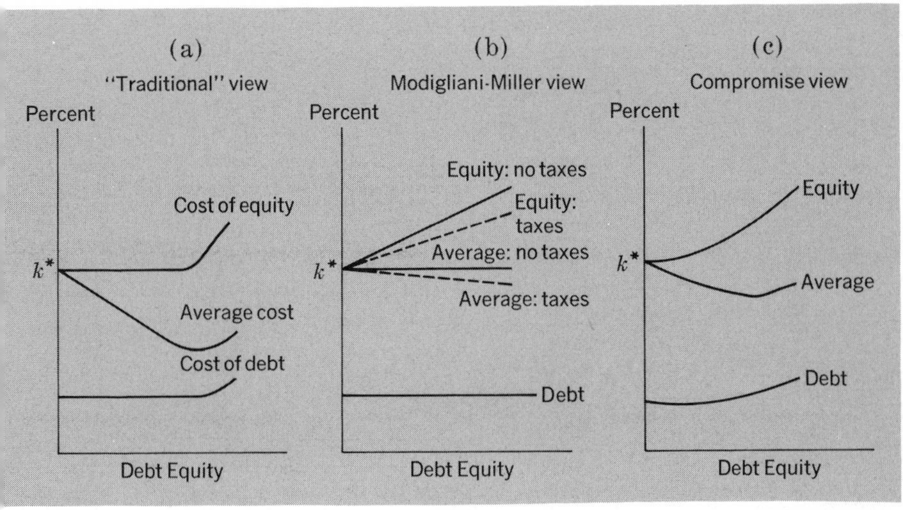

Figure A12–4 Alternative Views of the Relationship between the Use of Debt and the Cost of Capital

debt range than is suggested by the "traditional" view. In other words, over a fairly wide range of debt ratios, the average cost of capital is relatively insensitive to the debt ratio.

As might be expected, a_2 has a positive sign, indicating that investors are averse to risk as measured by the variance of earnings; a_4 had a negative sign, indicating that larger companies have a lower cost of capital than smaller ones.[14]

Some Uses of Cost of Capital Studies

The most obvious uses of cost of capital studies such as the one described above are (1) to obtain a cost of equity capital value to use in calculating the weighted cost of capital, which in turn is used in the capital budgeting decision; and (2) to increase a firm's understanding of the impact of leverage, dividend policy, and so forth on its cost of capital so that it may follow practices that minimize capital costs. Some other uses should also be pointed out.

1. Pricing in Regulated Industries. Prices are set by regulatory agencies in a number of important industries—electric and gas utilities, telephone,

[14] The size coefficient found in the Brigham and Gordon analysis was not very important, but the sample of firms included only large utilities listed on the NYSE. Other work suggests that, had the size range been larger, the size coefficient would have been more significant.

water, airline, railroad, and trucking are some of the more important ones. Prices (or *rates,* as prices are generally called in the utility industries) are set at levels that cover operating costs plus capital costs. It is obviously necessary to know both operating costs *and the cost of capital* before a meaningful rate schedule can be set. Because of this, a great deal of effort has been devoted to determining the cost of capital in utility industries.

2. Pricing by Government Contractors. Closely related to utility pricing is the determination of contract prices for defense and other government contract work. The theory behind government contracting is that the price paid should be sufficient to cover production costs plus a "fair" profit (with incentive schemes built in to induce cost minimization). A "fair" profit is generally considered to be determined by opportunity costs on similar risk investment—or the market-determined cost of capital. Accordingly, firms in the defense industry are very much concerned with their cost of capital.

3. Antitrust Considerations. Some of the first formal work on the cost of capital was done in connection with antitrust decisions requiring certain manufacturers—principally in the shoe machinery and computer industries—to sell as well as lease equipment. Previously these manufacturers had only leased, and their power to cancel leases and to supply servicing on the leased equipment was held to give them excessive monopoly power.

Although ordered to offer to sell as well as to lease equipment, it is obvious that the sale price could be set so high *vis à vis* the rental charges that no customer would elect to buy. There must be a "fair" relationship between the lease charges and the sale price. This "fair" relationship was determined to be such that the sales price was equal to the present value of the anticipated receipts under the lease contract, with the rental payments discounted at the cost of capital.

$$\text{Sales price} = \sum_{t=1}^{N} \frac{\mathrm{R}_t}{(1+k)^t}$$

where R_t is the anticipated rent, k is the average cost of capital, and N is the life of the leased asset. The rental payment schedules were readily available, and the lives of the leased assets could be estimated. The cost of capital was, thus, the pivotal issue in the pricing policies of the affected firms; this value had to be solved jointly by the affected companies and the Justice Department.

It is obvious that the cost of capital is a necessary ingredient in the pricing policy determination of *any* firm that offers lease plans or other forms of long-term sales financing, whether the company is operating under the eyes of the Justice Department or not. The fact that more and more firms are setting up sales financing plans has stimulated further work on the cost of capital.

Summary

In this appendix we have shown how the Gordon model is developed, described its use in theoretical research, and given some indications of how it can be and has been used for empirical studies of the cost of capital. The appendix is not meant to be anything more than suggestive; it does, however, give an idea of the kinds of developments that are taking place in the field of finance.

APPENDIX B TO CHAPTER 12 Other Views on the Cost of Capital Controversy

In Appendix A to Chapter 12 we summarized the basic nature of the Gordon model, one of the major works on the subject of the cost of capital. The other main stream of literature on valuation of the firm and determination of the cost of capital has been stimulated by the writings of Miller and Modigliani. We shall summarize some of their central formulations, developing further the general issues raised. We begin with their article on dividend policy to which reference was made in Chapter 12.[1]

Miller-Modigliani 1961 Model of Dividend Policy

Theoretically, under certainty and in the absence of tax advantages, it should make no difference whether a firm retains earnings or pays dividends which can then be reinvested in the firm by the stockholders. This has been demonstrated clearly by Miller and Modigliani in a formal paper that develops their analysis under the assumptions of certainty and of no tax advantages to retained earnings.

The formal development of their models results in two equations. The two equations are numbered 23 and 24 in their original article and are numbered B12–1 and B12–2 here.

$$(23) \qquad V(0) = \frac{X(0)}{\rho}\left[1 + \frac{k(\rho^* - \rho)}{\rho - k\rho^*}\right] = \frac{X(0)(1-k)}{\rho - k\rho^*} \qquad \text{(B12–1)}$$

$$(24) \qquad D_0(0)\sum_{t=0}^{\infty}\frac{(1+g)^t}{(1+\rho)^{t+1}} = \frac{D(0)}{\rho - g} = \frac{X(0)[1-k_r]}{\rho - g} \qquad \text{(B12–2)}$$

[1] M. H. Miller and F. Modigliani, "Dividend Policy, Growth, and the Valuation of Shares," *Journal of Business*, XXXIV (October 1961), 421–423.

The symbols have the meanings indicated in Table B12–1. The meaning of k deserves special analysis. Miller and Modigliani define k in the following statement: "Specifically, suppose that in each period t the firm has the opportunity to invest in real assets a sum $I(t)$ that is k percent as large as its total earnings for the period. . . ."[2]

Thus k is the ratio of investment per period to the firm's earnings per period. But k is composed of two parts, internal capital and external capital. This they explain in the following definitions:

g = the rate of growth of dividends per share, or, what amounts to the same thing, the rate of growth of dividends accruing to the shares of the current holders (i.e., $D_0(t) = D_0(0)[1 + g]^t$);

k_r = the fraction of total profits retained in each period (so that $D(t) = X(0)[1 - k_r]$);

$k_e = k - k_r$ = the amount of external capital raised per period, expressed as a fraction of profits in the period.[3]

They assert that both equations 23 and 24 (here, B12–1 and B12–2) are equal to the value of the firm. Hence they state that the meaning of g can be determined by setting the two equations equal to each other and solving for g. They express the value of g in equation B12–3, (their equation 25).

$$(25) \qquad g = k\rho^* \frac{1 - k_r}{1 - k} - k_e\rho \frac{1}{1 - k} \qquad \text{(B12–3)}$$

The meaning of these formulations may be clarified by a numerical example utilizing their equations. The illustrative facts are set out at the top of Table B12–1. Utilizing the Miller and Modigliani equations 23, 24, and 25, we show the relation between earnings and dividends in the lower part of Table B12–1.

It should be observed that regardless of the financing mix employed, under the assumptions of certainty and no tax advantages, and the additional assumption that $k = 0.4$, the total earnings of the firm are the same. This is to say that given the internal profitability rate of the firm and its initial earnings, the growth rate in earnings will depend only on the ratio of investment to total earnings per period and the number of time periods.

The relations between earnings, dividends, and the value of the firm may be further clarified by graphing the equations of Table B12–1 in Fig. B12–1. Total earnings are the same. Since Fig. B12–1 is on a semilogarithmic scale, the graph for total earnings (line A of Table B12–1)

[2] "Dividend Policy, Growth, and the Valuation of Shares, p. 421.

[3] "Dividend Policy, Growth, and the Valuation of Shares," p. 422.

TABLE B12–1 DIVIDEND POLICY, CERTAINTY MODEL, ALL EQUITY FINANCING

General symbols	*Illustrative values*
$X(0)$ = Total initial earnings of the firm.	= \$1,000
$D(0)$ = Total initial dividends of the firm.	
n = Total number of shares of common stock.	= 100
$x(0)$ = Initial earnings per share.	= \$10
$d(0)$ = Initial dividends per share.	
ρ = Market rate of return.	= 10 %
ρ^* = Internal rate of return.	= 20 %
t = Time.	
k = Ratio of investment to total earnings in time (t).	= 0.4
k_e = Investment financed from external sources.	
k_r = Investment financed from internal sources.	
ln = natural logarithm.	

	1. All internal financing. $k = 0.4$ $k_e = 0$ $k_r = 0.4$	2. All external financing. $k = 0.4$ $k_e = 0.4$ $k_r = 0$	3. Mixed financing. $k = 0.4$ $k_e = 0.1$ $k_r = 0.3$
A. Total earnings.	$lnX(t) = lnX(0) + k\rho^*t$ $lnX(t) = ln\$1{,}000 + 0.08t$	Same as A1.	Same as A1.
B. Total dividends.	$lnD(t) = lnX(0)(1 - k_r) + k\rho^*t$ $= ln\$600 + 0.08t$	$lnD(t) = lnX(0)(1 - k_r) + k\rho^*t$ $= ln\$1{,}000 + 0.08t$	$lnD(t) = lnX(0)(1 - k_r) + k\rho^*t$ $= ln\$700 + 0.08t$
C. Earnings per share.	$lnx(t) = lnx(0) + gt$ $g = k\rho^*$ $lnx(t) = ln\$10 + 0.08t$	$lnx(t) = lnx(0) + gt$ $g = \frac{k(\rho^* - \rho)}{1 - k}$ $lnx(t) = ln\$10 + 0.067t$	$lnx(t) = lnx(0) + gt$ $g = k\rho^* \frac{1 - k_r}{1 - k} - k_e\rho \frac{1}{1 - k}$ $lnx(t) = ln\$10 + 0.077t$
D. Dividends per share.	$lnd(t) = lnx(0)(1 - k_r) + gt$ g = Same as C1 $lnd(t) = ln\$6 + 0.08t$	$lnd(t) = lnx(0)(1 - k_r) + gt$ g = Same as C2 $lnd(t) = ln\$10 + 0.067t$	$lnd(t) = lnx(0)(1 - k_r) + gt$ g = Same as C3 $lnd(t) = ln\$7 + 0.077t$
E. Value of firm.	$V(0) = \frac{X(0)(1 - k)}{\rho - \rho^*k}$ $= \frac{\$600}{0.10 - 0.08} = \frac{\$600}{0.02}$ $= \$30{,}000$	Same as E1.	Same as E1.

SOURCE: Adapted from M. H. Miller and F. Modigliani, "Dividend Policy, Growth, and the Valuation of Shares," *Journal of Business*, XXXIV (October 1961), 423.

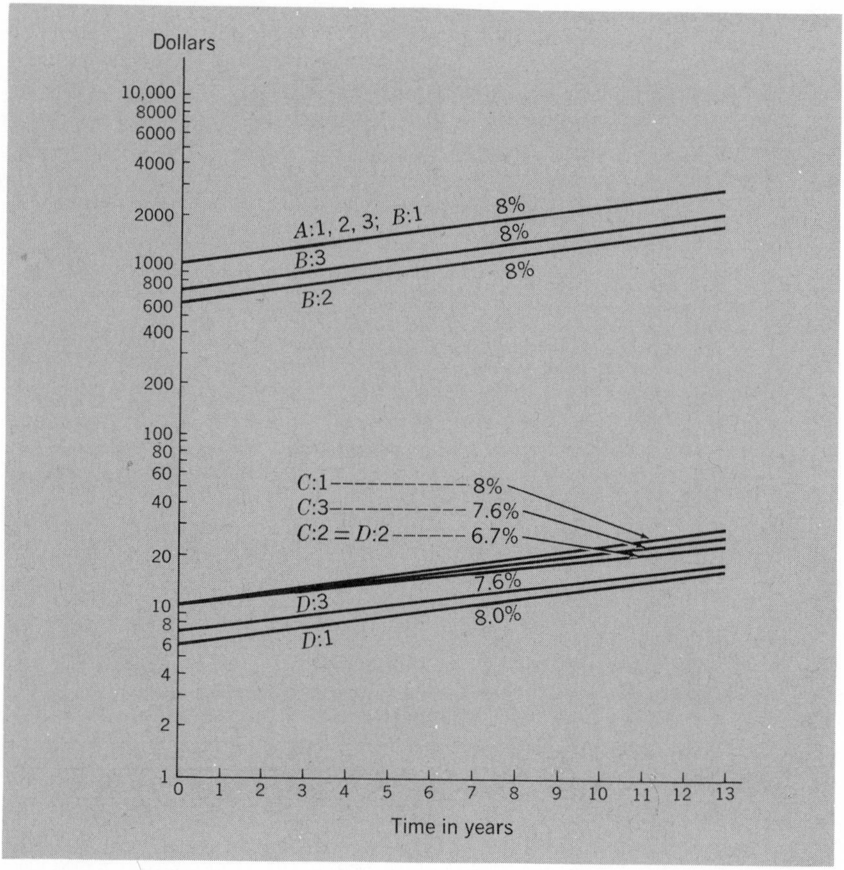

Figure B12–1 Growth of Total and Per Share Earnings and Dividends. (Data from Table B12–1.)

under the three assumptions of (1) all internal financing, (2) all external financing, and (3) mixed financing are all the same. Its intercept is $1,000 and it grows at 8 percent per annum.

Total dividends grow at the same rate. When all financing is external, total dividends are the same as total earnings. If some or all financing is internal, the intercept of the dividends line will be lower, as shown in B2 and B3 (Table B12–1).

While total dividends and earnings are less affected by the extent of external financing, dividends per share and earnings per share are greatly influenced because the extent of external equity financing determines the number of shares of stock that will be outstanding. In the all external financing case, the equations for both earnings per share and dividends per share are the same, with the lowest growth rate of all the cases, 6.7 percent per annum. The growth rate per share is highest for all internal financing, but the initial dividend is the lowest of the six cases on the per share basis.

Section E of Table B12–1 indicates that the value of the firm will be the same, independent of the method of financing under the assumptions of the model. The critical assumptions bear repeating: the amount of financing is independent of the financing mix, the amount of investment is independent of the source of financing, full certainty, and no tax advantages. But the price of the common stock per share will be influenced by the source of financing used for growth, since the initial earnings or dividends per share and their respective growth rates are thereby influenced.

The Miller-Modigliani formula can be used to illustrate that dividend policy does depend upon the relation between the firm's internal profitability rate and the market capitalization rate. If ρ^* is no greater than ρ, or if ρ^* is lower than ρ, the firm can increase its value by paying all of its earnings out in dividends. If ρ^* is greater than ρ, the firm will maximize its value by paying no dividends. Thus, we have demonstrated that the Miller-Modigliani formula in fact leads to the same dividend policy decisions as does the Gordon formula (and also the Walter formula). Indeed, in all certainty and infinite period dividend models, the above implications for dividend policy will hold.

But all of the foregoing is based on the assumption, among others, of no tax advantages. Under such assumptions, "dividends do not matter." However, dividends do matter when capital gains tax rates are lower than tax rates on personal income. This effect is large for a growth firm. A growth firm has investment opportunities that promise a higher profit return than can be obtained in the market on the average. Thus, the stockholders of growth firms would prefer to have their funds reinvested rather than to seek alternative market opportunities. The growth firm would suffer a price decline if it had to pay out earnings in dividends, subjected to personal income tax rates in excess of 25 percent, and then had to sell securities.[4]

For these reasons, growth firms have very high retention rates, typically paying out either no dividends or a dividend rate less than 20 percent of earnings. For industries and firms that grow no faster than the economy as a whole, dividends approximate a 50 percent payout range. If the firm is not a growth firm, its profit opportunities are not

[4] The illustration makes clear that the combination of taxes and an internal rate of return higher than the market rate may influence the firm's rate of investment and hence its value. In the absence of taxes, the extra expenses and leakages in seeking to recapture dividends to finance further growth make it advantageous for growth firms to retain a high percentage of earnings. Conversely, firms whose internal rate is below the market rate should not reinvest below the market rate. Their dividend payout rates are likely to be high or they may be repurchasing their own shares of common stock. Hence the relation between internal rates of return and market rates of return have implications for financing rates and dividend payout rates.

likely to be greater than those available to stockholders. For such firms, dividend changes are probably taken as indicators of expected changes in future earnings. The prices of these stocks probably will change in proportion to dividend changes. The higher dividend payouts of utilities (which run in the 60–80 percent range) are undoubtedly explained by two special factors: (1) utility commissions are reputed to give less weight to an investment base achieved by earnings retention than to one achieved by equity funds raised from the outside, (2) for a long time, investors regarded utilities as income stocks and therefore were responsive to dividend payouts.

The increased use of share repurchase merits comment in connection with dividend policy. In theory, because of the differential tax rates on dividends and capital gains, repurchase of shares is always superior to payment of a cash dividend to shareholders. The benefit is increased if the firm's marginal profitability rate is lower than its marginal cost of capital and the market price of its stock is depressed. If the firm's incremental internal profitability rate is higher than its marginal cost of capital, more will be gained by reinvesting the funds than by share repurchase. But even in such circumstances, share repurchase is better than utilizing an equivalent amount of cash for dividend payment.

Miller-Modigliani's 1966 Empirical Model

Modigliani and Miller's 1961 article on dividend policy was purely theoretical, but in 1966 they presented empirical tests of the theory (and also their theory of the effects of leverage on the cost of capital). This second study incorporates the effect of corporate income taxes but not the effects of personal income taxes. Because the symbols employed in the discussion of the role of corporate taxes are numerous and the concepts highly technical, we will begin our discussion with an illustrative income statement, Table B12–2, in order to show the numerical relations which the symbols represent.[5] The main distinction is between the concepts of earnings after taxes ($\bar{X}^t$) and tax-adjusted earnings $\bar{X}(1-t)$. The amount of earnings after taxes ($\bar{X}^t$) is obtained by adding the total interest payments to net income after taxes and interest.

[5] These symbols are employed throughout the three Modigliani-Miller articles on leverage. These articles, and the basic logic behind the development of their models, are summarized in the following discussion. The original articles contain an extended formal development of the mathematical aspects of their models, and a reader interested in testing his ability to work through highly formal mathematical elaboration of models from a set of abstract assumptions will find them of great interest. The articles are: 1. "The Cost of Capital, Corporation Finance and the Theory of Investments," *American Economic Review* (June 1958), 261–296; 2. "Taxes and the Cost of Capital: A Correction," *American Economic Review,* LIII (June 1963), 443–443; and 3. "Some Estimates of the Cost of Capital to the Electric Utility Industry," *American Economic Review,* LVI (June 1966), 333–390.

The concept of tax-adjusted earnings, $\bar{X}(1-t)$, takes into account the tax savings property of interest paid and adds back to net income the amount of interest paid less the tax shelter obtained by the interest payment.

First we will summarize their derivation of the structural equation,

TABLE B12–2 TERMINOLOGY FOR ANALYSIS OF TAX INFLUENCE

Income statement

Sales		\$2,000
Total operating costs		1,800
Net operating income (NOI)(EBIT)	$(\bar{X})$	200
Interest paid with $r = 5\%$	$(\bar{R})$	20
Net income before tax (EBT)		180
Tax at 0.4	(t)	72
Net income	$(\bar{\pi}^t)$	108

Illustrative relations

Taxes paid $t(\bar{X} - R) = 0.4(200 - 20) = \$72$.
$\bar{X}$ is defined as $\bar{X} = \bar{X}^t + t(\bar{X} - R)$.

$\bar{X}^t = \bar{\pi}^t + R$ $\quad \bar{X}^t$ = earnings after taxes
= expected profits after taxes plus interest payments
$= 108 + 20 = \$128$

$$\bar{X} = 128 + 72 = 200$$

$$\text{Tax-adjusted earnings} = \bar{X}(1-t) = \bar{X}^t - t\bar{R} = \bar{\pi}^t + \bar{R} - t\bar{R}$$

$$200(0.6) = 128 - 8$$

$$\bar{X}(1-t) = \bar{\pi}^t + (1-t)\bar{R}$$

$$120 = 108 + 12$$

employing the symbols introduced in Table B12–2 and set forth more fully in Table B12–3. Table B12–4 presents the derivation of Modigliani and Miller's equation 8 in their June 1966 article.[6] The derivation process indicated in Table B12–4 represents a series of definitions and algebraic substitutions from equations B12–3 through B12–9. Their equation

[6] "Some Estimates of the cost of Capital of the Electric Utility Industry," p. 341.

TABLE B12–3 KEY TO SYMBOLS

A =	Total assets.
b =	Average earnings retention rate.
C =	Cost of capital.
D =	Debts of the firm.
dA =	Purchase cost of assets acquired.
dS^n =	Market value of the additional securities issued to finance the investment.
dS^o =	Change in value of the holdings of the original owners.
g =	Compound growth rate.
$i = \bar{\pi}/S$ =	Return to equity.
L =	Target proportion of debt to the value of the firm.
P =	Preferred stock.
$\overline{Pdv}$ =	Expected preferred dividends.
$\bar{\pi}$ =	Expected net profits to the common shareholders.
$r(MM)$ =	Interest rate on debt or the market capitalization rate for sure streams.
ρ^* =	Profitability rate on new investments.
$\bar{R}$ =	Expected interest payments.
$\rho = \rho_k$ =	Market's capitalization rate for the expected value of uncertain, pure equity earnings streams of the type characteristic of risk class k.
S =	The market value of the common stock.
t =	The (constant) marginal and average rate of corporate taxation.
X =	The (uniform) income stream generated in perpetuity by assets presently held.
$\bar{X}$ =	A firm's expected total earnings.
U =	Random disturbance term.
V =	Equilibrium current market value.
V_u =	Market value of unlevered firm.
V_o =	Market value of debt.
T =	Number of years during which profitable opportunities yield a return greater than market capitalization rate, that is $\rho^* > \rho$.

6 (here, B12–8) is equivalent to their equation 31c, set forth in their tax correction article.[7] Miller and Modigliani's concluding statement in connection with equation 8 re-emphasizes the findings of the tax correction article: "Since the deductibility of interest payments thus makes the value of the firm a function of its financial policy, it must also make the required yield or cost of capital a function of financial policy.[8]

Equation 8 (B12–10) of Miller and Modigliani reflects the influence of leverage and taxes only. They next bring in the role of growth by defining C as the cost of capital in the sense of the required change in after-tax net operating earnings in response to an increase (growth)

[7] "Taxes and the Cost of Capital: A Correction," p. 438.

[8] "Some Estimates of the Cost of Capital to the Electric Utility Industry," p. 341.

in assets. In their article Miller and Modigliani formulate an expression for the current market value of the firm "by analogy to the solution we have derived for the certainty case. . . "[9] This is employed in equation 9d of Table B12–5 to obtain equation 10 (B12–12) by "analogy."

Miller and Modigliani explain the significance of their equation 10

TABLE B12–4 MILLER AND MODIGLIANI DERIVATION OF THE REQUIRED YIELD

(1)	$\bar{X} = \bar{X}^t + t(\bar{X} - R)$	Definition	(B12–3)
(1a)	$\bar{X}^t = \bar{X} - t(\bar{X} - R)$ $= \bar{X} - t\bar{X} + tR$	Solving from (B12–3)	(B12–3a)
(1b)	$(1 - t)\bar{X} = \bar{X}^t - tR$	Rearranging terms	(B12–3c)
(2)	$V_u \equiv \dfrac{(1 - t)\bar{X}}{\rho_k}$	Definition	(B12–4)
(3)	$V_0 \equiv \dfrac{tR}{r} = tD$	Definition	(B12–5)
(4)	$V = \dfrac{(1 - t)\bar{X}}{\rho_k} + tD$	From (B12–4) plus (B12–5)	(B12–6)
(5)	$V = \dfrac{X^t - tR}{\rho_k} + tD$	From (B12–3c)	(B12–7)
(6)	$V \equiv S + D + P$	Definition Substituting in (B12–8)	(B12–8) (B12–8a)
(7)	$dS^n + dP + dD = dA$	Definition from (B12–8)	(B12–9)
(8)	$\dfrac{dV}{dA} = \dfrac{dS^o}{dA} + \dfrac{dS^n}{dA} + \dfrac{dP}{dA} + \dfrac{dD}{dA} = \dfrac{dS^o}{dA} + 1$	From (B12–8) and (B12–9)	(B12–10)
	$= \dfrac{d\bar{X}}{dA}(1 - t)\dfrac{1}{\rho_k} + \dfrac{tdD}{dA}$	From (B12–5) and (B12–6)	

(here B12–12) by stating: ". . . the first two terms, as before, represent the capitalized value of the current tax-adjusted earning power plus the tax benefits on debt; and the last term is the contribution of value of the future growth potential."[10]

The authors then discuss a number of other factors which may potentially influence the value of the firm: "Because of this confounding

[9] They then make reference to their dividend article, "Dividend Policy, Growth, and the Valuation of Shares," pp. 421–422, footnote 15.

[10] "Some Estimates of the Cost of Capital to the Electric Utility Industry," p. 344.

TABLE B12–5 MILLER AND MODIGLIANI DERIVATION OF THE CURRENT MARKET VALUE OF THE FIRM

(9) $$C \equiv (1 - t)\frac{d\bar{X}}{dA} \qquad \text{(B12–11)}$$

substitute in (B12–11) from (B12–10)

(9a) $$C\frac{1}{\rho_k} + t\frac{dD}{dA} = \frac{dS^o}{dA} + 1 \qquad \text{(B12–11a)}$$

$$\frac{dS^o}{dA} \geq 0 \quad \text{if} \quad C\frac{1}{\rho} + t\frac{dD}{dA} \geq 1$$

(9b) Therefore solve for C when the expression is equal to 1, the necessary condition for $\frac{dS^o}{dA} \geq 0$.

$$C\frac{1}{\rho_k} + t\frac{dD}{dA} = 1 \quad \text{(From B12–11a)} \qquad \text{(B12–11b)}$$

(9c) $$C = \rho\left[1 - t\frac{dD}{dA}\right] \qquad \text{(B12–11c)}$$

(9d) $$V = \frac{\bar{X}}{\rho} + k\bar{X}\left(\frac{\rho^* - \rho}{\rho(1 + \rho)}\right)T \qquad \text{(B12–11d)}$$

(From footnote 15 in 1961 dividend article, pp. 421–422.)

By "analogy" to B12–11d, taking taxes into account and substituting C for ρ. At this point in their article Miller and Modigliani drop the subscript k from ρ.

(10) $$V = \frac{1}{\rho}\bar{X}(1 - t) + tD + k\bar{X}(1 - t)\left[\frac{\rho^* - C}{C(1 + C)}\right]T \qquad \text{(B12–12)}$$

(11) $$(V - tD) = a_o + a_1\bar{X}(1 - t) + a_2\overline{\Delta A} + U \qquad \text{(B12–13)}$$

where:

- a_o is an intercept term whose size and sign will measure any effects of scale on valuation.
- a_1 is the marginal capitalization rate for pure equity streams in the class.
- a_2 is a measure of the effects of growth potential on value.
- U is a random disturbance term.

$$\overline{\Delta A} = \left[\frac{\tfrac{1}{5}(A_t - A_{t-5})}{A_{t-5}}\right]A_t$$

= a linear five-year average of total assets times current total assets.

of the earnings and dividend coefficients, our approach here will be initially to omit the dividend variable entirely . . ."[11]

They then state that their theory of valuation leads to the structural equation set forth in their equation 11 (B12–13).

[11] "Some Estimates of the Cost of Capital to the Electric Utility Industry," p. 347.

Modigliani and Miller make the following observation: "Notice that since the theory implies that the coefficient of the leverage variable D is equal to the marginal tax rate t, we have so constrained it in the above equation by incorporating it with the dependent variable."[12]

In moving from equation 10 (B12–12) to their equation 11 (B12–13), Miller and Modigliani perform an interesting shift. Equation 10 (B12–12) was developed from a formal theoretical basis. Equation 11 (B12–13), however, is essentially empiricial in its content. Equation 11 (B12–13) states that the value of a firm is a function of leverage, tax-adjusted earnings, and a measure of the growth rate in the assets of the firm. Without the elaborate theoretical discussion, the essentially empirical equation 11 (B12–13) could readily have been set out for testing by regression analysis. Their two independent variables in equation 11 (B12–13) are the same as two of the four independent variables in the Gordon model set forth in equation A12–25 in Appendix A to Chapter 12 (but are measured differently as will be discussed below).

Next, Modigliani and Miller take up the problem of heteroscedasticity. They observe that the disturbance term, U, is approximately proportional to the size of the firm. They express the structural equation in its yield form, dividing through by $(V - tD)$, obtaining equation (12).

$$(12) \qquad \frac{\bar{X}(1-t)}{(V-tD)} = a_1' + a_0' \frac{1}{(V-tD)} + a_2' \frac{\overline{\Delta A}}{(V-tD)} + U' \qquad \text{(B12–14)}$$

But equation 12 (B12–14) suffers from the defect that the variable $(V - tD)$ appears in the denominator on both sides of the equation. This has the possible consequence of biasing the results. It might give coefficients of growth and size that are too high and an estimate of the cost of capital that is too low. Since Modigliani and Miller state that they have no way of determining how large such a bias is, they use this form only to check the results obtained in other ways.

They also divide equation 11 (B12–13) by the book value of total assets. Dividing through by A, the book value of total assets, provides equation 14 (B12–16).

$$(14) \qquad \frac{V - tD}{A} = a_0 \frac{1}{A} + a_1 \frac{\bar{X}(1-t)}{A} + a_2 \frac{\Delta A}{A} + U \qquad \text{(B12–16)}$$

When they turn to the actual empirical fitting of their structural equations they employ "an instrumental variable approach," implementing it "by means of a two-stage procedure formally equivalent to the two-stage least-squares method of Theil and Madansky."[13]

[12] "Some Estimates of the Cost of Capital to the Electric Utility Industry," p. 348.

[13] Miller and Modigliani, p. 353 and references cited there to Theil and Madansky.

Their two-stage least-squares estimates for 1957 of equations 14 (B12–16) and 12 (B12–14) are as follows:

$$(14)\quad \frac{V - tD}{A} = \underset{(0.46)}{16.1}\,\frac{\bar{X}^t - tR}{A} - \underset{(0.08)}{0.28}\,\frac{10^7}{A} + \underset{(0.23)}{1.36}\,\frac{\Delta A}{A} \quad [R = 0.88]$$

(B12–16)

$$(12)\quad \frac{\bar{X}^t - t\bar{R}}{V - tD} = \underset{(0.002)}{0.0592} + \underset{(0.04)}{0.166}\,\frac{10^6}{(V - tD)} - \underset{(0.02)}{0.0516}\,\frac{\Delta A}{(V - tD)}$$

(B12–14)

Finally, by substituting sample mean values into these equations and their derived functions, Miller and Modigliani develop estimates of the cost of capital. For 1957, for example, the average tax- and leverage-adjusted total earnings yield is:

$$\frac{\bar{X}^t - t\bar{R}}{V - tD} = 0.056$$

The associated cost of equity capital is 0.062 for 1957.

Modigliani and Miller's latest study highlights three issues: (1) the effect of leverage on the cost of capital; (2) the relative influence of dividends versus earnings on valuation and the cost of capital; and (3) the need to simultaneously optimize debt policy, dividend policy, the use of outside equity financing, and the capital budgeting decision. These issues are discussed below.

Leverage and Cost of Capital

With respect to leverage, in both their 1963 "tax correction" article and their 1966 "measurement" article, they recognize that, through tax savings, leverage reduces the cost of capital. The tax benefit from leverage continues with increased leverage. Thus the higher the leverage, the lower the firm's cost of capital. Since they do not admit of a rising cost of capital function at some high level of leverage, they suggest that firms would be induced by the tax advantage to use the maximum amount of debt. But firms obviously do not ordinarily use extremely high debt ratios.

Miller and Modigliani resort to the concept of a "target debt ratio" to explain the limit on increasing leverage. But a target debt ratio signifies some policy on the financing mix of debt and equity; this is what business finance has argued and what Miller and Modigliani have denied. They state that "The determination of the optimal value of L (the firm's target debt ratio) involves many difficult issues for which no completely well-worked-out theoretical analysis is yet available."[14] They imply that L is related, but not uniformly, to the "maximum permitted by lenders." This is an imprecise way of stating that the

[14] Myron J. Gordon, "Some Estimates of the Cost of Capital to the Electric

cost of capital, at some point, rises sharply with leverage. This in turn suggests an optimal debt to equity ratio.

Under the Modigliani and Miller formulation, the influence of taxes causes the cost of capital to decline continuously with increased leverage, but their theory fails to explain why firms should not operate with extremely high leverage ratios. But we have shown in Figure A12–4c that a view that represents a compromise between the traditional view and the Modigliani and Miller view does provide an explanation. Since, under this formulation, the cost of capital function for combinations of equity and debt financing falls and then rises, there exists an area of a lower cost of capital, representing a target or range of desired debt-equity proportions.

Additional reinforcement of the compromise view that we suggested in Appendix A to Chapter 12 is provided by the Miller and Modigliani data—this point was made so clearly by Gordon in a comment on the Miller and Modigliani paper that we quote it verbatim:[15]

> Under the reasoning that led to equation (3) the subtraction of τD and V completely accounts for the influence of leverage on the value of a corporation. Accordingly, with debt and preferred stock added to the equation's independent variables, their coefficients should not differ significantly from zero. This is what *MM* found with their electric utility sample. However, using a utility sample actually gave results that were against their leverage theorem, since regulatory agencies treat the income tax as an expense in determining the income a utility is allowed to earn. Only if their sample had consisted of nonregulated industrial companies would their results have been evidence in support of their theorem.

The point Gordon is making is that Miller and Modigliani hold that the only influence of leverage on the value of the firm is through the tax benefit of debt. When this is taken into account by the subtraction of tD from V, the addition of debt and preferred stock in the second-stage least-square estimates had no influence. In regulated industries, however, the rate of return allowed is *after* provision for payment of taxes by the utility firms, so the value of a regulated firm is not influenced by the tax benefit of debt. Thus, the indicated influence of debt on the value of firms must come from the "pure" leverage effect. By not taking the regulated status of their companies into account, Miller and Modigliani have inadvertently demonstrated that leverage does influence the value of the firm in the manner suggested by Panel c of Figure A12–4 in Appendix A to Chapter 12.

Utility Industry, 1954–1957: Comment," *American Economic Review* LVII (December 1967), 1267–1278.

[15] Myron J. Gordon, "Some Estimates of the Cost of Capital to the Electric Utility Industry, 1954–1957: Comment," *American Economic Review* LVII (December 1967), 1267–1278.

The Dividends versus Retained Earnings Controversy

The earnings versus dividends controversy was raised anew by the last Miller and Modigliani paper. We have indicated that, in a world of certainty and in the absence of personal income taxes, "dividends should make no difference." Miller and Modigliani have argued that even with personal income taxes the effects are still negligible. Gordon found that higher dividend payments increased the value of equity. However, in his empirical studies, growth is measured by some function of retained earnings. This has the effect of adding the regression coefficient of retained earnings to the regression coefficient for dividends, without affecting the standard error of the regression coefficient.[16] The result is to overstate the influence of dividends on value.

A study by Friend and Puckett sought to demonstrate that stock prices are an increasing function of retained earnings, rather than dividends.[17] The study attempted to avoid a number of possible sources of statistical bias by eliminating individual "firm effects" of random fluctuations in income, income measurement errors, and profitability of investment opportunities as assessed by the market.[18] The "firm effect" variable is measured by the difference between the firm's price-earnings ratio and the average price-earnings ratio for all firms in the sample. This difference is lagged one period and used in the regression equation. The effect of the adjustment procedures employed by Friend and Puckett is to shift some of the influence that dividends seemed to have on stock prices over to earnings; that is, their statistical analysis indicated that previous work had been based in favor of dividends.[19]

The latest study by Miller and Modigliani, as would be expected from their earlier theoretical article on dividend policy, suggested that earnings were more important than dividends. Because of the errors in measurement of earnings, Miller and Modigliani employ an instrumental variable approach for measuring earnings. Essentially, this method enables them to measure earnings by other variables to reduce the correlation of the error term of the regression equation with the independent variables (earnings).[20] In their Table 2, Miller and Modigliani present their first-stage least-squares regressions of earnings on the instrumental variables.[21] Their first test does not include dividends, and the multiple R's range from .13 to .31 for the three years studied. When

[16] The clearest demonstration of this point has been presented by Myron J. Gordon himself, *The Investment, Financing, and Valuation of the Corporation* (Homewood, Illinois: R. D. Irwin, Inc., 1962), pp. 141–143.

[17] Irwin Friend and Marshall Puckett, "Dividends and Stock Prices," *American Economic Review* LIV (September 1964), 656–682.

[18] Friend and Puckett, p. 666.

[19] Friend and Puckett, pp. 667–670.

[20] For a relatively concise presentation of the basic ideas, see K. Chu, *Principles of Econometrics* (Scranton, Penna.: International Textbook Co., 1968) pp. 107–111.

[21] Some Estimates of the Cost of Capital to the Electric Utility Industry," p. 361.

dividends are added to the instrumental variables, the multiple R's rise to a range of .64 to .73. This result suggests that their instrumental variable measure of earnings in fact substitutes dividends for earnings.[22]

Simultaneous Solution Requirement

Our own view is that additional empirical work is required to establish the relative influence of earnings and dividends on stock prices. As indicated in Chapter 12, we feel that an important variable is the prospective internal profitability rate on new investments compared with the average productivity of funds in the economy as a whole at that time. From a measurement standpoint, we emphasize the difficulty of separating the influence of dividends from their role in providing information on present and prospective levels of earnings.

We feel that progress will be furthered by models that explicitly recognize the need to optimize simultaneously leverage, dividend policy, and the firm's rate of growth, reflecting its internal profitability opportunities in relation to financing constraints.[23] Such a model was developed by Gordon in his testimony before the Federal Communications Commission on a rate of return for the American Telephone and Telegraph Company.[24] The model is summarized in Table B12–6. The return permitted by the Commission, X^*, determines Y, income per share. The influence on the market price per share of stock can be analyzed by varying the retention rate, the growth rate in assets, and leverage in relation to the permitted rate of return.[25] That combination can be selected which indicates maximization of the market price per share of the Company's stock. Some of the basic decision variables may be constrained by market opportunities or Commission determinations. This approach reflects Vickers' emphasis on the simultaneous solution of production and investment decisions within the limits of financing constraints.[26]

Other Leading Models

Eugene Lerner and Willard Carleton, in an important work, first popularized the now generally accepted principle of a simultaneous approach, seeking to optimize the central financial policy decision variables in

[22] Gordon, "Comment," p. 1273.

[23] See D. Vickers, *The Theory of the Firm* (New York: McGraw-Hill Book Company, 1968).

[24] F. C. C. Docket No. 16258, Staff Exhibit No. 17, 1967.

[25] For a brief explanation of this type of model, see M. J. Gordon, "Rate of Return on Equity Capital Under Regulation," presentation to the Institute of Public Utilities, Michigan State University (April 17, 1968).

[26] For a critique of Gordon's use of this framework, see J. F. Weston, "Discussion," Institute of Public Utilities, Michigan State University (April 17, 1968). Also see Craig G. Johnson, *A Critique of Cost of Capital Models,* Unpublished PhD dissertation, UCLA (August 1968), pp. 208–225.

relation to investment opportunities.[27] However, to date Lerner and Carleton have not presented empirical tests of their model, so their impact on the cost of capital controversy has been theoretical rather than empirical.

TABLE B12–6 GORDON AT&T MODEL

OBJECTIVE FUNCTION

$$P = 18.18D^{1.0}(1 + g)^{21.0}(1 + h)^{-0.30}(1 + w)^{-7.5}$$

INPUT VARIABLES

1. $D = (1 - b)Y$
2. $Y = W[X^* + h(X^* - i^*)]$
3. Test for $b = .4$, obtain value of w in: →

$$w = \frac{1}{W}\left[\left(\frac{qA}{1 + h^*}\right) - bY\right]$$

3a. $A = W(1 + h)$

If $w \lesseqgtr 0$, calculate b from:

$$b = \frac{qA}{Y(1 + h^*)}$$

otherwise use $b = .4$

4. $g = rb + ws$
5. $r = X^* + h(X^* - i)$
6. $S = 1 - \frac{W}{P}$ Theory

$S = 1 - \frac{.07}{X^*}$ Computer Program

For some q, maximize P

SYMBOLS	VALUES ASSUMED OR CALCULATED
P = market price per share	
Y = expected earnings per share on equity	
D = dividends per share	
b = retention rate	
g = growth in price per share	
h = average debt to equity	= .5
h^* = marginal debt to equity	= 2.0
W = book value per share	= $38.00
w = growth in equity from outside equity financing	
X^* = expected return on investment	
i^* = imbedded cost of debt	= 4.1%
i = marginal cost of debt	= 5.0%
A = total assets per share	
q = growth rate of assets	8%
r = permitted return on equity	7%

Another very important work is that of Alexander Robichek and Stewart Myers. The distinctive feature of Robichek and Myers' model

[27] Eugene M. Lerner and Willard T. Carleton. *A Theory of Financial Analysis* (New York: Harcourt, Brace & World, Inc., 1966).

is its careful attention to the nature of the risk variables.[28] Aspects of their contribution were summarized in Chapter 8 in connection with the discussion of their certainty equivalent concept. Like Lerner and Carleton, Robichek and Myers have not yet developed empirical results based on their own model; their strong arguments for the use of certainty equivalent adjustment factors rather than risk adjusted discount rates will doubtless stimulate empirical research.

Concluding Comment

It is our hope that the analysis of some alternative theories affecting the selection of optimal investment and policies will provide a basic foundation for further study of this large and growing literature. We have sought to emphasize the importance of the assumptions employed in the development of the model, the formulation of the theory or model, the selection of measurement procedures for testing the model, and the importance of understanding the implications of the statistical techniques employed.

[28] Alexander A. Robichek and Stewart C. Myers, *Optimal Financing Decisions* (Englewood Cliffs, N.J.: Prentice-Hall, Inc., 1965).

PART FIVE

WORKING CAPITAL MANAGEMENT

13

The Nature of Working Capital

Working capital refers to a firm's investment in short-term assets—cash, short-term securities, accounts receivable, and inventories. *Gross working capital* is defined as the firm's total current assets. *Net working capital* is defined as current assets minus current liabilities. If the term "working capital" is used without further qualification, it generally refers to gross working capital.

There are advantages and disadvantages to using the concept "working capital management." In the modern systems approach to business management everything is recognized to be related to everything else, and the operations of the firm are viewed as a total, integrated system. In this sense, it is artificial to study one segment of the firm, such as its current assets or its current liabilities. However, if one is really to understand the integrated whole, he must first understand the individual parts of the business firm. Therefore, it seems useful to break the total problem down and to analyze the component parts before taking an integrated view, as we do in Part VII.

IMPORTANCE OF WORKING CAPITAL MANAGEMENT

There are a number of aspects of working capital management that make it an important topic for study. Among them are the following.

TIME DEVOTED TO WORKING CAPITAL MANAGEMENT. Surveys indicate that the largest portion of a financial manager's time is devoted to the day-by-day internal operations of the firm; this may be appropriately subsumed under the heading "working capital management." Since so much time is spent on working capital decisions, it is appropriate that the subject be covered carefully in managerial finance courses.

INVESTMENT IN CURRENT ASSETS. Characteristically, current assets represent more than one-half the total assets of a business firm. Because they represent a large investment and because this investment tends to be relatively volatile, current assets are worthy of the financial manager's careful attention.

RELATIONSHIP BETWEEN SALES GROWTH AND CURRENT ASSETS. The relationship between sales growth and the need to finance current assets is close and direct. For example, if the firm's average collection period is 40 days and if its credit sales are $1,000 a day, it will have an investment of $40,000 in accounts receivable. If sales rise to $2,000 a day, the investment in accounts receivable will rise to $80,000. Sales increases produce similar immediate needs for additional inventories and perhaps for working cash balances. All these needs must be financed, and since they arise so quickly, it is imperative that the financial manager keep himself aware of developments in the working capital segment of the firm. Of course, continued sales increases will require additional long-term assets, and these fixed asset additions must also be financed. However, fixed asset investments, while critically important to the firm in a strategic long-run sense, do not generally have the same urgency as do current asset investments; this is seen in the following section.

IMPORTANCE FOR SMALL FIRMS. Working capital management is particularly important for small firms. A small firm may minimize its investments in fixed assets by renting or leasing plant and equipment. However, there is no way of avoiding an investment in cash, receivables, and inventories. Therefore, current assets are particularly significant for the financial manager of a small firm. Similarly, a small firm has relatively limited access to the long-term capital markets; therefore, it must necessarily rely heavily on trade credit and short-term bank loans, both of which affect net working capital by increasing current liabilities.

HE CASH CYCLE

Working capital management emphasizes the cash flow problems of a firm. Growing firms require new investment—immediate investment in current assets and, as full capacity is reached, investment in fixed assets as well. New investments must be financed. New financing carries with it commitments and obligations to service the capital obtained.[1] A growing, profitable firm is likely to require more cash for investments in receivables, inventories, and fixed assets. Therefore, a growing, profitable firm can have a cash flow problem. The nature of this problem, and the cause and effect relationship between working capital and sales, is illustrated in the following discussion, where the consequences of a series of transactions are traced.

Effects on the Balance Sheet

1. Two partners invest a total of $50,000 to create the Glamour Galore Dress Company. The plant is rented, but equipment and other fixed assets cost $30,000. The resulting financial situation is shown by Balance Sheet 1.

2. Glamour Galore receives an order to manufacture 10,000 dresses. The receipt of an order in itself has no effect on the balance sheet. However, in preparation for the manufacturing activity, the firm buys $20,000 worth of cotton cloth on terms of net 30 days. Without additional investment by the owners, total assets increase by $20,000, financed by the trade accounts payable to the supplier of the cotton cloth.

After the purchase, the firm spends $20,000 on labor for cutting the cloth to the required pattern. Of the $20,000 total cost, $10,000 is paid

[1] By "servicing" capital we refer to interest and repayment of principal on debt as well as dividends and retained earnings (the cost of equity capital) on common stocks.

BALANCE SHEET 1

ASSETS		LIABILITIES	
Current Assets			
Cash	$20,000		
Fixed Assets		Capital stock	$50,000
Plant and equipment	30,000	Total liabilities	
Total assets	$50,000	and net worth	$50,000

in cash and $10,000 is owed in the form of accrued wages. These two transactions are reflected in Balance Sheet 2.

Total assets increase to $80,000. Gross working capital is increased; net working capital, total current assets minus total current liabilities, remains constant. The current ratio declines to 1.67, and the debt ratio rises to 38 percent. The financial position of the firm is weakening. If it should seek to borrow at this point, Glamour Galore could not use the work-in-process inventories as collateral because a lender could find little use for partially manufactured dresses.

BALANCE SHEET 2

ASSETS		LIABILITIES	
Current Assets		Accounts payable	$20,000
Cash	$10,000	Accrued wages payable	10,000
Inventories:			
Work in process:			
Materials	20,000	Total current liabilities	$30,000
Labor	20,000		
Total current assets	$50,000	Capital stock	50,000
Fixed Assets			
Plant and equipment	30,000	Total liabilities	
Total assets	$80,000	and net worth	$80,000

3. In order to complete the dresses, additional labor costs of $20,000 are incurred and paid in cash. It is assumed that the firm desires to maintain a minimum cash balance of $5,000. Since the initial cash balance is $10,000, Glamour Galore must borrow an additional $15,000

from its bank to meet the wage bill. The borrowing is reflected in notes payable in Balance Sheet 3. Total assets rise to $95,000, with a finished goods inventory of $60,000. The current ratio drops to 1.4, and the debt ratio rises to 47 percent. These ratios represent a further weakening of the financial position.

BALANCE SHEET 3

ASSETS		LIABILITIES	
Current Assets		Accounts payable	$20,000
Cash	$ 5,000	Notes payable	15,000
Inventory:		Accrued wages payable	10,000
Finished goods	60,000		
Total current assets	$65,000	Total current liabilities	$45,000
Fixed Assets		Capital stock	50,000
Plant and equipment	30,000		
		Total liabilities	
Total assets	$95,000	and net worth	$95,000

4. Glamour Galore ships the dresses on the basis of the original order, invoicing the purchaser for $100,000 within 30 days. Accrued wages and accounts payable have to be paid now, so Glamour Galore must borrow an additional $30,000 in order to maintain the $5,000 minimum cash balance.

Note that in Balance Sheet 4, finished goods inventory is replaced

BALANCE SHEET 4

ASSETS		LIABILITIES	
Current Assets		Notes payable	$ 45,000
Cash	$ 5,000	Total current	
Accounts receivable	100,000	liabilities	$ 45,000
Total	$105,000	Capital stock	$ 50,000
Fixed Assets		Retained earnings	40,000
Plant and equipment	30,000	Total net worth	$ 90,000
		Total liabilities	
Total assets	$135,000	and net worth	$135,000

by receivables, with the markup reflected as retained earnings. This causes the debt ratio to drop to 33 percent. Since the receivables are carried at selling price, the current assets increase to $105,000 and the current ratio rises to 2.3. Compared with the conditions reflected in Balance Sheet 3, most of the financial ratios show improvement. However, the absolute amount of debt is large.

Whether the firm's financial position is really improved depends upon the credit worthiness of the purchaser of the dresses. If the purchaser is a good credit risk, Glamour Galore may be able to borrow further on the basis of the accounts receivable.

5. The firm receives payment for the accounts receivable, pays off the bank loan, and is now in the highly liquid position shown by Balance Sheet 5. If a new order for 10,000 dresses is received, it will have no

BALANCE SHEET 5

ASSETS		LIABILITIES	
Current Assets		Capital stock	$50,000
Cash	$60,000	Earned surplus	40,000
Fixed Assets			
Plant and equpment	$30,000		
Total assets	$90,000	Total liabilities and net worth	$90,000

effect on the balance sheet, but a cycle similar to the one described above will begin.

The idea of the cash cycle can now be generalized. An order that requires the purchase of raw materials is placed with the firm. The purchase in turn generates accounts payable. As labor is applied, work-in-process inventories build up. To the extent that wages are not fully paid at the time labor is used, accrued wages will appear on the liability side of the balance sheet. As goods are completed, they move into finished goods inventories. The cash needed to pay for the labor to complete the goods may make it necessary for the firm to borrow.

Finished goods inventories are sold, usually on credit, which gives rise to accounts receivable. As the firm has not received cash, this point in the cycle represents the peak in financing requirements. If the firm did not borrow at the time finished goods inventories were at their maximum, it may do so as inventories are converted into receivables by credit sales. Income taxes, which were not considered in the example, can add to the problem. As accounts receivable become cash, short-term obligations can be paid off.

How Sales Require Financing

How the process just described results in the need for increased financing as the volume of sales rises can be illustrated by actual data for the Radio Corporation of America (RCA) during 1949–1964 (Table 13–1). During the first ten years of this period, sales rose by $800 million,

TABLE 13–1 RADIO CORPORATION OF AMERICA, 1949–1964
(dollars in millions)

				PERCENTAGE OF INCREASE	
	1949	1958	1964	1949–1958	1958–1964
Sales	$400	$1,200	$1,800	200	50
Current assets	150	480	800	220	67
Net plant and equipment	75	200	300	167	50
Total	225	680	1,100	202	62
Current liabilities	60	175	310	192	77
Long-term debt	40	250	300	525	20
Shareholders' equity	140	300	525	114	75
Total	$240	$ 725	$1,135	202	57

SOURCE: *RCA Annual Report, 1958–1964*. Totals do not balance because only the significant items were taken from the report.

which represents a 200 percent increase. Current assets increased by 220 percent, net plant and equipment by only 167 percent. The $800 million increase in sales gave rise to the need to finance a $330 million increase in current assets and a $125 million increase in net fixed assets. Thus current assets rose by about 40 percent of the increase in sales, and net fixed assets at somewhat over 15 percent of the increase in sales. Stated differently, for every $10 million increase in sales, RCA had to finance an additional $4 million in current assets and $1.5 million in net fixed assets.

During the decade covered by the RCA data, increased operating assets were financed about two thirds by debt and one third by shareholders' equity. Long-term debt increased by 525 percent, and thus working capital increased from $90 million to $305 million.

The data for 1949–1958 may be compared with those for the subsequent six years, thus testing to see if the generalizations made from the early years hold for the latter period. Since a shorter period is involved and since the base amount of the figures is larger, the percentage figures are smaller. However, there is strong confirmation of the generalizations made with respect to the decade between 1948 and 1958. During the later period, 1958 through 1964, sales increased by 50 percent and total assets by 62 percent. Note again the close correspondence between the percentage increase in sales and the percentage increase in financing requirements. When sales increased by 50 percent, net plant and equipment also increased by precisely 50 percent. Current assets increased by 67 percent.

An interesting contrast is provided by the methods of financing growth. In the earlier period, current liabilities increased by about the same percentage as sales increased. However, in that earlier period, long-term debt increased by over 500 percent, while net worth increased by somewhat over 100 percent. In the years 1958–1964, long-term debt increased by a much smaller percentage than did sales, and net worth increased by a much larger percentage.

These data, drawn from RCA's actual experience, illustrate the close relationship between changes in the level of sales and changes in financing requirements. This close relationship holds not only over long periods but also during short-term fluctuations in sales as well.

Financing Patterns

The influence of sales on current asset levels was illustrated above. Over the course of several cycles, the fluctuations in sales will be accompanied in most industries by a rising long-term trend. Figure 13–1 shows the consequences of such a pattern.[2] Total permanent assets increase steadily in the form of current and fixed assets. Increases of this nature should be financed by long-term debt; by equity; by "spontaneous" increases in liabilities such as accured taxes and wages; and by accounts receivable, which naturally accompany increasing sales. However, temporary increases in assets can be covered by short-term liabilities. The distinction between temporary and permanent asset levels may be difficult to make in practice, but it is neither illusory nor unimportant. Short-term financing to finance long-term needs is dangerous. A profit-

[2] Seasonal influences are omitted for the sake of simplicity.

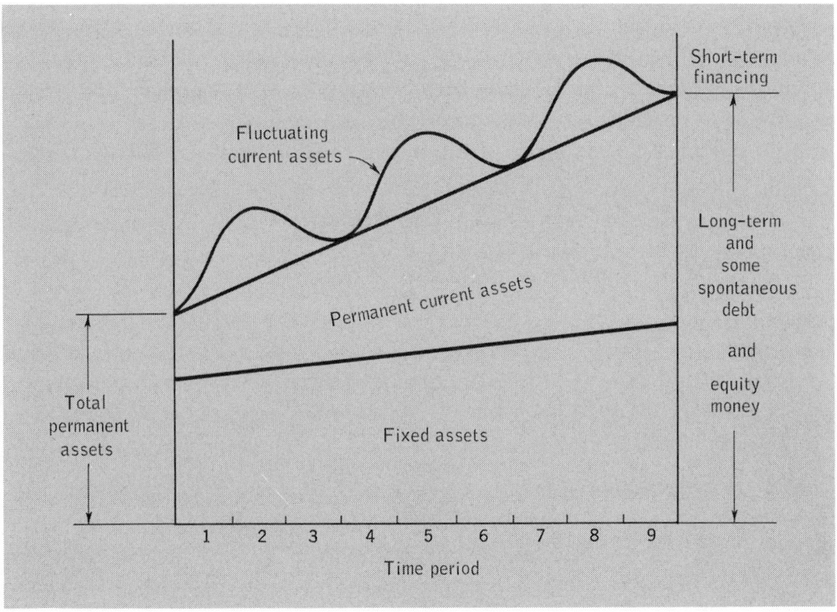

Figure 13–1 Fluctuating versus Permanent Assets

able firm may become unable to meet its cash obligations if funds borrowed on a short-term basis have become tied up in permanent asset needs.

PRODUCT LIFE CYCLE

An important aspect of working capital management is the recognition of cash flows over the life cycle of individual products. A new product or new firm typically experiences an initial period of cash flow deficits that must be financed from external sources. A typical product life cycle cash flow is shown in Table 13–2 and Figure 13–2, and is described below.

Net cash flow are small and negative while the firm completes the necessary preliminary organization activities leading to engineering outlays and preparations for manufacturing activities. When manufacturing begins, inventories of raw materials, work in process, and finished goods are generated before sales are made. Sales result in receivables, so some additional time may elapse before a positive cash flow begins.

An illustrative pattern is indicated in Table 13–2. After two years, when the preliminary studies have been completed, $15,000 has been spent. Engineering and manufacturing activities begin in 1968, and actual production and sales are started in 1969. Net cash flows are still negative at the end of 1970, at which time negative cash flows of $305,000 have

TABLE 13–2 GOODMAN MANUFACTURING CORPORATION PRODUCT LIFE CYCLE CASH FLOW AND RATE OF RETURN ANALYSIS

			PRESENT VALUES AT 20%		PRESENT VALUES AT 32%	
Year	Net Cash Flows	Cumulative Cash Flows	Present Value Factor at 20%	Present value of inflows or (outflows)	Present Value Factor at 32%	Present Value
1966	($5,000)	($5,000)	0.833	(4,165)	0.758	(3,790)
1967	(10,000)	(15,000)	0.694	(6,940)	0.574	(5,740)
Completion of preliminary studies						
1968	(50,000)	(65,000)	0.579	(28,950)	0.435	(21,750)
1969	(200,000)	(265,000)	0.482	(96,400)	0.329	(65,800)
1970	(40,000)	(305,000)	0.402	(16,080)	0.250	(10,000)
Positive cash flows begin						
1971	30,000	(275,000)	0.335	10,050	0.189	5,670
1972	50,000	(225,000)	0.279	13,950	0.143	7,150
1973	225,000	—	0.233	52,425	0.108	24,300
1974	250,000	250,000	0.194	48,500	0.082	20,500
1975	300,000	550,000	0.162	48,600	0.062	18,600
1976	350,000	900,000	0.135	47,250	0.047	16,450
1977	200,000	1,100,000	0.112	22,400	0.036	7,200
1978	200,000	1,300,000	0.083	16,600	0.027	5,400
1979	100,000	1,400,000	0.078	7,800	0.021	2,100
1980	50,000	1,450,000	0.065	3,250	0.016	800
Net present value				$118,290		$1,090

been accumulated. This represents a total amount that the organizers of the firm, or product managers responsible for new product activities, must recognize as a total investment outlay.

By 1971, positive cash flows begin. At first they are relatively small; then, with product acceptance, they become large. By 1973, positive cash inflows are substantial and cumulative cash flows on a nondiscounted basis become zero.

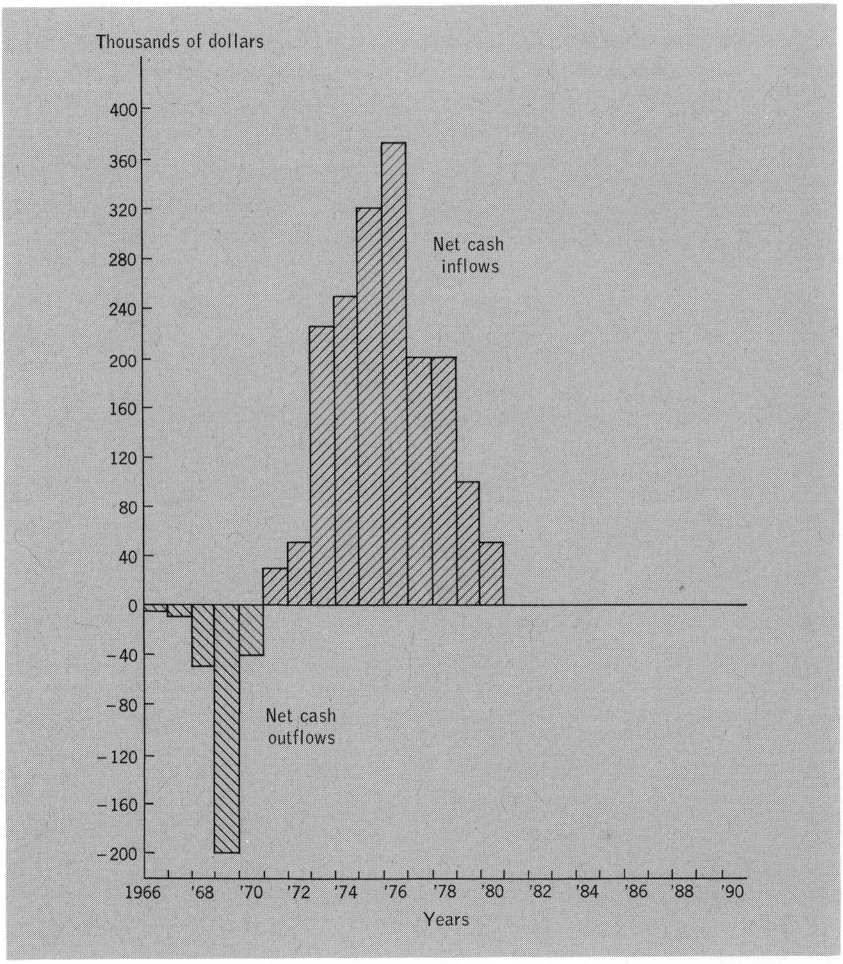

Figure 13–2 Cash Flows over the Product Life Cycle

The remainder of Table 13–2 illustrates how the material of Chapters 6 through 11 can be integrated with cash flow analysis. Present value factors are applied to the cash outflows, cash inflows, and cumulative present values of cash flows. A discount factor of 20 percent is applied, because this new product activity involves considerable estimating risks. It will be noted in the table that positive cash flows are not generated until some eight years after preliminary analysis of the product potential has begun. It is not implied that it always takes 8 to 10 years to begin to achieve positive cash flows. However, for the successful launching of many new products, such a development period is not unusual. In an industry of fast-moving technology or in relatively simple indus-

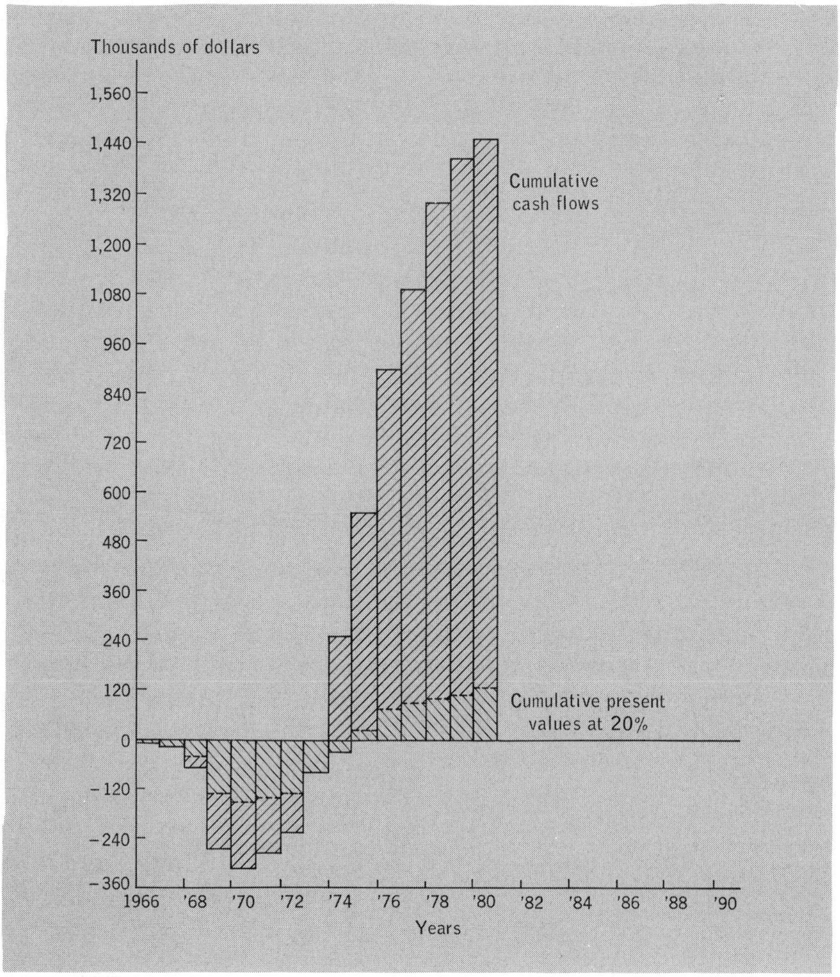

Figure 13–3 Cumulative Cash Flows over the Product Life Cycle

tries such as wholesale or retail trade, the duration of the life cycle may be substantially compressed.

On the basis of the discounted cash flows, a "breakeven" is not achieved until the tenth year (see Figure 13–3). From that point on, positive net cash flows from the project are achieved. The success of this product invites competition, so in the year of maximum profits, 1976, it begins to attract additional capacity into the industry. As a consequence, profit margins and total profits begin to decline. By the end of 1980, profits have declined to the point where serious consideration should be given to abandoning business activity in this particular product line.

It will be noted that over the 15-year product life cycle analyzed, in which a 20 percent discount factor was applied, the cumulative net present value of the project is $118,290. Analysis indicates that this project would provide a substantial cumulative positive present value of returns. The internal rate of return of this product life cycle is approximately 32 percent.

The main emphasis of this exposition, however, has been to illustrate the cash requirements of new project activities. The necessity for taking into consideration the heavy cash outlays required before beginning engineering and manufacturing activities is frequently overlooked. Also, there is often inadequate understanding of the cash requirements for financing raw material purchases and labor payrolls used to build up the initial work in process and finished goods inventories. In addition, an investment in receivables is required. The total amount of cash outflows in the period over which negative cash flows are incurred is frequently large, requiring a careful analysis to avoid a cash crisis before positive cash flows begin. For new product activity, therefore, the typical short-term monthly cash budget analysis should certainly be augmented by a product life-cycle cash flow analysis.

CONTROLLING INVESTMENT IN CASH AND MARKETABLE SECURITIES

The starting point in controlling the investment in assets is effective control of cash and cash equivalent. Cash equivalent includes marketable securities—for example, short-term government securities—characteristically held for liquidity purposes. These interest-bearing liquid assets can be converted to cash rapidly if the firm should need additional funds. "Cash" is primarily held as balances with commercial banks, largely in the form of demand deposits. Approximately 85 to 90 percent of all transactions in the United States are accomplished through the use of "cash" in the form of demand deposits.[3]

[3] A comment on the growing use of credit cards and the approach of the so-called checkless, cashless society is appropriate. As an increasing number of transactions are made with credit cards, individuals need smaller cash balances. If and when computerized transactions between accounts is feasible—A makes a purchase from B and instructs a computer to make a transfer from his balance to that of B—the

Businesses or individuals have three primary motives for holding cash: (1) the transactions motive, (2) the precautionary motive, and (3) the speculative motive.

The transactions motive for holding cash is to enable the firm to conduct its ordinary business—making purchases and sales. The types of flows described for Glamour Galore indicate the kinds of needs involved in the transactions use of cash. In some lines of business, such as the utilities, where billings can be cycled throughout the month, cash inflows can be scheduled and synchronized closely with the need for the outflow of cash. Hence, we expect the cash-to-revenues ratio or cash-to-total-assets ratio for utility firms to be relatively low. In retail trade, by contrast, a large number of transactions may actually be conducted by physical currency. As a consequence, retail trade requires a higher ratio of cash to sales and of cash to total assets.

The seasonality of a business may give rise to a need for cash for the purchase of inventories. For example, raw materials may be available only during a harvest season and may be perishable, as in the food-canning business. Or sales may be seasonal, as are department store sales around the Christmas and the Easter holidays, giving rise to an increase in needs for cash.

The two other traditional motives for holding "cash" are actually satisfied in large part by holdings of near-money assets—short-term government securities and the like. The precautionary motive relates primarily to the predictability of cash inflows and outflows. If the predictability is high, less cash or cash equivalent will need to be held against an emergency or any other contingency. Another factor that strongly influences the precautionary motive for holding cash is the ability to obtain additional cash on short notice when circumstances necessitate. Borrowing flexibility is primarily a matter of the strength of the firm's relations with banking institutions and other sources of potential augmentation of its cash holdings.

The speculative motive for holding cash is to be ready for profit-making opportunities that may arise. By and large, accumulations of cash for speculative purposes are not widely found. Holding cash is more a function of the behavior of individual investors. However, the cash and marketable securities account may rise to rather sizable levels as a temporary basis for accumulating the means of financing. A dramatic example of this was the rise in cash and marketable securities of Montgomery Ward in 1948 to $149 million, representing 22 percent of total

---

need for working balances of both businesses and individuals will be greatly reduced. Trends in this direction have already caused huge increases in the income velocity of money (national income/money supply), and all indications are for a continuation if not acceleration of the trend.

assets. Ward was counting on a post-World War II depression and built up cash to take advantage of the projected price level decline.[4]

ADVANTAGES OF ADEQUATE CASH

In addition to these general motives, sound working capital management requires maintenance of an ample amount of cash for several specific reasons. First, it is essential that the firm have sufficient cash to take trade discounts. The payment schedule for purchases is referred to as "the term of the sale." A commonly encountered billing procedure, or term of trade, allows a 2 percent discount if the bill is paid within 10 days, with full payment required in 30 days in any event. Since the net amount is due in 30 days, failure to take the discount means paying this extra 2 percent for using the money an additional 20 days. If you were to pay 2 percent for every 20-day period over the year, there would be eighteen such periods:

$$18 = \frac{360 \text{ days}}{20 \text{ days}}$$

This represents an annual interest rate of 36 percent.[5] Most firms are able to borrow at a rate substantially lower than 36 percent a year.

Second, since the current and acid test ratios are key items in credit analysis, it is essential that the firm, in order to maintain its credit standing, meet the standards of the line of business in which it is engaged. A strong credit standing enables the firm to purchase goods from trade suppliers on favorable terms and to maintain its line of credit with banks and other sources of credit.

Third, ample cash is useful for taking advantage of favorable business opportunities that may come along from time to time. Finally, the firm should have sufficient liquidity to meet emergencies, such as strikes, fires, or marketing campaigns of competitors.

Using the knowledge about the general nature of cash flows presented above, the financial manager may be able to improve the inflow-outflow

[4] After the fact, this turned out to be a big mistake as no depression occurred; Ward's principal competitor, Sears Roebuck, expanded rapidly and captured a large part of Ward's traditional market.

[5] The method of calculating the effective interest rate on accounts payable is described in Chapter 15.

pattern of cash. He can do so by better synchronization of flows and by reduction of float, as will be explained in the following two sections.

Synchronization of Cash Flows

As an example of synchronization, cash flows may be improved by more frequent requisitioning of funds by divisional offices from the firm's main or central office. A concrete illustration makes the point clearly.

> Some Gulf Oil Corporation divisional field offices, for instance, used to requisition funds once or twice a week; now the treasurer's office insists on daily requisitions, thus keeping some cash on tap as much as four days longer. John Shaw, assistant treasurer, told an American Management Association seminar last year that, on the basis of ten offices, each requiring $500,000 a week, these staggered requisitions free the equivalent of $10 million for one day each week. At 3 percent interest, this earns better than $42,000 a year.[6]

In addition, effective forecasting can reduce the investment in cash. The cash flow forecasting at Universal Commercial Investment Trust Credit Corporation illustrates this idea. An assistant treasurer forecasts planned purchases of automobiles by the dealers. He estimates daily the number of cars shipped to the 10,000 dealers who finance their purchases through Universal CIT. He then estimates how much money should be deposited in Detroit banks that day to pay automobile manufacturers. On one day he estimated a required deposit of $6.4 million; the actual bill for the day was $6.397 million, a difference of one-tenth of 1 percent. Although such close forecasting cannot be achieved by every type of firm, the system enables Universal CIT to economize on the amount of money it must borrow and thereby keeps interest expense to a minimum.

Reduction of Float

Another important method of economizing on the volume of cash required is by reduction of "float." Float refers to funds in transit between cities. Checks received from customers in distant cities are subject to two types of delays: the time required for the check to travel in the mail and the time required for clearing through the banking system.

To reduce these two types of float, a "lock-box plan" can be used. If our firm makes sales in large amounts at far distances, we can establish a lock box in a post office located in the customer's area. We can arrange to have customers send payments to the postal box in their city and then have a bank pick up the checks and deposit them in a special checking account. The bank then has the checks cleared in the

[6] *Business Week,* July 12, 1958.

local area and remits by wire to our bank of deposit. If our distant customers are scattered, we can establish the lock box in our local city and have the checks picked up by our bank. The bank begins the clearing process, notifying us that a check has been received. In this way the clearing process starts before our firm processes the check. By these methods, float may be reduced by one to five days. Examples of freeing funds in the amount of $1.5 million or more by these methods have been cited by firms.

The use of lock-box plans can be illustrated by citing an example. Northeast Airlines, a firm with headquarters in Boston, has heavy ticket sales through travel agencies in Miami. If the Miami travel agents paid for tickets by mailing checks to Boston, Northeast would deposit the checks in a Boston bank, which would then clear them through the Federal Reserve System. This would require that the checks be physically sent to the Miami bank on which they were written. After clearance, Northeast's Boston bank would be notified, and only then could Northeast use the funds. The lock-box plan avoids all the time lost in mailing checks to and from Boston and thus gives Northeast the use of funds as much as a week earlier than without the plan.

Investment of Funds

A firm may have cash to invest for a number of reasons. One is seasonal or cyclical fluctuations in business. As sales expand, inventories and receivables mount. As sales fall off, inventories and receivables decrease and become cash. Thus, during a seasonal or cyclical expansion, the firm will need to finance an increase in inventories and receivables. Some firms may borrow as their seasonal or cyclical needs for financing expand. Others, particularly firms in capital goods industries where fluctuations are violent, attempt to accumulate cash or near-cash during a downturn to be ready to finance an upturn in business volume.

Firms may also accumulate resources as a protection against a number of contingencies. When they make uninsurable product warranties, firms must be ready to meet claims that may arise. Firms in highly competitive industries must have resources to carry them through substantial shifts in the market structure. A firm in an industry in which new markets are emerging—for example, foreign markets—needs to have resources to meet developments; these funds may be on hand for fairly long periods.

Thus, because of uncertain contingencies, a firm may have cash funds to invest for a few weeks, a few months, a few years, or even indefinitely. Investment alternatives are available to meet the needs of the firm. Taking both yield and risk considerations into account, the alternatives are listed in Table 13–3.

TABLE 13–3 ALTERNATIVE MARKETABLE SECURITIES FOR INVESTMENTS

	APPROXIMATE MATURITIES*
U.S. Treasury bills	91–182 days
U.S. Treasury certificates	9–12 months
U.S. Treasury notes	1–5 years
Prime commercial paper	Varies, up to 270 days
Negotiable certificates of deposit†	Varies, up to 3 years
Savings certificates at commercial banks	6 months
Savings accounts at commercial banks	
Savings accounts at savings and loan associations	
Bonds and stocks of other corporations	
Bonds and stocks of the firm in question‡	

* The maturities are those at issue date. For outstanding securities, maturities varying almost by day or week are available.
† See Roy L. Reierson, "A New Money Market Instrument" (New York: Bankers Trust Company, March 24, 1961).
‡ See L. A. Guthart, "More Companies Are Buying Back Their Stock," *Harvard Business Review*, XLIII, March 1965, 40–45.

Depending on how long he anticipates holding the funds, the financial manager decides upon a suitable maturity pattern for his holdings. The numerous alternatives can be selected and balanced in such a way that he obtains the maturities and risks appropriate to the financial situation of his firm. Commercial bankers, investment bankers, and brokers provide the financial manager with detailed information on each of the forms of investments in the list. Since their characteristics change with shifts in financial market conditions, it would be misleading to attempt to give detailed descriptions of these investment outlets here. The financial manager must keep up to date on these characteristics. He should follow the principle of making investment selections that offer maturities, yields, and risks appropriate to his firm.

Because some funds are to be held for extended periods, they may be invested with the objective of a higher return than that available from government securities. Such investments may be made in the shares of other companies. "Mostly, however, these are investments pure and simple, not for the sake of control. They were purchased to put the buyer's surplus cash to work hard, producing a larger return than it could earn, say, in the government bond market."[7]

[7] "Part-Time Portfolios," *Forbes*, Vol. 95, (May 15, 1961), 16–17.

Investments in other companies follow several patterns. The percentage of ownership is characteristically small; thus it cannot be said that the dominant motive is control. Often the investments are made in firms in related industries. This practice is followed partly because the nature and outlook for such industries are better understood and partly because such investments may yield additional information useful for purchasing or sales activities. For example, suppliers to larger firms may often hold shares in the larger firms for the contacts that will be provided by shareholders' information and meetings. Clearly, control cannot be exercised by the smaller firm. However, the smaller firm may in this manner obtain market information that might otherwise be more difficult to obtain.

Optimizing Techniques

Models have been developed to determine the optimum, or most desirable, level of cash balances for a firm to hold. These "cash management models" are variations of the standard inventory model discussed in the next chapter. Rather than discuss them now, we defer a consideration of cash management models until after developing the concept of the general inventory model.

MANAGEMENT OF INVESTMENT IN RECEIVABLES

In the present chapter, the term "trade credit" refers to accounts *receivable,* and it involves both the credit used to support and expand sales and the resulting investment required of the firm. In Chapter 15, where its potentials and limitations as a source of funds are discussed, trade credit refers to accounts *payable.*

The ratio of receivables to sales generally is in the range from 8 to 12 percent for manufacturing firms, representing an average collection period of approximately one month. The ratio of receivables to total assets centers on about 16 to 20 percent. However, wide variations are experienced among firms, particularly when nonmanufacturing industries are included.

The major determinants of the level of receivables are (1) volume of credit sales, (2) seasonality of sales, (3) rules for credit limits, (4) terms of sales and credit policies of individual firms, and (5) collection policies. Variations in the ratios of receivables to sales (or the average collection periods) among firms reflect the differential impact of the factors listed above.

Variations in terms of sale reflect the customs of the line of business. A very important influence, however, is the perishability of the product. On the one hand, very short payment periods are found in the bakery products, milk products, and meat products industries. On the other hand, relatively high ratios of receivables to sales are observed in the construction, industrial machinery, agricultural machinery, office equipment, and printing and publishing industries. In addition, higher ratios of receivables to sales are found among larger firms, which obtain funds at lower cost and tend to be wholesalers of credit obtained from financial institutions and reloaned to smaller firms.

Credit Policy

The basis of a firm's credit policy is its industry's characteristic credit terms; generally, a firm must meet the terms provided by other firms in the industry. However, when a customer is a poor credit risk, the company giving the trade credit must be less lenient for its own protection. A central task in formulating credit policy is an evaluation of the credit worthiness of the potential customer.

To evaluate the credit risk, the credit manager considers the five Cs of credit: *character, capacity, capital, collateral, conditions.* Character refers to the probability that the customer will *try* to honor his obligations. This factor is of considerable importance, because every credit transaction implies a *promise* to pay. Will the creditor make an honest effort to pay his debts, or is he likely to try to get away with something? Experienced credit men frequently insist that the moral factor is the most important issue in a credit evaluation.

Capacity is a subjective judgment of the *ability* of the customer. This is gauged by his past record, supplemented by physical observation of the customer's plant or store and business methods. Capital is measured by the general financial position of the firm as indicated by a financial-ratio analysis, with special emphasis on the tangible net worth of the enterprise. Collateral is represented by assets that the customer may offer as a pledge for security of the credit extended to him. Finally, conditions refers to the impact of general economic trends on the firm or special developments in certain areas of the economy that may affect the customer's ability to meet his obligations.

The five Cs of credit represent the factors by which the credit risk is judged. Information on these items is obtained from the firm's previous experience with the customer, supplemented by a well-developed system of information-gathering groups. Two major sources of external information are available. The first is the work of the credit associations. By periodic meetings of local groups and by direct communication, information on experience with creditors is exchanged. More formally, credit interchange, a system developed by the National Association of Credit Management for assembling and distributing information on debtors' past performance, is provided. The interchange reports show the paying record of the debtor, industries from which he is buying, and the trading areas in which his purchases are being made.[8]

The second is the work of the credit-reporting agencies, the best known of which is Dun & Bradstreet. Agencies that specialize in coverage of a limited number of industries also provide information. Representative of these are the National Credit Office and the Lyon Furniture Mercantile Agency. Some of the services of Dun & Bradstreet are briefly described to indicate the nature of the information obtainable.

The Dun & Bradstreet Reference Book is published six times a year and covers the entire United States and Canada. Regional and state editions are also published. The Reference Book contains listings of firms and their credit ratings by town location. The credit ratings shown in Table 13–4 indicate both estimated financial strength and a composite credit appraisal. A credit appraisal of "high" indicates that financial affairs appear healthy and meet a number of important tests with reference to the five Cs of credit.

When the rating of a firm is less than high, the financial manager may wish to obtain more specific information from credit reports sold by Dun & Bradstreet. The credit reports follow the forms indicated in Table 13–5. They provide a summary of the main information about the customer: his credit rating and history, a discussion of the business operations and their location, financial information, and the payment experience. The payment experience indicates whether the customer takes discounts, whether he pays promptly, and by how many days he delays payment if he does not pay promptly. In the example shown in Table 13–5, the five entries in the Payments section indicate that five suppliers were queried by Dun & Bradstreet. The first column, HC, shows the highest credit that has ever been extended by each creditor. The next column shows how much is presently outstanding, while the third column gives any amounts presently past due. The terms "Disc' and "Ppt" indicate that the illustrative firm takes discounts where available and otherwise pays promptly.

The information in Tables 13–4 and 13–5 can be translated into risk classes, grouped according to the probability of risk associated with sales

[8] For additional information, see *Credit Management Handbook, Second Edition,* a publication of the National Association of Credit Management, (Homewood, Ill.: Irwin, 1965).

TABLE 13–4 KEY TO RATINGS

ESTIMATED FINANCIAL STRENGTH			COMPOSITE CREDIT APPRAISAL			
			High	Good	Fair	Limited
AA	Over	$1,000,000	A1	1	1½	2
A+	Over	750,000	A1	1	1½	2
A	$500,000 to	750,000	A1	1	1½	2
B+	300,000 to	500,000	1	1½	2	2½
B	200,000 to	300,000	1	1½	2	2½
C+	125,000 to	200,000	1	1½	2	2½
C	75,000 to	125,000	1½	2	2½	3
D+	50,000 to	75,000	1½	2	2½	3
D	35,000 to	50,000	1½	2	2½	3
E	20,000 to	35,000	2	2½	3	3½
F	10,000 to	20,000	2½	3	3½	4
G	5,000 to	10,000	3	3½	4	4½
H	3,000 to	5,000	3	3½	4	4½
J	Up to	3,000	J..... 3	3½	4	4½
K	Up to	3,000	K.... 3	3½	4	4½
L	Up to	3,000	L..... 3½	4	4½	5

K & L are being phased out

CLASSIFICATION FOR BOTH ESTIMATED FINANCIAL STRENGTH AND CREDIT APPRAISAL

Financial Strength Bracket		Explanation
1	$125,000 and Over	When only the numeral (1, 2, 3, or 4) appears, it is an indication that the estimated financial strength, while not definitely classified, is presumed to be within the range of the ($) figures in the corresponding bracket and that a condition is believed to exist which warrants credit in keeping with that assumption.
2	20,000 to 125,000	
3, 4	Up to 20,000	

4 is being phased out

"INV." shown in place of a rating indicates that the report was under investigation at the time of going to press. It has no other significance.

NOT CLASSIFIED OR ABSENCE OF RATING

The absence of a rating, expressed by two hyphens (- -), is not to be construed as unfavorable but signifies circumstances difficult to classify within condensed rating symbols. It suggests the advisability of obtaining a report for additional information.

ABSENCE OF A LISTING

The absence of a listing is not to be construed as meaning a concern is non-existent, has discontinued business, nor does it have any other meaning. The letters "NQ" on any written report mean "not listed in the Reference Book."

YEAR BUSINESS STARTED

The numeral shown is the last digit of the year date when the business was established or came under present control or management. Thus, 8 means 1958; 9 means 1959. No dates go past ten years. Thus the absence of a numeral indicates ten years or more. This feature is not used in connection with branch listings.

SOURCE: *Courtesy of Dun & Bradstreet, Inc.*

TABLE 13–5

Dun & Bradstreet REPORT RATING

SIC	D-U-N-S	DATE OF REPORT	STARTED	RATING
34 61	803-4520	CD 13 APR 21 19— N		
	ARNOLD METAL PRODUCTS CO	METAL STAMPINGS	1957	D 1

53 S MAIN ST
DAWSON MICH 66666
TEL 215 999-0000

SAMUEL B. ARNOLD
GEORGE T. ARNOLD } PARTNERS

SUMMARY

PAYMENTS	DISC PPT
SALES	$177,250
WORTH	$42,961
EMPLOYS	8
RECORD	CLEAR
CONDITION	SOUND
TREND	UP

PAYMENTS

HC	Owe	P Due	Terms	Apr 1 19—	Sold
3000	1500		1 10 30	Disc	Over 3 yrs
2500	1000		1 10 30	Disc	Over 3 yrs
2000	500		2 20 30	Disc	Old account
1000			30	Ppt	Over 3 yrs
500			30	Ppt	Over 3 yrs

FINANCE On Apr. 21 19— S. B. Arnold, Partner, submitted statement Dec 31 19—

Cash	$ 4,870	Accts Pay	$ 6,121
Accts Rec	15,472	Notes Pay (Curr)	2,400
Mdse	14,619	Accruals	3,583
Current	34,961	Current	12,104
Fixed Assets	22,840	Notes Pay (Def)	5,000
Other Assets	2,264	NET WORTH	42,961
Total Assets	60,065	Total	60,065

19— sales $177,250; gross profit $47,821; net profit $4,204. Fire Insurance mdse $15,000; fixed assets $20,000. Annual rent $3,000. Signed Apr 21 19— ARNOLD METAL PRODUCTS CO by Samuel B. Arnold, Partner Johnson Singer, CPA, Dawson

Sales and profits increased last year due to increased sub-contract work and this trend is reported continuing. New equipment was purchased last Sept for $8,000 financed by a bank loan secured by a lien on the equipment payable $200 per month. With increased capacity, the business has been able to handle a larger volume. Arnold stated that for the first two months of this year volume was $32,075 and operations continue profitable.

BANKING Medium to high four figure balances are maintained locally. An equipment loan is outstanding and being retired as agreed.

HISTORY Style registered Feb 1 1965 by partners. SAMUEL, born 1918, married. 1939 graduate of Lehigh University with B.S. degree in Mechanical Engineering. 1939–50 employed by Industrial Machine Corporation, Detroit, and 1950–56 production manager with Aerial Motors Inc., Detroit. Started this business in 1957. GEORGE, born 1940, single, son of Samuel. Graduated in 1963 from Dawson Institute of Technology. Served U.S. Air Force 1963–64. Admitted to partnership interest Feb 1965.

OPERATION Manufactures light metal stampings for industrial concerns and also does some work on a sub-contract basis for aircraft manufacturers. Terms net 30. 12 accounts. Five production, two office employees, and one salesman. LOCATION: Rents one-story cinder block building with 5,000 square feet located in industrial section in normal condition. Housekeeping is good.

4-21 (803 77) PRA

PLEASE NOTE WHETHER NAME, BUSINESS AND STREET ADDRESS CORRESPOND WITH YOUR INQUIRY. This report is furnished by DUN & BRADSTREET, Inc. in STRICT CONFIDENCE of your request under your subscription agreement for your exclusive use as a basis for credit, insurance, marketing and other business decisions and for no other purpose. DUN & BRADSTREET, Inc. does not guarantee the correctness of this report and shall not be liable for any loss or injury caused by the neglect or other act or failure to act on the part of said company and/or its agents in procuring, collecting or communicating any information

9R2-2(12-65)

Courtesy of Dun & Bradstreet, Inc.

to a customer. The combination of rating and supplementary information might lead to the following groupings of loss experience.

GROUP NUMBER	LOSS RATIO (IN PERCENTAGES)
1	None
2	0–½
3	½–1
4	1–2
5	2–5
6	5–10
7	10–20
8	over 20

If the selling firm has a 20 percent margin over the sum of direct operating costs and all delivery and selling costs, and if it is producing at less than full capacity, it may adopt the following credit policies. It may sell on customary credit terms to groups 1 to 5; sell to groups 6 and 7 under more stringent credit terms, such as cash on delivery; and require advance payments from group 8. As long as the bad debt loss ratios are less than 20 percent, the additional sales are contributing something to overhead.

Statistical techniques, especially regression analysis and discriminant analysis,[9] have been used with some success in judging credit worthiness. These methods serve best when individual credits are relatively small and a large number of borrowers are involved. Thus, they have worked best in retail credit, consumer loans, mortgage lending, and the like. As the increase in credit cards and similar procedures builds up, as computers are used more frequently, and as credit records on individuals and small firms are developed, statistical techniques promise to become much more important than they are today.[10]

[9] Discriminate analysis is similar to multiple regression analysis, except that it partitions a sample into two components on the basis of a set of characteristics. The sample, for example, might be loan applicants at a consumer loan company. The components into which they are classified might be those likely to make prompt repayment and those likely to default. The characteristics might be such factors as whether the applicant owns his home, how long he has been with his employer, and so forth.

[10] It has been said the biggest single deterent to the increased automation of credit processes is George Orwell's classic book, *1984,* in which he described the social dangers of centralized files of information on individuals. Orwell's omnipresent watcher, Big Brother, is mentioned frequently in Congressional sessions discussing mass storage of information relevant to credit analysis.

In reviewing credit extensions, the financial manager should not be guided by bad debt loss ratios alone. These must also be related to the potential contribution that additional sales have made to overhead costs. Accounts receivable represent an investment. The return on this investment can be calculated by taking the contribution to additional net earnings and determining the return from the investment in receivables, as in any capital budgeting problem.

UMMARY

The du Pont system described in Chapter 4 makes it clear that a high rate of return on investment is dependent upon controlling the size of the firm's investment. The purpose of this chapter was to examine methods of controlling the investment in current assets. Investment in current assets is important because current assets constitute more than one half the total assets of the firm. Moreover, the relationship between sales growth and the need for funds to finance current assets is close and direct. For small, undercapitalized firms, working capital management is particularly important, because, while investment in fixed assets may be minimized by renting or leasing equipment and plant, investment in receivables and inventories cannot be reduced to the same degree.

The Cash Cycle

The chapter began by making clear the cause-and-effect relationship between current assets, frequently called working capital, and sales. Inventories must be on hand before sales are made, so a higher anticipated level of sales requires an investment in inventories. Next, most sales are made on credit, so even after the sale has been completed the firm's investment is not returned *until accounts receivable have been collected.* A thorough understanding of the cash cycle will go a long way toward enabling us to understand the flows of funds within the firm and, consequently, when it will require funds and when they can be repaid.

Control of Investment in Current Assets

Current assets consist primarily of cash, marketable securities, accounts receivable, and inventories. Ways of determining just how much of the first three should be kept on hand were analyzed in some detail in this chapter; inventory control will be developed in the next chapter.

Cash and marketable securities are kept on hand for transaction purposes. There are clear advantages to having adequate cash on hand, but cash is a nonearning asset, so holding should be kept to the minimum necessary level.

Accounts receivable are an important element of current assets. The major determinants of the level of receivables are the volume of credit sales, terms of sales, credit policies, and collection policies. The financial manager should understand how these factors interact to determine receivables and how he can alter the factors to control the level of receivables.

QUESTIONS

13–1 How can better methods of communications make it less necessary for firms to hold large cash balances?

13–2 The highly developed financial system of the United States, with its myriad of different near-cash assets, has greatly reduced cash balance requirements by reducing the need for transactions balances. Discuss.

13–3 Assuming a firm's volume of business remained constant, would you expect it to have higher cash balances (demand deposits) during a tight-money or an easy-money period? Does this situation have any ramifications for federal monetary policy?

13–4 If a firm sells on terms of net 30 and its accounts are on the average 30 days overdue, what will its investment in receivables be if its credit sales approximate $720,000?

13–5 "It is difficult to judge the performance of many of our employees, but not that of the credit manager. If he's performing perfectly, credit losses are zero, and the higher our losses (as a percent of sales), the worse his performance." Evaluate the statement.

PROBLEMS

13–1 The Pettit Production Company sells 150,000 oil-pipe connector units at $25 a unit. The costs of production are shown below.

Selling price		$25
Cost of goods sold per unit		
Direct material	$8	
Direct labor	7	
Factory overhead	5	20
Gross margin		$ 5
General and administrative expenses	$1	
Selling expenses	1	2
Net profit per unit		$ 3

The firm is operating with one shift. By going to a second shift it can sell an additional 150,000 units at the $25 price. The additional sales will have a probable credit loss of 10 percent and will involve collection costs of $50,000. Total factory overhead will rise by \$250,000. General and administrative expenses are fixed (\$150,000); selling expenses are constant at \$1 a unit; and labor costs are fixed at \$7 a unit.

a) Based on the data given, should the additional credit sales be made?
(Work this problem using total rather than per unit figures.)
b) What other factors should be taken into account for such a decision?

13–2 The Pappas Machinery Company has sales of \$40 million a year in good years and \$25 million in poor years. Its fixed assets are \$12 million; receivables and inventories are 40 percent of sales; total assets are constant at \$30 million.

The firm must have liquidity because of substantial risks under product warranties. In addition, the firm must be ready to meet extended terms provided by foreign competitors.

a) How much cash does the firm have available for investment in good years? in poor years?
b) Suggest three kinds of investments to be used by this firm.

Selected References

Andrews, Victor L., "Captive Finance Companies," *Harvard Business Review* (July-August 1961), 80–92.

Bean, Virginia L., and Reynolds Griffith, "Risk and Return in Working Capital Management," *Mississippi Valley Journal of Business and Economics,* I (Fall 1966), 28–48.

Benishay, Haskel, "A Stochastic Model of Credit Sales Debt," *Journal of the American Statistical Association,* LXI (December 1966), 1010–1028.

———, "Managerial Controls of Accounts Receivable— A Deterministic Approach," *Journal of Accounting Research,* III (Spring 1965), 114–133.

Cyert, R. M., H. J. Davidson, and G. L. Thompson, "Estimation of the Allowance for Doubtful Accounts by Markov Chains," *Management Science,* VIII (April 1962), 287–303.

Eiteman, Wilford J., and James N. Holtz, "Working Capital Management," in Karl A. Boedecker, ed., *Essays on Business Finance* (4th ed.) (Ann Arbor, Mich.: Masterco Press, 1963).

Gole, V. L., "The Management of Working Capital," *Australian Accountant,* XXIX (June 1959), 319–329.

Griswold, J. A., *Cash Flow Through a Business* (Hanover, N. H.: Amos Tuck School of Business Administration, Dartmouth College, 1955).

Horn, Frederick E., "Managing Cash," *Journal of Accountancy,* CXVII.

Hunt, Alfred L., "Credit Management in the Electronic Accounting Era," *Controller,* XXVIII (August 1960), 374–375, 384.

Jacobs, Donald P., "The Marketable Security Portfolios of Nonfinancial Corporations: Investment Practices and Trends," *Journal of Finance,* XV (September 1960).

Johnson, Robert W., "More Scope for Credit Managers," *Harvard Business Review,* XXXIX (November-December 1961).

Kuehn, Hayden, "What a Credit Rating Signifies," *Banking,* LIII and LIV (December 1960 and January 1961), 80–82, 138; 79–82.

Leone, Edmund, "Techniques for Improving Cash Turnover," *Financial Executive,* XXXII (January 1964), 38–42.

Levy, Ferdinand K., "An Application of Heuristic Problem Solving to Accounts Receivable Management," *Management Science,* XII (February 1966), 236–244.

"Lock Box Banking—Key to Faster Collections," *Credit and Financial Management,* LXIX (June 1967), 16–21.

Myers, James H., and Edward W. Forgy, "The Development of Numerical Credit Evaluation Systems," *Journal of the American Statistical Association,* LVIII (September 1963), 799–806.

Park, Colin, and John W. Gladson, *Working Capital.* (New York: Macmillan, 1963).

Robbins, Sidney M., "Getting More Mileage Out of Cash," *NAA Bulletin* (September 1960).

Ross-Skinner, Jean, "The Profitable Art of Handling Corporation Cash," *Dun's Review* (May, 1962) 38–41, 109–111.

Seiden, Martin H., *The Quality of Trade Credit,* Occasional Paper 87 (New York: National Bureau of Economic Research, 1964).

Sisson, Roger L. and Norman L. Statland, "The Future of Computers in Credit Management," *Credit and Financial Management,* LXVII (May 1965), 13–15, 40, 44.

Soldofsky, Robert M., "A Model for Accounts Receivable Management," *N.A.A. Bulletin* (January 1966), pp. 55–58.

Vanderwicken, Peter, "More Firms Sustitute Drafts for Checks, To Pay, Collect Bills," *Wall Street Journal* (August 29, 1961), 1.

Vogel, Robert C., and G. S. Maddala, "Cross-Section Estimates of Liquid Asset Demand by Manufacturing Corporations," *Journal of Finance,* XXII (December 1967), 557–576.

Walker, Ernest W., "Towards a Theory of Working Capital," *Engineering Economist,* IX (January-February 1964), 21–35.

14

Inventory Control

Manufacturing firms generally have three kinds of inventories: raw materials, work in process, and finished goods. The levels of raw material inventories are influenced by anticipated production, seasonality of production, reliability of sources of supply, and efficiency of scheduling purchases and production operations.

Work-in-process inventory is strongly influenced by the length of the production period, which is the time between placing raw material in production and completing the finished product. Inventory turnover can be increased by decreasing the production period. One means of accomplishing this is perfecting engineering techniques to speed up the manufacturing process. Another means of reducing work in process is to buy items rather than make them.

The level of finished goods inventories is a matter of coordinating production and sales. The financial manager can stimulate sales by changing credit terms or by allowing credit to marginal risks. Whether the goods remain on the books as inventories or as receivables, the financial manager has to finance them. Many times, firms find it desirable to make the sale and thus take one step nearer to realizing cash. The potential profits can outweigh the additional collection risk.

Our primary focus in this chapter is on techniques for controlling the investment in inventories. These techniques, which are generally referred to as *inventory models,* have proved extremely useful in minimizing inventory requirements. As our examination of the du Pont system in Chapter 4 showed, any procedure that can reduce the investment required to generate a given sales volume may have a beneficial effect on the firm's rate of return, and, hence, on the value of the firm.

DETERMINANTS OF SIZE OF INVENTORIES

Although wide variations occur, inventory-to-sales ratios are generally concentrated in the 12 to 20 percent range, and inventory-to-total assets ratios are concentrated in the 16 to 30 percent range.

The major determinants of investment in inventory are the following: (1) level of sales, (2) length and technical nature of the production processes, and (3) durability versus perishability or style factor in the end product. Inventories in the tobacco industry are high because of the long curing process. Likewise, in the machinery-manufacturing industries, inventories are large because of the long work-in-process period. However, inventory ratios are low in coal mining and in oil and gas production because no raw materials are used, and the goods in process are small in relation to sales. Because of the seasonality of the raw materials, inventories are large in the canning industry.

With respect to the durability and style factors, large inventories are found in the hardware and the precious-metals industries because durability is great and the style factor is small. Inventory ratios are low in baking because of the perishability of the final product. Inventories are low in printing because the items are manufactured to order and require negligible finished inventories.

GENERALITY OF INVENTORY ANALYSIS

Within limits set by the economics of a firm's industry, there exists a potential for improvement in inventory control from the use of computers and operations research. Although the techniques are far too diverse and complicated for a complete treatment in this text, the financial manager should be prepared to make use of the contributions of specialists who have developed effective procedures for minimizing the investment in inventory.

Illustrative of the techniques at the practical level is the following:

> Raytheon's new system works like this: Tabulator cards are inserted in each package of five electronic tubes leaving Raytheon's warehouse. As the merchandise is sold, the distributor collects the cards and files his replacement order without doing paper work. He simply sends in the cards, which are identified by account number, type of merchandise, and price of the units he orders.
>
> Western Union Telegraph Co. equipment accepts the punched cards and transmits information on them to the warehouse, where it is duplicated on other punched cards. A typical order of 5,000 tubes of varying types can be received in about 17 minutes, Raytheon says. It can be assembled in about 90 minutes and delivered to Boston's Logan Airport in an additional 45 minutes. Orders from 3,000 miles away can be delivered within 24 hours, a saving of 13 days in some cases.[1]

Managing assets of all kinds is basically an inventory-type problem—the same method of analysis applies to cash and fixed assets, as well as to inventories themselves. First, a basic stock must be on hand to balance inflows and outflows of the items, with the size of the stock depending upon the patterns of flows, whether regular or irregular. Second, because the unexpected may always occur, it is necessary to have safety stocks on hand. They represent the little extra to avoid the costs of not having enough to meet current needs. Third, additional amounts may be required to meet future growth needs. These are anticipation stocks. Related to anticipation stocks is the recognition that there are optimum purchase sizes, defined as *economical ordering quantities*. In borrowing money, or in buying raw materials for production, or in purchasing plants and equipment, it is cheaper to buy more than just enough to meet immediate needs.

With the foregoing as a basic foundation, the theoretical basis for determining the optimal investment in inventory can be developed and illustrated as in Figure 14–1. Some costs rise with larger inventories—included here would be warehousing costs, interest on funds tied up in inventories, insurance, obsolescence, and so forth. Other costs decline with larger inventories—included here would be the loss of profits resulting from sales lost because of running out of stock, costs of production interruptions caused by inadequate inventories, possible purchase discounts, and so on.

Those costs that decline with higher inventories are designated by

[1] Roger B. Rowand, "Tactics Vary as Firms Try to Cut Warehouse Costs, Speed Service," *Wall Street Journal* (May 26, 1961), 1, 11.

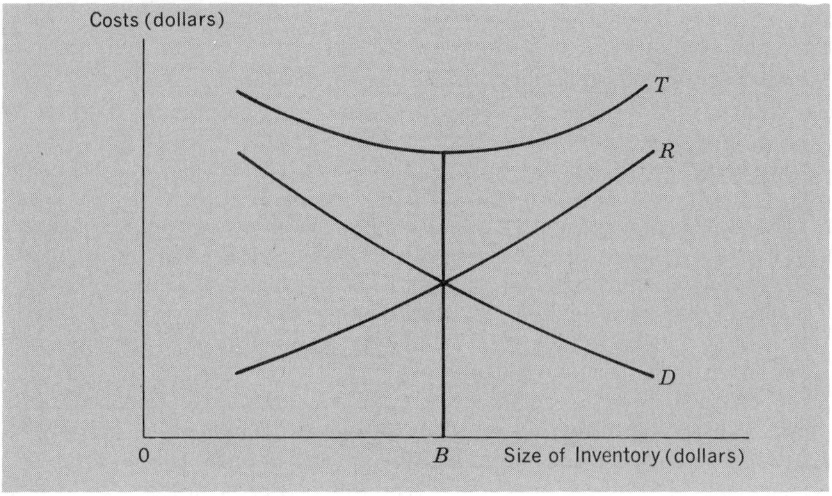

Figure 14–1 Determination of Optimum Investment in Inventory

curve D in Figure 14–1, while those that rise with larger inventories are designated by line R. Line T is the total of lines R and D, and it represents the cost of ordering and holding inventories. At the point where the *slope* of the R line is equal to the *slope* of the D line (that is, where *marginal* rising costs are equal to *marginal* declining costs, which will not necessarily be at the intersection of the R and D lines), the T line is at a minimum. This represents the optimum size of inventory investment.

This type of inventory investment analysis has wide applicability. In can be applied to investment in cash, receivables, and fixed assets, as well as to inventories. On the one hand, consider the investment in plant and equipment. If a large investment is made in specialized equipment, variable production costs per unit will be reduced. On the other hand, such additional investment in plant and equipment produces higher depreciation and capital costs. So, again, some costs decline and some rise with size of investment in plant and equipment. Therefore, an optimum investment point can be found.[2]

The concept can also be applied to decisions on the replacement of capital assets. For example, suppose we are considering when to replace a fleet of trucks. If we had costs ($) on the vertical axis and years on the horizontal axis, capital costs would decline as the number of years

[2] Since the investment in plant and equipment is of more than one-year duration, extending in some cases to 20-years or more, not only must the type of analysis indicated by Figure 14–1 be taken into account, but the time value of money and the interest factor must be considered. This type of analysis was covered in Chapters 6 and 7.

a truck is used increases (the cost of the truck minus the salvage value, divided by the years the truck is used represents the capital cost) but maintenance costs would increase. At the point where maintenance costs and capital costs are equal, the total cost of operating the fleet of trucks is at a minimum. This is the optimum replacement point, or the optimum length of time to use a truck.

IVENTORY ECISION MODELS

The generalized statements in the preceding section can be made much more specific. In fact, it is usually possible to specify the curves shown in Figure 14–1, at least to a reasonable approximation, and to actually find the minimum point on the total cost curve. In this section, we develop the procedure for finding this optimum inventory level, using an example to illustrate the procedure. Since whole courses (in operations research programs) are devoted to inventory control techniques and since a number of books have been written on the subject, we obviously cannot deal with inventory decision models in a very complete fashion. The model we do develop, however, is probably more widely used—even by quite sophisticated firms—than any other, and it can readily be expanded to encompass any refinements one cares to make.

Nature of the Problem

Assume the Norgaard Company expects to achieve a sales volume, S, of 1,000 widgets during 1970, and that Norgaard is quite confident of hitting this target. Further, these sales are expected to be evenly distributed over the year, so inventories will decline smoothly and gradually. Widgets are purchased for $10 each. No inventory is on hand at the start of the year, and none will be held at year's end.

Under these circumstances, the Norgaard Company could place one order for 1,000 units at the start of the year. If it did, the average inventory, A, would be equal to

$$
\begin{aligned}
A &= \frac{\text{Order Quantity } (Q) + \text{Ending Inventory}}{2} \\
&= \frac{S + \text{Ending Inventory}}{2} \qquad (14\text{–}1) \\
&= \frac{1{,}000 + 0}{2} = 500 \text{ units}
\end{aligned}
$$

Alternatively, Norgaard could place two orders for 500 each, in which case average inventories would be

$$A = \frac{500 + 0}{2} = 250,$$

four orders of 250 each for an average inventory of 125, and so on.

Thus we can see that average inventories are a function of the number of orders placed per year, N. Specifically, when the number of orders placed is incorporated into the calculation, equation 14–1 becomes

$$A = \frac{S/2}{N} \tag{14-1a}$$

Rearranging terms, we find

$$N = \frac{S}{2A}$$

By ordering more frequently (increasing N), Norgaard can reduce its average inventory further and further.

How far should inventory reductions be carried? Smaller inventories involve lower *carrying costs*—cost of capital tied up in inventories, storage costs, insurance, and so on—but, since a smaller average inventory implies more frequent orders, higher *ordering costs* are involved—costs of placing orders, shipping and handling, and so on. The first step in the process of building an inventory model is to specify those costs that rise and those that decline with higher levels of inventory.

Classification of Costs

Table 14–1 gives a listing of some typical costs that are associated with carrying inventories. In the table, we have broken costs down into three categories: those associated with holding inventories, those associated with running short of inventory, and those associated with ordering and receiving inventories.

Although they may well be the most important element, we shall disregard the second category of costs—the costs of running short—at this point. These costs will be considered at a later stage, when we add "safety stocks" to the inventory model. Further, we shall disregard quantity discounts, although it is easy enough to adjust the basic model to include discounts. The costs that remain for consideration at this stage, then, are carrying costs and ordering costs.

CARRYING COSTS. Carrying costs generally rise in direct proportion to the average amount of inventory carried, and this is the case with the Norgaard Company. For example, Norgaard's cost of capital is 10 percent, and the purchase price per unit of inventory, P, is \$10. Therefore, the "interest" cost of carrying inventories is \$1.00 per unit, calculated as ($.1 \times \$10 = \$1.00$) or, in total, carrying costs are $\$1(A)$. Similarly, depreciation is estimated to amount to 5 percent, so the depreciation cost of carrying inventory is \$.5 per unit or a total of $\$.5(A)$. Lumping together these and Norgaard's other costs of carrying inventory produces a total of \$2.50 per unit, or $\$2.50(A)$, for the total carrying costs. Defining the cost per unit as C, we can, in general, find the total carrying costs as

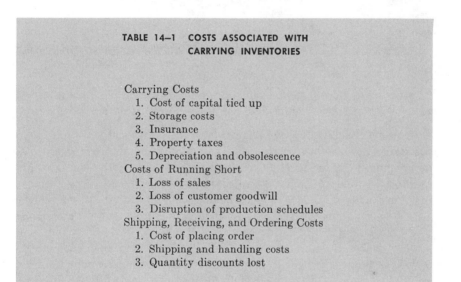

TABLE 14–1 COSTS ASSOCIATED WITH CARRYING INVENTORIES

Carrying Costs
1. Cost of capital tied up
2. Storage costs
3. Insurance
4. Property taxes
5. Depreciation and obsolescence

Costs of Running Short
1. Loss of sales
2. Loss of customer goodwill
3. Disruption of production schedules

Shipping, Receiving, and Ordering Costs
1. Cost of placing order
2. Shipping and handling costs
3. Quantity discounts lost

$$K = \text{total carrying costs} = C(A). \qquad (14\text{–}2)$$

If Norgaard elects to order only once a year, average inventories will be $1{,}000/2 = 500$ and the cost of carrying the inventory will be $\$2.50 \times 500 = \$1{,}250$. If the company orders twice a year, carrying costs will decline to \$625, and so on.

In an unpublished study, the U.S. Department of Commerce estimated that, on the average, manufacturing firms have an annual cost of carrying inventories that equals 25 percent of original inventory cost. This percentage is broken down as follows:

Obsolescence	10.00%
Depreciation	5.00
Interest (1965)	6.00
Handling	2.50
Property taxes	.50
Insurance	.25
Storage	.75
Total	25.00%

These costs obviously vary from situation to situation but, with carrying costs of this magnitude, inventories deserve careful attention.

SHIPPING, RECEIVING, AND ORDERING COSTS. Although carrying costs are entirely variable and rise in direct proportion to the average size of inventories, ordering costs are partly fixed and partly variable. For example, the cost of *placing* an order—interoffice memos, long distance telephone calls, and so on—may be fixed, so the total cost of placing orders may simply be the cost of placing an order times the number of orders placed. Shipping and receiving costs, on the other hand, generally involve a minimum fixed charge plus a variable component.[3]

We can lump together all fixed costs of placing and receiving an order and define them as F. Norgaard's total fixed cost per order, for example, may be \$100. The company's variable cost of ordering, shipping, and receiving, V, depends upon the number of units ordered and amounts to \$1.00 per unit ordered.

Combining the fixed and variable components of ordering costs, we obtain the following equation for R, the total cost of placing and receiving orders:

$$R = F \cdot N + V \cdot S \tag{14–3}$$

where F = fixed costs per order; N = number of orders placed; V = variable cost per unit ordered; and S = sales = total number of units ordered

[3] The fixed-versus-variable components in ordering costs can be confusing, so some elaboration on this point might be useful. First, *in toto,* ordering costs are considered to be a variable cost—if the firm does not place any orders, it does not incur any ordering costs. However, some of the costs of each order are fixed and some are variable. It is this fact—that a component of a *variable* cost is *fixed*—that occasionally causes confusion.

during the year. Since $N = S/2A$, we may rewrite equation 14–3 as

$$R = F\left(\frac{S}{2A}\right) + V \cdot S \qquad (14\text{–}4)$$

To illustrate, if $F = \$100$, $S = 1{,}000$, $A = 250$, and $V = \$1.00$, then

$$R = \$100(2) + \$1(1{,}000) = \$1{,}200$$

TOTAL INVENTORY COSTS. Inventory carrying costs as defined in equation 14–2 and ordering costs as defined in equation 14–4 may be combined to find total inventory costs, T, as follows:

$$T = K + R$$

$$T = C \cdot A + F\left(\frac{S}{2A}\right) + V \cdot S \qquad (14\text{–}5)$$

Recognizing that $A = Q/2$, or one half the size of each order, equation 14–5 may be rewritten as:

$$T = C\left(\frac{Q}{2}\right) + F\left(\frac{S}{Q}\right) + V \cdot S$$

$$T = C\left(\frac{Q}{2}\right) + \frac{F \cdot S}{Q} + V \cdot S \qquad (14\text{–}6)$$

The next step is to locate an optimal order quantity, or the value of Q that minimizes T. This optimal quantity, or the *economic order quantity* (EOQ) as it is generally called, is found by differentiating equation 14–6 with respect to Q, setting the derivative equal to zero, and obtaining:[4]

$$\text{EOQ} = \sqrt{\frac{2FS}{C}} \qquad (14\text{–}7)$$

[4] Proof: differentiate equation 14–6 with respect to Q and set equal to zero, then solve for Q:

$$\frac{\partial T}{\partial Q} = \frac{C}{2} - \frac{FS}{Q^2} = 0$$

$$\frac{C}{2} = \frac{FS}{Q^2}$$

$$Q^2 = \frac{2FS}{C}$$

$$Q = \sqrt{\frac{2FS}{C}}$$

In the Norgaard case, we find the EOQ, to be

$$\begin{aligned}\text{EOQ} &= \sqrt{\frac{2(\$100)(1000)}{2.50}}\\ &= \sqrt{\frac{200{,}000}{2.5}}\\ &= \sqrt{80{,}000}\\ &\approx 280 \text{ units}\end{aligned}$$

If this quantity is ordered 4 times a year ($1000/280 \approx 4$), or every three months, total costs of ordering and carrying inventories, calculated from equation 14–6, will be:

$$\begin{aligned}T &= C\left(\frac{Q}{2}\right) + \frac{FS}{Q} + VS\\ &= \$2.50(140) + \frac{(\$100)(1000)}{280} + \$1(1000)\\ &= \$350 + \$357 + \$1000\\ &= \$1{,}707\end{aligned}$$

This is the lowest possible cost of ordering and carrying the required inventories.

Equation (14–7) gives us the optimum, or cost minimizing, order quantity for given levels of sales (S), inventory carrying costs (C), and fixed order costs (F). Knowing the EOQ and continuing our assumption of zero beginning and ending inventory balances, we find the optimal average inventory as:[5]

$$A = \frac{\text{EOQ}}{2} = \frac{280}{2} = 140$$

Norgaard will, thus, have an average inventory investment of 140 units at \$10 each, or \$1,400.

With this background, it will be useful to examine a further example

[5] If we maintain a "safety stock" of inventory to guard against shipping delays, unexpectedly heavy demand, and so on, then average inventories will be higher by this amount and inventory costs will be higher by C times this amount. The nature of safety stocks will be considered in a subsequent section.

of the use of the EOQ model and some of the implications of the model itself.

Illustration of the Use of the EOQ Model

Assume the following values are determined to be appropriate for a particular firm:

S = Sales = 100 units
P = Purchase price = \$1
C = Carrying cost = 20 percent of inventory value = \$.20/unit
F = Fixed cost of ordering = \$10

substituting these values into equation 14–7 we obtain:

$$\begin{aligned} \text{EOQ} &= \sqrt{\frac{2FS}{C}} \\ &= \sqrt{\frac{2 \times 10 \times 100}{.2}} \\ &= 100 \text{ units} \end{aligned}$$

Intuitively, we would suppose that the higher the ordering or processing costs, the less frequently orders should be placed. However, the higher the carrying costs of inventory, the more frequently stocks should be ordered. These two features are incorporated in the formula. Notice also that if sales had been estimated at 200 units, the EOQ would have been 144 and the average inventory 72 versus 50 with sales of 100 units. Thus, a doubling of sales leads to less than a doubling of inventories.

The formula may be utilized to determine the EOQ and the average inventory under a series of assumptions with regard to values of the variables, as is shown in Table 14–2. The results of the calculations are charted in Figure 14–2. The graph shows sales and the corresponding average level of inventories as a series of lines somewhat curved over. The height and the slope of each line are different; they depend upon the values of such critical factors as order processing costs and inventory carrying costs. But the significant fact from the standpoint of the financial manager is that a stable and dependable relation exists between sales and inventories when the strategic variables influencing inventory policy are known. The financial manager can work with the production department in determining the EOQ. From the EOQ he can develop financial standards for inventory levels.

TABLE 14–2 RELATION BETWEEN SALES AND INVENTORY LEVELS RESULTING FROM USE OF ECONOMICAL ORDERING QUANTITY

SITUATION NUMBER									
I		II		III		IV		V	
P = \$1 C = \$.20 F = \$10		P = \$1 C = \$.20 F = \$5		P = \$1 C = \$.10 F = \$10		P = \$1 C = \$.05 F = \$10		P = \$1 C = \$.30 F = \$20	
S	A	S	A	S	A	S	A	S	A
1,000	158	1,000	112	1,000	224	1,000	316	1,000	183
2,000	224	2,000	158	2,000	316	2,000	447	2,000	258
3,000	274	3,000	194	3,000	387	3,000	548	3,000	316
4,000	316	4,000	224	4,000	447	4,000	632	4,000	365
5,000	354	5,000	250	5,000	500	5,000	707	5,000	408
6,000	387	6,000	274	6,000	548	6,000	774	6,000	447

S = level of sales in units.
A = average level of inventories in units.

Use of economic ordering quantity models not only contributes to sound inventory management but also provides a basis for projecting requirements for investment in inventories.[6] In other words, sound asset management results in stable relations, which facilitate forecasts of financing requirements.

Extension of the EOQ Model to Include "Safety Stocks"

The EOQ model as we have developed it thus far assumes that sales can be forecast perfectly and that usage is evenly distributed over the year. Further, the model assumes that orders are placed and received with no delays whatever.

The implications of these assumptions are graphed in Figure 14–3. The Thompson Company, with a demand of 1,000 units per year and an EOQ of 28, places 36 orders each year, or one every 10 days. With a zero beginning and ending inventory balance, the maximum inventory

[6] The newer operations research techniques for inventory control that have been investigated by the authors also result in stable relationships between sales and the size of investments.

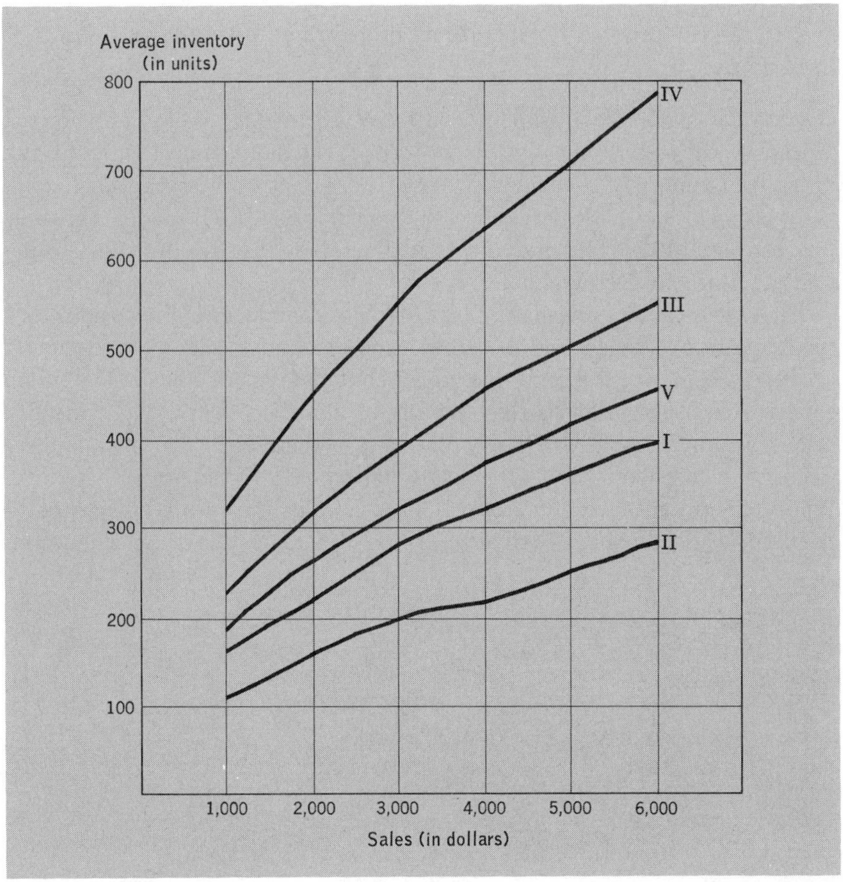

Figure 14–2 Relation between Inventory and Sales Based on the Formula for the Economical Order Quantity

is 28 units and the average is 14 units. The slope of the line in Figure 14–3 measures the daily rate of usage; in this case, 2.8 units of inventory are used each day. The usage line is shown as a step function in the first period, then smoothed in subsequent periods for convenience.

ORDER POINT. We can relax the assumption of instantaneous order and delivery. Assume Thompson requires five days to place an order and take delivery. The company must, then, have a five-day stock, or 14 units (lead time $\times$ daily usage $= 5 \times 2.8 = 14$) on hand when it places an order. The stock that is required to be on hand at time of order is defined as the *order point;* when inventories dip to this point, a new order is placed. If Thompson's inventories control process is automated, the computer will generate an order when the stock on hand falls to 14 units.[7]

SAFETY STOCK. To this point we have assumed that usage (demand) is known with certainty and is uniform throughout time, and that the order lead time never varies. Either or both of these assumptions could be incorrect, so it is necessary to modify the EOQ model to allow for this possibility. This modification generally takes the form of adding a *safety stock* to average inventories.

The safety stock concept is illustrated in Figure 14–4. First, note that the slope of the usage line measures expected daily usage. The company *expects* a usage of 2.8 units each day but, let us assume, a maximum conceivable usage of twice this amount, or 5.6 units each day. It initially orders 42 units, the EOQ of 28 plus a safety stock of 14 units. Subsequently, it reorders the EOQ, 28 units, whenever the inventory level falls to 28 units, the safety stock of 14 units plus the 14 units expected to be used while awaiting delivery of the order. Notice that Thompson

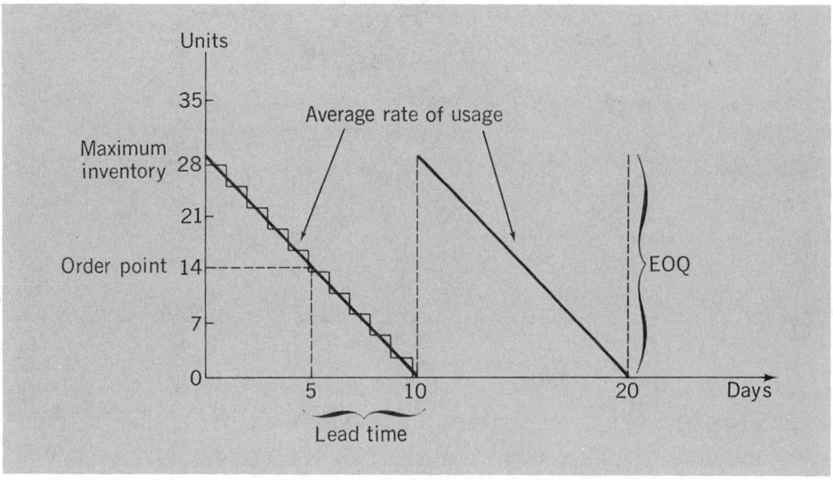

Figure 14–3 Demand Forecast with Certainty

[7] We should note that if a new order must be placed before a subsequent order is received—that is, if the normal delivery lead time is longer than the time between orders—then what might be called a "goods in transit" inventory builds up. This complicates matters somewhat, but the simplest solution to the problem is to deduct goods in transit when calculating the order point. In other words, the order point would be calculated as

$$\text{order point} = \text{lead time} \times \text{daily usage} - \text{goods in transit}$$

This situation arises in Problem 14–2 at the end of this chapter.

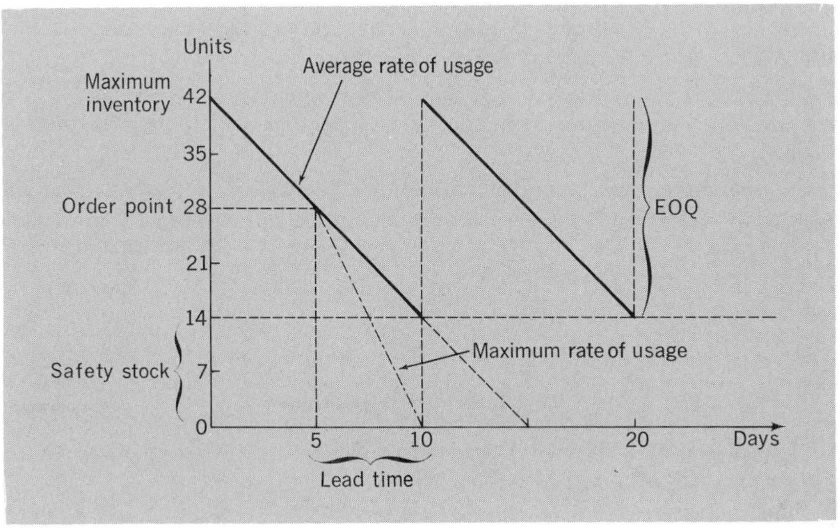

Figure 14–4 Safety Stock to Account for Uncertainty

could, over the five-day delivery period, sell 5.6 units a day ($^{28}/_{5}$ days = 5.6 units/day), or double its normal expected sales. This maximum rate of usage is shown by the steeper line in Figure 14–4. The event that made possible this higher maximum rate of usage, of course, was the introduction of a *safety stock* of 14 units.

The safety stock is also useful to guard against delays in receiving orders. The expected delivery time is five days; however, with a 14 unit safety stock, Thompson could maintain sales at the expected rate for an additional five days if shipping delays held up an order.

The optimum safety stock increases with (1) the uncertainty of demand forecasts, (2) the costs in terms of lost sales and lost goodwill that result from inventory shortages, and (3) the probability of delays in receiving shipments; it decreases with the cost of carrying the extra inventory. The actual calculation of optimum safety stocks varies from situation to situation, but it depends upon these four factors.[8]

Cash Management as an Inventory Problem

In Chapter 5, when cash budgeting was considered, we indicated that firms generally have "minimum desired cash balances." Then, in discussing cash management in Chapter 13, we considered the various factors that influence cash holdings; we did not, however, attempt to specify

[8] For a more detailed calculation of safety stocks, see Arthur Snyder, "Principles of Inventory Management," *Financial Executive*, XXXII (April 1964).

optimum cash balances. Optimum cash balances can be found by the use of inventory-type models such as those discussed in this chapter. In fact, cash management, together with inventory controls, is perhaps the area of financial management where mathematical tools have proved most useful.

Sophisticated cash management models recognize the uncertainty inherent in forecasting both cash inflows and cash outflows. Inflows are represented, in effect, by the "orders" in our inventory model; they come principally from (1) receipts, (2) borrowing, and (3) sale of securities. Outflows are represented by our "average inventory usage line" in Figures 14–3 and 14–4. The primary "carrying cost" of cash is the opportunity cost of having funds tied up in nonearning assets (or in low yielding near-cash items), the principal "ordering costs" are brokerage costs associated with borrowing funds or converting marketable securities into cash.

Since cash management models are so similar to the inventory model developed above, we shall not describe them in detail in the text. However, four models—one developed by Baumol, one by Miller and Orr, one by Beranek, and one by White and Norman—are discussed in the Appendix to this chapter.

SUMMARY

Inventories—raw materials, work in process, and finished goods—are necessary in most businesses. Rather elaborate systems for controlling the level of inventories have been designed. These systems frequently use computers for keeping records of all the items in stock; an inventory control model that considers anticipated sales, ordering costs, and carrying costs can be used to determine EOQs for each item.

The basic inventory model recognizes that certain costs (carrying costs) rise as average inventory holdings increase, but that certain other costs (ordering costs and stock-out costs) fall as average inventory holdings rise. These two sets of costs comprise the total cost of ordering and carrying inventories, and the EOQ model is designed to locate an optimal order size that will minimize total inventory costs.

The basic EOQ model is a certainty model—that is, it assumes that a regular pattern of behavior always occurs. Uncertainty is introduced by the addition of safety stocks to account for delays in receiving orders, as well as for greater-than-anticipated demand.

An inventory-model approach can also be taken to the management of cash balances. Several such models are described in the Appendix to this chapter.

QUESTIONS

14–1 Explain how a firm may reduce its investment in inventory by having its supplier hold raw materials inventories and its customers hold finished goods inventories. What are the limitations of such a policy?

14–2 What factors are likely to reduce the holdings of inventory in relation to sales in the future? What factors will tend to increase the ratio? What, in your judgment, is the net effect?

14–3 What are the probable effects of the following on inventory holdings?

a) Manufacture of a part formerly purchased from an outside supplier.

b) Greater use of air freight.

c) Increase, from 7 to 17, in the number of styles produced.

d) Your firm receives large price reductions from a manufacturer of bathing suits if they are purchased in December and January.

14–4 Inventory decision models are designed to facilitate the minimization of the cost of obtaining and carrying inventory. Describe the basic nature of the fundamental inventory control model, discussing specifically the nature of increasing costs, decreasing costs, and total costs. Illustrate your discussion with a graph.

14–5 The basic EOQ model assumes (1) a constant rate of usage and (2) a known and fixed lead time in ordering. Describe how the model can be modified to make allowance for uncertainty in each of these factors.

PROBLEMS

14–1 The following relations for inventory purchase and storage costs have been established by analysis for the Irwin Manufacturing Corporation.

1. Orders must be placed in multiples of 100 units.
2. Requirements for the year are 50,000 units. (Use 50 weeks in a year for calculations.)
3. Carrying cost is 30 cents per unit.
4. Purchasing cost per order is $18.75.
5. Desired safety stock is 3,000 units (on hand initially).
6. Two weeks are required for delivery.

a) What is the economical order size?

b) What is the optimal number of orders to be placed?

c) At what inventory level should a reorder be made?

14–2 Jenjo Sales Company is a retail distributor of living-room furniture. As a small firm, with sales under $1,000,000 a year, it has estimated that its cost of capital is a high 16 percent. The firm employes 20 salesmen who average two orders a week. From this information the proprietor, Hank Morris, has estimated his sales volume for the coming year to be 2,000 units. There is some seasonal variation; sales decrease before Christmas, Easter, and Labor Day, as consumers divert their income to the purchase of gifts, clothes, and vacations—Morris ignores this in his preliminary inventory planning for the coming year.

In preparing his inventory plans, Morris reviews the following data: Average cost per living-room ensemble is $150; depreciation and obsolescence on inventory is estimated at ½ of 1 percent a *month;* fire, theft, and all-hazards insurance coverage costs ½ of 1 percent a *year;* the current property tax rate is 1 percent a *year.* Each living-room set requires 20 square feet of storage space, and warehousing is available at $.12 a square foot per month.

Morris' cost accountant has provided data revealing that shipping, receiving, and ordering costs are as follows: interoffice memos $3 an order; air mail letter $2 per order (requires 4 weeks for delivery) or long distance telephone call $7 per order (requires 2 weeks for delivery); other fixed costs per order total $1. All other shipping, receiving, and handling costs amount to $3 per unit ordered. The desired safety stock is one week's requirements. (Use 50 weeks in a year for your calculations.)

a) Specify values for each element of inventory cost:
   (1) Inventory carrying costs per unit
   (2) Inventory ordering costs per unit
b) What is the value of the economical order size for each method of ordering?
c) What is the optimal number of orders to be placed for each method of ordering?
d) At what inventory level should a reorder be made? (See footnote 7, page 480, before working this part of the problem.)
e) What is the total cost of ordering and carrying inventories under each of the two methods? Use the equation $T = CA + FN + VS$.
f) Why is V omitted from the EOQ solution formula?
g) When should telephone orders be placed with 2 week delivery, rather than mail orders for 4 week delivery? (Use 50 weeks in a year for calculations.)

Selected References

Anderson, Clay J., "Managing the Corporate 'Money' Position," *Business Review,* Philadelphia: Federal Reserve Bank of Philadelphia (March 1961), 3–10.

Archer, Stephen H., "A Model for the Determination of Firm Cash Balances," *Journal of Financial and Quantitative Analysis,* I (March 1966), 1–11.

Baumol, William J., "The Transactions Demand for Cash: An Inventory Theoretic Approach," *Quarterly Journal of Economics,* LXV (November 1952), 545–556.

Beranek, William, "Financial Implications of Lot-Size Inventory Models," *Management Science,* XIII (April 1967), 401–408.

Bierman, Harold, Jr., and Alan K. McAdams, *Management Decisions for Cash and Marketable Securities.* (Ithaca, N.Y.: Graduate School of Business, Cornell University, 1962.)

Buchan, Joseph, and Ernest Koenigsberg, *Scientific Inventory Management.* (Englewood Cliffs, N.J.: Prentice-Hall, 1963.)

Hadley, G., and T. M. Whitin, *Analysis of Inventory Systems.* (Englewood Cliffs, N.J.: Prentice-Hall, 1963.)

Magee, John F., "Guides to Inventory Policy," I, II, and III, *Harvard Business Review* (January-February 1956), 34, 49–60; (March-April 1956), 49–60; (May-June), 103–116 and 57–70.

Miller, Merton H., and Daniel Orr, "A Model of the Demand for Money by Firms," *Quarterly Journal of Economics,* LXXX (August 1966), 413–435.

Snyder, Arthur, "Principles of Inventory Management," *Financial Executive,* XXXII (April 1964).

Starr, Martin K., and David W. Miller, *Inventory Control: Theory and Practice.* (Englewood Cliffs, N.J.: Prentice-Hall, 1962.)

Vienott, Arthur F., Jr., "The Status of Mathematical Inventory Theory," *Management Science,* XII (July 1966), 745–777.

APPENDIX TO CHAPTER 14
Cash Management Models[1]

Inventory-type models have been constructed to aid the financial manager in determining his firm's optium cash balances. Four such models—those developed by Baumol, Miller and Orr, Beranek, and White and Norman are presented in this appendix.

[1] We would like to acknowledge the assistance of Richard A. Samuelson in the preparation of this appendix.

The Baumol Model[2]

The classic article on cash management by William J. Baumol applies the EOQ model to the cash management problem. Although Baumol's article emphasized the macroeconomic implications for monetary theory, he recognized the implications for business finance and set the stage for further work in this area. In essence, Baumol recognized the fundamental similarities of inventories and cash from a financial viewpoint. In the case of inventories, there are ordering and stock-out costs that make it expensive to keep inventories at a zero level by placing orders for immediate requirements only. But there are also costs involved with *holding* inventories, and an optimal policy balances off the opposing costs of ordering and holding inventory.

With cash and securities the situation is very similar. There are order costs in the form of clerical work and brokerage fees when making transfers between the cash account and an investment portfolio. On the other side of the coin, there are holding costs consisting of interest foregone when large cash balances are held to avoid the costs of making transfers. Further, there are also costs associated with running out of cash, just as there are in the case of inventories. As with inventories, there is an optimal cash balance that minimizes these costs.

In its most operational form, the Baumol model assumes that a firm's cash balances behave, over time, in a saw-tooth manner, as shown in Figure A14–1. Receipts come in at periodic intervals, such as time 0, 1, 2, 3, and so forth; expenditures occur continuously throughout the periods. Since the model assumes certainty, the firm can adopt an optimal policy that calls for investing I dollars in a short-term investment portfolio at the beginning of each period, then withdrawing C dollars from the

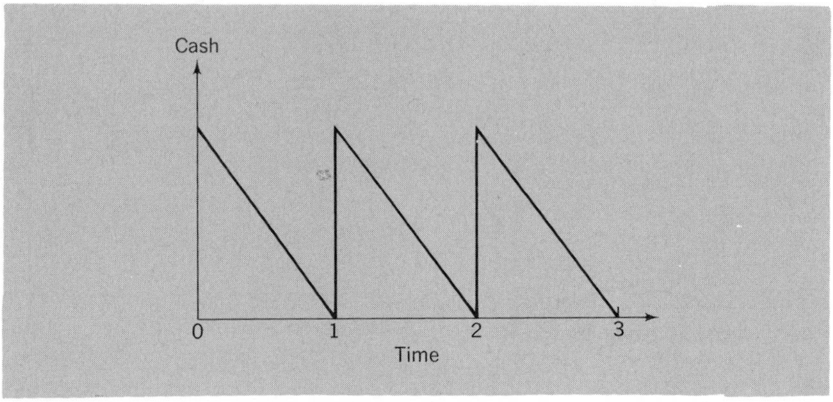

Figure A14–1 Baumol's Pattern of Receipts and Expenditures

[2] William J. Baumol, "The Transactions Demand for Cash: An Inventory Theoretic Approach," *Quarterly Journal of Economics,* LXVI (November 1952), 545–556.

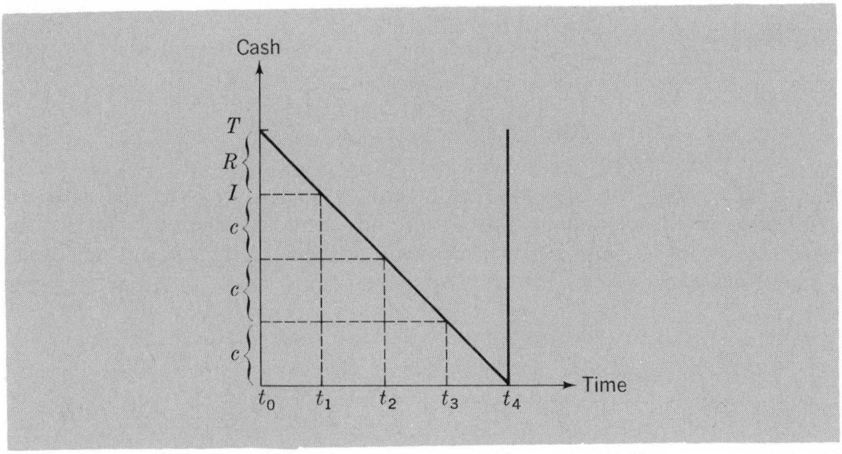

Figure A14–2 Baumol's Transfers from Securities to Cash

portfolio and placing it in the cash account at regular intervals during the period. The model must, of course, take into account both the costs of investment transactions and the costs of holding cash balances.

The decision variables facing the financial manager for a single period can be illustrated in Figure A14–2. At the beginning of the period, he has an amount of cash equal to T. A portion of the initial cash, $R = T - I$, is retained in the form of cash, and the balance, I, is invested in a portfolio of short-term liquid assets that earns a rate of return, i. The retained cash, R, is sufficient to meet expenditures during the period from t_0 to t_1. At time t_1, an additional C dollars will be transferred from the investment portfolio to the cash account to cover expenditures for the period from t_1 to t_2; C dollars will again be withdrawn at times t_2 and t_3. At t_4, receipts of T dollars again flow into the cash account, and the same process is repeated during the following period.

If the disbursements are assumed to be continuous, then $R = T - I$ dollars withheld from the initial cash receipt will serve to meet payments during $(T - I)/T$, a fraction of the period between receipts. Further, since the average cash holding for that time will be $(T - I)/2$, the interest cost (opportunity cost) of withholding that money will be

$$\left(\frac{T-I}{2}\right) i \left(\frac{T-I}{T}\right)$$

where i is the interest rate on invested funds. A brokerage fee is required to invest the I dollars invested, and this fee is equal to $b_d + k_d I$, where b_d and k_d are fixed and variable costs, respectively, of making deposits (investments).

The cost of obtaining cash for the remainder of the period is found, similarly, to be

$$\left(\frac{C}{2}\right) i \left(\frac{I}{T}\right) + \left(b_w + k_w C\right) \frac{I}{C}$$

The first term is the interest (opportunity) cost of holding the average amount $C/2$ of cash over the subperiod, and the second term is the brokerage cost of making withdrawals from the investment account.

Combining these component costs, the total cost function is given by:

$$Z = \left(\frac{T - I}{2}\right) i \left(\frac{T - I}{T}\right) + b_d + k_d I + \left(\frac{C}{2}\right) i \left(\frac{I}{T}\right) + (b_w + k_w C) \frac{I}{C} \tag{A14–1}$$

The optimal value for C is found by differentiating this function A14–1 with respect to C and setting the derivative equal to zero. This gives

$$C = \sqrt{\frac{2b_w T}{i}} \tag{A14–2}$$

R, the optimum cash balance to withold from the initial receipt, is found by differentiating equation A14–1 with respect to I, obtaining

$$R = T - I = C + T\left(\frac{k_w + k_d}{i}\right) \tag{A14–3}$$

The financial manager, in order to minimize costs, will then withhold R dollars from the initial receipts to cover expenditures for the beginning of the period and will withdraw C dollars from his investment portfolio I/C times per period.

While the Baumol model captures the essential elements of the problem, its restrictive assumptions about the behavior of cash inflows and outflows are probably more applicable to an individual's situation than to a business firm's. For the firm, inflows are likely to be less lumpy, and outflows are likely to be less smooth. Instead, the behavior of cash balances might resemble the pattern of Figure A14–3. Daily changes in the cash balance may be up or down, following an irregular and somewhat unpredictable pattern. When the balance drifts upward for some length of time, a point is reached at which the financial officer orders a transfer of cash to the investment portfolio, and the cash balance is returned to some lower level. When disbursements exceed receipts for some period of time, investments are sold and a transfer is made

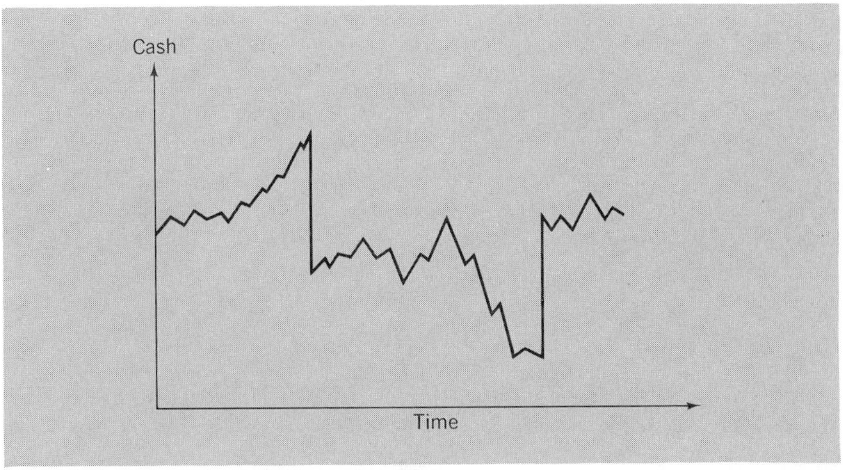

Figure A14–3 Pattern of Receipts and Expenditures for a Firm

to the cash account to restore the cash balance to a higher level. If this particular behavior is typical, then the certainty assumptions of the Baumol model are too restrictive to make it operational.

The Miller-Orr Model[3]

Recently Merton Miller and Daniel Orr expanded the Baumol model by incorporating a stochastic generating process for periodic changes in cash balances so that the cash pattern resembles that shown in Figure A14–3. In contrast to the completely deterministic assumptions of the Baumol model, Miller and Orr assume that net cash flows behave as if they were generated by a "stationary random walk." This means that changes in the cash balance over a given period are random, in both size and direction, and form a normal distribution as the number of periods observed increases. The model allows for a priori knowledge, however, that changes at a certain time have a greater probability of being either positive or negative.

The Miller-Orr model is designed to determine the time and size of transfers between an investment account and the cash account according to a decision process illustrated in Figure A14–4. Changes in cash balances are allowed to wander until they reach some level h at time t_1; they are then reduced to level z, the "return point," by investing $h - z$ dollars in the investment portfolio. Again the cash balance wanders aimlessly until it reaches the minimum balance point, r, at t_2, at which time enough earning assets are sold to return the cash balance to its return point, z. The model is based on a cost function similar to

[3] Merton H. Miller and Daniel Orr, "A Model of the Demand for Money by Firms," *Quarterly Journal of Economics,* LXXX (August 1966), 413–435.

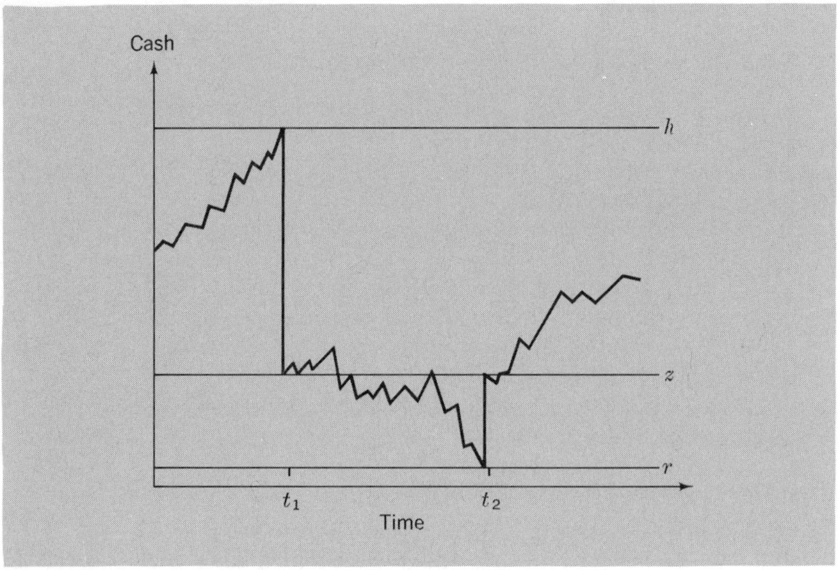

Figure A14–4 The Miller-Orr Cash Management Model

Baumol's, and it includes elements for the cost of making transfers to and from cash and for the opportunity cost of holding cash. The upper limit, h, which cash balances should not be allowed to surpass, and the return point, z, to which the balance is returned after every transfer either to or from the cash account, are computed so as to minimize the cost function. The lower limit is assumed to be given, and it could be the minimum balance required by the banks in which the cash is deposited.

The cost function for the Miller-Orr model can be stated as $E(c) = bE(N)/T + iE(M)$, where $E(N)$ = the expected number of transfers between cash and the investment portfolio during the planning period; b = the cost per transfer; T is the number of days in the planning period; $E(M)$ = the expected average daily balance; and i = the daily rate of interest earned on the investments. The objective is to minimize $E(c)$ by choice of the variables h and z, the upper control limit and the return point, respectively.

The solution as derived by Miller and Orr becomes

$$z^* = \left(\frac{3b\sigma^2}{4i}\right)^{1/3} \qquad \text{(A14–4)}$$
$$h^* = 3z^*$$

for the special case where p (the probability that cash balances will increase) equals .5, and q (the probability that cash balances will decrease) equals .5. The variance of the daily changes in the cash balance is represented by σ^2. As would be expected, a higher transfer cost, b, or variance, σ^2, would imply a greater spread between the upper and lower control limits. In the special case where $p = q = \frac{1}{2}$, the upper control limit will always be 3 times greater than the return point.

Miller and Orr tested their model by applying it to nine months of data on the daily cash balances and purchases and sales of short-term securities of a large industrial company. When the decisions of the model were compared to those actually made by the treasurer of the company, the model was found to produce an average daily cash balance which was about 40 percent *lower* ($160,000 for the model and $275,000 for the treasurer). Looking at it from another side, the model would have been able to match the $275,000 average daily balance with only 80 transactions as compared to the treasurer's 112 actual transactions.

As with most inventory control models, its performance depends not only on how well the conditional predictions (in this case the expected number of transfers and the expected average cash balance) conform to actuality, but also on how well the parameters are estimated. In this model, b, the transfer cost, is sometimes difficult to estimate. In the study made by Miller and Orr, the order costs included such components as "(a) making two or more long-distance phone calls plus fifteen minutes to a half-hour of the assistant treasurer's time, (b) typing up and carefully checking an authorization letter with four copies, (c) carrying the original of the letter to be signed by the treasurer and (d) carrying the copies to the controller's office where special accounts are opened, the entries are posted and further checks of the arithmetic are made."[4] These clerical procedures were thought to be in the magnitude of $20 to $50 per order. In the application of their model, however, Miller and Orr did not rely on their estimate for order costs; instead they tested the model using a series of "assumed" order costs until the model used the same number of transactions as did the treasurer. They could then determine the order cost implied by the treasurer's own action. The results were then used to evaluate the treasurer's performance in managing the cash balances, and, as such, provided valuable information to the treasurer.

The treasurer found, for example, that his action in purchasing securities was often inconsistent. Too often he made small-lot purchases well below the minimum of $h–z$ computed by the model, while at other times he allowed cash balances to drift to as much as double the upper control limit before making a purchase. If it did no more than give the treasurer some perspective about his buying and selling activities, the model was used successfully.

[4] Merton H. Miller and Daniel Orr, *An Application of Control Limit Models to the Management of Corporate Cash Balances,* Proceedings of the Conference on Financial Research and Its Implications for Management, Alexander A. Robichek, ed. (New York: Wiley, 1967).

The Beranek Model[5]

William Beranek has devoted a chapter in his text, *Analysis for Financial Decisions,* to the problem of determining the optimal allocation of available funds between the cash balance and marketable securities. His approach differs from Baumol's in that he includes a probability distribution for expected cash flows and a cost function for the loss of cash discounts and deterioration of credit rating when the firm is caught short of cash. The decision variable in Beranek's model is the allocation of funds between cash and investments at the beginning of the period. Withdrawals from investment are assumed possible only at the end of each planning period.

According to Beranek, it is more helpful for the analysis of cash management problems to regard cash *disbursements* as being directly controllable by management and relatively lumpy and to regard *receipts* as being uncontrollable and continuous. In the certainty case this pattern of cash balance behavior would be the reverse of the saw-tooth pattern assumed by Baumol, and it would look similar to the pattern illustrated in Figure A14–5. To rationalize this approach one can argue that institutional customs and arrangements might cause cash outflows to be concentrated at periodic intervals. Wages and salaries are ordinarily paid weekly or monthly, credit terms for merchandise purchases may allow payment on the tenth and final days of the month, and other significant outflows such as tax and dividend payments will be concentrated at regular intervals. Insofar as cash outflows are controllable and recur in a cyclical manner, the financial manager can predict his needs for cash over a planning period and can invest a portion of the funds that are not expected to be needed during the period.

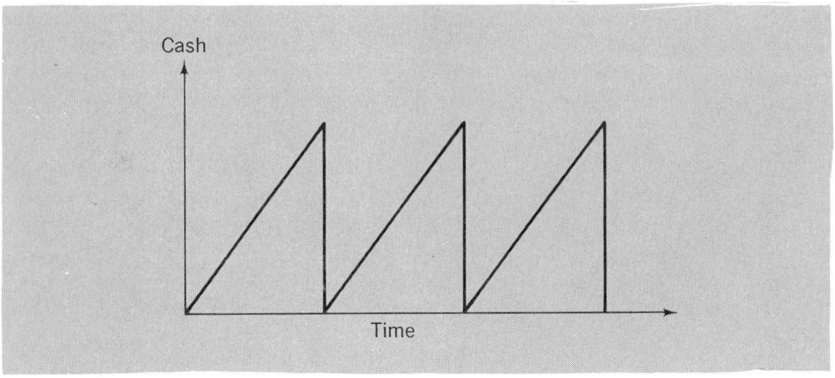

Figure A14–5 Beranek's Pattern of Receipts and Expenditures

[5] William Beranek, *Analysis for Financial Decisions* (Homewood, Ill. Irwin, 1963), pp. 345–387.

In Beranek's model, the financial manager is regarded as having total resources of k dollars available at the beginning of a planning period. He expects his net cash drain (receipts less disbursements) at the end of the period to be y dollars (either positive or negative), with a probability distribution $g(y)$. His objective of maximizing returns by investment in securities is constrained by transactions costs and the risk of being short of cash when funds are needed for expenditures. "Short costs" are regarded by Beranek as consisting of cash discounts foregone and the deterioration of the firm's credit rating when it is unable to meet payments in time. It might be more realistic, however, to think of "short costs" as the cost of borrowing on a line of credit, since the company would undoubtedly prefer short-term borrowing to foregoing cash discounts or allowing its credit rating to deteriorate.

Given the probability distribution of net cash flows, the costs of running short of cash, and the opportunity cost of holding cash balances, Beranek develops a cost function and differentiates it to find the optimal initial cash balance, or the amount of cash that should be on hand at the start of the period. His solution calls for setting the cash balance at a level where, if this critical level is set, the cumulative probability of running short of cash is equal to the ratio d/a, where d = net return on the investment portfolio and a = incremental cost of being short \$1 of cash. Stated in other words, this means that the financial manager should continue shifting resources from the opening cash balance to securities until the expectation that the ending cash balance will be below the critical minimum is equal to the ratio of the incremental net return per dollar of investment to the incremental short cost per dollar.

The White and Norman Model[6]

D. J. White and J. M. Norman developed a model for an English insurance company very similar in spirit to the Beranek model. Investment decisions are assumed to be considered periodically, and cash inflows from premiums and outflows for claims and expenses are assumed to fluctuate randomly according to some known distribution. In addition, another cash outflow for "call-offs" by the stockbrokers is assumed to have an independent distribution function. A penalty rate on overdrafts (borrowings), analagous to Beranek's short-cost function, is also included in the model, while transactions costs are ignored (or implicitly considered in the net rate of return on investments). The opening cash balance that maximizes expected wealth at the end of the period is the relevant decision variable. The optimal solution is a function of Beranek's d, the incremental return per dollar of investment, and the interest rate on overdrafts.

[6] D. J. White and J. M. Norman, "Control of Cash Reserves," *Operational Research Quarterly,* 16, No. 3 (September 1965).

A Comparison of the Models

The models described in this appendix differ in various details but more essentially in the emphasis given to certain costs effecting their solutions. The Baumol and Miller-Orr models give critical emphasis to the costs arising from transfers between the cash account and the investment portfolio. They ignore the alternative of borrowing and concentrate on the liquidation of investments to meet the needs for cash outflows. The Beranek and White-Norman models, however, give critical emphasis to the costs arising from the shortage of cash (the cost of borrowing, from one viewpoint), while transactions costs are only indirectly considered. The latter models ignore the alternative of liquidating investments to meet cash needs. A model that directly incorporates both the possibility of borrowing and the possibility of holding a portfolio of liquid assets would be desirable, since it is not clear that liquidation of investments would always be preferable to borrowing, or vice versa.

Of all the models, the Miller-Orr version appears to be the easiest to implement, if for no other reason than that its decision rules are so simple. Decision models are more likely to be used when their application is easily understood by management. In addition, the Miller-Orr decision model's planning period covers a longer period of time, so it would not have to be revised as often as the Beranek and Norman-White models. In the Beranek and Norman-White versions, information must be fed into the model and a decision derived each time a transfer between cash and securities is being considered. While this must be counted as a disadvantage of these models, it could result in better decisions by making the models more responsive to conditions existing at the time decisions are made.

The Miller-Orr model has an element of flexibility, however, that should not be overlooked. Expectations that cash balances are more likely to either increase or decrease over a given period can be incorporated into the calculation of the optimal values for the decision variables. Thus, if a business is subject to seasonal trends, the optimal control limits can be adjusted for each season by using different values for p and q, the probabilities that cash will increase and decrease, respectively.

The Miller-Orr model is built on the assumption that cash balances behave as if they were generated by a random walk. To the extent that this assumption is erroneous, the model would be of little use to management. If the timing of cash outflows (and perhaps even cash inflows) can be controlled significantly by management, then a model of the Beranek or Norman-White type may be more suitable. In this case, management should not have too much difficulty in forming the subjective probability distributions that are needed for these models. In reality, it would probably be true that cash flows are partly random and partly controllable, so that the applicability of any of the models could only be determined by testing them with actual data.

It should be remembered that decision models of the type discussed in this paper are not intended to be applied blindly. There are, of course, difficulties in estimating parameters and probabilities, as has been pointed out. But even more important, there is often information available to the financial manager that is not directly incorporated into the model. Thus, a model, acting ignorantly and unaware of other relevant information, might provide completely erroneous advice. On the other hand, despite their restrictive assumptions and errors, decision models often perform very well if they capture the essential elements in a decision problem. They should not, however, be used as the final answer to any particular decision; rather, cash management models should be used as a guide to intelligent decision-making, tempered with the manager's own good judgment.

Selected References

Baumol, William J., "The Transactions Demand for Cash: An Inventory Theoretic Approach," *Quarterly Journal of Economics,* LXVI (November 1952).

Beranek, William, *Analysis for Financial Decision,* (Homewood, Ill. Irwin, 1963), pp. 345–381.

Eppen, Gary D., and Eugene F. Fama, "Solutions for Cash-Balance and Simple Dynamic-Portfolio Problems," *Journal of Business,* 41, No. 1 (January 1968), 94–112.

Lutz, Friedrich and Vera Lutz, *The Theory of Investment of the Firm,* (Princeton, N.J.: Princeton University Press, 1951), pp. 205–211.

Miller, Merton H. and Daniel Orr, *An Application of Control Limit Models to the Management of Corporate Cash Balances,* Proceedings of the Conference on Financial Research and Its Implications for Management, Stanford University, Alexander A. Robichek, ed. (New York: Wiley, 1967).

Miller, Merton H. and Daniel Orr, "A Model of the Demand for Money by Firms," *Quarterly Journal of Economics,* (August 1966), 413–435.

Tobin, J., "The Interest Elasticity of Transactions Demand for Cash," *Review of Economics and Statistics,* XXXVIII (August 1956), 241–247.

White, D. J. and J. M. Norman, "Control of Cash Reserves," *Operational Research Quarterly,* 16, No. 3 (September 1965).

15

Major Sources of Short-Term Financing

In Chapter 13 we traced the flow of cash through an illustrative business firm and discussed certain broad principles for managing investments in current assets. We then formalized current asset management somewhat in Chapter 14, where inventory models were considered. In the present chapter we take up the main forms of short-term credit, considering both the characteristics and the source of this credit.

Short-term credit is defined as debt originally scheduled for repayment within one year; in other words, short-term credit is equal to current liabilities minus the current maturities of long-term debt. The three major sources of funds with short maturities are discussed in this chapter. Ranked in descending order by volume of credit supplied to business, the main sources of short-term financing are (1) trade credit between firms, (2) loans from commercial banks, and (3) commercial paper. To some degree these sources also supply funds for longer terms, but their primary importance in short-term financing justifies treatment at this point.

RADE CREDIT[1]

In the ordinary course of events, a firm buys its supplies and materials on credit from other firms, recording the debt as an *account payable.* Accounts payable, or trade credit, as it is commonly called, is the largest single category of short-term credit, and it represents about 40 percent of the current liabilities of nonfinancial corporations. This percentage is somewhat larger for smaller firms; since small companies may not qualify for financing from other sources, they rely rather heavily on trade credit.

Trade credit is a "spontaneous" source of financing in that it arises from ordinary business transactions. For example, suppose a firm makes average purchases of $2,000 a day on terms of net 30. On the average it will owe 30 times $2,000, or $60,000 to its suppliers. If its sales, and consequently its purchases, double, accounts payable will also double to $120,000. The firm will have spontaneously generated an additional $60,000 of financing. Similarly, if the terms of credit are extended from 30 to 40 days, accounts payable will expand from $60,000 to $80,000; thus, lengthening the credit period as well as expanding sales and purchases generates additional financing requirements.

Credit Terms

The terms of sales, or credit terms, describe the payment obligation of the buyer. The four main factors that influence the length of credit terms are outlined below.

1. ECONOMIC NATURE OF PRODUCT. Commodities with high sales turnover are sold on relatively short credit terms; the buyer resells the product rapidly, generating cash that enables him to pay the supplier. Groceries have a high turnover, but perishability also plays a role. The

[1] In Chapter 13, we discussed trade credit from the point of view of minimizing investment in current assets. In the present chapter we look at "the other side of the coin," viewing trade credit as a *source* of financing rather than as a *use* of financing. In Chapter 14, the use of trade credit by our customers resulted in an asset investment called "accounts receivable." In the present chapter, the use of trade credit gives rise to a short-term obligation generally called "accounts payable."

credit extended for fresh fruits and vegetables might run from 5 to 10 days, whereas the credit extended on canned fruits and vegetables would more likely be 15 to 30 days. Terms for items that have a slow retail turnover, such as jewelry, may run six months or longer.

2. SELLER CIRCUMSTANCES. Financially weak sellers must require cash or exceptionally short credit terms. For example, farmers sell livestock to meat-packing companies on a cash basis. In some industries, variations in credit terms can be used as a sales promotion device. Although the use of credit as a selling device endangers sound credit management, the practice does occur, especially when the seller's industry has excess capacity. Also, a large seller could use his position to impose relatively short credit terms. However, the reverse appears more often in practice; that is, financially strong sellers are suppliers of funds to smaller firms.

3. BUYER CIRCUMSTANCES. In general, financially sound retailers who sell on credit may, in turn, receive slightly longer terms. Some classes of retailers regarded as selling in particularly risky areas (such as clothing) receive extended credit terms, but they are offered large discounts to encourage early payment.

4. CASH DISCOUNTS. A cash discount is a reduction in price based on payment within a specified period. The costs of not taking cash discounts often exceed the rate of interest at which the buyer can borrow, so it is important that a firm be cautious in its use of trade credit as a source of financing—it could be quite expensive.[2] If the firm borrows and takes the cash discount, the period during which accounts payable remain on the books is reduced. The effective length of credit is thus influenced by the size of discounts offered.

ILLUSTRATIVE CREDIT TERMS. Credit terms typically express the amount of the cash discount and the date of its expiration, as well as the final due date. Probably the most frequently encountered terms are 2/10, net 30. In other words, if payment is made within 10 days

[2] The following equation may be used for calculating the cost of not taking discounts:

$$\text{cost} = \frac{\text{discount percent}}{(100 - \text{discount percent})} \times \frac{360}{(\text{final due date} - \text{discount period})}$$

The denominator in the first term (100 — discount percent) equals the funds made available by not taking the discount. To illustrate, the cost of not taking a discount when the terms are 2/10, net 30 is computed.

$$\text{cost} = \frac{2}{98} \times \frac{360}{20} = 0.0204 \times 18 = 36.72\%$$

of the invoice date, a 2 percent cash discount is allowed. If the cash discount is not taken, payment is due 30 days after the date of invoice. The cost of not taking cash discounts can be substantial, as shown here.

CREDIT TERMS	COST OF CREDIT IF CASH DISCOUNT NOT TAKEN
1/10, net 20	36.36%
1/10, net 30	18.18%
2/10, net 20	73.44%
2/10, net 30	36.72%

Employment of Trade Credit

Trade credit has double-edged significance for the firm. It is a source of credit for financing purchases and a way to use funds by which a firm finances credit sales to customers. For example, if a firm sells on the average $3,000 of goods a day with an average collection period of 40 days, it will have accounts receivable at any balance sheet date of approximately $120,000.

If the firm buys $2,000 worth of materials a day and the balance is outstanding for 20 days, accounts payable will average $40,000. The firm is extending net credit of $80,000, the difference between accounts receivable and accounts payable.

It is important, therefore, that the firm make the maximum use of trade credit as a source of funds, but at the same time it should minimize the extent to which its own funds are tied up in accounts receivable.

Advantages of Trade Credit as Source of Financing

Trade credit, a customary part of doing business in most lines of activity, is convenient and informal. A firm that does not qualify for credit from a financial institution may receive trade credit because previous experience has familiarized the seller with the credit-worthiness of his customer. As the seller knows the merchandizing practices of the line of business, he is usually in a good position to judge the capacity of his customer and the risk of selling to him on credit. The amount of trade credit fluctuates with the buyer's purchases, subject to any credit limits that may be operative.

Whether trade credit costs more or less than other forms of financing is a moot question. Sometimes trade credit can be surprisingly expensive to the buyer. The user often does not have other alternative forms of financing available, and the costs to the buyer may be commensurate with the risks to the seller. But in some instances trade credit is used simply because the user may not realize how expensive it is. In such circumstances careful financial analysis may lead to the substitution of alternative forms of financing for trade credit.

At the other extreme, trade credit may represent a virtual subsidy or sales promotion device offered by the seller. The authors know, for example, of cases where manufacturers quite literally supplied *all* the financing for new firms by selling on credit terms substantially longer than those of the new company. In one instance a manufacturer, anxious to obtain a dealership in a particular area, made a loan to the new company to cover operating expenses during the initial phases and geared the payment of accounts payable to cash receipts. Even in such instances, however, the buying firm must be careful that it is not really paying a hidden financing cost in the form of higher product prices than could be obtained elsewhere.[3]

SHORT-TERM FINANCING BY COMMERCIAL BANKS

Commercial bank lending appears on the balance sheet as *notes payable* and is second in importance to trade credit as a source of short-term financing. Banks occupy a pivotal position in the short-term and intermediate-term money markets. Their influence is greater than appears from the dollar amounts they lend, because the banks provide marginal funds. As a firm's financing needs grow, the banks are called upon to provide the additional funds. If the request is denied, often the alternative is to slow down the rate of growth or to cut back operations.

Characteristics of Loans from Commercial Banks

The main characteristics of lending patterns of commercial banks are briefly described.

FORMS OF LOANS. A single loan obtained from a bank by a business firm is not different in principle from a loan obtained by an individual. In fact, it is often difficult to distinguish a bank loan to a small business from a personal loan. A single loan is obtained by signing a conventional

[3] For numerous examples, see Robert P. Hungate, "Inter-business Financing" (Unpublished Ph.D. dissertation, University of California, Los Angeles, January 1961).

promissory note. Repayment is made in a lump sum at maturity (when the note is due) or in installments throughout the life of the loan.

A *line of credit* is a formal or an informal understanding between the bank and the borrower concerning the maximum loan balance the bank will allow the borrower. For example, a bank loan officer may indicate to a financial manager that the bank regards his firm as "good" for up to $80,000 for the forthcoming year. Subsequently, the manager signs a promissory note for $15,000 for 90 days—he is said to be "taking down" $15,000 of his total line of credit. This amount is credited to the firm's checking account at the bank. At maturity, the checking account will be charged for the amount of the loan. Interest may be deducted in advance or paid at maturity of the loan. Before repayment of the $15,000, the firm may borrow additional amounts up to $65,000.

A more formal procedure may be followed if the firm is quite large. To illustrate, Chrysler Corporation arranged a line of credit for over $100 million with a group of banks. The banks were formally committed to lend Chrysler the funds if they were needed. Chrysler, in turn, paid a commitment fee of approximately ¼ of 1 percent on the unused balance of the commitment to compensate the banks for tying up their funds.

SIZE OF LOANS. Banks make loans of all sizes. The bulk of loans from commercial banks by dollar amount is obtained by firms with total assets of $5 million and more. But, by number of loans, firms with total assets of $50,000 and less account for about 40 percent of bank loans.

MATURITY. Commercial banks concentrate on the short-term lending market. Short-term loans make up about two thirds of bank loans by dollar amount, whereas "term loans" (loans with maturities longer than one year) make up only one third.

SECURITY. If a potential borrower is a questionable credit risk or if his financing needs exceed the amount that the loan officer of the bank considers to be prudent on an unsecured basis, some form of security is required. More than one half the dollar value of bank loans is secured; the forms of security are described later in this chapter. In terms of the number of bank loans, two thirds are secured or endorsed by a third party who guarantees payment of the loan in the event the borrower defaults.

MINIMUM BALANCE. Banks typically require that a regular borrower maintain a minimum checking account balance equal to 15 or 20 percent of the outstanding loan. These balances, which are commonly called *compensating balances*, are a method of raising the effective interest rate. For example, if a firm needs $80,000 to pay off outstanding obligations, but must maintain a 20 percent compensating balance, it must borrow $100,000 to be able to obtain the required $80,000. If the stated interest rate is 5 percent, the effective cost is actually 6¼ percent—$5,000 divided by $80,000 equals 6.25 percent.[4]

REPAYMENT OF BANK LOANS. Because the bulk of bank deposits is subject to withdrawal on demand, commercial banks seek to prevent firms from using bank credit for permanent financing. A bank may therefore require its borrowers to "clean up" their short-term bank loans for at least one month each year. If a firm is unable to become free of bank debt at least part of each year, it is using bank financing for permanent needs and should develop additional sources of long-term or permanent financing.

COST OF COMMERCIAL BANK LOANS. Loans from commercial banks generally run about 4 to 7 percent, with the effective rate depending upon the characteristics of the firm and the level of interest rates in the economy. If the firm can qualify as a "prime risk" because of its size and financial strength, the rate of interest will be one half to three quarters of 1 percent above the rediscount rate charged by federal reserve banks to commercial banks. On the other hand, a small firm with below average financial ratios may be required to provide collateral security and to pay an effective rate of interest of 10 percent or more.

Determination of the effective or true rate of interest on a loan depends upon the stated rate of interest and the method of charging interest by the lender. If the interest is paid at the maturity of the loan, the stated rate of interest is the effective rate of interest. If the bank deducts the interest in advance (*discounts* the loan), the effective rate of interest is increased. On a $10,000 loan for one year at 5 percent, the discount is $500 and the borrower obtains the use of only $9,500. The effective rate of interest is

$$\frac{\$500}{\$9{,}500} = 5.3\%$$

If the loan is repaid in twelve monthly installments, the effective rate of interest is even higher. In this event the borrower pays $500 for the use of about one half the amount he receives. The amount received is $10,000 or $9,500, depending upon the methods of charging interest, but the *average* amount outstanding during the year is only

[4] Note, however, that if the compensating balance is set as a minimum monthly *average*, and if the firm would maintain this average anyway, the compensating balance requirement does not entail higher effective rates.

$5,000 or $4,750. If interest is paid at maturity, the effective rate would be approximately

$$\frac{\$500}{\$5{,}000} = 10\%$$

Under the discounting method, the effective cost of the installment loan would be approximately

$$\frac{\$500}{\$4{,}750} = 10.53\%$$

The point to note here is that interest is paid on the *original* amount of the loan, not on the amount actually outstanding (the declining balance), and this causes the effective interest rate to be approximately double the stated rate.

Choice of Bank or Banks

Banks have close relations with their borrowers. Since there is considerable personal contact over the years, the business problems of the borrower are frequently discussed; thus the bank often provides informal management counseling services. A potential borrower seeking bank relations should recognize the important differences among banks as potential sources of funds. These differences can be summarized into the following seven points.

1. Banks have different basic policies toward risk. Some banks are inclined to follow relatively conservative lending practices, others engage in what are properly termed "creative banking practices." The policies reflect partly the personalities of officers of the bank and partly the characteristics of the bank's deposit liabilities. Thus a bank with fluctuating deposit liabilities in a static community will tend to be a conservative lender. A bank whose deposits are growing with little interruption may follow "liberal" credit policies. A large bank with broad diversification over geographical regions or among industries served can obtain the benefit of combining and averaging risks. Thus, marginal credit risks that might be unacceptable to a small bank or to a specialized unit bank can be pooled by a branch banking system to reduce the over-all risks of a group of marginal accounts.

2. Some bank loan officers are active in providing counsel and in stimulating development loans with firms in their early and formative years.

Certain banks have specialized departments to make loans to firms expected to become growth firms. The personnel of these departments can provide considerable counseling to customers.

3. Banks differ in the extent to which they will support the activities of the borrower in bad times. This characteristic is referred to as the degree of *loyalty* of the banks. Some banks may put considerable pressure on a business to liquidate its loans when the firm's outlook becomes clouded, whereas others will stand by the firm and work diligently to help it attain a more favorable condition.

4. The fourth characteristic by which banks differ is the degree of deposit stability. Instability arises not only from fluctuations in the level of deposits but also from the composition of deposits. Deposits can take the form of demand deposits (checking accounts) or time deposits (savings accounts, certificates of deposit, Christmas clubs). Total deposits tend to be more stable when time deposits are substantial. Differences in deposit stability go a long way toward explaining differences in the extent to which the banks are willing or able to help the borrower work himself out of difficulties or even crises.

5. Banks differ greatly in the degree of loan specialization. Larger banks have separate departments specializing in different kinds of loans, such as real estate, installment loans, and commercial loans, among others. Within these broad categories there may be a specialization by line of business, such as steel, machinery, or textiles. The strengths of smaller banks are likely to reflect the nature of the business and the economic environment in which the banks operate. They tend to become specialists in specific lines, such as oil, construction, and agriculture, to name a few. The borrower can obtain more creative cooperation and more active support if he goes to the bank that has the greatest experience and familiarity with his particular type of business. The financial manager should therefore choose his bank with care. A bank that is excellent for one firm may be unsatisfactory for another.

6. The size of a bank can be an important characteristic. Since the maximum loan a bank can make to any one customer is generally limited to 10 percent of capital accounts (capital stock plus surplus accounts), it will generally not be appropriate for large firms to develop borrowing relationships with small banks.

7. With the heightened competition between commercial banks and other financial institutions, the aggressiveness of banks has increased. Modern commercial banks now offer a wide range of financial and business services. Most large banks have business development departments that provide counseling to firms and serve as intermediaries on a wide variety of their requirements.

COMMERCIAL PAPER

Nature

Commercial paper consists of promissory notes of *large* firms and is sold primarily to other business firms, insurance companies, pension funds, and banks. Although the amounts of commercial paper outstanding are less than 5 percent of bank loans outstanding, this form of financing is important to particular lines of business.

Maturity and Cost

Maturities of commercial paper vary from two to six months, with an average of about five months. The rates on prime commercial paper vary, but they are generally about ½ of 1 percent below those on prime business loans.

Use

The use of the open market for commercial paper is restricted to a comparatively small number of concerns that are exceptionally good credit risks. Dealers prefer to handle the paper of concerns whose net worth is $5 million or more and whose annual borrowing exceeds $500,000.

Appraisal of Use

A large number of advantages are claimed for the commercial paper market. (1) It permits the broadest and most advantageous distribution of paper. (2) It provides more funds at lower rates than do other methods. (3) The borrower avoids the inconvenience and expense of financing arrangements with a number of institutions, each of which requires a compensating balance. (4) Publicity and prestige accrue to the borrower as his product and his paper become more widely known. (5) Finally, the commercial paper dealer frequently offers valuable advice to his clients.

A basic limitation of the commercial paper market is that the size of the funds available is limited to the excess liquidity that corporations, the main suppliers of funds, may have at any particular time. Another disadvantage is that a debtor who is in temporary financial difficulty receives little consideration, because commercial paper dealings are impersonal. Bank relations, on the other hand, are much more personal; a bank is much more likely to help a good customer weather a temporary storm than is a commercial paper dealer.

USE OF SECURITY IN SHORT-TERM FINANCING

It is ordinarily better to borrow on an unsecured basis, as the bookkeeping costs of secured loans are often high, but frequently a potential borrower's credit rating is not sufficiently strong to justify the loan. If the loan can be secured by the borrower's putting up some form of collateral to be claimed by the lender in the event of default, then the lender may extend credit to an otherwise unacceptable firm. Similarly, a firm that could borrow on an unsecured basis may elect to use security if it finds that this will induce lenders to quote a lower interest rate.

Several different types of collateral can be employed—marketable stocks or bonds, land or buildings, equipment, inventory, and accounts receivable. Marketable securities make excellent collateral, but few firms hold portfolios of stocks and bonds. Similarly, real property (land and buildings) and equipment are good forms of collateral, but they are generally used as security for long-term loans. The bulk of secured short-term business borrowing involves the pledge of short-term assets—accounts receivable or inventories. These two types of loans are described in the following two sections.

FINANCING ACCOUNTS RECEIVABLE

Accounts receivable financing involves either the *pledge* or the *sale* of receivables. The pledging of accounts receivable is called *accounts receivable discounting.* The process is characterized by the fact that the lender takes the receivables but has recourse to the borrower (seller); if the person or the firm that bought the goods does not pay, the selling firm must take the loss. In other words, the risk of default on the accounts receivable pledged remains with the borrower. Also, the buyer of the goods is not ordinarily notified about the discounting of the receivables. The financial institution that lends on the security of accounts receivable will generally be either a commercial bank or one of the large industrial finance companies such as CIT, Commercial Credit, Heller, and the like.

Factoring, the second basic type of receivables financing, is the purchase of accounts receivable by the lender without recourse to the borrower (seller). The buyer of the goods is notified of the transfer and makes payment directly to the lender. Since the factoring firm assumes the risk of default on bad accounts, it must do the credit checking; so it may be fairly said that factors provide not only money but also a credit department for the borrower. Incidentally, the same financial institutions that discount accounts receivable also serve as factors. Thus, depending on the circumstances and the wishes of the borrower, a financial institution will provide either form of receivables financing.

Procedure for Discounting Accounts Receivable

The financing of accounts receivable is initiated by a legally binding agreement between the seller of the goods and the financing institution. The agreement sets forth in detail procedures to be followed and legal obligations of both parties. Once the working relation has been established, the seller will periodically take a batch of invoices to the financing institution. The lender reviews the invoices and makes an appraisal of the buyers. Invoices of companies that do not meet the lender's credit standards will not be accepted for discounting. The financial institution seeks to protect itself at every phase of the operation. Selection of sound invoices is the essential first step in safeguarding the financial institution. If the buyer of the goods does not pay the invoice, the bank still has recourse against the seller of the goods. However, if many buyers default, the seller will doubtlessly be unable to meet his obligation to the financial institution.

Accounts receivable financing is, to a considerable extent, a mass financing operation in which large numbers of invoices or accounts receivable are handled. The smaller the average size of the invoice, the greater the administrative work for the financing institution. Before World War II, the average loan balance outstanding for approximately half the borrowers using accounts receivable financing was less than $100,000, indicating that firms using accounts receivable financing were typically small firms. The development of accounts receivable financing has therefore contributed to the financing of small business.

Procedure for Factoring Accounts Receivable

The procedure for factoring is somewhat different from that for discounting. Again, an agreement between the seller and the factor is made to specify legal obligations and procedural arrangements. When the seller receives an order from a buyer, a credit approval slip is written and immediately sent to the factoring company for a credit check. If the factor does not approve the sale, the seller will generally refuse to fill the order. This procedure informs the seller prior to the sale about the buyer's credit-worthiness and acceptability to the factor. If the sale is approved, shipment is made and the invoice is stamped to notify the buyer to make payment directly to the factoring company.

The factor performs three functions in carrying out the normal procedure as outlined above: (1) credit checking, (2) lending, and (3) risk bearing. The seller can select various combinations of these functions by changing provisions in the factoring agreement. For example, a small or a medium-sized firm can avoid establishing a credit department. The factor's service might well be less costly than a department that may have excess capacity for the firm's credit volume. At the same time, if the firm uses part of the time of a noncredit specialist to perform credit checking, lack of education, training, and experience may result in excessive losses.

The seller may utilize the factor to perform the credit-checking and risk-taking functions but not the lending function. The following procedure will be carried out on receipt of a $10,000 order. The factor checks and approves the invoices. The goods are shipped on terms n/30. Payment is made to the factor, who remits to the seller. But assume that the factor has received only $5,000 by the end of the credit period. He must still remit $10,000 to the seller (less his fee, of course). If the remaining $5,000 is never paid, the factor sustains a $5,000 loss.

Now consider the more typical situation in which the factor performs a lending function by making payment in advance of collection. The goods are shipped and, even though payment is not due for 30 days, the factor immediately makes funds available to the seller. Suppose $10,000 of goods is shipped; the factoring commission for credit checking is 2½ percent of the invoice price, or $250; and the interest expense is computed at a 9 percent annual rate on the invoice balance, or $75.[5] The seller's accounting entry will read as follows.

[5] Since the interest is only for one month, we take $\frac{1}{12}$ of the stated rate, 9 percent, and multiply this by the $10,000 invoice price.

$$\tfrac{1}{12} \times 0.09 \times \$10{,}000 = \$75$$

Note that the effective rate of interest is really above 9 percent, because the borrower does not get the full $10,000. In many instances, however, the factoring

Cash	$9,175	
Interest expense	75	
Factoring commission	250	
Reserve: due from factor on collection of account	500	
Accounts receivable		$10,000

The $500 "due from factor on collection of account" in the entry is a reserve established by the factor to cover disputes between sellers and buyers on damaged goods, goods returned by the buyers to the seller, and failure to make outright sale of goods. The amount is paid to the seller firm when the factor collects on the account.

Factoring is normally a continuous process instead of the single cycle described above. The seller of the goods receives orders; he transmits the purchase orders to the factor for approval; on approval, the goods are shipped; the factor advances the money to the seller; the buyers pay the factor when payment is due; and the factor periodically remits any excess reserve to the seller of the goods. Once a routine is established, a continuous circular flow of goods and funds takes place between the seller, the buyers of the goods, and the factor.

Cost of Receivables Financing

Accounts receivable discounting and factoring services are convenient and advantageous, but they can be costly. The credit-checking commission is 1 to 3 percent of the amount of invoices accepted by the factor. The cost of money is reflected in the interest rate of 6 to 10 percent charged on the unpaid balance of the funds advanced by the factor. Where the risk to the factor is excessive, he purchases the invoices (either with or without recourse) at discounts from face value.

Evaluation of Receivables Financing

It cannot be said categorically that accounts receivable financing is always either a good or a poor method of raising funds for an individual business. Among the advantages is, first, the flexibility of this source of financing. As the sales of a firm expand and it needs more financing, a larger volume of invoices is generated automatically. Because the dollar amounts of discounted invoices vary directly with sales, the amount of readily available financing increases. Second, receivables or invoices provide security for a loan that a firm might otherwise be unable to obtain. Third, factoring provides the services of a credit department

contract would call for interest to be computed on the invoice price *less* the factoring commission and the reserve account.

that might otherwise be available to the firm only under much more expensive conditions.

Accounts receivable financing also has disadvantages. First, when invoices are numerous and relatively small in amount, the administrative costs involved may render this method of financing inconvenient and expensive. Second, the firm is using a highly liquid asset as security. For a long time, accounts receivable financing was frowned upon by most trade creditors. In fact, such financing was regarded as confession of a firm's unsound financial position. It is no longer regarded in this light, and many sound firms engage in receivables discounting or factoring. However, the traditional attitude causes some trade creditors to refuse to sell on credit to a firm that is discounting its receivables on grounds that to do so removes from the trade creditor a possible source of repayment.

Economically, the increased use of receivables financing has represented a substantial contribution to the financing of small businesses. It makes possible the financing of smaller firms and marginal credit risks for which other financing might not be available.

Future Use of Receivables Financing

We might make a prediction at this point—in the future, accounts receivable financing will increase in relative importance. Computer technology is rapidly advancing toward the point where credit records of individuals and firms can be kept in computer memory units. Systems have been devised so that a store can have a unit on hand that, when an individual's magnetic credit card is inserted into a box, gives a signal that his credit is "good" and that a bank is willing to "buy" the receivable created when the store completes the sale. The cost of handling invoices will be greatly reduced over present-day costs because the new systems will be so highly automated. This will make it possible to use accounts receivable financing for very small sales, and it will reduce the cost of all receivables financing. The net result will be a marked expansion of accounts receivable financing.

INVENTORY FINANCING

A relatively large volume of credit is secured by business inventories. If a firm is a relatively good credit risk, the mere existence of the inventory may be a sufficient basis for receiving an unsecured loan. If the firm is a relatively poor risk, the lending institution may insist upon security, which often takes the form of a chattel mortgage on the inventory. Alternatively, trust receipts or field warehouse receipts can be used to secure the loan. These methods of using inventories as security are discussed below.

Chattel Mortgage Security[6]

The chattel mortgage gives the lending institution a lien against property of the borrower. The chattel mortgage is sometimes inconvenient if the lending institution is really worried about the credit position of the borrowing firm, because, in order to establish a valid chattel mortgage, a meticulous description of the items and recordation with the county recorder may be required. Inventory description and legal control are difficult if the inventory is fluid. For example, a fruit and vegetable canner has inventory on hand from which he makes sales and into which additional inventories flow as the canning process takes place. In order to maintain the continuous legal validity of the chattel mortgage, a change in the inventory's items might require a change in the description of the inventory. Furthermore, in some jurisdictions a chattel mortgage on stock in trade is invalid.

Trust Receipts

Because of the weaknesses of the chattel mortgage, another type of security is used, the trust receipt. A trust receipt is an instrument acknowledging that the borrower holds the goods in trust for the lender. When trust receipts are used, the borrowing firm, on receiving funds from the lender, conveys a trust receipt for the goods. The goods can be stored in a public warehouse or held on the premises of the borrower. The trust receipt provides that the goods are held in trust for the lender or are segregated in the borrower's premises on behalf of the lender, and proceeds from the sale of goods held under trust receipts are transmitted to the lender at the end of each day.

One defect of trust receipt financing is the requirement that a trust receipt must be issued for specific goods. For example, if the security is bags of coffee beans, the trust receipts would have to indicate the bags by number. In order to validate its trust receipts, the lending institution will have to send a man to the premises of the borrower to see that the bag numbers are correctly listed. Furthermore, complex legal

[6] A Uniform Commercial Code has been devised to make inventory financing, among other things, a much simpler process. Under the code, which has already been adopted by many states, inventories can be pledged without the necessity of identifying individual items.

requirements of trust receipts require the attention of a bank officer. Problems are compounded if borrowers are widely separated geographically from the lender. To offset these inconveniences, field warehousing is coming into wide use as a method of securing loans with inventory.

Field Warehouse Financing

Like trust receipt and chattel mortgage financing, warehouse financing uses inventory as security. A public warehouse represents an independent third party engaged in the business of storing goods. Sometimes a public warehouse is not practical because of the bulkiness of goods and the expense of transporting them to and from the borrower's premises. Field warehouse financing represents an economical method of inventory financing in which the warehouse is established at the place of the borrower. To provide inventory supervision, the lending institution employs a third party in the arrangement, the field warehousing company. This company acts as the control (or supervisory) agent for the lending institution.

A field warehouse can be illustrated very simply. Suppose that a potential borrower has stacked iron in an open yard on his premises. A field warehouse can be established if a field warehousing concern places a temporary fence around the iron and erects a sign which says "This is a field warehouse supervised and conducted by the Smith Field Warehousing Corporation." These are minimal conditions, of course.

The example illustrates the two elements in the establishment of a warehouse: (1) public notification of the field warehouse arrangement and (2) supervision of the field warehouse by a custodian of the field warehouse concern. When the field warehousing operation is relatively small, the second condition is sometimes violated by hiring an employee of the borrower to supervise the inventory. This practice is viewed as undesirable by the lending institution because there is no control over the collateral by a person independent of the borrowing concern.[7]

The field warehouse financing operation is described best by a specific illustration. Assume that a tomato canner is interested in financing his operations by bank borrowing. The canner has sufficient funds to finance

[7] This lack of independent control was the main cause of the breakdown that resulted in the huge losses connected with the loans to the Allied Crude Vegetable Oil Company headed by Anthony (Tino) DeAngelis. American Express Field Warehousing Company hired men from Allied's staff as custodians. Their dishonesty was not discovered because of another breakdown—the fact that the American Express touring inspector did not actually take a physical inventory of the warehouses. As a consequence, the swindle was not discovered until losses running into the hundreds of millions of dollars had been suffered. Cf. Norman C. Miller, *The Great Salad Oil Swindle,* (Baltimore, Md.: Penguin Books, 1965), pp. 72–77.

15 to 20 percent of his operations during the canning season. These funds are adequate to purchase and process an initial batch of tomatoes. As the cans are put into boxes and rolled into the storerooms, the canner needs additional funds for both raw materials and labor.

Because of the credit rating of the canner, the bank decides that a field warehousing operation is necessary to secure its lending. The field warehouse is established, and the custodian notifies the lending institution of the description by number of the boxes of canned tomatoes in storage and under his control. Thereupon the lending institution establishes for the canner a deposit on which he can draw. From this point on, the bank finances the operations. The canner needs only enough cash to initiate the cycle. The farmers bring more tomatoes; the canner processes them; the cans are boxed, and the boxes are put into the field warehouse; field warehouse receipts are drawn up and sent to the bank; the bank establishes further deposits for the canner based on the receipts; the canner can draw on the deposits to continue the cycle.

Of course, the canner's ultimate objective is to sell the canned tomatoes. As the canner receives purchase orders, he transmits them to the bank and the bank directs the custodian to release the inventories. It is agreed that, as remittances are received by the canner, they will be turned over to the bank. These remittances by the canner pay off the loans made by the bank.

Typically, a seasonal pattern exists. At the beginning of the tomato harvesting and canning season, the canner's cash needs and loan requirements begin to rise and reach a maximum by the end of the canning season. It is hoped that, just before the new canning season begins, the canner has sold a sufficient volume to have paid off the loan completely. If for some reason the canner has had a bad year, the bank may carry him over another year to enable him to work off his inventory.

Acceptable Products

In addition to canned foods, which account for about 17 percent of all field warehouse loans, many other product inventories provide a basis for field warehouse financing. Some of these are miscellaneous groceries, which represent about 13 percent; lumber products, about 10 percent; and coal and coke, about 6 percent.

These products are relatively nonperishable and are sold in well-developed, organized markets. Nonperishability protects the lender, if he should have to take over the security. For this reason a bank would not make a field warehousing loan on such perishables as fresh fish. However, frozen fish, which can be stored for a long time, can be field warehoused. An organized market aids the lender in disposing of an inventory which it takes over. Banks are not desirous of going into the canning or the fish business. They want to be able to dispose of an inventory within a matter of hours and with the expenditure of a minimum amount of time.

Cost of Financing

The fixed costs of a field warehousing arrangement are relatively high; this type of financing is therefore not suitable for an extremely small firm. If a field warehouse company sets up the field warehouse itself, it will typically set a minimum charge of about $350 to $600 a year, plus about 1 or 2 percent of the amount of credit extended to the borrower. In addition, the financing institution will charge from 6 to 10 percent interest. The minimum size of a field warehousing operation requires an inventory of about $100,000.

Appraisal

There are several advantages in the use of field warehouse financing as a source of funds for business firms. First, the amount of funds available is flexible, because the financing is tied to the growth of inventories, which in turn is related directly to financing needs. Second, the field warehousing arrangement increases the acceptability of inventories as loan collateral. Some inventories would not be accepted by a bank as security without a field warehousing arrangement. Third, the necessity for inventory control, safekeeping, and the use of specialists in warehousing has resulted in improved warehouse practices. The services of the field warehouse companies have often saved money for the firm in spite of the costs of financing mentioned above. The field warehouse company may suggest inventory practices which reduce the labor that the firm has to employ, and reduce inventory damage and loss as well.

The major disadvantage of a field warehousing operation is the fixed cost element, which reduces the feasibility of this form of financing for small firms.

SUMMARY

Short-term credit is defined as debt originally scheduled for repayment within one year. This chapter has discussed the three major sources of short-term credit—trade credit between firms, loans from commercial banks, and commercial paper.

Trade Credit

Trade credit, represented by accounts payable, is the largest single category of short-term credit and is especially important for smaller firms. Trade credit is a *spontaneous source of financing* in that it arises from ordinary business transactions; as sales increase, so does the supply of financing from accounts payable.

Although trade credit is a most useful method of financing, it is important that the financial manager be aware of its implicit cost. If discounts are offered for prompt payment, as they very often are, then the cost of not taking the discount amounts to an interest payment. Under certain common discount procedures, the implicit interest cost of not taking discounts is quite high. For example, under terms of 2/10, net 30, where a 2 percent discount is allowed if payment is made within 10 days and the account is payable within 30 days, if the discount is not taken, the implicit interest cost is over 36 percent.

Bank Credit

Bank credit occupies a pivotal position in the short-term money market. Banks provide the marginal credit that allows firms to expand more rapidly than is possible through retained earnings and trade credit; to be denied bank credit often means that a firm must slow its rate of growth.

Bank loans are generally represented by *notes payable.* The loan itself is frequently arranged prior to the time it is needed—this is called *establishing a line of credit.* To insure that loan customers are also deposit customers, and also to raise the effective rate of interest on loans, banks frequently require minimum deposit balances known as *compensating balances.* When used, compensating balances are generally set at about 15 to 20 percent of the outstanding amount of the loan.

Bank interest rates are quoted in three ways—regular compound interest, discount interest, and installment interest where the interest charges are computed on the original amount of the loan rather than on the outstanding balance. Regular interest needs no adjustment—it is "correct" as stated. Discount interest requires a small upward adjustment to make it comparable to regular compound interest rates. Installment interest rates require a large adjustment, and frequently the true interest rate is double the quoted rate for an installment loan.

Commercial Paper

Bank loans are personal in the sense that the financial manager meets with the banker, discusses the terms of the loan with him, and reaches an agreement that involves direct and personal negotiation. Commercial paper, however, although it is physically quite similar to a bank loan, is sold in a broad, impersonal market. A California firm might, for example, sell commercial paper notes to a bank in the Midwest.

Only the very strongest firms are able to use the commercial paper markets—the nature of these markets is such that the firm selling the paper must have a reputation so good that buyers of the paper are willing to buy the paper without any sort of credit check. *Interest rates* in the commercial paper market are the lowest available to business borrowers.

A disadvantage of commercial paper *vis-â-vis* bank credit, however, is that if a firm gets into any kind of temporary trouble, it will be completely excluded from the commercial paper market. Commercial banks, on the other hand, are frequently willing to lend support to a long-time customer even when it is having problems. This can be a big advantage to bank credit.

Use of Security in Short-Term Financing

It is ordinarily better to borrow on an unsecured basis, but frequently a potential borrower's credit rating is not sufficiently strong to justify the loan. If the loan can be secured by the borrower's putting up some forms of collateral to be claimed by the lender in the event of default, the lender may extend credit to an otherwise unacceptable firm. The most common types of collateral used for short-term credit are inventories and accounts receivable.

Accounts receivable financing can be done either by *pledging the receivables* (discounting) or by selling them outright, frequently called *factoring*. When the receivables are pledged, the borrower retains the risk that the person or firm who owes the receivable will not pay; this risk is typically passed on to the lender when factoring is involved. Because the factor takes the risk of default, he will typically investigate the purchaser's credit; therefore, the factor can perform three services—a lending function, a risk-bearing function, and a credit-checking function. When receivables are pledged, the lender typically performs only the first of these three functions. Consequently, factoring is generally quite a bit more expensive than is pledging accounts receivable.

Inventory loans are rather difficult to administer under most circumstances. For certain types of inventory, however, the technique known as *field warehousing* is used to provide adequate security to the lender. Under a field warehousing arrangement, the inventory is under the physical control of a warehouse company, which releases the inventory only on order from the lending institution. Canned goods, lumber, steel, coal, and other standardized products are the type of goods usually covered in field warehouse arrangements.

QUESTIONS

15–1 It is inevitable that firms will obtain a certain amount of their financing in the form of trade credit, which is, to some extent, a free source of funds. What are some other factors that lead firms to use trade credit?

15–2 "Commercial paper interest rates are always lower than bank loan rates to a given borrower. Nevertheless, many firms perfectly capable of selling commercial paper employ higher cost bank credit." Discuss the statement, indicating (a) why commercial paper rates are lower than bank rates and (b) why firms might use bank credit in spite of its higher cost.

15–3 "Trade credit has an explicit interest rate cost if discounts are available but not taken. There are also some intangible costs associated with the failure to take discounts." Discuss.

15–4 What are some of the reasons that lead firms to offer high cash discounts?

15–5 A large manufacturing firm that had been selling its products on a 3/10, n/30 basis changed its credit terms to 1/20, n/90. What changes might be anticipated on the balance sheets of the manufacturer and its customers?

15–6 The availability of bank credit is more important to small firms than to large ones. Why is this so?

15–7 What factors should a firm consider in selecting its primary bank? Would it be feasible for a firm to have a primary deposit bank (the bank where most of its funds are deposited) and a different primary loan bank (the bank where it does most of its borrowing)?

15–8 Indicate whether each of the following changes would raise or lower the cost of accounts receivable financing, and why:

a) The firm eases up on its credit standards in order to increase sales.
b) The firm institutes a policy of refusing to make credit sales if the amount of the purchase (invoice) is below \$100. Previously, about 40 percent of all invoices were below \$100.
c) The firm agrees to give recourse to the finance company for all defaults.
d) The firm, which already has a recourse arrangement, is merged into a larger, stronger company.
e) A firm without a recourse arrangement changes its terms of trade from net 30 to net 90.

15–9 Would a firm that manufactures specialized machinery for a few large customers be more likely to use some form of inventory financing or some form of accounts receivable financing? Why?

15–10 "A firm that factors its accounts receivable will look better in a ratio analysis than one that discounts its receivables." Discuss.

15–11 Why would it not be practical for a typical retailer to use field warehousing?

15–12 For each of the following, list one industry, together with your reasons for including it, that might be expected to use each type of credit:

a) Field warehousing
b) Factoring
c) Accounts receivable discounting
d) Trust receipts
e) None of these

PROBLEMS

15–1 What is the equivalent annual interest rate that would be lost if a firm failed to take the cash discount under each of the following terms?

a) 1/15, n/30
b) 2/10, n/60
c) 3/10, n/60
d) 2/10, n/40
e) 1/10, n/40

15–2 Given below is the balance sheet of the Consolidated Credit Corporation as of December 31, 1968.

CONSOLIDATED CREDIT CORPORATION
BALANCE SHEET
December 31, 1968
(in millions of dollars)

Cash	$ 60	Bank loans	$ 220
Net receivables	2,280	Commercial paper	775
Marketable securities	120	Others	335
Repossessions	3	Total due within a year	$1,330
Total current assets	$2,463	Long-term debt	940
Other assets	137	Total shareholders' equity	330
Total assets	$2,600	Total claims	$2,600

a) Calculate commercial paper as a percent of short-term financing, as a percent of total-debt financing, as a percent of all financing.
b) Why do finance companies such as Consolidated Credit use commercial paper to such a great extent?
c) Why do they use both bank loans and commercial paper?

15–3 The Kaplan Corporation had sales of $1.5 million during 1968 and earned a 2 percent return after taxes on total assets.

Although its terms of purchase are 30 days, its accounts payable represent 60 days' purchases. The president of the company is seeking to increase the company's bank borrowings in order to become current in meeting trade obligations.

The company's balance sheet is shown here.

KAPLAN CORPORATION
BALANCE SHEET
December 31, 1968

Cash	$ 20,000	Accounts payable	$ 200,000
Accounts receivable	100,000	Bank loans	200,000
Inventory	480,000	Accruals	100,000
Current assets	600,000	Current debt	500,000
Land and buildings	200,000	Mortgage on real estate	200,000
Equipment	200,000	Common stock, par 10 cents	100,000
		Retained earnings	200,000
Total assets	$1,000,000	Total liabilities and net worth	$1,000,000

a) How much bank financing is needed to become immediately current on trade credit?

b) Would you as a bank loan officer make the loan? Why?

15–4 The Mattson Plastics Company has been growing rapidly. It is suffering from insufficient working capital, however, and has therefore become slow in paying bills. Of its total accounts payable, $100,000 is overdue. This threatens its relationship with its main supplier of powders used in the manufacture of various kinds of insulation materials for aircraft and missiles. Over 80 percent of its sales are to six large defense contractors. Its balance sheet, sales, and net profit for the year ended December 31, 1969, are shown here.

MATTSON PLASTICS
BALANCE SHEET
December 31, 1969

Cash	$ 30,000	Trade credit	$ 250,000
Receivables	450,000	Bank loans	200,000
Inventories		Accruals	50,000
Raw material	40,000		
Work in process	200,000	Total current debt	500,000
Finished goods	60,000	Chattel mortgages	300,000
		Capital stock	100,000
Total current assets	780,000	Surplus	100,000
Equipment	220,000		
Total assets	$1,000,000	Total liab. and net worth	$1,000,000
Sales	$2,050,000		
Profit after taxes	100,000		

a) If the same ratio of sales to total assets continues and if sales increase to $2.550 million, how much nonspontaneous financing will be required?
b) The bank is reluctant to loan Mattson Plastics more than $150,000 to $200,000 on an unsecured basis. Why?
c) Could Mattson obtain more funds by use of inventory financing? Explain.
d) Would receivables financing be a possibility for Mattson? Explain.
e) *Assuming the facts listed below,* on the average what is the total amount of receivables outstanding at any time? How much cash does the firm actually receive by factoring the average amount of receivables? What is the average duration of advances, on the basis of 360 days a year? What is the total cost of the financing? What is the effective annual financing charge (percentage) paid on the money received?
   1) Receivables turn over five times a year.
   2) Cash sales amount to $50,000.
   3) The factor requires an 8 percent reserve for returns and disputed items.
   4) The factor also requires a 2 percent commission to cover the costs of credit checking.
   5) There is a 6 percent annual interest charge based on receivables less any reserve requirements and commissions. This payment is made at the beginning of the period and is deducted from the advance.

15–5 The Warren Company manufactures plastic toys. It buys raw materials, manufactures the toys in the spring and summer, and ships them to department stores and toy stores by the late summer or early fall. Warren factors its receivables. If it did not, the following would be its situation. For example, in October 1968, the balance sheet of Warren would have looked like this.

WARREN COMPANY
PRO FORMA BALANCE SHEET
October 31, 1968

Cash	$ 100,000	Accounts payable	$3,000,000
Receivables	3,000,000	Notes payable	2,000,000
Inventory	2,000,000	Accruals	200,000
		Total current debt	5,200,000
Total current assets	5,100,000	Common stock	500,000
		Mortgages	1,000,000
Fixed assets	2,000,000	Retained earnings	400,000
Total assets	$7,100,000	Total claims	$7,100,000

Warren provides advanced dating on its sales; thus its receivables are not due for payment until January 31, 1969. However, Warren would have been overdue on some $2 million of its accounts payable if the above situation actually existed.

Warren has an agreement with a finance company to factor the receivables. The factoring company charges a flat commission of 2 percent, plus 6 percent per year interest on the outstanding balance; it deducts a reserve of 8 percent for returned and damaged materials. Interest and commission are paid in advance. No interest is charged on the reserved funds or on the commission.

a) Show the balance sheet of Warren on October 31, 1968, giving effect to the purchase of all the receivables by the factoring company and the use of the funds to pay accounts payable.

b) If the $3 million is the average level of outstanding receivables and if they turn over 4 times a year (hence the commission is paid 4 times a year), what are the total dollar costs of financing and the effective annual interest rate?

15–6 The Karalus Company is a producer of building materials. The demand for its products is highly seasonal, concentrated in the spring and summer months. Its own production is therefore highly uneven.

Karalus could profitably allow a 10 percent trade discount to distributors if they were willing to accept deliveries during the slack season. The 10 percent concession would be advantageous to the distributors. However, as the distributors are generally underfinanced, they cannot accept deliveries without outside financing.

Outline a program of field warehousing to provide financing for the distributors.

Selected References

"Accounts Receivable Lending—Credit at the Margin," *Business Conditions,* Federal Reserve Bank of Chicago (March 1958).

Addison, Edward T., "Factoring: A Case History," *Financial Executive,* XXI (November 1963) 32–33.

Agemian, Charles A., "Maintaining an Effective Bank Relationship," *Financial Executive,* XXXII (January 1964), 24–28.

Baxter, Nevins D. and Harold T. Shapiro, "Compensating Balance Requirements: The Results of a Survey," *Journal of Finance,* XIX (September 1964), 483–496.

———, *The Commercial Paper Market.* (Princeton, N.J.: Princeton University Press, 1964).

Beckman, T. N., and R. Bartel, *Credit and Collections: Management and Theory,* 7th ed. (New York: McGraw-Hill, 1962).

———, "Interest Rates, Liquidity, and the Financing of Captive Finance Companies," *National Banking Review* II, No. 4, (June 1965), pp. 461–481.

"Commercial Paper," *Money Market Instruments,* (Cleveland: Federal Reserve Bank of Cleveland, 1965), pp. 41–47.

Gibson, W. E., "Compensating Balance Requirements," *National Banking Review,* II (March 1965), 298–311.

Guttentag, J. M. and R. G. Davis, "Compensating Balances," *Monthly Review,* Federal Reserve Bank of New York, XLIII (November 1961), 205–210.

Hayes, Douglas A., *Bank Lending Policies: Issues and Practices.* (Ann Arbor, Mich.: University of Michigan Press, 1964), Chapter 5.

Laudadio, Leonard, "Size of Bank, Size of Borrower, and the Rate of Interest," *Journal of Finance,* XVIII (March 1963), 20–28.

Lent, G. E., *The Changing Structure of Commercial Banking, Tuck* Bulletin XXIV (Hanover, N.H.: Dartmouth College, 1960).

Mayer, Thomas, "Trade Credit and the Discriminatory Effects of Monetary Policy," *National Banking Review,* III (June 1966), 543–545.

Moore, Carroll G., "Factoring—A Unique Important Form of Financing and Service," *Business Lawyer,* XIV (April 1959), 703–727.

Palamara, Francis J., "Commercial Financing: An Economic Tool," *Financial Executive,* XXXII (January 1964), 52–54.

"Prime Commercial Paper," *Monthly Review,* Federal Reserve Bank of Richmond, (July 1964), 8–10.

Robichek, A. A., D. Teichroew, and J. M. Jones, "Optimal Short Term Financing Decisions," *Management Science,* XII (September 1965), 1–36.

Robinson, Roland I., *The Management of Bank Funds,* Parts III and IV (New York: McGraw-Hill, 1962).

Rogers, Robert W., "Warehouse Receipts and Their Use in Financing," *Bulletin of the Robert Morris Associates,* XLVI (April 1964).

Selden, Richard T., *Trends and Cycles in the Commercial Paper Market* (New York: National Bureau of Economic Research, 1963).

Stewart, William C., "How Business Picks Banks," *Burroughs Clearing House,* XLIV (January 1960), 33–35, 80.

Wojnilower, Albert M., *The Quality of Bank Loans.* (New York: National Bureau of Economic Research, 1962).

16

Intermediate-Term Financing

Intermediate-term financing is defined as debt originally scheduled for repayment in more than one year but in less than five years. Anything shorter is a current liability and falls in the class of short-term credit, while obligations due in five or more years are thought of as long-term debt. This distinction is arbitrary, of course—we might just as well define long-term credit as credit starting with a maturity of 10 or more years. However, the one-to-five year distinction is commonly used, so we shall follow it here.

The major forms of intermediate-term financing include (1) *term loans,* (2) *conditional sales contracts, and* (3) *lease financing*. These types of credit are described in the present chapter.

TERM LOANS

A term loan is a business loan with a maturity of more than one year. There are exceptions to the rule, but ordinarily term loans are retired by systematic repayments (often called *amortization payments*) over the life of the loan.

Security, generally in the form of a chattel mortgage on equipment, is often employed, but the larger, stronger companies are able to borrow on an unsecured basis.

The primary lenders on term credit are commercial banks; life insurance companies; and, to a lesser extent, pension funds. Bank loans are generally restricted to maturities of between one and five years, while insurance companies and pension funds make the bulk of their term loans for between 5 and 15 years. Therefore, insurance company term loans are generally long-term, not intermediate-term, financing. Sometimes, when relatively large loans ($10 million and up) are involved, banks and insurance companies combine to make a loan, with the bank taking the short maturities and the insurance company the long maturities. Some specific features of term loans are discussed in the following sections.

Repayment Schedule

The repayment, or amortization, schedule is a particularly important feature of practically all term loans, so it is useful to describe how it is determined. The purpose of amortization, of course, is to have the loan repaid gradually over its life rather than falling due all at once. Amortization forces the borrower to retire the loan slowly, thus protecting both the lender and the borrower against the possibility that the borrower will not make adequate provisions for retirement during the life of the loan.

To illustrate how the amortization schedule is determined, let us assume that a firm borrows $1,000 on a 10-year term loan, that interest is computed at 5 percent on the declining balance, and that the principal and interest are to be paid in ten equal installments. What is the amount of each of the ten annual payments? To find this value we must use the present value concepts developed in Chapter 6.

First, notice that the lender advances $1,000 and receives in turn a 10-year annuity of R dollars each year. In the section headed Annual Receipts from an Annuity in Chapter 6 we saw that these receipts could be calculated as

$$R = \frac{A_n}{\text{IF}}$$

where R is the annual receipts, A_n is the present value of the annuity, and IF is the appropriate interest factor found either in Table 6–5 or in Appendix Table A–4. Substituting the $1,000 for A_n and the interest factor for a 10-year, 5 percent annuity, or 7.722, for IF, we get

$$R = \frac{\$1{,}000}{7.722} = \$130$$

Therefore, if our firm makes ten annual installments of $130 each, it will have retired the $1,000 loan and provided the lender a 5 percent return on his investment.

Table 16–1 breaks down the annual payments into interest and repayment components and, in the process, proves that level payments of $130 will, in fact, retire the $1,000 loan and give the lender his 5 percent return. This breakdown is important for tax purposes, as the interest payments are deductible.

TABLE 16–1 TERM LOAN REPAYMENT SCHEDULE

YEAR		TOTAL PAYMENT	INTEREST*	AMORTIZATION REPAYMENT	REMAINING BALANCE
1		$ 130	$ 50	$ 80	$920
2		130	46	84	836
3		130	42	88	748
4		130	38	92	656
5		130	34	96	560
6		130	28	102	458
7		130	23	107	351
8		130	18	112	239
9		130	13	117	122
10		130	8	122	0
	Totals	$1,300	$300	$1,000	

* Interest for the first year is 0.05 × $1,000 = $50; for the second year it is 0.05 × $920 = $46; and so on. The numbers are not exact because of rounding errors.

Characteristics of Term Loans

SIZE OF LOAN. The typical term loan is small in terms of its dollar amount. Most commercial bank term loans are from $100,000 to $250,000. About 50 percent of life insurance loans run from about $1 million to $5 million. Commercial banks typically make smaller and shorter term loans; life insurance companies make larger and longer term loans on the average, although they also make a few short-term loans.

SIZE OF BORROWERS. It has been estimated that 90 percent of the term loans made by commercial banks are to small firms with assets of less than $5 million. Most of the term and direct loans made by insurance companies are to larger firms.

INDUSTRY OF THE BORROWER. Earlier surveys have indicated that nearly 40 percent of term loans were confined to two major industry groups: (1) transportation, communication, and other public utilities and (2) petroleum, coal, chemicals, and rubber. These two groups also showed the highest ratio of term-to-total bank borrowing. This reflects the large proportion of their assets having relatively long service lives. By contrast, the smaller users of term credit were commodity dealers and sales finance companies, which have small fixed investment. A 1957 survey showed that the greatest relative increase in term loans was in trade, construction, and real estate—small firms growing rapidly.

MATURITY. For commercial banks, the term loan runs five years or less, typically three years. For insurance companies, the most typical maturities have been 10 to 15 years. This difference reflects the fact that liabilities of commercial banks are shorter term than are those of insurance companies. As we pointed out above, banks and insurance companies occasionally cooperate in their term lending. For example, if a firm (usually a large one) seeks a 15-year term loan, a bank may take the loan for the first five years and an insurance company for the last 10 years.

COLLATERAL. Commercial banks have required security on about 60 percent of the volume and 90 percent of the number of term loans made. They have taken as security mainly stocks, bonds, machinery, and equipment. Insurance companies also have required security on nearly a third of their loans, frequently using real estate as collateral on the longer loans.

OPTIONS. In recent years institutional investors have increasingly taken compensation in addition to fixed interest payments on directly negotiated loans. The most popular form of additional compensation is an option to buy common stock, "the option being in the form of detachable warrants permitting the purchase of the shares at stated prices over a designated period."[1]

USE OF FUNDS BY BORROWERS. During an earlier period, more than 50 percent of direct loans were used to refund outstanding bonds sold originally at higher interest rates. More recently, direct loans have pro-

[1] C. M. Williams and H. A. Williams, "Incentive Financing," *Harvard Business Review,* XXXVIII (March-April 1960), 124.

vided primarily working capital and, secondarily, plant and equipment financing.

REPAYMENT PROVISIONS. Most term loans are repayable in equal installments. Only a small percentage of the loans have any balloon segment of repayment at the end. Term loans are geared specifically to the ability of the firm to meet a certain repayment, or amortization, schedule. It is possible to prepay term loans ahead of schedule, but a prepayment penalty equal to from 1 to 5 percent of the outstanding balance is usually assessed in such cases.

Terms of Loan Agreements

The term loan assures funds to the borrower, and he will not be faced with an inability to renew his loan if his needs for funds continue. Offsetting the advantages of having the assured use of funds for a period of from 3 to 20 years is a set of disadvantages that grow out of the inherent nature of the term loan. On a 90-day loan, since the commercial bank has the option to renew or not renew, the bank can take the occasion to reexamine the situation of the borrower. If it has deteriorated unduly, the loan officer simply does not renew the loan. On a term or direct loan, however, the bank or insurance company has committed itself for a period of years. Thus, there are certain restrictive provisions in the loan agreement designed to protect the lender for the duration of the loan. The most important of the typical restrictive provisions are listed below.

CURRENT RATIO. The current ratio must be maintained at some specified level—2½ to 1, 3 to 1, 3½ to 1, depending upon the borrower's line of business. Net working capital must be maintained at some minimum.

ADDITIONAL FIXED ASSETS. There are restrictions on the amount of additional fixed assets that may be purchased by the borrower in the future. The lender seeks to protect himself against the borrower's sinking his funds excessively in fixed investments.

ADDITIONAL LONG-TERM DEBT. Typically, there are prohibitions against incurring additional long-term indebtedness except with the permission of the lender. Furthermore, the lender does not permit the pledge of assets without the permission of the lender. Moreover, the loan agreement prohibits the borrower from assuming any contingent liabilities, such as guaranteeing the indebtedness of a subsidiary. Finally, the loan agreement probably restricts the borrower from signing long-term leases beyond specified amounts.

MANAGEMENT. The loan agreement may require that any major changes in management personnel, or in its composition, must be approved by the lender. The loan agreement requires life insurance on the principals of the business, especially if they are key personnel. In addition, the loan agreement may provide for the creation of a voting trust or a granting of proxies for a specified period to ensure that the management of the company will be under the control of the group on which the lender has relied in making the loan.

FINANCIAL STATEMENTS. The lender will require the borrower to submit periodic financial statements for his review.

This list does not exhaust all the kinds of terms found in loan agreements, but it is illustrative. It serves to indicate the kind of protective provisions the bank or insurance company seeks to embody in the loan agreement.

Cost of Term Loans

Another major aspect of term lending is its cost. As with other forms of lending, the interest rate on term loans varies with the size of the loan and the quality of the borrower. Surveys show that on term loans of less than $500 the interest rate may run up to 15 percent. On loans of $1 million and above, term loan rates have been close to the prime rate. The size of the loan often reflects the quality of the borrower as well as the fixed cost involved in making small loans.

The interest rate may be related to the Federal Reserve rediscount rate. Often the loan agreement specifies that the interest rate will be based on the average of the rediscount rate in the borrower's Federal Reserve district during the previous three months, generally ½ percent to 1 or 2 percent above the rediscount rate. In other words, the loan rate can fluctuate during the life of the loan and is often tied to the rediscount rate. It may also be geared to the published prime rate charged by New York City banks.

Economic Aspects of Long-Term Loans

It is useful to comment on several aspects of the broader economic significance of long-term loans.

1. The long-term loan may make the economy less vulnerable to forced liquidation. Since the loan is not subject to renewal every 90 days, there is less danger of forced liquidation of loans accumulating during a depression when lenders become pessimistic and the financial position of the borrower deteriorates.

2. It brings insurance companies into direct lending to business. Before the 1930s, insurance companies invested in business primarily by buying bonds. In such a situation, the insurance company was simply one among other bondholders; now the relation is direct. The insurance company has considerable stability in its own liabilities. The flow of cash into an insurance company is highly predictable, and the danger of a wave of cash surrenders of life insurance policies during a recession has proved historically to be very small.[2] The insurance company, therefore, is in a position to allow an extension to a borrower if he gets into difficulties. This arrangement makes the economy less vulnerable to forced liquidation or to a continuous chain of liquidations in one area that forces liquidation in another, causing a downward spiral in the economy.

3. The term loan increases the availability of longer term debt for smaller businesses. However, it does not completely solve the small-business financing problem, because it does not represent equity funds (the funds are not left in the business permanently). Since amortization of the loan on a systematic basis is required, the small firm has the money only for a limited period and must have substantial cash throw-off ability in order to handle the term loan. The term loan does, however, extend the period over which the small business firm can grow by plowing back earnings.

ONDITIONAL ALES ONTRACTS

Conditional sales contracts are used to finance a substantial portion of the new equipment purchased by American business firms. Under the sales contract, the buyer agrees to buy a particular piece of equipment and to pay for it in installments over a one-to-five-year period. Until payment is completed, the seller of the equipment continues to hold title to the equipment. This fact gives rise to the name *conditional* sales contract—the sale is conditional upon satisfactory completion of

[2] This statement must be qualified somewhat. In a period of extremely tight money, as was the case in 1966, insurance company policy loans (loans secured by the cash surrender value of policies) rise dramatically. The interest rate on policy loans is fixed, hence it does not rise with interest rates in general. This fixed rate is set high enough so that not too much policy loan borrowing occurs during "normal" times. However, policy loans become relatively attractive as the general level of interest rates rises; in periods of extremely tight-money, policy loans can constitute a serious cash drain for insurance companies.

the payments. While the contract is being paid off, the purchaser has possession of the equipment and uses it in his business. Also, it is typical for the firm that sold the equipment, a manufacturer or dealer, to sell the entire conditional sales contract to a bank or a finance company. What we have, in effect, is a long-term accounts receivable financing arrangement.

Procedure

Assume that a dentist needs a high-speed drill and that he has 30 percent of the purchase price. He makes the arrangements for the purchase from the manufacturer, and he agrees to finance the remaining 70 percent of the purchase price through a finance company or a bank. The dentist signs a conditional sales contract, which schedules payments based on the income he expects to earn. The payments are established exactly like those examined under the term-loan arrangement.

The conditional sales contract may be signed with the manufacturer, who sells it to a finance company or a bank. The financing institution usually requires a recourse agreement from the manufacturer for several reasons. The vendor (manufacturer) wants his money when the equipment leaves his factory. If the equipment is returned or repossessed, however, the manufacturer is in a better position than the financing institution to recondition and sell it. A financing institution cannot be expected to recondition a wide variety of specialized equipment. However, in a conditional sales contract it is usual to require that the financing institution repossess and return the equipment to the manufacturer within 60 days after the first default.

Products, Terms, and Appraisal

PRODUCTS. Many kinds of equipment purchases are financed under conditional sales contracts. In descending order of frequency they are factory equipment, hotel and restaurant fixtures, equipment for beauty and barber shops, equipment for buses and trailers, medical equipment, diners and dining equipment, and bowling alley equipment. Studies of the credit positions of firms using installment equipment financing reveal that a high proportion of them are small firms with low credit ratings.

TERMS. The terms of installment equipment financing are influenced mainly by the length of life of the equipment purchased. The down payment runs around one third of the equipment purchase price, and the maturity generally runs from two to three years. The cost of equipment financing is relatively high—usually 6 percent of the orginal amount discounted on the face amount of the contract, an effective rate of interest of 14 or 15 percent giving consideration to both the discount and the installment loan features of the contract. On heavy machinery purchased by prime credit risks, the effective rate may run as low as 8 or 9 percent.

APPRAISAL. The main advantage of conditional sales financing is that it increases the ability of small firms to purchase equipment. Since the equipment generally produces income, the cash flow thus generated provides for repayment of the loan. In this sense the loan is self-liquidating. While the interest costs are high in an absolute sense, they may be low when related to the profitability of the equipment thereby acquired. The major limitation of conditional sales contract equipment financing is that it is by necessity limited to only the fixed asset portion of the assets of the firm.

LEASE FINANCING

Firms are generally interested in *using* buildings and equipment, not in owning them per se. One way of obtaining the use of facilities and equipment is to buy them, but an alternative is to lease rather than own. Prior to the 1950s, leasing was generally associated with real estate—land and buildings—but today it is possible to lease virtually any kind of fixed asset.

Leasing takes several different forms, the most important of which are sale and leaseback, service leases, and straight financial leases. These three major types of leasing are described below.

Sale and Leaseback

Under a sale and leaseback arrangement, a firm owning land, buildings, or equipment sells the property to a financial institution and simultaneously executes an agreement to lease the property back for a specified period under specific terms. If real estate—land or buildings—is involved, the financial institution is generally a life insurance company; if the property consists of equipment and machinery, the *lessor* could be an insurance company, a commercial bank, or a specialized leasing company.

Note that the seller, or lessee, immediately obtains the purchase price put up by the buyer, or lessor. At the same time, the seller-lessee retains the use of the property. This parallel is carried over to the lease payment schedule. Under a mortgage loan arrangement, the financial institution would receive a series of equal payments just sufficient to amortize the loan and provide the lender with a specified rate of return on his investment. The nature of the calculations was described above under the term loan arrangement. Under a sale and leaseback arrangement, the lease payments are set up in exactly the same manner—the payments are sufficient to return the full purchase price to the financial institution, in addition to providing it with a stated return on its investment.

Service Leases

Service or operating leases include both financing and maintenance services. International Business Machines Corporation is one of the pioneers of the service lease contract; computers, together with automobiles and trucks, are the primary types of equipment involved in service leases.

Another important characteristic of the service lease is the fact that it is frequently not fully amortized. In other words, the payments required under the lease contract are *not* sufficient to recover the full cost of the equipment. Obviously, however, the lease contract is written for considerably less than the expected life of the leased equipment, and the lessor expects to recover his cost in subsequent renewal payments or upon disposal of the leased equipment.

A final feature of the service lease is the fact that such leases frequently contain a cancellation clause giving the lessee the right to cancel the lease and return the equipment before the expiration of the basic lease agreement. This is an important consideration for the lessee, for it means that he can return the equipment if technological developments render it obsolete.

Financial Leases

A strict financial lease is one that does *not* provide for maintenance services, is *not* cancelable, and is fully amortized (that is, the lessor receives rental payments equal to the full price of the leased equipment). The lessor is generally an insurance company, if real estate is involved, and a commercial bank or specialized leasing company, if the leased property is equipment. The typical arrangement involves the following steps:

1. The firm that will use the equipment selects the specific items it wants and negotiates the price and delivery terms with the manufacturer or the distributor.
2. Next, the user firm arranges with a bank or a leasing company to buy the equipment from the manufacturer or the distributor,

> and the user firm simultaneously executes an agreement to lease the equipment from the financial institution. The terms call for full amortization of the financial institution's cost, plus a return of from 6 to 10 percent a year on the unamortized balance. The lessee is generally given an option to renew the lease at a reduced rental on expiration of the basic lease, but he does not have the right to cancel the basic lease without completely paying off the financial institution.

These leases are almost exactly the same as sale and leaseback arrangements, the only difference being that the leased equipment is new and the lessor buys it from a manufacturer or a distributor rather than from the user-lessee. A sale and leaseback may, then, be thought of as a special type of financial lease.

Internal Revenue Service Requirements for a Lease

The full amount of the annual lease payments are deductible for income tax purposes *provided the Internal Revenue Service agrees that a particular contract is a genuine lease and not simply an installment loan called a lease.* This makes it important that a lease contract be written in a form acceptable to the Internal Revenue Service. The following are the major requirements for bona fide lease transactions from the standpoint of the IRS:

1. The term must be less than 30 years, otherwise the lease is regarded as a form of sale.
2. The rent must represent a reasonable return to the lessor, "reasonable" being in the range of 6 to 10 percent on the investment.
3. The renewal option must be bona fide, and this requirement can best be met by giving the lessee the first option to meet an equal bona fide outsider offer.
4. There shall be no repurchase option; if there is, the lessee should merely be given parity with an equal outside offer.

Cost Comparison

For an understanding of the possible advantages and disadvantages of lease financing, the cost of leasing must be compared with the cost of owning the equipment. In the typical case a firm that contemplates the acquisition of new equipment must also think about how to finance the equipment. When financing is necessary, the three major alternatives are (1) a term loan secured by a chattel mortgage on the equipment, (2) a conditional sales contract, and (3) a lease arrangement.

To judge the cost of leasing, we must make a comparison of leasing versus the two borrow-to-purchase alternatives.

This comparison is best carried out in the manner presented in Table 16–2. Here it is assumed that the firm is acquiring a piece of equipment costing $1,000 and that it has the choice of borrowing the $1,000 at 5 percent, to be repaid in ten annual installments of $130 each, or of leasing the machine for $130 a year. (Under the lease arrangement the firm is paying a 5 percent implicit interest rate; this is the rate the lessor is earning.)

Note that the decision to acquire the machine is not at issue here—this decision was made previously as part of the capital budgeting process. Here we are concerned simply with whether to obtain the use of the machine by a lease or by a purchase. However, if the effective cost of the lease is substantially lower than the cost of debt—and, as will be explained later in this chapter, this could occur for a number of reasons, including the ability to use more debt financing if leasing is employed—then the cost of capital used in capital budgeting would have to be recalculated and, perhaps, projects formally deemed unacceptable might become acceptable.

Columns 2 through 5 show the payment schedule for the loan—note that this section is identical with the schedule shown in Table 16–1 for a term loan and that it would apply equally well to a 10-year conditional sales contract payment schedule. Column 6 gives the annual depreciation charges, assuming the firm owns the equipment and depreciates it on a straight line basis. Column 7 gives the total tax deductible expense, interest plus depreciation charges. These tax deductions reduce the tax bill by one half the amount of the deductions, assuming a 50 percent tax rate; this gives rise to the tax savings recorded in column 8. Now the total cash outlay associated with the borrow-purchase arrangement is the annual loan payment recorded in column 2; this is the gross cash outflow. Deducting the tax savings shown in column 8 from the payments in column 2 gives the net cash cost of owning shown in column 9.

Assuming that the leasing company—which might well be the same bank that is willing to make the term loan—is willing to accept a 5 percent return on its investment, the annual lease payments must be $130, the same as those under the loan arrangement. This entire payment is deductible for income tax purposes, so the after-tax cost of the lease is $65 a year for 10 years. This figure is shown in column 10.

Column 9 shows the firm's net cash outlay each year if it elects to borrow the money and purchase the machine, while column 10 shows the net cash outflow if it elects the lease alternative. Subtracting column 9 from column 10 gives the cash flow advantage—plus or minus—to

TABLE 16–2 COMPARISON OF COST OF LEASING VERSUS BUYING

(1)	(2)	(3)	(4)	(5)	(6)	(7)	(8)	(9)	(10)	(11)	(12)	(13)
	COMPUTING NET COST OF OWNING											
	Applicable to Loan											
Year	*Total Payment*	*Interest*	*Amortization Payment*	*Remaining Balance*	*Depreciation*	*(3) + (6) Tax Deductible Expense*	*½ (7) Tax Saving*	*(2) − (8) Net Cost of Owning*	*Lease Cost after Tax*	*(10) − (9) Advantage to Owning*	*2½% Present Value Factor*	*(11) × (12) Present Value of Advantage to Owning*
1	$ 130	$ 50	$ 80	$920	$ 100	$ 150	$ 75	$ 55	$ 65	10	0.976	9.76
2	130	46	84	836	100	146	73	57	65	8	0.952	7.62
3	130	42	88	748	100	142	71	59	65	6	0.929	5.57
4	130	38	92	656	100	138	69	61	65	4	0.906	3.62
5	130	34	96	560	100	134	67	63	65	2	0.884	1.77
6	130	28	102	458	100	128	64	66	65	(1)	0.862	(.86)
7	130	23	107	351	100	123	62	68	65	(3)	0.841	(2.52)
8	130	18	112	239	100	118	59	71	65	(6)	0.821	(4.93)
9	130	13	117	122	100	113	56	74	65	(9)	0.801	(7.21)
10	130	8	122	—	100	108	54	76	65	(11)	0.781	(8.59)
Totals	$1,300	$300	$1,000	—	$1,000	$1,300	$650	$650	$650			4.23

Assumptions:

1) The firm can borrow $1,000 at 5% to be repaid in ten equal annual installments.
   The annual payments are computed as:
   a) Interest factor for 10 years, 5% annuity = 7.722
   b) Required annual payment = $1,000 ÷ 7.722 = $130
2) The firm can arrange to finance its $1,000 equipment purchase under a 10-year lease plan calling for an annual rental of $130.
3) The equipment is worthless at the end of 10 years.
4) The firm uses straight-line depreciation.

Note: If the equipment was expected to have a salvage value at the end of 10 years, this amount would constitute a *negative* payment (a receipt) and would reduce the net cost of owning. The salvage value would be deducted from the "net cost of owning" figure in column 9 for the tenth year.

owning versus leasing. This figure is recorded in column 11, which shows that owning involves smaller annual cash outlays in each of the first five years but that leasing requires smaller cash flows during the last five years.

We can no more add dollars payable in one year to those payable in another than we can add apples to oranges. We must, therefore, put the annual cash flow differentials between leasing and borrowing on a common basis; this requires converting them to present values. Column 12 gives the interest factors for 2½ percent, the firm's after-tax cost of debt.[3] These interest factors, when multiplied by the cash flow differentials shown in column 11, give the present value of the differentials; these figures are given in column 13.

When column 13 is summed, we have the net present value of the advantage to owning. This figure can be either plus or minus. A positive result, as in the example, indicates that it is cheaper for the firm to borrow and purchase than it is to lease. A negative result would suggest that leasing has the advantage over buying.

What would happen to the relative cost of leasing versus owning if the example was modified to allow for accelerated depreciation? Accelerated depreciation would produce a higher tax shield, hence lower taxes, in the early years. This would reduce the net cost of owning (column 9) in the early years and raise it later on. Since the lease cost after tax (column 10) is unaffected, the result would be to increase the advantage to owning (column 11) in the early years and to lower it in the later years. When the analysis is carried through to the Present Value column, the final result of accelerated depreciation would be to make owning relatively more attractive than it already is.

Raising the cost of capital factor (column 12) would have the same effect as switching to accelerated depreciation. The advantage of leasing comes in the later years, which are the ones that would be penalized most heavily by a higher cost of capital factor. The net result would be to increase the advantage of owning.

However, a table similar to Table 16–2, constructed from the lessor's point of view, would show that leases provide higher returns than loans, other things the same, because under a lease the lessor can take advan-

[3] As a technical point, we should state that the discount factor that should be applied is *not* the weighted cost of capital. Rather, it is the cost of debt. The logic behind this statement is explained in the excellent article "The Refunding Decision," by Oswald D. Bowlin in the March 1966 issue of *The Journal of Finance*. In brief, Bowlin points out that in comparing two financial alternatives there is essentially no risk to the firm in obtaining the savings attributable to one alternative over the other. This being the case, a discount rate that reflects the low risk is preferable to one that reflects the firm's average risk. For this reason, we have chosen to use the after-tax debt rate rather than the weighted cost of capital.

tage of the accelerated depreciation. In such a situation the lessor is permitted some profit flexibility in setting lease terms, and competition among leasing companies could reduce the costs of leasing.

TABLE 16–3 VARIATIONS IN ASSUMED CONDITIONS AND THEIR IMPLICATIONS FOR COSTS OF OWNING VERSUS LEASING

ASSUMED CONDITIONS	CONSEQUENCES
Use of accelerated depreciation	Costs of owning lower
Implicit interest rates higher in leasing	Costs of leasing higher
Large residual values	Costs of owning lower
Rapid obsolescence	Costs of leasing lower

It may be useful to summarize some of the variations and their implications for the evaluation of owning versus leasing, and this is done in Table 16–3. The material in the table summarizes frequently encountered arguments about advantages and disadvantages of leasing. Each assumed condition is subject to substantial qualification or error. Each will be considered in turn.

USE OF ACCELERATED DEPRECIATION. It is often argued that because of the ability to use accelerated depreciation methods, owning must be less expensive than leasing. Such an argument does not take into account the competitive aspects of the money and capital markets. Competition will force tax advantages, such as accelerated depreciation, to be shared between lessor and lessee. This relates to the point made just above. The payments pattern under leasing can be quite flexible. Thus, any opportunities available to equipment owners will have to be reflected in the competitive system of rates charged by leasing companies.

IMPLICIT INTEREST RATES HIGHER IN LEASING. The statement is frequently made that leasing always involves higher interest rates. This argument is of doubtful validity. First, when the nature of the lessee as a credit risk is considered, there may be no difference. Second, it is difficult to separate the money costs of leasing from the other services that may be embodied in a leasing contract. If, because of its specialist operations, the leasing company can perform the nonfinancial services, such as maintenance of the equipment, at lower cost than the lessee or some other institution could perform them, the effective cost of leasing may be lower than for funds obtained from borrowing or other sources. The efficiencies of performing specialized services may thus enable the leasing company to operate by charging a lower total cost than the lessor would have to pay for the package of money plus services on any other basis.

LARGE RESIDUAL VALUES. One important point that must be mentioned in connection with leasing is that the lessor owns the property at the expiration of the lease. The value of the property at the end of the lease is called the *residual value*. Superficially, it would appear that where residual values are large, owning will be less expensive than leasing. However, even this obvious advantage of owning is subject to substantial qualification. On leased equipment, the obsolescence factor is likely to be so large that it is doubtful whether residual values will be of a great order of magnitude. If residual values appear favorable, competition between leasing companies and other financial sources, and competition among leasing companies themselves, will force leasing rates down to the point where the potentials of residual values are fully recognized in the leasing contract rates. Thus, the existence of residual values on equipment is not likely to result in materially lower costs of owning. However, in connection with decisions whether to lease or to own land, the obsolescence factor is not involved except to the extent of deterioration in areas with changing population or use patterns. In a period of optimistic expectations about land values, there may be a tendency to overestimate rates of increase in land values. As a consequence, the current purchase of land may involve a price so high that the probable rate of return on owned land may be relatively small. Under this condition, leasing may well represent a more economical way of obtaining the use of land than owning. Conversely, if the probable increase in land values is not fully reflected in current prices, it will be advantageous to own the land.

Thus it is difficult to generalize whether current residual values or increases in the value of the land are likely to make the present cost of leasing higher or lower than the cost of owning. Generalization is impossible—the results depend on whether the individual firm has opportunities to take advantage of overoptimistic or overpessimistic evaluations of future value changes by the market as a whole.

RAPID OBSOLESCENCE. Another fallacy is the idea that leasing costs will be lower because of the rapid obsolescence of some kinds of equipment. If the obsolescence rate on equipment is high, leasing costs must reflect such a rate. Thus, in general terms, it might be argued that neither residual values nor obsolescence rates can basically affect the cost of owning versus leasing.

In connection with leasing, however, it is possible that certain types of leasing companies may be well equipped to handle the obsolescence problem. For example, the Clark Equipment Company is a manufacturer, reconditioner, and specialist in materials handling equipment and has its own sales organization and system of distributors. This may enable Clark to write favorable leases for equipment. If the equipment becomes obsolete to one user, it may still be satisfactory for other users with different materials handling requirements, and Clark is ably situated to locate these other users.

Similarly, Management Assistance, Inc., provides an integrated operation in connection with the leasing of data processing equipment; it reconditions and maintains the equipment, in addition to providing a lease finance service. Data processing equipment that is obsolete for one firm may represent the most efficient (least cost) method of performing accounting functions in another firm. The active organization of Management Assistance, Inc., can thus shift the equipment to the user to whom it represents the most efficient method of performing the tasks required.

These illustrations indicate how the leasing company, by combining lending with other specialized services, may reduce the social costs of obsolescence and increase effective residual values. By such operations the total cost of obtaining the use of such equipment is reduced. Possibly other institutions that do not combine financing and other specialist functions, such as manufacture, reconditioning, servicing, and sales, may, in conjunction with financing institutions, perform the over-all functions as efficiently and at as low cost as do integrated leasing companies. However, this is a factual matter depending upon the relative efficiency of the competing firms in different lines of business and different kinds of equipment. To determine which combination of methods results in the lower costs, an analysis along the lines of the pattern outlined in Table 16–2 is required. Aside from the strictly quantitative considerations that would be reflected in such a table, it is useful to consider some of the possible qualitative advantages of leasing.

Possible Advantages of Leasing

TAX DEDUCTIONS. One factor that shows up clearly in the cost calculation is tax deduction differentials between leasing and buying. If the lease is written for a relatively short period, it will have very large, *deductible* payments in the early years and smaller renewal payments in later years. In a sense, this amounts to a very rapid write-off, which is advantageous. However, the Internal Revenue Service rightly disallows as deductions lease payments under leases (1) that call for a rapid amortization of the lessor's costs and (2) that have a relatively low renewal or purchase option.

INVESTMENT TAX CREDIT. The investment tax credit is computed as a percentage of the initial cost of long-term assets, but is limited by the firm's computed taxes. For example, if the tax credit is 7 percent of new investment and if new investment is $10 million, the tax credit is $700,000. But if operating income is so low that taxes are running only $100,000 annually, the tax credit cannot be fully utilized.

Many companies are finding that their rapid rate of asset expansion, their low profits, or a combination of the two makes it impossible to use the entire amount of their tax credit. In these instances it may be possible to lease from a large bank or other supplier of lease funds, letting the lessor take the tax credit as purchaser of the asset. The lessee obtains a low implicit interest rate on the lease in return for giving up the investment tax credit. United Airlines undertook such an arrangement in 1964 when it leased some $25 million worth of jet engines from a group of six major banks. If this advantage is present and is of sufficient importance, it will be brought out in the cost calculations.

INCREASED CREDIT AVAILABILITY. Two possible situations may exist to give leasing an advantage to firms seeking the maximum degree of financial leverage. First, it is frequently stated that firms can obtain more money for longer terms under a lease arrangement than under a secured loan agreement for the purchase of a specific piece of equipment. Second, leasing may not have as much of an impact on future borrowing capacity as borrowing and buying of equipment. This point is illustrated by examining the balance sheets of two hypothetical firms, A and B, in Table 16–4.

TABLE 16–4 BALANCE SHEET EFFECTS OF LEASING

BEFORE ASSET INCREASE				AFTER ASSET INCREASE							
Firms A and B				Firm A				Firm B			
Total assets	100	Debt	50	Total assets	200	Debt	150	Total assets	100	Debt	50
		Equity	50			Equity	50			Equity	50
Totals	100		100	Totals	200		200	Totals	100		100

Initially, the balance sheets of both firms are identical, and they both have debt ratios of 50 percent. Next, they each decide to acquire assets costing $100. Firm A borrows $100 to make the purchase, so an asset and a liability go on its balance sheet, and its debt ratio is increased to 75 percent. Firm B leases the equipment. The lease may call for as high or even higher fixed charges than the loan, and the obligations assumed under the lease can be equally or more dangerous to other creditors; the fact that the debt ratio of firm B is lower may enable it to obtain additional credit from other lenders. The amount of the annual rentals is shown as a note to the financial statements, but all available evidence suggests that credit analysts give less weight to firm B's lease than to firm A's loan.

This illustration indicates quite clearly a weakness of the debt ratio—if two companies are being compared and if one leases a substantial amount of equipment, then the debt ratio as we calculate it does not accurately show their relative leverage positions. It is, therefore, necessary to examine such cash flow figures as the "times fixed charges covered" ratio when making a comparative analysis of two or more firms.[4]

JMMARY

Intermediate-term financing is defined as debt originally scheduled for repayment in more than one year but less than 5 years. Anything shorter is a current liability, while obligations due in 5 or more years are thought of as long-term debt. The major forms of intermediate-term financing include (1) *term loans,* (2) *conditional sales contracts,* and (3) *lease financing.*

Term Loans

A term loan is a business credit with a maturity of more than one year but less than 15 years. There are exceptions to the rule, but ordinarily term loans are retired by systematic repayments (amortization payments) over the life of the loan. Security, generally in the form of a chattel mortgage on equipment, is often employed; the larger, stronger companies are able to borrow on an unsecured basis. Commercial banks and life insurance companies are the principal suppliers of term loan credit. Commercial banks typically make smaller, shorter term loans; life insurance companies grant larger, longer term credits.

The interest cost of term loans, like rates on other credits, varies with the size of the loan and the strength of the borrower. For small loans to small companies, rates may go up as high as 10 percent; for large loans to large firms, the rate will be close to prime. Since term loans run for long periods, during which interest rates can change radically, many loans have variable interest rates, with the rate set at a certain level above the prime rate or above the Federal Reserve rediscount rate.

Another aspect of term loans is the series of *protective covenants* contained in most loan agreements. The lender's funds are tied up for

[4] To help alleviate this problem, the accounting profession has given serious thought to capitalizing leases and showing them as both an asset and a liability on the balance sheet. The likelihood of this actually being done in the near future is remote, however. Cf. J. Myers, *Reporting of Leases in Financial Statements* (New York: American Institute of Certified Public Accountants, 1961).

a long period, and during this time the borrower's situation can change markedly. To protect himself, the lender will include in the loan agreement stipulations that the borrower will maintain his current ratio at a specified level, limit acquisitions of additional fixed assets, keep his debt ratio below a specified level, and so on. These provisions are necessary from the lender's point of view, but they necessarily restrict the borrower's actions.

Conditional Sales Contracts

Conditional sales contracts continue to be a major method by which firms obtain the use of equipment. Under the sales contract, the buyer agrees to buy a particular piece of equipment and to pay for it in installments over a one-to-five year period. Until payment is completed, the seller of the equipment continues to hold title to the equipment; thus the completion of the sale is *conditional* upon completion of the payments.

The cost of financing under sales contracts is relatively high—usually 6 percent of the original balance discounted on the face amount of the contract, an effective rate of interest of 14 or 15 percent. On heavy machinery purchased by prime credit risks the rate may run as low as 8 to 9 percent.

Lease Financing

Leasing has long been used in connection with the acquisition of equipment by railroad companies. In recent years it has been extended to a wide variety of equipment. In the absence of major tax advantages, whether or not leasing is advantageous turns primarily on the firm's ability to acquire funds by other methods. Leasing has the advantage of a smaller down payment and increased opportunities for tax savings, and it probably increases the over-all availability of nonequity financing to the firm.

However, a leasing contract is very close to a straight-debt arrangement and uses some of the firm's debt-carrying ability. Also, the rental is a fixed obligation. Because of the importance of residual value, it will generally be advantageous to a firm to own its land and buildings. Because of the obsolescence factor, the residual value considerations may be less important in connection with the acquisition of equipment. Leasing of equipment may therefore continue to grow in importance.

QUESTIONS

16–1 "The type of equipment best suited for leasing has a long life in relation to the length of the lease; is a removable, standard product that could be used by many different firms; and is easily identifiable. In short, it is the kind of equipment that could be repossessed and sold readily. However, we would be quite happy to write a 10-year lease on paper towels for a firm such as General Motors." Discuss the statement.

16–2 On the basis of (a) the factors that make leasing a desirable means of financing and (b) your knowledge of the characteristics of different industries, name three industries that might be expected to use lease financing. Discuss.

16–3 Leasing is often called a hedge against obsolescence. Under what conditions is this actually true?

16–4 Is leasing in any sense a hedge against inflation for the lessee? for the lessor?

16–5 What characteristics of railroad equipment certificates make them prime investment securities?

16–6 One of the alleged advantages of leasing is that it keeps liabilities off the balance sheet, thus making it possible for a firm to obtain more leverage than it otherwise could. This raises the question of whether or not both the lease obligation and the asset involved should be capitalized and shown on the balance sheet. Discuss the pros and cons of capitalizing leases and the related assets.

16–7 A firm is seeking a term loan from a bank. Under what conditions would it want a fixed interest rate, and under what condition would it want the rate to fluctuate with the prime rate?

16–8 Under what conditions would a "balloon note" be advantageous to a borrower?

PROBLEMS

16–1 Suggest the form and source of financing for the following situations:

a) A manufacturer, after a long search for a particular type of equipment he needed, finally found it. The seller demanded cash in full or the deal was off, but the manufacturer had only enough cash for 20 percent of the total required.

b) A hardware dealer saw profits ahead if he could immediately stock up on certain items at favorable prices. He needed additional funds of $75,000 to take advantage of the opportunity.

c) An appliance dealer had recently moved to larger quarters. He needed $120,000 to finance additional inventory to handle increased business.

d) The growing business of a retail butcher on a busy thoroughfare warranted the cost of modernizing for customer convenience and more attractive display. The owner needed $3,000 to pay in full for items not eligible under FHA Title I financing.

e) An established partnership needed to purchase a heavy crane with special attachments that would increase earnings about $2,000 a month. The partnership was in the contracting business. It was able to make a one third down payment, but did not have the balance of $60,000.

f) An automobile mechanic purchased a service station at a relatively low cost because of its previous poor earnings record. He had saved about $5,000, which he invested in the business and which mostly represented payment for equipment acquired. Increased volume necessitated employment of two men, and the owner required additional funds of $3,000 to carry inventory and meet payrolls.

g) A small manufacturer in the woodwork business with a record of stable earnings needed $500,000 to buy additional productive equipment to handle orders for houseware items that had become in short supply. The mortgage on his plant had been partially paid off.

16–2 The Altman Department Store is considering a sale and leaseback of its major property, consisting of land and a building, because it is 35 days late on 80 percent of its accounts payable. The recent profit record and the balance sheet of Altman are shown below. Profit before taxes in 1969 is $25,000; after taxes, $14,000.

ALTMAN DEPARTMENT STORE
BALANCE SHEET
December 31, 1969
(in thousands of dollars)

Cash		$ 200	Accounts payable	$1,000
Receivables		1,000	Bank loans, 6%	1,000
Inventories		1,300	Other current liabilities	500
Total current assets		2,500	Total current debt	2,500
Land	$800		Common stock	1,000
Building	500		Retained earnings	500
Fixtures and equipment	200			
Net fixed assets		1,500		
Total assets		$4,000	Total claims	$4,000

Annual depreciation charges are $40,000 a year on the building and $50,000 a year on the fixtures and equipment.

The land and building could be sold for a total of $2.3 million. The annual net rental will be $170,000.

a) How much capital gains tax will Altman pay if the land and building are sold?
b) Compare the current ratio before and after the sale and leaseback if the net proceeds are used to "clean up" the bank loans and to reduce accounts payable and other current liabilities.
c) If the lease had been in effect during 1969, what would Altman's profit for 1969 have been?
d) What are the basic financial problems facing Altman? Will the sale and leaseback operation solve them?

16–3 The Johnson Company is faced with the decision whether to purchase or to lease a new fork-lift truck. The truck can be leased on a five-year contract for $1,000 a year, or it can be purchased for $4,000. The lease includes maintenance and service. The salvalge value of the truck five years hence is $1,000. The company uses the sum-of-the-years'-digits method of depreciation. If the truck is owned, service and maintenance charges (a deductible cost) would be $250 a year. This cost should be added to the out-of-pocket expenses of owning (shown in the Total Payment column of your worksheet). The company can borrow at 6 percent and has a 50 percent tax rate.

Answer the questions shown below under each of the following alternative assumptions:

1) The firm borrows the $4,000 at an interest rate of 6 percent, and 3 percent is used as the discount factor in comparing the costs of leasing versus owning. (Assume the $4,000 loan is paid back in installments, not in a lump sum.) Taxes are 50 percent.
2) The firm borrows the $4,000 at an interest rate of 6 percent, which is used in computing the interest cost of owning, but the firm's 10 percent cost of capital is used in calculating the present values of the cash flows involved in leasing versus owning. Taxes are 50 percent.

a) Which method of acquiring the use of equipment should the company choose?
b) What factors could alter the results indicated by the quantitative analysis based on the above facts?
c) Discuss the use of 3 percent versus 10 percent as the discount factor.

Selected References

Andrews, Victor L., "Captive Finance Companies," *Harvard Business Review*, XLII (July-August 1964), 80–92.

Arlt, C. T., Jr., "Member Bank Term Lending to Business, 1955–57," *Federal Reserve Bulletin*, XLV (April 1959), 353–368.

Bower, Richard S., Frank C. Herringer, and J. Peter Williamson, "Lease Evaluation," *Accounting Review* XLI, 2 (April 1966), 257–265.

Brigham, Eugene F., "Equipment Lease Financing," *Bankers Magazine,* 149 (Winter 1966), 65–75.

———, "The Impact of Bank Entry on Market Conditions in the Equipment Leasing Industry" *National Banking Review,* II (September 1964), 11–26.

Budzeika, George, "Term Lending by New York City Banks," *Essays in Money and Credit,* Federal Reserve Bank of New York.

———, "The Maturity of Loans at New York City Banks," *Monthly Review,* XLIX (January 1967), 10–14. (New York: Federal Reserve Bank of New York.)

———, "Term Lending by New York City Banks in the 1960's," *Monthly Review,* XLIX (October 1967), 199–203. (New York: Federal Reserve Bank of New York.)

Gant, Donald R., "A Critical Look at Lease Financing," *Controller,* XXIX (June 1961).

———, "Illusion in Lease Financing," *Harvard Business Review,* XXXVII (March-April 1959), 121–142.

Griesinger, Frank K., "Pros and Cons of Leasing Equipment," *Harvard Business Review,* XXXIII (March-April 1955), 75–89.

Hamel, Henry G., "Another Look at Leasing," *Business Management Record,* XIV (November 1963), 47–52.

———, *Leasing in Industry* (New York: National Industrial Conference Board, 1968), Studies in Business Policy, No. 127.

Hayes, Douglas A., *Bank Lending Policies: Issues and Practices,* (Ann Arbor, Mich.: Bureau of Business Research, University of Michigan, 1964), Chapter 6.

Knutson, Peter H., "Leased Equipment and Divisional Return on Capital," *N.A.A. Bulletin,* XLIV (November 1962), 15–20.

Law, Warren A., and M. Colyer Crum, *Equipment Leasing and Commercial Banks* (Chicago, Ill.: Association of Reserve City Bankers, 1963).

Leasing of Industrial Equipment. (Washington, D.C.: Machinery and Allied Products Institute, 1965.)

McLean, James H., "Economic and Accounting Aspects of Lease Financing," *Financial Executive,* XXXI (December 1963), 18–23.

Moore, George S., "Term Loans and Interim Financing," in Benjamin Haggott Beckhart (ed.), *Business Loans of American Commercial Banks* (New York: Ronald, 1959), pp. 208–282.

Myers, John H., *Reporting of Leases in Financial Statements* (New York: American Institute of Certified Public Accountants, 1962).

Nelson, A. Thomas, "Capitalized Leases—The Effect on Financial Ratios," *Journal of Accountancy,* CXVI (July 1963), 49–58.

Opinions of the Accounting Principles Board, No. 5 (New York: American Institute of Certified Public Accountants, 1964).

Robinson, Roland I., *The Management of Bank Funds* (New York: McGraw-Hill, 1962).

Rogers, Dean E., "An Approach to Analyzing Cash Flow for Term Loan Purposes," *Bulletin of Robert Morris Associates,* XLVIII (October 1965), 79–85.

Shillinglaw, Gordon, "Accounting for Leased Property by Capitalization," *NAA Bulletin,* XXXIX (June 1958), 31–45.

Thurlin, W. Bernard, "Own or Lease? Underlying Financial Theory," *Financial Executive,* XXXII (April 1964), 23–31.

Vancil, Richard F., "Lease or Borrow: New Method of Analysis," *Harvard Business Review,* XXXIX (September-October 1961).

———, "Lease or Borrow: Steps in Negotiation," *Harvard Business Review,* XXXIX (November-December 1961), 238–59.

———, and Robert N. Anthony, "The Financial Community Looks at Leasing," *Harvard Business Review,* XXXVII (November-December 1959), 113–130.

Weston, J. Fred, and Rupert Craig, "Understanding Lease Financing," *California Management Review,* II (Winter 1960), 67–75.

Zises, Alvin, "Disclosure of Long-Term Leases," *Journal of Accountancy,* CXI (February 1961), 37–47.

PART SIX

LONG-TERM FINANCING

17

The Market for Long-Term Securities

Short- and intermediate-term financial markets were discussed in Chapters 15 and 16. We now examine the markets in which long-term securities—stocks, bonds, warrants, and convertibles—are traded; we consider efficient procedures for the financial manager to follow when raising funds by selling long-term securities. This background is necessary for an understanding of the characteristics and uses of the long-term financing instruments described in Chapters 18 through 20.

SECURITY MARKETS

There are two broad types of security markets—the *organized exchanges,* typified by the New York Stock Exchange, and the less formal *over-the-counter markets.*[1] Since the organized exchanges have actual physical market locations and are easier to describe and understand, we shall consider them first. With this background it will be easier to comprehend the nature of the over-the-counter market.

Organized Security Exchanges

The organized security exchanges are tangible, physical entities. Each of the larger ones occupies its own building, has specifically designated members, and has an elected governing body—its Board of Governors. Members are said to have seats on the exchange, although everybody stands up. These seats, which are bought and sold, represent the right to trade on the exchange. In 1968, seats on the New York Stock Exchange (NYSE) sold at a record high of $500,000.

Most of the larger stock brokerage firms own seats on the exchanges and designate one of the officers of the firm as a member of the exchange. The designated officer occupies the seat. The exchanges are open daily, and the members meet in a large room equipped with telephones and telegraphs that enable each brokerage house member to communicate with the officers of his firm throughout the country.

Like other markets, a security exchange facilitates communication between buyers and sellers. For example, a Merrill Lynch, Pierce, Fenner, and Smith (the largest brokerage firm) office in Atlanta might receive an order from a customer to buy 100 shares of General Motors stock. Simultaneously, a brokerage house in Denver might receive an order from a customer to sell 100 shares of GM. Each broker would communicate by wire with his firm's representative on the NYSE. Other brokers throughout the country are also receiving customer orders to buy and sell GM, and they are also communicating with their own exchange members. The exchange members with *sell orders* offer the shares for sale, which are bid for by the members with *buy orders*. Thus, the exchanges operate as *auction markets.*[2]

Special procedures are available for handling large blocks of securities. For example, if a firm like General Motors, whose stock is already listed on the NYSE, plans to sell a new issue of stock, the exchange

[1] There is also a "private" market in which the borrowing firm goes directly to the lending institutions; this is the market for *private placements or direct placements,* as it is frequently called. The primary instrument used in this market is the *term* loan, described in Chapter 16.

[2] This discussion is highly simplified. The exchanges have members known as "specialists," who facilitate the trading process by keeping an inventory of shares of the stocks in which they specialize. If a buy order comes in at a time when no sell order arrives, the specialist may sell off some of his inventory. Similarly, if a sell order comes in, the specialist will buy and add to his inventory.

has facilities that make it easier for the market to absorb the new issue. Similarly, if a large mutual fund or pension fund wants to sell a large block of a listed stock, procedures are available that facilitate the sale without putting undue pressures on the stock price.

Two practices said to contribute to effectively functioning securities markets—*margin trading and short selling*—should be noted briefly.

Margin trading involves the buying of securities on credit. For example, when margin requirements are 80 percent, 100 shares of a stock selling for $100 a share can be bought by putting up in cash only $8,000, or 80 percent of the purchase price, and borrowing the remaining $2,000. The stockbroker lends the margin purchaser the funds, retaining custody of the stock as collateral. Margin requirements are determined by the Federal Reserve Board (the Fed). When the Fed judges that stock market activity and prices are unduly stimulated by easy credit, it raises margin requirements and thus reduces the amount of credit available for the purchase of stocks. On the other hand, if the Fed desires to stimulate the market as a part of its over-all monetary policy operations, it reduces margin requirements. The last change in margin requirements prior to publication of this book was in June 1968, when the margin was raised from 70 to 80 percent. The last change prior to that was in 1963, when margins were raised from 50 to 70 percent.

Short selling means selling a security that is not owned by the seller at the time of sale. Short selling is usually performed in anticipation of a decline in the market price. For example, a stock selling at $40 may be sold short. Suppose that in two months the market drops to $30. The short seller can buy at $30 and make delivery on stock which he sold at $40. The seller borrows the stock from his broker; often the broker has the stock because others of his customers either have purchased it on margin or have left the securities in the brokerage house's name—a so-called street name. The advantage claimed for short selling is that it increases the number of participants operating in the market and thereby reduces fluctuations in stock prices. This is, however, a controversial subject.

Insofar as margin trading and short selling provide for a more continuous market, they encourage stock ownership and have two beneficial effects. (1) They broaden the ownership of securities by increasing the ability of people to buy securities. (2) They provide for a more active market; more active trading makes for narrower price fluctuations. However, when a strong speculative psychology grips the market, margin trading can be a fuel that feeds the speculative fervor. Short selling can also aggravate pessimism on the downside. However, there are restrictions on short selling that provide that a short sale may not be made at a price lower than on the last previously recorded sale. Current rules on short selling limit speculative and manipulative practices. Similarly, flexible margin requirements have had salutary effects on the use of credit in stock market transactions.

Benefits Provided by Security Exchanges

Organized security exchanges provide important benefits to businesses in at least four ways.

1. Security exchanges facilitate the investment process because they provide a marketplace in which to conduct transactions efficiently and relatively inexpensively. Investors are thus assured that they will have a place in which to sell their securities, if they decide to do so. The increased liquidity thus provided by the exchanges makes investors willing to accept a lower rate of return on securities than they would otherwise require. This means that exchanges lower the cost of capital to businesses.

2. By providing a market, exchanges create an institution in which continuous transactions test the values of securities. The purchases and sales of securities record judgments on the values and prospects of companies and their securities. Companies whose prospects are judged favorable by the investment community will have higher values, facilitating new financing and growth.

3. Security prices are relatively more stable because of the operation of the security exchanges. Organized markets improve liquidity by providing continuous markets which make for more frequent, but smaller, price changes. In the absence of organized markets, price changes would be less frequent but more violent.

4. The securities markets aid in the digestion of new security issues and facilitate their successful flotation.

OVER-THE-COUNTER SECURITY MARKETS

In contrast to the formal security exchanges, the over-the-counter market is a nebulous, intangible organization. Perhaps an explanation of the name "over the counter" will help clarify exactly what this market is. The exchanges operate as auction markets—buy and sell orders come in more or less simultaneously, and the exchanges are used to match these orders. But if a stock is traded less frequently, perhaps because it is the stock of a new or a small firm, few buy and sell orders come in and matching them within a reasonable length of time would be difficult. To avoid this problem, brokerage firms maintain an inventory of the stocks. They buy when individual investors wish to sell, and sell when investors want to buy. At one time the inventory of securities was kept in a safe and, when being bought and sold, the stocks were literally passed "over the counter."

Today, over-the-counter markets are defined as all facilities that provide for security transactions not conducted on the organized exchanges. These facilities consist primarily of (1) the relatively few brokers who hold inventories of over the counter securities and who are said to "make a market" in these securities and (2) the thousands of brokers who act as agents in bringing these dealers together with investors.

The majority of stocks in terms of the number of issues are traded over the counter. However, the stocks of larger companies are listed on the exchanges, and it is estimated that two-thirds of the dollar volume of stock trading takes place on the exchanges. The situation is reversed in the bond market. Although the bonds of a number of the larger companies are listed on the NYSE bond list, in excess of 95 percent of bond transactions take place in the over-the-counter market. The reason for this is that bonds typically are traded among the large financial institutions—for example, life insurance companies and pension funds—and these institutions deal in very large blocks of securities. It is relatively easy for the over-the-counter bond dealers to arrange the transfer of large blocks of bonds among the relatively few holders of the bonds. It would be impossible to conduct similar operations in the stock market among the literally millions of large and small stockholders.

ECISION O LIST TOCK

The exchanges require firms to meet certain requirements before their stock can be listed. These requirements relate to size of the company, number of years in business, earnings record, number of shares outstanding and their market value, and the like. In general, requirements become higher as we move from the regional exchanges toward the NYSE.

The firm itself makes the decision to seek to list or not list its securities on an exchange. Typically, the stocks of new and small companies are traded over the counter—there is simply not enough activity to justify the use of an auction market for such stocks. As the company grows, establishes an earnings record, expands the number of shares outstanding, and increases its list of stockholders, it may decide to apply for listing on one of the regional exchanges. For example, a Chicago company might list on the Midwest Stock Exchange, or a West Coast company might list its stock on the Pacific Coast Exchange. As the company grows still more, and as its stock becomes distributed throughout the country, it may seek a listing on the American Stock Exchange, the smaller of the two national exchanges. Finally, if it reaches a position as one of the nation's leading firms, it could switch to the Big Board, the New York Stock Exchange.

Assuming a company qualifies, it is generally felt that listing is beneficial both to it and to its stockholders. Listed companies receive a certain amount of free advertising and publicity, and their status as a listed company enhances their prestige and reputation. This probably has a beneficial effect on the sales of the products of the firm, and it certainly is beneficial in terms of lowering the required rate of return on the common stock. Investors respond favorably to increased information, increased liquidity, and increased prestige; by providing investors with these services in the form of listing their companies' stocks, financial managers lower their firms' cost of capital.[3]

NATURE OF INVESTMENT BANKING

In the American economy, saving is performed by one group of persons while investing is performed by another. ("Investing" is used here in the sense of actually putting money into plant, equipment, and inventory, not "investing" in the sense of buying securities.) Thus, savings are placed with financial intermediaries who, in turn, make the funds avail-

[3] Two industries, banking and insurance, have a tradition against listing their stocks. The historic reason given by banks was that they were afraid that a falling market price of their stocks would lead depositors to think the bank itself was in danger and, thus, cause a run on the bank. Some basis for such fears may have existed before the creation of the Federal Deposit Insurance Corporation in 1935, but the fear is no longer justified. The other reason for banks not listing has to do with reporting financial information. The exchanges require that quarterly financial statements be sent to all stockholders; banks have been reluctant to provide financial information. Increasingly, bank regulatory agencies are requiring public disclosure of additional financial information. As this trend continues, it is expected that banks will increasingly seek listing on exchanges. A notable first is the Chase Manhattan Bank, which was listed on the New York Stock Exchange in 1965.

able to firms wishing to acquire plant and equipment and to hold inventories.

One of the major institutions performing this channeling role is known as *investment banking*. The term "investment banker" is somewhat misleading in that investment bankers are neither investors nor bankers. That is, they do not invest their own funds permanently, nor are they repositories for individuals' funds, as are commercial banks or savings banks. What, then, *is* the nature of investment banking? In defining any set of institutions, a functional rather than a descriptive definition is required; for example, an elephant is best defined in terms of appearance, but a shovel is best defined in terms of what it does. Investment banking is best defined in terms of what investment bankers do.

The many activities of investment bankers may be described first in general terms and then with respect to specific functions. The historical and traditional function of the investment banker has been to act as the middleman in channeling driblets of savings and funds of individuals into the purchase of business securities, primarily bonds. The investment banker does this by purchasing and distributing the new securities of individual companies. Specifically, the investment banker performs the following functions.

Underwriting

Underwriting is the insurance function of bearing the risks of adverse price fluctuations during the period in which a new issue of securities is being distributed. The nature of the underwriting function of the investment banker can best be conveyed through an example. A business firm needs $10 million. It selects an investment banker, conferences are held, and the decision is made to issue $10 million of bonds. An underwriting agreement is drawn up; on a specific day, the investment banker presents the company with a check for $10 million (less commission). In return, the investment banker receives bonds in denomination of $1,000 each, which he sells to the public.

The company receives the $10 million before the investment banker has sold the bonds. Between the time the investment banker pays the firm the $10 million and the time he has sold the bonds, the investment banker bears all the risk of market price fluctuations in the bonds. Conceivably, it can take the investment banker 10, 20, 30 days, 6 months, or longer to sell bonds. If in the interim the bond market collapses, the investment banker will be carrying the risk of loss in the sale of the bonds. There have been dramatic instances of bond market collapses within one week after an investment banker has bought $50 million or $100 million of bonds.

But the individual firm does not need to be concerned about the risk of market price fluctuations while the investment banker is selling the bonds. The firm has received its $10 million. *One fundamental economic function of the investment banker, then, is to underwrite the risk of a decline in the market price between the time the investment banker transmits the money to the firm and the time the bonds are placed in the hands of their ultimate buyers.* For this reason, the investment banker is often called an underwriter: he is an underwriter of risk during the distribution period.

Distribution

The second function of the investment banker is securities marketing. The investment banker is a specialist who has a staff and dealer organization to distribute securities. The investment banker can, therefore, perform the physical distribution function more efficiently and more economically than could an individual corporation. Sporadically, whenever it wished to sell an issue of securities, each corporation would find it necessary to establish a marketing or selling organization. This would be a very expensive and ineffective method of selling securities. The investment banker has a permanent, trained staff and dealer organization continuously available to distribute the securities. In addition, the investment banker's reputation for selecting good companies and pricing securities fairly builds up a broad clientele over a period, further increasing the ease with which he can sell securities.

Advice and Counsel

Since the investment banker is engaged in the origination and sale of securities, through experience he becomes an expert in advising about terms and characteristics of securities that will appeal to investors. The advice and guidance of the investment banker in determining the characteristics and provisions of securities so that they will be successfully marketed is valuable. Furthermore, the reputation of the investment banker, as a seller of the securities, depends upon the subsequent performance of the securities. Therefore, he will often sit on the boards of directors of firms whose securities he has sold. In this way he is able to provide continuing financial counsel and to increase the firm's probability of success.

Such, then, are the main economic functions provided by investment bankers. The investment houses engage in a wide variety of activities to provide many other services to business firms, but the other activities will best be understood after a more complete description of the investment banking operation is given.

INVESTMENT BANKING OPERATION

To understand clearly the investment banking function it is useful to trace the history of a new issue of securities.[4]

Pre-underwriting Conferences

First, the members of the issuing firm and the investment banker hold pre-underwriting conferences. At these conferences they discuss the amount of capital to be raised, the type of security to be issued, and the terms of the agreement.

Memorandums will be written by the treasurer of the issuing company, describing alternative proposals suggested at the conferences. Meetings of the board of directors of the issuing company will be held to discuss the alternatives and to attempt to reach a decision.

At some point, the issuer enters an agreement with the investment banker that a flotation will take place. The investment banker will then begin to conduct what is called an underwriting investigation. If the company is proposing to purchase additional assets, the underwriter's engineering staff will make an engineering analysis of the proposed asset acquisition. A public accounting firm will be called upon to make an audit of the issuing firm's financial situation. In addition, the public accounting firm will aid in the preparation of the registration statements for the Securities and Exchange Commission (SEC) in connection with these issues.

A firm of lawyers will be called in to give interpretations and judgments about legal aspects of the flotation. In addition, the originating underwriter, who will be the manager of the subsequent underwriting syndicate, will make an exhaustive investigation of the prospects of the company.

When the investigations are completed, but before registration with

[4] The process described here relates primarily to situations where the firm doing the financing picks an investment banker, then negotiates with him over the terms of the issue. An alternative procedure, used extensively only in the public utility industry, is for the selling firm to specify the terms of the new issue, then to have investment bankers bid for the entire new issue by use of *sealed bids*. The very high fixed costs that an investment banker must incur to thoroughly investigate the company and its new issue rule out sealed bids except for the very largest issues. The type of operation described in this section is called *negotiated underwriting;* competition is keen among underwriters, of course, to develop and maintain working relations with business firms.

the SEC, an underwriting agreement will be drawn up by the investment banker. Terms of the tentative underwriting agreement may be modified through discussions between the underwriter and the issuing company. Finally, agreement will be reached on all underwriting terms except the actual price of the securities.

Registration Statement

A registration statement will then be filed with the SEC. The commission requires a 20-day waiting period, during which time its staff analyzes the registration statement to determine whether there are any omissions or misrepresentations of fact. The SEC may file exceptions to the registration statement or may ask for additional information from the issuing company or the underwriters during the 20-day waiting period. During this period, the investment bankers are not permitted to offer the securities for sale, although they may print preliminary prospectuses with all the information customarily contained in a prospectus, except the offering price.

Setting the Price of the Securities

The actual price the underwriter pays the issuer is not generally determined until the close of the registration period. There is no universally followed practice, but one common arrangement for a new issue of stock calls for the investment banker to buy the securities at a prescribed number of points below the closing price on the last day of registration. For example, suppose the stock of XYZ Company has a current price of $38 and has sold in a range of $35 to $40 a share during the previous three months. The firm and the underwriter agree that the investment banker will buy 200,000 new shares at $2.50 below the closing price on the last day of registration. If the stock closes at $36 on the day the SEC releases the issue, then the firm will receive $33.50 a share. Typically, such agreements have an escape clause that provides for the contract to be voided if the price of the securities ends below some predetermined figure. In the illustrative case, this "upset" price might be set at $34 a share. Thus, if the closing price of the shares on the last day of registration is $33.50, the issuing firm will have an option of withdrawing from the agreement.

The preceding arrangement holds, of course, only for additional offerings of the stock of firms whose old stock was previously traded. When a company "goes public" for the first time, the investment banker and the firm will negotiate on a price in accordance with the valuation principles described in Chapter 10. But, since the value of an individual stock is very much dependent upon the state of the general market, the *final* price on a new issue is established at the close of the SEC waiting period.

The investment banker will have an easier job if the issue is priced low and has a high yield. The issuer of the securities naturally wants as high a price and as low a yield as possible. Some conflict of interest on price therefore arises between the investment banker and the issuer. If the issuer is financially sophisticated and looks to comparisons with similar issues of securities, the investment banker is forced to price close to the market.

The Underwriting Syndicate

The investment banker with whom the issuing firm has conducted its discussions will not typically handle the purchase and distribution of the issue alone unless the issue is a very small one. If the sums of money involved are large and the risk of price fluctuation substantial, the investment banker forms a syndicate in an effort to minimize the amount of risk he carries. A syndicate is a temporary association for the purpose of carrying out a specific objective. The nature of the arrangements for a syndicate in the underwriting and sale of a security through an investment banker may best be understood with the aid of Figure 17–1.

The managing underwriter invites other investment bankers to participate in the transaction on the basis of their knowledge of the particular

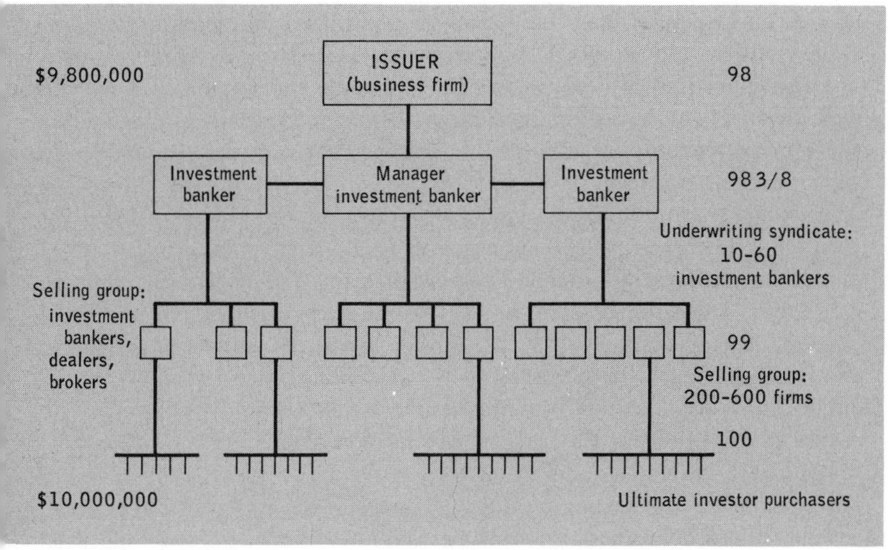

Figure 17–1 Diagram of Sales of $10 Million of Bonds through Investment Bankers

kind of offering to be made and on the basis of their strength and dealer contacts in selling securities of the type involved in the issue.

Each investment banker has business relations with other investment bankers and dealers; thus, each investment banker has a selling group consisting of himself and other investment bankers and dealers. Some firms combine all these characteristics. For example, the firm of Merrill Lynch, Pierce, Fenner and Smith, Inc., underwrites some issues and manages the underwriting of others. On still other flotations it will be invited by the manager to join in the distribution of the issue. It also purchases securities as the dealer and carries an inventory of these securities. It publishes lists of securities it has for sale. In addition to being a dealer, Merrill Lynch, of course, carries on substantial activity as a broker. An individual investment firm may carry on all these functions, just as a department store sells many different types of merchandise.

But there are also firms with a narrower range of functions—specialty dealers, specialty brokers, and specialty investment counselors. Thus, in the financial field there is specialization of financial functions as well as department store types of operations. A *dealer* purchases securities outright, holds them in inventory as a grocery store would hold its inventory, and sells them at whatever price he can get. He may benefit from price appreciation or he may suffer a loss on declines, as any merchandiser does. A *broker,* on the other hand, takes orders for purchases and transmits them to the proper exchange; his gain is the commission he charges for the service.

Syndicates are used in the distribution of securities for three reasons. (1) A single investment banker may be financially unable to handle a large issue alone. (2) The originating house may desire to spread the risk even if it is financially able to handle the issue alone. (3) The utilization of several selling organizations, as well as other underwriters, permits an economy of selling effort and expense and encourages broader, nationwide distribution.

Participating underwriters and dealers are provided with full information on all phases of these financing transactions, and they share in the underwriting commission. To show how the underwriting commission is shared, let us illustrate how a two-point spread would be divided. An investment banker buys $10 million worth of bonds to be sold at par, or $1,000 each. If the investment banker receives a two-point spread, he will buy the bonds from the issuer at 98; thus, he must pay the issuer $9.8 million for the issue of $10 million. Typically, on a two-point spread, the manager-underwriter will receive the first ¼ of 1 percent for originating and managing the syndicate. Next, the entire underwriting group will receive about ¾ of 1 percent. Members of the selling group receive about 1 percent as a sales commission.

If the manager of the underwriting group makes a sale to an ultimate purchaser of the securities, he will receive the ¼ percent as manager, ¾ percent as underwriter, and 1 percent as the seller—the full 2 percent. If he wholesales some of the securities to members of the selling group who make the ultimate sale, the latter will receive the 1 percent selling commission, and the manager will receive the other 1 percent for managing and underwriting the issue. If the issue is managed by one firm, underwritten by a second, and sold by a third, the 2 percent commission is divided, with 1 percent going to the selling firm, ¾ percent to the underwriter, and ¼ percent to the manager of the underwriting group.

Ordinarily, each underwriter's liability is limited to his agreed-upon commitment. For example, if an investment banker participates in a $20 million offering and agrees to see to it that $5 million of the securities are sold, his responsibility ends when he sells his $5 million.

Selling Group

The selling group is formed primarily for the purpose of distributing securities; it consists of dealers, who take relatively small participations from the members of the underwriting group. The underwriters act as wholesalers; members of the selling group act as retailers. The number of houses in a selling group depends partly upon the size of the issue. A selling group may have as many as 300 to 400 dealers; for example, the one for Communications Satellite Corporation consisted of 385 members.

The operation of the selling group is controlled by the *selling group agreement,* which usually covers the following major points.

DESCRIPTION OF THE ISSUE. The description is set forth in a report on the issue, the *prospectus,* which fully describes the issue and the issuer.

CONCESSION. Members of the selling group subscribe to the new issue at a public offering price less the concession given to them as a commission for their selling service. In the preceding example, this was 1 percent.

HANDLING REPURCHASED SECURITIES. The selling group agreement provides that no member of the selling group be permitted to sell the securities below the public offering price. The syndicate manager invariably pegs the quotation in the market by placing continuous orders to buy at the public offering price. A careful record is kept of bond or stock certificate numbers so that repurchased bonds may be identified with the member of the selling group who sold them. General practice is to cancel the commission on such securities and add brokerage costs incurred in the repurchase. Repurchased securities are then placed with other dealers for sale.[5]

DURATION OF SELLING GROUP. The most common provision in selling group agreements is that the group has an existence of 30 days, subject to earlier termination by the manager. The agreement may be extended, however, for an additional 80 days by members representing 75 percent of the selling group.

Offering and Sale

After the selling group has been formed, the actual offering proceeds. Publicity in advance of the offering date is developed. Advertising material for release as soon as permissible is prepared. The actual day of the offering is chosen with a view to avoiding temporary congestion in the security market and other unfavorable events or circumstances.

The formal public offering is called "opening the books," an archaic term reflecting ancient customs of the investment banking trade. When the books are opened, the manager accepts subscriptions to the issue from both selling group participants and outsiders who may wish to buy.

If the demand for the issue is great, the books may be closed immediately. An announcement is then made that the issue is oversubscribed. However, when the reception is not strong, the books may remain open for an extended period.

Market Stabilization

During the period of the offering and distribution of securities, the manager of the underwriting group typically stabilizes the price of the issue. The duration of the price-pegging operation is usually 30 days. The price is pegged by placing orders to buy at a specified price in the market. The pegging operation is designed to prevent a cumulative downward movement in the price if it should soften. A downward price shift would result in losses for all members of the underwriting group. As the manager of the underwriting group has the major responsibility, he assumes the task of pegging the price.

If the market deteriorates during the offering period, the investment banker carries a rather substantial risk. For this reason, the pegging operation may not be sufficient to protect the underwriters. In the Pure

[5] Without these repurchase arrangements, a member of the selling group could sell his share of the securities on the open market instead of to new purchasers. Since the pegging operation is going on, there would be a ready market for the securities; consequently, a penalty is necessary to avoid thwarting of the syndicate operation.

Oil Company issue of $44 million convertible preferred stock of September 3, 1937, at 100, only $1 million of shares were sold by the underwriters. At the conclusion of the underwriting agreement, initial trading took place at 74, giving the investment bankers a loss of over $11 million ($43 million × 26 percent). Not until 1941, did the stock again sell as high as 90. In the Textron issue of June 1967, the offering was reduced from $100 million to $50 million because of market congestion, and yet 5 percent of the bonds were unsold after the initial offering. Other similar cases can be cited.

It has been charged that pegging the price during the offering period constitutes a monopolistic price-fixing arrangement. However, investment bankers reply that not to peg the price would increase the risk and therefore the underwriting cost to the issuer. On balance, it appears that the pegging operation is a socially useful function. The danger of monopolistic pricing is avoided, or at least mitigated substantially, by competitive factors. If an underwriter attempts to set a monopolistic price on a particular issue of securities, the investor can turn to thousands of other securities not involved in price-pegging operations. The degree of control over the market by the underwriter in a price-pegging operation seems to be negligible.

Costs of Flotation

The cost of selling new issues of securities can be put into perspective by Table 17–1. The table summarizes the data on cost of flotation in

TABLE 17–1 COSTS OF FLOTATION, 1951–1955
(costs expressed as percentage of gross proceeds)

	DEBT			PREFERRED STOCK			COMMON STOCK		
Size of Issue (in millions of dollars)	Underwriting Commission	Other Expenses	Total Costs	Underwriting Commission	Other Expenses	Total Costs	Underwriting Commission	Other Expenses	Total Costs
Under 0.5	—	—	—	—	—	—	21.0	6.2	27.2
0.5–0.9	7.5	4.0	11.5	8.7	4.0	12.7	17.1	4.6	21.7
1.0–1.9	5.8	2.4	8.2	6.0	2.0	8.0	11.2	2.3	13.5
2.0–4.9	2.4	1.4	3.8	3.8	1.0	4.8	8.5	1.5	10.0
5.0–9.9	1.0	0.8	1.8	2.9	0.8	3.7	5.3	0.9	6.2
10.0–19.9	0.9	0.6	1.5	2.4	0.5	2.9	5.2	0.5	5.7
20.0–49.9	0.9	0.5	1.4	2.8	0.4	3.2	5.0	0.4	5.4
50.0 and over	0.9	0.3	1.2	2.1	0.4	2.5	—	—	—

SOURCES: Securities and Exchange Commission, *Cost of Flotation of Corporate Securities*, 1951–1955 (Washington, D.C.: U.S. Government Printing Office, June 1957).

the last available report on the subject by the SEC. Although these data are rather old, the figures are still appropriate; important generalizations can be drawn from them.

1. The cost of flotation for common stock is greater than for preferred stocks, and the costs of both are greater than the cost of flotation for bonds.
2. The costs of flotation as a percentage of the gross proceeds are greater for small issues than for large ones.

What are the reasons for these relationships? The explanations are found in the amount of risk involved and in the job of physical distribution. Bonds are generally bought in large blocks by a relatively few institutional investors, whereas stocks are bought by millions of individuals. For this reason the distribution job is greater for common stock, and the expenses of marketing it are greater.

The explanation for the variation in cost with the size of issue is also easily found. In the first place, certain fixed expenses are associated with any distribution of securities. Four items of expense account for 85 percent of the cost of flotation. Many of these expenses are fixed—the underwriting investigation, the preparation of the registration statement, legal fees, and so forth. Since they are relatively large and fixed, their percentage of the total cost of flotation runs high on small issues.

Second, small issues are typically those of relatively less well-known firms. The underwriting expenses may be larger than usual, because the danger of omitting vital information is greater for a small firm. Furthermore, the selling job is greater. More salesmen must exert greater effort to sell the securities of a less well-known firm. For these reasons the underwriting commission, as a percentage of the gross proceeds, is relatively high for small issues.

It has been charged that the expenses of flotation have become high since the SEC, created in 1934, began requiring that relatively elaborate registration statements be filed prior to selling securities. An analysis of the costs of flotation has been made, breaking them down into costs associated with registration and those not affected by it. Underwriting commissions account for about 65 percent of the total cost of flotation. Registration expenses account for about 30 percent, and expenses not affected by registration account for the remainder, or about 5 percent. Registration expenses as a percentage of the gross proceeds are relatively minor and do not vary greatly with the size of flotation. Costs partly affected by registration—printing, engraving, legal, accounting, and engineering costs—do increase somewhat in percentage as the size of flotation decreases. The other costs are relatively minor.

These data demonstrate convincingly that the high percentage costs of flotation on small issues are not caused by discrimination against small issues. The fixed expenses of flotation are large when expressed as a percentage of the proceeds on small issues.

In addition to the factors discussed above, flotation costs are also influenced by whether or not the issue is a rights offering, and if it is, by the extent of the underpricing.[6] If rights are used and if the underpricing is substantial, then the investment banker bears little risk of inability to sell the shares. Further, very little selling effort will be required in such a situation. These two factors combine to enable a company to float new securities to its own stockholders at a relatively low cost.

EGULATION 'F SECURITY RADING

The operations of investment bankers, the exchanges, and the over-the-counter markets described in the previous sections of this chapter are significantly influenced by a series of federal statutes enacted during and after 1933. The financial manager is affected by these laws for several reasons. (1) Corporate officers are subjected to additional liabilities. (2) The laws affect the ease and costs of financing. (3) They also affect the behavior of the money and capital markets in which the corporations' securities are sold and traded. (4) Investors' willingness to buy securities is influenced by the existence of safeguards provided by these laws.

Securities Act of 1933

The first of the securities acts, the Securities Act of 1933, followed Congressional investigations after the stock market collapse of 1929–1932. The reasons motivating the act were (1) the large losses to investors, (2) the failures of many corporations on which little information had been provided, and (3) the misrepresentations that had been made to investors.

The basic objective of the Securities Act of 1933 was to provide for both *full disclosure* of relevant information and a *record of representations*. It seeks to achieve these objectives by the following means.

[6] "Rights offerings" involve the sale of stock to existing stockholders. This topic is discussed extensively in Chapter 18.

1. It applies to all interstate offerings to the public (some exemptions are government bonds and bank stocks) in amounts of $300,000 or more.

2. Securities must be reigstered at least 20 days before they are publicly offered. The registration statement provides financial, legal, and technical information about the company. A prospectus summarizes this information for use in selling the securities. If information is inadequate or misleading, the SEC will delay or stop the public offering.

3. After the registration has become effective, the securities may be offered if accompanied by the prospectus. Preliminary or "red herring" prospectuses may be distributed to potential buyers during the waiting period.

4. Any purchaser who suffers a loss may sue for damages if the registration statement or prospectus contains misrepresentations or omissions of material facts. Liabilities and severe penalties may be imposed on the issuer, its officers, directors, accountants, engineers, appraisers, underwriters, and others who participated in the preparation of the registration statement.

The act provides for full disclosure. It also has resulted in a procedure for obtaining a record of representations.

Securities Exchange Act of 1934

The Securities Exchange Act of 1934 extends the disclosure principle as applied to new issues by the act of 1933 to trading in already issued securites (the "secondhand" securities market). It seeks to accomplish this by the following measures.

1. It establishes a Securities and Exchange Commission (the Federal Trade Commission had been administering the act of 1933).

2. It provides for registration and regulation of national securities exchanges. Companies whose securities are listed on an exchange must file reports similar to registration statements with both the SEC and the stock exchange and provide periodic reports as well.

3. It provides control over corporate "insiders." Officers, directors, and major stockholders of a corporation must file monthly reports of changes in holdings of the stock of the corporation. Any short-term profits from such transactions may have to be paid to the corporation, if stockholders take legal action.

4. The act gives the SEC the power to prohibit manipulation by such devices as pools (aggregations of funds used to affect prices artificially), wash sales (sales between members of the same group to record artificial transaction prices), and pegging the market. "Put-and-call" transactions were made subject to regulation.

5. The SEC is given control over the proxy machinery and practices.

6. Control over the flow of credit into security transactions is established by giving the Board of Governors of the Federal Reserve System the power to control margin requirements.

It will be noted that these powers extend only to listed securities. Many feel that the powers should be extended also to unlisted securities.

Mutual Fund Regulated - 1940 act
Advisor's are Regulated

APPRAISAL OF REGULATION OF SECURITY TRADING

Why should security transactions be regulated? If a valid answer exists, it is found in the argument that a great body of relevant knowledge is necessary for an informed judgment of the value of a security. Moreover, security values are subject to great gyrations, which influence stability and business conditions generally. Hence, social well-being requires that orderly markets be promoted.

The objectives of the regulation may be summarized into three points:

1. To protect the amateur investor from fraud and to provide him with a basis for more informed judgments
2. To control the volume of bank credit to finance security speculation
3. To provide orderly markets in securities

Progress has been made on all three counts. There has been some cost in the increased time and expense involved in new flotations by companies. Although these burdens have not been as large as some persons have claimed, room for improvement exists. The regulations are powerless to prevent investors from investing in unsound ventures or to prevent stock prices from skyrocketing during booms and falling greatly during periods of pessimism. But requirements for increased information have been of great value.

From the standpoint of the financial manager, regulation has twofold significance. It affects the costs of issuing securities and also the effectiveness of the operation of the securities markets. With regard to the first, the data on costs of flotation reviewed above indicate that such costs have, in fact, been increased by regulation requirements. The increase, however, appears to have been only moderate except for smaller issues. The enactment of the regulatory acts of the 1930s restored public confidence in the securities markets and paved the way for renewed wide public participation in the securities markets with the post-World War II recovery in spending power. The net effect of regulation has therefore been to facilitate the raising of capital by business.

SUMMARY

Securities are traded both on *exchanges* and in the *over-the-counter market.* The stocks of larger industrial and utility companies are generally listed on an exchange, while stocks of financial institutions and bonds of practically all firms are traded over the counter. From the standpoint of the financial manager, listing on an exchange seems advantageous for seasoned issues. The over-the-counter market may aid in the seasoning process until the security can meet the requirements for listing.

The investment banker provides middleman services to both the seller and the buyer of new securities. He helps plan the issue, underwrites it, and handles the job of selling the issue to the ultimate investor. The cost of the service to the issuer is related to the magnitude of the total job the banker must perform to place the issue. The investment banker must also look to the interests of his brokerage customers; if these investors are not satisfied with the banker's products, they will deal elsewhere.

The financial manager should be familiar with the federal laws regulating the issuance and trading of securities, because they influence his liabilities and affect financing methods and costs. Regulation of securities trading seeks (1) to provide information that investors can utilize as a basis for judging the merits of securities, (2) to control the volume of credit used in securities trading, and (3) to provide orderly securities markets. The laws, however, do not prevent either purchase of unsound issues or wide price fluctuations. They raise somewhat the costs of flotation but have probably decreased the cost of capital by increasing public confidence in the securities markets.

Flotation costs are lowest for bonds, higher for preferred stocks, and highest for common stock. Larger companies have lower flotation costs than smaller ones for each type of security, and most companies can cut their stock flotation costs by issuing the new securities to stockholders through rights offerings.

QUESTIONS

17–1 State several advantages to a firm that lists its stock on a major stock exchange.

17–2 Would you expect the cost of capital of a firm to be affected if it changed its status from one traded over the counter to one traded on the New York Stock Exchange? Explain.

17–3 Evaluate the following statement: "Short selling is fundamentally a form of gambling; it is simply betting that a stock's price will decline. Buying stocks, on the other hand, is more in the nature of true investment; stock is purchased in order to receive a dividend return on the invested capital. Consequently, if we do not wish to see Wall Street turned into an eastern Las Vegas, all short selling should be forbidden."

17–4 Evaluate the following statement: "The fundamental purpose of the federal security laws dealing with new issues is to prevent investors, principally small ones, from sustaining losses on the purchase of stocks."

17–5 Suppose two firms were each selling $10 million of common stock. The firms are identical—that is, they are of the same size, are in the same industry, have the same leverage, and have other similarities—except that one is publicly owned and the other is closely held. Would their costs of flotation be the same? If different, state the probable relationships. If the issue were $10 million of bonds, would your answer be the same?

17–6 Define these terms: brokerage firm, underwriting group, selling group, and investment banker.

17–7 Each month the Securities and Exchange Commission publishes a report of the transactions made by the officers and directors of listed firms in their own companies' equity securities. Why do you suppose the SEC makes this report?

17–8 The SEC forbids officers and directors to sell short the shares of their own company. Why do you suppose this rule is on the books?

17–9 Prior to 1933, investment banking and commercial banking were both carried on by the same firm. In that year, however, the Banking Act required that these functions be separated. Based on your knowledge of investment banking and commercial banking, discuss the pros and cons of this forced separation.

17–10 Before entering a formal agreement, investment bankers investigate quite carefully the companies whose securities they underwrite; this is especially true of the issues of firms going public for the first time. Since the bankers do not themselves plan to hold the securities but plan to sell them to others as soon as possible, why are they so concerned about making careful investigations? Does your answer to the question have any bearing on the fact that investment banking is a very difficult field to "break into"?

17–11 If competitive bidding was required on all security offerings, would flotation costs be higher or lower? Would the size of the issuing firm be material in determining the effects of required competitive bidding?

17–12 Since investment bankers price new issues in relation to outstanding issues, should a spread exist between the yields on the new and the outstanding issues? Discuss this matter separately for stock issues and bond issues.

17–13 What is there about the nature of insurance companies that causes them to make, on the average, (a) longer term loans, and (b) larger loans, than commercial banks?

17–14 What problems are raised by the increasing purchase of equities by institutional investors?

PROBLEMS

17–1 Listed below are salient facts on the terms of sale of several securities sold through investment bankers in recent years. All facts are taken from prospectuses issued in connection with the sales. Explain the differences in underwriting costs between the groups and among the firms within each group.

	Securities Issued			
Company Name, Business, Industry Characteristics	*Date*	*Size (in millions of dollars)*	*Unit Price to Public (in dollars)*	*Total Under-writing Cost (in percentages)*
I. Bonds				
A. Nonconvertible				
1. General Motors Acceptance Corporation. Organized 1919. Finances distribution of new cars and dealers' installment sales of General Motors products. Industry is competitive, discount rates fluctuate depending on competitive factor. 4½%, due 1985.	Nov. 1963	150.00	995.00	0.875
2. The Western Union Telegraph Company. Organized 1851. Furnishes communication services throughout the United States. Provides the only public telegraph message service. Competitive with telephone and mail. 5%, due 1982.	Mar. 1964	75.00	1,005.00	1.46
3. The Maston Company, Inc. Organized				

	Securities Issued			
Company Name, Business, Industry Characteristics	*Date*	*Size (in millions of dollars)*	*Unit Price to Public (in dollars)*	*Total Underwriting Cost (in percentages)*
in 1923. Provides commercial and industrial loans up to three years. 5½%, due 1977.	Apr. 1962	5.00	1,000.00	2.29
B. Convertible with rights				
1. Litton Industry, Inc. Organized 1953. Manufacturing and sales business, commercial and military electrical systems. Industry is highly competitive and subject to changes in defense budget. 3½%, due 1987. Market price common: $138; conversion price: $160 until 1972, thereafter $170.	Apr. 1962	50.70	1,000.00	1.70*
2. Brunswick Corporation. Organized 1907. Principal product is bowling supplies. Company is one of the two leading manufacturers in its field. 4½%, due 1981. Market price common: $47; conversion price: $51.	Jan. 1961	25.60	1,000.00	2.06*
3. Chock Full O' Nuts. Organized 1932. Operates a chain of counter-service restaurants. Restaurants principally located in the Borough of Manhattan, New York City. 4½%, due 1981. Market price common: $26; conversion price: $28.50.	Aug. 1961	7.00	1,000.00	4.07*
C. Convertible: nonrights				
1. Union Oil Company of California. Organ-				

Company Name, Business, Industry Characteristics	Securities Issued *Date*	*Size (in millions of dollars)*	*Unit Price to Public (in dollars)*	*Total Under-writing Cost (in percentages)*
ized 1890. Engaged in substantially all branches of oil industry. The oil industry is characterized by intensive competition. 4¼%, due 1991. Market price common: $55; conversion price: $65.	June 1961	60.00	1,000.00	1.26
2. Baxter Laboratories, Inc. Organized 1931. One of the leading pharmaceutical companies in the manufacture and sale of parental solutions. Industry is extremely competitive. 4%, due 1982. Market price common: $31; conversion price: $38.	Apr. 1962	10.00	1,020.00	2.29
3. Standard Motor Products, Inc. Organized 1926. Engaged in the manufacture and sale of replacement parts for electrical and fuel systems, mainly for motor vehicles. Primary market is the automobile industry. 4¾%, due 1984. Market price common: $13; conversion price: $15.	Apr. 1964	3.00	1,000.00	4.27
II. Nonconvertible Preferred Stock				
1. Brockton Edison Company. Organized 1883. A Massachusetts electric utility serving an aggregate population of about 200,000. Is a member of the hold-				

	Securities Issued			
Company Name, Business, Industry Characteristics	*Date*	*Size (in millions of dollars)*	*Unit Price to Public (in dollars)*	*Total Underwriting Cost (in percentages)*
ing company system of Eastern Utilities Associates. No competition within its territory. 4.64%.	Oct. 1963	6.00	1,019.78	1.64
III. Common Stock				
A. With Rights				
1. Bank of America. Organized 1904. Provides banking services in California. Operates the largest system of branch banks in the nation. Market price: bid, \$65.88, ask, \$69.75; subscription price: \$59.	Nov. 1961	94.4	59.00	1.19*
2. The Western Casualty and Surety Company. Organized 1924. Engaged in the underwriting of all major types of insurance except life. In 1960, ranked forty-seventh among 115 leading insurance company groups of all types. Market price: bid, \$60.50, ask, \$62; subscription price: \$57.	Mar. 1962	10.7	57.00	1.96*
3. The Akron-Dime Banks. Organized in 1960 from the consolidation of the Dime Bank and the Bank of Akron. The Dime Bank was organized in 1900 and the Bank of Akron Company in 1918. Bank has 11 offices serving Summit County, Ohio. Is the second largest of 6 commercial banks in				

Company Name, Business, Industry Characteristics	Securities Issued			
	Date	*Size (in millions of dollars)*	*Unit Price to Public (in dollars)*	*Total Underwriting Cost (in percentages)*
the county. Market price: bid, $34, ask, $35; subscription price: $26.	June 1965	1.7	26.00	1.92*
B. Nonrights				
1. Communications Satellite Corporation. Organized 1963. Plans to establish and operate a global commercial communication satellite system. Authorized by the Communication Satellite Act of 1962, but not an agency of the United States government. No previous market price.	June 1964	200.0	20.00	2.3
2. Delta Air Lines, Inc. Organized 1930. Engaged in air transportation of persons, property, and mail. Industry is regulated by the government. Market price: $38.	Apr. 1962	7.6	37.25	6.38
3. Hudson Wholesale Groceries, Inc. Organized 1918. Engaged primarily in the procurement, warehousing, and sale of groceries and nonfood items to supermarkets, discount stores, and neighborhood grocery stores. No previous market price.	May 1962	0.8	8.00	19.25

* The starred figures represent the minimum cost of financing, assuming that the subscription is fully subscribed. This cost will increase if the underwriter is required to buy any unsubscribed stock. In general, the subscription price is sufficiently below the market price to insure complete subscription. This point is discussed in more detail in Chapter 18.

17–2 Match each firm in list 1 with the most appropriate source of financing found in list 2, and set forth the key factors determining your choice. (There is no one right answer to this problem. Judgment is required, and where judgment is called into play, different people will reach different conclusions.)

List 1

a) Firm selling a large volume of small- and medium-sized orders to numerous medium-sized firms. Working capital position and ownership investment relatively small.

b) Medium-sized firm producing plastic toys. Profitability good, but dependent on independence of action by two owners. Growth good, requiring substantial investment in inventories of specialized packaging materials.

c) Medium-sized firm in growing industry. Needs a 15-to-20-year loan of $2 million; needs funds quickly; professional, financial, and business analysis indicates that the firm's outlook is promising.

d) Two scientists with strong technical competence have an idea for developing a product. Only technical experts could appraise the soundness of the idea. Need management guidance and encouragement as well as financing.

e) Large, highly reputable firm in the steel industry with expansion needs. Good credit rating with a 60 percent debt ratio. Fairly high price/earnings ratio.

f) Firm has large seasonal needs for funds in the autumn of each year.

g) Textile firm with declining profits because of competition of lower labor costs in other regions of the United States. Considering relocation in low-cost labor areas in cities interested in attracting new industry.

List 2

1. Commercial bank
2. Investment bankers
3. Life insurance company
4. Finance companies
5. Equity markets
6. Suppliers
7. Investment-development companies or Small Business Investment Company (SBIC).
8. Community-development companies
9. Friends and relatives

17–3 Excerpts from prospectuses, with particular focus on the underwriter agreements, are given below for three firms.

a) What differences do you find in the underwriting costs and agreements?

b) How do you explain the differences?

A summary of the financial information on the companies follows:

	Speedee Mart, Inc.	*Spiegel, Inc.*	*Beckman Instruments, Inc.*
Total assets, end of 1960	$2.3*	$291.3*	$39.0*
Net worth, end of 1960	0.7	64.2	19.5
Sales			
1958	0.097	152.7	39.8
1960	0.253	268.8	54.3
Net Income after taxes			
1958	0.018	5.0	(0.946)
1960	0.023	11.8	3.1

* Dollar amounts in millions

Speedee Mart, Inc. 90,000 shares, common stock, without par value.

	Price to Public	*Underwriting Discounts and Commissions*	*Proceeds to Company*
Per share	$ 6	$ 0.60	$ 5.40
Total	540,000	54,000.00	486,000.00

DESCRIPTION OF BUSINESS

Speedee Mart, Inc. (the "company"), whose principal offices are located at 7988 Normal Avenue, La Mesa, California, was incorporated in California on April 10, 1956. It is engaged in the business of enfranchising others (franchises) to manage and operate retail food stores under the name "Speedee Mart." From October 2, 1960, 51 stores have been doing business under franchises as herein described and the company was in varying stages of establishing 33 additional stores.

Speedee Mart markets are located primarily in areas where they provide convenient neighborhood food-shopping facilities away from metropolitan shopping centers. In a sense, these convenience markets, which are open from 7 A.M. to 11 P.M., seven days a week, are in competition with several national supermarket chain store organizations, local chain stores, and large independent food stores, as well as other neighborhood markets. The Speedee Mart stores do not, however, purport to compete for the large weekly shopping trade, but rather to provide a convenient place for customers to make purchases for daily needs. The company believes that it meets supermarket prices on items comprising a majority of its sales volume.

UNDERWRITING

The underwriter, J. A. Hogle & Company, 132 South Main Street, Salt Lake City, Utah, has made a firm commitment, subject to the terms and conditions of the underwriting agreement (a copy of which is filed as an exhibit to the registration statement), to purchase all the shares of the company offered hereby. The company has been advised by the underwriters that the common stock is proposed to be offered by the underwriter for sale initially at the public offering price set forth on the cover page of this prospectus. Concessions to selected dealers may be allowed in an amount not exceeding 35 cents a share, of which 15 cents a share may be reallowed to other dealers, provided such reallowance is retained. The public offering price and the concessions and reallowances to dealers may be changed by the underwriter after the initial public offering, by reason of changes in market conditions.

SOURCE: Prospectus, J. A. Hogle & Company, January 31, 1961.

Spiegel, Inc., $40,000,000, 5¼% debentures, dated April 1, 1961; due April 1, 1983.

	Price to Public	*Underwriting Discounts and Commissions*	*Proceeds to Company*
Per unit	100%	1.5%	98.5%
Total	$40,000,000	$600,000	$39,400,000

DESCRIPTION OF BUSINESS

The company is engaged, and intends to continue to engage, in the sale of merchandise by mail. Customers are offered three ways to buy: cash with order, 30-day charge, and monthly payments. The company is believed to sell a substantially larger proportion of its total volume on the monthly payment plan than any other national retailer of general merchandise does.

The company expects to continue to concentrate its efforts in the specialized techniques of catalogue credit promotion, credit acceptance, collections, and credit finance. Experience has demonstrated that monthly payment selling is more profitable than selling for cash. Monthly payment customers tend to buy more frequently and in larger amounts than do cash customers. In addition, after being charged with the company's total interest expense, the servicing of the credit accommodation now contributes materially to consolidated profit.

UNDERWRITING

Subject to the terms and conditions set forth in the underwriting agreement, the company has agreed to sell to each of the underwriters named below, and each of the underwriters for whom Wertheim & Company is acting as representative has severally agreed to purchase, at the price set forth on the cover page of this prospectus, the principal amount of debentures set opposite its name.

The nature of the underwriting commitments is such that the several underwriters are obligated, subject to certain conditions, to purchase all the debentures offered hereby. In the event of default by any underwriter, the underwriting agreement provides that in certain circumstances other underwriters may be substituted or the agreement terminated.

The company has been advised by Wertheim & Company that in connection with the sale of the debentures by the underwriters, concessions may be allowed to other dealers not in excess of 0.25 percent.

SOURCE: Prospectus, Wertheim & Company, April 12, 1961.

Beckman Instruments, Inc. 69,993 shares, common stock, par value $1 a share.

The company hereby offers to the holders of its common stock the right to subscribe for additional shares of its common stock at the rate of one additional share for each 20 shares held of record on the close of business on March 28, 1961, all as more fully set forth herein.

	Subscription Price	*Underwriting Commissions*	*Proceeds to Company*
Per share	$ 114	Min. $ 2.00	Max. $ 112.00
		Max. 5.40	Min. 108.60
Total	7,972,362	Min. 139,866.00	Max. 7,832,496.00
		Max. 377,638.20	Min. 7,594,723.80

DESCRIPTION OF BUSINESS

The company and its subsidiaries are engaged in the business of designing, developing, manufacturing, and selling precision instruments for scientific, industrial, medical, and laboratory use.

UNDERWRITING

In the underwriting agreement, the several underwriters, represented by Lehman Brothers, have agreed, subject to the terms and conditions therein set forth, to purchase from the company all the shares of common stock offered hereby not purchased on exercise of rights, at the subscription price set forth on the cover page of this prospectus. For their respective commitments the underwriters are to receive compensation as set forth below and on the cover page of this prospectus. Reference is made to the underwriting agreement filed as an exhibit to the registration statement.

The company has agreed to pay the underwriters $2 a share with respect to each share of common stock offered hereby, plus $3.40 a share on all shares (herein called the "unsubscribed stock") not purchased on the exercise of rights or which are purchased by the underwriters on the exercise of rights purchased by them. The minimum underwriting commissions and maximum proceeds to the company shown on the cover page of this prospectus are based on the assumption that all shares of common stock offered hereby will be subscribed for by other than the underwriters, and the maximum underwriting commissions and minimum proceeds to the company are based on the assumption that none of such shares will be so subscribed for.

If the aggregated sales price of all unsubscribed stock sold by the several underwriters during the period of the subscription offer and within 30 days thereafter is in excess of the aggregate subscription price of the unsubscribed stock, the underwriters will pay to the company 50 percent of such excess. Such excess is to be computed after deducting all costs and expenses (including selling concessions, brokerage commissions, and transfer taxes) and any losses paid or incurred, directly or indirectly, by the underwriters in connection with the distribution of the unsubscribed stock, the purchase of rights (whether

Name	
Lehman Brothers	20.00
A. C. Allyn and Company, Inc.	6.00
Ball, Burge & Kraus	2.00
J. Barth & Company	2.00
Bear, Stearns & Company	8.00
Blyth & Company, Inc.	8.00
Burnham and Company	2.00
Eastman Dillon, Union Securities & Company	8.00
Goodbody & Company	2.00
Hayden, Stone & Company	4.50
Hornblower & Weeks	4.50
Paine, Webber, Jackson & Curtis	4.50
Paribas Corporation	8.00
Peltason, Tenebaum Company	2.00
Shearson, Hammill & Company	4.50
Stein Bros. & Boyce	2.00
Sutro & Company	2.00
Wagenseller & Durst, Inc.	2.00
Dean Witter & Company	8.00
Total	100.00

or not exercised), stabilization operations, overallotments, short sales, and related transactions. For the purpose of this paragraph, unsubscribed stock not sold or contracted to be sold by the underwriters on the date on which such 30-day period terminates will be deemed to have been sold on such date of termination at the weighted average of the sales prices of the common stock of the company on the New York Stock Exchange on such date.

Lehman Brothers has advised the company that the underwriters may offer shares of common stock as set forth on the cover page of this prospectus, that initially they may allow concessions not in excess of $2.50 a share to certain dealers, and that the underwriters and such dealers initially may reallow concessions not in excess of 50 cents a share to other dealers. Such concessions to dealers may be changed by the representative.

SOURCE: Prospectus, Lehman Brothers, March 28, 1961.

Selected References

Andrews, Victor L., "The Supply of Loanable Funds from Non-Insured Corporate, State-, and City-Administered Employee Pension Trusts," *Journal of Finance,* XVI (May 2, 1961), 328–350.

Archer, Stephen H., and LeRoy G. Faerber, "Firm Size and the Cost of Equity Capital," *Journal of Finance,* XXI (March 1966), 69–84.

Bloch, Ernest, "Pricing a Corporate Bond Issue: A Look Behind the Scenes," *Essays in Money and Credit.* (New York: Federal Reserve Bank of New York, 1964), pp. 72–76.

Browne, Dudley E., "The New SEC Regulations—and the Future of Financing Relations," *Financial Executive,* XXXIII (July 1965), 15–16.

Cohan, Avery B., "Yields on New Underwritten Corporate Bonds," *Journal of Finance,* XVII (December 1962), 585–605.

———, *Private Placements and Public Offerings: Market Shares Since 1935.* (Chapel Hill, School of Business Administration, University of North Carolina, 1961.)

Conklin, George T., "Direct Placements," *Journal of Finance,* VI (June 1951), 85–123.

"Direct Placement of Corporate Debt," *Economic Review* (March 1965) (Federal Reserve Bank of Cleveland).

Eiteman, David K., "The S.E.C. Special Study and the Exchange Markets," *Journal of Finance,* XXI (May 1966), 311–323.

Friend, Irwin, "Broad Implications of the S.E.C. Special Study," *Journal of Finance,* XXI (May 1966), 324–332.

Friend, Irwin, G. W. Hoffman, and W. J. Winn, *The Over-the-Counter Securities Market* (New York: McGraw-Hill, 1958).

Miller, G. R., "Long-Term Business Financing from the Underwriter's Point of View," *Journal of Finance,* XVI (May 1961), 280–290.

Nair, Richard S., "Investment Banking: Judge Medina in Retrospect," *Financial Analysts Journal,* XVI (July-August 1960), 35–40.

Robinson, Roland, and H. Robert Bartell, Jr., "Uneasy Partnership: SEC/NYSE," *Harvard Business Review,* XLIII (January-February 1965), 76–88.

Soldofsky, Robert M., "The Size and Maturity of Direct Placement Loans," *Journal of Finance,* XV (March 1960), 32–44.

Stuebner, E. A., "The Role of the Investment Banker in Arranging Private Financing," *Business Lawyer,* XVI (January 1961), 377–385.

Sullivan, Brian, "An Introduction to 'Going Public'," *Journal of Accountancy* (November 1965).

Waterman, M. H., *Investment Banking Function.* (Ann Arbor, Mich.: Bureau of Business Research, University of Michigan, 1958.)

Winter, E. L., "Cost of Going Public," *Financial Executive,* XXXI (September 1963), 30–32.

18

Common Stock

Common equity or, if unincorporated enterprises are considered, partnership or proprietorship interests constitute the first source of funds to a new business and the base of support for existing firms' borrowings. Accordingly, our discussion of specific forms of long-term financing will begin with an analysis of common stock.

APPORTIONMENT OF INCOME, CONTROL, AND RISK

The nature of equity ownership depends upon the form of the business organization. The central problem revolves around an apportionment of certain rights and responsibilities among those who have provided the funds necessary for the operation of the business.

The rights and responsibilities attaching to equity consist of positive considerations—income potential and control of the firm—and negative considerations—loss potential, responsibility, and personal liability.

General Rights of Holders of Common Stock

The rights of holders of common stock in a business corporation are established by the laws of the state in which the corporation is chartered and by the terms of the charter granted by the state. The characteristics of charters are relatively uniform on many matters, including the following.

COLLECTIVE RIGHTS. Certain collective rights are usually given to the holders of common stock. Some of the more important rights allow stockholders (1) to amend the charter with the approval of the appropriate officials in the state of incorporation; (2) to adopt and amend bylaws; (3) to elect the directors of the corporation; (4) to authorize the sale of fixed assets; (5) to enter into mergers; (6) to change the amount of authorized common stock; and (7) to issue preferred stock, debentures, bonds, and other securities.

SPECIFIC RIGHTS. Holders of common stock also have specific rights as individual owners. (1) They have the right to vote in the manner prescribed by the corporate charter. (2) They may sell their stock certificates, their evidence of ownership, and in this way transfer their ownership interest to other persons. (3) They have the right to inspect the corporate books.[1] (4) They have the right to share residual assets of the corporation on dissolution; however, the holders of common stock are last among the claimants to the assets of the corporation.

Apportionment of Income

There are two important positive considerations involved in equity ownership: income and control. The right to income carries risks of loss. Control also involves responsibility and liability. In an individual proprietorship, using only funds supplied by the owner, the owner has a 100 percent right to income and control and to loss and responsibility. As soon as the proprietor incurs debt, however, he has entered into contracts that place limitations on his complete freedom to control the firm and to apportion the firm's income.

In a partnership, these rights are apportioned among the partners in an agreed manner. In the absence of a formal agreement, a division is made by the laws of the locality. But the more significant issues arise concerning the rights of the owners of a business corporation.

[1] Obviously, a corporation cannot have its business affairs disturbed by allowing every stockholder to go through any record that he would like to inspect. A corporation could not wisely permit a competitor who happened to buy shares of its common stock to look at all the corporation records. There must be, and there are, practical limitations to this right.

Apportionment of Control

Through the right to vote, holders of common stock have legal control of the corporation. As a practical matter, however, in many corporations the principal officers constitute all, or a majority of, the members of the board of directors. In such circumstances the board of directors may be controlled by the management, rather than vice versa. Management control, or control of a business by others than its owners, results. However, numerous examples demonstrate that stockholders can reassert their control when dissatisfied. In recent years, proxy battles with the aim of altering corporation policies have occurred fairly often.

As receivers of residual income, holders of common stock are frequently referred to as the ultimate entrepreneurs in the firm. They are the ultimate owners and they have the ultimate control. Presumably the firm is managed on behalf of its owners, the holders of common stock, but there has been much dispute about the actual situation. The point of view has been expressed that the corporation is an institution with an existence separate from the owners, and that the corporation exists to fulfill certain functions for stockholders as only one among other important groups, such as workers, consumers, and the economy as a whole. This view doubtlessly has some validity, but it should also be noted that ordinarily the officers of a firm are also large stockholders. Furthermore, more and more firms are tying officers' compensation in with the firm's profit performance either by granting executives stock purchase options or by giving bonuses. These actions are, of course, designed to make management more stockholder-oriented.

Apportionment of Risk

The fact that, on liquidation, holders of common stock are last in the priority of claims signifies that the portion of capital they contribute provides a cushion for creditors if losses occur on dissolution. The equity-to-total-assets ratio indicates the percentage by which assets may shrink in value on liquidation before creditors will incur losses.

For example, compare two corporations, A and B, with the balance sheets shown in Table 18–1. The ratio of equity to total assets in corporation A is 80 percent. Total assets would therefore have to shrink by 80 percent before creditors would lose money. By contrast, in corporation B the extent by which assets may shrink in value on liquidation before creditors lose money is only 40 percent.

Since the average equity-to-total-assets ratio for all manufacturing is approximately two thirds, a substantial equity cushion ordinarily exists. For some industries, such as airline transport and aircraft manufac-

TABLE 18–1 BALANCE SHEETS FOR CORPORATIONS A AND B

CORPORATION A				CORPORATION B			
		Debt	$ 20			Debt	$ 60
		Equity	80			Equity	40
Total assets	$100	Total claims	$100	Total assets	$100	Total claims	$100

turing, however, the equity cushion is only about one-third of total assets. Further, individual firms within industries can have abnormally high or low debt ratios.

COMMON STOCK FINANCING

Before undertaking an evaluation of common stock financing it is desirable to describe some of its additional important characteristics. These topics include (1) the nature of voting rights, (2) the nature of the pre-emptive right, (3) the significance of par value, and (4) variations in the forms of common stock.

Nature of Voting Rights

For each share of common stock owned, the holder has the right to cast a vote at the annual meetings of stockholders of the corporation or at such special meetings as may be called.

PROXY. Provision is made for the temporary transfer of this right to vote by an instrument known as a proxy. A proxy is defined as a transfer of the right to vote. The transfer is limited in its duration, typically for a specific occasion such as the annual meeting of stockholders.

The SEC supervises the use of the proxy machinery and issues frequent rules and regulations seeking to improve its administration. SEC supervision is justified for several reasons. First, if the proxy machinery is left wholly in the hands of management, there is a danger that the incumbent management will be self-perpetuated. Second, if it is made easy for minority groups of stockholders and opposition stockholders to oust management, there is danger that small groups of stockholders may gain control of the corporation for temporary advantages or place their friends in management positions. Sometimes, the minority may be seeking the prizes that go along with controlling the corporation, for example, income from real estate.

ELIGIBILITY TO VOTE. In certain situations there may be some doubt about who has the right to vote. For example, in a *hypothecation of securities* (where securities are pledged as collateral for a loan), does the pledger or the lender have the right to vote? The law provides that in a simple hypothecation situation the pledger of the stock, rather than the lender, retains the right to vote. In a trust situation, where the donor has placed the stock in the hands of a trustee to be controlled for the benefit of the beneficiary, three possible parties might have the right to vote: the donor, the trustee, and the beneficiary. The law provides that the trustee shall have the right to vote.

Proxies may be mailed to stockholders of record of a specified date—for example, April 10. The voting may relate to an annual meeting to be held one month later, May 10. In the interim the stock may be sold. Who has the right to be proxy: the stockholder of record on April 10 or the new stockholder? Technically, the stockholder of record has the right to vote. He has the proxy and he may keep it. However, the new buyer may, and should, request the proxy from the seller.

CUMULATIVE VOTING. A method of voting that has come into increased prominence is cumulative voting.[2] Cumulative voting for directors is required in 22 states, including California, Illinois, Pennsylvania, Ohio, and Michigan. It is permissive in 18, including Delaware, New York, and New Jersey. Ten states make no provision for cumulative voting.

Cumulative voting permits multiple votes for a single director. For example, suppose six directors are to be elected. The owner of 100 shares can cast 100 votes for each of the six openings. Cumulatively, then, he has 600 votes. When cumulative voting is permitted, the stockholder may accumulate his votes and cast 600 votes for *one* director, instead of 100 each for *six* directors. Cumulative voting is designed to enable a minority group of stockholders to obtain some voice in the control of the company by electing at least one director to the board.

The nature of cumulative voting is illustrated by use of a well-known formula.

$$r = \frac{d \times S}{D + 1} + 1 \qquad (18\text{–}1)$$

[2] For an excellent discussion of all aspects of cumulative voting, see C. M. Williams, *Cumulative Voting for Directors* (Boston: Graduate School of Business Administration, Harvard University, 1951).

r = number of shares required to elect a desired number of directors
d = number of directors stockholder desires to elect
S = total number of shares of common stock outstanding and entitled to vote[3]
D = total number of directors to be elected

The formula may be made more meaningful by an example. The ABC company will elect six directors. There are 15 candidates and 100,000 shares entitled to a vote. If a group desires to elect two directors, how many shares must it have?

$$r = \frac{2 \times 100{,}000}{6 + 1} + 1 = 28{,}572 \qquad (18\text{–}2)$$

Observe the significance of the formula. Here, a minority group wishes to elect one-third of the board of directors. They can achieve their goal by owning less than one third the number of shares of stock.[4]

The question may be put in another way. Assuming that a group holds 40,000 shares of stock in this company, how many directors would it be possible for the group to elect, following the rigid assumptions of the formula? The formula can be used in its present form or can be solved for d and expressed as

$$d = \frac{(r - 1)(D + 1)}{S} \qquad (18\text{–}3)$$

Inserting the figures, the calculation would be

$$d = \frac{39{,}999 \times 7}{100{,}000} = 2.8 \qquad (18\text{–}4)$$

The 40,000 shares could elect 2.8 directors. Since directors cannot exist as fractions, the group can elect only two directors.

[3] An alternative that may be agreed to by the contesting parties is to define S as the number of shares *voted,* not authorized to vote. This procedure, which in effect gives each group seeking to elect directors the same percentage of directors as their percentage of the voted stock, is generally followed. When it is followed, a group that seeks to gain control with a minimum investment must estimate the percentage of shares that will be voted, then obtain control of more than 50 percent of that number.

[4] Note also that at least 14,287 shares must be controlled to elect one director. As far as electing a director goes, any number less than 14,287 constitutes a useless minority.

As a practical matter, suppose that in the above situation the total number of shares is 100,000. Hence 60,000 shares remain in other hands. The voting of all the 60,000 shares may not be concentrated. Suppose the 60,000 shares (cumulatively, 360,000 votes) not held by our group are distributed equally among 10 candidates, 36,000 shares held by each candidate. If our group's 240,000 votes are distributed equally for each of six candidates, we could elect all six directors even though we do not have a majority of the stock.

In actuality, it is difficult to make assumptions about how the opposition votes will be distributed. What is shown here is a good example of game theory. One rule involved in the theory of games is to assume that your opponents will do the worst they can do to you and to counter with actions to minimize the maximum loss. This is the kind of assumption followed in the formula. If your opposition concentrates its votes in the optimum manner, what is the best you can do to work in the direction of your goal? Other plausible assumptions can be substituted if one has sufficient facts to support alternative hypotheses about the behavior of his opponents.

Pre-emptive Right

The pre-emptive right gives holders of common stock the first option to purchase additional issues of common stock. In some states the pre-emptive right is made a part of every corporate charter. In other states it is necessary to insert the pre-emptive right specifically in the charter.

The purpose of the pre-emptive right is twofold. First, it protects the power of control of present stockholders. If it were not for this safeguard, the management of a corporation under criticism from stockholders could prevent stockholders from removing it from office by issuing a large number of additional shares at a very low price and purchasing these shares itself. Management would thereby secure control of the corporation to frustrate the will of the current stockholders.

The second, and by far the more important, protection that the pre-emptive right affords stockholders regards dilution of value. An example may clarify this. Assume that 1,000 shares of common stock with a market value of $100 are outstanding, making the total market value of the firm $100,000. An additional 1,000 shares are sold at $50 a share, or for $50,000, thus raising the total market value of the firm to $150,000. When the total market value is divided by the new total shares outstanding, a value of $75 a share is obtained. Thus, selling common stock at below market value will dilute the price of the stock and be detrimental to present stockholders and beneficial to those who purchased the new shares. The pre-emptive right prevents such occurrences. This point will be discussed at length later in this chapter.

Par Value versus No-Par Value

SOME DISTINCTIONS. Some distinctions need to be made among different concepts of value. *Par value* is the nominal value of common stock. It is the value arbitrarily stated on the shares. *Book value,* the concept that has been used here, is the historical value of the common stock. Book value per share is calculated by adding the balance sheet value of the common stock, plus earned surplus, plus capital surplus, and dividing this sum by the number of shares outstanding. If there is a goodwill account on the left-hand side of the balance sheet, the analyst may or may not deduct the goodwill item, depending upon whether it generates superior earning power. *Market value,* as explained in Chapter 10, is the prevailing price paid for a share of common stock as registered in transactions between buyers and sellers of common stock. Intrinsic value, or economic value, is not an objective amount. It represents a judgment of the long-run value of the common stock as determined by fundamental economic forces.

These distinctions facilitate analysis of the use of par value, the trend toward no-par value, and the reversal of that trend. Originally, the purpose of a par value was to protect creditors. It was to insure that the full amount of payment for common stock had actually been received by the company. By clearly stating a par value on the balance sheet, the creditors of the company had the assurance that, if the full amount had not been paid in, they had the right to levy deficiency judgments against the present holders of common stock.

For example, A buys a $100 par value stock *from the company* for $65. On insolvency he is liable up to $35 to a subsequent assessment by creditors. This deficiency assessment right holds even though A may have subsequently sold his stock. For example, B purchases the stock from A for $115, an amount that exceeds par value by $15. The deficiency assessment liability of $35 is acquired by B, because the company has never received the full par value of the stock. The deficiency provision follows stock ownership.

Having a high par value can cause other problems. For example, suppose a firm sells stock for $100 par at the time it is organized. Years later, the market price may be well below par—say $50. Now suppose the company has some good investment opportunities, but to take advantage of them it must raise funds by selling common stock. However, the market price of the stock is only $50, so this sets the practical maximum at which new shares can be sold. But if new shares are sold *by the company* at only $50, purchasers would be liable for a deficiency judgment. This, in turn, makes it impractical to sell new common stock.

NO-PAR STOCK. Because of deficiency assessments and other reasons, no-par stock was developed. No-par stock was first permitted by a New

York State statute in 1912. When no-par stock is issued, it is carried on the balance sheet at the price at which the stock is sold or at some other stated value. Sometimes when no-par stock is sold, a paid-in surplus is created. For example, assume 1,000 shares are sold at $10 a share, a total of $10,000. The stated value of the common stock sold may be stated, quite arbitrarily, as $8,000 with a paid-in surplus of $2,000.

No-par stock has several advantages. First, it avoids the problem of deficiency assessments. Second, it avoids misleading the investor who may feel that par value has some significance; the fact that par value is stated on the common stock certificate may lead some unwary and uninformed investors to feel that somehow the intrinsic worth of the stock is represented by its stated par value. Third, it may increase the marketability of the stock, since the company can sell additional shares of common stock at any time at whatever price the stock will bring.

Some possible disadvantages of no-par stock should also be examined. First, it is sometimes said that no-par stock may lead to possible manipulation of the accounts. Stock may be sold at $10 a share and carried on the books at $8, with a paid-in surplus for the difference. Unsophisticated investors might think this represents *earned* surplus and thus shows that the company is operating profitably. However, creation of surplus can also occur with par stock. For example, a company may sell stock at $8 a share, establishing a par value of $5 a share and showing the difference of $3 as paid-in surplus. Therefore, whether stock is par value or no-par value has little fundamental influence on possible manipulation.

Second, if stock is sold at a price below the present stated value, or book value of no-par stock, the value of the old stock may be diluted. But the book value of par stock can also be diluted if it is sold at less than book value. Typically, par value is less than book value; if a company has an earned surplus, the book value of its stock will be greater than the par value.

For some years, no-par stock was taxed at $100 value for stock transfer tax purposes. This resulted in a trend toward the use of low-par stocks of $1 to $5. However, the stock transfer tax is now based on market prices. Hence, no general advantage for the use or nonuse of a nominal value for common stock exists.

Forms of Common Stock

CLASSIFIED COMMON STOCK. Classified common stock was used extensively in the late 1920s, sometimes in ways that misled investors. During that period Class A common stock was usually nonvoting, and Class B was typically voting. Thus promoters could control companies by selling large amounts of Class A stock while retaining Class B stock.

In more recent years there has been a revival of Class B common for sound purposes. It is used by a small, new company seeking to acquire funds from outside sources. Common Stock A is sold to the public, and typically pays dividends of a consistent amount; it has full voting rights. Common stock B, however, is retained by the organizers of the company, but dividends are not paid on it until the company has established its earning power. By the use of the classified stock, the public can take a position in a conservatively financed growth company without sacrificing income.

FOUNDERS' SHARES. Founders' shares are somewhat like Class B stock except that they carry *sole* voting rights and, typically, do not have the right to dividends for a number of years. Thus the organizers of the firm are able to maintain complete control of the operations in the crucial initial development of the firm. At the same time, other investors are protected against excessive withdrawals of funds by owners.

EVALUATION OF COMMON STOCK AS A SOURCE OF FUNDS

Thus far, the chapter has covered the main characteristics of common stock, frequently referred to as equity shares in the company. By way of a summary of the important aspects of common stock, common stock financing will be appraised from the standpoint of the issuer.

Advantages

First, common stock does not entail fixed charges. If the company generates the earnings, it can pay common stock dividends. In contrast to bond interest, however, there is no legal obligation to pay dividends.

Second, common stock carries no fixed maturity date.

Third, since common stock provides a cushion against losses for creditors, the sale of common stock increases the credit-worthiness of the firm.

Fourth, common stock may at times be sold more easily than debt. Common stock may appeal to certain investor groups for two reasons:

(1) it typically carries a higher yield than does preferred stock or debt, and (2) it provides the investor with a better hedge against inflation than do straight preferred stock and bonds, because it represents the ownership in the firm. Ordinarily common stock increases in value when the value of real assets rises during an inflationary period.

Disadvantages

First, the sale of common stock extends voting rights or control to the additional stockowners who are brought into the company. For this reason, among others, additional equity financing is often avoided by small and new firms. The owner-managers may be unwilling to share control of their companies with outsiders.

Second, common stock gives more owners the right to share in income. The use of debt may enable the firm to utilize funds at a fixed low cost, whereas common stock gives equal rights to new stockholders to share in the net profits of the firm.

Third, as we saw in Chapter 17, the costs of underwriting and distributing common stock are usually higher than those for underwriting and distributing preferred stock or debt. Flotation costs for selling common stock are characteristically higher because (1) the costs of investigating an equity security investment are higher than investigating the feasibility of a comparable debt security and (2) stocks are more risky, which means equity holdings must be diversified, which in turn means that a given dollar amount of new stock must be sold to a greater number of purchasers than the same amount of debt.

Fourth, as we saw in Chapter 11, the component cost of common stock is typically less than that of debt. Therefore, if the firm has less debt than is called for in the optimum captial structure, the cost of common equity is high.

Fifth, common stock dividends are not deductible as an expense for calculating the corporation's income subject to the federal income tax, but bond interest is deductible. The impact of this factor is reflected in the relative cost of equity capital *vis à vis* debt capital.

Other Aspects of Equity Financing

Common stock also should be considered from a social standpoint. Common stock is a desirable form of financing because it renders business firms, hence a major segment of the economy, less vulnerable to the consequences of declines in sales and earnings. If sales and earnings decline, common stock financing involves no fixed charges, the payment of which might force the firm into reorganization or bankruptcy.

However, there is another aspect of common stock financing that may have less desirable social consequences. Common stock prices fall in recessions, and this causes a rise in the cost of equity capital.[5] The rising cost of equity raises the over-all cost of capital, which in turn reduces investment. This reduction further aggravates the recession. However, an expanding economy is accompanied by rising stock prices, and with rising stock prices comes a drop in the cost of capital. This, in turn, stimulates investment, which may add to a developing inflationary boom. In summary, a consideration of its effects on the cost of capital suggests that stock financing may tend to amplify cyclical fluctuations.

Just how these opposing forces combine to produce a net effect is unknown, but the authors believe that the first is the stronger; that is, stock financing tends to stabilize the economy.

HE USE OF IGHTS IN INANCING[6]

If the pre-emptive right is contained in a particular firm's charter, then it must offer any new common stock to existing stockholders. If the charter does not prescribe a pre-emptive right, the firm has a choice of making the sale to its existing stockholders or to an entirely new set of investors. If the sale is to the existing stockholders, the stock flotation is called a *rights offering*. Each stockholder is issued an option to buy a certain number of the new shares, and the terms of the option are contained on a piece of paper called a *right*. Each stockholder receives one right for each share of stock he owns. The advantages and disadvantages of rights offerings are described in this section.

HEORETICAL ELATIONSHIPS

Several issues confront the financial manager who is deciding on the details of a rights offering. The various considerations can be made clear by the use of illustrative data on the Southeast Company, whose balance sheet and income statement are given in Table 18–2.

[5] See Table 10–1.

[6] Much of the material for this section was obtained from J. R. Nelson, *Rights* (Unpublished PhD dissertation, University of California, Los Angeles, 1961).

TABLE 18–2 SOUTHEAST COMPANY BALANCE SHEET BEFORE RIGHTS OFFERING

		Total debt, 5%	$ 40,000,000
		Common stock ($10 par)	10,000,000
		Retained earnings	50,000,000
Total assets	$100,000,000	Total liabilities and capital	$100,000,000

SOUTHEAST COMPANY
PARTIAL INCOME STATEMENT

Total earnings	$10,000,000
Interest on debt	2,000,000
Income before taxes	8,000,000
Taxes (50% assumed)	4,000,000
Earnings after taxes	4,000,000
Earnings per share (1,000,000 shares)	$4
Market price of stock (price earnings ratio of 25 assumed)	$100

Southeast earns $4 million after taxes and 1 million shares are outstanding, so earnings per share are $4. The stock sells at 25 times earnings, or for $100 a share. The company plans to raise $10 million of new equity funds through a rights offering and decides to sell the new stock to shareholders for $50 a share. The questions now facing the financial manager are:

1. How many rights will be required to purchase a share of the newly issued stock?
2. What is the value of each right?
3. What effect will the rights offering have on the price of the existing stock?

Each of these questions will now be analyzed.

Number of Rights to Purchase a New Share

Southeast plans to raise $10 million in new equity funds and to sell the new stock at a price of $50 a share. Dividing the subscription price into the total funds to be raised gives the number of shares to be issued.

$$\text{number of new shares} = \frac{\text{funds to be raised}}{\text{subscription price}} = \frac{\$10{,}000{,}000}{\$50}$$
$$= 200{,}000 \text{ shares}$$

The next step is to divide the number of new shares into the number of previously outstanding shares to get the number of rights required to subscribe to one share of the new stock. Note that stockholders always get one right for each share of stock they own.

$$\text{number of rights needed to buy a share of the stock} = \frac{\text{old shares}}{\text{new shares}} = \frac{1{,}000{,}000}{200{,}000} = 5 \text{ rights}$$

Therefore, a stockholder will have to surrender five rights plus $50 dollars to get one of the newly issued shares. Had the subscription price been set at $95 a share, 9.5 rights would have been required to subscribe to each new share, while only one right would have been needed if the price had been set at $10 a share.

Value of a Right

It is clearly worth something to be able to buy for less than $100 a share of stock selling for $100. The right provides this privilege, so the right must have a value. To see how the theoretical value of a right is established, we will continue with the example of the Southeast Company, assuming that it will raise $10 million by selling 200,000 new shares at $50 a share.

First, notice that the *market value* of the old stock was $100 million—$100 a share times 1 million shares. (The book value is irrelevant.) When the firm sells the new stock, it brings in an additional $10 million. As a first approximation, we assume that the market value of the common stock increases by exactly this $10 million. Actually, the market value of all the common stock would go up by more than $10 million if investors think the company will be able to invest these funds at a yield substantially in excess of the cost of equity capital, but by less than $10 million if investors are doubtful of the company's ability to put the new funds to work profitably in the near future.

Under the assumption, the total market value of the common stock after the new issue will be $110 million. Dividing this new value by the new total number of shares outstanding, 1.2 million, we obtain a new market value of $91.67 a share. Therefore, we see that after the financing has been completed, the price of the common stock will have fallen from $100 to $91.67.

Since the rights give the stockholders the privilege of buying for only $50 a share of stock that will end up being worth $91.67, thus saving $41.67, is $41.67 the value of each right? The answer is "no," because five rights are required to buy one new share; we must divide $41.67 by 5 to get the value of each right. In the example each one is worth $8.33.

Ex Rights

Rights are handled much like dividends in some regards. Recall that dividends go with the stock until the ex-dividend date, which is four days prior to the stock of record date. Rights are treated similarly when the old stock is traded prior to the issuance of the new stock but after the announcement of the financing. For example, on October 15, Southeast Company might announce the terms of the new financing, stating that rights will be mailed out on December 1 to stockholders of record as of the close of business on November 15. Anyone buying the old stock on or before November 11 will receive the rights; anyone buying the stock on or after November 12 will *not* receive the rights. Thus, November 12 is the *ex-rights date;* before November 12 the stock sells *rights on.* In the case of Southeast Company, the *rights on price* is $100, the *ex-rights price* is $91.67.

Formula Value of the Rights

RIGHTS ON. Equations have been developed for determining the value of rights without going through all the procedures described above. (See footnote 7 at the end of this section.) While the stock is still selling rights on, the value at which the rights will sell when they are issued can be found by use of the following formula:

$$\text{value of one right} = \frac{\text{market value of stock, rights on} - \text{subscription price}}{\text{number of rights required to purchase one share plus 1}}$$

$$R = \frac{M_o - S}{N + 1} \tag{18–5}$$

Here M_0 is the rights-on price of the stock, S is the subscription price, N is the number of rights required to purchase a new share of stock, and R is the value of one right. Substituting in the appropriate values for the Southeast Company,

$$R = \frac{\$100 - \$50}{5 + 1} = \frac{\$50}{6} = \$8.33$$

This agrees with the value of the rights as found by the long procedure.

EX RIGHTS. Suppose you are a stockholder in the Southeast Company. When you return to the United States from a trip to Europe, you read about the rights offering in the newspaper. The stock is now selling ex rights for $91.67 a share. How can you calculate the theoretical value of a right? Simply using the following formula, which follows the logic described in preceding sections, you can determine the value of each right to be \$8.33:

$$\text{value of one right} = \frac{\text{market value of stock ex rights} - \text{subscription price}}{\text{number of rights required to purchase one share}}$$

$$R = \frac{M_e - S}{N} \tag{18–6}$$

$$R = \frac{\$91.67 - \$50}{5} = \frac{\$41.67}{5} = \$8.33$$

Here M_e is the ex-rights price of the stock.[7]

EFFECTS ON POSITION OF STOCKHOLDERS

A stockholder has the choice of exercising his rights or selling them. If he has sufficient funds and if he wants to buy more shares of the company's stock, the stockholder will exercise the rights. If he does

[7] Equation 18–5 follows directly from the verbal explanation. Equation 18–5 can be derived from equation 18–6 as follows:

1. Note that

$$M^e = M_o - R \tag{18–7}$$

2. Substitute equation 18–7 into equation 18–5, obtaining

$$R = \frac{M_o - R - S}{N} \tag{18–8}$$

3. Simplify equation 18–8 as follows, ending with equation 18–5. This completes the derivation.

$$R = \frac{M_o - S}{N} - \frac{R}{N}$$

$$R + \frac{R}{N} = \frac{M_o - S}{N}$$

$$R\left(\frac{N + 1}{N}\right) = \frac{M_o - S}{N}$$

$$R = \frac{M_o - S}{N} \cdot \frac{N}{N + 1}$$

$$R = \frac{M_o - S}{N + 1} \tag{18–5}$$

not have the money or does not want to buy more stock, he will sell his rights. In either case, provided the formula values of the rights hold true, the stockholder will neither benefit nor lose by the rights offering. This statement can be made clear by considering the position of an individual stockholder in the Southeast Company.

The stockholder had 10 shares of stock before the rights offering. The 10 shares had a market value of $100 a share, so the stockholder had a total market value of $1,000 in the company's stock. If he exercises his rights, he will be able to purchase two additional shares at $50 a share, a new investment of $100; his total investment is now $1,100. He now owns 12 shares of his company's stock, which, after the rights offering, has a value of $91.67 a share. The value of his stock is $1,100, exactly what he has invested in it.

Alternatively, if he sold his 10 rights, which have a value of $8.33 a right, he would receive $83.30. He would now have his original 10 shares of stock plus $83.30 in cash. But his original 10 shares of stock now have a market price of $91.67 a share. The $916.70 market value of his stock plus the $83.30 in cash is the same as the original $1,000 market value of stock with which he began. From a purely mechanical or arithmetical standpoint, the stockholder neither benefits nor gains from the sale of additional shares of stock through rights. Of course, if he forgets to exercise or sell his rights or if brokerage costs of selling the rights are excessive, then a stockholder can suffer a loss. But, in general, the issuing firm makes special efforts to minimize brokerage costs, and adequate time is given to enable the stockholder to take some action, so losses are minimal.

Relation between Market Price and Subscription Price

We can now investigate the factors influencing the use of rights and, if they are used, the level at which the subscription price will be set. The articles of incorporation of the Southeast Company permit it to use rights or not, depending on whether it judges their use to be advantageous to the company and its stockholders. The financial vice-president of the company is considering three alternative methods of raising the additional sum of $10 million.

ALTERNATIVE I. Southeast Company could sell additional shares through investment bankers to the public at approximately $100 a share, the company netting approximately $96 a share; thus, it would need to sell 105,000 shares in order to cover the underwriting commission.

ALTERNATIVE II. The company could sell additional shares through rights, using investment bankers and paying a commission of 1 percent on the total dollar amount of the stock sold plus ¾ percent on all shares unsubscribed and taken over by the investment bankers. Allowing for the usual market pressure when common stock is sold, the new shares would be sold at a 15 percent discount, or at $85. Thus, 125,000 additional shares would be offered through rights. With eight rights, an additional share could be purchased at $85.

We should note that stockholders are given the right to subscribe to any unexercised rights on a pro rata basis. To illustrate, suppose a stockholder owns 10 percent of the stock in a firm that is selling new shares through a rights offering. If 30 percent of the total new shares offered are not subscribed (that is, if 30 percent of the rights are not exercised), then our 10 percent stockholder could, if he so desired, buy 10 percent of the unsubscribed shares. Only shares not subscribed to on an original or secondary basis are sold to the underwriters and subjected to the ¾ percent additional commission.

ALTERNATIVE III. The company could sell additional shares through rights at $10 a share. Investment bankers would not be employed at all. The number of additional shares of common stock to be sold would be one million. For each right held, existing stockholders would be permitted to buy one share of the new common stock.

Under alternative I, investment bankers are used. Rights would not be utilized at all. In this circumstance the underwriting commission, or flotation cost, is approximately 4 percent. In alternative II, where rights are used with a small discount, the underwriting commission is reduced, because the discount removes much of the risk of not being able to sell the issue. The underwriting commission consists of two parts—1 percent on the original issue and an additional ¾ of 1 percent commission on all unsubscribed shares the investment bankers are required to take over and sell. Thus, the actual commission will range somewhere between 1 percent and 1¾ percent.

Under alternative III, the subscription price is $10 a share. With such a large concession the company does not need to use investment bankers at all, because the rights are certain to have value and to be either exercised or sold.

Which of the three alternatives is superior?

Alternative I will provide a wider distribution of the securities sold, thus lessening any possible control problems. Also, it provides the assurance from the investment bankers that the company will receive the $10 million involved in the new issue. The company pays for these services in the form of underwriting charges. The stock price, after the issue, should be approximately $100.

Under alternative II, by utilizing rights, underwriting expenses are reduced. There is also a small reduction in the unit price per share, from \$100 to \$98 a share. Also, since the rights do have a low value, some stockholders may neither exercise them nor sell them, thus suffering a loss.[8] Because existing stockholders will buy some of the new shares, the distribution is likely to be less wide. Because of the underwriting contract, under alternative II the firm is also assured of receiving the funds sought.

Alternative III involves no underwriting expense, and it results in a substantial decrease in the unit price of shares. Initially, however, the shares will be less widely distributed. Note that alternative III has a large stock-split effect, which results in a much lower final stock price per share. Many people feel that there is an optimal stock price—one that will produce a maximum total market value of the shares—and that this price is generally in the range of \$30 to \$60 a share. If this is the feeling of Southeast's directors, they may believe that alternative III permits them to reach this more desirable price range, while at the same time reducing flotation costs on the new issue. Also, since the rights have a substantial value, few stockholders will fail either to exercise or to sell them, so there should be a minimum of stockholder loss from inaction.

The three alternatives are summarized below.

	ADVANTAGES	DISADVANTAGES
Alternative I	1. Wider distribution 2. Certainty of receiving funds	1. High underwriting costs
Alternative II	1. Smaller underwriting costs 2. Lower unit price of shares 3. Certainty of receiving funds	1. More narrow distribution
Alternative III	1. No underwriting costs 2. Substantial decrease in unit price of shares	1. More narrow distribution

The alternative that is most advantageous depends upon the company's needs. If the company is strongly interested in a wider distribution of its securities, alternative I is preferable. If it is most interested in reducing the unit price of its shares and is confident that the lower unit price will induce wider distribution of its shares, alternative III will be chosen.

[8] The value of each right is computed as

$$R = \frac{\$100 - \$85}{8 + 1} = \frac{\$15}{9} = \$1.67$$

The value of the stock, after financing, is \$100 — \$1.67 = \$98.33 a share.

If the company's needs are moderate in both directions, alternative II may offer a satisfactory compromise. Whether rights will be used and the level of the subscription price both depend upon the needs of the company at a particular time.

Exercise of Rights

Interestingly enough, it is expected that a small percentage of stockholders may neglect to exercise their rights or to sell them. In an offering in 1955, the holders of 1½ percent of the shares of General Motors common stock did not exercise their rights.[9] The loss involved to these stockholders was $1.5 million. Those who failed to exercise their rights in a number of offerings during 1955 held from 1.5 to 2.75 percent of the shares of stock outstanding. In an AT&T issue in that year, the loss to shareholders who neglected to exercise their rights was $960,000.[10]

Market Price and Subscription Price

Measured from the registration date for the new issue of the security, the average percentage by which the subscription prices of new issues were below their market prices was 22.8 percent during the years 1946–1947 and 15.3 percent during the years 1956–1957. Examples of price concessions of 40 percent or more are observed in a small percentage of issues. The most frequently encountered discounts are from 10 to 20 percent.

Effect on Subsequent Behavior of Market Price of Stock

It is often stated that new issues of stock through rights will depress the price of the existing common stock of the company. To the extent that a subscription price in connection with the rights offering is lower than the market price, there will be a "stock split effect" on the market price of the common stock. With the prevailing market price of Southeast Company's stock at $100 and a $10 subscription price, the new market price will probably drop to $55.

But the second question is whether, because of the rights offering, the actual new market price will be $55 or lower or higher. Again, empirical analysis of the movement in stock prices during rights offerings indicates that generalization is not practical. What happens to the market prices of the stock ex rights and after the rights trading period depends upon the prospects of the issuing company.

[9] E. A. Grimm, "The Money You Save May Be Your Own," *Exchange,* XVI (December 1955), 17–20.

[10] Grimm, pp. 17–20.

SIGNIFICANCE OF RIGHTS BEHAVIOR

To this point the material on rights has sought to develop an understanding of the nature and behavior of rights and their values. Much of this may have appeared to be from the standpoint of the investor. But such an approach is necessary to uncover the basic properties of rights. With this understanding as a background, it is now possible to focus directly on the significance of the use of rights in formulating financing policies. This material may be conveniently organized in terms of advantages to the use of rights.

Advantages of Use of Rights in New Financing

It has been seen that the pre-emptive right gives the shareholders the protection of preserving their pro rata share in the earnings and surplus of the company. The firm also benefits. By offering new issues of securities to the existing stockholders, it increases the likelihood of a favorable reception for the stock. By their ownership of common stock in the company, these investors have already indicated a favorable evaluation of the company. They may be receptive to the purchase of additional shares, particularly when the additional reasons indicated below are taken into account.

The shares purchased with rights are subject to lower margin requirements. For example, margin requirements since June 13, 1968 have been 80 percent; in other words, a person buying listed stocks must have at least $80 of his own funds for every $100 of securities purchased. However, if shares of new issues of stocks are purchased with rights, only $25 per $100 of common stock purchased must be furnished by the investor himself; he is permitted by law to borrow (if feasible) up to 75 percent of the purchase price. Furthermore, the absence of a clear pattern in the price behavior of the adjusted market price of the stocks and rights before, during, and after the trading period may enhance interest in the investment possibilities of the instruments.

These factors may offset the tendency toward a downward pressure on the price of the common stock occurring at the time of a new issue.[11]

[11] The downward pressure develops because of an increase in the supply of securities without a necessarily equivalent increase in the demand. Generally, it is a temporary phenomenon, and the stock tends to return to the theoretical price after a few months. Obviously, if the acquired funds are invested at a very high

With the increased interest and advantages afforded by the rights offering, the "true" or "adjusted" downward price pressure may actually be avoided.

A related advantage is that the flotation costs to an issuer associated with a rights offering will be lower than the costs of a public flotation. Costs referred to here are cash costs. For example, the flotation costs of industrial issues of common stock in 1955 were 9 percent on public issues compared with 3.8 percent of the proceeds to the company on rights offerings.[12] Underpricing on rights offerings increases their "costs" to 20.6 percent. However, the underpricing is not a cash outlay and, as we have seen, the underpricing accrues to stockholders by making their rights more valuable.

The financial manager may obtain positive benefits from underpricing. Since a rights offering is a stock split to a certain degree, it will cause the market price of the stock to fall to a level lower than it otherwise would have been. But stock splits will increase the number of shareholders in a company by bringing the price of a stock into a more attractive trading level. Furthermore, because a rights offering is an indirect stock split, it may result in additional dividends for the stockowners.

Finally, the total effect of the rights offering may be to stimulate an enthusiastic response from stockholders and the investment market as a whole, with the result that opportunities for financing become more attractive to the firm. Thus, the financial manager may be able to engage in common stock financing at lower costs and under more favorable terms.

SUMMARY

In this chapter, a number of characteristics of common stock financing have been presented. The advantages and disadvantages of external equity financing, compared with the use of preferred stock and debt, have been described. The purpose of the descriptive background material has been to provide a basis for making sound decisions when financing by common stock is being considered as a possible alternative.

Chapters 9, 10, and 11 have already provided a framework for analyzing the advantages and limitations to the use of debt financing versus equity financing. The more specific aspects influencing financing decisions

---

rate of return, the stock price benefits; if the investment does not turn out well, the stock price suffers.

[12] H. W. Stevenson, *Common Stock Financing* (Ann Arbor: University of Michigan, 1957), p. 61.

will now be considered. Among the numerous factors involved, eight have particular importance:

1. Patterns of sales and profits
2. Growth rate of sales and profits
3. Existing financial position
4. Age of firm
5. Control considerations
6. Cash flow requirements
7. Costs
8. Restrictions associated with the financing agreement

An important factor influencing financing decisions is the industry of the firm. In part, a firm's industry determines many of the above characteristics. The industry characteristics will strongly influence the asset structure, which in turn will influence the extent to which the firm will have collateral or meet other requirements of particular forms of financing.

With respect to the eight factors listed, some favor common stock financing, others favor other forms. The influence of each factor will now be discussed.

If sales and profit patterns are highly volatile, such as in the durable-goods industries, common stock financing is favored. Rarely will firms with serious profit instability employ significant amounts of long-term debt. The risks of having to meet fixed charges will be too large.

The existing financial position of the company in relation to its optimal or "target" capital structure is another crucial factor determining whether common stock will be employed. If the maximum debt ratio considered safe for the line of business is 50 percent and the firm already has a ratio of 60 percent, common stock financing will be indicated.

If the firm is new, it may have difficulty finding creditors willing to lend large sums on a long-term basis. The age of the firm may make equity financing the only available source. If the firm is established and its existing common stock is widely held, common stock financing will not raise problems of maintaining control of the company.

The absence of fixed interest or rental payments and the fact that there are no maturity and no sinking fund requirements will make future cash flows more stable with common stock financing. Although common stock is expected to pay dividends at some time, dividend payments are ordinarily not legally required, particularly if the earnings of the firm have been small.

The relative costs of common stock financing may be favorable at a particular point in time. If both stock prices and interest rates appear to be high, stock financing may be indicated. The converse is also true, of course; Chapter 23 deals specifically with the timing of debt and equity issues.

Finally, debt financing may carry important disadvantages, such as loan agreements with restrictions on the management, including the requirement to maintain the current ratio at some prescribed level. Debt financing may call for collateral that is not available in the required amount or kind.

This discussion of eight factors important for decisions whether to use common stock financing when long-term funds are required may be regarded as a check list. Some factors will favor the use of common stock, but all need not be present to justify the selection of common stock. When some, but not all, of the conditions favoring common stock are present, the financial manager must exercise judgment in making the final decision. Differences in recommendations may arise because the decision, in part, depends upon such uncertain factors as the future level of the firm's sales and profits.

It is also important to note that one *cannot* go through the eight factors, decide that six or even seven favor common stock, and recommend common stock over debt. The one factor that favors debt may be dominant in the particular case—it may override all those favoring common stock. In other words, here, just as in all other aspects of financial management, analytical tools provide a basis for the exercise of judgment.

The chapter also discussed the key decisions confronting the financial manager when he considers a rights offering and indicated the major features bearing on such decisions. Rights offerings may be used effectively by financial managers to increase the goodwill of shareholders. If the new financing associated with the rights represents a sound decision—one likely to result in improved earnings for the firm—a rise in stock values will probably result. The use of rights will permit shareholders to preserve their positions or to improve them. However, if investors feel that the new financing is not well advised, the rights offering may cause the price of the stock to decline by more than the value of the rights.

Because the rights offering is directed to existing shareholders, it may be possible to reduce the costs of floating the new issue.

A major decision for financial managers in a rights offering is to set the subscription price, or the amount of the concession from the existing market price of the stock. Formulas reflecting the static effects of a rights offering indicate that neither the stockholders nor the company benefits or loses from the price changes. The rights offering has the effect of a stock split. The level set for the subscription price will, to a great degree, reflect the objectives and effects of a stock split.

The subsequent price behavior of the rights and the common securities in the associated new offering will reflect the earnings and dividends prospects of the company, as well as the underlying developments in the securities markets. The new financing associated with the rights offering may be an indicator of prospective growth in the sales and earnings of the company. The stock-split effects of the rights offering may be used to alter the company's dividend payments. The effects of these developments on the market behavior of the rights and the securities before, during, and after the rights trading period will reflect the expectations of investors toward the outlook for earnings and dividends per share.

QUESTIONS

18–1 What percentage could total assets shrink in value on liquidation before creditors incurred losses in each of the following cases:
a) Equity to total asset ratio, 50 percent
b) Debt to equity ratio, 50 percent
c) Debt to total asset ratio, 40 percent

18–2 Distinguish between stated value and par value.

18–3 What factors, if any, are relevant to the decision to use par-value common stock versus no-par value stock?

18–4 What difficulties do small firms encounter in raising equity capital?

18–5 What characteristics of a new common stock issue would make its purchase more attractive to prospective investors?

18–6 How many shares must a minority group possess in order to assure election of two directors if nine new directors will be elected and 200,000 shares are outstanding? Assume cumulative voting exists.

18–7 Should the pre-emptive right entitle stockholders to purchase convertible bonds before they are offered to outsiders?

18–8 Are there advantages for a corporation to have its securities listed on more than one exchange?

18–9 What are the reasons for not letting officers and directors of a corporation make short sales in their company's stock?

18–10 It is frequently stated that the primary purpose of the pre-emptive right is to allow individuals to maintain their proportionate share of the ownership and control of a corporation. Just how important do you suppose this consideration is for the average stockholder of a firm whose shares are traded on the New York or American stock exchanges? Is the pre-emptive right likely to be of more importance to stockholders of closely held firms?

18–11 How would the success of a rights offering be affected by a declining stock market?

18–12 What are some of the advantages and disdvantages of setting the subscription price on a rights offering substantially below the current market price of the stock?

18–13 Is a firm likely to get a wider distribution of shares if it sells new stock through a rights offering or directly to underwriters? Why would a company be interested in getting a wider distribution of shares?

PROBLEMS

18–1 The Green Field Company is principally engaged in the business of growing, processing, and marketing a variety of canned and frozen vegetables and is a major company in this field. High-quality products are produced and marketed at premium prices.

During each of the past several years the company's sales have increased and the needed inventories have been financed from short-term sources. The officers have discussed the idea of refinancing their bank loans with long-term debt or common stock. A common stock issue of 310,000 shares sold at this time (present market price is $24 a share) would yield $7 million after expenses. This same sum could be raised by selling 12-year bonds with an interest rate of 6½ percent and a sinking fund to retire the bonds over their 12-year life.

Canning Industry Financial Ratios

Current ratio (times)	2.2
Sales to total assets (times)	2.0
Sales to inventory (times)	5.6
Average collection period (days)	22.0
Current debt/total assets (percent)	25–30
Long-term debt/total assets (percent)	10–15
Preferred/total assets (percent)	0.5
Net worth/total assets (percent)	60–65
Profits to sales (percent)	2.3
Net profits to total assets (percent)	4.0
Profits to net worth (percent)	8.4
Expected growth rate of earnings and dividends (percent)	6.5

GREEN FIELD COMPANY
CONSOLIDATED BALANCE SHEET
March 31, 1969*
(in millions of dollars)

Current assets	$47	Accounts payable	$ 4	
Fixed plant and equipment	19	Notes payable	12	
Other assets	4	Accruals	5	
		Total current liabilities		$21
		Long-term debt, 5%		21
		Preferred stock	3	
		Common stock	4	
		Retained earnings	21	
		Net worth		28
Total assets	$70	Total claims on assets		$70

* The majority of harvesting activities do not begin until late April or May.

GREEN FIELD COMPANY
CONSOLIDATED STATEMENT OF INCOME
Year Ended March 31
(in millions of dollars)

	1966	1967	1968	1969
Net sales	$75.0	$78.2	$97.6	$115.7
Cost of goods sold	48.7	52.2	65.1	76.8
Gross profit	26.3	26.0	32.5	38.9
Other expenses	20.6	22.0	27.0	29.5
Operating income	5.7	4.0	5.5	9.4
Other income (net)	(1.1)	(1.4)	(1.9)	(3.1)
Earnings before tax	4.6	2.6	3.6	6.3
Taxes	2.4	1.1	1.8	3.2
Net profit	2.2	1.5	1.8	3.1
Preferred dividend	0.1	0.1	0.1	0.1
Earnings available to common stock	$ 2.1	$ 1.4	$ 1.7	$ 3.0
Earnings per share	$ 1.05	$ 0.70	$ 0.85	$ 1.50
Cash dividends per share	0.43	0.48	0.53	0.60
Price range for common stock				
High	22.00	23.00	22.00	27.00
Low	10.00	14.00	17.00	21.00

a) Should Green Field refinance the short-term loans? Why?
b) If the bank loans should be refinanced, what factors should be considered in determining which form of financing to use?

This question should not be answered in terms of precise cost of capital calculations. Rather, a more qualitative and subjective analysis is appropriate. The only calculations necessary are some simple ratios. Careful interpretation of these ratios is necessary, however, to understand and discuss the often complex, subjective judgment issues involved.

18–2 Pitney-Bowes has been practically the sole manufacturer of postage meters, which it leases or sells outright. Postage meters accounted for half of all the United States postage used by 1959. In addition, the company makes and sells a variety of mailing and business machines.

A few years ago the company incurred $6 million in short-term bank loans because of the expansion of its Stamford plant and offices. The officers of Pitney-Bowes discussed the desirability of refinancing the bank loans with long-term debt or common stock. Underwriters informed them that 20-year, 5½ percent sinking fund debentures or 200,000 shares of common stock could be sold to raise the desired funds. As the common stock was selling above

$40 per share, the company could receive about $8,000,000 net from the sale of 200,000 shares. Financial data are shown below.

PITNEY-BOWES, INC.
CONSOLIDATED BALANCE SHEET
December 31, 1959*
(in millions of dollars)

Current assets	$21	Accounts payable	$ 4	
Fixed plant and equipment	29	Notes payable, 5%	6	
		Income taxes payable	3	
		Other accruals	2	
		Total current liabilities		$15
		Prepaid rental income (net)		7
		Promissory notes, 3¾%, due in 1967		4
		Cumulative preferred stock, $50 par, 4¼%		1
		Common stock, $2 par value	8	
		Capital surplus	4	
		Retained earnings	11	
		Net worth		23
Total assets	$50	Total claims on assets		$50

* The balance sheet and income statement figures have been altered to simplify the calculations.

PITNEY-BOWES, INC.
CONSOLIDATED STATEMENT OF INCOME
Year Ended December 31
(in millions of dollars)

	1956		1957		1958		1959	
Sales (net)		17		17		20		22
Rental and service income		26		29		31		33
Operating income		43		46		51		55
Cost of products sold	7		7		9		9	
Depreciation on rental equipment	2		3		3		3	
Selling, administrative, and other expenses	26		27		30		33	
		35		37		42		45
Net operating income		8		9		9		10
Income taxes		4		5		5		5
Net profit for the period		4		4		4		5
Earnings per share of common		1.00		1.00		1.00		1.25
Cash dividends per common share		0.50		0.52		0.53		0.60
Price range for common stock								
High		24		24		33		45
Low		15		15		18		35

Manufacturing Industry Financial Ratios

Current ratio (times)	2.0
Sales to total assets (times)	___
Sales to inventory (times)	9.0
Average collection period (days)	___
Current debt/total assets (percent)	20–25
Long-term debt/total assets (percent)	6–10
Preferred/total assets (percent)	___
Net worth/total assets (percent)	65–70
Profits to sales (percent)	4–6
Net profits to total assets (percent)	10–12
Profits to net worth (percent)	13–15
Expected growth in earnings and dividends (percent)	7.5

a) Should Pitney-Bowes have refunded the short-term bank loan? Why?

b) If you were to refinance the short-term loan, what factors would enter into your consideration of the two alternatives?

c) Indicate which means of refinancing you would suggest.

This question should not be answered in terms of precise cost of capital calculations. Rather, a more qualitative and subjective analysis is appropriate. The only calculations necessary are some simple ratios. Careful interpretation of these ratios is necessary, however, to understand and discuss the often complex, subjective judgment issues involved.

18–3 The common stock of the Industrial Research Company is selling for $99 on the market. The stockholders are offered one new share at a subscription price of $75 for every three shares held. What is the value of each right?

18–4 Lewis has 20 shares of Northwood Industries. The market price per share is $70. The company now offers stockholders one new share to be purchased at $40 for every five shares held.

a) Determine the value of each right.

b) Assume that Lewis (1) uses 15 rights and sells the other 5, or (2) sells 20 rights at the market price you have calculated. Prepare a statement showing the changes in his position under the above assumptions.

18–5 National Appliance Company common stock is priced at $43 a share on the market. Notice is given that stockholders may purchase one new share at a price of $25 for every five shares held. You hold 80 shares at the time of notice.

a) At approximately what price will each right sell on the market?

b) Why will this be the approximate price?

c) What effect will the issuance of rights have on the original market price? Why?

18–6 The Wilson Company has the following balance sheet and income statement:

THE WILSON COMPANY
BALANCE SHEET BEFORE RIGHTS OFFERING

		Total debt, (5%)	$ 5,000,000
		Common stock ($20 par value)	2,000,000
		Retained earnings	3,000,000
Total assets	$10,000,000	Total liabilities and capital	$10,000,000

Earnings rate: 10% on total assets	
Total earnings	$1,000,000
Interest on debts	250,000
Income before taxes	750,000
Taxes (40% rate assumed)	300,000
Earnings after taxes	$ 450,000
Earnings per share	$ 4.50
Dividends per share (56%)	$ 2.50
Price/earnings ratio	20 times
Market price per share	$90.00

The Wilson Company plans to raise an additional $4 million through a rights offering. The additional funds will continue to earn 10 percent. The price/earnings ratio is assumed to remain at 20 times, dividend payout will continue to be 56 percent, and the 40 percent tax rate will remain in effect. (Do not attempt to use the formulas given in the chapter for this problem. Additional information is given here which violates the "other things constant" assumption inherent in the formula.)

a) Assuming subscription prices of $20, $40, and $60 a share:
   (1) How many additional shares of stock will have to be sold?
   (2) How many rights will be required to purchase one new share?
   (3) What will be the new earnings per share?
   (4) What will be the new market price per share?
   (5) Selling stock through a rights offering with the subscription price set below the current market price has an effect that is somewhat similar to a stock split or stock dividend. A stock split of approximately what degree would have the same effect on earnings per share as does the rights offering under each of the three subscription prices?
   (6) What will be the new dividend per share if the dividend payout ratio is maintained?

b) What is the significance of your results?

Selected References

Barry, Eugene P., *The Financing of Stock Issues with Preemptive Rights* (New York: Shields & Company, March 1948).

Chamberlain, John, "Why It's Harder and Harder to Get a Good Board," *Fortune* (November 1966).

Donaldson, Gordon, "Financial Goals: Management vs. Stockholders," *Harvard Business Review,* XLI (May-June 1963), 116–129.

Duvall, Richard M., and Douglas V. Austin, "Predicting the Results of Proxy Contests," *Journal of Finance,* XX (September 1965), 467–471.

Evans, G. H., Jr., "The Theoretical Value of a Stock Right," *Journal of Finance,* X (March 1955), 55–61. See comments on this article by Stephen H. Archer and by William Beranek in *Journal of Finance,* XI (September 1956), 363–370.

"1958 Rights Financing Profitable to Share Owners," *Exchange,* XX (March 1959), 8–9.

Lowe, H. D., "The Classification of Corporate Stock Equities," *Accounting Review,* XXXVI (July 1961), 425–433.

Nelson, J. Russell, "Price Effects in Rights Offerings," *Journal of Finance,* XX (December 1965), 647–650.

O'Neal, F. H., "Minority Owners Can Avoid Squeeze-Outs," *Harvard Business Reveiw,* XLI (March-April 1963), 150–152.

Sametz, Arnold W., "Trends in the Volume and Composition of Equity Financing," *Journal of Finance,* XIX (September 1964), 450–469.

Stevenson, Harold W., *Common Stock Financing* (Ann Arbor, Mich.: University of Michigan, 1957).

Williams, Charles M., *Cumulative Voting for Directors* (Boston: Graduate School of Business Administration, Harvard University, 1951).

19

Fixed Income Securities: Debt and Preferred Stock

The major factors underlying the decision to use financial leverage were set out in Part IV. It was noted that the use of leverage magnifies returns on common stock. Up to a point—with the particular point varying with the characteristics of the firm's line of activity—additional leverage is advantageous in terms of (1) maximizing the market value of the common stock and (2) minimizing the average cost of capital. Beyond that point, which was defined as the "optimal debt ratio," or the "optimum capital structure," additional debt raises the cost of capital and lowers the value of the firm.

In the theoretical discussion of leverage, we abstracted from reality by explaining the concepts largely in terms of one homogeneous type of fixed income security, "debt." In fact, there are a myriad of fixed income securities: long- and short-term, secured and unsecured, marketable and nonmarketable, participating and nonparticipating, senior and junior, and so on.

Different classes of investors favor different types of securities, and tastes change over time. An astute financial manager knows how to "package" his securities at a given point in time to make them most attractive to the most potential investors and thereby keep his cost of capital to a minimum. We have already analyzed the major types and forms of short-term and intermediate-term debt financing. This chapter deals with the two most important types of long-term fixed income securities, bonds and preferred stocks.

INSTRUMENTS OF LONG-TERM DEBT FINANCING

For an understanding of long-term forms of financing, some familiarity with technical terminology is necessary. However, the presentation will be limited to only that descriptive material necessary to analyze important problems and to formulate financial policies. The discussion of long-term debt therefore begins with an explanation of several important instruments.

Eight Key Concepts

BOND. Most people have had some experience with short-term promissory notes. A *bond* is a long-term promissory note.

MORTGAGE. A *mortgage* represents a pledge of designated property for a loan. Under a *mortgage bond* the corporation pledges certain real assets as security for the bond. A mortgage bond is therefore secured by real property.[1] The pledge is a condition of the loan.

DEBENTURE. A *debenture* is long-term debt unsecured in the sense that it lacks a pledge of any specific property. However, like other general creditor claims, it is secured by any property not otherwise pledged.

FUNDED DEBT. *Funded debt* is simply long-term debt. When a firm is said to be planning to "fund" its floating debt, it will replace short-

[1] There are also *chattel mortgages,* which are secured by personal property, but these are generally intermediate-term instruments.

term securities by long-term securities. Funding does not imply placing money with a trustee or other repository; it is simply part of the jargon of finance and means long term.

INDENTURE. Since a bond is a long-term promissory note, a long-term relation between borrower and lender is established in a document called an *indenture*. When it is a matter of an ordinary 60- or 90-day promissory note, few new developments are likely to occur in the life or affairs of the borrower to endanger repayment. The lender looks closely at the borrower's current position because current assets are the main source of repayment. A bond, however, is a long-time contractual relationship between the issuer of the bond and the bondholders; over such an extended period the bondholder has cause to worry that the firm's position might change materially.

In the ordinary common stock or preferred stock certificate or agreement, the details of the contractual relation can be summarized in a few paragraphs. The bond indenture, however, may be a document of several hundred pages covering a large number of factors that will be important to the contractual parties. It discusses the form of the bond and the instrument. It provides a complete description of property pledged. It specifies the authorized amount of the bond issue. It contains protective clauses or *covenants,* which are detailed and which usually include limits on indebteness, restrictions on dividends, and a sinking fund provision. Generally a minimum current ratio requirement during the bond indebtedness, as well as provisions for redemption or call privileges, are also added.

TRUSTEE. Not only is a bond of long duration, but the issue is also likely to be of substantial size. Before the rise of the large aggregations of savings through insurance companies or pension funds, no single buyer was able to buy an issue of such size. Bonds were therefore issued in denominations of $1,000 each and were sold to a large number of purchasers. To facilitate communication between the issuer and the numerous bondholders, another device was instituted, the *trustee,* who is the representative of the bondholders. He is presumed to act at all times for their protection and on their behalf.

Any legal person, including a corporation, is considered competent to act as a trustee. Typically, however, the duties of the trustee are handled by a department of a commercial bank.

The trustee has three main responsibilities. (1) The trustee certifies the issue of bonds. This duty involves making certain that all the legal requirements for drawing up the bond contract and the indenture have been carried out. (2) The trustee polices the behavior of the corporation in its performance of the responsibilities set forth in the indenture provision. (3) The trustee is responsible for taking appropriate action on behalf of the bondholders if the corporation defaults on payment of interest or principal.

It is said that in a large number of the corporate bond defaults in the early 1930s, trustees did not act in the best interests of the bondholders. The trustees did not conserve the assets of the corporation effectively. Often they did not take early action, so that corporation executives continued their salaries and disposed of assets under conditions favorable to themselves but detrimental to the bondholders. Assets pledged as security for the bonds were sold; specific security was, thus, no longer available. The result in many instances was that holders of mortgage bonds found themselves more in the position of general creditors than in that of secured bondholders.

As a consequence of such practices, the Trust Indenture Act of 1939 was passed in order to give more protection to bondholders. It provides that trustees must be given sufficient power to act on behalf of bondholders. The indenture must fully disclose rights and responsibilities and must not be deceptive. There is provision for changes in the indenture at the option of the bondholders. A specific requirement of prompt, protective action on the part of the trustees for bondholders on default is made. Provision is made for making certain that an arm's-length relation exists between the issuing corporation and the trustee. The obligor may not own more than 10 percent of the common stock of the trustee, nor the trustee more than 5 percent of the voting stock of the obligor. Finally, the corporation must make periodic reports to trustees to enable them to carry out their protective responsibilities.

CALL PROVISION. A call provision gives the issuing corporation the right to call in the bond for redemption. If it is used, the call provision generally states that the company must pay an amount greater than the par value of the bond, with this additional sum being defined as the *call premium*. The call premium is typically set equal to one year's interest if the bond is called during the first year, with the premium declining at a constant rate each year thereafter. For example, the call premium on a $1,000 par value, 20-year, 6 percent bond would generally be $60 if called during the first year, $57 if called during the second year (calculated by reducing the $60 (or 6 percent) premium by $\frac{1}{20}$), and so on.

As will be pointed out later in this chapter, the call privilege is valuable to the firm but potentially detrimental to an investor, especially if the bond is issued in a period when interest rates are thought to be cyclically high. Accordingly, the interest rate on a new issue of callable bonds will exceed that on a new issue of noncallable bonds. For example, on May 28, 1968, Monongahela Power Co. sold an issue of AA rated bonds to yield 7.375 percent. These bonds were callable immediately. On the same day, Union Oil of California sold an issue of AA rated bonds to yield 6.720 percent. Union Oil's bonds were noncallable for 10 years. Investors were apparently willing to accept a .655 percent lower interest rate on Union Oil's bonds for the assurance that the relatively high (by historic standards) rate of interest would be earned for at least 10 years. Monongahela Power, on the other hand, had to incur a .655 percent higher annual interest rate for the privilege of calling the bonds in the event of a subsequent decline in interest rates. The analysis for determining when to call an issue will be considered later in this chapter.

SINKING FUND. A *sinking fund* is a provision that facilitates the orderly retirement of a bond issue (or, in some cases, an issue of preferred stock). Typically, the sinking fund provision requires the firm to buy and retire a portion of the bond issue each year. Sometimes the stipulated sinking fund payment is tied to sales or earnings of the current year, but usually it is a mandatory fixed amount. If it is mandatory, a failure to meet the sinking fund payment causes the bond issue to be thrown into default and possibly leads the company into bankruptcy. Obviously, then, a sinking fund can constitute a dangerous cash drain to the firm.

In most cases the firm is given the right to handle the sinking fund in either of two ways: (1) it may call a certain percentage of the bonds at a stipulated price each year—for example, 2 percent of the original amount at a price of $1,050—with the actual bonds, which are numbered serially, being determined by a lottery; or (2) it may spend the funds provided by the sinking fund payment to buy the bonds on the open market. The firm will do whichever results in the greatest reduction of outstanding bonds for a given expenditure. Therefore, if interest rates have risen (and the price of the bonds has fallen), the firm will choose the open market alternative. If interest rates have fallen and bond prices have risen, the company will elect to use the option of calling bonds.

It must be recognized that the call provision of the sinking fund may at times work to the detriment of bondholders. If, for example, the bond carries a 7 percent interest rate, and if yields on similar securities are 4 percent, the bond will sell for well above par. A sinking fund call at par would thus greatly disadvantage some bondholders. This would apply to bonds *subsequent* to their initial issue, however; on balance, securities that provide for a sinking fund and continuing redemption are likely to be offered initially on a lower yield basis than are securities without such a fund. Since sinking funds provide additional protection to investors, bonds with this feature are likely to sell initially at higher prices; hence, they have a lower cost of capital to the issuer.

SECURED LONG-TERM DEBT

Secured long-term debt may be classified according to (1) the priority of claims, (2) the right to issue additional securities, and (3) the scope of the lien.

Priority of Claims

1. A senior mortgage is a mortgage with prior claims on assets and earnings. Senior railroad mortgages have been called the mortgages next to the rail, implying that they have the first claim on the land and assets of the railroad corporations.

2. A junior mortgage is a subordinate lien, such as a second or a third mortgage. It is a lien or claim junior to others.

Right to Issue Additional Securities

Mortgage bonds may also be classified with respect to the right to issue additional obligations pledging already encumbered property.

In the case of a *closed-end mortgage,* a company may not sell additional bonds, beyond those already issued, secured by the property specified in the mortgage. For example, assume that a corporation with plant and land worth $5 million has a $2 million mortgage on these properties. If the mortgage is closed end, no more bonds having first liens on this property may be issued. Thus a closed-end mortgage provides greater security to the bond buyer. The ratio of the amount of the senior bonds to the value of the property will not be increased by subsequent issues.

If the bond indenture is silent on this point, it is called an *open-end mortgage.* Its nature may be illustrated by the facts of the example cited. Against property worth $5 million, bonds of $2 million are sold. If an additional first mortgage bond of $1 million is subsequently sold, the property has been pledged for a total of $3 million bonds. If, on liquidation, the property sold for $2 million, the original bondholders would receive 67 cents on the dollar. If the mortgage had been closed end, they would have been fully paid.

Most characteristic is the *limited open-end mortgage.* Its nature may be indicated by continuing the example. A first mortgage bond issue of $2 million is sold secured by the property worth $5 million. The indenture provides that an additional $1 million worth of bonds—or an additional amount of bonds up to 60 percent of the original cost of the property—may be sold. Thus, the mortgage is open only up to a certain point.

These are some ways in which the limited feature of an open-end mortgage may be expressed. The limited open-end mortgage is flexible in that it provides for the issuance of additional securities. At the same time, it limits this right; thus the original bondholder is protected.

Scope of the Lien

Bonds may also be classified with respect to the scope of their lien. When it is a matter of a *specific lien,* the security for a first mortgage or a second mortgage is a specifically designated property. A lien is granted on certain described property. On the other hand, a *blanket mortgage* pledges all real property currently owned by the company. The definition of real property is land and those things affixed thereto. Hence a blanket mortgage would not be a mortgage on cash, accounts receivables, or inventories, because these items are regarded as personal property. A blanket mortgage gives more protection to the bondholder than does a specific mortgage because it provides a claim on all real property owned by the company.

UNSECURED BONDS

Debentures

The debenture is an unsecured bond and, as such, provides no lien on specific property as security for the obligation. Debenture holders are therefore general creditors whose claim is protected by property not otherwise pledged. The advantage of debentures from the standpoint of the issuer is that he leaves his property unencumbered for subsequent financing. However, in practice the use of debentures depends on the nature of the firm's assets and its general credit strength.

If the credit positions of the borrowing companies in an industry are exceptionally strong, these firms can issue debentures—they simply do not need specific security. However, the credit position of a company may be so weak that it has no alternative to the use of debentures—all its property may already be encumbered. American Telephone & Telegraph's vast financing program since the end of World War II has been mainly through debentures, both convertible and straight debentures. AT&T is such a strong institution that it does not have to provide security for its debt issues.

Debentures are also often issued by companies in industries where it would not be practical to provide a lien through a mortgage on fixed assets. An example of such an industry would be the large mail order houses, which characteristically do not have large fixed assets in relation to their total assets. The bulk of their assets is in the form of inventory, which is not satisfactory security for a mortgage lien.

Subordinated Debentures

The term *subordinate* means below or inferior. Thus, subordinated debt has claims on assets after unsubordinated debt in the event of liquidation. Debentures may be subordinated to designated notes payable—usually bank loans—or to any or all other debt. In the event of liquidation or reorganization, the debentures cannot be paid until senior debt *as named in the indenture* has been paid. Senior debt typically does not include trade accounts payable. How the subordination provision strengthens the position of senior-debt holders is shown in Table 19–1.

Where $200 is available for distribution, the subordinated debt has a claim of one half of $100, or $50. However, this claim is subordinated to the bank debt (senior debt) and is added to the $100 claim of the bank. As a consequence, 75 percent of the bank's original claim is satisfied.

Where $300 is available for distribution, the $75 allocated to the subordinated debt is divided into two parts: $50 goes to the bank and the other $25 remains for the subordinated-debt holders. In this situation, the senior bank debt holders are fully paid off, 75 percent of other debt is paid, and the subordinated debt receives only 25 percent of its claim.

Subordination is frequently required. Alert credit managers of firms supplying trade credit, or commercial bank loan officers, typically will insist upon subordination, particularly where debt is owed to the principal stockholders or officers of a company.

Preferred stock, in comparison to subordinated debt, suffers from the disadvantage that preferred stock dividends are not deductible as an expense for tax purposes. The interest on subordinated debentures is an expense for tax purposes. Some people have referred to subordinated

TABLE 19–1 ILLUSTRATION OF LIQUIDATING PAYMENTS TO SENIOR DEBT, OTHER DEBT, AND SUBORDINATED DEBT

FINANCIAL STRUCTURE	(1) BOOK VALUE	(2) PERCENT OF TOTAL DEBT	(3) INITIAL ALLOCATION	(4) ACTUAL PAYMENT	(5) PERCENT OF ORIGINAL CLAIM SATISFIED
I. $200 available for claims on liquidation					
Bank debt	$200	50	$100	$150	75
Other debt	100	25	50	50	50
Subordinated debt	100	25	50	0	0
Total debt	400	100	$200	$200	
Net worth	300				0
Total	$700				
II. $300 available for claims on liquidation					
Bank debt	$200	50	$150	$200	100
Other debt	100	25	75	75	75
Subordinated debt	100	25	75	25	25
Total debt	400	100	$300	$300	
Net worth	300				0
Total	$700				

STEPS: 1. Express each type of debt as a percentage of total debt (column 2).
2. Multiply the debt percentages (column 2) by the amount available, obtaining the initial allocations shown in column 3.
3. The subordinated debt is subordinate to bank debt. Therefore, the initial allocation to subordinate debt is added to the bank debt allocation until it has been exhausted or until the bank debt is finally paid off. This is given in column 4.

debentures as being much like a special kind of preferred stock, the dividends of which are deductible as an expense for tax purposes. Subordinated debt has therefore become an increasingly important source of corporate capital.

The reasons for the use of subordinated debentures are clear. They offer a considerable tax advantage over preferred stock, and yet they do not restrict the ability of the borrower to obtain senior debt as would be the case if all debt sources were on an equal basis.

Subordinated debentures are further stimulated by periods of tight money when commercial banks may require a greater equity base for short-term financing. Subordinated debentures provide a greater equity cushion for loans from commercial banks or other forms of senior debt. The use of subordinated debentures also illustrates the development of hybrid securities which emerge to meet changing situations that develop in the capital market.

The amount of subordinated debt that may be employed is limited, as is the amount of any form of debt. The rule of thumb employed by investment bankers in connection with industrial issues of subordinated debentures appears to be about $2 of net worth for each $1 of subordinated debt.

Income Bonds

Income bonds typically arise from corporate reorganizations. These bonds pay interest only if income is actually earned by the company because the company, having gone through reorganization, has been in difficult financial circumstances. Interest is not a fixed charge; the principal, however, must be paid when due.

Income bonds are like preferred stock in that management is not required to pay interest if it is not earned. However, they differ from preferred stock in that if interest has been earned, management is usually required to pay it. In recent years, income bonds have been increasingly used as a source of ordinary financing.[2]

The main characteristic and distinct advantage of the income bond is that interest is payable only if the company achieves some earnings. Since earnings calculations are subject to differing interpretations, the indenture of the income bond carefully defines income and expenses. If it did not do so, long, drawn-out litigation might result.

Some income bonds are cumulative for a limited number of years (if interest is not paid, it "accumulates" and must be paid at some future date); others are cumulative for the first three to five years, after which time they become noncumulative. Some issues are fully cumulative.

Income bonds usually contain sinking fund provisions to provide for their retirement. The payments to the sinking funds range between ½ and 1 percent of the face amount of the original issue. Because the sinking fund payments are typically dependent on earnings, a fixed-cash drain on the company is avoided.

Sometimes income bonds are convertible. There are sound reasons for their being convertible if they arise out of a reorganization. Creditors who receive income bonds in exchange for defaulted obligations have

[2] See S. M. Robbins, "A Bigger Role for Income Bonds," *Harvard Business Review*, XXXIII (November-December 1955), 100–114.

a less desirable position than they had before. Since they have received something based on an adverse and problematical forecast of the future of the company, it is appropriate that if the company should prosper, income bondholders should be entitled to participate. When income bonds are issued in situations other than reorganization, the convertibility feature is a "sweetener" likely to make the issue more attractive to prospective bond buyers.

Typically, income bonds do not have voting rights when they are issued. Sometimes bondholders are given the right to elect one, two, or some specified number of directors if interest is not paid for a certain number of years.

Income bonds have been used instead of preferred stock in situations other than reorganization. Armour & Company has made repeated use of such bonds.[3] In 1943, Armour used subordinated income bonds to substitute for a preferred stock issue. At the close of 1954, Armour replaced convertible preferred stock with dividend arrearages by 5 percent cumulative income bonds subordinated to other debt with a warrant to buy common stock. The replacement of preferred stock by income bonds resulted in a substantial tax saving for the company.

CHARACTERISTICS OF LONG-TERM DEBT

From Viewpoint of Holder

A critical framework for analyzing the position of any security holder in a corporation includes aspects of risk, control, and income.

RISK. Debt is favorable to the holder because it gives him priority both in earnings and in liquidation. Debt also has a definite maturity and is protected by the covenants of the indenture.

INCOME. The bondholder has a fixed return; except in the case of income bonds, interest payments are not contingent on the level of earnings of the company. However, debt does not participate in any superior earnings of the company, and gains are limited in magnitude. Frequently, long-term debt is callable. If bonds are called, the investor receives funds that must be reinvested to be kept active.

CONTROL. The bondholder usually does not have the right to vote. Yet there are periods when a substantial portion of bonds sold are convertible bonds. If bonds are convertible into common stock, under certain

[3] Robbins, p. 106.

conditions the bondholder may obtain the position of an equity holder rather than a debt holder.

An over-all appraisal of the characteristics of long-term debt indicates that it is strong from the standpoint of risk, has limited advantages with regard to income, and is weak with respect to control.

From Viewpoint of Issuer

ADVANTAGES. (1) The cost of debt is definitely limited. Bondholders do not participate in superior profits if earned.

(2) Not only is the cost limited, but it is also lower than the cost of common or preferred stock.

(3) The owners of the corporation do not share control of the corporation when debt financing is used.

(4) The interest payment on debt is deductible as a tax expense.

(5) Flexibility in the financial structure of the corporation may be achieved by inserting a call provision in the indenture of the debt.

DISADVANTAGES. (1) Debt is a fixed charge; there is greater risk if the earnings of the company fluctuate, because the corporation may be unable to meet these fixed charges.

(2) As was seen in Chapter 10, higher risk brings higher capitalization rates on equity earnings. Thus, even though leverage is favorable and raises earnings per share, the higher capitalization rates attributable to leverage may drive the common stock value down.

(3) Debt usually has a definite maturity date. Because of the fixed maturity date, the financial officer must make provision for repayment of the debt.

(4) Since long-term debt is a commitment for a long period, such debt involves risk; the expectations and plans on which the debt was issued may change. The debt may prove to be a burden, or it may prove to have been advantageous. For example, if income, employment, and the price level fall greatly, the assumption of a large amount of debt may prove to have been an unwise financial policy. The railroads are always given as an example in this regard. They were able to meet their ordinary operating expenses during the 1930s but were unable to meet the heavy financial charges they had undertaken earlier, when the prospects for the railroads looked more favorable than they turned out to be.

(5) In a long-term contractual relationship, the indenture provisions are likely to be much more stringent than they are in a short-term credit agreement. Hence the firm may be subject to much more disturbing and crippling restrictions in the indenture of a long-term debt arrangement than would be the case if it had borrowed on a short-term basis or had issued common stock.

(6) There is a limit on the extent to which funds can be raised through long-term debt. Some of the generally accepted standards of financial policy dictate that the debt ratio shall not exceed certain limits. These standards of financial prudence set limits or controls on the extent to which funds may be raised through long-term debt.

ECISIONS ON USE OF ONG-TERM DEBT

The foregoing discussion of the various forms of debt illustrates an important principle in business finance: Any form of financing arrangement is likely to be developed as the economic environment and the needs of firms require. The only limitations are the imaginations of the issuers and investment bankers and the needs of investors—and these permit a wide degree of variation in securities forms.

The conditions favoring the use of long-term debt when a number of alternative methods of long-term financing are under consideration include the following:

1. Sales and earnings are relatively stable or a substantial increase in sales and earnings is expected in the future, providing substantial benefit to the use of leverage.
2. A substantial rise in the price level is expected in the future, making it advantageous for the firm to incur debt that can be repaid with cheaper dollars.
3. The existing debt ratio is relatively low for the line of business.
4. Management thinks the price of the common stock in relation to that of bonds is temporarily depressed.
5. Sale of common stock would involve problems of maintaining the existing control pattern in the company.

NATURE OF PREFERRED STOCK

Preferred stock has claims or rights ahead of common stock. The preference may be a prior claim on earnings, it may take the form of a prior claim on assets in the event of liquidation, or it may take a preferential position with regard to both earnings and assets.

Hybrid Form

The hybrid nature of preferred stock becomes apparent when one tries to classify it in relation to bonds and common stock. The priority feature and the (generally) fixed dividend indicate that preferred stock is similar to bonds. Payments to the preferred stockholders are limited in amount so that the common stockholders receive the advantages (or disadvantages) of leverage. However, if the preferred dividends are not earned, the company can forgo paying them without danger of bankruptcy. In this characteristic, preferred stock is similar to common stock. Moreover, failure to pay the stipulated dividend does not cause default of the obligation, as does failure to pay bond interest.

Debt and Equity

In some kinds of analysis, preferred stock is treated as debt. For example, if the analysis is being made by a potential stockholder considering the earnings fluctuations induced by fixed-charge securities, preferred stock would be treated as debt. Suppose, however, that the analysis is by a bondholder studying the firm's vulnerability to *failure* brought on by declines in sales or in income. Since the dividends on preferred stock are not a fixed charge in the sense that failure to pay them would represent a default of an obligation, preferred stock represents a cushion; it provides an additional equity base. From the point of view of *stockholders,* it is a leverage-inducing instrument much like debt. From the point of view of *creditors*, it constitutes additional net worth. Preferred stock may therefore be treated either as debt or as equity, depending on the nature of the problem under consideration.

MAJOR PROVISIONS OF PREFERRED STOCK ISSUES[4]

The possible characteristics, rights, and obligations of any specific security vary widely, and a point of diminishing returns is quickly reached in a descriptive discussion of different kinds of securities. As economic circumstances change, new kinds of securities are manufactured. The possibilities are numerous. The kinds and varieties of securi-

[4] Much of the data in this section is taken from a recent study by Donald E. Fischer and Glenn A. Wilt, Jr., "Non-Convertible Preferred Stocks as a Financing Instrument," *Journal of Finance,* XXIII (September 1968), 611–624.

ties are limited chiefly by the imagination and ingenuity of the managers formulating the terms of the security issues. It is not surprising, then, that preferred stock can be found in a variety of forms. One need only look at the main terms and characteristics in each case and examine the possible variations in relation to the kinds of situations or circumstances in which they could occur, as is done below.

Priority in Assets and Earnings

Many provisions in a preferred stock certificate are designed to reduce risk to the purchaser relative to the risk carried by the holder of common stock. Preferred stock usually has priority with regard to earnings and assets. Two provisions designed to prevent undermining these preferred stock priorities are often found. The first states that, without the consent of the holders of the preferred stock, there can be no subsequent sale of securities having a prior or equal claim on earnings. The second provision seeks to hold earnings in the firm. It requires a minimum level of retained earnings before common stock dividends are permitted. In order to assure the availability of liquid assets that may be converted into cash for the payment of dividends, the maintenance of a minimum current ratio may also be required.

Par Value

Unlike common stock, preferred stock usually has a par value; this par value is a meaningful quantity. First, it establishes the amount due to the preferred stockholders in the event of a liquidation. Second, the preferred dividend is frequently stated as a percentage of the par value. For example, J. I. Case has preferred stock outstanding that has a par value of $100, and the dividend is stated to be 7 percent of par. It would, of course, be just as appropriate for the Case preferred stock to state simply that the annual dividend is $7, and on many preferred stocks the dividends are stated in this manner rather than as a percentage of par value.

Cumulative Dividends

A high percent of dividends on preferred stocks is cumulative—all past preferred dividends must be paid before common dividends may be paid. The cumulative feature is therefore a protective device. If the preferred stock was not cumulative, preferred and common stock dividends could be passed by for a number of years. The company could then vote a large common stock dividend, but only the stipulated payment to preferred stock. Suppose the preferred stock with a par value of $100 carried a 7 percent dividend. Suppose the company did not pay dividends for several years, so that it accumulated an amount that would enable it to pay in total about $50 in dividends. It could pay one $7 dividend to the preferred stock and a $43 dividend to the common stock. Obviously, this device could be used to evade the preferred position that the holders of preferred stock have tried to obtain. The cumulative feature prevents such evasion. Note, however, that compounding is absent in most cumulative plans. In other words, the arrearages themselves earn no return.

Arrearages on preferred stock would make it difficult to resume dividend payments on common stock for a long time. To avoid delays in resuming common stock dividend payments, a compromise arrangement with the holders of common stock is likely to be worked out.

A package offer is one possibility; for example, a recapitalization plan may provide for an exchange of shares. The arrearage will be wiped out by the donation of common stock with a value equal to the amount of the preferred stock arrearage, and the holders of preferred stock are thus given an ownership share in the corporation. Whether this ownership share is worth anything depends on the future earnings prospects of the company. In addition, resumption of current dividends on the preferred may be promised.

The advantage to the company of substituting common stock for dividends in arrears is that it can start again with a clean balance sheet. If earnings recover, dividends can be paid to the holders of common stock without making up arrearages to the holders of preferred stock. The original common stockholders, of course, will have given up a portion of their ownership of the corporation.

Convertibility

Approximately 40 percent of the preferred stock that has been issued in recent years is convertible into common stock. For example, one share of a particular preferred stock could be convertible into 2.5 shares of the firm's common stock at the option of the preferred shareholder. The nature of convertibility is discussed in Chapter 20.

Other Infrequent Provisions

Some of the other provisions occasionally encountered among preferred stocks include the following:

VOTING RIGHTS. Sometimes a preferred stock is given the right to vote for directors. When this feature is present, it generally permits the preferred to elect a *minority* of the board, say three out of nine directors. The voting privilege becomes operative only if the company has not paid the preferred dividend for a specified period, for example, 6, 8, or 10 quarters.

PARTICIPATING. A rare type of preferred stock is one that participates with the common stock in sharing the firm's earnings. The following factors generally relate to participating preferred stocks: (1) the stated preferred dividend is paid first—for example, $5 a share; (2) next, income is allocated to common stock dividends *up to* an amount equal to the preferred dividend—in this case, $5; (3) any remaining income is shared equally between the common and preferred stockholders.

SINKING FUND. Some preferred issues have a sinking fund requirement. When they do, the sinking fund ordinarily calls for the purchase and retirement of a given percentage of the preferred stock each year.

MATURITY. Preferred stocks almost never have maturity dates on which they must be retired. However, if the issue has a sinking fund, this effectively creates a maturity date.

CALL PROVISION. A call provision gives the issuing corporation the right to call in the preferred stock for redemption. If it is used, the call provision generally states that the company must pay an amount greater than the par value of the preferred stock, with this additional sum being defined as the *call premium*. For example, a $100 par value preferred stock might be callable at the option of the corporation at $105 a share.

EVALUATION OF PREFERRED STOCK AS A SOURCE OF FINANCING

Appraisal from Viewpoint of Issuer

ADVANTAGES. An important advantage of preferred stock from the viewpoint of the issuer is that, in contrast to bonds, the obligation to make fixed interest payments is avoided. Also, a firm wishing to expand because its earning power is high may obtain higher earnings for the original owners by selling preferred stock with a limited return rather than by selling common stock.

By selling preferred stock the financial manager avoids the provision of equal participation in earnings that the sale of additional common stock would require. Preferred stock also permits a company to avoid sharing control through participation in voting. In contrast to bonds, it enables the firm to conserve mortgageable assets. Since preferred stock typically has no maturity and no sinking fund, it is more flexible than bonds.

DISADVANTAGES. There are several disadvantages associated with preferred stock. Characteristically, it must be sold on a higher yield basis than that for bonds.[5] Preferred stock dividends are not deductible as a tax expense, a characteristic that makes their cost differential very great in comparison with that of bonds. As we have seen in Chapter 11, the after-tax cost of debt is approximately half the stated coupon rate for profitable firms. The cost of preferred, however, is the full percentage amount of the preferred dividend. This fact has greatly reduced the use of preferred stocks in recent years.[6]

Appraisal from Viewpoint of Investor

In fashioning securities, the financial manager needs to consider the investor's point of view. Frequently it is asserted that preferred stocks have so many disadvantages both to the issuer and to the investor that they should never be issued. Nevertheless, preferred stock is issued in substantial amounts. In fact, between 1930 and 1950, more preferred stock than common stock was issued and sold.

ADVANTAGES. From the viewpoint of the investor, preferred stock provides the following advantages. (1) Preferred stocks provide reasonably steady income. (2) Preferred stockholders have a preference over common stockholders in liquidation; numerous examples can be cited where the prior-preference position of holders of preferred stock saved them from losses incurred by holders of common stock. (3) Many corporations (for example, insurance companies) like to hold preferred stocks as investments because 85 percent of the dividends received on these shares is not taxable.

[5] Historically, a given firm's preferred stock generally carried higher rates than its bonds because of the greater risk inherent in preferred stocks from the holder's viewpoint. However, as is noted below, the fact that preferred dividends are largely exempt from the corporate income tax has made them attractive to corporate investors. In recent years, high-grade preferreds, on average, have sold on a lower yield basis than high-grade bonds. In 1965, Fischer and Wilt found that bonds had a yield 0.39 percentage points above preferred stocks. Thus, a very strong firm could sell preferreds to yield about 0.4 percent less than bonds.

[6] By far the most important issuers of nonconvertible preferred stocks are the utility companies. For these firms, taxes are an expense for rate-making purposes—that is, higher taxes are passed on to the customers in the form of higher prices—so tax deductibility is not an important issue. This explains why utilities issue about 85 percent of all nonconvertible preferreds.

DISADVANTAGES. Some disadvantages to investors are also present. (1) Although the holders of preferred stock bear a substantial portion of ownership risk, their returns are limited. (2) Price fluctuations in preferred stock are far greater than those in bonds, yet yields on bonds are frequently higher than those on preferred stock. (3) There is no legally enforceable right to dividends. (4) Accrued dividend arrearages are seldom settled in cash comparable to the amount of the obligation that has been incurred.

Recent Trends

Because of the nondeductibility of preferred stock dividends as a tax expense, many companies have retired their preferred stock. Often debentures or subordinated debentures will be offered to preferred stockholders in exchange. The interest on the debentures is deductible as a tax expense, while preferred stock dividends are not deductible.

No longer applicable

When the preferred stock is not callable, the company must offer terms of exchange that are sufficiently attractive to induce the preferred stockholders to agree to the exchange. Characteristically, bonds or other securities in an amount somewhat above the recent value of the preferred stock will be issued in exchange. Sometimes bonds equal in market value to the preferred stock will be issued, along with additional cash or common stock to provide an extra inducement to the preferred stockholders. Sometimes the offer will be bonds equal to only a portion of the current market value of the preferred with an additional amount, represented by cash or common stock, that will bring the total amount offered to the preferred stockholders to something over its market value as of a recent date.

U.S. Steel's replacement of its 7 percent preferred stock in 1965 illustrates one of these exchange patterns. U.S. Steel proposed that its 7 percent preferred stock be changed into 4⅝ percent 30-year bonds at a rate of $175 principal amount of bonds for each preferred share. On August 17, 1965, when the plan was announced, the preferred stock was selling at $150. By September 29, 1965, the preferred stock was selling for $170. U.S. Steel also announced that the conversion would increase earnings available to common stock by $10 million yearly, or 18 cents a share at 1965 federal income tax rates; this was sufficient inducement to persuade the company to give the preferred stockholders the added $20 a share.

Tax considerations have reduced the use of preferred stock. But a countertrend has been the use of convertible preferred stock in mergers.[7]

[7] Convertibles are discussed in detail in Chapter 20 and financial aspects of mergers in Chapter 21.

The reasoning here also involves taxes. The owners of the acquired firm frequently are willing to sell out because they are seeking to get away from the worries associated with ownership and management. Consequently, they can be more easily induced to sell out if they are offered a fixed income security. But if bonds (or cash) are offered for the shares of the acquired firm the selling stockholders may pay a capital gains tax on any proceeds received in excess of their cost basis. Frequently, this would involve a heavy capital gains tax liability. If the exchange is convertible preferred stock of the acquiring company for common stock of the acquired firm, the exchange can qualify for exemption on the capital gains liability. In this manner the stockholders of the acquired firm can receive a fixed income security, avoid an immediate capital gains liability, and receive additional benefits from the conversion feature if the price of the acquiring firm's common stock rises.

The use of convertible preferreds has been most noticeable among merger-minded conglomerate corporations. These conglomerates are frequently growth companies with low dividend payout policies, and they frequently buy out firms that have been paying substantial dividends. If the merger was accomplished by an exchange of stock, the stockholders of the acquired company would suffer a reduction in their dividend receipts. The use of a convertible preferred can avoid this dividend dilution and thus enhance the chances that the acquired firm's stockholders will approve the merger.

DECISION-MAKING ON USE OF PREFERRED STOCK

The circumstances favoring the use of preferred stock can now be distilled from the foregoing analysis. As a hybrid security type, the use of preferred stock is favored by conditions that fall between those favoring the use of common stock and those favoring the use of debt.

When a firm's profit margin is high enough to more than cover preferred stock dividends, it will be advantageous to employ leverage. However, if the firm's sales and profits are subject to considerable fluctuations, the use of debt with fixed interest charges may be unduly risky. Preferred stock may offer a happy compromise. The use of preferred stock will be strongly favored if the firm already has a debt ratio that is heavy relative to the reference level maximum for the line of business.

Relative costs of alternative sources of financing are always important considerations. When the market prices of common stocks are relatively low, the costs of common stock financing are relatively high; this has been shown in Chapter 10. The costs of preferred stock financing follow interest rate levels more than common stock prices; in other words, when interest rates are low, the cost of preferred stock is also likely to be low. When the costs of fixed income instruments such as preferred stock are low and the costs of variable value securities such as common stock are high, the use of preferred stock is favored.

Preferred stock may also be the desired form of financing when the use of debt would involve excessive risk or when the issuance of common stock would result in problems of control for the dominant ownership group in the company.

REFUNDING A BOND OR PREFERRED STOCK ISSUE[8]

Suppose a company sells bonds or preferred stock at a time when interest rates are relatively high. Provided the issue is callable, as many are, the company can sell a new issue of low yielding securities and use the proceeds to retire the high rate issue. This is called a *refunding operation.*

The decision to refund a security issue is analyzed in much the same manner as a capital budgeting expenditure. The costs of refunding—the "investment outlay"—are (1) the call premium paid for the privilege of calling the old issue and (2) the flotation costs involved in selling the new issue. The annual receipts, in the capital budgeting sense, are the interest payments that are saved each year; for example, if interest expense on the old issue is $1 million while that on the new issue is $700,000, the $300,000 saving constitutes the annual benefits.

In analyzing the advantages of refunding, the net present value method is the recommended procedure—discount the future interest savings back to the present and compare the discounted value with the cash outlays associated with the refunding. *In the discounting process, the interest rate on the new debt, not the average cost of capital, should be used as the discount factor.* The reason for this is that there is no risk to the savings—their value is known with complete certainty, which is quite unlike most capital budgeting decisions. Because no risk is involved

[8] For an excellent discussion of refunding, see O. D. Bowlin, "The Refunding Decision," *Journal of Finance,* XXI (March 1966), 55–68.

in the refunding, a low discount rate should be used. The following example illustrates the calculations needed in a refunding operation decision.

The Culver City Company has outstanding a $60 million, 20-year bond issue, carrying a 6½ percent interest rate. The bond indenture carries a call provision making it possible for the company to retire the bonds by calling them in at a 6 percent premium. Investment bankers have assured the company that it could sell an additional $60 to $70 million worth of 20-year bonds at an interest rate of 5 percent. Predictions are that interest rates are unlikely to fall below 5 percent. Flotation costs of the new issue will amount to $2,650,000. Should the company refund the $60 million worth of bonds?

Step 1 What is the investment outlay required to refund the issue?
- a) Call premium: 0.06 × $60,000,000 = $3,600,000
- b) Flotation costs of new issue: $2,650,000
- c) Total costs: $6,250,000

Step 2 What are the annual savings?
- a) Old bonds: $60,000,000 × 0.065 = $3,900,000
- b) New bonds: $60,000,000 × 0.050 = 3,000,000
- c) Savings = $ 900,000

Step 3 What is the present value of the savings?
- a) 20-year annuity factor at 5 percent: 12.462
- b) PV of $900,000 a year for 20 years: 12.462 × $900,000 = $11,215,800

CONCLUSION. Since the present value of the receipts ($11,215,800) exceeds the required investment ($6,250,000), the issue should be refunded.

Two other points should be made. First, since the $900,000 savings is an absolutely riskless investment, its present value is found by discounting at the firm's most riskless rate—its cost of debt. Second, since the refunding operation is advantageous to the firm, it must be disadvantageous to bondholders—they must give up their 6½ percent bond and reinvest in one yielding 5 percent. This points out the danger of the call provisions to bondholders and explains why, at any given time, bonds without a call provision command higher prices than callable bonds[9]

[9] Cf. F. C. Jen and J. E. Wert, "The Effects of Call Risk on Corporate Bond Yields," *Journal of Finance,* XXII (December 1967) 637–652; and G. Pye, "The Value of Call Deferment on a Bond: Some Empirical Results," *Journal of Finance,* XXII (December 1967), 623–636.

SUMMARY

A *bond* is a long-term promissory note. A *mortgage bond* is secured by real property. An *indenture* is an agreement between the firm issuing a bond and the numerous bondholders, represented by a *trustee.*

Secured long-term debt differs with respect to (1) the priority of claims, (2) the right to issue additional securities, and (3) the scope of the lien provided. These characteristics determine the amount of protection provided to the bondholder by the terms of the security. Giving the investor more security will induce him to accept a lower yield but will restrict the future freedom of action of the issuing firm.

The main forms of unsecured bonds are (1) *debentures,* (2) *subordinated debentures,* and (3) *income bonds.* Holders of debentures are unsecured general creditors. Subordinated debentures are junior in claim to bank loans. Income bonds are similar to preferred stock in that interest is paid only when earned.

The characteristics of long-term debt determine the circumstances under which it will be used when alternative forms of financing are under analysis. The cost of debt is limited, but it is a fixed obligation. Bond interest is an expense deductible for tax purposes. Debt carries a maturity date and may require sinking fund payments to prepare for extinguishing the obligation. Indenture provisions are likely to include restrictions on the freedom of action of the management of the firm.

The nature of long-term debt encourages its use under the following circumstances:

1. Sales and earnings are relatively stable.
2. Profit margins are adequate to make trading on the equity advantageous.
3. A rise in profits or the general price level is expected.
4. The existing debt ratio is relatively low.
5. Common stock price/earnings ratios are low in relation to the levels of interest rates.
6. Control considerations are important.
7. Cash flow requirements under the bond agreement are not burdensome.
8. Restrictions of the bond indenture are not onerous.

Although seven of the eight factors may favor debt, the eighth can swing the decision to the use of equity capital. The list of factors is, thus, simply a check list of things to consider when deciding upon bonds versus stock; the actual decision is based on a judgment about the relative importance of the several factors.

The *characteristics of preferred stock* vary with the requirements of the situation under which it is issued. However, certain patterns tend to remain. Preferred stocks usually have priority over common stocks with respect to earnings and claims on assets in liquidation. Preferred stocks are usually cumulative; they have no maturity but are sometimes callable. They are typically nonparticipating and have only contingent voting rights.

The advantages to the issuer are limited dividends and no maturity. These advantages may outweigh the disadvantages of higher cost and the nondeductibility of the dividends as an expense for tax purposes. But their acceptance by investors is the final test of whether they can be sold on favorable terms.

Companies sell preferred stock when they seek the advantages of trading on the equity but fear the dangers of the fixed charges on debt in the face of potential fluctuations in income. If debt ratios are already high or if the costs of common stock financing are relatively high, the advantages of preferred stock will be reinforced.

The use of preferred stock has declined significantly since the advent of the corporate income tax because preferred dividends are not deductible for income tax purposes while bond interest payments are deductible. However, in recent years there has been a strong shift back to a new kind of preferred stock—convertible preferred, used primarily in connection with mergers. If cash or bonds are given to the stockholders of the acquired company, they are required to pay capital gains taxes on any gains that might have been realized. However, if convertible preferred stock is given to the selling stockholders, this constitutes a tax-free exchange of securities. The selling stockholders can obtain a fixed income security and at the same time postpone the payment of capital gains taxes.

QUESTIONS

19–1 There are many types of bonds—for example, mortgage, debentures, collateral trust—and varying maturities for each type. What are some factors that determine the particular type of bond a company should use?

19–2 A sinking fund is set up in one of two ways: (1) the corporation makes annual payments to the trustee, who invests the proceeds in securities (frequently government bonds) and uses the accumulated total to retire the bond issue on maturity; (2) the trustee uses the annual payments to retire a portion of the issue each year, either calling a given percentage of the issue by a lottery and paying a specified price per bond or buying bonds on the open market, whichever is cheaper. Discuss the advantages and disadvantages of each procedure from the viewpoint of both the firm and the bondholders.

19–3 Why is a financial institution such as a bank, instead of an individual, a better choice for a bond trustee?

19–4 Since a corporation often has the right to call bonds at will, do you believe individuals should be able to demand repayment at any time they so desire?

19–5 What are the relative advantages and disadvantages of issuing a long-term bond during a recession versus during a period of prosperity?

19–6 On September 24, 1965, Missouri Pacific $4\frac{3}{4}$ percent income bonds due in 2020 were selling for $770, while the company's $4\frac{1}{4}$ percent first mortgage bonds due in 2005 were selling for $945. Why would the bonds with the lower coupon sell at a higher price? (Each has a $1,000 par value.)

19–7 When a firm sells bonds, it must offer a package acceptable to potential buyers. Included in this package of terms are such features as the issue price, the coupon interest rate, the term to maturity, any sinking fund provisions, and other features. The package itself is determined through a bargaining process between the firm and the investment bankers who will handle the issue. What particular features would you, as a corporate treasurer, be especially interested in, and which would you be most willing to give ground on, under each of the following conditions:

a) You believe that the economy is near the peak of a business cycle.

b) Long-run forecasts indicate that your firm will have heavy cash inflows in relation to cash needs during the next 5 to 10 years.

c) Your current liabilities are presently low, but you anticipate raising a considerable amount of funds through short-term borrowing in the near future.

19–8 Bonds are less attractive to investors during periods of inflation because a rise in the price level will reduce the purchasing power of the fixed-interest payments and also of the principal. Discuss the advantages and disadvantages to a corporation of using a bond whose interest payments and principal would increase in direct proportion to increases in the price level (an inflation-proof bond).

19–9 If preferred stock dividends are passed for several years, the preferred stockholders are frequently given the right to elect several members of the board of directors. In the case of bonds that are in default on interest payments, this procedure is not followed. Why does this difference exist?

19–10 Preferred stocks are found in almost all industries, but one industry is the really dominant issuer of preferred shares. What is this industry, and why are firms in it so disposed to use preferred stock?

19–11 From the point of view of the issuing firm, what are some of the advantages of preferred stock?

19–12 If the corporate income tax was abolished, would this raise or lower the amount of new preferred stock issued?

19–13 Investors buying securities have some expected or required rate of return in mind. Which would you expect to be higher, the required rate of return (before taxes) on preferred stocks or on common stocks (a) for individual investors and (b) for corporate investors (for example, insurance companies)?

19–14 Do you think the before-tax required rate of return is higher or lower on very high-grade preferred stocks or on bonds (a) for individual investors and (b) for corporate investors?

19–15 Discuss the pros and cons of a preferred stock sinking fund from the point of view (a) of the issuing corporation and (b) of a preferred stockholder.

19–16 For purposes of measuring a firm's leverage, should preferred stock be classified as debt or as equity? Does it matter if the classification is being made (a) by the firm itself, (b) by creditors, or (c) by equity investors?

PROBLEMS

19–1 The Raymond Company has a $100,000 long-term bond issue outstanding. This debt has an additional 10 years to maturity and bears a coupon interest rate of 8 percent. The firm now has the opportunity to refinance the debt with 10-year bonds at a rate of 6 percent. Further declines in the interest rate are not anticipated. The bond redemption premium (call premium) on the old bond would be $5,000; issue costs on the new would be $6,000. If tax effects are ignored, should the firm refund the bonds?

19–2 In early 1970, the Harris Instrument Corporation planned to raise an additional $100 million for financing plant additions and for working capital. Harris manufactures precision instruments and tools.

Investment banks state that the company could sell common stock at a market price of $25.60 a share to net $25, or it could sell sinking fund debentures to yield 4 percent. Costs of flotation would be slightly higher for common stock but not enough to influence the decision.

The balance sheet and the income statement of Harris Instrument prior to the financing are given below.

HARRIS INSTRUMENT CORPORATION
BALANCE SHEET
March 31, 1970
(in millions of dollars)

Current assets	$250	Accounts payable	$ 20
Investments	25	Notes payable to banks	80
Net fixed assets	125	Taxes	40
		Other current liabilities	35
		Total current liabilities	$175
		Long-term debt	100
		Common stock, $1 par	25
		Earned surplus	100
Total assets	$400	Total claims	$400

HARRIS INSTRUMENT CORPORATION
INCOME STATEMENT
FOR YEAR ENDED March 31, 1970
(in millions of dollars)

Sales	$700
Net income before taxes, 10%	70
Interest on debt	6
Net income subject to tax	64
Tax, 50%	32
Net income after tax	32

a) Assuming that net income before interest and taxes remains at 10 percent of sales, calculate earnings per share under both the stock financing and debt financing alternatives at sales levels of $200, $400, $600, $800, and $1,000 million.
b) Make a break-even chart for the earnings under a.
c) Using a price/earnings ratio of 20 times, calculate the market value per share of common stock under both the stock financing and debt financing alternatives.
d) Make a break-even chart of the market value per share of the company for c.
e) *If the use of debt caused the price/earnings ratio to fall to 12.5*, what would the market value per share of common stock become under the debt financing alternatives in the range of sales being considered?
f) Make a break-even chart for e, keeping a price/earnings ratio of 20 for equity financing.
g) Using the data and assumptions set out, which form of financing should Harris adopt? Why? (Answer in terms of both the quantitative factors listed above and the qualitative factors discussed in the chapter.)

19–3 The Brockton Steel Company is planning a capital improvement program to provide greater efficiency and versatility in its operations. It is estimated that by mid-1970 the company will need to raise $50 million. Brockton is a leading steel producer with an excellent credit rating.

You are asked to set up a program for obtaining the necessary funds. Using the following information, indicate the best form of financing. Some of the items you should include in your analysis are profit margins, relative costs, control, cash flows, ratio analysis, and *pro forma* analysis.

Brockton's common stock is selling at $80 a share. The company could sell debt (25 year) at 4.5 percent or preferred stock at 5 percent.

Steel Industry Financial Ratios

Current ratio (times)	2.1
Sales to total assets (times)	1.8
Coverage of fixed charges	7.0
Average collection period (days)	42.0
Current debt/total assets (percent)	20–25
Long-term debt/total assets (percent)	10.0
Preferred/total assets (percent)	0–5
Net worth/total assets	65–70
Profits to sales (percent)	3.3
Profits to total assets (percent)	6.0
Profits to net worth (percent)	9.5
Expected growth rate in earnings and dividends	5.3

BROCKTON STEEL COMPANY
CONSOLIDATED BALANCE SHEET
December 31, 1969
(in millions of dollars)

Assets		
Current	$190	
Other investments	35	
Properties (net)	285	
Deferred assets	10	
Total assets		$520
Liabilities		
Current	$ 80	
Long-term debt, 4.44%	45	
Total liabilities		$125
Common stock, $10 par	80	
Capital surplus	75	
Retained income	220	
Reserves	20	
Total net worth		395
Total liabilities and net worth		$520

BROCKTON STEEL COMPANY
CONSOLIDATED INCOME STATEMENT
For Years Ended December 31, 1967, 1968, and 1969
(in millions of dollars)

	1967	1968	1969
Sales	$610	$455	$540
Other income	5	5	5
Total	615	460	545
Costs and expenses	530	400	480
Income before taxes	85	60	65
Federal income tax	43	30	32
Net income	42	30	33
Cash dividends	23	23	23
Interest on long-term debt	1.0	1.3	2.0
Depreciation	20	16	17
Shares outstanding (widely held)	7,850,000		

19–4 In late 1969 the Frontier Edison Company of Massachusetts sought to raise $4 million to refinance present preferred stock issues at a lower rate. The company is a member of the Western Utilities Associates Holding Company system. The company could sell additional debt at 5 percent, preferred stock at 4.64 percent, or common stock at $80 a share. How should the com-

Public Utilities Financial Ratios

Current ratio (times)	1.00
Interest earned (before taxes) (times)	4.0
Sales to total assets (times)	0.3
Average collection period (days)	28.0
Current debt/total assets (percent)	5–10
Long-term debt/total assets (percent)	45–50
Preferred/total assets (percent)	10–15
Common equity/total assets (percent)	30–35
Earnings before interest and taxes to total assets (percent)	5.9
Profits to common equity (percent)	10.1
Expected growth in earnings and dividends (percent)	4.625

FRONTIER EDISON COMPANY
BALANCE SHEET
July 31, 1969
(in millions of dollars)

Cash	$ 0.5	Current liabilities	$ 2.0
Receivables	1.0	Long-term debt, 3.5%	18.0
Material and supplies	0.8	Preferred stock, 5.60%	4.0
Total current	2.3	Common stock, $25 par value	7.5
		Paid-in surplus	4.4
Net property	37.7	Earned surplus	4.1
Total assets	$40.0	Total claims	$40.0

pany raise the money? Relevant financial information is provided below.

This question should not be answered in terms of precise cost of capital calculations. Rather, a more qualitative and subjective analysis is appropriate. The only calculations necessary are some simple ratios. Careful interpretation of these ratios is necessary, however, to understand and discuss the often complex, subjective judgment issues involved.

FRONTIER EDISON COMPANY
INCOME STATEMENT
For Year Ended July 31, 1969
(in millions of dollars)

Operating revenues	\$12.6
Operating expenses (incl. taxes)	10.5
Net operating income	2.1
Interest deductions	0.6
Net income	1.5
Earnings per share	\$ 5.00
Dividends per share	\$ 3.50

19–5 Genesco, Inc., is a manufacturer of apparel and footwear. Although principally a manufacturer of shoes, it has in recent years acquired a number of companies that make men's and women's apparel.

The company seeks to retire its 4.5 percent unsecured notes due in 1970 and its outstanding 5 percent notes due in 1971. A substantial amount of funds (\$10 million) from new financing is earmarked for additions to working capital and retirement of short-term bank notes as they mature. Genesco can issue new debt at 5½ percent, a preferred stock issue at 4.5 percent, or common stock at \$30 a share. Total new financing is expected to be \$20 million. How should the company raise the money? Relevant financial data are given below, and some have been slightly changed.

Footwear Industry Financial Ratios

Current ratio (times)	2.2
Sales to total assets (times)	2.3
Sales to inventory (times)	6.1
Average collection period (days)	46.0
Current debt/total assets (percent)	30.0
Long-term debt/total assets (percent)	10.0
Preferred/total assets (percent)	0–10
Common equity/total assets (percent)	50–60
Profits to sales (percent)	2.3
Net profits to total assets (percent)	5.0
Profits to common equity (percent)	9.0
Expected growth in earnings and dividends (percent)	3.33

GENESCO, INC.
CONSOLIDATED BALANCE SHEET
July 31, 1969
(in millions of dollars)

Current assets	$150	Current liabilities	$ 40
Plant and equipment (net)	28	Long-term debt	60
Other assets	22	Preferred stock $4.50	10
		Common stock $1 par value	3
		Paid-in capital	42
		Retained earnings	45
Total assets	$200	Total claims	$200

GENESCO, INC.
CONSOLIDATED INCOME STATEMENT
For Year Ended July 31, 1969
(in millions of dollars)

Net sales and other income	$400
Cost of sales and expenses	381
Earnings before interest and taxes	19
Taxes and interest ($3)	10
Net income	9
Earnings per share	3
Dividends	2

This question should not be answered in terms of precise cost of capital calculations. Rather, a more qualitative and subjective analysis is appropriate. The only calculations necessary are a few simple ratios. Careful interpretation of these ratios is necessary, however, to understand and discuss the often complex, subjective judgment issues involved.

Selected References

Bowlin, Oswald D., "The Refunding Decision," *Journal of Finance,* XXI, (March 1966), 55–68.

Cohan, Avery B., "Yields on New Underwritten Corporate Bonds, 1935–1958," *Journal of Finance,* XXVII (December 1962), 585–605.

Donaldson, Gordon, "In Defense of Preferred Stock," *Harvard Business Review,* XL (July-August 1962), 123–136.

———, "New Framework for Corporate Debt Policy," *Harvard Business Review,* XL (March-April 1962), 117–131.

Everett, Edward, "Subordinated Debt—Nature and Enforcement," *Business Lawyer,* XX (July 1965), 953–987.

Fischer, Donald E. and Glenn A. Wilt, Jr., "Non-Convertible Preferred Stock as a Financing Instrument, 1950–1965," *Journal of Finance,* XXIII (September 1968), 611–624.

Fisher, Lawrence, "Determinants of Risk Premiums on Corporate Bonds," *Journal of Political Economy,* LXVII (June 1959), 217–237.

Halford, Frank A., "Income Bonds," *Financial Analysts Journal,* XX (January-February 1964), 73–79.

Hickman, W. B., *Corporate Bonds: Quality and Investment Performance,* Occasional Paper 59 (New York: National Bureau of Economic Research, 1957).

Jen, Frank C., and James E. Wert, "The Value of the Deferred Call Privilege," *National Banking Review,* III (March 1966), 369–378.

——— and ———, "The Effects of Call Risk on Corporate Bond Yields," *Journal of Finance,* XXII (December 1967), 637–652.

Johnson, Robert W., "Subordinated Debentures: Debt That Serves as Equity," *Journal of Finance,* X (March 1955), 1–16.

Pye, Gordon, "The Value of the Call Option on a Bond," *Journal of Political Economy,* LXXIV (April 1966), 200–205.

———, "The Value of Call Deferment on a Bond: Some Empirical Results," *Journal of Finance,* XXII (December 1967), 623–636.

Robbins, Sidney M., "A Bigger Role for Income Bonds," *Harvard Business Review,* XXXIII (November-December 1955), 100–114.

Spiller, Earl A., Jr., "Time-Adjusted Breakeven Rate for Refunding," *Financial Executive,* XXXI (July 1963), 32–35.

Weingartner, H. Martin, "Optimal Timing of Bond Refunding," *Management Science,* XIII (March 1967), 511–524.

Winn, Willis J., and Arleigh Hess, Jr., "The Value of the Call Privilege," *Journal of Finance,* XIV (May 1959), 182–195.

20

Warrants and Convertibles

Thus far in the discussion of long-term financing, we have examined the nature of common stock, preferred stock, and long-term debt. We also saw how offering common stock through the use of rights can facilitate low-cost stock flotations. In this chapter, we see how the financial manager, through the use of warrants and convertibles, can make his company's securities attractive to a broader range of investors, thereby lowering his cost of capital.

WARRANTS

A *warrant* is an option to buy a stated number of shares of stock at a specified price. For example, Trans World Airlines has warrants outstanding that give the warrant holders the right to buy one share of TWA stock at a price of $22 for each warrant held. The warrants gen-

TABLE 20–1 ILLUSTRATIVE LIST OF WARRANTS LISTED ON AMERICAN STOCK EXCHANGE

Name of Company	Price on 7/24/67		Option to Purchase Common Shares		Date Option Expires	Theoretical Value	Premium†
	Common	Warrants	No.	Price			
Allegheny Airlines	20	15	1.0	$10.50	5/1/69	$ 9.50	$ 5.50
Allegheny Corp.	11 3/8	8 5/8	1.0	3.75	Perpetual	7.63	0.99
Atlas Corp.	5 5/8	3	1.0	6.25	Perpetual	0.00	3.00
Braniff Airways	65 3/4	30	1.0	73.00	12/1/86	0.00	30.00
General Acceptance Corporation	29 1/4	11 1/4	1.0	20.00	10/31/69	9.25	2.00
Hilton Hotels Corp.	38	19 3/4	1.0	46.00	10/15/70	0.00	19.75
Indian Head Corp.	29 1/2	14 1/2	1.0	20.00	5/15/70	9.50	5.00
Jefferson Lake Petrochemicals	39 1/2	30 1/2	1.04	10.00	6/1/71	30.68	(0.18)
Martin Marietta	24 1/2	29 1/8	2.73	16.50	11/1/68	21.84	7.28
McCrory	21	6 5/8	1.0	20.00	3/15/76	1.00	5.62
National General	16 1/2	7	1.0	15.00	5/15/74	1.50	5.50
Pacific Petroleum	16 1/4	5	1.1	19.00	3/13/68	0.00	5.00
Sperry Rand	34 1/4	10 1/2	1.08	28.00	9/15/67	6.75	3.75
Textron, Inc.*	73	57 3/8	1.0	15.00	5/1/84	58.00	(0.62)
Trans World Airlines	64 1/2	46 7/8	1.0	22.00	12/1/73	42.50	4.38
Tri-Continental Corporation	27 7/8	48	2.54	8.88	Perpetual	48.31	(0.31)
United Industrial Corp.	15 1/4	3 3/8	.05	17.00	11/15/69	0.00	3.38
Uris Buildings	24 3/4	15 5/8	1.06	12.50	5/1/75	12.98	2.64

* Price at which common may be purchased increases by $2.50 in 1969, 1974, and 1979.
† Price of warrant minus theoretical value.

erally expire on a certain date—TWA's warrants expire on December 1, 1973—although some have perpetual lives. An illustrative list of warrants is shown in Table 20–1.

Theoretical Value of a Warrant

Warrants have a calculated or theoretical value and an actual value or price that is determined in the marketplace. The theoretical value is found by use of the following equation.

$$\text{theoretical value} = \left(\begin{matrix}\text{market price}\\ \text{of}\\ \text{common stock}\end{matrix} - \begin{matrix}\text{option}\\ \text{price}\end{matrix}\right) \times \begin{matrix}\text{number of shares each}\\ \text{warrant entitles owner}\\ \text{to purchase}\end{matrix}$$

For example, a TWA warrant entitles the holder to purchase one share of common stock at $22 a share. If the market price of the common stock is $64.50, the formula price of the warrant may be obtained as follows:

$$(\$64.50 - \$22) \times 1.0 = \$42.50$$

Actual Price of a Warrant

Generally, warrants sell above their theoretical values. For example, when TWA stock was selling for $64.50, the warrants had a theoretical value of $42.50 but were selling at a price of $46.87. This represented a premium of $4.37 above the theoretical value.

A set of TWA stock prices, together with actual and theoretical warrant values, is given in Table 20–2 and plotted in Figure 20–1. At any stock price below $22, the theoretical value of the warrant is zero; beyond $22, each $1 increase in the price of the stock brings with it a $1 increase in the theoretical value of the warrant.[1] The actual market price of the warrants lies above the theoretical value at each price of the common stock. Notice, however, that the premium of market price over theoretical value declines as the price of the common stock increases. For example, when the common sold for $22 and the warrants had a zero theoretical value, their actual price and the premium was $9. As the price of the stock rises, the theoretical value of the warrants matches the increase dollar for dollar, but for a while the market price of the warrant climbs less rapidly and the premium declines. The pre-

[1] The formula gives a *negative* theoretical value when the stock is selling for less than the option price. This makes no sense, so we define the theoretical value to be zero when the stock is selling for less than the option price.

mium is $9 when the stock sells for $22 a share, but it declines to $1 by the time the stock price has risen to $75 a share. Beyond this point the premium seems to be constant.

Why do you suppose this pattern exists? Why should the warrant ever sell for more than its theoretical value, and why does the premium decline as the price of the stock increases? The answer lies in the specula-

TABLE 20–2 THEORETICAL AND ACTUAL VALUES OF TWA WARRANTS AT DIFFERENT MARKET PRICES

	VALUE OF WARRANT		
Price of Stock	Theoretical	Actual Price	Premium
$ 0.00	$ 0.00	Not Available	—
22.00	0.00	$ 9.00	$9.00
23.00	1.00	9.75	8.75
24.00	2.00	10.50	8.50
33.67	11.67	17.37	5.70
52.00	30.00	32.00	2.00
75.00	53.00	54.00	1.00
100.00	78.00	79.00	1.00
150.00	128.00	Not Available	—

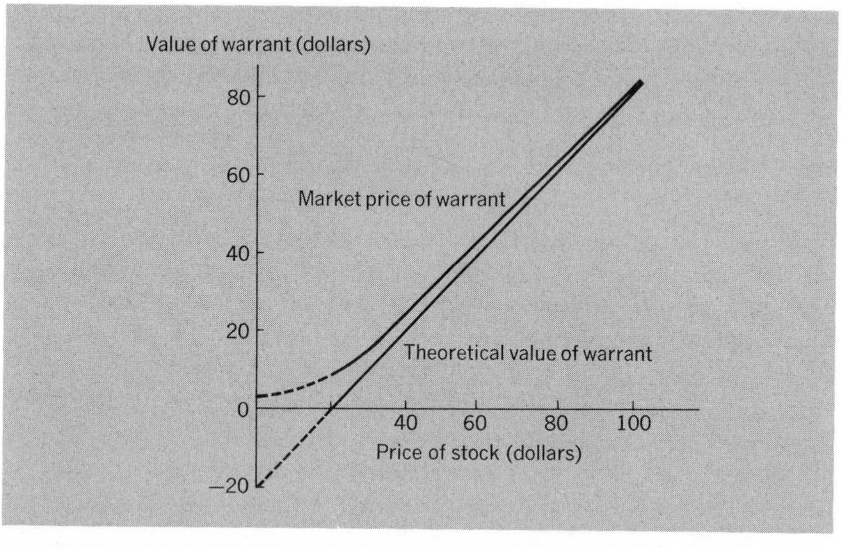

Figure 20–1 Theoretical and Actual Values of TWA Warrants at Different Common Stock Prices

tive appeal of warrants—they enable a person to gain a high degree of personal leverage when buying securities. To illustrate, suppose TWA warrants always sold for exactly their theoretical value. Now suppose you are thinking of investing in the company's common stock at a time when it is selling for $25 a share. If you buy a share and the price rises to $50 in a year, you have made a 100 percent capital gain. However, had you bought the warrants at their theoretical value ($3 when the stock sells for $25), your capital gain would have been $25 on a $3 investment, or 833 percent. At the same time, your total loss potential with the warrant is only $3, while the potential loss from the purchase of the stock is $25. However, a $3 decline in the stock price produces only a 12 percent loss if the stock is purchased and a 100 percent loss if you buy the warrant. The huge capital gains potential, combined with the loss limitation, is clearly worth something—the exact amount that it is worth to investors is the amount of the premium.

But why does the premium decline as the price of the stock rises? The answer here is that both the capital gains leverage effect and the loss protection feature decline at high stock prices. For example, if you are thinking of buying the stock at $75 share, the theoretical value of the warrants is $53. If the stock price doubles to $150, the theoretical value of TWA warrants goes from $53 to $128. The percentage capital gain on the stock is still 100 percent, but the percentage gain on the warrant declines from 833 percent to 142 percent. Also, notice that the loss potential on the warrant is much greater when the warrant is selling at high prices. These two factors, the declining leverage impact and the increasing danger of losses, explain why the premium diminishes as the price of the common stock rises.

Use of Warrants in Financing

Warrants are generally used by small, rapidly growing firms as "sweeteners" when selling either debt or preferred stocks. Such firms frequently are regarded by investors as being highly risky, so their bonds could be sold only if the firms are willing to accept extremely high rates of interest and very restrictive indenture provisions. However, giving warrants along with the bonds enables investors to share in the company's growth if it does, in fact, grow and prosper; therefore, investors are willing to accept a lower bond interest rate and less restrictive indenture provisions. A bond with warrants has some of the characteristics of debt and some of the characteristics of equity. It is a hybrid security that provides the financial manager with an opportunity to expand his mix of securities, appeal to a broader group of investors, and thus possibly lower his firm's cost of capital.

Also, notice that warrants can bring in additional funds. The option price is generally set 15 to 20 percent above the market price of the stock at the time of the bond issue. If the firm does grow and prosper and if its stock price rises above the option price at which shares may be purchased, warrant holders will surrender their warrants and buy stock at the stated price. This happens for several reasons. First, it will surely happen if the warrants are about to expire with the market price of the stock above the option price. Second, it will happen voluntarily as the company raises the dividend on the common stock. No dividend is earned on the warrant, so it provides no current income. However, if the common stock pays an attractive dividend, it provides an attractive dividend yield. This induces warrant holders to exercise their option to buy the stock. Third, warrants sometimes have *stepped-up option prices*. For example, the Williamson Scientific Company has warrants outstanding with an option price of $25 until December 31, 1975, at which time the option price rises to $30. If the price of the common stock is above $25 just before December 1975, many warrant holders will exercise their option before the stepped-up price takes effect.

One desirable feature of warrants is that they generally bring in additional funds only if these funds are needed. If the company grows and prospers, causing the price of the stock to rise, the warrants are exercised and bring in needed funds. If the company is not successful and cannot profitably employ additional money, the price of its stock will probably not rise sufficiently to induce exercise of the options.

CONVERTIBLES[1]

Convertible securities are bonds or preferred stocks that are exchangeable, at the option of the holder, under specified terms and conditions. The *conversion ratio* gives the number of shares of common stock the holder of the convertible receives when he surrenders his security on conversion, and the *conversion price* is the effective price paid for the common stock when conversion occurs.

The relationship between the conversion ratio and the conversion price is illustrated by the Adams Electric Company $1,000 par value convertible debentures. At any time prior to July 1, 1989, a debenture holder

[1] The text material on convertibles is supplemented by Appendix A, which presents a theoretical model of convertible issues, and by Appendix B, which reports on a survey of convertible bonds issued in the period 1961–1963.

can turn in his bond and receive in its place 20 shares of common stock; therefore, the conversion ratio is 20 shares for one bond. The bond has a par value of $1,000, so the holder is giving up this amount when he converts. Dividing the $1,000 by the 20 shares received gives a conversion price of $50 a share.

$$\text{conversion price} = \frac{\text{par value of bond}}{\text{shares received}} = \frac{\$1{,}000}{20} = \$50$$

The conversion price and the conversion ratio are established at the time the convertible bond is sold. Generally, these values are fixed for the life of the bond, although sometimes a stepped-up conversion price is used.[2] Litton Industries' convertible debentures, for example, are convertible into 12.5 shares until 1972, into 11.76 shares from 1972 until 1982, and into 11.11 shares from 1982 until they mature in 1987. The conversion price thus starts at $80, rises to $85, then to $90. Litton's convertibles, like most, are callable at the option of the company.

Like warrant option prices, the conversion price is characteristically set from 10 to 20 percent above the prevailing market price of the common stock at the time the convertible issue is sold. Exactly how the conversion price is established can best be understood after examining some of the reasons why firms use convertibles.

Relative Use of Convertibles

A study by C. James Pilcher[3] on the use of convertibles, during the period 1933 through 1952, showed that 182 convertible debentures were issued during the 20-year period. Another study, made by the late Robert R. McKenzie[4] of New York University, estimated that 419 issues were

[2] Another factor that may cause a change in the conversion price and ratio is a standard feature of practically all convertibles—the clause protecting the convertible against dilution from stock splits, stock dividends, and the sale of common stock at low prices (as in a rights offering). The typical provision states that no common stock can be sold at a price below the conversion price, and that the conversion price must be lowered (and the conversion ratio raised) by the percentage amount of any stock dividend or split. For example, if Adams Electric had a two-for-one split, the conversion ratio would automatically be adjusted to 40 and the conversion price lowered to $25. If this protection was not contained in the contract, a company could completely thwart conversion by the use of stock splits and dividends. Warrants are similarly protected against dilution.

[3] C. J. Pilcher, *Raising Capital with Convertible Securities* (Ann Arbor: Bureau of Business Research, University of Michigan, 1955).

[4] Robert R. McKenzie, "Convertible Securities, 1956–1965," Quarterly Review of Economics and Business, VI (Winter 1966), 41–48.

placed in the 10-year period 1956–1965. Thus, there has been a pronounced increase in the use of convertibles in more recent years.

There were clear and definite advantages to investors who bought convertibles in the post-World War II period. This was a time of great uncertainty. Many economists were forecasting a major postwar recession, while others were forecasting an unprecedented boom. The use of convertibles permitted the investor to hedge against both. In the event of a postwar collapse, he had the protection of his senior position. But if a boom and inflation caused common stock prices to soar, the convertible would rise with the price of the common stock. Thus, convertibles offered the investor both lower risk and speculative potentialities—a hedge against both deflation and inflation. Note, however, that the coupon interest rate on a convertible is *always* lower than the interest rate of an equivalent nonconvertible bond. Accordingly, an investor who buys a convertible gives up interest income in the hope of a capital gain.

A sampling of the price behavior of convertibles issued in 1962 shows that by 1965 the market price of the common stock was approximately 150 percent of the conversion price. In other words, the market price of the stock rose approximately 50 percent above its market price at the time the convertibles were issued. Correspondingly, through 1965 there were marked profits for people who bought convertibles at the time they were originally issued. Note also, however, that profits would have been even greater had the holders of these convertibles purchased the common stock for which they were exchangeable. The reason is that the conversion price is set higher than the initial market price of the common stock.

Reasons for Use of Convertibles

Convertibles offer advantages to corporations as well as to individual investors. The most important of these advantages are discussed below.

As a sweetener when selling debt. Sometimes a company can sell debt with reasonable interest rates and protective covenants only by giving investors a chance to share in potential capital gains; convertibles, like bonds with warrants, offer this possibility.

To sell common stock at prices higher than those now prevailing. Many companies actually want to sell common stock, not debt, but feel that the price of the stock is temporarily depressed. Management may know, for example, that earnings are depressed because of a strike but that they will snap back during the next year and pull the price of the stock up with them. To sell stock now would require giving up more shares to raise a given amount of money than management thinks is necessary. However, setting the conversion price 15 to 20 percent above the present market price of the stock will require giving up 15 to 20 percent fewer shares when the bonds are converted than would be required if stock was sold directly.

Notice, however, that management is counting on the stock price rising above the conversion price to make the bonds actually attractive in conversion. If the stock price does not rise and conversion does not occur, then management is saddled with debt.

How can the company be sure that conversion will occur when the price of the stock rises above the conversion price? Characteristically, convertibles have a provision that gives the issuing firm the opportunity of calling the convertible at a specified price. Suppose the conversion price is $50, the conversion ratio is 20, the market price of the common stock has risen to $60, and the call price on the convertible bond is $1,050. If the company called the bond (by giving the usual notification of 20 days), bondholders could either convert into common stock with a market value of $1,200 or allow the company to redeem the bond for $1,050. Naturally, bondholders prefer $1,200 to $1,050, so conversion occurs. The call provision therefore gives the company a means of forcing conversion, provided that the market price of the stock is greater than the conversion price.

To have low-cost captial during a construction period. Another advantage from the standpoint of the issuer is that a convertible issue may be used as a temporary financing device. During the years 1946 through 1957, American Telephone & Telegraph Company sold $10 billion of convertible debentures. By 1959 about 80 percent of these convertible debentures had been converted into common stock. AT&T could not have sold straight debt in this amount because its financial structure would have been unbalanced. On the other hand, if AT&T had simply issued large amounts of common stock periodically, there would have been price pressure on its stock because the market is slow to digest large blocks of stock.

By using convertible debentures, which provided for a lag of some six to nine months before they were converted into common stock, AT&T received relatively cheap money to finance growth. Transmission lines and telephone exchange buildings must first be built to provide the basis for ultimately installing phones. While AT&T is installing transmission lines and telephone exchange buildings, these investments are not earning any money. Therefore it was important to AT&T to minimize the cost of money while these installations were being made. After six to nine months had elapsed and these installations were translated into telephones that were bringing in revenues, AT&T was better able to pay the regular common stock dividend. Thus, convertibles provide for stages in financing by a firm.

Disadvantages of Convertibles

From the standpoint of the issuer, convertibles have a possible disadvantage. Although the convertible stock gives the issuer the opportunity to sell common stock at a price 15 to 20 percent higher than it could otherwise be sold, if the common stock greatly increases in price the issuer may find that he would have been better off if he had waited and simply sold the common stock. Further, if the company truly wants to raise equity capital and if the price of the stock declines after the bond is issued, then it is stuck with debt.

But the plain fact of the matter may well be that the company has no alternative, especially if it is a small and growing company. A sufficient investment demand in the company's debt securities or preferred stock may not be present. For this reason the company may be virtually forced to use convertibles. In this kind of situation the convertibles perform a very useful function in that they enable management to raise additional debt and equity money and maintain control in the company.

DECISIONS ON THE USE OF WARRANTS AND CONVERTIBLES

The Winchester Company, an electronic circuit and component manufacturer with assets of $12 million, illustrates a typical case where convertibles are useful.

Winchester's profits have been depressed as a result of its heavy expenditures on research and development for a new product. This situation has held down the growth rate of earnings and dividends; the price/earnings ratio is only 18 times, as compared with an industry average of 22. At the current $2 earnings per share and P/E of 18, the stock is selling for $36 a share. The Winchester family owns 70 percent of the 300,000 shares outstanding, or 210,000 shares. It would like to retain majority control, but cannot buy more stock.

The heavy R&D expenditures have resulted in the development of a new type of printed circuit that management believes will be highly profitable. Five million dollars is needed to build and equip new production facilities, and profits will not start to flow in to the company for some 18 months after construction on the new plant is started. Winchester's debt amounts to $5.4 million, or 45 percent of assets, well above the 25 percent industry average. Present debt indenture provisions restrict the company from selling additional debt unless the new debt is subordinate to that now outstanding.

Investment bankers inform J. H. Winchester, Jr., the financial vice-president, that subordinated debentures cannot be sold unless they are convertible or have warrants attached. Convertibles or bonds with warrants can be sold with a 5 percent coupon interest rate if the conversion price or warrant option price is set at 15 percent above the present market price of $36, or at $41 a share. Alternatively, the investment bankers are willing to buy convertibles or bonds with warrants at a 5½ percent interest rate and a 20 percent conversion premium, or a conversion (or exercise) price of $43.50. If the company wants to sell common stock directly, it can net $33 a share.

Which of the alternatives should Winchester choose? First, note that if common stock is used, the company must sell 151,000 shares ($5 million divided by $33). Combined with the 90,000 shares held outside the family, this amounts to 241,000 shares versus the Winchester holdings of 210,000, so the family will lose majority control if common stock is sold.

If the 5 percent convertibles or bonds with warrants are used and the bonds are converted or the warrant is exercised, 122,000 new shares will be added. Combined with the old 90,000, the outside interest will then be 212,000, so again the Winchester family will lose majority control. However, if the 5½ percent convertibles or bonds with warrants are used, then after conversion or exercise only 115,000 new shares will be created. In this case the family will have 210,000 shares versus 205,000 for outsiders; absolute control will be maintained.

In addition to control, using the convertibles or warrants also benefits earnings per share in the long run—the total number of shares is less because fewer new shares must be issued to get the $5 million, so earnings per share will be higher. Before conversion or exercise, however, the firm has a considerable amount of debt outstanding. Adding $5 million raises the total debt to $10.4 million against a new total assets of $17 million, so the debt ratio will be over 61 percent versus the 25 percent industry average. This could be dangerous. If delays are encountered in bringing the new plant into production, if demand does not meet expectations, if the company should experience a strike, if the economy should go into a recession—if any of these things occurs—the company will be extremely vulnerable because of the high debt ratio.

In the present case, the decision was made to sell the 5½ percent convertible debentures. Two years later, earnings climbed to $3 a share, the P/E ratio to 20, and the price of the stock to $60. The bonds were called, but, of course, conversion occurred. After conversion, debt amounted to approximately $5.5 million against total assets of $17.5 million (some earnings had been retained), so the debt ratio was down to a more reasonable 31 percent.

Convertibles were chosen rather than bonds with warrants for the following reason. If a firm has a high debt ratio and its near-term prospects are favorable, it can anticipate a rise in the price of its stock and thus be able to call the bonds and force conversion. Warrants, on the other hand, have a stated life, and even though the price of the firm's stock rises, the warrants may not be exercised until near their expiration date. If, subsequent to the favorable period (during which convertibles could have been called), the firm encounters less favorable developments and the price of its stock falls, the warrants may lose their value and never be exercised. The heavy debt burden will then become aggravated. Therefore, the use of convertibles gives the firm greater control over the timing of future capital structure changes. This factor is of particular importance to the firm if its debt ratio is already high in relation to the risks of its line of business.

USE OF OPTIONS IN SMALL BUSINESS FINANCING

Most of the principles of financing are equally applicable to large and small firms. However, one aspect of small business financing has received considerable attention—the fact that organizers and owners of small businesses are often reluctant to share control of the firm as it grows. This presents problems, for growth brings with it the need to obtain additional funds. Small firms characteristically do not present a record of earnings or stability that justifies long-term debt financing, and the sale of equity shares would result in dilution of ownership and control.

This basic dilemma of small business financing can be eased considerably by the use of convertibles and warrants, the subject of the present chapter. Until the necessary background on convertibles and warrants had been set forth, we could not present a rounded discussion of small business financing. We can now do so. The use of convertibles and warrants enables a small firm to raise long-term debt money from the capital markets and at the same time provide investors in such securities with a degree of participation in the potential increase in equity values. Since the convertibles and warrants provide for future purchase of the common stock at a price usually at a premium over the current common stock price, the extent of dilution of control by the present owners is diminished to some degree.

Investment Banker Sponsorship of Small Firms

With the background of the use of options such as convertibles and warrants, it is now possible to discuss another important aspect of investment banker operations since the mid-1950s. One of the barriers to small firms' security issues has been the high cost of flotation, which until the mid-1950's according to SEC data, averaged around 20 percent of gross proceeds. Since the mid-1950s, warrants have been used to reduce direct flotation costs on both equity and debt issues for small firms. A common practice among investment bankers has been to reduce their commission from 20 percent to about 5 to 10 percent and to receive warrants to purchase up to 10 percent of the common stock of the small firm. With these kinds of inducements, investment bankers have vigorously sponsored small equity issues and have maintained a continued program of financing for small firms, especially those with good growth potential.

Small Business Investment Companies

The original intention of the Small Business Investment Company (SBIC) Act of 1958 was to create, with federal government financing help, institutions that would provide funds to small business firms on a debt basis with the added inducement of equity participation through the use of convertibles and warrants. Since the adoption of the act in 1958, the SBICs have gone through alternate periods of optimistic and pessimistic evaluations of their prospects. Both government regulations providing for the nature and extent of government assistance and the investment powers of the SBICs have undergone a series of changes. Throughout all these changes, two broad policies have characterized the operations of the small business investment corporations. First, they emphasize convertible securities and obligations with warrants, giving the SBIC a residual equity position in the companies to which funds are provided. Second, they emphasize the provision for SBIC management counsel, for which a fee is charged.

In order to promote small business financing, the SBICs were granted advantageous tax provisions. Dividends received by the SBICs from their small business investments are 100 percent deductible from the SBIC's income, compared with 85 percent for ordinary corporations. Losses from convertible debentures of the stocks into which these are converted can be treated as losses chargeable against ordinary income, not against capital gains. SBICs are exempt from penalties for improper accumulation of income if they meet certain requirements. Also, investors in SBICs may treat their own stock losses as ordinary losses chargeable against ordinary income. In keeping with the spirit of the act, the

SBICs are under the administrative control of the Small Business Administration (SBA).

OTHER ACTIVITIES OF THE SMALL BUSINESS ADMINISTRATION

Since one of the activities of the Small Business Administration (SBA) was discussed in connection with the SBIC program, it may be useful to round out the discussion by describing some of the other important activities of the Small Business Administration.

Scope of Operations of the SBA

The Small Business Administration helps small business firms in a number of ways. It aids small business in obtaining a fair share of government contracts, and it also emphasizes assistance in management and production problems. These two objectives recognize that a substantial number of small business firms need management counseling and assistance. In addition, the SBA actively aids small firms with their financial problems; this aspect of SBA operations will be emphasized here.

For business loans, the SBA defines a small business as one that is independently owned and operated and is nondominant in its field. Specific standards depend upon the industry of the firm. Any manufacturing concern is defined as small if it employs 250 or fewer persons, and it is defined as large if it employs more than 1,000 persons. However, if a manufacturing concern operates in an industry that has few competitors and if it has less than 5 percent of sales, it may be called a small business; American Motors is classed as a small business under this definition. A wholesale concern is classified as small if its yearly sales are $5 million or less. Most retail businesses and service trades are defined as small if their total annual receipts do not exceed $1 million. A business operating under a franchise may obtain a loan if the SBA can be assured that the firm is not a large business through its affiliation with the franchiser. The Department of Commerce estimates that, as of the end of 1966, 95 percent of all firms were classified as small businesses. There is, therefore a wide scope for SBA operations.

Loan Policies and Types

By law, the SBA makes loans to small business concerns only when financing is not available to them on reasonable terms from other sources.

The SBA loans are of two types: direct and participating. In a direct loan, there is no participation by a private lender—the loan is made directly by the SBA to the borrower. In participating loans, the SBA joins with a bank or other private lending institution in making a loan to a small business firm.

A participating loan may be made under a loan guarantee or on an immediate basis. A participating loan on a *guarantee basis* provides that the SBA will purchase its guaranteed portion of the outstanding balance of the loan if the borrower defaults. When the SBA participates in a loan on an *immediate basis,* it purchases immediately a fixed percentage of the original principal amount of the loan. By law, the SBA may not enter into an immediate participation if it can arrange a guaranteed loan.

SUMMARY

Both warrants and convertibles are forms of options used in financing business firms. The use of long-term options such as warrants and convertibles is encouraged by an economic environment combining prospects of both boom or inflation and depression or deflation. The senior position of the securities protects against recessions. The option feature offers the opportunity for participation in rising stock prices.

Both the convertibility privilege and warrants are used as "sweeteners." The option privileges they grant may make it possible for small companies to sell debt or preferred stock which otherwise could not be sold. For large companies, the "sweeteners" result in lower costs of the securities sold. In addition, the options provide for the future sale of the common stock at prices higher than could be obtained at the time. The options thereby permit the delayed sale of common stock at more favorable prices.

The exercise of convertibles by their holders does not ordinarily bring additional funds to the company. The exercise of warrants will provide these funds.[5] The conversion of securities will result in reduced debt ratios. The exercise of warrants will strengthen the equity position but will still leave the debt or preferred stock on the balance sheet. In comparing the use of convertibles with senior securities carrying warrants, a firm with a high debt ratio should choose convertibles. A firm with a moderate or low debt ratio may employ warrants.

Options such as warrants and convertibles have been increasingly used

[5] An outstanding exception is the convertible debenture issued by AT&T since the end of World War II. For each $100 principal amount of debentures, an additional $35 to $45 (varying with the issue) was required to obtain one share of common stock.

to facilitate small business financing. One of the ways in which options have stimulated investment banker sponsorship of small firms has been in reducing the cash expenses of floating new issues of securities. SEC data showed that for a number of years flotation costs on small issues averaged as high as 20 percent of gross proceeds. The use of options has caused cash flotation costs to be reduced. The characteristic pattern has been for the investment banker to charge a commission of 5 to 10 percent of gross proceeds plus taking warrants exercisable at the issue price on up to 10 percent of the number of new shares issued.

Another institutional arrangement that encouraged the use of options in the financing of small business resulted from the establishment of Small Business Investment Corporations in 1958. The SBICs were empowered to make debt investments in small business and to take warrants and conversion features as an inducement for making the loans.

In addition to their operations through SBICs, the Small Business Administration has provided financing to small business firms in a number of ways. First, the SBA helps small businesses obtain government contracts. Second, the SBA has emphasized management counseling to small business. Finally, the SBA itself makes two types of loans to small business—direct loans to borrowers and participating loans through other financial institutions. Participating loans are either *immediate* loans in which a fixed percentage of the loan is made by the SBA to the small business, the remainder of the funds being supplied by a bank, or a loan *guarantee* under which the SBA will purchase its guaranteed portion if the borrower defaults.

QUESTIONS

20–1 Why do warrants typically sell at prices greater than their theoretical values?

20–2 Why do convertibles typically sell at prices greater than their theoretical values (the higher of the conversion value or straight-debt value)? Would you expect the percentage premium on a convertible bond to be more or less than that on a warrant? (The percentage premium is defined as the market price minus the theoretical value, divided by the market price.)

20–3 What effect does the trend in stock prices (subsequent to issue) have on a firm's ability to raise funds (a) through convertibles and (b) through warrants?

20–4 If a firm expects to have additional financial requirements in the future, would you recommend that it use convertibles or bonds with warrants? Why?

20–5 How does a firm's dividend policy affect each of the following?
a) The value of long-term warrants
b) The likelihood that convertible bonds will be converted
c) The likelihood that warrants will be exercised

20–6 Evaluate the following statement: "Issuing convertible securities represents a means by which a firm can sell common stock at a price above the existing market."

20–7 Why do corporations often sell convertibles on a rights basis?

PROBLEMS

20–1 The Dixon Manufacturing Company's capital consists of 8,000 shares of common stock and 4,000 warrants, each good to buy two shares of common at $80 a share. The warrants are protected against dilution (that is, the subscription price is adjusted downward in the event of a stock dividend or if the firm sells common stock at less than the $80 exercise price). The company issues rights to buy one new share of common at $60 for every two shares held. With the stock selling rights on at $90, compute:
a) The theoretical value of the rights before the stock sells ex rights
b) The new subscription price of the warrant after the rights issue

20–2 The Marfield Electronics Corporation was planning to finance an expansion in the summer of 1970. The principal executives of the company were agreed that an industrial company of this type should finance growth by means of common stock rather than by debt. However, they felt that the price of the company's common stock did not reflect its true worth, so they were desirous of selling a convertible security. They considered a convertible debenture but feared the burden of fixed interest charges if the common stock did not rise in price to make conversion attractive. They decided on an issue of convertible preferred stock.

The common stock was currently selling at $60 a share. Management projected earnings for 1970 at $4 a share and expected a future growth rate of 8 percent a year. It was agreed by the investment bankers and the management that the common stock would sell at 20 times earnings, the current price-earnings ratio.
a) What conversion price should be set by the issuer?
b) Should the preferred stock include a call-price provision? Why?

20–3 Marfield Electronics, Inc., has the following balance sheet:

BALANCE SHEET 1

Current assets	$ 50,000	Current debt	$ 20,000
Net fixed assets	50,000	Common stock, par value $2	20,000
		Earned surplus	60,000
Total assets	$100,000	Total claims	$100,000

a) The firm earns 20 percent on total assets before taxes (assume a 50 percent tax rate). What are earnings per share?
b) If the price/earnings ratio for the company's stock is 20 times, what is the market price of the company's stock?
c) What is the book value of the company's stock?

In the following few years, sales are expected to double and the financing needs of the firm will double. The firm decides to sell debentures to meet these needs. It is undecided, however, whether to sell convertible debentures or debentures with warrants. The new balance sheet would appear as follows:

BALANCE SHEET 2

Current assets	$100,000	Current debt	$ 40,000
Net fixed assets	100,000	Debentures	60,000
		Common stock, par value $2	20,000
		Earned surplus	80,000
Total assets	$200,000	Total claims	$200,000

The convertible debentures would pay 5 percent interest and would be convertible into 25 shares of common stock for each $1,000 debenture. The debentures with warrants would carry a 6 percent coupon and entitle each holder of a $1,000 debenture to buy 20 shares of common stock at $40. Richard Marfield owns 80 percent of Electronics before the financing.

d) Assume that convertible debentures are sold and all are later converted. Show the new balance sheet, disregarding any changes in retained earnings.

BALANCE SHEET 3

		Current debt	______
		Debentures	______
		Common stock, par value $2	______
		Paid-in surplus	______
		Earned surplus	______
Total assets	______	Total claims	______

e) Complete the firm's income statement after the debentures have all been converted:

INCOME STATEMENT

Net income after all charges except debenture interest and before taxes (20% of total assets)	________
Debenture interest	________
Federal income tax, 50%	________
Net income after taxes	________
Earnings per share after taxes	________

f) Now, instead of convertibles, assume that debentures with warrants were issued. Assume further that the warrants were all exercised. Show the new balance sheet figures.

BALANCE SHEET 4

		Current debt	________
		Debentures	________
		Common stock, par value $2	________
		Paid-in surplus	________
		Earned surplus	________
Total assets	________	Total claims	________

g) Complete the firm's income statement after the debenture warrants have all been exercised.

INCOME STATEMENT

Net income after all charges except debenture interest and before taxes	________
Debenture interest	________
Taxable income	________
Federal income tax	________
Net income after taxes	________
Earnings per share after taxes	________

20–4 The Baker Company has grown rapidly during the past five years. Recently its commercial bank has urged the company to consider increasing permanent financing. Its bank loan had risen to $200,000, carrying 6 percent interest. Baker has been 30 to 60 days late in paying trade creditors.

Discussions with an investment banker have resulted in the suggestion to raise $400,000 at this time. Investment bankers have assured Baker that the following alternatives will be feasible (flotation costs will be ignored):

Alternative 1: Sell common stock at $8.

Alternative 2: Sell convertible bonds at a 6 percent coupon, convertible into common stock at $10.

Alternative 3: Sell debentures at a 6 percent coupon, each $1,000 bond carrying 100 warrants to buy common stock at $10.

Additional information is given below.

BAKER COMPANY
BALANCE SHEET
December 31, 1969

		Current liabilities	$350,000
		Common stock, par $1.00	100,000
		Retained earnings	50,000
Total assets	$500,000	Total liabilities and capital	$500,000

BAKER COMPANY
INCOME STATEMENT
December 31, 1969

Sales	$1,000,000
All costs except interest	900,000
Gross profit	$ 100,000
Interest	12,000
Profit before taxes	$ 88,000
Taxes at 50%	44,000
Profits after taxes	$ 44,000
Shares	100,000
Earnings per share	$0.44
Price/earnings ratio	20×
Market price of stock	$8.80

E. E. Baker, the president owns 68 percent of the common stock of Baker Company and wishes to maintain control of the company.

a) Show the new balance sheet under each of the alternatives. For alternatives 1 and 2, show the balance sheet after conversion of the debentures or exercise of warrants. Assume that one half the funds raised will be used to pay off the bank loan and one half to increase total assets.
b) Show Baker's control position under each alternative, assuming Baker does not purchase additional shares.
c) What is the effect on earnings per share of each of the alternatives, if it is assumed that profits before interest and taxes will be 20 percent of total assets?
d) What will be the debt ratio under each alternative?
e) Which of the three alternatives would you recommend to Baker, and why?

Selected References

Ayers, Herbert F., "Risk Aversion in the Warrants Market," *Industrial Management Review,* V (Fall 1963), 45–53.

Baumol, William J., Burton G. Malkiel, and Richard E. Quandt, "The Valuation of Convertible Securities," *Quarterly Journal of Economics,* LXXX (February 1966), 48–59.

Bladen, Ashly, *Techniques for Investing in Convertible Bonds.* (New York: Salomon Bros. & Hutzler, 1966.)

Brigham, Eugene F., "An Analysis of Convertible Debentures: Theory and Some Empirical Evidence," *Journal of Finance,* XXI (March 1966), 35–54.

Broman, Keith L., "The Use of Convertible Subordinated Debentures by Industrial Firms 1949–1959," *Quarterly Review of Economics and Business,* III (Spring 1963), 65–75.

Hayes, Samuel L., III, "New Interest in Incentive Financing," *Harvard Business Review,* XLIV (July-August 1966), 99–112.

McKenzie, Robert R., "Convertible Securities, 1956–1965," *Quarterly Review of Economics and Business,* VI (Winter 1966), 41–48.

Pease, Fred, "The Warrant—Its Power and Its Hazards," *Financial Analysts Journal,* XIX (January-February 1963), 25–32.

Poensgen, Otto H., "The Valuation of Convertible Bonds," Parts I and II, *Industrial Management Review,* VI and VII (Fall 1965 and Spring 1966), 77–92 and 83–98.

Samuelson, Paul A., "Rational Theory of Warrant Pricing," *Industrial Management Review,* VI (Spring 1965), 13–31.

Shelton, John P., "The Relation of the Price of a Warrant to the Price of its Associated Stock," *Financial Analysts Journal,* XXIII (May-June and July-August 1967), 143–151 and 88–99.

Skelly, William S., *Convertible Bonds—A Study of Their Suitability for Commercial Bank Bond Portfolios.* (New York: Salomon Bros. & Hutzler, 1959.)

Sprenkle, Case, "Warrant Prices as Indicators of Expectations," *Yale Economic Essays,* I (1961), 179–232.

Weil, Roman L., Jr., Joel E. Segall, and David Green, Jr., "Premiums on Convertible Bonds," *Journal of Finance,* XXIII (June 1968), 445–464.

Williams, B. S. and Marvin Letwat, "Underwritten Calls of Industrial

Convertible Securities, 1950–1961," *Quarterly Review of Economics and Business,* III (Winter 1963), 71–77.

Williams, Howard A. and Charles M. Williams, "Incentive Financing—A New Opportunity," *Harvard Business Review,* XXXVIII (March-April 1960), 123–134.

APPENDIX A TO CHAPTER 20 Some Theoretical Aspects of Convertible Securities[1]

A convertible security is a hybrid, having some of the characteristics of common stocks and some of those of bonds or preferred stocks. Investors expect to earn an interest yield as well as a capital gains yield; moreover, the corporation recognizes that it incurs an interest cost and a potential dilution of equity when it sells convertibles. In this appendix, we develop a theoretical model to combine these two cost components, present some empirical data on the use of convertibles, and discuss the conditions under which convertibles should be issued.

A Model of Convertible Bonds

The essential features of a convertible bond may be described by reference to Figure A20–1. While the figure may be given either an *ex*

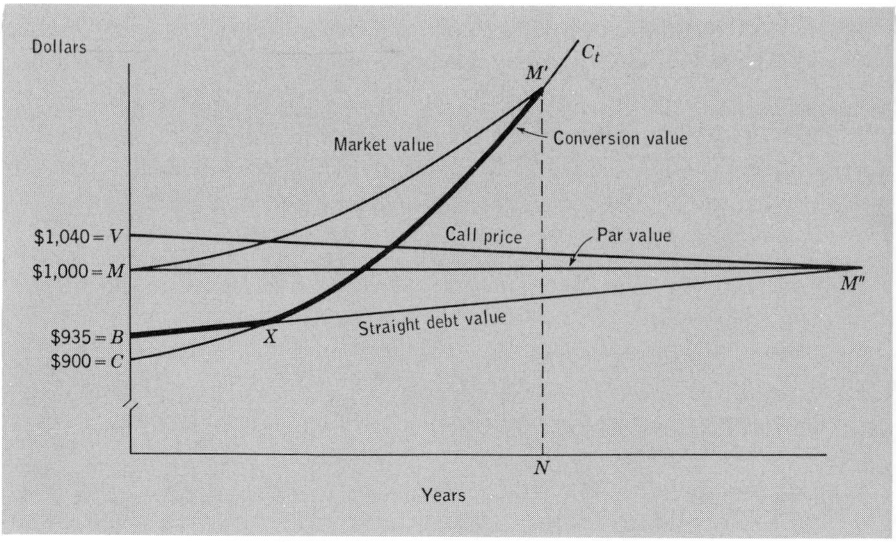

Figure A20–1 Hypothetical Model of a Convertible Bond

[1] For a more detailed treatment of the theory of convertibles, see Eugene F. Brigham, "An Analysis of Convertible Debentures: Theory and Some Empirical Evidence," *Journal of Finance,* XXI (March 1966), 35–54. This appendix is based on that article.

post or *ex ante* interpretation, at this point it is more convenient to think of it *ex post*. In other words, the conditions described are assumed to have occurred.

The hypothetical bond was sold for M dollars in year t_o, and this initial price was also the par (and maturity) value. The bond was callable at the option of the corporation, with the call price originating at V, somewhat above par, and declining linearly over the term to maturity to equal M'' at maturity.

The original conversion value (C) was established by multiplying the market price of the stock at the time of issue by the number of shares into which the bond may be converted (the conversion ratio). The stock price grew at a constant rate (g), causing the conversion value curve (CC_t) to rise at this same rate. This established the curve CC_t, which shows the conversion value at each point in time. All of this is expressed by equation A20–1.

$$C_t = P_o(1 + g)^t R \qquad \text{(A20–1)}$$

where:

C_t = conversion value at time t
P_o = initial price of the common stock = \$45 per share
g = rate of growth of the stock's price = 4%
R = conversion rate, or number of shares received on conversion = 20

The initial conversion value of the bond, when $t = 0$, is simply \$45 × 20, or \$900. One year later it is \$45(1.04)(20) = \$936; after two years it has risen to \$973.44; and so on. Had growth turned out to be zero, CC_t would have been a horizontal line; had it been negative, CC_t would have declined; and had growth been uneven, CC_t would not have been a smooth curve, and equation A20–1 would have been more complicated.

In addition to its value in conversion, the bond also had a straight-debt value, or the price at which the bond would sell if it did not have the conversion option, at each point in time that was determined by the following equation:

$$B_t = \sum_{K=1}^{(T-t)} \frac{I}{(1 + i)^K} + \frac{M''}{(1 + i)^{(T-t)}} \qquad \text{(A20–2)}$$

where:

B_t = convertible bond's value as a straight debt instrument at time t
T = original term to maturity, 20 years
K = time subscript from year t to year T
i = market rate of interest on equivalent risk, pure debt issues, 4½%
I = dollars of interest paid each year, \$40 = 4% of M
M'' = bond's redemption value at maturity, \$1,000, the par value

Equation A20–2 calculates the bond value B_t from each point t to the maturity date, T. It is a present value calculation with an annuity component I and a final value M''. In the early years of its life, the annuity component dominates the total value; in the later years, B_t is dominated by M''. If $I = iM$, then $B_t = M$; but in the illustrative case, as is typically true, $I < iM$ with the consequence that $B_t < M$ prior to the maturity date. In Figure A20–1, the values of B_t are shown by the line BM; B_o is seen to be \$935 in the illustrative case.

Note that the conversion value and the straight debt value combine to establish a lower bound for the price of the bond. Logically, the bond could not sell for less than its value as straight debt (BM''), and if it should fall below the conversion value (CC_t) arbitragers would enter the market, short the stock, and cover their short positions by buying and converting bonds. This latter process would continue until the market price of the bond is driven up to its conversion value. The higher of these two floors dominates, with the discontinuous curve BXC_t forming the effective market value floor.

The curve designating the market value (MM') lies above the line of basic value (BXC_t) over most of the range but converges with BXC_t in year N. The rationale behind this price action is developed in the following two subsections.

Why the Market Value Exceeds the BXC_t Floor

The spread between MM' and BXC_t, which represents the premium marginal investors[2] are willing to pay for the conversion option, may be explained by several factors. First, since the convertible bond may be converted into common stock if the company prospers and the stock price rises, it usually commands a premium over its value as straight debt (that is, the right of conversion has a positive value). Second, the convertible bond usually commands a premium over its conversion value because, by holding convertibles, an investor is able to reduce his risk exposure. To illustrate, suppose someone buys the hypothetical bond for \$1,000. At the time, it is convertible into 20 shares of stock with a market price of \$45, giving a conversion value of \$900. If the stock market turns sharply down and the stock price falls to \$22.50 per share, a stock investor would suffer a 50 percent loss in value. Had he held a convertible bond, its price would have fallen from \$1,000 to the bond value floor, BM'' in Figure A20–1, which is at least \$935. Hence, holding the convertible entails less risk than holding common stock; this also causes convertibles to sell at a premium above their conversion value.

[2] Marginal investors, often called "the market," are defined as those just willing to hold the bond at its going price. These investors are, in fact, the ones who actually determine the level of the bond's price.

Why the Market Value Approaches the Conversion Value

The MM' curve in Figure A20–1 rises less rapidly than the CC_t curve, indicating that the market value approaches the conversion value as the conversion value increases. This empirically validated fact is caused by three separate factors. First, and probably most important, the bondholders realize that the issue is callable; if it is in fact called, they have the option of either surrendering for redemption or converting. In the former case, they receive the call price; in the latter, they receive stock with a value designated by C_t. If the market price of the bond is above either of these values, the holder is in danger of a potential loss in wealth in the event of a call; this fact prevents wide spreads between MM' and BXC_t whenever the market value exceeds the call price.

The second factor driving MM' toward CC_t is related to the loss protection characteristic of convertibles. Barring changes in the interest rate on the firm's straight-debt securities, the potential loss on a convertible is equal to the spread between MM' and BM''. Since this spread increases at high conversion values, the loss potential also increases, causing the premium attributable to the loss protection to diminish.

The third factor causing the gap between MM' and CC_t to close has to do with the relationship between the yield on a convertible and that on the common stock for which it may be exchanged. The yield on most common stocks consists of two components: a dividend yield and a capital gain yield. In the next section, it is shown that convertibles also have two yield components, one from interest payments and one from capital gains. After some point, the expected capital gain is the same for both instruments, but the current yield on the bond declines *vis-à-vis* that on the common stock because dividends on growing stocks typically rise while interest payments are fixed. This causes the gap between MM' and CC_t to close and would eventually lead to a negative premium except for the fact that voluntary conversion occurs first.

Convertible Yields

The actual rate of return earned on a convertible is found by solving equation A20–3 for k, the internal rate of return:

$$M = \sum_{t=1}^{N} \frac{I}{(1+k)^t} + \frac{\text{TV}}{(1+k)^N} \qquad \text{(A20–3)}$$

where:

M = price paid for bond

I = dollars of interest received per year

TV = terminal value of bond: call price if surrendered on call; maturity value if redeemed; conversion value if converted; or market price if sold

N = number of years bond was held

k = internal rate of return

The equation is purely definitional; it simply states that if one paid M dollars for a convertible bond, held it for N years and received a series of interest payments plus a terminal value, then he has received a return on his investment equal to k.[3]

The *ex ante* yield on a convertible (k^*) is probabilistic—it is dependent upon a set of variables subject to probability distributions and hence must itself be a random variable. It is possible, however, to define each of the determinants of k^* in terms of its mean expected value; $E(g)$, for example, is the expected value of the growth rate in the stock's price over N years. For simplicity, $E(g)$ and other random variables are shortened to g, TV, and so on. With the variables defined in this manner, it is possible to work sequentially through two equations to find the expected rate of return on a convertible bond.

Remembering that bondholders are assumed to cash out in year N, presumably reinvesting the terminal value received in some other security, the determinants of TV may be established: (1) the corporation's policy in regard to calling the bond to force conversion; or (2) the investor's decision to hold the bond until it is called, to sell it, or to voluntarily convert.

CORPORATION'S CALL POLICY. It will be shown in the empirical section that corporations issuing convertible bonds generally have policies regarding just how far up the CC_t curve they will allow a bond to go before calling to force conversion. These policies range from calling as soon as they are "sure" conversion will take place (this generally means a premium of about 20 percent over the call price) to never calling at all. If the policy is never to issue a call, however, the firm generally relies on the dividend-interest differential to cause voluntary conversion.

It is apparent that call policy has a very direct influence on the TV figure used in equation A20–3. Naturally, expectations about call policy influence the expected rate of return on a convertible bond.

INVESTORS' CASH-OUT POLICY. This factor is similar to the corporate call policy in that it sets a limit on how far up the CC_t curve an investor is willing to ride. The decision is influenced by the interest-dividend relationship, by the investor's aversion to risk (recall that risk due to a stock price decline increases as one moves up the CC_t curve), and by his willingness to hold securities providing low current yields. To simplify, it is assumed that investors are willing to ride higher up CC_t, given the dividend-interest relationship, than the firm is willing to let them ride; hence, corporate call policy supersedes investor cash-out policy.

[3] Three simplifications are made in this analysis. First, taxes are ignored. Second, the problem of reinvestment rates is handled by assuming that all reinvestment is made at the internal rate of return. Third, it is assumed that the bondholder does not hold stock after conversion; he cashes out, as would be true of an institutional investor precluded from holding common stock.

Years the Bond Is Held

As was seen, the path of the conversion value curve is traced out by equation A20–1.

$$C_t = P_o(1 + g)^t R \qquad \text{(A20–1)}$$

Recognizing that $R = M/P_c$, where P_c is defined as the conversion price of the shares, equation (A20-1) may be rewritten:

$$C_t = \frac{P_o}{P_c}(1 + g)^t M \qquad \text{(A20–4)}$$

Setting equation A20–4 equal to the TV defined by corporate policy (for example, $1,200 if a 20 percent premium is used), one finds:

$$\text{TV} = \frac{P_o}{P_c}(1 + g)^N M \qquad \text{(A20–5)}$$

Now, converting to logarithmic form and solving for N, one obtains:

$$N = \frac{(\log P_c - \log P_o) + (\log \text{TV} - \log M)}{\log (1 + g)} \qquad \text{(A20–6)}$$

Equation A20–6 may be interpreted as follows. First, an inspection of equation A20–3, which was used to find the realized internal rate of return (k), reveals that for given values of M, I, and TV, smaller values of N produce larger values of k. In other words, for a given interest component and a given capital gains component, the faster the capital gain is realized, the larger the internal rate of return. From equation A20–6 it is seen that N is smaller as the differentials between log P_c and log P_o, and between log TV and log M, decline and the larger the rate of growth.[4] P_o, P_c, and M are all known with certainty at $t = 0$, while TV (defined by corporate policy), g, and N are expected, probabilistic values.

With these definitions and equations, consider how an investor might look upon *ex ante* convertible bond yields. The following is the calculating sequence. First, the investor (or potential investor) has expectations about the variables on the right side of equation A20–6. Specifically, he knows P_c, P_o, and M; he has expectations about the values of TV

[4] Since log X − log Y is equal to X/Y, these log differentials could be expressed as ratios of the absolute values. In other words, N is smaller as the ratios P_c/P_o and TV/M become smaller.

and g.[5] This information may be used to solve equation A20–6 for N. With N estimated, the potential investor has all the data necessary to solve equation A20–3 for k^*, the expected yield on the bond.

Market Equilibrium

When convertible bonds are initially offered to the public, they are typically priced at par (usually $1,000).[6] If the terms of the issue, in combination with investor expectations about the other key variables, produce an expected rate of return just equal to the marginal investor's required rate of return on investments with this degree of risk (his opportunity cost, in a sense), then the bond will just clear the market. The price will not run up in the manner of a "hot issue" nor will it fall after underwriters have ceased stabilization. In the unlikely event that investor expectations are borne out exactly, the conversion value will follow a predicted CC_t curve, the market price will follow a predicted MM' curve, the firm will call the bond at the predicted TV, and investors will realize a yield k^*.

An Illustrative Case

To illustrate the material in this and the preceding section, it is useful to present an example. Suppose that a firm's stock price has been rising and is expected to continue rising by 4 percent a year; that the firm is known to have called convertibles in the past when the conversion value exceeded the par value by 20 percent; and that its common stock is currently selling for $45 per share. If the firm then offers a debenture that pays 4 percent interest and is convertible into 20 shares of stock for sale at par, $1,000 (the conversion price is thus $50, or $1,000/20), a potential investor could calculate the years to conversion by substitut-

[5] A word about TV and g is in order. In a later section, it is shown that corporations do have policies with regard to calling to force conversion, and investors are able to make forecasts about the *minimum* conversion value at which the bond is likely to be called. Further, somewhat strong institutional constraints tend to prohibit firms from calling bonds until this minimum value has been reached.

The growth rate of the common stock is much less predictable; it, too, can be estimated. One approach is simply to extrapolate past share price growth, adjusted in whatever manner the investor thinks appropriate. Alternatively, one can recognize that stock price growth is dependent upon earnings and dividend growth and that these are dependent upon retained earnings, the rate of return at which retained earnings can be invested, and the amount of leverage employed by the firm (among other things). In this appendix, no attempt is made to specify the manner in which investors measure expected growth.

[6] It must be made very clear that the discussion at this point is related to publicly offered bonds, not to those offered through rights to existing stockholders. There are quite fundamental differences, which are discussed later, between rights offerings and issues sold to the general public.

ing the expected values in equation A20–6. He would find N approximately equal to eight years.[7] With this estimate of the years, the bond will remain outstanding, the investor could then substitute in equation A20–3 and solve for k^*. For the values in the example, this would be approximately 6 percent.[8] If this *ex ante* yield is equal to or greater than the investor's required rate of return on investments with the same (estimated) risk, then he would buy the bonds. If the marginal investor's opportunity cost is just met, the issue price will be stable.[9]

Impact of Convertibles on Stockholders

Since the desirability of using convertibles is probabilistic, thus necessarily subjective, it is difficult to reach any very general conclusions. It is, however, possible to describe specific circumstances under which using convertibles appears to be advantageous *ex ante* and conversely. Fortunately, the basic assumptions needed for this analysis seem to apply to most of the firms that returned the questionnaire described in Appendix B to this chapter.

Target debt/equity ratio. The first assumption is that the firm has a long-run target debt/equity ratio, and that this target ratio is independent of the decision to use or not to use convertibles. Further, when convertibles are used, they are classified as debt until converted, at which point they are classed as equity for purposes of calculating the target debt ratio.

Financial alternatives. The firm is assumed to be capable of obtaining funds in the desired mix; that is, it is able to borrow or sell stock in whatever amounts are necessary to maintain its target debt ratio. Further, market conditions are assumed to be such that it may deviate, within the limits of its annual outside financing needs, from the target ratio at any time. In other words, it can finance with debt one year and with equity the next, oscillating about the target ratio rather than maintaining it exactly. The decision to use debt or equity in any given year will depend upon conditions in the security markets and on the relationship between the actual and the target debt/equity ratios.

While questionnaire responses and interviews suggested that this assumption is approximately correct for the large, listed firms in the sample, it is probably not true for smaller companies. For small, nonlisted businesses, the flotation costs of stock are probably substantially higher

[7]
$$N = \frac{(\log \$50 - \log \$45) + (\log \$1200 - \log \$1000)}{\log (1.04)} \approx 8$$

[8]
$$\$1{,}000 = \sum_{t-1}^{8} \frac{\$40}{(1 + k^*)^t} + \frac{\$1200}{(1 + k^*)^8} \text{ when } K^* = 6\%$$

[9] In the case of rights offerings, bonds are generally underpriced; consequently, they sell at a premium over par immediately after issue.

than the costs of selling bonds. Further, it may be that the convertibles of small companies sell in a broader market than their common stock and therefore reduce the fear of loss of control. Finally, if a small firm sells a block of stock, there is more likelihood that it will cause a subsequent break in the market price than if a sale is made by a larger firm whose stock sells in a broader market. These possibilities must be explored in greater detail before the analysis may be applied to small firms.

Capital budget. It is further assumed that the firm has determined its capital budget. This decision is not presumed to be made independently of the over-all cost of capital, but it is presumed to be made independently of the method of financing during the current year. In other words, using or not using convertibles will have no impact on the level of investment (other than whatever secondary effects convertibles might have on future investment through their impact on the cost of capital).

Required rate of return. The "marginal investor" is assumed to have a required rate of return which he expects to earn on the firm's shares (and convertibles). This return varies over time; at any given time it varies among firms in accordance with their "riskiness," which is defined as the variance of the expected rate of return. The required rate of return on shares is expected to be realized from the dividend yield plus a capital gain, while that on convertibles is expected to come from interest payments plus capital gains.

Various conditions. Suppose a firm's long-run plans indicate that new outside funds—both debt and equity—will be required in each future year as far ahead as has been forecast. The necessary equity capital can be raised (1) by the sale of common stock; (2) by the sale of debt now and refunding later with an equity issue (this will cause a temporary deviation from the target debt ratio); or (3) by the sale of convertibles which, when converted, will provide the required equity. If convertibles are sold, they may be used in either of two ways. First, the firm can sell both straight and convertible debt in the current year and thus have more debt than is called for by the target ratio, with this situation being rectified when conversion occurs. Alternatively, it can sell both common stock and debt in the current year to maintain the target debt ratio but make part of the debt convertible. This current issue of convertible debt, when converted, will thus provide for part of the future equity requirements. (The converted debt will, of course, be replaced to maintain the target debt ratio.)

Operating within the assumptions specified above, which choice is best? For firms interested in their stockholders, the best choice is that which maximizes the wealth of existing shareholders. This amounts to selecting the financing package that (consistent with the target debt ratio) minimizes the number of new shares that must be given up, *ex ante,* to raise the necessary equity funds. This, in turn, depends upon management's judgment versus that of the market about the "proper level" of share prices.

Stock "fairly priced." If the firm's management and the "market" are in agreement (1) about the firm's prospects for growth and (2) about its appropriate risk class, then they must also be in agreement about the current price of the stock. Under such circumstances, there is no reason to think that any one of the choices is clearly superior to any other. The institutional factors discussed above—the demand for convertibles generated by margin requirements and limitations on institutional holdings of common stocks—may be sufficient to create an advantage for convertibles; this, however, is not at all clear. Aside from this possible point, the use or nonuse of convertibles would appear to be a matter of indifference when the stock is thought to be fairly priced.

Stock undervalued. If management deems its stock to be undervalued—presumably because it thinks the market is overly pessimistic about the firm's growth prospects or risk class, or is simply undervaluing all equities at the particular time—then the best financing decision is to issue debt. Later on, when the stock price has risen, sufficient equity will be issued to return to the target debt ratio. Convertibles are a better choice than common stock, but using them is still not as good as using straight debt. That component of the convertible's expected return that investors plan to receive from the common stock is, presumably, undervalued. This means the firm must set the conversion price relatively low or the coupon rate relatively high in order to sell the bonds.

Stock overvalued. If the stock is overvalued, exactly the reverse holds true. Financing should be with common stock, but convertibles are a better choice than straight debt.

SUMMARY

The major findings of this appendix may be summarized as follows. First, the graphic model showed that a convertible bond has a market value floor which is set by the higher of its straight debt or conversion value. Typically, the bond will sell above this floor because (1) of a capital gains potential coupled with a degree of protection against losses due to a drop in stock prices and (2) of institutional constraints (described in Appendix B to this chapter) against the purchase of stock.

A convertible's *ex ante* yield is dependent upon expectations about the following: (1) growth rates; (2) firm's policy on calling to force conversion; (3) conversion ratio; (4) price of the shares at time of issue; and (5) coupon interest rate. If this *ex ante* yield, as computed by marginal investors, differs from their required rate of return, the bond will go to a premium or a discount immediately after issue.

The *ex ante* desirability of using convertibles depends on management's views about impending movements in the price of its stock *vis-à-vis* the market's views. If management believes its stock to be relatively overpriced, then financing with stock is best, convertibles second best, and straight debt worst. Just the reverse holds if the stock is thought to be undervalued. If management agrees with the market (or refuses to take a stand), the choice of financing under a set of reasonable assumptions turns out to be immaterial. Note, however, that *ex post* a firm using convertibles will always have intermediate financing results. Since convertibles lie between debt and equity, a firm using them is "hedging its bets."

There are, however, some perhaps important institutional factors that might render convertible financing advantageous in a more positive sense. To the extent that certain investors who really want to make equity commitments are able to buy convertibles but not common stock, the demand curve for convertibles may be shifted to the right. This shift, in turn, would lower the cost of convertible capital *vis-à-vis* directly sold common stock. The extent of this phenomenon was not investigated, but it may well be important at times. In addition, the conclusions stated apply only to larger, publicly owned corporations. The use of convertibles by smaller firms was not investigated, but there are reasons for believing that convertible securities might offer special advantages to smaller companies with less financial flexibility than to the large firms in the sample studied.

APPENDIX B TO CHAPTER 20 Empirical Data on Convertible Bond Usage

To gain insights into the corporate planning that lies behind the decision to issue convertibles, as well as to determine the characteristics of convertible bonds themselves, a sample of issues was examined and a detailed questionnaire was sent to the issuing firms. During the period 1961 to 1963, 215 publicly offered convertible bonds having a value of $1,080 million were sold to the public.[1] Of this total, $820 million, or 76 percent, were sold by 42 listed companies; these 42, shown in Table B20–1, were chosen for the sample.[2] Because of the selection process, the remarks in this section refer only to the use of convertibles by large corporations.

Statistics on the Sample

Table B20–2 gives information on the sample companies and on the characteristics of the bonds themselves. Section A shows that the issues ranged in size from $2.5 million to $60 million, with the majority falling in the $5 million to $20 million classes. Industrial firms predominated; the fact that convertibles were not used to any extent by utilities, which

[1] "Corporate Financing Directory," *Investment Dealers' Digest* (February 1965).

[2] One firm, Crowell-Collier, had two convertible issues during the period, so there are actually 43 bonds in the sample. Twenty-two firms, or 52 percent, completed the questionnaire.

TABLE B20–1 LIST OF COMPANIES IN SAMPLE

1. Air Reduction Company
2. Allied Stores Corp.
3. American Distilling Company
4. American Machine and Foundry Company
5. Armour and Company
6. Ashland Oil and Refining Company
7. Automatic Canteen Company of America
8. Baxter Laboratories, Inc.
9. Belco Petroleum Corp.
10. Berman Leasing Company
11. Brunswick Corporation
12. Canada Dry Corp.
13. Chock Full O'Nuts Corp.
14. City Products Corp.
15. Collins Radio Company
16. Continental Baking Company
17. Control Data Corp.
18. Crowell-Collier Publishing Company
19. FMC Corp.
20. General Acceptance Corp.
21. Holly Sugar Corp.
22. Hunt Foods and Industries, Inc.
23. International Silver Company
24. Interstate Department Stores
25. Keystone Steel and Wire Company
26. Lafayette Radio Electronics Corp.
27. Litton Industries
28. McCall Corp.
29. National Airlines, Inc.
30. Nopco Chemical Company
31. Northern Indiana Public Service Company
32. Occidental Petroleum Corp.
33. Ryder System, Inc.
34. Stokely-Van Camp, Inc.
35. Stouffer Foods Corp.
36. Symington Wayne Corp.
37. Thor Power Tool Company
38. Union Oil Company of California
39. United Aircraft Corp.
40. U.S. Freight Company
41. Vornado, Inc.
42. Xerox Corp.

TABLE B20–2 STATISTICS ON THE SAMPLE OF CONVERTIBLE BONDS

		Issues	
A. Size of issue	Dollars (Millions)	Number	Percent
	2.5–4.9	3	7
	5.0–9.9	16	37
	10.0–19.9	11	26
	20.0–29.9	5	12
	30.0–39.9	4	9
	40.0–60.0	4	9
B. Category	Industrial	37	86
	Transportation	4	9
	Public utility	1	2
	Finance	1	2
C. Maturity	Years to Maturity		
	15	5	12
	20	25	58
	21	1	2
	22	2	5
	25	7	16
	30	3	7
D. Quality rating	S & P Rating		
	A	3	7
	BBB	11	26
	BB	20	46
	B	9	21
E. Coupon rate	$3\frac{1}{8}$–$3\frac{1}{2}$	2	5
	$3\frac{5}{8}$–4	4	9
	$4\frac{1}{8}$–$4\frac{1}{2}$	17	40
	$4\frac{5}{8}$–5	16	37
	$5\frac{1}{8}$–$5\frac{1}{2}$	2	5
	$5\frac{5}{8}$–$6\frac{1}{2}$	2	5
F. Rights offering	Offered to stockholders	23	53
	Not offered to stockholders	20	47
G. Stepped-up conversion price	Price stepped up	8	19
	Not stepped up	35	81
H. Sinking fund provision	Sinking fund	38	88
	No sinking fund	5	12
I. Underwriting data	Number of Issues per Underwriter	Underwriters	
	13	1	
	5	1	
	2	3	
	1	5	
	1	9	

have been doing much new financing, is significant. Section C shows that maturities ranged from 15 to 30 years, with 20 and 25 years being most frequent.

The bond ratings ranged from A to B, with 67 percent falling below BBB, the lower limit of "investment-grade" securities.[3] However, the fact that the convertible issues were generally rated low *should not* be interpreted as meaning that the firms' straight debt was also low rated. All but two of the convertible issues were subordinated—generally to all existing and future long- and short-term debt. This clearly caused the convertibles to be rated well below the straight debt issues of the same companies.

About one-half of the issues were sold through rights offerings; 19 percent employed a stepped-up conversion price; and 88 percent had a sinking fund provision.[4] It is not shown in the table, but all the bonds had essentially the same call provisions—they were callable immediately after issue with the call premium starting at the coupon interest rate and declining by ¼ percent a year to par. Relatively high concentration was found from the underwriting data, with Lehman Brothers acting as principal underwriter for nine issues, and Eastman Dillion, Union Securities for five.

Reasons for Using Convertibles

When a firm sells convertibles, it does so for one of two primary reasons: (1) it wants equity capital and believes that convertibles are an expedient way of selling common stock; or (2) it desires debt but finds that by adding the convertible feature, interest costs are reduced substantially. Of the firms replying to the questionnaire, 73 percent were primarily interested in obtaining equity, while 27 percent used convertibles to "sweeten" debt issues. The bonds of this latter group generally carried the lower ratings, which was to be expected.[5]

Financing Alternatives

To gain insights into other sources of funds and their costs, the following question was asked: "At the time you decided to use convertibles,

[3] BB bonds "are regarded as lower medium grade. They have only minor investment characteristics." *Standard & Poor's Bond Guide.*

[4] The typical sinking fund provision does not commence for some 10 years after issue; it requires the corporation to deliver funds to the trustee, who uses the funds to acquire bonds by lottery at par or through open market purchase, whichever is cheaper. It gives the firm the right to deliver bonds acquired in conversion rather than money. Generally, the sinking fund amortizes from 50 to 80 percent of the total amount of bonds.

[5] Recall that the firms in the sample are large, all listed on either the New York Stock or the American stock exchange. Had the sample been extended to smaller, financially weaker companies, it is likely that a larger percentage would have indicated that convertibles were used to "sweeten" debt issues.

what alternatives were available for raising *the same amount of funds as was obtained from selling convertibles?"* All companies indicated that common stock could have been sold at net prices ranging from 2 to 5 percent below the market price, the larger discounts being applicable to small firms and to those needing large sums of money relative to the value of their outstanding shares. It is worth noting that neither in the questionnaire responses nor in subsequent interviews with selected firms was a fear indicated that a common stock issue would have brought on the danger of a break in the market price of the stock. The feeling seemed to hold that the market could absorb a stock issue the size of the convertible debenture offering. All but two respondents indicated that straight debt could have been sold. When rates on straight debt were mentioned, they ranged from ½ to 1 percent above those on the convertible issue.

In summary, the relatively large, listed corporations in the sample were by no means forced to use convertibles. They generally had the opportunity of selling either straight debt or stock, both at "reasonable" costs; they deliberately chose to employ convertibles.

Conversion Policy

It was pointed out in the preceding Appendix that a firm's policy with regard to forcing conversion by calling the issue is one of the vital determinants of the rate of return to bondholders. In order that something might be learned about this factor, the firms were asked about their conversion policy on the questionnaire, and the sample of bonds was examined to see when conversion actually was forced.

The question and the responses to it are shown in Table B20–3. Almost a quarter of the companies stated that their policy was to force conversion as soon as the conversion value exceeded the call price by about 20 percent. Another 23 percent indicated that they would encourage voluntary conversion by raising dividends.[6] The remaining 54 percent of the respondents either did not plan to force conversion at all or else had no clearly defined policy.

These responses have been borne out reasonably well by actual experience. Of the 43 bonds in the sample, 20 had reached the point where the conversion value exceeded the call price by at least 20 percent. Six of these bonds, or 30 percent, had been called by March 1965.

[6] One of these firms returned a schedule showing the way voluntary conversion occurred in its case. In September 1964, the common dividend was raised by 25 percent. At this point bondholders would receive about 15 percent more income from dividends on conversion than in interest on the bonds. The conversion value was approximately equal to the market value and exceeded the call price by about 30 percent. Between the time of the dividend increase and the record date of the next quarterly dividend, some 50 percent of the bonds were converted voluntarily, and the company indicated that these conversions were continuing as additional bondholders recognized the income differential.

Institutional Factors Making Convertibles Attractive

Questionnaire responses and interviews suggested that two strictly institutional phenomena may serve to make convertibles a relatively attractive form of financing. First, a number of institutional investors—life insurance companies, certain pension funds, and banks, for example—are severely restricted in their ability to hold common stocks. The investment officers of many of these institutions are thought to feel that it would be desirable to have more equities than regulations permit. Convertible bonds provide these intermediaries with a method of indirectly holding more equities than the law permits.

TABLE B20–3 CONVERSION POLICIES

"Which of the following most nearly reflects your company's policy with regard to conversion?"

	NO.	PERCENT
1. Force conversion by calling as soon as you are "sure" the bonds will actually be converted, not redeemed. (Please indicate by how much conversion value must exceed call price.)	5	23
2. Encourage conversion by increasing common stock dividends, thus making the yield on common higher than that on bonds.	5	23
3. Have not encouraged conversion at all, but would force conversion prior to selling a new debt issue.	2	9
4. Do not plan to force or encourage conversion at all.	7	31
5. Other. (Please explain.)	3	14
	22	100

NOTE: The three companies checking "other" have no established conversion policy.

The second institutional factor has to do with margin requirements. Stockbrokers suggest that there exists a class of investors who desire to obtain more leverage than is available under current margin requirements. Many convertible bonds could be bought on a 20 percent or lower margin as against one of 70 percent on listed common stocks. Margin requirements on convertibles vary, but the figures given here held when the questionnaire was mailed in 1965. In the fall of 1968 the margin requirement on convertibles was 60 percent versus 80 percent on common stocks.

To the extent that high-leverage investors and restricted institutions are important factors in the market, it is possible that this might, in effect, shift to the right the supply curve for funds placed in the convertible market, thus lowering the cost of capital convertibles. This is, in fact, what many advocates of convertibles suggest.[7] Although it may be true, there is no reason whatever to suppose that the supply shift could not be matched by an equal demand shift on the part of corporate borrowers, thus eliminating the supposed advantage attributed to convertibles. Indeed, is it not possible that corporations could be "oversold" on the use of convertibles, thus causing them to demand an excessive amount of funds through such issues and making the cost of convertible capital relatively more expensive than other types? This condition is completely speculative, of course. There is no evidence to indicate whether these institutional factors create a favorable or unfavorable situation for convertibles. The institutional effects are probably favorable, on balance, but decidedly of second order importance.

[7] For example, see W. S. Skelly, *Convertible Bonds: A Study of Their Suitability for Commercial Bank Bond Portfolios* (New York: Salomon Bros. & Hutzler, 1959).

PART SEVEN

VALUATION IN MERGERS AND CORPORATE READJUSTMENT

21

External Growth: Mergers and Holding Companies

Growth is vital to the well-being of a firm; without it, a business cannot attract able management because it cannot give them recognition in promotions and challenging creative activity. Without able executives, the firm is likely to decline and die. Much of the material in the previous chapters dealing with analysis, planning, and financing has a direct bearing on the financial manager's potential contribution to the growth of a firm. However, because of the central importance of the growth requirement, the present chapter is focused on strategies for promoting it.

Merger activity has played an important part in the growth of firms in the United States, and financial managers are required both to appraise the desirability of a prospective purchase and to participate directly in evaluating the respective companies involved in a merger.[1] Consequently, it is essential that the study of financial management provide the background necessary for effective participation in merger negotiations and decisions.

Financial managers—and intelligent laymen—also need to be aware of the broader significance of mergers. Despite the heightened merger activities in the 1920s, again after World War II, and during the mid-1960s, recent merger movements have neither approached the magnitude nor had the social consequences of the mergers that took place from 1890 to 1905. During this period, more than 200 major combinations were effected, resulting in the concentration that has characterized the steel, tobacco, and other important industries. Regardless of the business objectives and motives of merger activity, the social and economic consequences of mergers must also be taken into account.

REASONS FOR SEEKING GROWTH

One of the objectives of growth, whether by external acquisitions or by internal development, is large size for the purpose of achieving economies of large-scale operations. Economies of scale result from the following factors.

RESEARCH. Research activities are especially crucial in today's dynamic economy. The large firm can finance large-scale research which may benefit a great number of its diverse operations. But suppose a large firm is broken into 10 units. Could not the 10 units each contract to hire research from a research organization? It is true that research in the large firm is often conducted by executives hired on a salary basis, and independent research firms do sell their services on a fee basis. There are some kinds of research, however, that are the unique contribution of the large firm.

For example, suppose that a large firm which spends $50 million a year on research is divided into ten firms, each of which could allocate $5 million a year for research. If each of these ten firms hires the services of a research organization, each would attempt to buy $5 million worth of research designed to give it a competitive advantage over its nine

[1] As we use the term, "merger" means any combination that forms one economic unit from two or more previous ones. For legal purposes there are distinctions between the various ways these combinations can occur, but our emphasis is on fundamental business and financial aspects of mergers or acquisitions.

rivals and any other firms in the industry. It seems reasonable to suppose that certain kinds of research could not be purchased by the $5 million a year but could be achieved by the $50 million budget.

Modern large-scale business organizations represent the combination of centralized and decentralized decisions. Research is an activity performed most efficiently when centralized. Although the amounts of money spent on research are relatively small, its significance is critical for the progress of the firm.

TOP-MANAGEMENT SKILLS. Related to indivisibility of research expenditures is the value of the highly able executive. The very competent individual is another one of the indivisible factors that make for an advantage of large-scale operations. It cannot be denied that many decisions are decentralized; for many matters, delegation of authority to committees and subordinates takes place. However, some of the centralized decisions and the catalytic process of a great mind on policy matters are of pervasive and powerful influence on the growth pattern and performance of an organization.

OPERATING ECONOMIES. Often there are other economies of multiproduct operations. Lower salary ratios may be achieved by consolidating certain departments (accounting, marketing, advertising, switchboard, clerical); marketing costs may be lowered by consolidating salesmen covering the same territory for several companies, thus reducing the total number of salesmen required; production savings may come from the ability to utilize large, high-output machinery or to obtain quantity discounts on purchases.

RISK REDUCTION. Still another important factor is the risk reduction of multiplant operations, which is heightened by the tax structure. If a new firm attempts an innovation or a new product line and fails, the loss may force it out of business completely. However, if an established firm attempts a change or an innovation, any loss can be offset against assured income from other sources. The higher the tax rate, the higher the proportion of the innovation costs borne by taxes. This is another reason why multiproduct and multiplant firms confer economic advantages, not only on the firm itself but also on the economy as a whole, in terms of the potential rate of economic progress.

MARKET CAPITALIZATION RATES. While it is not strictly an operating economy, the fact that the earnings of larger economic units are capitalized at lower rates and, hence, produce higher market values has stimulated many mergers. The securities of larger firms have better marketability, these firms are more able to diversify and thus reduce risks, and they are generally better known. All these factors lead to higher price/earnings ratios. As a result, it may be possible to consolidate firms and have the resulting market value greater than the sum of their individual values, even if there is no increase in aggregate earnings. To illustrate, three companies may each be earning $100 and selling at 10 times earnings, for a total market value of ($100) (10) (3) equals $3,000. When these companies combine, the new company may obtain a Stock Exchange listing or take other actions to improve the price of its stock. If so, the price/earnings ratio may rise to 15, in which case the market value of the consolidated firm would be $4,500.[2]

The five factors just discussed provide a plausible rationale for the existence and operation of larger multiproduct and multiplant enterprises.

MERGERS VERSUS INTERNAL GROWTH

Many of the objectives of size and diversification may be achieved either through internal growth or by external growth through acquisitions and mergers. In the post-World War II period, considerable diversification was achieved by many firms through external acquisition. The reasons for utilizing external acquisition instead of internal growth to achieve diversification may be briefly indicated.

SPEED. New facilities may be acquired more quickly through mergers. New products, new processes, new plants, and new productive organizations can be acquired in a fully operative condition by a merger.

COST. The desired facilities may be obtained more cheaply by purchasing the ownership stock of each existing company. For many reasons, the securities of a company may be selling below the replacement costs of the firm's assets. For example, stock market prices were relatively depressed from 1946 to 1953, and the market values of common stocks were low in relation to earnings levels. A basis was provided for developing favorable merger terms.

The mergers in the steel industry in the period immediately following 1946 are good examples of this influence. A steel company could add new capacity much more cheaply by buying another company than by

[2] The market capitalization rate is related to the cost of equity, as was explained in Chapter 11. A lower capitalization rate results in a lower cost of capital. Therefore, the same actions that raise the market value of the equity also lower the firm's cost of new capital.

building new plants to achieve the same increase in capacity. Furthermore, the speed factor mentioned above was important here. The duration of the seller's market in steel was unknown. The sooner a steel company could acquire additional facilities and get them into operation for making sales, the more likely it would be to benefit from the favorable market conditions.

Related to this is the objective of obtaining the services of desired personnel. Sometimes the inducement of higher compensation to attract an outstanding individual or management group might be either unduly expensive or useless. Simply buying the company that employs these people may prove to be the most effective means of obtaining their services. In such circumstances, a merger may be the only practicable method of obtaining the kind of superior management talent or technical skill that the acquiring firm is seeking to obtain.

FINANCING. Sometimes it is possible to finance an acquisition when it is not possible to finance internal growth. A large steel plant, for example, involves a large investment. Steel capacity may be acquired in a merger through an exchange of stock more cheaply than it can be obtained by buying the facilities themselves. Sellers may be more willing to accept the stock of the purchaser in payment for the facilities sold than would investors in a public distribution. The use of stock reduces cash requirements for the acquisition of assets.

RISK. The desired new product, new process, or new organization may be developed with less uncertainty of investment loss. The purchased facility may already have demonstrated its revenue-yielding capacity.

STABILIZING EFFECTS. A merger may represent the most effective method of achieving stability and progress at a given stage of industrial development. It may represent the most efficient method of combining facilities and disposing of obsolete and inefficient properties, as was probably true at some stages in the development of industries such as railroad transport, air transport, banking, agricultural implements, and steel.

TAXES. Without question, the high level of taxation was a factor in the postwar period. A study by a Harvard group[3] indicates that taxes appear to have been a major reason for the sale of about one-third of the firms acquired by merger. Inheritance taxes precipitated these sales in some cases; in others, the advantage of buying a company with a tax loss, which was discussed in Chapter 2, provided the motivation.

[3] J. K. Butters, J. Lintner, and W. L. Cary, *Effects of Taxation: Corporate Mergers* (Boston, Mass.: Division of Research, Graduate School of Business Administration, Harvard University, 1951).

COMPETITIVE ADVANTAGES. The development of new products and market areas may be accomplished through mergers. Firms in the early stages of development can in this way avoid combating difficult competition or remedy a management weakness. A market control may be obtained more rapidly with less risk through mergers than by internal expansion. The merger of two large firms may result in market dominance by the combined firms and may therefore be prevented by the antitrust authorities.

Regardless of the motives or objectives of mergers from a business standpoint, the consequences of the market-control position of the acquiring company may lead to intervention by governmental regulatory agencies. Hence, it is not enough for the financial manager to consider only the business aspects of the merger. He must also consider the effects on market control. If the merger will have potentially adverse effects on competition, there is a strong likelihood that government action will be interposed against the merger.

TERMS OF MERGERS

For every merger actually consummated, a number of other potentially attractive combinations fail during the negotiating stage. In some of these cases, negotiations are broken off when it is revealed that the companies' operations are not compatible. In others, tangible benefits would result, but the parties are unable to agree on the merger terms. Of these terms, the most important is the price paid by the acquiring firm for the firm acquired. Factors that influence this important aspect of a merger are now considered.

Effects on Price and Earnings

A merger carries potentialities for either favorable or adverse effects on earnings, market prices of shares, or both. Previous chapters have shown that investment decisions should be guided by the effects on market values and that these effects should in turn be determined by the effects on future earnings and dividends. These future events are difficult to forecast, however, so stockholders as well as management give considerable weight to the immediate effects of a contemplated merger on earnings per share. Directors of companies will often state, "I do not know how the merger will affect the market price of the shares of my company because so many forces influencing market prices are at work. But the effect on earnings per share can be seen directly."

An example will illustrate the effects of a proposed merger on earnings per share and thus suggest the kinds of problems that are likely to arise. Assume the following facts for two companies:

	COMPANY A	COMPANY B
Total earnings	$20,000	$50,000
Number of shares of common stock	5,000	10,000
Earnings per share of stock	$ 4.00	$ 5.00
Price/earnings ratio per share	15×	12×
Market price per share	$ 60.00	$ 60.00

Suppose the firms agree to merge, with B, the surviving firm, acquiring the shares of A by a one-for-one exchange of stock. The exchange ratio is determined by the respective market prices of the two companies. Assuming no increase in earnings, the effects on earnings per share are shown in the following tabulation:

		EARNINGS PER SHARE	
	Shares of Company B Owned after Merger	Before Merger	After Merger
A's stockholders	5,000	$4	$4.67
B's stockholders	10,000	5	4.67
Total	15,000		

Since total earnings are $70,000 and a total of 15,000 shares will be outstanding after the merger has been completed, the new earnings per share will be $4.67. Earnings will increase by 67 cents for A's stockholders, but they will decline by 33 cents for B's.

The effects on market values are less certain. If the combined companies sell at the 15 times price/earnings ratio of company A, the new market value per share of the new company will be $70. In this case, shareholders of both companies will have benefited. This result comes about because the combined earnings are now valued at a multiplier of 15, whereas prior to the merger a portion of the earnings was valued at a multiplier of 15 and a portion valued at a multiplier of 12.

If, on the other hand, the earnings of the new company are valued at B's multiplier of 12, the indicated market value of the shares will be $56. The shareholders of each company will have suffered a $4 dilution in market value.

Because the effects on market value per share are less certain than those on earnings per share, the impact on earnings per share tends to be given greater weight in merger negotiations. Because of this, the following analysis also emphasizes effects on earnings per share, while recognizing that maximizing market value is the valid rule for investment decisions.

If the merger takes place on the basis of earnings, neither earnings dilution nor earnings appreciation will take place. This follows from the results shown below:

		EARNINGS PER OLD SHARE	
	Shares of Company B Owned after Merger	Before Merger	After Merger
A shareholders[4]	4,000	$4	$4
B shareholders	10,000	5	5
Total	14,000		

It is clear that the equivalent earnings per share after the merger are the same as before the merger. The effects on market values will depend upon whether the 15-times multiplier of A or the 12-times multiplier of B prevails.

Of the numerous factors affecting the valuation of the constituent companies in a merger, all must ultimately be reflected in the earnings per share or market price of the companies. Hence, all the effects on the earnings position or wealth position of stockholders are encompassed by the foregoing example. The discussion may, therefore, turn to a con-

[4] Based on earnings, the exchange ratio is 4:5; that is, company A's shareholders receive four shares of B stock for each five shares of A stock they own. Earnings per share of the merged company is $5, but since A's shareholders now own only 80 percent of the number of their old shares, their equivalent earnings per *old* share is the same $4. For example, suppose one of A's stockholders formerly held 100 shares. He will own only 80 shares of B after the merger, and his total earnings will be 80 × $5 = $400. Dividing their $400 total earnings by the number of shares they formerly owned, 100, gives the $4 per *old* share.

sideration of the factors that will influence the terms on which an acquisition or a merger is likely to take place. Both quantitative and qualitative factors receive consideration.

Quantitative Factors Affecting Terms of Mergers

Five factors have received the greatest emphasis in arriving at merger terms:

Earnings and growth rates	Market values
Dividends	Book values
Net current assets	

Analysis is typically based on the per share values of the foregoing factors. The relative importance of each factor and the circumstances under which each is likely to be the most influential determinant in arriving at terms will vary. The nature of these influences is now described.

EARNINGS AND GROWTH RATES. Both expected earnings and capitalization rates (P/E ratios) are important in determining the values that will be established in a merger. The analysis necessarily begins with historical data on the firms' earnings, whose past growth rates, future trends, and variability are important determinants of the earnings multiplier, or P/E ratio, that will prevail after the merger.

How future earnings growth rates affect the multiplier can be illustrated by extending the preceding example. First, we know that high P/E ratios are commonly associated with rapidly growing companies. Since company A has the higher P/E ratio, it is reasonable to assume that its earnings are expected to grow more rapidly than those of company B. Suppose A's expected growth rate is 10 percent and B's 5 percent. Looking at the proposed merger from the point of view of company B and its stockholders and assuming that the exchange ratio is based on present market prices, it can be seen that B will suffer a dilution in earnings when the merger occurs. However, B will be acquiring a firm with more favorable growth prospects; hence its earnings after the merger should increase more rapidly than before. In fact, the new growth rate may turn out to be a weighted average of the growth rates of the individual firms, weighted by their respective total earnings before the merger. In the example, the new expected growth rate is 6.43 percent.

With the new growth rate it is possible to determine just how long it will take company B's stockholders to regain the earnings dilution. That is, how long will it take earnings per share to be back to where they would have been without the merger? This can be determined

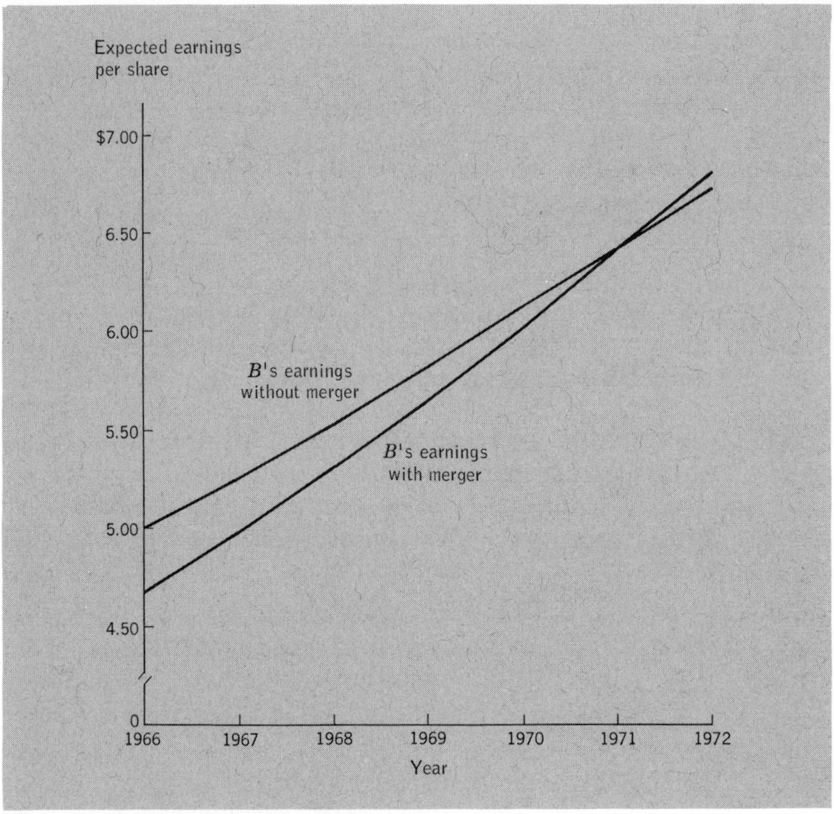

Figure 21–1 Effect of Merger on Future Earnings

graphically from Figure 21–1.[5] Without the merger, B would have initial earnings of $5 a share, and these earnings would have grown at a rate of 5 percent a year. With the merger, earnings drop to $4.67 a share, but the rate of growth increases to 6.43 percent. Under these conditions, the earnings dilution is overcome after five years; from the fifth year on, B's earnings will be higher, assuming the merger is consummated.

This same type of relationship could be developed from the point of view of the faster growing firm. Here there would be an immediate earnings increase but a reduced rate of growth. Working through the analysis would show the number of years before the earnings accretion would be eroded.

[5] The calculation could also be made algebraically by solving for N in the following equation: $E_1(1+g_1)^N = E_2(1+g_2)^N$, where E_1 = earnings before the merger, E_2 = earnings after the merger, g_1 and g_2 are the growth rates before and after the merger, and N is the break-even number of years.

It is apparent that the critical variables are (1) the respective rates of growth of the two firms; (2) their relative sizes, which determine the actual amount of the initial earnings per share dilution or accretion, as well as the new weighted average growth rate; (3) the firms' P/E ratios; and (4) the exchange ratio. These factors interact to produce the resulting pattern of earnings per share for the surviving company. It is possible to generalize the relationships somewhat;[6] for our purposes, it is necessary simply to note that in the bargaining process the exchange ratio is the variable that must be manipulated in an effort to reach a mutually satisfactory earnings pattern.

DIVIDENDS. Dividends, because they represent the actual income received by stockholders, may influence the terms of merger. However, as the material in Chapter 17 indicates, dividends are likely to have little influence on the market price of companies with a record of high growth and high profitability. For example, some companies, such as Litton Industries, have not yet paid cash dividends but command market prices representing a high multiple of current earnings. At the end of 1964, Litton was selling at a multiplier of approximately 40 times. However, for utility companies and for companies in industries where growth rates and profitability have declined, the dollar amount of dividends paid may have a relatively important influence on the market price of the stock. Dividends may therefore influence the terms on which these companies would be likely to trade in a merger.

MARKET VALUES. The price of a firm's stock reflects expectations about its future earnings and dividends, so one might expect current market values to have a strong influence on the terms of a merger. However, one could predict that the value placed on a firm in an acquisition is likely to exceed its current market price for a number of reasons. (1) If the company is in a depressed industry, its stockholders are likely to overdiscount the dismal outlook for the company; this will result in a very low current market price. (2) The prospective purchaser may be interested in acquiring the company for the contribution that it may make to the acquiring company. Thus, the acquired company is worth more to an informed purchaser than it is in the general market. (3) Stockholders are offered more than current market prices for their stock as an inducement to sell.

BOOK VALUE PER SHARE. Book values are now generally considered to be relatively unimportant in determining the value of a company,

[6] For a generalization, as well as for a more detailed examination of the interrelations, see D. F. Folz and J. Fred Weston, "Looking Ahead in Evaluating Proposed Mergers," *N.A.A. Bulletin* (April 1962).

and they merely represent the historical investments that have been made in the company. These historical investments may have little relation to current values or prices. At times, however, especially when book values substantially exceed market values, they may well have an impact on merger terms. The book value is an index of the amount of physical facilities made available in the merger. Despite a past record of low earning power, it is always possible that, under effective management, a firm's assets may once again achieve normal earning power. If this is the case, the market value of the company will rise. Because of the potential contribution of physical properties to improved future earnings, book values may have an important influence on actual merger or acquisition terms.

NET CURRENT ASSETS PER SHARE. Net current assets (current assets minus current liabilities) per share are likely to have an influence on merger terms because they represent the amount of liquidity that may be obtained from a company in a merger. In the postwar textile mergers, net current assets were very high, and this was one of the characteristics making them attractive to the acquiring firms. By buying a textile company, often with securities, an acquiring company was in a position to look for still other merger candidates, paying for the new acquisition with the just-acquired liquidity. In this same connection, if the acquired company is debt-free, the acquiring firm may be able to borrow the funds required for the purchase, using the acquired firm's assets and earning power as security for the loan.

Relative Importance of Quantitative Factors

Attempts have been made to determine statistically the relative weights assigned to each of these factors in actual merger cases. However, these attempts have been singularly unsuccessful—in one case, one factor seems to dominate, in another some other determinant appears to be most important. This absence of consistent patterns among the quantitative factors suggests that qualitative forces are also at work, and we now turn our attention to these more nebulous variables.

Qualitative Influences

Sometimes the most important influence on the terms of a merger is a business consideration not reflected at all in historical quantitative data. A soundly conceived merger is one in which the combination produces what may be called a *synergistic*, or "two-plus-two-equals-five" effect. By the combination, more profits result than could be achieved by the individual firms operating separately.

For example, in the 1953 merger between Merck and Company and Sharp and Dohme, it was said that each company complemented the other in an important way. Merck had a strong reputation for its research organization. Sharp and Dohme had a most effective sales organization. The combination of these two pharmaceutical companies added strength to both. Another example is the merger in late 1954 between Carrier Corporation and Affiliated Gas Equipment, Inc. The merger enabled the combined company to provide a complete line of air-conditioning and heating equipment. The merger between Hilton Hotels and Statler Hotels led to economies in the purchase of supplies and materials. One Hilton executive estimated that the savings accruing simply from the combined management of the Statler Hotel in New York and Hilton's New York Hotel amounted to $700,000 a year. The bulk of the savings were in laundry, food, advertising, and administrative costs.

The qualitative factors may also reflect other influences. The merger or acquisition may enable one company to obtain general management ability that it lacks but which the other company possesses. Another factor may be the acquisition of a technically competent scientific or engineering staff. One of the companies may have fallen behind in the technological race and may need to combine with another company if it expects to catch up at all. In such a situation, the company lacking the technical competence possessed by the other firm may be willing to pay a substantial premium over previous levels of earnings, dividends, or market or book values.

The purpose of the merger may be to develop a production capability a firm does not possess. Some firms are strong in producing custom-made items with high-performance characteristics, yet these firms, on entering new markets, must make use of mass-production techniques. If the firm has had no experience in mass-production techniques, this skill may have to be obtained by means of a merger. The firm may perhaps need to develop an effective sales organization. For example, some of the companies previously oriented to the defense market, such as the aircraft companies, found that they had only a limited industrial sales organization; merger was the solution to the problem.

The foregoing are the kinds of qualitative considerations that may have an overriding influence on the actual terms of merger, and the values of these contributions are never easy to qualify. The all-encompassing question, of course, is how these factors will affect the contribution of each company to future earnings per share in the combined operation. The historical data and the qualitative considerations described, in addition to judgment and bargaining, combine to determine merger terms.

ACCOUNTING POLICIES IN MERGERS[7]

After merger terms have been agreed upon, the financial manager must be familiar with the principles for recording the financial results of the merger and for reflecting the initial effect on the earnings of the surviving firm. This section deals with these matters.

The financial statements of the survivor in a merger must follow the regulations and supervision of the Securities and Exchange Commission. The SEC's requirements follow the recommendations of professional accounting societies on combinations, but interpretations of actual situations require considerable financial and economic analysis.

Both the SEC and the *Accounting Research Bulletin No. 48* make a distinction between two forms of mergers, "purchase" and "pooling of interests." Three main tests must be met to establish that a "pooling of interests" has occurred:

1. The net worth of the two firms must be roughly the same size at the time of combination.
2. The relative asset sizes of the two firms must be approximately equal.
3. Both managements must continue to carry on important functions in the resulting firm.

In a purchase, an important part of one or more of the ownership interests is absorbed, and the other tests of pooling of interests are not met.

In practice it is difficult to distinguish between purchase and merger, especially when combinations show characteristics of each. However, the SEC spends long hours in conferences with representatives of registrants discussing the financial treatment of combinations.

Another aspect of the distinction between purchase and pooling of interests relates to the creation of goodwill. In a purchase, the excess (or deficit) over the book value of net worth purchased is set up as goodwill, and capital surplus is increased (or decreased) accordingly. In a pooling of interests, any premium over book value is charged against capital surplus. As a consequence, the combined total assets after a pooling represents a simple sum of the asset contributions of the constituent companies.

[7] The material in this section is rather technical and is generally covered in accounting courses. The section may be omitted without loss of continuity.

If the merger is handled as a purchase, the acquired firm is treated as an investment, just as would the acquisition of any other capital asset. The goodwill, or difference between the purchase price and the acquired net worth, is considered to be "depreciable." Goodwill must therefore be written off against earnings over some "reasonable" period, just as any other depreciable asset must be written off. (However, goodwill written off is not deductible for tax purposes.) Therefore, if a merger is treated as a purchase, reported profits will be lower than if it is handled as a pooling of interests. This is the reason that most firms prefer pooling of interest to purchase, and it is also the reason for the SEC's interest in the accounting method followed.

These general statements may be made more meaningful by concrete illustrations of first a purchase and then a pooling of interests.

Financial Treatment of a Purchase

The financial treatment of a purchase may best be explained by use of a hypothetical example. The Mammoth Company has just purchased the Petty Company under an arrangement known as a *purchase*. The facts are as given in Table 21–1, which also shows the financial treatment. The illustration conforms to the general nature of a purchase. Measured by total assets, the Mammoth Company is 20 times as large as Petty, while its total earnings are 15 times as large. Assume that the terms of the purchase will be one share of Mammoth for two shares of Petty, based on the prevailing market value of their shares of common stock. Thus in terms of Mammoth's stock, Mammoth is giving to Petty's stockholders $30 of market value and $7 of book value for each share of Petty stock. Petty's market value is $30 a share and its book value is $3 a share. The total market value of Mammoth paid for Petty is $60,000. The goodwill involved may be calculated as follows:

Value given by Mammoth	$60,000
Net worth of Petty purchased	6,000
Goodwill	$54,000

The $54,000 goodwill represents a debit in the Adjustments column and is carried to the *pro forma* balance sheet. The *pro forma* balance sheet is obtained by simply adding the balance sheets of the constituent companies.

The other adjustments to complete the entry are described below.

Common stock, Petty	$ 1,000	
Retained earnings, Petty	5,000	
Goodwill	54,000	
Common stock, Mammoth		$ 4,000
Capital surplus, Mammoth		56,000

A total value of $60,000 has been given by Mammoth. This amount represents a payment of $1,000 for the common stock of Petty, $5,000 for the retained earnings, and $54,000 goodwill. The corresponding credit is the 1,000 shares of Mammoth given in the transaction at their par value of $4 a share, resulting in a credit of $4,000. Capital surplus

TABLE 21–1 FINANCIAL TREATMENT OF A PURCHASE

	Mammoth Company	Petty Company	ADJUSTMENTS Debit	ADJUSTMENTS Credit	*Pro Forma* Balance Sheet
Assets					
Current	$ 80,000	$ 4,000			$ 84,000
Other assets	20,000	2,000			22,000
Net fixed assets	100,000	4,000			104,000
Intangible assets			$54,000		54,000
Total assets	$200,000	$10,000			$264,000
Liabilities and net worth					
Current liabilities	$ 40,000	$ 4,000			$ 44,000
Long-term debt	20,000				20,000
Common stock	40,000	1,000	1,000	$ 4,000	44,000
Capital surplus	20,000			56,000	76,000
Retained earnings	80,000	5,000	5,000		80,000
Total	$200,000	$10,000			$264,000

Explanation	Mammoth	Petty
Par value per share common stock	$4	$0.50
Number of shares outstanding	10,000	2,000
Book value per share	$14	$3
Total earnings	$30,000	$2,000
Earnings per share	$3	$1
Price/earnings ratio	20×	30×
Market value per share	$60	$30

of Mammoth is increased by $56,000. When these adjustments are carried through to the *pro forma* balance sheet, total assets are increased from the combined total of $210,000 by the $54,000 increase in goodwill; the result is new total assets of $264,000. Total tangible assets, however, still remain $210,000.

The effects on earnings per share for stockholders in each company are now shown.

Total earnings	\$32,000
Total shares	11,000
Earnings per share	\$2.91
For Petty Shareholders	
New earnings per share[8]	\$1.46
Before-purchase earnings per share	\$1.00
Accretion per share	\$0.46
For Mammoth Shareholders	
Before-purchase earnings per share	\$3.00
New earnings per share	2.91
Dilution per share	\$0.09

Total earnings represent the combined earnings of Mammoth and of Petty. The total shares are 11,000, because Mammoth has given one share of stock for every two shares of Petty previously outstanding. The new earnings per share are therefore \$2.91. The calculation of earnings accretion or dilution proceeds on the same principles as the calculations set forth earlier in the chapter. The results require two important comments, however.

It will be noted that although the earnings accretion per share for Petty is \$0.46, the earnings dilution per share for Mammoth is relatively small, only 9 cents per share. The explanation is that the size of Mammoth is large in relation to that of Petty. This example also illustrates a general principle—when a large company acquires a small one, it can afford to pay a high multiple of earnings per share of the smaller company. In the present example, the price/earnings ratio of Petty is 30, whereas the price/earnings ratio of Mammoth is 20. If the acquiring company is large relative to the acquired firm, it can pay a substantial premium and yet suffer only small dilution in its earnings per share.

It is, however, unrealistic to assume that the same earnings on total assets will result after the merger. After all, the purpose of the merger is to achieve something that the two companies could not have achieved alone. When in late 1953, Philip Morris & Company purchased Benson & Hedges, maker of Parliament, a leading filter-tip brand, it was buying the ability and experience of Benson & Hedges. By means of this merger, Philip Morris & Company was able to make an entry into the rapidly growing filter-cigarette business more quickly than it could otherwise have done. The combined earnings per share were likely to have been higher.

[8] Petty shareholders, after the one for two exchange, have only one half as many shares as before the merger. Therefore their earnings per *old* share are \$2.91 ÷ 2 = \$1.46. The example does not reflect the write-off of goodwill.

In the previous illustration, it will be noted that the earnings rate on the tangible assets of Mammoth is 15 percent and on the total assets of Petty is 20 percent. Let us now assume that the return on total tangible assets of the combined companies rises to 20 percent. With the same total shares of 11,000 outstanding, the new earnings per share will be $3.82. Thus there will be accretion of $2.82 for the Petty shareholders, a rise of almost three dollars per share. Here, however, there will be an accretion of 82 cents for the Mammoth shareholders as well.

Another general principle is illustrated. If the purchase of a small company adds to the earnings of the consolidated enterprise, earnings per share may increase for both participants in the merger. Even if the merger results in an initial dilution in earnings per share of the larger company, the merger may still be advantageous. The initial dilution in the earnings per share may be regarded as an investment. The investment will have a payoff at some future date in terms of increased earnings per share of the consolidated company.

Treatment of Goodwill

In a purchase, goodwill is likely to arise; since goodwill represents an intangible asset, its treatment is subject to the exercise of judgment. It will therefore be useful to set out a few generalizations on good practice with respect to the treatment of goodwill.

1. When goodwill is purchased, it should not be charged to surplus immediately on acquisition. Preferably, goodwill should be written off against income and should go through the income statement. Since goodwill is to be written off against income, it would not be appropriate to write it off entirely on acquisition, because an immediate write-off would be of such magnitude that distortion of earnings for that year would result.

2. The general view is not to write off purchased goodwill by charges to capital surplus. Purchased goodwill is supposed to represent, and to be reflected in, a future rise of income. It should be written off against income rather than against capital surplus. If goodwill is set up and capital surplus is created where no actual goodwill exists, it would be appropriate to write off such goodwill; such writing off, however, is more in the nature of correcting an error.[9]

3. When goodwill is purchased, an estimate should be made of its period of life. Annual charges, based on the estimated life of the goodwill, should then be made against income, to amortize the goodwill over the estimated period of the usefulness of the goodwill purchased.

[9] W. W. Werntz, "Intangibles in Business Combinations," *Journal of Accountancy,* CIII (May 1957), 47–48.

4. If the life of intangibles does not appear to be limited, no systematic write-off is required. However, a conservative policy may justify a systematic write-off in amounts that will not distort income.

When goodwill is purchased, it should be treated as the purchase of any other valid asset. It should be written off to the extent that the value represented by any part of goodwill has a limited life, as is likely to be the situation. In a free enterprise economy, the existence of high profits represented by superior earning power attracts additional resources into that line of business. The growth of capacity and the increase in competition are likely to erode the superior earning power over time.

Financial Treatment of Pooling of Interests

When a business combination is a *pooling of interests* rather than a purchase, the accounting treatment is simply to combine the balance sheets of the two companies. Goodwill will not ordinarily arise in the consolidation.

The financial treatment may be indicated by another example, which reflects the facts as they are set forth in Table 21–2. In order to focus on the critical issues, the balance sheets are identical in every respect. However, a difference in the amount and rate of profit (after interest) of the two companies is indicated.

Book value per share is $24. The amount of profit after interest and taxes is $40,000 for company A and $20,000 for company B. Earnings per share are therefore $8 and $4, respectively. The price/earnings ratio is 15 for A and 10 for B, so that the market price of stock for A is $120 and for B $40. The working capital per share is $10 in each instance. The dividends per share are $4 for A and $2 for B.

For the example, assume that the terms of the merger would reflect either earnings or market price per share. If the terms of merger are based on earnings, 15,000 shares of stock will be outstanding. Total earnings are $60,000. The number of shares of stock in the new company AB is 15,000; hence, earnings per share in the company will be $4. As the owners of company A receive two shares, they are receiving the equivalent of $8 per share of stock that they originally held. Stockholders of both A and B have experienced neither earnings dilution nor earnings accretion.

When the terms of exchange are based on market price per share, the terms of exchange are 3 to 1. The number of shares of stock outstanding increases to 20,000, so that earnings per share become $3. The stockholders in company A now each receive three shares of stock with earnings per share of $3. Nine dollars of earnings per original share represents

TABLE 21–2 FINANCIAL TREATMENT OF POOLING OF INTEREST

	A	B	Adjustments or Ratios		NEW FIRM AB IF EXCHANGE BASIS IS 2/1	3/1
Current assets	$100,000	$100,000			$200,000	$200,000
Fixed assets	100,000	100,000			200,000	200,000
Total assets	$200,000	$200,000			$400,000	$400,000
Current liabilities	$ 50,000	$ 50,000			$100,000	$100,000
Long-term debt	30,000	30,000			60,000	60,000
Total debt	80,000	80,000			160,000	160,000
Common stock, par value $10	50,000	50,000		$ 50,000* 100,000†	150,000	200,000
Capital surplus	60,000	60,000	$ 50,000* 100,000†		70,000	20,000
Earned surplus	10,000	10,000			20,000	20,000
Total claims on assets	$200,000	$200,000			$400,000	$400,000
Number of shares of stock	5,000	5,000			15,000	20,000
Book value	$ 24.00	$ 24.00	1.0			
Amount of profit after interest and taxes	$ 40,000	$ 20,000			$ 60,000	$ 60,000
Earnings per share	$8	$4	2.0		4.0	3.0
Price/earnings ratio	15	10				
Market price of stock	$120	$40	3.0			
Working capital per share	$10	$10	1.0			
Dividends per share	$4	$2	2.0			
Exchange ratio No. 1—earnings basis	2/1	1/1	2/1			
Equivalent earnings per share	$8	$4				
Exchange ratio No. 2—price basis	3/1	1/1				
Equivalent earnings per share	$9	$3				

* = 2/1 ratio basis. † = 3/1 ratio basis.

an accretion of $1 for the stockholders of company A. The earnings per share of $3 for the stockholders of company B represents dilution of $1 a share.

The general principle is that when terms of merger are based on the market price per share and the price/earnings ratios of the two companies are different, earnings accretion and dilution will occur. The company with a higher price/earnings ratio will attain earnings accretion; the company with the lower price/earnings ratio will suffer earnings dilution. If the sizes of the companies are greatly different, the effect on the larger company will be relatively small, whether in earnings dilution or in earnings accretion. The effect on the smaller company will be large.

HOLDING COMPANIES

In 1889, New Jersey became the first state to pass a general incorporation law permitting corporations to be formed for the sole purpose of owning the stocks of other companies. This law was the origin of the holding company. The Sherman Act of 1890, which prohibits combinations or collusion in restraint of trade, gave an impetus to holding company operations as well as to outright mergers and complete amalgamations, because companies could do as one company what they were forbidden to do, by the terms of the act, as separate companies.

Many of the advantages and disadvantages of holding companies are no more than the advantages and disadvantages of large-scale operations already discussed in connection with mergers and consolidations. Whether a company is organized on a divisional basis or with the divisions kept as separate companies does not affect the basic reasons for conducting a large-scale multiproduct, multiplant operation. However, the holding company form of large-scale operations has different advantages and disadvantages from those of completely integrated divisionalized operations.

Advantages

CONTROL WITH FRACTIONAL OWNERSHIP. Through a holding company operation a firm may buy 5, 10, or 50 percent of the stock of another corporation. Such fractional ownership may be sufficient to give the acquiring company effective working control or substantial influence over the operations of the company in which stock ownership has taken place. An article in the *New York Times* of November 16, 1958, makes this point clearly.

> Working control is often considered to entail more than 25 percent of the common stock, but it can be as low as 10 percent if the stock is widely distributed. One financier says that the attitude of management is more important than the number of shares owned, adding that "if they think you can control the company, then you do." In addition, control on a very slim margin can be held through friendship with large stockholders outside the holding company group.

Sometimes holding company operations represent the initial stages of the transformation of an operating company into an investment company, particularly when the operating company is in a declining industry. When the sales of an industry begin to fall off permanently and the firm begins to liquidate its operating assets, it may use these liquid funds to invest in industries having a more favorable growth potential. An illustration of this is provided by the same *New York Times* article.

> Former investment banker Gordon W. Wattles, who holds many corporate directorships, is the architect of the pyramid built on Century Investors and Webster Investors. The former was once an aviation investment concern, while the latter began as a cigar maker.

ISOLATION OF RISKS. Because the various operating companies in a holding company system are separate legal entities, the obligations of any one unit are separate from the obligations of the other units. Catastrophic losses incurred by one unit of the holding company system are therefore not transmitted as claims on the assets of the other units.

Although this is the customary generalization of the nature of a holding company system, it is not completely valid. In extending credit to one of the units of a holding company system, an astute financial manager or loan officer will look through the holding company veil and require a guarantee or a claim on the assets of all the elements in a complete holding company system. Therefore, to some degree, the assets in the various elements of a holding company are joined. The advantage remains to the extent that unanticipated catastrophies that may occur to one unit in a holding company system will not be transmitted to the other units.

APPROVAL NOT REQUIRED. If a holding company group is seeking to obtain effective working control of a number of companies, it may quietly purchase a portion of the stock of the companies in which it is interested. This is a completely informal operation, and the permission or approval of the stockholders of the acquired company or companies is not required. Thus the guiding personalities in a holding company operation are not dependent upon negotiations and approval of the other interest groups in order to obtain their objectives.

TENDER OFFERS. In a tender offer, one party, generally a corporation seeking a controlling interest in another corporation, asks the stockholders of the firm it is seeking to control to submit, or "tender," their shares in exchange for a specified price. The price is generally stated as so many dollars per share of acquired stock, although it can be stated in terms of shares of stock in the acquiring firm. The tender offer is a direct appeal to stockholders, so the tender need not be cleared with the management of the acquired firm. Tender offers have been used for a number of years, but the pace greatly accelerated after 1965.

If one firm wishes to gain control over another, the acquiring firm typically approaches the to-be-acquired firm's management and seeks its approval of the merger. If approval cannot be obtained, the company wishing to gain control can appeal directly to stockholders by means of the tender offer, unless the management of the to-be-acquired firm holds enough stock to retain control. If the potential acquiring firm has reason to believe that the to-be-acquired firm's management will not approve the merger, it may use a tender offer without ever informing the to-be-acquired firm's management of its intentions. In this situation, the potential acquirer will frequently buy the stock of the acquired firm in the name of a stockbroker ("street name") to conceal its intentions. Because of the frequency of tender offers and because of the views of some that (1) the recent merger trend is leading to "too much concentration" in the economy and (2) the feeling that tender offers are somehow "unfair" to the managements of firms acquired through this vehicle, Congressional investigations were conducted during 1967 with the idea of obtaining information that could be used to legislate controls over the use of tender offers. The controls most likely to be imposed are the following: (1) The acquiring firm must give 30 days' notice of its intentions to make the acquisition to both the management of the acquired firm and to the SEC. (2) When substantial blocks are purchased through tender offers (or through open market purchases—that is, on the stock exchange), the beneficial owner of the stock must be disclosed together with the name of the party putting up the money for the transaction.

The example of Tenneco's acquisition of Kern County Land Company illustrates many of these points. First, Kern was a relatively old, conservatively managed company whose assets consisted largely of oil properties and agricultural land together with some manufacturing subsidiaries. Many informed investors believed that Kern's assets had a potential long-run value in excess of its current market price. Occidental Petroleum, a relatively aggressive company, made an investigation of Kern's assets and decided to make a tender offer for the company. At that time, Kern's market price was about $60 a share, while the price Occidental decided to offer Kern's stockholders was $83.50 a share. According to Kern's management, Occidental's management got in touch with the former over a weekend and informed Kern that the tender offer would be made the following Monday.

Kern's management resisted the offer. Because the published statements of Occidental indicated that it felt Kern's undervalued position was partly the result of an unaggressive management, Kern's management could anticipate being replaced in the event that Occidental effected the takeover. One could anticipate that Kern's management would resist the takeover, and it did indeed. Kern's president wrote a letter to stockholders condemning the merger and published the letter as an advertisement in the *Wall Street Journal.* His position was that Kern's stock was indeed valuable, but it was worth more than had been offered by Occidental Petroleum.

How would Kern County's stockholders react to this exchange? In the first place, the stock had been selling at about $60 a share, and now they were offered $83.50 a share. One might anticipate that stockholders would accept the tender unless Kern's management could do something to keep the price above $83.50. What Kern did was to obtain "marriage proposals" from a number of other companies. Kern's management reported to the newspapers—while Occidental's tender offer was still outstanding—that it had received a substantial number of proposals calling for the purchase of Kern's stock at a price substantially in excess of $83.50.

The offer Kern's management finally accepted—and presumably the one giving Kern's stockholders the highest price—was from Tenneco Corporation. Tenneco offered one share of a new $5.50 convertible preferred stock for each share of Kern's stock. The market value of this convertible preferred was estimated at the time of Tenneco's offer to be worth about $105 a share. Further, Kern's stockholders would not have to pay capital gains tax on this stock at the time of the exchange. (Had they acepted Occidental's offer, the difference between $83.50 and the cost of their stock would be taxable income to Kern's stockholders.) According to newspaper reports, Tenneco planned to keep Kern's existing management after the merger was completed.

The Kern-Tenneco merger was completed in the fall of 1967. Tenneco owns the Kern stock and is thus a holding company, with Kern being one of its operating subsidiaries.

Disadvantages

PARTIAL MULTIPLE TAXATION. Provided the holding company owns at least 80 percent of a subsidiary's voting stock, the Internal Revenue regulations permit the filing of consolidated returns, in which case dividends received by the parent are not taxed. However, if less than 80 percent of the stock is owned, returns may not be consolidated, but 85 percent of the dividends received by the holding company may be deducted. With a tax rate of 48 percent, this means that the effective tax on intercorporate dividends is 7.2 percent. This partial double taxation somewhat offsets the benefits of holding company control with limited ownership, but whether the penalty of 7.2 percent of dividends received is sufficient to offset other possible advantages is a matter that must be decided in individual siutations.

RISKS OF EXCESSIVE PYRAMIDING. While pyramiding magnifies profits if the operations are successful, as was seen in the trading-on-the-equity analysis, it also magnifies losses. The greater the degree of pyramiding, the greater the degree of risk involved for any degree of fluctuations in sales or earnings of the company. This is one of the potential disadvantages of pyramiding operations through holding companies.

EASE OF ENFORCED DISSOLUTION. In the case of a holding company operation that falls into disfavor with the U.S. Department of Justice, it is relatively easy to require dissolution of the relation by disposition of stock ownership. A clear case in point is the recent requirement that du Pont dispose of its 23 percent stock interest in General Motors Corporation. The acquisition took place in the early 1920s. Because there was no fusion between the corporations, there were no difficulties, from an operating standpoint, in requiring the separation of the two companies. However, if complete amalgamation had taken place, it would have been much more difficult to break up the company after a lapse of so many years.

Leverage in Holding Companies

The problem of excessive leverage is worthy of further note, for the degree of leveraging in certain past instances has been truly staggering. For example, in the 1920s, Samuel Insull and his group controlled electric utility operating companies at the bottom of a holding company pyramid by a 1/20 of 1 percent investment. As a ratio, this represents 1/2000. In other words, $1 of capital at the top holding company level controlled $2,000 of assets at the operating level. A similar situation existed in the railroad field. It has been stated that Robert R. Young, with an investment of $254,000, obtained control of the Allegheny system consisting of total operating assets of $3 billion.

The nature of leverage in a holding company system and its advantages and disadvantages are illustrated by the hypothetical example developed in Table 21–3. As in the previous examples, although this

TABLE 21–3 LEVERAGE IN A HOLDING COMPANY SYSTEM

	HOLDING COMPANY 2		
Common stock B of holding company 1	5,000	Debt	2,000
		Preferred stock	1,000
		Common stock: class A*	1,000
		Common stock: class B	1,000
	HOLDING COMPANY 1		
Common stock B of Operating Company	100,000	Debt	50,000
		Preferred stock	10,000
		Common stock: class A*	30,000
		Common stock: class B	10,000
	OPERATING COMPANY		
Total assets	2,000,000	Debt	1,000,000
		Preferred stock	150,000
		Common stock: class A*	650,000
		Common stock: class B	200,000

* Common stock A is nonvoting.

is a hypothetical case, it illustrates actual situations. One thousand dollars of class B common stock of holding company 2 controls $2 million of assets at the operating company level. Further leverage could, of course, have been postulated in this situation by setting up a third company to own the common stock B of holding company 2.

Table 21–4 shows the results of holding company leverage on gains and losses at the top level. In the first column it is assumed that the operating company earns 12 percent before taxes on its $2 million of assets, while in the second column it is assumed that the return on assets is 8 percent. The operating and holding companies are the same ones described in Table 21–3.

TABLE 21–4 RESULTS OF HOLDING COMPANY LEVERAGE ON GAINS AND LOSSES

Assume that each company pays: 4% on debt
5% on preferred stock
8% on common stock A

	EARNINGS BEFORE TAXES	
Operating Company	12%	8%
Amount earned	$240,000	$160,000
Less		
Tax*	100,000	60,000
Available to meet fixed charges	140,000	100,000
Debt interest	40,000	40,000
Preferred stock	7,500	7,500
Common stock A	52,000	52,000
Total charges	99,500	99,500
Available to common B	40,500	500
Dividends to common B	40,000	500
Holding Company 1		
Amount earned	20,000	250
Less		
Tax (0.5 × 0.15 × $18,000)*	1,350	0
Available to meet fixed charges	18,650	250
Debt interest	2,000	2,000
Preferred stock	500	500
Common stock A	2,400	2,400
Total charges	4,900	4,900
Available to common B	13,750	loss
Dividends to common B	10,000	
Holding Company 2		
Amount earned	5,000	
Less		
Taxes (0.5 × 0.15 × $4,920)*	369	
Available to meet fixed charges	4,631	
Debt interest	80	
Preferred stock	50	
Common stock A	80	
Total	210	
Available to common B	4,421	
Percent return on common B	442%	

* Tax computed on earnings less interest charges at a 50% tax rate. Since earnings are entirely in the form of inter-corporate dividends, only 15% of them are taxable.

A return of 12 percent on the operating assets of $2 million represents a total profit of $240,000. The debt interest of $40,000 is deducted from this amount, and the 50 percent tax rate applies to the remainder. The amount available to common stock after payment of debt interest, preferred stock dividends, and an 8 percent return to the nonvoting common stock A is $40,500. Assuming a $40,000 dividend payout, the amount earned on the assets of holding company 1 is $20,000. If the same kind of analysis was followed through, the amount available to the common stock B in holding company 2 would be $4,421. This return is on an investment of $1,000, representing a return on the investment in common stock B of holding company 2 of about 440 percent. The power of leverage in a holding company system can indeed be great.

On the other hand, if a decline in revenues caused the pretax earnings to drop to 8 percent of the total assets of the operating company, the results would be disastrous. The amount earned under these circumstances is $160,000. After deducting the bond interest, the amount subject to tax is $120,000, resulting in a tax of $60,000. The after-tax-but-before-interest earnings are $100,000. The total prior charges are $99,500, leaving $500 available to common stock B. If all earnings are paid out in dividends to common stock B, the earnings of holding company 1 are $250. This is not enough to meet the debt interest. The holding company system would be forced to default on the debt interest of holding company 1 and, of course, holding company 2.

This example illustrates the potentiality for tremendous gains in a holding company system. It also illustrates that a small decline in earnings on the assets of the operating companies would be disastrous.

SUMMARY

Growth is vital to the well-being of a firm, for without it a business cannot attract able management because it cannot give men recognition in promotions and challenging creative activity. Mergers have played an important part in the growth of firms, and since financial managers are required both to appraise the desirability of a prospective merger and to participate in evaluating the respective companies involved in the merger, the present chapter has been devoted to background materials on merger decisions.

One of the objectives of growth, whether by external acquisitions or by internal development, is large size for the purpose of achieving economies of scale. Economies of scale result from the following factors.

Research. Certain types of research can be performed best by large firms.

Top-management skills. Skilled executives are an extremely scarce commodity, and it is often economical to spread their talents over a relatively large enterprise.

Operating economies. For some types of production, the average cost per unit of output is lower when large-scale plants and distribution systems are used.

Risk reduction. Risk is reduced by diversification in large enterprises. Tax considerations add to the importance of this factor.

Market capitalization rates. Market capitalization rates are lower for larger firms.

While the size necessary to take advantage of these aspects of economies of scale may be attained by internal expansion, there are certain advantages to growth by merger.

Speed. Growth may be attained much more rapidly by merger than by internal expansion.

Cost. Frequently, the cost of expansion is lower if new facilities and talents are obtained by merger.

Financing. Sometimes it is possible to finance an acquisition when it is not possible to finance internal growth.

Risk. Risks may be reduced by acquiring a going concern rather than starting a new division.

Stabilizing effects. Certain economies may arise that result in stabilizing a particular industry. The railroad mergers in the late 1960s may be cited as an example.

Taxes. Taxes appear to have been a factor in about one-third of all mergers.

Competitive advantages. A merger of two firms may combine their strengths or balance their strengths and their weaknesses.

Market control. Two firms may combine to coordinate their price and output decisions. The vigor of competitive processes and antitrust actions make the accomplishment of this result highly unlikely in recent years.

Terms of Mergers

The most important term that must be negotiated in a merger arrangement is the price the acquiring firm will pay for the acquired business. Some of the factors that influence this decision are given below.

Earnings. Present earnings and expected future earnings after the merger, which are reflected in expectations about the effects of the merger on the surviving firm's *growth rate,* are perhaps the most important determinants of the price that will be paid for a firm that is being acquired.

Market prices. Current market prices are the second most important determinant of prices in mergers.

Book value. Depending on whether or not asset values are indicative of the approximate value of the merged firm, book values may exert an important influence on the terms of the merger.

Net current assets. Net current assets are an indication of the amount of liquidity being purchased in a merger, and this can be an important factor.

The factors listed above are all *quantitative;* qualitative, or nonmeasurable, factors are sometimes the overriding determinant of merger terms. Qualitative considerations may suggest that *synergistic,* or "two-plus-two-equals-five," effects may be present to a sufficient extent to warrant paying more for the acquired firm than the quantitative factors would suggest.

If the terms of merger reflect the respective earnings per share of the two companies, neither earnings dilution nor earnings accretion will result. If the exchange terms are based on the market price of the shares of the company and if the prevailing price/earnings ratios of the two companies differ, earnings accretion and dilution are likely to result. Any initial earnings dilution may be offset by the improved earnings of the combined operation. After a period, appreciation of earnings per share for all the constituent companies in the merger may be achieved.

Accounting Policies and Mergers

A merger may be treated as either a *purchase* or a *pooling of interests.* Generally, in a purchase, a larger firm takes over a smaller one and assumes all management control. The amount actually paid for the smaller firm is reflected in the acquiring firm's balance sheet; if more was paid for the acquired firm than the book value of its assets, goodwill is reflected on the acquiring firm's financial statements. In a pooling of interests, the merged firms are generally of about the same size; both managements carry on important functions after the merger. The total assets of the surviving firm are equal to the sum of the assets of the two independent companies, so no goodwill is created.

Holding Companies

In mergers, one firm disappears. However, an alternative is for one firm to buy all or a majority of the common stock of another and to run the acquired firm as an operating subsidiary. When this occurs, the acquiring firm is said to be a *holding company.* A number of advantages arise when a holding company is used:

Control with fractional ownership. It may be possible to control the acquired firm with a smaller investment than would be necessary if a merger were to occur.

Isolation of risks. Each firm in a holding company is a separate legal entity, and the obligations of any one unit are separate from the obligations of the other units.

Approval not required. Stockholder approval is required before a merger can take place. This is not necessary in a holding company situation.

There are also some disadvantages to holding companies, some of which are:

Partial multiple taxation. If the holding company does not own 80 percent of the subsidiary's stock and does not file consolidated tax returns, it is subject to taxes on dividends received from the subsidiary.

Risks from excessive pyramiding. The leverage effects possible in holding companies can subject the holding company to a great deal of risk.

Ease of dissolution. The Antitrust Division of the U.S. Department of Justice can much more easily force the breakup of a holding company situation than it can the dissolution of two completely merged firms.

QUESTIONS

21–1 The number of mergers tends to fluctuate with business activity, rising when GNP rises and falling when GNP falls. Why does this relationship exist?

21–2 A large firm has certain advantages over a smaller one. What are some of the *financial* advantages of large size?

21–3 What are some of the potential benefits that can be expected by a firm that merges with a company in a different industry?

21–4 Mergers can often be important to rapidly growing firms. How?

21–5 Distinguish between a holding company and an operating company. Give an example of each.

21–6 Which appears to be more risky, the use of debt in the holding company's capital structure or the use of debt in the operating company? Why?

21–7 Is the public interest served by an increase in merger activity? Give arguments both pro and con.

21–8 Would the book value of a company's assets be considered the absolute minimum price to be paid for a firm? Why? Is there any value that would qualify as an absolute minimum?

21–9 Discuss the situation where one firm, California Motors, for example, calls off merger negotiations with another, American Space Labs, because the latter's stock price is overvalued. What assumption concerning dilution is implicit in the above situation?

21–10 Thus far, many methods by which a company can raise additional capital have been discussed. Can a merger or a purchase be considered a means of raising additional equity capital? Explain.

21–11 A particularly difficult problem regarding business combinations has been whether to treat the new company as a purchase or as a pooling of interests.

a) What criteria can be set down to differentiate between these two forms of business combinations?

b) Would you as a stockholder in one of the firms prefer a purchase or a pooling arrangement? Why?

c) Which combination would you prefer if you were a high-ranking manager in one of the firms?

21–12 The question 21–11 discusses purchases and pooling arrangements. Why is it important to make a distinction between these two combination forms?

21–13 Are the negotiations for merger or purchase agreements more difficult if the firms are in different industries or in the same industry? if they are about the same size or quite different in size? Why?

21–14 How would the existence of long-term debt in a company's financial structure affect its valuation for merger purposes? Could the same be said for any debt account regardless of its maturity?

21–15 During 1964–1965, the Pure Oil Company was involved in merger negotiations with at least three other firms. The terms of these arrangements varied from a transfer of stock to a direct cash purchase of Pure Oil. Discuss the relative advantages to a corporation of paying for an acquisition in cash or in stock.

21–16 In late 1968 the SEC and the New York Stock Exchange each issued sets of rulings on disclosure of information which, in effect, required that firms disclose the fact that they have entered into merger discussions as soon as they start such discussions. Since the previous procedure had been to delay disclosure until it was evident that there was a reasonably good expectation the merger under discussion would actually go through (and not to bring the matter up at all if the merger died in the early stages), it can safely be predicted that, in a statistical sense, a larger percentage of perspective mergers will be "abandoned" in the future than in the past.

a) Why do you suppose the new rulings were put into effect?

b) Will the new rulings have any adverse effects? Why?

PROBLEMS

21–1 Given the following balance sheets:

H COMPANY
CONSOLIDATED BALANCE SHEET

Cash	$ 800	Borrowings	$ 600
Other current assets	600	Common stock	1,000
Net property	1,000	Surplus	800
Total assets	$2,400	Total claims on assets	$2,400

A COMPANY
BALANCE SHEET

Current assets	$200	Net worth	$400
Net property	200		
Total assets	$400	Total net worth	$400

a) The holding company, H, buys the operating company, A, with "free" cash of $400. Show the new consolidated balance sheet for H after the acquisition.

b) Instead of buying A, H buys operating company B with free cash of $600. The balance sheet of B follows:

B COMPANY
BALANCE SHEET

Current assets	$ 400	Borrowings	$ 400
Net property	600	Net worth	600
Total assets	$1,000	Total claims on assets	$1,000

Show the new consolidated balance sheet for H after acquisition of B.

c) What are the implications of your consolidated balance sheets for measuring the growth of firms resulting from acquisitions?

21–2 H Company is a holding company owning the entire common stock of Minor Company and Operating Company. The balance sheet as of December 31, 1969, for each subsidiary is identical with the following one.

BALANCE SHEET
December 31, 1969

Current assets	$3,000,000	Current liabilities	$ 500,000
Fixed assets, net	2,000,000	First mortgage bonds (4%)	1,000,000
		Preferred stock (5%)	1,000,000
		Common stock	2,000,000
		Surplus	500,000
Total assets	$5,000,000		$5,000,000

Each operating company earns $550,000 annually before taxes and before interest and preferred dividends. A 50 percent tax rate is assumed.

a) What is the annual rate of return on each company's net worth (common stock plus surplus)?

b) Construct a balance sheet for H Company based on the following assumptions: (1) The only asset of the holding company is the common stock of the two subsidiaries; this stock is carried at par (not book) value. (2) The holding company has $700,000 of 4 percent coupon debt and $1,300,000 of 6 percent preferred stock.

c) What is the rate of return on the book value of the holding company's common stock?

d) How could the rate of return in c be increased?

e) What investment is necessary to control the three companies under the assumptions of the initial conditions?

f) If ownership of 25 percent of the holding company's common stock ($2 million of common) could control all three firms, what percentage would this be of the total assets?

21–3 You are given the following data on two companies:

TERMS OF MERGER ANALYSIS

	Company A	*Company B*	*Adjustments or Ratio*	*Consolidated Statement*
Current assets	$120,000	$120,000		1. ______
Fixed assets	80,000	80,000		2. ______
Total assets	$200,000	$200,000		3. ______
Current liabilities	$ 60,000	$ 60,000		4. ______
Long-term debt	40,000	40,000		5. ______
Total debt,* 5%	$100,000	$100,000		6. ______
Common stock, par value $5	$ 50,000	$ 50,000	1. ______	7. ______
Capital surplus	40,000	40,000	2. ______	8. ______
Earned surplus	10,000	10,000	3. ______	9. ______
Total claims on assets	$200,000	$200,000		10. ______
			Ratios	
(1) Number of shares of stock	10,000	10,000		1. ______
(2) Book value per share	______	______	1. ______	2. ______
(3) Amount of profit before interest and taxes†	$ 65,000	$ 25,000		3. ______
(4) Earnings per share	______	______	2. ______	4. ______
(5) Price/earnings ratio	20	15		
(6) Market price of stock	______	______	3. ______	
(7) Working capital per share	______	______	4. ______	
(8) Dividends per share, 50% payout	______	______	5. ______	
(9) Exchange ratio	______	______	6. ______	(A/B)
(10) Equivalent earnings per old share	______	______		

* Average rate on interest-bearing and noninterest-bearing debt combined.
† Assume a 50 percent tax rate.

a) What in your judgment would be a reasonable basis for determining the terms at which shares in company A and in company B would be exchanged for shares in the new AB company? What exchange ratio would you recommend and why?

b) Use the market price of stock relation as the basis for the terms of exchange of stock in the old company for stock in the new company (2 shares of AB for 1 share of A, or ½ share of AB for 1 share of B). Then complete all calculations for filling in all the blank spaces, including the adjustments for making the consolidated statement. Treat this problem as a situation that the SEC and accountants would refer to as a pooling of interests.

21–4 The Alpha Company has just purchased the Beta Company under an arrangement known as a purchase. The purchase was made by stock in a settlement based exactly on the indicated market prices of the two firms. The data on the two companies are given below.

a) Fill in the blank spaces and complete the Adjustments and *Pro Forma* Balance Sheet columns, and show the journal entries for the stock purchase. Give an explanation for your entries.

b) Calculate earnings dilution or accretion for both companies on the assumption that total earnings are unchanged.

c) Calculate the earnings dilution or accretion on the assumption that the return on combined tangible assets rises to 20 percent after interest and taxes.

d) Comment on your findings.

	Alpha	*Beta*	*Adjust-ments*	Pro Forma *Balance Sheet*
Current assets	$ 900,000	$14,000		
Other assets	300,000	10,000		
Fixed assets	800,000	16,000		
Intangibles				
Total assets	$2,000,000	$40,000		
Current liabilities	$ 400,000	$16,000		
Long-term debt	300,000			
Common stock	400,000	4,000		
Capital surplus	300,000			
Retained earnings	600,000	20,000		
Total claims	$2,000,000	$40,000		
Par value	$ 8.00	$ 1.00		
Number of shares	______	______		
Total earnings available to common	$ 250,000	$16,000		
Book value	______	______		
Earnings per share	______	______		
Price/earnings ratio	10 times	25 times		
Market value per share	______	______		

21–5 Every merger agreement is subject to negotiation between the companies involved. One significant indicator of the compensation received by the acquired company is the respective market prices of the companies' stocks relative to the merger items. Some actual merger data are given below.

Calculate the percent premium or discount received by the acquired company, using market prices as the criteria. Compare the results of your calculations based on the stock prices of the two previous quarters with that of your results based on the prices immediately preceding the merger. Which is the proper measure of the actual discount or premium received: the one indicated by the earlier stock prices or the one indicated by the stock prices immediately preceding the merger? Explain.

	Company	*Date*	*Terms*	*Market Price Two Quarters before Merger* (*A*)	(*B*)	*Market Price Preceding Merger* (*A*)	(*B*)
1	(A) Celanese Corp. (B) Champlain Oil	9/21/64	2 shares of Celanese for every 3 shares of Champlain	62	34	67	42
2	(A) Cities Service Co. (B) Tennessee Corp.	6/14/63	0.9 shares (2.25 pref.) for each Tenn. Corp. share (common)	65	48	61	55
3	(A) Ford Motor Co. (B) Philco Corp.	12/11/61	1 share of Ford for every 4½ shares of Philco	81	22	113	25
4	(A) General Telephone (B) Sylvania Elec.	3/5/59	Share for share basis	52	46	69	69

Selected References

Alberts, William W., and Joel E. Segall (eds.), *The Corporate Merger.* (Chicago: University of Chicago Press, 1966.)

Ansoff, H. Igor, and J. Fred Weston, "Merger Objectives and Organization Structure," *Quarterly Review of Economics and Business,* II (August 1962), 49–58.

Austin, Douglas V., "A Defense of the Corporation Pirate," *Business Horizons* (Winter 1964), 51–58.

Barr, Andrew, "Accounting Aspects of Business Combinations," *Accounting Review,* XXXIV (April 1959), 175–181.

Bock, Betty, *Mergers and Markets.* (New York: National Industrial Conference Board, Inc., 1962, 1964.)

Bosland, Chelcie C., "Stock Valuation in Recent Mergers: A Study of Appraisal Factors," *Trusts and Estates* (June, July, and August 1955).

Butters, J. Keith, John Lintner, and William L. Cary, *Effects of Taxation: Corporate Mergers.* (Boston: Division of Research, Graduate School of Business Administration, Harvard University, 1951.)

Crane, Roger R., "The Place of Scientific Techniques in Mergers and Acquisitions," *Controller,* XXIX (July 1961).

Drayton, Clarence I., Jr., Craig Emerson, and John D. Griswold, *Mergers and Acquisitions: Planning and Action.* (New York: Financial Executives Research Foundation, Inc., 1963.)

Folz, David F., and J. Fred Weston, "Looking Ahead in Evaluating Proposed Mergers," *NAA Bulletin,* XLIII (April 1962), 17–27.

Gort, Michael, *Diversification and Integration in American Industry.* (Princeton, N.J.: Princeton University Press, 1962.)

Jaenicke, Henry R., "Management's Choice to Purchase or Pool," *Accounting Review,* XXXVII (October 1962), 758–765.

Kaplan, A. D. H., "The Current Merger Movement Analyzed," *Harvard Business Review,* XXXIII (May-June 1955), 91–98.

Kelly, Eamon M., *The Profitability of Growth Through Mergers.* (Pa.: Pennsylvania State University, 1967.)

Kinard, Hargett Y., "Financing Mergers and Acquisitions," *Financial Executive,* XXXI (August 1963), 13–16.

McCarthy, George D., "Premeditated Merger," *Harvard Business Review,* XXXIX (January-February 1961.)

Mace, Myles L., and George G. Montgomery, Jr., *Management Problems of Corporate Acquisitions.* (Boston: Division of Research, Graduate School of Business Administration, Harvard University, 1962.)

Reilly, Frank K., "What Determines the Ratio of Exchange in Corporate Mergers?" *Financial Analysts Journal,* XVIII (November-December 1962), 47–50.

Sapienza, S. R. "Business Combinations—A Case Study," *The Accounting Review,* XXXIX (January 1963), 91–101.

———, "Pooling Theory and Practice in Business Combinations," *Accounting Review* (April 1962).

Silberman, Irwin H., "A Note on Merger Valuation," *Journal of Finance,* XXIII (June 1968), 528–534.

Smalter, Donald J. and Roderic C. Lancey, "P/E Analysis in Acquisition Strategy," *Harvard Business Review,* XLIV (November-December 1966), 85–95.

Tincher, William R., "Yardsticks for Evaluating Corporate Acquisitions," *Management Review* (October 1964), 33–45.

Weston, J. Fred, "Reply," *Journal of Finance,* XXIII (June 1968), 535–536.

———, *The Role of Mergers in the Growth of Large Firms.* (Berkeley: University of California Press, 1953.)

Wise, T. A. "How McDonnell Won Douglas," *Fortune* (March 1967).

22

Failure, Reorganization, and Liquidation

Thus far the text has dealt with issues associated mainly with the growing, successful enterprise. Not all businesses are so fortunate, however, so we must examine financial difficulties, their causes, and their possible remedies. This material is significant for the financial manager of successful, as well as potentially unsuccessful, firms. The successful firm's financial manager must know his firm's rights and remedies as a creditor and must participate effectively in efforts to collect from financially distressed debtors. Conversely, the financial manager must know how to handle his own firm's affairs if financial difficulties arise. Often such understanding may mean the difference between loss of ownership of the firm and rehabilitation of the operation as a going enterprise.

THE FIRM'S LIFE CYCLE

The life cycle of an industry or firm is often depicted as an S-shaped curve, as shown in Figure 22–1. The figure repre-

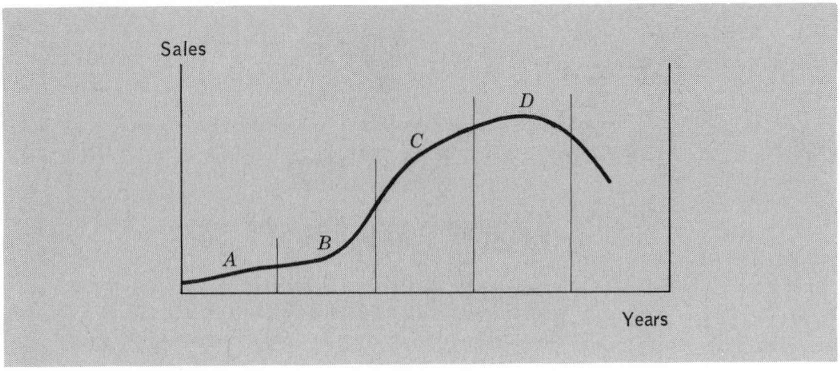

Figure 22–1 Hypothetical Life Cycle of a Firm

sents a hypothetical life cycle of a representative firm. Although it is an oversimplification, it provides a useful framework for analysis. The hypothesis represented by the four-stage life-cycle concept is based on a number of assumptions. It assumes competent management in the growth periods and insufficient management foresight prior to the decline phase. Obviously, one of management's primary goals is to prolong phase *B* and completely forestall phase *D*, and a great many firms are apparently successful in these endeavors.

If an industry experiences the period of decline, financial readjustment problems will arise, affecting most firms in the industry. In addition, specific events may result in business failure—for example, a prolonged strike, a fire not adequately covered by insurance, or a bad decision on a new product.

FAILURE

Although failure can be defined in several ways, according to various applications of the term, it does not necessarily result in the collapse and dissolution of a firm.

Economic Failure

Failure in an economic sense usually signifies that a firm's revenues do not cover costs. Another formulation states that a firm has failed if the rate of earnings on the historical cost of investment is less than the firm's cost of capital. According to still another possible definition, a firm can be considered a failure if its actual returns have fallen below expected returns. There is no consensus on the definition of failure in an economic sense.[1]

Financial Failure

Failure from a financial standpoint is a less ambiguous term than the concept of economic failure. Financial failure signifies insolvency; even here, however, two aspects are generally recognized.

1. A firm can be considered a failure if it is insolvent in the sense that it cannot meet its current obligations as they come due, even though its total assets may exceed its total liabilities.
2. A firm is a failure or is bankrupt if its total liabilities exceed a fair valuation of its total assets. The "real" net worth of the firm is negative.

When we use the word "failure" hereafter, we include both of these aspects.

CAUSES OF FAILURE

According to data compiled regularly by Dun & Bradstreet, Inc., the yearly rate of failure per 10,000 firms was about 50 immediately prior to World War II.[2] In the years immediately following World War II, the failure rate was low, about 20 to 30 per 10,000 firms, because of the vigorous rate of business activity in making up the war postponements of production. In recent years the failure rate has risen to 60 per 10,000 firms, reflecting the resumption of stronger competition between firms.

The liability per failure averaged about $20,000 prewar but has risen to nearly $100,000 in recent years. The Dun & Bradstreet compilations

[1] In still another economic sense, a firm that goes bankrupt may not be a failure at all. To illustrate, suppose someone starts a business to *attempt* to develop a product that, if successful, will produce very large returns and, if unsuccessful, will result in a total loss of invested funds. The entrepreneur *knows* that he is taking a risk but thinks the potential gains are worth the chance of loss. If the loss in fact results, then it was expected (in a probability sense).

[2] *The Failure Record through 1965* (New York: Dun & Bradstreet, Inc. 1966), p. 3.

also indicate that about 60 percent of these firms fail during the first five years of their lives, and another 25 percent fail during the second five years.[3]

Different studies assign the causes of failure to different factors. The Dun & Bradstreet compilations assign these causes as follows:

CAUSE OF FAILURE	PERCENTAGE OF TOTAL
Neglect	4
Fraud	2
Disaster	1
Management incompetence	91
Unknown	2

A number of other studies of failures may be generalized into the following groupings:[4]

CAUSE OF FAILURE	PERCENTAGE OF TOTAL
Unfavorable industry trends (secular)	20
Management incompetence	60
Catastrophes	10

Both classifications presumably include the effects of recessions and place the resulting failures in the category of managerial incompetence. This method is logical—managements should be prepared to operate in environments in which recessions take place and should frame their policies to cope with downturns as well as to benefit from business upswings.

A number of financial remedies are available to management when it becomes aware of the imminence or occurrence of insolvency.

1. Extension
2. Composition
3. Reorganization

[3] *The Failure Record,* p. 12.

[4] See studies referred to in A. S. Dewing, *The Financial Policy of Corporations* (New York: Ronald, 1953), Vol. II, Chap. 28.

4. Liquidation
   a) Assignment
   b) Bankruptcy

These remedies are described in the remainder of this chapter in the order listed.

EXTENSION AND COMPOSITION

Extension and composition are discussed together because they both represent voluntary concessions by creditors. *Extension postpones* the date of required payment of past-due obligations. *Composition* voluntarily *reduces* the creditor's claim on the debtor. Both have the purpose of keeping the debtor in business and of avoiding court costs. Although creditors absorb a temporary loss, the recovery is often greater than if one of the formal procedures had been followed, and the hope is that a stable customer will emerge.

Procedure

A meeting of the debtor and his creditors is held. The creditors appoint a committee consisting of four or five of the largest creditors and one or two of the smaller ones. These meetings are typically arranged and conducted by adjustment bureaus associated with local credit managers' associations or by trade associations. The factors are presented in a general statement to the adjustment bureaus.

After a meeting is held at the adjustment bureau and it is judged that the case can be worked out, the bureau assigns investigators to make an exhaustive report. The bureau and the creditors' committee use the facts of the report to formulate a plan for adjustment of claims. Another meeting between the debtor and the creditors is then held in an attempt to work out an extension or a composition or a combination of the two. Subsequent meetings may be required to reach final agreements.

Necessary Conditions

At least three conditions are usually necessary to make an extension or composition feasible:

1. Debtor is a good moral risk
2. Debtor shows ability to make a recovery
3. General business conditions are favorable to recovery

Extension

An extension is preferred by creditors in that it provides for payment in full. The debtor buys current purchases on a cash basis and pays off his past balance over an extended time. In some cases, creditors may agree not only to extend time of payment but also to subordinate existing claims to new debts incurred in favor of vendors extending credit during the period of the extension. The creditors must have faith that the debtor will solve his problems. Because of the uncertainties involved, however, creditors will want to exercise controls over the debtor while waiting for their claims to be paid.

As examples of controls, the committee may insist that an assignment (turnover of assets to the creditors' committee) be executed, to be held in escrow in case of default. Or if the debtor is a corporation, the committee may require that stockholders transfer their stock certificates into an escrow until repayment as called for under the extension has been completed. The committee may also designate a representative to countersign all checks. Furthermore, the committee may obtain security in the form of notes, mortgage, or assignment of accounts receivable.

Composition

In a composition a pro rata cash settlement is made. Creditors receive from the debtor in cash a uniform percentage of the obligations. The cash received is taken as full settlement of the debt. The ratio may be 10 percent or higher. Bargaining will take place between the debtor and the creditors over the savings that result in avoiding certain costs associated with the bankruptcy: costs of administration, legal fees, investigators, and so on. In addition to financial considerations, the debtor gains in that the stigma of bankruptcy is avoided, and thus he may be induced to part with most of the savings that result from avoiding bankruptcy.

Combination Settlement

Often the bargaining process will result in a compromise involving both an extension and a composition. For example, the settlement may provide for a cash payment of 25 percent of the debt and six future installments of 10 percent each. Total payment would thereby aggregate 85 percent. Installment payments are usually evidenced by notes. Creditors will also seek protective controls.

Appraisal of Voluntary Settlements

The advantages of voluntary settlements are informality and simplicity. Investigating, legal, and administrative expenses are held to a minimum. The procedure is the most economical and results in the largest return to creditors.

One possible disadvantage is that the debtor is left in control of his business. This situation may involve legal complications or erosion of assets still operated by the debtor. However, numerous controls are available to give the creditors protection.

A second disadvantage is that small creditors may take a nuisance role in that they may insist on payment in full. As a consequence, settlements typically provide for payment in full for claims under $50 or $100. If a composition is involved and all claims under $50 are paid, all creditors will receive a base of $50 plus the agreed-on percentage of the balance of their claims.

REORGANIZATION

Reorganization is a form of extension or composition of the firm's obligations. However, the legal formalities are much more involved than the procedures thus far described. Regardless of the legal procedure followed, the reorganization processes have several features in common.

1. The firm is insolvent either because it is unable to meet cash obligations as they come due or because claims on the firm exceed its assets. Hence, some modifications in the nature or amount of the firm's obligations must be made. A scaling down of terms or amounts must be formulated. This procedure may represent scaling down fixed charges or converting short-term debt into long-term debt.
2. New funds must be raised for working capital and for property rehabilitation.
3. The operating and managerial causes of difficulty must be discovered and eliminated.

The procedures involved in effecting a reorganization are highly legalistic and are, in fact, thoroughly understood only by attorneys who specialize in bankruptcy and reorganization. We shall therefore confine our remarks to the general principles involved.

A reorganization is, in essence, a composition, a scaling down of claims. In any composition, two conditions must be met: (1) the scaling down must be fair to all parties and (2) in return for the sacrifices, the likelihood of successful rehabilitation and profitable future operation of the firm must be feasible. These are the standards of *fairness* and *feasibility,* which are analyzed further in the next section.

FINANCIAL DECISIONS IN REORGANIZATIONS

When a business becomes insolvent, a decision must be made whether to dissolve the firm through liquidation or to keep it alive through reorganization.[5] Fundamentally, this decision depends upon a determination of the value of the firm if it is rehabilitated versus the value of the sum of the parts if the firm is dismembered.

Liquidation values depend upon the degree of specialization of the capital assets used in the firm and, hence, their resale value. In addition, liquidation itself involves costs of dismantling, including legal costs. Successful reorganization also involves costs. Typically, better equipment must be installed, obsolete inventories must be disposed of, and improvements in management must be made.

Net liquidation values are compared with the value of the firm after reorganization, net of the costs of rehabilitation. The procedure that promises the higher returns to the creditors and owners will be the course of action favored. Often the greater indicated value of the firm in reorganization, compared with its value in liquidation, is used to force a compromise agreement among the claimants in a reorganization, even when they feel that their relative position has not been treated fairly in the reorganization plan.

In reorganizations both the SEC and the courts are called upon to determine the *fairness* and the *feasibility* of proposed plans of reorganization.[6] In developing standards of fairness in connection with such reorganizations, both the courts and the SEC have adhered to two court decisions which established precedent on these matters.[7]

[5] This discussion is based on the excellent treatment by N. S. Buchanan, *The Economics of Corporate Enterprise* (New York: Holt, Rinehart and Winston, 1940), pp. 363–388.

[6] The federal bankruptcy laws specify that reorganization plans be worked out by court-appointed officials and be reviewed by the Securities and Exchange Commission.

[7] *Case v. Los Angeles Lumber Products Co.,* 308 U.S. 106 (1939) and *Consolidated Rock Products Co. v. duBoise,* 213 U.S. 510 (1940). Securities and Exchange Commission, Seventeenth Annual Report, 1951 (Washington, D.C.: U.S. Government Printing Office), p. 130.

Standards of Fairness

The basic doctrine of fairness states that claims must be recognized in the order of their legal and contractual priority. Junior claimants may participate only to the extent that they have made an additional cash contribution to the reorganization of the firm.

The carrying out of this concept of fairness involves the following steps:

1. An estimate of future sales must be made.
2. An analysis of operating conditions must be made so that the future earnings on sales can be estimated.
3. A determination of the capitalization rate to be applied to these future earnings must be made.
4. The capitalization rate must be applied to the estimated future earnings to obtain an indicated value of the properties of the company.
5. Provision for distribution to the claimants must then be made.

ILLUSTRATIVE CASE. The meaning and content of these procedures may best be set out by the use of an actual example of reorganization involving the Northeastern Steel Corporation.

Table 22–1 gives the balance sheet of the Northeastern Steel Corporation as of March 31, 1957. The company had been suffering losses running to $2.5 million a year, and on February 1, 1957, it filed a petition for reorganization with a federal court. The court, in accordance with the law, appointed a disinterested trustee. On June 13, 1957, the trustee filed with the court a plan of reorganization, which was subsequently analyzed by the SEC.

The trustee found that the company could not be internally reorganized, and he concluded that the only feasible program would be to combine Northeastern with an established producer of stainless and alloyed steel. Accordingly, the trustee solicited the interest of a number of steel companies. Late in March 1957, Carpenter Steel Company showed an interest in Northeastern. On June 3, 1957, Carpenter made a formal proposal to take over the $6 million of 4½ percent first-mortgage bonds of Northeastern, to pay $250,000 taxes owed by Northeastern, and to pay 40,000 shares of Carpenter Steel common stock to the company. Since the stock had a market price of $75 a share, the value of the stock was equivalent to $3 million. Thus, Carpenter was offering this sum, plus the $6 million takeover and the $250,000 taxes, a total of $9.2 million on assets that had a net book value of $16.7 million.

TRUSTEE'S PLAN. The trustee's plan, based on 40,000 shares at $75 equaling $3 million, is shown in Table 22–2. The total claims of the unsecured creditors equal $10 million. However, the amounts available total only $3 million. Thus, each claimant would be entitled to receive 30 percent before the adjustment for subordination. Before this adjustment, holders of notes payable would receive 30 percent of their claim of $250,000, or $75,000. However, the debentures are subordinated to *the notes payable,* so an additional $175,000 would be transfered to notes payable from the subordinated debentures. In the last column of Table 22–2, the dollar claims of each class of debt are restated in terms

TABLE 22–1 NORTHEASTERN STEEL CORPORATION
BALANCE SHEET
March 31, 1957
(amounts in millions)

Current assets	$ 3.50
Net property	12.50
Miscellaneous assets	0.70
Total assets	$16.70
Accounts payable	$ 1.00
Taxes	0.25
Notes payable	0.25
Other current liabilities	1.75
4½% First-mortgage bonds, due 1970	6.00
6% Subordinated debentures, due 1975	7.00
Common stock ($1)	1.00
Paid-in capital	3.45
Earned surplus	(4.00)
Total liabilities and capital	$16.70

of the number of shares of Carpenter common stock received by each class of unsecured creditors.

SEC EVALUATION. The Securities and Exchange Commission, in evaluating the proposal from the standpoint of fairness, made the following analysis. The SEC began with an evaluation of the prospective value of Northeastern Steel (Table 22–3). After a survey and discussion with various experts, they arrived at estimated sales of Northeastern Steel Corporation of $25 million a year. It was further estimated that the profit margin on sales would equal 6 percent, thus giving an indicated future earnings of $1.5 million a year.

The SEC analyzed price/earnings ratios for comparable steel companies and arrived at 8 times future earnings for a capitalization factor.

TABLE 22–2 NORTHEASTERN STEEL CORPORATION TRUSTEE'S PLAN

PRIOR CLAIMS	AMOUNT	RECEIVES
Taxes	$ 250,000	Cash paid by Carpenter
First mortgage, 4½%, 1970	6,000,000	Same assumed by Carpenter

TRUSTEES' PLAN FOR REMAINDER OF CLAIMS

Valuation based on 40,000 shares at $75 equals $3 million, or 30% of $10 million liabilities.

CLAIMS	AMOUNT	30 PERCENT × AMOUNT OF CLAIM	CLAIM AFTER SUBORDINATION	NO. OF SHARES OF COMMON STOCK
Notes payable	$ 250,000	$ 75,000	$ 250,000	3,333
General unsecured creditors	2,750,000	825,000	825,000	11,000
Subordinated debentures	7,000,000	2,100,000	1,925,000	25,667
	$10,000,000	$3,000,000	$3,000,000	40,000

TABLE 22–3 NORTHEASTERN STEEL CORPORATION SEC EVALUATION OF FAIRNESS

VALUATION	
Estimated sales of Northeastern Steel Corp.	$25,000,000 per year
Earnings at 6% of sales	1,500,000
Price/earnings ratio of 8 times earnings	12,000,000
Mortgage assumed, $6,000,000	6,000,000
Net value	$ 6,000,000

CLAIMS	AMOUNT	CLAIM	CLAIM AFTER SUBORDINATION
Notes payable	$ 250,000	$ 150,000	$ 250,000*
General unsecured creditors	2,750,000	1,650,000	1,650,000
Subordinated debentures (subordinate to notes payable)	7,000,000	4,200,000	4,100,000*
Totals	$10,000,000	$6,000,000	$6,000,000
Total available	6,000,000		
Percentage of claims	60%		

* Notes payable must be satisfied before subordinated debentures receive anything.

Multiplying 8 by $1.5 million gave an indicated total value of the company of $12 million. Since the mortgage assumed by Carpenter Steel was $6 million, a net value of $6 million is left for the other claims. This value is exactly double that of the 40,000 shares of Carpenter Steel stock paid for the remainder of the company. Because the SEC felt that the value of these claims was $6 million rather than $3 million, the SEC concluded that the trustee's plan for reorganization did not meet the test of fairness. It will be noted that under both the trustee's plan and the SEC plan, the holders of common stock would receive nothing, while the holders of the first-mortgage bond were paid in full.

Because no better alternative offer could be obtained, the proposal of Carpenter Steel was accepted despite the SEC disagreement with the valuation. This example illustrates how the implementation of the standard of fairness is actually applied in a reorganization plan.

Standards of Feasibility

The primary test of feasibility is that the fixed charges on the income of the corporation after reorganization are amply covered by earnings or, if a value for a firm that is to be sold is established, that a buyer at that price can be found. Adequate coverage of fixed charges for a company that is to continue in operation generally requires an improvement in earnings or a reduction of fixed charges, or both.

POLICIES REQUIRED. Among the actions that will have to be taken to improve the earning power of the company are the following:

1. Where the quality of management has been inefficient and inadequate for the task, new talents and abilities must be brought into the company if it is to operate successfully subsequent to the reorganization.
2. If inventories have become obsolete to a considerable degree, the useless inventory should be disposed of and the operations of the company streamlined.
3. Sometimes the plant and the equipment of the firm need to be modernized before it can operate and compete successfully on a cost basis.
4. Reorganization may also require an improvement in production, marketing, advertising, and other functions, to enable the firm to compete successfully and earn satisfactory profits.
5. Sometimes it is necessary to develop new product activity of the firm so that it can move from areas where economic trends have become undesirable into areas where the growth and stability potential is greater.

APPLICATION OF FEASIBILITY TESTS. Referring again to the Northeastern Steel Corporation example, the SEC observed that the reorganization involved taking over the properties of the Northeastern Steel Corporation by the Carpenter Steel Company. It judged that the direction and aid of the Carpenter Steel Company would remedy the production and operating deficiencies that had troubled Northeastern Steel. Whereas the debt-to-assets ratio of Northeastern Steel had become unbalanced, the Carpenter Steel Company went into the purchase with only a moderate amount of debt. After the consolidation had taken place, the total debt of Carpenter Steel was approximately $17.5 million compared with total assets of more than $63 million. Thus the debt ratio of 27 percent after the reorganization was not unreasonable.

The net income after taxes of Carpenter Steel had been running at a level of approximately $6 million. The interest on the debt of Carpenter Steel would be $270,000 on the long-term debt and, taking other borrowings into account, would total a maximum of $600,000 a year. The $6 million profit after taxes would therefore provide a 10-times coverage of fixed charges; this exceeds the standard of 8 times set forth in Chapter 9.

Notice that the question of feasibility would have been irrelevant (from the standpoint of the SEC) had Carpenter Steel offered $3 million in cash rather than in stock. It is the SEC's function to protect the interests of Northeast Steel's creditors. Since they are being forced to take common stock in another firm, the SEC must look into the feasibility of the transaction. However, if Carpenter had made a cash offer, the feasibility of Carpenter's own operation after the transaction was completed would have been none of the SEC's concern. Notice that the SEC feasibility study is much more important if a small, weak firm buys the assets of a reorganized firm for stock than if the purchase is made by a stronger firm. Thus, the SEC would be more concerned with the feasibility of a takeover of Northeast by Wesbrig Corporation than it would if General Motors made the takeover.

LIQUIDATION PROCEDURES

Liquidation of a business takes place when the estimated value of the firm is greater "dead than alive."

Assignment is a liquidation procedure that does not go through the courts, although it can be used to achieve full settlement of claims on the debtor. *Bankruptcy* is a legal procedure carried out under the jurisdiction of special courts in which a business firm is formally liquidated and claims of creditors are completely discharged.

Assignment

Assignment (as well as bankruptcy) takes place when the debtor is insolvent and the possibilities of restoring profitability so remote that the enterprise should be dissolved—that is, when the firm is "worth more dead than alive." Assignment is a technique for liquidating a debtor and yielding a larger amount to the creditors than is likely to be achieved in formal bankruptcy.

Technically, there are three types of assignments:

1. Common law assignment
2. Statutory assignment
3. Assignment plus settlement

COMMON LAW ASSIGNMENT. The common law provides for an assignment whereby a debtor transfers his title to assets to a third person, known as an assignee or a trustee. The trustee is instructed to liquidate the assets and to distribute the proceeds among the creditors on a pro rata basis.

Typically, an assignment is conducted through the adjustment bureau of the local credit managers' association. The assignee may liquidate the assets through what is known as a bulk sale, which is a public sale through an auctioneer. The auction is preceded by sufficient advertising so that there will be a number of bids at the auction. Liquidation may also be by a piecemeal auction sale conducted on the premises of the assignor by a competent licensed auctioneer, rather than by a bulk sale. On-premises sales are particularly advantageous in the liquidation of large machine shops or manufacturing plants.

The common law assignment, as such, does not discharge the debtor from his obligations. If a corporation goes out of business and does not satisfy all its claims, there will still be claims against the corporation, but in effect the corporation has ceased to exist. The people who have been associated with the corporation can then proceed to organize another corporation free of the debts and obligations of the previous corporation. There is always the danger, however, that the court may look through the corporate veil and hold the individuals responsible. It is therefore usually important to obtain a statement from creditors that claims have been completely settled. Such a statement is, of course, even more important for a nonincorporated business.

Although a common law assignment has taken place, the assignee, in drawing up checks paying the creditors, may write on the check the requisite legal language to make the payment a complete discharge of the obligation. There are technical legal requirements for this process, which are best carried out with the aid of a lawyer, but essential is a statement that endorsement of this check represents acknowledgment of full payment for the obligation.

STATUTORY ASSIGNMENT. Statutory assignment is similar in concept to common law assignment. Legally, it is carried out under state statutes regulating assignment; technically, it requires more formality. The debtor executes an instrument of assignment, which is recorded. This recordation provides notice to all third parties. A court is utilized: the court appoints an assignee and supervises the proceedings, including the sale of the assets and distribution of the proceeds. As in the common law assignment, the debtor is not automatically discharged from the balance of his obligations. He can discharge himself, however, by printing the requisite statement on the settlement checks.

ASSIGNMENT PLUS SETTLEMENT. Both the common law assignment and the statutory assignment may take place with recognition and agreement beforehand with the creditors that the assignment will represent a complete discharge of obligation. Normally, the debtor will communicate with the local credit managers' association. The adjustment bureau of the association will arrange a meeting of all the creditors. A trust instrument of assignment is drawn up. The adjustment bureau is designated to dispose of the assets, which are sold through regular trade channels, by bulk sales, by auction, or by private sales. The creditors will, typically, leave all responsibility for the liquidation procedure with the assignee, the adjustment bureau of the local credit managers' association.

Having disposed of the assets and obtained funds, the adjustment bureau will then distribute the dividends pro rata among the creditors, with the designation on the check that this is in full settlement of the claims on the debtor. Ordinarily, a release is not agreed upon prior to the execution of the assignment. After full examination of the facts, the creditors' committee will usually make a recommendation for the granting of a release following the execution of the assignment. If releases are not forthcoming, the assignor may, within four months of the date of the assignment, file a voluntary petition in bankruptcy. In this event, the assignment is terminated and the assignee must account and report to the trustee and the referee in bankruptcy, and deliver to the trustee all assets in the estate (usually by that time assets have been reduced to cash).

Assignment has substantial advantages over bankruptcy. Bankruptcy through the courts involves much time, legal formalities, and accounting and legal expenses. An assignment saves the substantial costs of bankruptcy proceedings, and it may save time as well.

Furthermore, an assignee usually has much more flexibility in disposing of property than does a bankruptcy trustee. He may be more familiar with the normal channels of trade. Since he takes action much sooner, before the inventories become more obsolete, he may achieve better results.

BANKRUPTCY

Although the bankruptcy procedures leave room for improvement, the Federal Bankruptcy Acts themselves represent two main achievements. (1) They provide safeguards against fraud by the debtor during liquidation and at the same time provide for an equitable distribution of the debtor's assets among his creditors. (2) Insolvent debtors may discharge all their obligations and start new businesses unhampered by a burden of prior debt.

Prerequisites for Bankruptcy

A voluntary petition of bankruptcy may be filed by the debtor. But if an involuntary petition of bankruptcy is to be filed, three conditions must be met.

1. The total debts of the insolvent must be $1,000 or more.
2. If the debtor has less than 12 creditors, any one of the creditors may file the petition if the amount owed him is $500 or more. If there are 12 or more creditors, the petition must be signed by three or more creditors with provable total claims of $500 or more.
3. Within the four months preceding, the debtor must have committed one or more of the six acts of bankruptcy.

Acts of Bankruptcy

The six acts of bankruptcy can be summarized briefly.

1. CONCEALMENT OR FRAUDULENT CONVEYANCE. Concealment constitutes hiding assets with intent to defraud creditors. Fraudulent conveyance is transfer of property to a third party without adequate consideration and with intent to defraud creditors.

2. PREFERENTIAL TRANSFER. A preferential transfer is the transfer of money or assets by an insolvent debtor to a creditor, giving the creditor a greater portion of his claim than other creditors would receive on liquidation.

3. LEGAL LIEN OR DISTRAINT. If an insolvent debtor permits any creditor to obtain a lien on his property and fails to discharge the lien within 30 days, or if the debtor permits a landlord to distrain (to seize property that has been pledged as security for a loan) for nonpayment of rent, he has committed an act of bankruptcy. In this way creditors, by obtaining a lien, may force an insolvent but obdurate debtor into bankruptcy.

4. ASSIGNMENT. If a debtor makes a general assignment for the benefit of his creditors, an act of bankruptcy likewise exists. Again, this enables creditors who have become distrustful of the debtor in the process of assignment to transfer the proceedings to a bankruptcy court. As a matter of practice, typically in common law assignments, creditors will require that a debtor execute a formal assignment document to be held in escrow, to become effective if informal and voluntary settlement negotiations fail. If they do fail, the assignment becomes effective and the creditors have their choice of throwing the case into the bankruptcy court.

5. APPOINTMENT OF RECEIVER OR TRUSTEE. If an insolvent debtor permits the appointment of a receiver or a trustee to take charge of his property, he has committed an act of bankruptcy. In this event, the creditors may remove a receivership or an adjustment proceeding to a bankruptcy court.

6. ADMISSION IN WRITING. If the debtor admits in writing his inability to pay his debts and his willingness to be judged bankrupt, he has committed an act of bankruptcy. The reason for this sixth act of bankruptcy is that debtors are often unwilling to engage in voluntary bankruptcy because it carries some stigma of avoidance of obligations. Sometimes therefore, negotiations with a debtor reach an impasse. Admission in writing is one of the methods of forcing the debtor to commit an act of bankruptcy and of moving the proceedings into a bankruptcy court, where the debtor will no longer be able to reject all plans for settlement.

Adjudication and the Referee

On the filing of the petition of involuntary bankruptcy, a subpoena is served on the debtor. There is usually no contest by the debtor, and the court adjudges him bankrupt. On adjudication, the case is transferred by the court to a referee in bankruptcy. A referee in bankruptcy is generally a lawyer appointed for a specified term by the judge of the bankruptcy court to act in his place after adjudication.

In addition, on petition of the creditors, the referee in voluntary proceedings, or the judge in involuntary proceedings, may appoint a receiver, who serves as the custodian of the property of the debtor until the appointment of a trustee. This arrangement was developed because a long period elapses between the date of the filing of a petition in bankruptcy and the election of a trustee at the first creditors' meeting. To safeguard the creditors' interest during this period, the court, through either the referee or the judge, may appoint a receiver in bankruptcy. The receiver in bankruptcy has full control until the trustee is appointed.

First Creditors' Meeting: Election of Trustee

At the first meeting of the creditors, a trustee is elected. If different blocks of creditors have a different candidate for trustee, the election may become drawn out. Frequently, the trustee will be the adjustment bureau of the local credit managers' association. At this first meeting the debtor may also be examined for the purpose of obtaining necessary information.

Subsequent Procedure

The trustee and the creditors' committee act to convert all assets into cash. The trustee sends a letter to people owing the debtor money, warning that all past-due accounts will result in instant suit if immediate payment is not made, and if necessary he will institute such suit. Appraisers are appointed by the courts to set a value on the property. With the advice of the creditors' committee and by authorization of the referee, the merchandise is sold by approved methods. As in an assignment, auctions may be held.

Property may not be sold without consent of the court at less than 75 percent of the appraised value that has been set by the appraisers appointed by the court. Cash received from the disposition of the property is used first to pay all expenses associated with the proceedings of the bankruptcy. The trustee will then pay any remaining funds to the claimants.

Final Meeting and Discharge

When the trustee has completed his liquidation and has sent out all the claimants' checks, he makes an accounting, which is reviewed by the creditors and the referee. After all the payments have been made by the trustee, the bankruptcy is discharged and the debtor is released from all debts.

If the hearings before the referee indicate the probability of fraud, the FBI is required to undertake an investigation. If fraud was not committed and the bankruptcy is discharged, the debtor is again free to engage in business. Since business is highly competitive in many fields, he will probably not have great difficulty in obtaining credit again. Under the National Bankruptcy Act, however, a debtor may not be granted a discharge more often than at six-year intervals.

Priority of Claims on Distribution of Proceeds of a Bankruptcy

The order of priority of claims in bankruptcy is as follows:

1. Costs of administrating and operating the bankrupt estate.
2. Wages due workers if earned within three months prior to the filing of the petition in bankruptcy. The amount of wages is not to exceed $600 a person.
3. Taxes due the United States, state, county, or any other governmental agency.
4. Secured creditors with the proceeds of the sale of specific property pledged for a mortgage.
5. General or unsecured creditors. This claim consists of the remaining balances after payment to secured creditors from the sale of specific property, and includes trade credit, bank loans, and debenture bonds. Holders of subordinated debt fall in this category, but they must turn over required amounts to the holders of senior debt.
6. Preferred stock.
7. Common stock.

To illustrate how this priority of claims works out, let us take a specific example. The balance sheet of the bankrupt firm is shown in Table 22–4. Assets total $90 million. The claims are those indicated on the right-hand side of the balance sheet. It will be noted that the subordinated debentures are subordinated to the notes payable to commercial banks.

Now assume that the assets of the firm are sold. The following amounts are realized on liquidation:

Current assets	$28,000,000
Net property	5,000,000
Total	$33,000,000

The order of priority of payment of claims is shown by Table 22–5. Fees and expenses of administration typically are about 20 percent of gross proceeds. In this example they are assumed to be $6 million. Next in priority are wages due workers, which total $700,000. The total amount of taxes to be paid is $1.3 million. Thus far the total paid from the $33 million is $8 million. The first mortgage is then paid from the net proceeds of $5 million from the sale of fixed property, leaving $20 million available to the general creditors.

TABLE 22–4 BANKRUPT FIRM BALANCE SHEET

Current assets	$80,000,000	Accounts payable	$20,000,000
Net property	$10,000,000	Notes payable (due bank)	10,000,000
		Accrued wages, 1,400 @ $500	700,000
		U.S. taxes	1,000,000
		State and local taxes	300,000
		Current debt	$32,000,000
		First mortgage	$ 6,000,000
		Second mortgage	1,000,000
		Subordinated debentures*	8,000,000
		Long-term debt	$15,000,000
		Preferred stock	2,000,000
		Common stock	26,000,000
		Capital surplus	4,000,000
		Earned surplus	11,000,000
		Net worth	$43,000,000
	$90,000,000	Total	$90,000,000

* Subordinated to $10 million notes payable to the First National Bank.

The claims of the general creditors total $40 million. Since $20 million is available, each claimant would receive 50 percent of his claim before the subordination adjustment. The subordination adjustment requires that the subordinated debentures turn over to the notes to which they are subordinated all amounts received until the notes are satisfied. In this situation, the claim of the notes payable is $10 million, but only $5 million is available. The deficiency is $5 million. After transfer by the subordinated debentures of $4 million, there remains a deficiency of $1 million, which will be unsatisfied. It will be noted that 90 percent of the bank claim is satisfied, whereas only 50 percent of other unsecured claims will be satisfied. These figures illustrate the usefulness of the

TABLE 22–5 BANKRUPT FIRM
ORDER OF PRIORITY OF CLAIMS

DISTRIBUTION OF PROCEEDS ON LIQUIDATION

1. Proceeds of sale of assets	$33,000,000
2. Fees and expenses of administration of bankruptcy	$ 6,000,000
3. Wages due workers earned three months prior to filing of bankruptcy petition	700,000
4. Taxes	1,300,000
	$25,000,000
5. First mortgage, paid from net property	5,000,000
6. Available to general creditors	$20,000,000

Claims of General Creditors	Claim (1)	Application of 50 Percent (2)	After Subordination Adjustment (3)	Percentage of Original Claims Received (4)
Unsatisfied portion of first mortgage	$ 1,000,000	$ 500,000	$ 500,000	92
Unsatisfied portion of second mortgage	1,000,000	500,000	500,000	50
Notes payable	10,000,000	5,000,000	9,000,000	90
Accounts payable	20,000,000	10,000,000	10,000,000	50
Subordinated debentures	8,000,000	4,000,000	0	0
	$40,000,000	$20,000,000	$20,000,000	56

NOTES: 1. Column (1) is the claim of each class of creditor. Total claims equal $40 million.
2. From line 6 in the top part of the table we see that $20 million is available. This sum, divided by the $40 million of claims, indicates that general creditors will receive 50 percent of their claims. This is shown in column (2).
3. The debentures are subordinated to the notes payable. Four million dollars is transferred from debentures to notes payable in column (3).
4. Column (4) shows the results of dividing the column (3) figure by the original amount given in Table 22–4, except for first mortgage, where $5 million paid on sale of property is included. The 56 percent total figure includes the first mortgage transactions, that is, ($20,000,000 + $5,000,000) ÷ ($40,000,000 + $5,000,000) = 56%.

subordination provision to the security to which the subordination is made. Since no other funds remain, the claims of the holders of preferred and common stock are completely wiped out.

Studies of the proceeds in bankruptcy liquidations reveal that unsecured creditors receive, on the average, about 15 cents on the dollar.

Consequently, where assignment to creditors is likely to yield more, assignment is to be preferred to bankruptcy.

SUMMARY

Problems associated with the decline and failure of a firm, as well as methods of rehabilitating or liquidating one that has failed, were the subjects treated in this chapter. The major cause of failure is incompetent management. Bad managers should, of course, be removed as promptly as possible; if failure has occurred, a number of remedies are open to the interested parties.

The first question to be answered is whether the firm is better off dead or alive—whether it should be liquidated and sold off piecemeal or rehabilitated. Assuming the decision is made that the firm should survive, it must be put through what is called a *reorganization.* Legal procedures are always costly, especially in the case of a business failure. Therefore, if it is at all possible, both the debtor and the creditors are better off if matters can be handled on an informal basis rather than through the courts. The informal procedures used in reorganization are (1) *extension,* which postpones the date of settlement, and (2) *composition,* which reduces the amount owed.

If voluntary settlement through extension or composition is not possible, the matter is thrown into the courts. If the court decides on reorganization rather than liquidation, it will appoint a trustee (1) to control the firm going through reorganization and (2) to prepare a formal plan of reorganization. The plan, which must be reviewed by the SEC, must meet the standards of *fairness* to all parties and *feasibility* in the sense that the reorganized enterprise will stand a good chance of surviving rather than being thrown back into the bankruptcy courts.

The application of standards of fairness and feasibility developed in this chapter are tools to determine the probable success of a particular plan of reorganization. The concept of fairness involves the estimation of sales and earnings and the application of a capitalization rate to the latter to determine the appropriate distribution to each claimant.

The *feasibility test* examines the ability of the new enterprise to carry the fixed charges resulting from the reorganization plan. The quality of management and the company's assets must be assured. Production and marketing may also require improvement.

Finally, where liquidation is treated as the only solution to the debtor's insolvency, the creditors should attempt procedures that will net them the largest recovery. *Assignment* of the debtor's property is the cheaper and the faster procedure. In addition, there is more flexibility in disposing of the debtor's property and thus providing larger returns. *Bankruptcy* provides formal procedures in liquidation to safeguard the debtor's property from fraud and provides equitable distribution to the creditors. The procedure is long and cumbersome. In addition, the debtor's property is generally poorly managed during bankruptcy proceedings unless the trustee is closely supervised by the creditors.

QUESTIONS

22–1 "A certain number of business failures is a healthy sign. If there are no failures, this is an indication (1) that entrepreneurs are overly cautious, hence not as inventive and as willing to take risks as a healthy, growing economy requires, (2) that competition is not functioning to weed out inefficient producers, or (3) that both situations exist." Discuss, giving pros and cons.

22–2 How can financial analysis be used to forecast the probability of a given firm's failure? Assuming that such analysis is properly applied, can it always predict failure?

22–3 Why do creditors usually accept a plan for financial rehabilitation rather than demand liquidation of the business?

22–4 Would it be possible to form a profitable company by merging two companies both of which are business failures? Explain.

22–5 Distinguish between a reorganization and a bankruptcy.

22–6 Would it be a sound rule to liquidate whenever the liquidation value is above the value of the corporation as a going concern? Discuss.

22–7 Why do liquidations of all types usually result in losses for the creditors or the owners, or both? Would partial liquidation or liquidation over a period limit their losses? Explain.

22–8 Are liquidations likely to be more common for public utility, railroad, or industrial corporations? Why?

PROBLEMS

22–1 The financial statements of the Blough Publishing Company for 1969 were as shown on page 748.

A recapitalization plan is proposed in which each share of the \$4 preferred will be exchanged for one share of \$1.60 preferred (stated value, \$25) plus one 6 percent subordinated income debenture (stated principal, \$50). The \$7 preferred would be retired from cash.

a) Show the *pro forma* balance sheet (in millions of dollars) giving effect to the recapitalization and showing the new preferred at its stated value and the common stock at its par value.
b) Present the *pro forma* income statement (in millions of dollars carried to two decimal places).
c) How much does the firm increase income available to common stock by the recapitalization?
d) How much less is the required pretax earnings after the re-

BLOUGH PUBLISHING COMPANY
BALANCE SHEET
December 31, 1969
(in millions of dollars)

Current assets	$ 40	Current liabilities	$ 14
Investments	16	Advance payments for subscriptions	26
Net fixed assets	51	Reserves	2
Goodwill	5	$4 preferred stock, $75 par (600,000 shares)	45
		$7 preferred stock, no par (300,000 shares, callable at $100)	3
		Common stock, par value of $1 (3,000,000 shares outstanding)	3
		Retained earnings	19
Total assets	$112	Total claims	$112

BLOUGH PUBLISHING COMPANY
CONSOLIDATED STATEMENT OF INCOME AND EXPENSE
For Year Ended December 31, 1969
(in millions of dollars)

Operating income		$180.0
Operating expense		172.0
Net operating income		$ 8.0
Other income		1.0
Other expense		0.0
Earnings before income tax		$ 9.0
Income tax at 50 percent		4.5
Income after taxes		$ 4.5
Dividends on $4 prior preferred stock	$2.4	
Dividends on $7 preferred stock	0.2	2.6
Income available for common stock		$ 1.9

capitalization compared to those before the change? Required earnings is that amount that is just enough to meet fixed charges, debenture interest, and/or preferred dividends in this case.

e) How is the debt-to-net-worth position of the company affected by the recapitalization?

f) Would you vote for the recapitalization if you were a holder of the $4 prior preferred stock?

22–2 The Perfecto Instrument Company produces precision instruments. The company's products are designed and manufactured according to specifications set out by its customers and are highly specialized.

Declines in sales and increases in development expenses in recent years resulted in a large deficit by the end of 1969.

PERFECTO INSTRUMENT COMPANY
BALANCE SHEET
December 31, 1969
(in thousands of dollars)

Current assets	$ 500	Current liabilities	$ 600
Fixed assets	500	Long-term debt (unsecured)	300
		Capital stock	200
		Earned surplus or (deficit)	(100)
Total assets	$1,000	Total claims	$1,000

Independent assessment led to the conclusion that the company would have a liquidation value of about $600,000. As an alternative to liquidation, the management concluded that a reorganization was possible with additional investment of $300,000. The management was confident of eventual success of the company and stated that the additional investment would restore earnings to $150,000 a year after taxes and before fixed charges. The appropriate multiplier to apply is 8 times. The management is negotiating wth a local investment group to obtain the additional investment of $300,000. If the funds are obtained, the holders of the long-term debt would be given one half the common stock in the reorganized firm in place of their present claims.

PERFECTO INSTRUMENT COMPANY
SALES AND PROFITS
1966–1969
(in thousands of dollars)

Year	*Sales*	*Net Profit After Tax Before Fixed Charges*
1966	$3,500	$350
1967	$3,200	300
1968	$1,900	(100)
1969	$1,800	(150)

Should the creditors agree to the reorganization or should they force liquidation of the firm?

22–3* On September 13, 1956, a voluntary petition for reorganization under Chapter X of the Bankruptcy Act was filed by Green River Steel Corporation in the U.S. District Court for the Western District of Kentucky, Owensboro Division. The petition was approved and a trustee was named. On November 12, 1956, the trustee filed a plan for reorganization with the court.

* Based on SEC Reorganization Release No. 1940. *In the matter of Green River Steel Corporation, Debtor, in proceedings for the reorganization of a corporation pursuant to Chapter X of the Bankruptcy Act* (Washington, D.C.: January 24, 1957), pp. 1–25. Facts altered and rounded to facilitate calculations.

GREEN RIVER STEEL COMPANY
BALANCE SHEET
July 31, 1956
(in thousands of dollars)

Assets		Current liabilities	
Current assets	$ 4,000	4½% mortgage due RFC ($2,100 past due)	$ 4,000
Net property account	9,000	Notes payable to banks	1,000
		Accounts payable	1,500
		Interest due to RFC	1,000
		Accruals	200
		Total current liab.	$ 7,700
		Long-term debt	
		4½% mortgage due RFC	$ 4,500
		Deferred interest	300
		3½% debentures, due 1961	4,000
		Interest accrued on 3½% debentures	18
		Total long-term debt	$ 8,818
		Capital stock	
		Common (10 cents par)	7
		Paid-in surplus	80
		Earned surplus (deficit)	(3,605)
Total assets	$13,000	Total claims	$13,000

On November 22, 1950, Green River Steel was incorporated under the laws of Kentucky for the purpose of engaging in the production and sale of semifinished steel products. In July 1953, Green River started operations. In early 1954, when the plant was ready to produce at its rated capacity, the entire industry was hit by a recession. In addition, the company lacked working capital as shown by the balance sheet below.

All attempts to secure additional funds failed. In spite of the difficulties, there has been a steadily improving trend in both sales and net profits.

However, with the entire $4 million principal amount of one of the mortgage notes held by RFC falling due on January 1, 1957, it was obvious to the management that the company could not meet its obligations.

GREEN RIVER STEEL COMPANY
SALES AND PROFITS, 1954–1956
(in thousands of dollars)

Year Ended	*Net Sales*	*Net Operating Profit Before Interest Charges*	*Net Profits*
July 31, 1954	$ 5,413	(1,603)	(2,185)
July 31, 1955	10,790	47	575
July 31, 1956	17,270	826	204

The trustee's plan of reorganization was based on an offer by Jessop Steel Company. The trustee's plan follows:

1) The United States, as the holder of RFC notes, will receive a new first-mortgage note in the principal amount of $9.8 million at the date of consummation, maturing 18 years thereafter and bearing interest at 3 percent a year for the first 3 years and 4½ percent a year thereafter.
2) The holders of outstanding debentures will receive, in exchange for each $1,000 principal amount and the interest accumulated thereon to the date of consummation, a new $1,000 income subordinated debenture note, maturing 25 years thereafter and bearing interest if earned, but noncumulative, of 2 percent for the third through the sixth years, 2½ for the seventh and eighth years, and 3½ percent thereafter. The new debentures will be subordinate (a) to a $9.8 million first-mortgage note, (b) to new 10-year notes payable to Jessop in the principal amount of not less than $1.5 million, and (c) to bank loans of $3 million.
3) The holders of the common stock of the debtor will receive in exchange for each 10 shares of such stock one share of common stock of Jessop. New common stock will be issued by Green River to Jessop, which will become the sole stockholder of the reorganized enterprise.
4) The trustee's plan provides for the issuance of 10-year notes to Jessop in exchange for cash advanced to the debtor in the principal amount of $1.5 million at the consummation date, maturing in 10 years and bearing interest of 4 percent a year.
5) The plan also provides for sinking funds for the retirement of the first-mortgage note, the 10-year note, and the new debentures.

The *pro forma* liabilities and net worth, giving effect to the trustee's plan, are:

Notes payable to banks	$3,000	
Accounts payable	1,500	
Accruals	200	
Current liabilities		$ 4,700
First mortgage due RFC	$9,800	
10-year note to Jessop	1,500	
Subordinated income debentures	4,000	
Long-term debt		15,300
Common stock, par value $10	$3,000	
Capital surplus	1,000	
Net worth		4,000
Total claims		$24,000

The *pro forma* statement is based on continuing the accounts payable at $1.5 million, on increasing the bank loans to $3 million, and on additional investment of $1.5 million by Jessop Steel.

a) What is the value of the assets of Green River less the new capital invested in the business?
b) Using the capitalization of income method, if the sales of Green River rise to $30 million, the profit rate on sales (before interest) is 7 percent and the price/earnings ratio is 8, what is the amount of the total assets of Green River after reorganization?
c) What is the amount of total assets of Green River if sales are $25 million but all other conditions are as in b?
d) Assume that sales of Green River are $25 million but that the profit rate rises to 8 percent. What is the amount of total assets of Green River now?
e) Because Jessop Steel would become the sole owner of Green River, does it make any difference whether Jessop's $1.5 million is treated as debt or as ownership investment?
f) What is your appraisal of the fairness of the proposed reorganization plan?
g) What is your opinion of the feasibility of the reorganization plan?

22–4 On May 10, 1969, the Simpson Company filed an involuntary petition in bankruptcy, having defaulted interest on its outstanding debt. At this date, it issued the following balance sheet.

SIMPSON COMPANY
BALANCE SHEET
May 10, 1969

Cash	$ 10,000	Accounts payable	$ 500,000
Receivables	190,000	Notes payable, 8%	500,000
Inventory	800,000	First mortgage, 5%	1,000,000
Machinery	2,000,000	Second mortgage, 6%	1,000,000
Plant	5,000,000	Debentures, 6%	2,000,000
Surplus	1,000,000	Preferred stock, 7%	1,000,000
		Common stock	3,000,000
Total	$9,000,000	Total	$9,000,000

The Simpson Company, after the necessary reorganization, can earn $320,000. You have determined that 8 percent is an appropriate capitalization rate.

a) State your plan of reorganization, using (1) absolute priority doctrine and (2) relative priority doctrine.
b) Defend both your plans for (1) "fairness" in legal connotation and (2) "feasibility" in legal connotation.

22–5 The Pomona Pipe Company has suffered several years of operating losses. Because of the unfavorable outlook for the firm, it goes into bankruptcy and is dissolved.

POMONA PIPE COMPANY
BALANCE SHEET
September 30, 1969
(last balance sheet before dissolution)

Cash	$ 20,000	Accounts payable	$ 1,000,000
Accounts receivable	100,000	Loans from banks	2,000,000
Inventories	2,000,000	Property taxes	5,000
Building	10,000,000	Accrued wages*	60,000
Equipment	5,000,000	Federal income taxes	5,000
		First mortgage on building	4,000,000
		Second mortgage on building	2,000,000
		Subordinated convertible debentures†	1,000,000
		Preferred stock	3,000,000
		Common stock	3,000,000
		Retained earnings	1,050,000
Total	$17,120,000	Total	$17,120,000

* Incurred during the last two months, no claim exceeds $600.
† Subordinated to bank loan only.

On liquidation, the following amounts are received from respective items:

Cash	$ 20,000
Receivables	50,000
Inventories	1,000,000
Building	5,000,000
Equipment	2,000,000

What would be the priority of payment, and how much would each class of creditor receive?

Selected References

"Allocation of Securities in Corporate Reorganization: Claims Measurement through Investment Value Analysis," *Yale Law Review*, LXI (May 1952), 656–685.

Altman, Edward I., "Financial Ratios, Discriminant Analysis, and the Prediction of Corporate Bankruptcy," *Journal of Finance*, XXIII (September 1968), 589–610.

Baldwin, W. H., "McKesson and Robbins Reorganization," *Harvard Business Review*, XX (Spring 1942), 473.

Billyou, D. F., "Priority Rights of Security Holders in Bankruptcy Reorganizations: New Directions," *Harvard Law Review*, LXVII (February 1954), 553–590.

Blum, Walter J., and Wilbur G. Katz, "Depreciation and Enterprise Valuation," *University of Chicago Law Review,* XXXII (Winter 1965).

———, "Full Priority and Full Compensation in Corporate Reorganizations," *University of Chicago Law Review,* XXV (Spring 1958), 417–444.

Calkins, Francis J., "Corporate Reorganization under Chapter X: A Post-Mortem," *Journal of Finance,* III (June 1948), 19–28.

———, "Feasibility in Plans of Corporate Reorganizations under Chapter X," *Harvard Law Review,* LXI (May 1948), 763–781.

The Failure Record through 1963: A Comprehensive Failure Study (New York: Dun & Bradstreet, Inc., Business Economics Department, 1964).

Fergusson, D. A., "Preferred Stock Valuation in Recapitalizations," *Journal of Finance,* XIII (March 1958), 48–69.

Fraine, Harold G., and Robert H. Mills, "Effect of Defaults and Credit Deterioration on Yields of Corporate Bonds," *Journal of Finance,* XVI (September 1961), 423–434.

Guthmann, H. G., "Absolute Priority in Reorganization," *Columbia Law Review,* XLV (September 1945), 739–754.

Michaelson, A. M., "Business Purpose and Tax-free Reorganization," *Yale Law Review,* LXI (January 1952), 14–44.

O'Leary, P. M., "The Role of Banking Groups in Corporate Reorganizations," *American Economic Review,* XXVIII (June 1939), 337–344.

Walter, James E., "Determination of Technical Insolvency," *Journal of Business,* XXX (January 1957), 30–43.

Watson, E. T. P., "Distribution of New Securities in Section 77 Reorganizations," *Journal of Finance,* V (December 1950), 337–367.

Weintraub, Benjamin, and Levin Harris, *Practical Guide to Bankruptcy and Debtor Relief.* (Englewood Cliffs, N.J.: Prentice-Hall, 1964.)

Wren, H. G., "Feasibility and Fairness in Section 20b Reorganizations," *Columbia Law Review,* LII (June 1952), 715–745.

PART EIGHT

AN INTEGRATED VIEW OF FINANCIAL MANAGEMENT

23

The Timing of Financial Policy

This chapter deals with the timing of financial policy. Variations in the relative cost and availability of funds require comparison of the changes in the cost and availability of equity money, long-term money, and short-term money over time. Fluctuations in the level of business activity produce a number of impacts on the firm. For good timing of financial policy, the financial manager must take into account prospective changes in asset requirements that will have to be financed over time. He must also consider prospective prices and returns from capital assets. Finally, he must plan his needs to meet future maturing obligations.

SIGNIFICANCE TO FINANCIAL MANAGEMENT

The significance of financial timing of firms is suggested by the following comments in *Business Week:*

> Since 1951, when the Federal Reserve won the right to pursue an independent monetary policy, the cost and availability of money have been a constant problem for corporate management. At times, as in the tight money squeeze of 1957, it has been a major worry.
>
> Company treasurers resented the high rates that banks charge on loans, and they resented even more banks' insistence that they hold compensating balances, depriving them of the full use of their borrowed money. And because they feared that rates would go even higher and that credit might not be available at all, they stepped up their demands—which had the effect of further tightening an already tight situation.[1]

The concern of financial managers over the cost of money in 1960 was mild compared with their reactions to the "credit crunch" that developed in August 1966 and again in the summer and fall of 1967. This is evidenced by another quotation from *Business Week* seven years later.

> Even a modest increase in monetary restraint will be hard for most companies to handle. Ever since the end of last year's credit drought, companies have worked hard to rebuild liquidity.
>
> However, there's a "difference between actual and desired liquidity," says an economist for a major New York City bank, "and companies haven't succeeded in loosening up balance sheets."
>
> In contrasting money market conditions that lie ahead with 1966, economists stress the expected impact of inflation itself. During late 1966, the wholesale price index remained relatively stable. But if price increases get larger in coming months, interest rates are almost sure to climb.
>
> "People who borrow under conditions of sharp inflation are willing to pay any amount for money," says Milton Friedman of the University of Chicago, "and people who lend ask high rates to protect themselves from loss of purchasing power." If the Fed doesn't tighten, Friedman expects prices to rise by at least 5% and possibly 7% during 1968 and predicts that interest rates will be in the 9% to 10% range."[2]

Financial managers are concerned with variations in money and capital market conditions—sharp changes in the cost and availability of funds have been experienced in the past, and similar fluctuations will undoubtedly be experienced in the future.

Table 23–1 gives an indication of the pattern of interest changes in the U.S. economy during the period of 1929–1966. One outstanding characteristic of interest rate behavior is made most clear by the table—the wide magnitude of the changes in the price of money over the years.

[1] "Where the Credit Pinch Hurts," *Business Week* (February 27, 1960), 65.
[2] "Is a Money Crunch on Its Way?" *Business Week* (September 29, 1967), 36.

For example, the borrowing rate on four to six months commercial paper, which is the best indication of the cost of short-term money to large corporations, reached a low of 0.53 percent in 1941. By 1953, this rate stood at 2.52 percent, but it declined to 1.58 percent during the business recession of the following year. In the early 1960s prime commercial paper rates rose to over 3 percent, and during the credit stringency of 1966 the rate reached 6 percent. It had declined to 4.75 percent by September 1967, but was back up to 6 percent by December 1968. Incidentally, at the latter date the prime rate on negotiated bank loans was 6¾ percent and the rate on Treasury bills was about 6¼ percent.

Yields on high grade long-term corporate bonds have fluctuated similarly, but not to the same degree. For example, the corporate AAA bond rate reached a low of 2.53 percent in 1946. It rose to over 3 percent in 1953 and, after declining to 2.90 percent during the business downturn of 1954, climbed to 4.41 percent by 1960. During August 1966, yields on AAA corporates rose above 5½ percent, and the rise continued in 1967. By the fall of 1968, new AAA issues were yielding over 7 percent.

This brief review of fluctuations in short-term and long-term interest rates is sufficient to demonstrate that fluctuations in the cost of capital to business represents one of the most volatile of the inputs purchased by firms. Within relatively short time periods, money costs have fluctuated by over 100 percent.

The significance of fluctuations in interest rates is seen to be especially important when one considers the large amounts of financing that may be involved. On July 11, 1967, Texaco came to the market with a $200 million offering of bonds due in 1997, carrying a rating of AAA and a coupon of 5¾ percent. On August 30, 1967, Alcoa issued $125 million of similarly rated bonds sold to yield 6.07 percent. Had Texaco waited another month to issue its bonds and incurred a ¼ percent higher cost, this would have represented a difference in interest charges of $500,000 a year.

While the cost variations associated with interest rate fluctuations are substantial, the greatest significance of interest rates is their role as an index of the availability of funds. A period of high interest rates reflects a period of tight money, which is in turn associated with tight reserve positions at commercial banks. At such times, interest rates will rise, of course, but there are conventional limits on interest rates. As a consequence, a larger quantity of funds is demanded by borrowers than banks are able to make available. Banks therefore begin to ration funds among prospective borrowers by continuing lines of credit to traditional customers but restricting loans to new borrowers or those whose credit standards are not as strong.

TABLE 23–1 BOND YIELDS AND INTEREST RATES, 1929–1966
(percent per year)

	U.S. GOVERNMENT SECURITIES				CORPORATE BONDS (MOODY'S)					
Year or Month	3-Month Treasury Bills	9–12 Month Issues	3–5 Year Issues	Taxable Bonds	AAA	BAA	High-grade Municipal Bonds (Standard & Poor's)	Average Rate on Short-term Bank Loans to Business—Selected Cities	Prime Commercial Paper, 4–6 Months	Federal Reserve Bank Discount Rate
1929	—	—	—	—	4.73	5.90	4.27	—	5.85	5.16
1930	—	—	—	—	4.55	5.90	4.07	—	3.59	3.04
1931	1.402	—	—	—	4.58	7.62	4.01	—	2.64	2.11
1932	0.879	—	—	—	5.01	9.30	4.65	—	2.73	2.82
1933	0.515	—	2.66	—	4.49	7.76	4.71	—	1.73	2.56
1934	0.256	—	2.12	—	4.00	6.32	4.03	—	1.02	1.54
1935	0.137	—	1.29	—	3.60	5.75	3.40	—	0.75	1.50
1936	0.143	—	1.11	—	3.24	4.77	3.07	—	0.75	1.50
1937	0.447	—	1.40	—	3.26	5.03	3.10	—	0.94	1.33
1938	0.053	—	0.83	—	3.19	5.80	2.91	—	0.81	1.00
1939	0.023	—	0.59	—	3.01	4.96	2.76	2.1	0.59	1.00
1940	0.014	—	0.50	—	2.84	4.75	2.50	2.1	0.56	1.00
1941	0.103	—	0.73	—	2.77	4.33	2.10	2.0	0.53	1.00
1942	0.326	—	1.46	2.46	2.83	4.28	2.36	2.2	0.66	1.00
1943	0.373	0.75	1.34	2.47	2.73	3.91	2.06	2.6	0.69	1.00
1944	0.375	0.79	1.33	2.48	2.72	3.61	1.86	2.4	0.73	1.00

1945	0.375	0.81	1.18	2.37	2.62	3.29	1.67	2.2	0.75	1.00
1946	0.375	0.82	1.16	2.19	2.53	3.05	1.64	2.1	0.81	1.00
1947	0.594	0.88	1.32	2.25	2.61	3.24	2.01	2.1	1.03	1.00
1948	1.040	1.14	1.62	2.44	2.82	3.47	2.40	2.5	1.44	1.34
1949	1.102	1.14	1.43	2.31	2.66	3.42	2.21	2.68	1.49	1.50
1950	1.218	1.26	1.50	2.32	2.62	3.24	1.98	2.69	1.45	1.59
1951	1.552	1.73	1.93	2.57	2.86	3.41	2.00	3.11	2.16	1.75
1952	1.766	1.81	2.13	2.68	2.96	3.52	2.19	3.49	2.33	1.75
1953	1.931	2.07	2.56	2.94	3.20	3.74	2.72	3.69	2.52	1.99
1954	0.953	0.92	1.82	2.55	2.90	3.51	2.37	3.61	1.58	1.60
1955	1.753	1.89	2.50	2.84	3.06	3.53	2.53	3.70	2.18	1.89
1956	2.658	2.83	3.12	3.08	3.36	3.88	2.93	4.20	3.31	2.77
1957	3.267	3.53	3.62	3.47	3.89	4.71	3.60	4.62	3.81	3.12
1958	1.839	2.09	2.90	3.43	3.79	4.73	3.56	4.34	2.46	2.16
1959	3.405	4.11	4.33	4.08	4.38	5.05	3.95	5.00	3.97	3.36
1960	2.928	3.55	3.99	4.02	4.41	5.19	3.73	5.16	3.85	3.53
1961	2.378	2.91	3.60	3.90	4.35	5.08	3.46	4.97	2.97	3.00
1962	2.778	3.02	3.57	3.95	4.33	5.02	3.18	5.00	3.26	3.00
1963	3.157	3.28	3.72	4.00	4.26	4.86	3.23	5.01	3.55	3.23
1964	3.549	3.76	4.06	4.15	4.40	4.83	3.22	4.99	3.97	3.55
1965	3.954	4.09	4.22	4.21	4.49	4.87	3.27	5.06	4.38	4.04
1966	4.881	5.17	5.16	4.65	5.13	5.67	3.82	6.00	5.55	4.50

SOURCE: *The Annual Report of the Council of Economic Advisers* (Washington, D.C.: U.S. Government Printing Office, 1967), p. 272.
Note: Rates are annual averages; variations within a given year can be pronounced.

Small firms will characteristically have greater difficulty obtaining financing during periods of tight money. Even among large borrowers, the bargaining position of the financial institutions is stronger in a period of tight money. It is a lender's market rather than a borrower's market. As a consequence, the restrictive conditions in term loan agreements are likely to be more onerous when the demand for funds is high.

Interest rates are therefore of very great significance to financial managers as an index to the availability of funds. For small- and medium-sized firms, a period of rising interest rates may indicate increasing difficulty in obtaining any financing at all. Or, if financing is obtained, it will be obtained at a higher cost and under less favorable conditions.

A period of tight money will have a particularly heavy impact on the utilities and other heavy industries, state and local governments, and the housing and construction sectors. For the heavy, long-term investments made in these areas, the impact of interest rates on profitability is likely to be very great.

The preceding paragraphs have described the conditions that exist when money is tight and interest rates are high. The situation is just the reverse when money is easy. Then funds are readily available at low costs and under relatively unrestrictive loan agreements.

DATA ON RELATIVE COSTS OF FINANCING OVER TIME

It has been seen that the cost of money can vary widely over the business cycle. In addition, costs of different forms of financing differ, and the timing of shifts in the cost of money and in the relative cost of financing by different sources changes over time. Detailed data are presented to provide a factual foundation for decision making in choosing between the alternatives available to financial managers. The data in Figure 23–1 present stock yields since 1912.

Cost of Equity Funds

Both earnings/price ratios and dividend yields on common stocks have exhibited wide fluctuations. Earnings/price ratios have been as high as 16 percent and as low as 5 to 6 percent, excluding years when earnings were negative. Dividend/yield ratios have also fluctuated widely, not

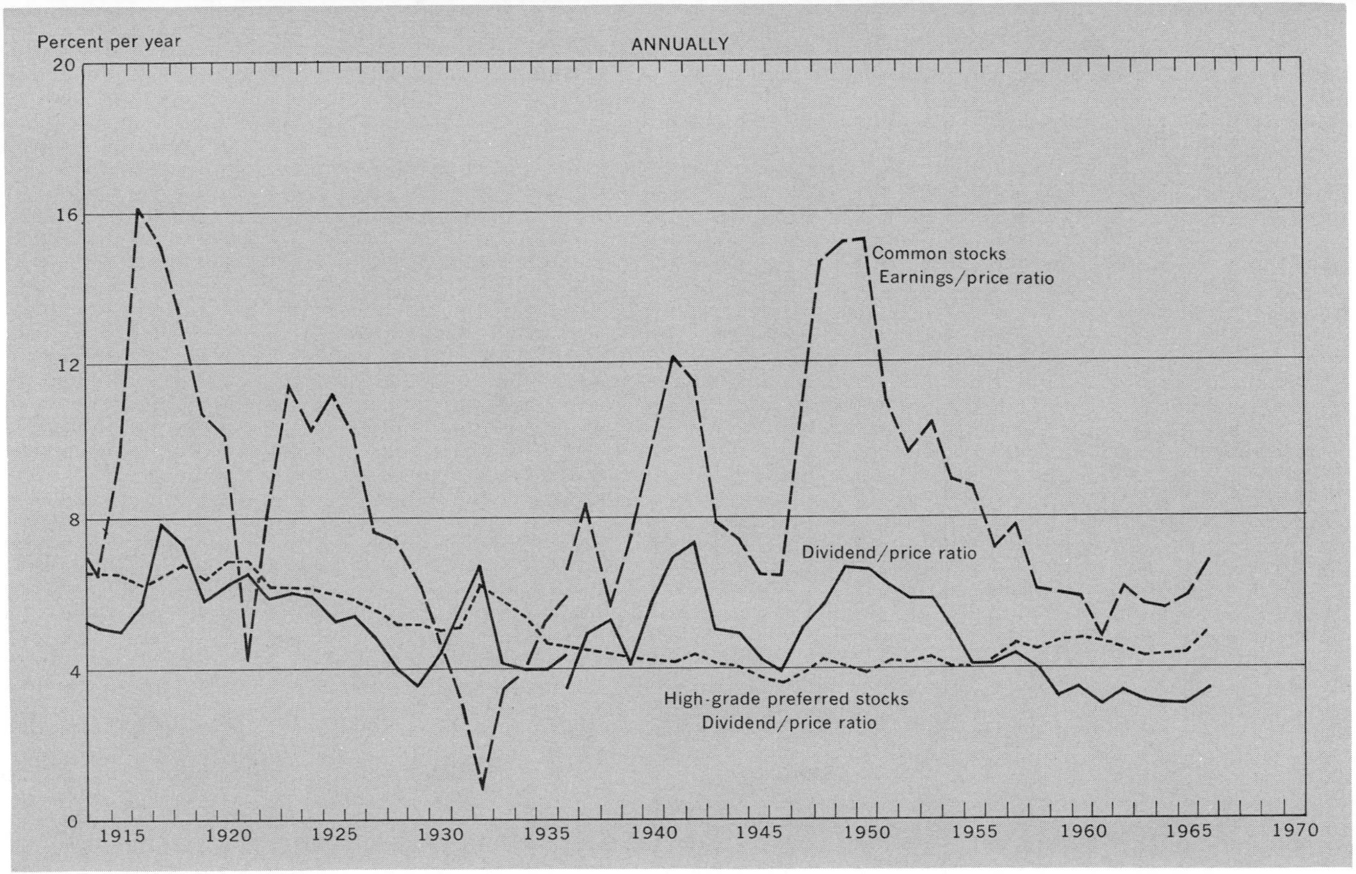

Figure 23–1 Stock Yields SOURCE: Historical Supplement to *Federal Reserve Chart Book on Financial and Business Statistics*, p. 37.

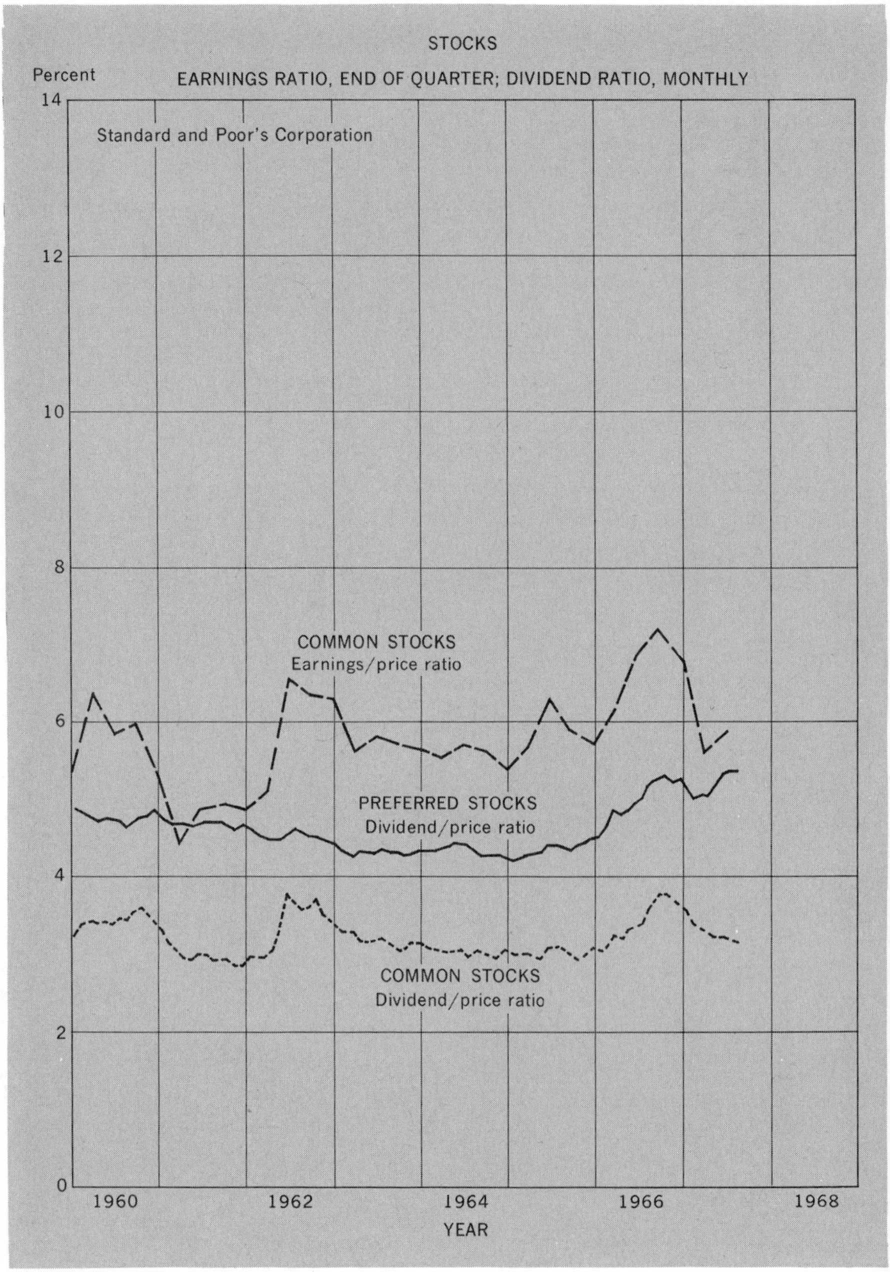

Figure 23–2 Security Yields

SOURCE: *Federal Reserve Chart Book on Financial and Business Statistics*, September 1967, p. 27.

as much because dividends have fluctuated greatly but because the price factor in the denominator has gyrated widely.

The pattern in recent years is shown more clearly in Figure 23–2, which is an enlargement of the segment of Figure 23–1 from 1960 through the first half of 1967. Common stock earnings/price ratios during the 1960s have averaged about 6 percent, ranging from 4.5 to 7.1 percent. Common stock dividend yields fluctuated between 3 and 3.75 percent during this same period. Preferred stocks yields have shown more moderate fluctuations than either earnings/price ratios or dividend yields. Since the late 1950s, preferred stock dividend yields have been about 2 percentage points higher than common stock dividend yields, reflecting the market's expectation that common stock earnings, dividends, and stock prices will grow and provide capital gains to supplement the dividend yield.

Relationship between Long-Term and Short-Term Interest Rates[3]

One of the important elements in the financial manager's timing decisions is an understanding of the relationship between long-term and short-term interest rates. Long-term interest rates are rates on securities with maturities in excess of 5 years. Short-term interest rates are those on securities with maturities of under one year.

Figure 23–3 graphs the relationship between long-term and short-term interest rates. In some periods, short-term interest rates were higher than long-term interest rates; this was true in late 1959 and late 1966, when the money market was extremely tight. These data refute the theory set out by some distinguished economists, who argued on the basis of the evidence of the 1930s that short-term rates of interest are always lower than long-term rates. Their case was based on the reasoning that long-term securities represent a greater degree of risk than do short-term securities. These economists argued that because of the greater risk involved in holding long-term bonds, long-term rates would always be higher than short-term rates. Their reasoning was partially sound, as there is greater risk to holding long-term securities than short-term securities. For one thing, the longer the maturity of the security in an uncertain economic environment, the greater the danger that the firm that issued it may not make an effective adaptation to its environment and, therefore, may not be able to meet its obligations in 10, 15, or 20 years. In addition, the *prices* of long-term bonds are much more volatile than short-term bond prices when interest rates change; the reason for this is largely arithmetic and was described in Chapter 10.

[3] The relationship between long- and short-term interest rates—generally referred to as *the term structure* of interest rates—is developed in summary fashion here and in some detail in the Appendix to this chapter.

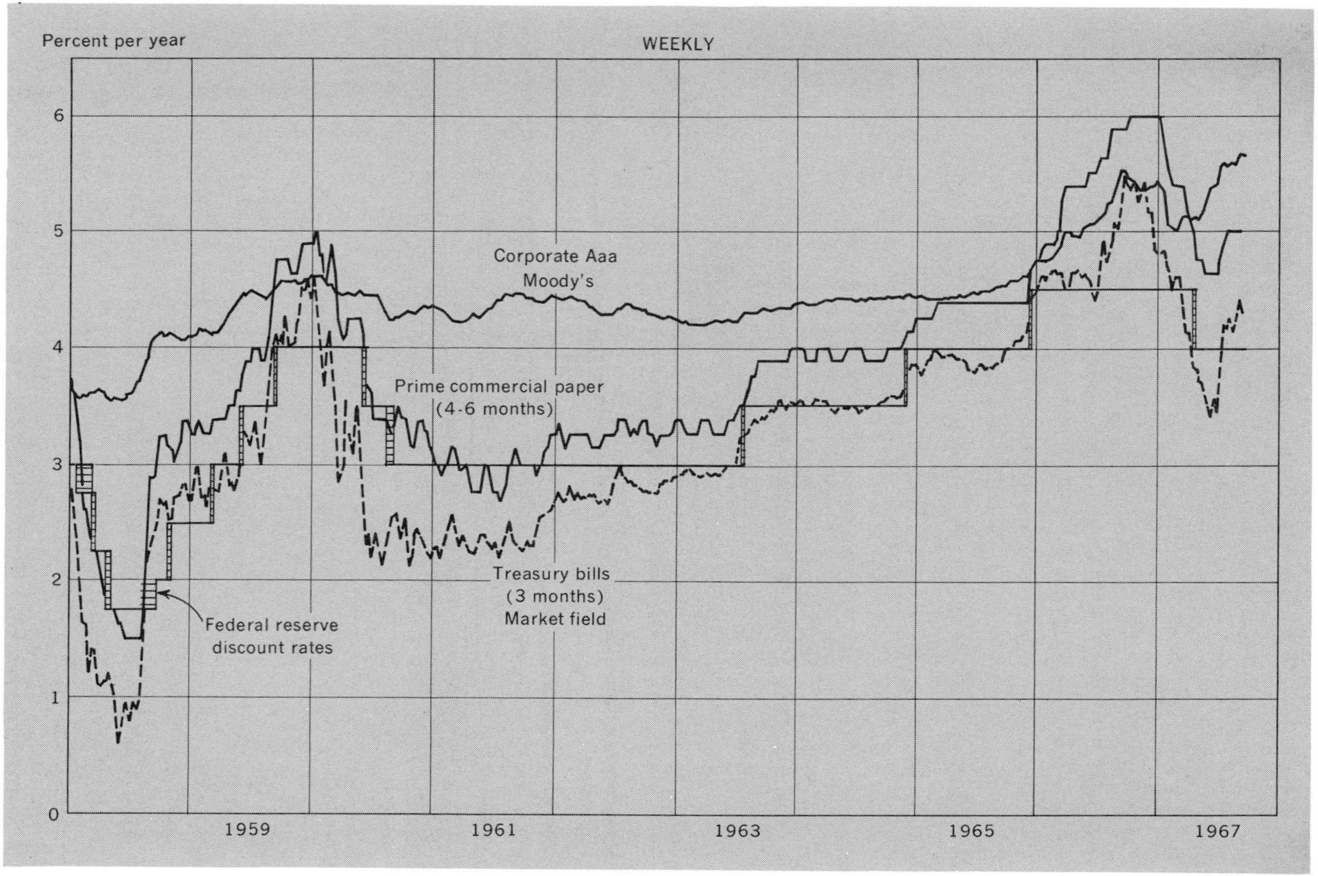

Figure 23–3 Long-Term and Short-Term Interest Rates SOURCE: *Federal Reserve Chart Book on Financial and Business Statistics*, September, 1967, p. 23

However, many other kinds of uncertainties are faced by the firm and the investor, and these other considerations may dominate at some point in time.

One of these uncertainties is the pattern of changes in the supply and demand of loanable funds over time. When the supply of funds is tight relative to the demand for them at prevailing prices, there will be strong pressure for short-term interest rates to rise. Short-term interest rates reflect current supply-and-demand situations. Long-term interest rates reflect an average of supply-and-demand conditions over the life of the security. This characteristic accounts for the fact that short-term interest rates are much more volatile than long-term interest rates (Figure 23–3).

A theory (economists call it the *expectations theory*) has been put forth that long-term interest rates may appropriately be regarded as an average of short-term interest rates. Thus the relationship between long rates and short rates will depend upon what is happening to the future of short-term interest rates, as illustrated by Table 23–2. In section A it is assumed that short-term interest rates rise 1 percent each year, beginning at 2 percent in year 1. The corresponding long-term interest rate in year 1 for a five-year period can be approximated by taking a simple arithmetic average of the five short-term rates, 4 percent. Thus, in year 1, the long-term rate would be double the short-term rate.

TABLE 23–2 RELATIONSHIP BETWEEN SHORT-TERM AND LONG-TERM INTEREST RATES

	A		B	
Year	5-Year Note	Short-Term Rates	5-Year Note	Short-Term Rates
1	4	2	4	6
2		3		5
3		4		4
4		5		3
5		6		2

Consider, however, the situation under section B. Here, in a tight-money situation in year 1, short-term rates are 6 percent; they are expected to decline by 1 percent each year. The average of these rates would be the same as in section A, because the numbers are identical—their order is simply reversed. Now, however, the long-term rate of 4 percent lies below the short-term rate of 6 percent.

These examples do not prove the relation between short-term rates and long-term rates. They do, however, illustrate the pattern that would exist if the only factor operating was expected changes in interest rate movements, themselves reflecting a broad group of supply-and-demand factors. However, many other uncertainty factors do operate on the market. Some of these include differences in the risks of loss and failure among individual business firms, in the economic outlook for different industries, in the degree to which price-level changes affect different products in industries, and in the impact that changes in government legislation will have on different firms in an industry.

Interest Rate Structure

The discussion now turns to an analysis of the wide range of relations between money costs in the postwar period. The basic data on bond yields and interest rates since 1929 for ten categories of instruments were presented in Table 23–1. The table indicates that when a person speaks of "the interest rate," he is in fact referring to an interest rate structure, or cost-of-money structure.

The data in Table 23–1 indicate the range of variations *between* rates on different securities at any moment of time, variations in rates on a particular security over time, and changes in the structure of rates through time. It provides the basic factual background for money cost patterns that will be discussed later. Furthermore, it provides a factual foundation for evaluating the timing of financial policy of firms during the post-World War II period. Reference to the table may be made when solving the problems at the end of this chapter.

As a starting point toward understanding the patterns exhibited in Table 23–1, the data are graphed in Figures 23–4 and 23–5. Figure 23–4 illustrates the relationship between interest rates on 20-year Treasury bonds and three-month Treasury bills over the post-World War II cycles. The relative costs typically spread widely apart during business downturns (the shaded areas) and tend to narrow during business upswings. Not only does the spread vary over time, but the absolute level also varies over time. It will be observed also that the movements in short-term rates are much more volatile than movements in long-term interest levels.

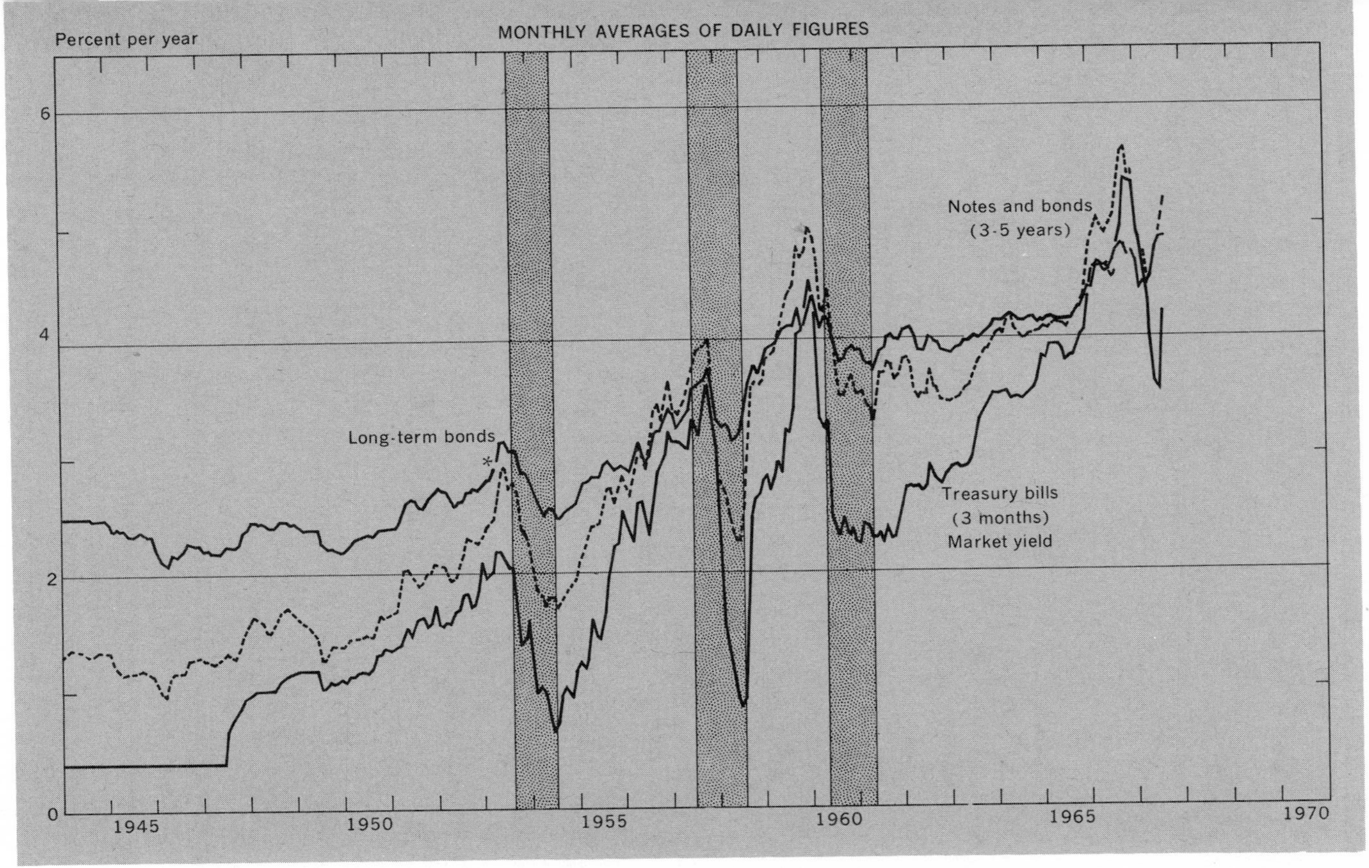

Figure 23–4 **Yields on U.S. Government Securities. Shaded areas represent periods of business contraction as defined by the cyclical reference dates of the National Bureau of Economic Research** SOURCE: *Federal Reserve Chart Book on Financial and Business Statistics*, September 1967, p. 25

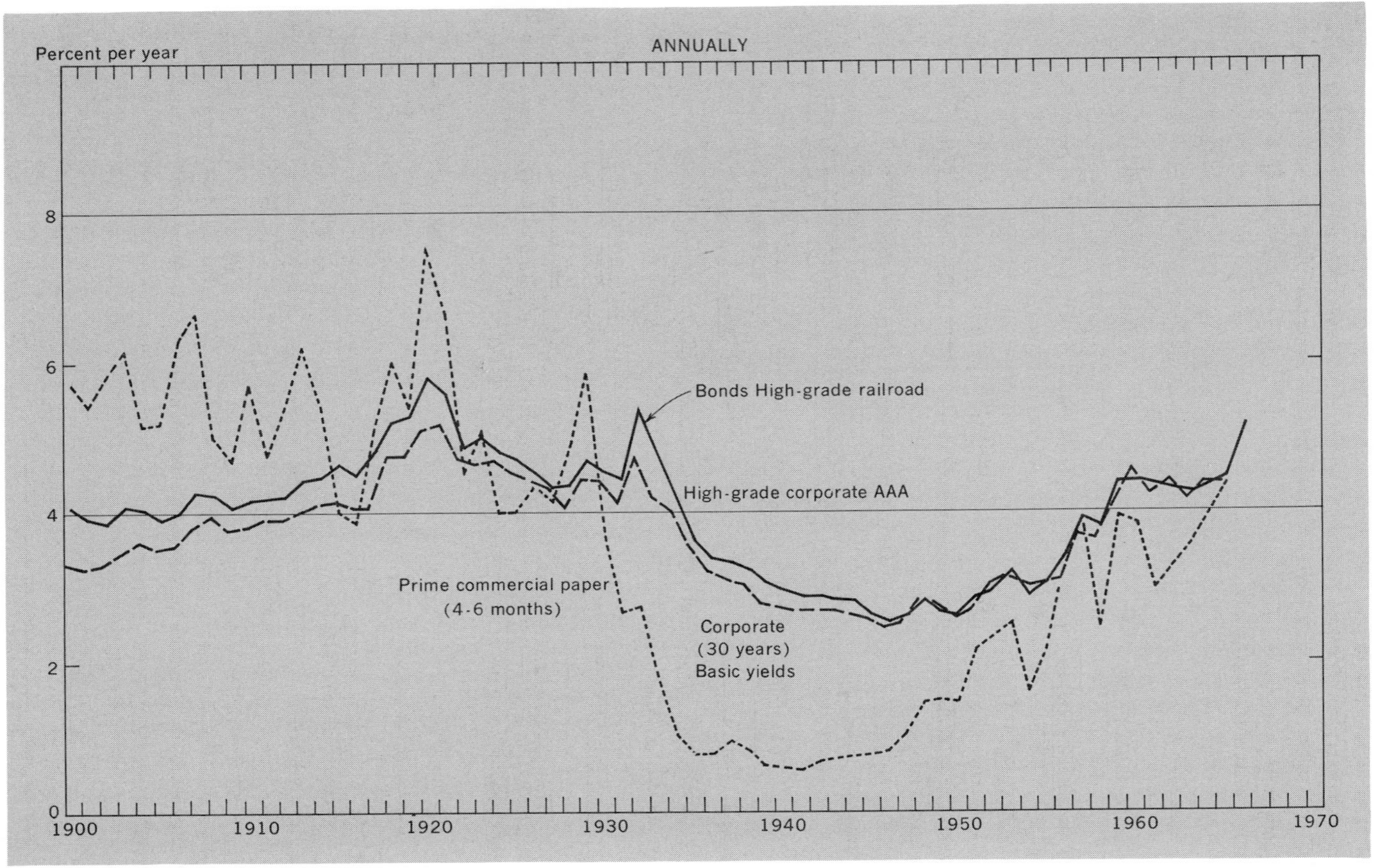

Figure 23–5 Long-Term and Short-Term Interest Rates SOURCE: *Federal Reserve Chart Book on Financial and Business Statistics*, September 1967, p. 23.

Further aspects are presented in Figure 23–5, which presents movements over time in prime commercial paper rates and rates on corporate Triple A bonds. With this abundant factual material on the movements of the cost of money, some generalizations may now be made and systematic patterns observed.

CHARACTERISTIC PATTERNS IN COST OF MONEY

The general nature of the relationships between long- and short-term interest rates and between rates and GNP are shown in Figure 23–6. Short-term interest rates show the widest amplitude of swings. Long-term interest rates are not as sensitive as short-term rates—short-term rates move more quickly than long-term rates. The costs of debt money tend generally to lag movements in general business conditions, both at the peak and at the trough. But the movements of long-term rates lag more than short-term rates. The significance of points A and B in the figure will be explained in a later section.

The cost of equity funds may best be approximated by equity yields, dividends plus capital gains. To understand the behavior of equity yields, the behavior of earnings, dividends, and prices must be analyzed. Corporate earnings are highly volatile. They lead the business cycle both on the upturn and on the downturn, and dividends follow earnings. Prices of common stocks anticipate changes in corporate earnings. Prices of equities are also influenced by money market conditions. Owing to the gradual tightening in money market conditions as expansion continues, bond yields rise and attract money out of stocks and into bonds, causing the prices of equities to turn down before corporate profits reach their peak. Hence, the cost of equity financing turns up because firms receive lower prices for the stocks they sell. In other words, the cost of equity capital begins to rise in the later stages of the business cycle.

If the financial manager is to apply these guidelines effectively, he must know the current stage of the financial cycle whenever he contemplates the acquisition of funds. A forecast of interest rate movements is therefore required. As an approach to laying a framework and foundation for forecasting interest rates, two kinds of material are covered: (1) broad trends to provide a basic foundation and (2) data for short-term forecasting.

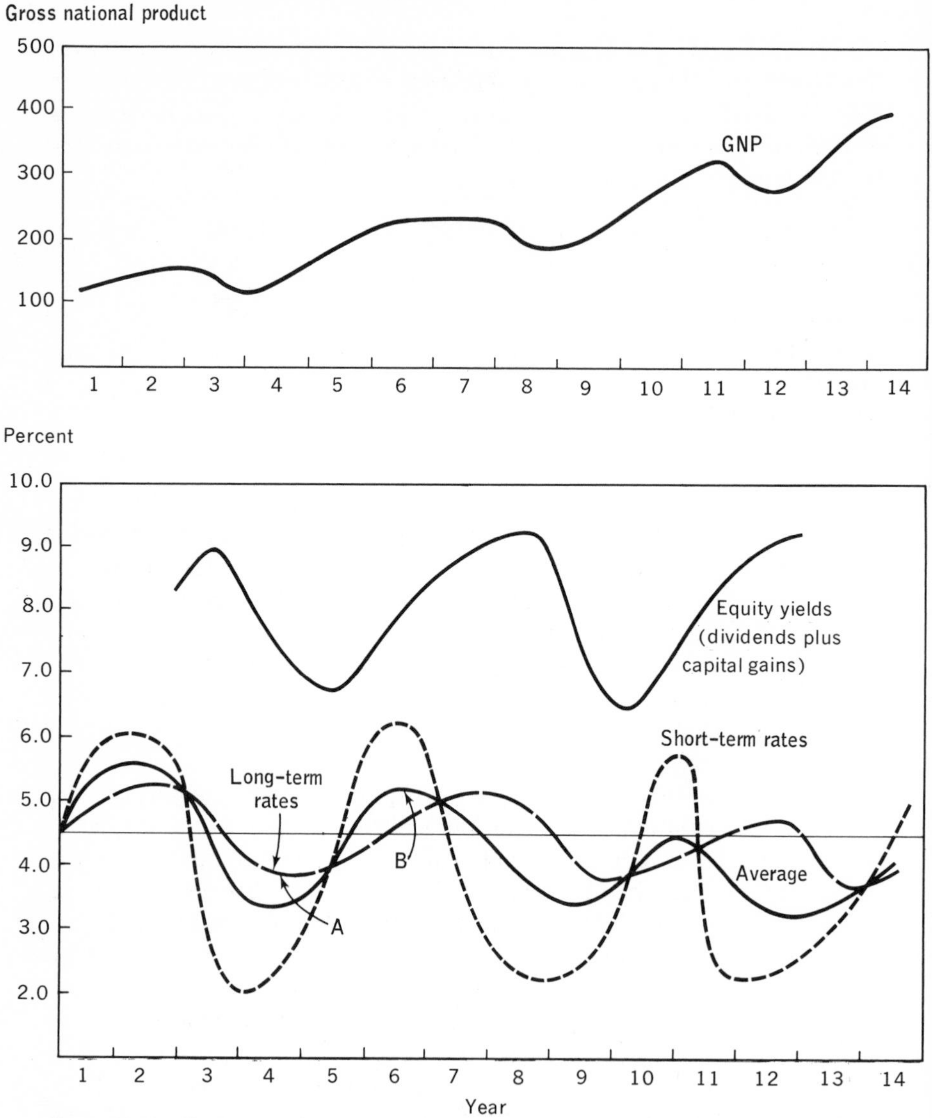

Figure 23–6 Illustrative Relation between Movements of Gross National Product and Interest Rates

PATTERNS IN FUND FLOWS

Within the broad framework described above, the forecaster of short-term movements in interest rates must look at immediate prospects for changes in the short-run supply and demand for funds. In the analysis of the supply and demand for funds, attention will be focused first on the supply of savings. National savings have averaged about 13½ percent of the net national product.[4] Personal savings account for 70 to 75 percent of total savings, with corporate savings making up the remaining 20 to 25 percent of total national savings. National income statistics presented on a current basis generally show personal savings as a percentage of disposable personal income running at about a 6-to-7 percent rate.

There has been an increase in the amount of indirect savings. Indirect savings are transmitted through a financial intermediary (banks, insurance companies, investment funds, pension funds) by the saver to the ultimate user. This percentage has risen from about 25 percent between 1900 and 1929 to about 40 percent in the 1950s and 1960s. Thus a considerable portion of saving does not bring the user and the saver into direct contact.

Another aspect of saving of some significance is that contractual saving, in which the saver makes a long-term commitment to save (for example, life insurance, pensions, mortgage repayments) has risen from 10 percent of the total amount of individual savings around 1900 to 20 percent in the 1920s and well over 50 percent in the 1950s and 1960s. Savings are therefore less subject to discretionary decisions by individuals on a current basis than they were in the past.

The principal uses of funds have been nonfinancial corporate bonds and stocks, real estate mortgages, state and local government net debt, and federal government and agency debt. These are mainly long-term funds. The principal uses of short-term funds have been consumer credit and various types of bank loans, principally short-term bank loans to business. Thus the principal competitors to business borrowers are residential real estate mortgages and federal, state, and local government borrowings.

External long-term corporate financing can be divided into three major categories: common stock, preferred stock, and bonds and notes. Until the bull market in stocks began to surge in 1953, bonds and notes accounted for about 80 percent of external financing (Table 23–3). In recent years, common stock financing has fluctuated markedly, rising in bull market years such as 1961 and declining in weak markets such as 1965 and 1966.

After 1964, bond financing again increased to over 85 percent of financing. Since convertibles, when initially offered, are counted in the bond and preferred stock categories, the great increase in convertible

[4] These data and related material are taken from the *Conference on Savings and Residential Financing, 1958 Proceedings* (United States Savings and Loan League, September 1958). The present data are taken from the paper by Raymond W. Goldsmith, "The Supply of Savings."

TABLE 23–3 CORPORATE SECURITIES OFFERED FOR CASH SALE IN THE UNITED STATES,* 1934–1967

YEAR	COMMON STOCK (MILLIONS OF DOLLARS)	COMMON STOCK (PERCENTAGES)	PREFERRED STOCK (MILLIONS OF DOLLARS)	PREFERRED STOCK (PERCENTAGES)	BONDS AND NOTES (MILLIONS OF DOLLARS)	BONDS AND NOTES (PERCENTAGES)	TOTALS (MILLIONS OF DOLLARS)
1934	19	4.8	6	1.5	372	93.7	397
1935	22	0.9	86	3.7	2,224	95.4	2,332
1936	272	6.0	271	5.9	4,028	88.1	4,572
1937	285	12.4	406	17.6	1,618	70.0	2,310
1938	25	1.2	86	4.0	2,044	94.8	2,155
1939	87	4.0	98	4.5	1,980	91.5	2,164
1940	108	4.1	183	6.8	2,386	89.1	2,677
1941	110	4.1	167	6.3	2,390	89.6	2,667
1942	34	3.2	112	10.4	917	86.4	1,062
1943	56	4.8	124	10.6	990	84.6	1,170
1944	163	5.1	369	11.5	2,670	83.4	3,202
1945	397	6.6	758	12.6	4,855	80.8	6,011
1946	891	12.9	1,127	16.3	4,882	70.8	6,900
1947	779	11.8	762	11.6	5,036	76.6	6,577
1948	614	8.7	492	7.0	5,973	84.3	7,078
1949	736	12.2	425	7.0	4,890	80.8	6,052
1950	811	12.8	631	9.9	4,920	77.3	6,361
1951	1,212	15.7	838	10.8	5,691	73.5	7,741
1952	1,369	14.4	564	5.9	7,601	79.7	9,534
1953	1,326	14.9	489	5.5	7,083	79.6	8,898
1954	1,213	12.7	816	8.6	7,488	78.7	9,516
1955	2,185	21.3	635	6.2	7,420	72.5	10,240
1956	2,301	21.0	636	5.8	8,002	73.2	10,939
1957	2,516	19.5	411	3.2	9,957	77.3	12,884
1958	1,334	11.6	571	4.9	9,653	83.5	11,558
1959	2,027	20.8	531	5.4	7,190	73.8	9,748
1960	1,664	16.4	409	4.0	8,081	79.6	10,154
1961	3,294	25.0	450	3.4	9,420	71.6	13,165
1962	1,314	12.3	422	3.9	8,969	83.8	10,705
1963	1,022	8.4	342	2.8	10,872	88.8	12,237
1964	2,679	19.2	412	3.0	10,865	77.8	13,957
1965	1,547	9.7	725	4.5	13,720	85.8	15,992
1966	1,940	10.5	570	3.1	15,908	86.4	18,418
1967	1,959	8.0	885	3.5	21,954	88.5	24,798

* Gross proceeds.
SOURCE: SEC Statistical Bulletins.

financing causes the role of fixed-charge financing to be greater than it actually is on a longer term basis. Most convertibles will be converted into common stock, so it is somewhat misleading to classify convertible financing with regular preferred stock or debt issues. Thus there is a bias in the table.

FORECASTING THE LEVEL OF INTEREST RATES

Although profound and impressive studies of the theory of interest rates have been made, from the practical standpoint it is necessary merely to assess the future behavior of the major supply-and-demand factors. The major categories of the sources and uses of funds for the economy are set out in Table 23–4. By projecting the sources and uses of funds in different categories, the direction of the pressure on interest rates can be estimated.[5]

The table can be used in the following way. Historical patterns can be established to show uses and sources of funds in relation to the growth of the economy as a whole as measured by GNP. When in any particular year the demand for funds grows faster than the supply in relation to historical patterns, interest rates are likely to rise. These extra funds are supplied by drawing on the commercial banking system, which is the pivot in the financial mechanism. Whenever the demand for funds must be met by drawing on the commercial banking system to a greater-than-normal degree, interest rates rise.

The data for 1966 present an interesting pattern. Statistics for 1966 reflect the impact of the tight money policy followed by the Federal Reserve System during most of the year. As a consequence of this policy, the total supply of funds in 1966 *decreased* by over $10 billion from the $61.6 billion total of 1965. The realized use (demand) for funds necessarily declined by a like amount, but it is estimated that at least $20 billion of unsatisfied demands for funds existed during 1966.

Another significant statistic in the table is the rise in the supply of funds from Individuals and Miscellaneous; funds from this source rose by almost $6 billion during 1966, and a further increase of $13 billion was estimated for 1968. With tight money, the ability of the commercial

[5] Compilations of studies of these kinds are facilitated by the flow of funds data developed by the Federal Reserve System, published in the monthly *Federal Reserve Bulletin.*

TABLE 23–4 DEMAND AND SUPPLY FOR CREDIT (billions $)

DEMAND	1961	1962	1963	1964	1965	1966	1967E	1968E
Mortgages (after Agency purchases)	18.9	21.9	26.7	25.6	25.1	17.5	19.5	20.5
Corporate Bonds	5.2	4.9	5.6	6.6	8.1	11.1	15.2	13.1
Term Loans	1.0	1.4	2.0	2.8	5.3	4.8	3.5	4.2
State and Local Securities	5.0	5.3	6.3	5.6	7.1	5.6	9.0	9.2
Foreign Bonds	0.5	0.9	1.1	0.9	1.2	0.9	0.9	0.8
Investment Demand, Long Term	30.6	34.4	41.7	41.5	46.8	39.9	48.1	47.8
Other Bank Loans (ex Term and Mortgages)	4.6	8.6	9.1	10.8	14.3	8.2	7.5	8.5
U.S. Government Debt (Publicly Held)*	5.8	6.1	2.5	3.2	0.5	2.9	3.2	12.2
Total Demand	41.0	49.1	53.3	55.5	61.6	51.0	58.8	68.5
SUPPLY†								
Savings Banks	2.2	3.0	3.6	4.1	3.6	2.5	4.7	3.5
Savings and Loan Associations	9.4	10.4	13.0	10.9	9.3	4.3	7.3	6.0
Life Insurance Companies	4.9	5.3	5.9	6.4	6.6	7.1	7.0	7.0
Fire and Casualty Insurance Companies	0.9	0.9	0.9	0.8	1.0	1.1	1.0	1.1
Private Pension Funds	1.5	1.7	1.9	2.1	2.1	1.9	2.1	2.3
Public Retirement Funds	2.1	2.2	2.5	2.7	2.9	3.2	3.7	4.0
Mutual Funds	0.2	0.7	−0.1	0.4	0.4	0.9	0.1	0.3
Nonbank Institutions	21.2	24.2	27.7	27.4	25.9	21.0	25.9	24.2
Commercial Banks	15.9	19.2	18.8	21.5	27.9	17.2	35.0	30.0
Corporations, State and Local Governments, Foreigners	−0.6	2.1	2.5	−0.5	0.6	−0.2	−3.0	0.5
Individuals and Miscellaneous	4.5	3.6	4.3	7.1	7.2	13.0	0.9	13.8
Total Supply	41.0	49.1	53.3	55.5	61.6	51.0	58.8	68.5

* Includes direct debt, Federal agencies and public corporation sales.
† Excludes funds for equities, cash, and miscellaneous demands not tabulated above.
SOURCE: Henry Kaufman, "Pressure on Capital and Money Markets," *Commercial and Financial Chronicle*, 206 (October 5, 1967), p. 24.

banks and other financial institutions to supply funds is restricted relative to demand. This produces high interest rates, and these high rates induce individuals, businesses, and others to make their surplus funds available to borrowers. Thus the supply of funds is augmented from nonbanking sources, but only at substantially higher interest rates.

The importance of monetary and fiscal policy when making forecasts of interest rate movements has been suggested. The nature of these governmental influences is now briefly treated.

FEDERAL RESERVE POLICY

No discussion of interest rate behavior would be complete without an analysis of the role of the central bank, which in the United States is the Federal Reserve System. The central bank is equipped with a set of powers having a significant influence on the operations of commercial banks, whose loan and investment activities in turn have an important influence on the supply of money. Of these powers the most powerful, and hence the one used most sparingly, is *changing reserve requirements*. The one most often used, which can be applied in a more direct and pinpointed fashion, is *changing the pattern of open-market operations*. Changes in the *discount rates* are likely to have more of a psychological influence than direct quantitative effects.

Changes in discount rate levels are shown in the last column of Table 23–1. These changes represent the announcement by Federal Reserve authorities that a change in economic conditions has taken place calling for a future tightening or easing of monetary conditions, signaled by the direction of change in the discount rate. The data in Table 23–1 demonstrate that increases in the Federal Reserve bank discount rate have been associated with rising interest rate levels.

Selective controls over real estate and consumer credit have been enforced periodically, but experience with them is not sufficient to determine whether the Federal Reserve authorities can effectively utilize these instruments of selective credit control. Changes in stock margin requirements have been used to counter strong movements in stock prices and probably perform some useful role. However, the underlying influences which determine stock prices are so strong and pervasive that changes in margin requirements typically are not of sufficient power to determine the future course of stock market prices.

FISCAL POLICY

The fiscal policy of the federal government has considerable impact on the movements in interest rates. A cash budget deficit represents a stimulating influence by the federal government, and a cash surplus exerts a restraining influence from the government-spending sector of the economy. However, this generalization must be modified to reflect the way a deficit is financed and by the way a surplus is used. To have the most stimulating effect, the deficit should be financed by sale of securities through the banking system, particularly the central bank—this provides a maximum amount of bank reserves and permits a multiple expansion in the money supply. To have the most restrictive effect, the surplus should be used to retire bonds held by the banking system, particularly the central bank, thus reducing bank reserves and causing a multiple contraction in the supply of money.

The impact of Treasury financing programs will be different at different times. Ordinarily, when the Treasury needs to draw on funds from the money market, it competes with other potential users of funds; the result may be a rise in interest rate levels. However, the desire to hold down interest rates also influences Treasury and Federal Reserve policy. To ensure the success of a large new offering, Federal Reserve authorities may temporarily ease money conditions, a procedure that will tend to soften interest rates. If the Treasury encounters resistance in selling securities in the nonbanking sector, securities may be sold in large volume to the commercial banking system, which expands its reserves and thereby increases the monetary base. This change in turn tends to lower the level of interest rates.

The interaction of monetary and fiscal policies is illustrated by the events since the early 1960s. Figure 23–7 presents the pattern of growth rates in gross national product both in current dollars and in constant dollars since 1959. Gross national product in current dollars increased at a 6.8 percent compound annual rate from the first quarter of 1961 through the fourth quarter of 1964. Real national product during the same period increased at a 5.4 percent annual rate, indicating that price inflation was about 1.4 percent a year. When growth in GNP rose to a 9.9 percent rate during 1965, the economy was able to achieve a growth in real product of 7.7 percent, indicating a 2.2 percent price inflation.

The role of monetary and fiscal policies during these periods is suggested by Figure 23–8. In the earlier period with moderate growth in

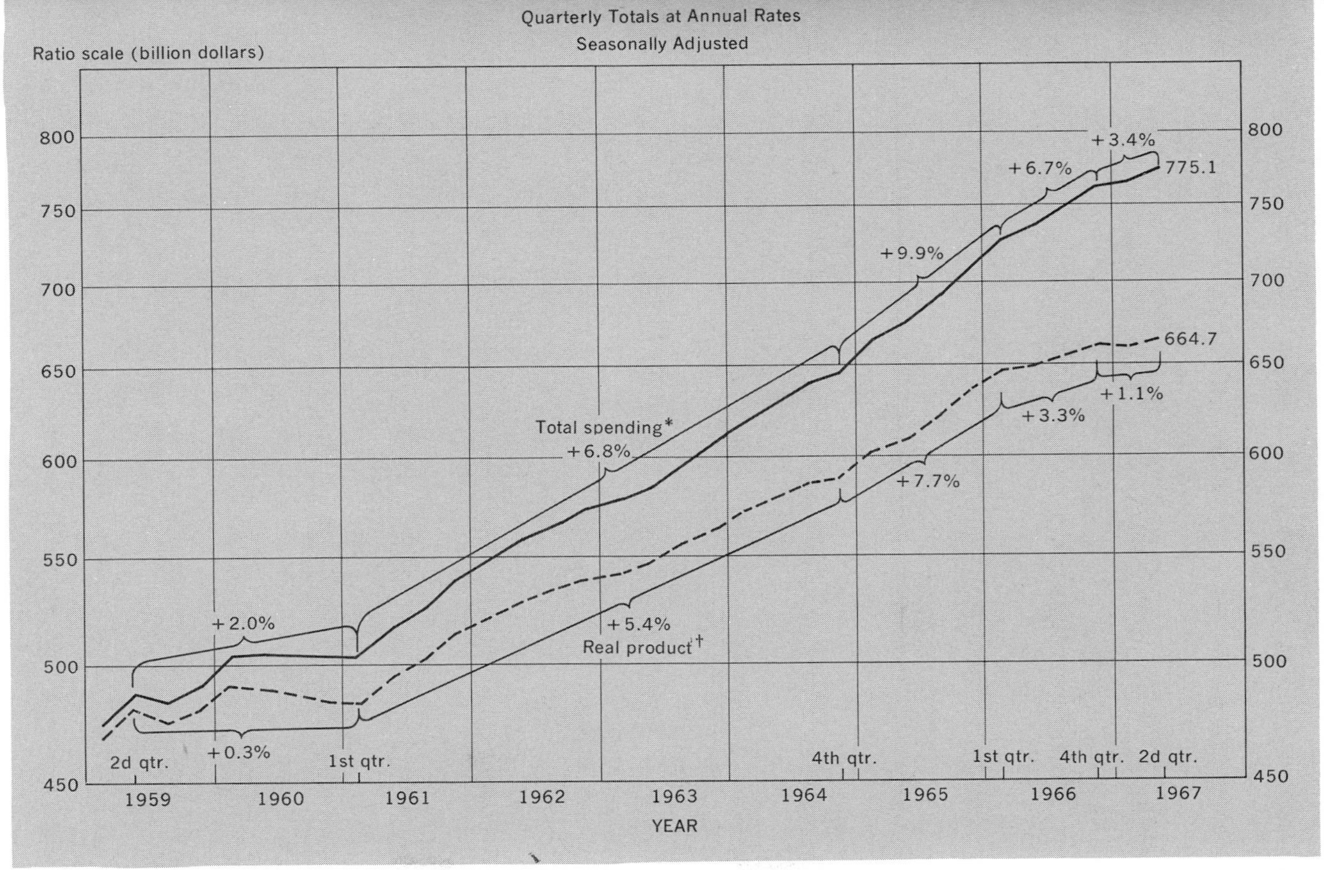

Figure 23–7 **Demand and Production** SOURCE: U.S. Department of Commerce. Prepared by Federal Reserve Bank of St. Louis.

*GNP in current dollars. †GNP in 1958 dollars.

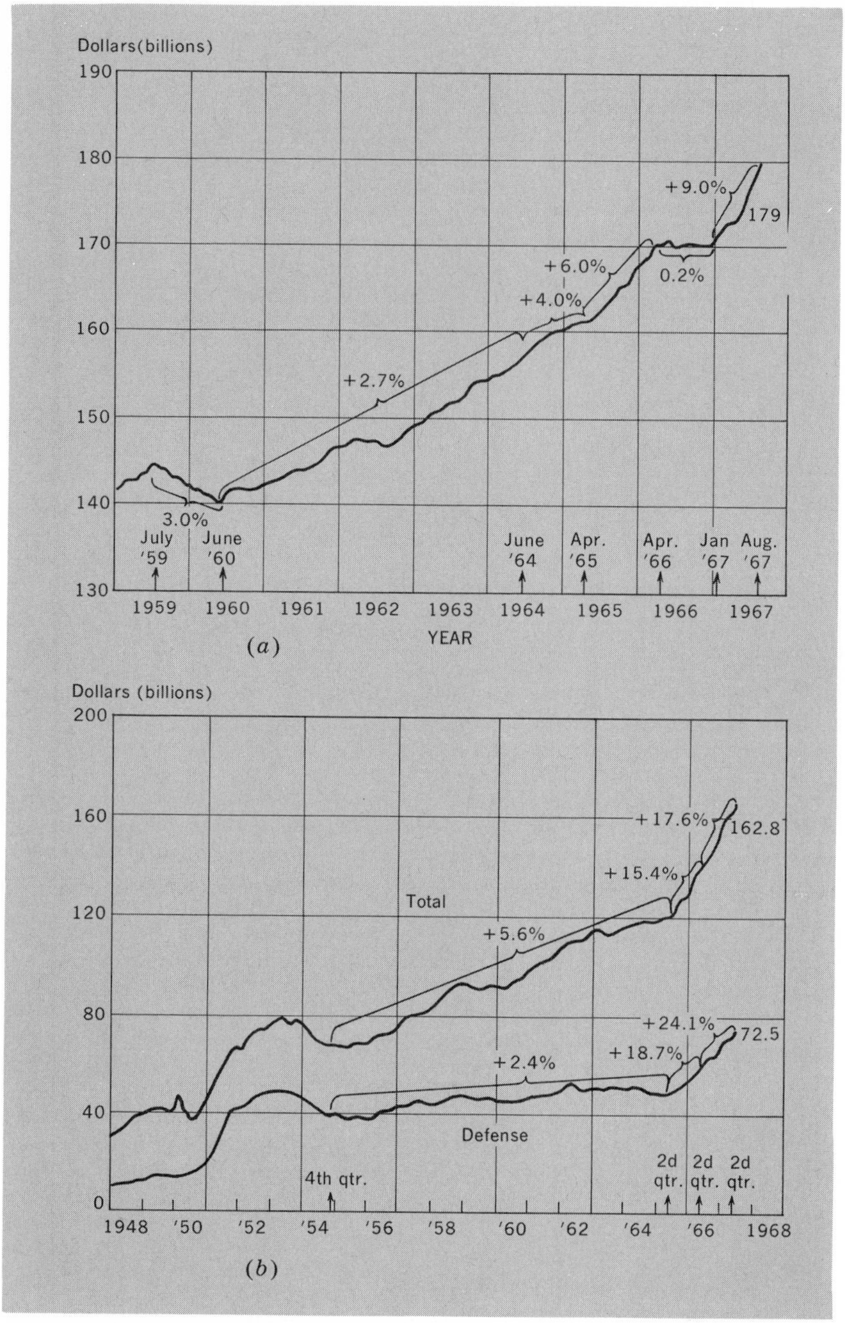

Figure 23–8 *upper* **Money Stock;** *lower* **Federal Government Expenditures—National Income Accounts Budget. Percentages are annual rates of change between periods indicated. They are presented as an aid in comparing most recent developments with past trends.**

SOURCE: Federal Reserve Bank of St. Louis, *Monthly Review*, September 1967, 5, 6.

GNP, both the monetary stock and federal government expenditures grew at moderate rates. During 1965, however, the rate of increase in the monetary stock jumped from about 3 percent to about 6 percent a year. Defense spending increased 18.7 percent in this one year, causing total federal government spending to rise by almost the same percentage. Fearing that the rate of inflation would increase, in 1966 the Federal Reserve System caused the money stock to shrink at a 2 percent annual rate. This produced a reduction in the annual growth rate of GNP from about 9 percent during the fourth quarter of 1966 to a rate of about 3.4 percent in the second quarter of 1967. Since defense spending increased at a 24.1 percent annual rate between the second quarter of 1966 and the second quarter of 1967, the slowdown in GNP growth must have occurred in the nondefense sector of the economy.

To combat the decline in the GNP growth rate, the Fed allowed the money stock to grow at a 9 percent annual rate during early 1967. This action by the monetary authorities exerted an expansionary influence on the economy; it brought with it, however, fears of more inflation and another tight-money period, which resulted in a considerable amount of anticipatory long-term financing by corporate financial managers.

Events in the money and capital markets during the latter part of 1968 demonstrate that the financial crunch of the summer of 1966 was not an isolated occurrence. Financial managers have had to face up to dealing with financial markets which have reflected the effects of inflation since 1965 and the *expectations* of continued inflation. With inflationary expectations, major impacts on financial markets take place.

Suppliers of funds become increasingly reluctant to place their funds in fixed-return securities, and do so only at rates of interest that include a premium for loss of purchasing power. Sources of straight debt financing begin to dry up; increasingly, debt instruments must carry equity features such as convertibility or warrants. Direct placements and directly negotiated mortgages on income properties also require equity participation features. Since the escalation in Vietnam in mid-1965, bond prices had been in a downward trend. Bond dealers found it increasingly difficult to carry on their operations. A quotation from the *New York Times* illustrates the problem: "For the nation, these doubts of bond dealers carry a serious warning that inflation must be slowed from its present rate. If it isn't, normal methods of financing economic growth will have to be discarded and replaced with different ways of raising capital, some economists fear."[6]

Interest rates in late 1968 and early 1969 reached their highest postwar levels. To stop inflationary expectations, the monetary-fiscal au-

[6] John H. Allan, "Why Bond Men Are Losing Sleep," *New York Times,* December 39, 1968, Section 3, p. 1.

thorities have found it necessary to pursue highly restrictive policies. Either they will "put the brake to the floor" or carry on steadily increasingly restraint over a sustained period. A period of inflation and the policies required to cope with inflation thus confront financial managers with new challenges. They must effectively combine debt and equity features in a given financing. The timing of financing must put the firm in a position to be independent of the need for external funds during financial crunches. The financial manager must also judge the length and severity of restrictive policies to determine whether interest rates have reached a peak or a plateau.

These events of 1966 through 1968 are described to illustrate different types of economic conditions and to show that fluctuations in money costs and availability, which have confronted financial managers in past decades, are still present and will continue to challenge the knowledge and judgment of these men in the years ahead. The financial manager will find it necessary and desirable to keep in close touch with federal budgetary developments and the nature of governmental policy, particularly interactions between fiscal and monetary policies, in order to judge trends in costs of money.[7] This subject deserves much more detailed and analytical treatment than can be given here, for it is of great significance for sound decision making by financial managers.

IMPLICATION OF COST OF MONEY PATTERNS FOR TIMING OF FINANCIAL POLICY

Variations in the cost of money and its availability are likely to be of great significance for decisions by financial managers. The importance of the sound timing of financial policy is further underscored by the mistakes observed in practice.[8]

Financial managers have tended to shift from short-term funds to long-term funds too late during the business upswing. Characteristically, firms have relied on short-term financing during the early stages of

[7] Useful sources of current information in addition to the monthly issues of the *Federal Reserve Bulletin* are *Economic Indicators,* prepared for the Joint Economic Committee of the U.S. Congress by the President's Council of Economic Advisers, and *Business Cycle Developments,* prepared by the Bureau of the Census of the U.S. Department of Commerce. Both of the latter publications are available on a subscription basis from the Superintendent of Documents, Government Printing Office, Washington, D.C., 20402.

[8] For illustrations, see J. Weston, "Financial Implications of Growth," *Controller,* (March 1958), 118–120.

a business upswing. The reason for this can clearly be seen from Figure 23–5. The cost of short-term money remains below the cost of long-term money until well into the boom. Furthermore, as recovery takes place, the major need for funds is for working capital purposes. Although these needs are permanent, as has been demonstrated previously, many financial managers in the past have tended to regard the financing of working capital as only a temporary use of funds.

As a consequence, the acquisition of long-term funds has been delayed until relatively late in the business upswing. Specifically, long-term funds have been acquired at point *B* in Figure 23–6 rather than at point *A*. At point *B*, there is an apparent logic in obtaining long-term funds rather than short-term funds. Compared with acquiring long-term funds at point *A*, the timing of the acquisition of long-term funds is unsound. It leads to obtaining long-term funds at a $4\frac{1}{4}$ percent rate, when they could have been obtained at something like a $3\frac{3}{4}$ percent rate earlier in the upswing. Another advantage of obtaining the funds at point *A* is that credit conditions are relatively much easier at this stage, and the terms under which funds may be acquired are likely to be much less onerous than they will be near the peak of the boom.

It is likely, therefore, that by making proper financial requirement projections, as described earlier, and by keeping historical perspective on the growth of the economy and the pattern of interest rate behavior, financial managers can improve the timing of their acquisition of debt funds. They can lower the cost and improve the terms of financing by obtaining long-term funds early in the upswing. As the upturn in business conditions improves, the firm will have the benefit of trading on the equity with the use of long-term debt money.

Before the peak of the business upswing, the firm may properly sell equity securities, replacing some of its debt. By selling equities near the highs of common stock prices, the firm is able to increase its equity base to the degree necessary to facilitate the sale of additional long-term debt money at the low point of the next business cycle.

Although all the strategies of the timing of financial policy are not encompassed by this brief overview, it does serve to focus attention on the need for awareness of changes in the cost of different forms of money during different stages of fluctuations in the level of business activity.

SUMMARY

In general, the financial manager should seek to time the acquisition of funds for his business enterprise in relation to trends and cycles in general business and in interest rates. At the beginning of a business upswing it is likely to be advantageous to raise funds through long-term debt sources. Although short-term rates are lower than long-term rates at this stage of the cycle, the magnitude of swings in short-term rates is large. In the later stages of a business upswing, short-term rates exceed long-term rates, and both are much higher. Qualitative aspects of financing reflected in credit terms will also be considerably more favorable if long-term borrowing is arranged during the beginning of the upswing. The firm will also obtain larger benefits from trading on the equity.

Later in the upswing, the equity markets are likely to be strong. Equity financing should be used for expansion and for replacing long-term debt financing arranged early in the upswing. At this time, interest rates will be relatively high, and equity yields relatively low. This situation allows refunding of debt issues and builds the equity base for protection during the downswing and for trading on the equity during the next upswing.

QUESTIONS

23–1 "It makes good sense for a firm to fund its floating debt, because this relieves the possibility that it will be called upon to pay off debt at an awkward time. However, from the standpoint of cost, it is always cheaper to use short-term debt than long-term debt." Discuss the statement.

23–2 Historical data indicate that more than twice as much capital is raised yearly by selling bonds than by selling common stocks. Does this indicate that corporate capital structures are becoming overburdened with debt?

23–3 Distinguish between the money market and the capital market. How are they related?

23–4 Is the Federal Reserve's tight money policy restraining the country's economic growth? Discuss the pros and cons from the corporation's viewpoint.

23–5 Why do interest rates on different types of securities vary widely?

23–6 What does GNP represent? Why are its level and growth significant to the financial manager?

23–7 Figure 23–5 indicates that short-term interest rates were higher than long-term interest rates for most of the period 1900–1930. Is there any reason to believe that this relationship may again prevail during the period 1970–1980?

23–8 Are short-term rates of any value in forecasting the rates for the long-term market?

PROBLEMS

23–1 In mid-1958 the Central Company made a reappraisal of its sales forecasts for the next one, two, and five years. It was clear that the product development program which had been under way for the previous five years was now coming to fruition. The officers of Central were confident that a sales growth of 12 to 15 percent a year (on a compound basis) for the next five years was strongly indicated unless general business declined.

The Central Company has total assets of $10 million. It has a debt-to-total assets ratio of 29 percent. Since it has been spending heavily on research and development during the past five years, its profits have been depressed and the stock has not been favorably regarded by investors.

The Central Company learned that it could borrow on a short-term basis at 2.5 percent (the rate for prime commercial paper at mid-1958 was 1.6 percent) and sell some common stock or float some nonconvertible long-term bonds at 4 percent. Central financed by selling $2 million of common stock (the maximum to avoid control problems) and by short-term loans at the lower rates until early 1960, when it found that its growing financial requirements could not be met by short-term borrowing. Its need for financing was so great that Central sold $10 million convertible debentures at 5.5 percent (the rate on prime commercial paper at this time was almost 5 percent) and with terms requiring a strong current ratio and limitations on fixed assets purchases. The price of its common stock had quadrupled by mid-1959 but had dropped by 10 percent in early 1960.

Evaluate the timing of the selection of forms of financing by the Central Company.

23–2 In July 1958, as the economy in general was emerging from the 1957–1958 downturn and the Flexible Container Corporation's business was resuming its strong growth in sales, Fred Bolden, the treasurer, concluded that the firm would require more working capital financing during the year ending June 30, 1959. Below are the historical and *pro forma* income statements and balance sheets of the Flexible Container Corporation.

How should the financing needs be met? Why? (Although the $800 *pro forma* financial requirements are shown in the long-term section of the balance sheet, they can be met with either long- or short-term funds.)

FLEXIBLE CONTAINER CORPORATION
BALANCE SHEETS
1958 and 1959, *Pro Forma*
(in thousand dollars)

Assets	1958	1959
Cash	$ 200	$ 600
Receivables	800	1,200
Inventories	1,000	1,600
Total current assets	$2,000	$3,400
Fixed assets, net	1,000	2,000
Total assets	$3,000	$5,400
Liabilities and Capital		
Accounts payable	300	500
Accruals	100	200
Reserves for taxes	600	800
Total current liabilities	$1,000	$1,500
Additional financing needed	0	800
Common stock, $10 par	1,000	1,000
Surplus	1,000	2,100
Total liabilities and capital	$3,000	$5,400

FLEXIBLE CONTAINER CORPORATION
INCOME STATEMENTS
For Years Ended June 30, 1958 and 1959

	1958	1959
Sales, net	$10,000	$14,000
Cost of sales	8,000	10,000
Gross profit	2,000	4,000
Operating expenses	1,000	1,500
Operating profit	1,000	2,500
Other income, net	200	100
Profits before taxes	1,200	2,600
Taxes	600	1,300
Net profit after taxes	600	1,300
Dividends	100	200
Retained earnings	$ 500	$ 1,100

Selected References

Eisner, Robert, "Factors Affecting the Level of Interest Rates," in *Savings and Residential Financing* (Chicago: U.S. Savings and Loan League, 1968), 28–40.

Frazer, W. J., Jr., "Some Factors Affecting Business Financing," *Southern Economic Journal,* XXV (July 1958), 33–47.

Freund, William C. "The Dynamic Financial Markets," *Financial Executive,* XXXIII (May 1965), 11–26, 57–58.

Freund, William C., and Edward D. Zinbarg, "Application of Flow of Funds to Interest-Rate Forecasting," *Journal of Finance,* XVIII (May 1963), 231–248.

Friedman, Milton, "Factors Affecting the Level of Interest Rates," in *Savings and Residential Financing* (Chicago: U.S. Savings and Loan League, 1968), 10–27.

Grossman, Herschel I., "The Term Structure of Interest Rates," *Journal of Finance,* XXII (December 1967), 611–622.

Johnson, N. O., "Financing Industrial Growth," *Journal of Finance,* XII (May 1957), 264–271.

Johnson, Ramon E., "Term Structures of Corporate Bond Yields as a Function of Risk of Default," *Journal of Finance,* XXII (May 1967), 313–345.

Kessel, Reuben A., *Cyclical Behavior of the Term Structure of Interest Rates* (New York: National Bureau of Economic Research, 1965).

Meltzer, Allan H., "Mercantile Credit, Monetary Policy, and Size of Firms," *Review of Economics and Statistics,* XLII (November 1960), 429–437.

Meiselman, David, "The Policy Implications of Current Research in the Term Structure of Interest Rates," in *Savings and Residential Financing* (Chicago: U.S. Savings and Loan League, 1968) 84–97.

Ritter, L. S., *Money and Economic Analysis,* 3d ed. (New York: Houghton Mifflin, 1967).

Robinson, Roland I., *Money and Capital Markets* (New York: McGraw-Hill, 1964).

Tussing, A. Dale, "Can Monetary Policy Influence the Availability of Credit?" *Journal of Finance,* XXI (March 1966), 1–14.

Van Horne, James, "Interest-Rate Expectations, the Shape of the Yield Curve, and Monetary Policy," *Review of Economics and Statistics,* XLVIII (May 1966), 211–215.

———, "Interest-Rate Risk and the Term Structure of Interest Rates," *Journal of Political Economy,* LXXIII (August 1965), 344–351.

Woodworth, G. Walter, *The Money Market and Monetary Management* (New York: Harper & Row, 1965).

APPENDIX TO CHAPTER 23
Term Structure of Interest Rates

The *term structure of interest rates* describes the relationship between interest rates and loan maturity. When measuring the term structure, we generally use yields on U.S. Government securities. The term structure on other instruments, however, varies similarly.

Figure A23–1 shows the term structure of rates in two recent years, 1963 and 1966. In the lower curve, for 1963, we see a pattern of rising yields—the shorter the maturity, the lower the rate of interest. This rising yield structure has been typical for most years since 1930. The higher curve, for 1966, shows a yield curve that rises for the first two years and declines as the term to maturity increases.

In addition to illustrating the changing term structure of interest rates, Figure A23–1 also reveals a shift in the "level of rates." Between May 1963 and May 1966, the interest rate on all government securities—long term and short term—rose. The upward movement is defined as an increase in the *general level of interest rates.*[1]

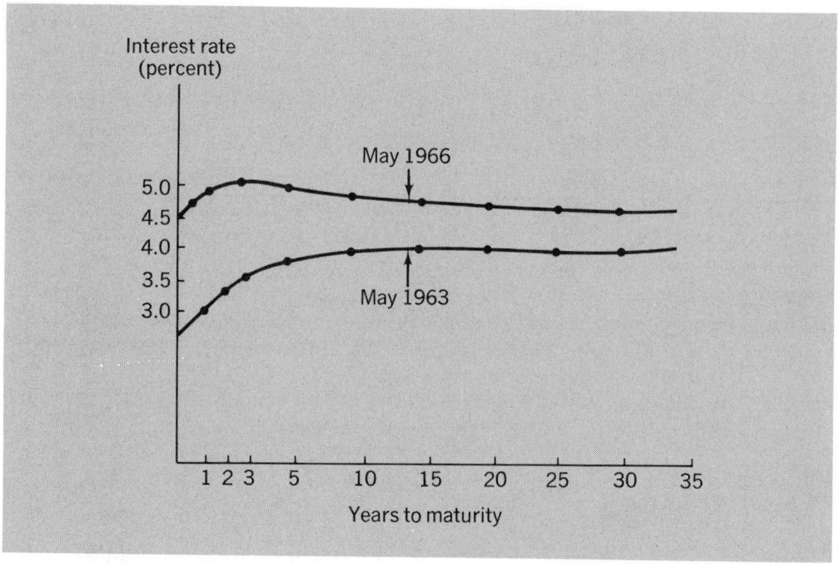

Figure A23–1 Term Structure of Rates on U.S. Government Securities, May 1963 and May 1966

[1] In addition to the level and term structure of rates on a given class of securities—in this case, government securities—there is also the pattern of relationships among different classes of securities. The interrelationships between various classes of securities—for example, mortgages, government bonds, corporates, and bank business loans—is not discussed here. In general, movements in the term structure and level of rates are similar for most classes of securities.

Historical Yield Curves

Figure A23–2 shows the yields on U.S. Government securities of various maturities for the period 1944 through 1967. Three maturities are shown—three-month treasury bills, three- to five-year notes, and long-term bonds. Several features of the figure should be noted:

1. At the beginning of the time span under observation—the World War II period and the immediate postwar years—the spread between short-term and long-term rates was relatively constant and very large.
2. Interest rates rose during the period 1947 to 1953, and the spread also narrowed during these six years.
3. Interest rates fell in the latter part of 1953 and reached a trough in 1954. During this period of decline, the spread between long- and short-term governments widened.
4. Interest rates rose substantially from mid-1954 through mid-1957. Simultaneously, the gap between short- and long-term governments narrowed; at the 1957 peak, the yields on three- to five-year notes exceeded the yields on long-term governments.
5. Rates declined dramatically from mid-1957 to mid-1958, and during this period the spread between short- and long-term securities exceeded any other shown on the graph before or after that date.
6. Interest rates climbed markedly from 1958 to 1959; again, the spread narrowed, and at the 1959 peak the rates on long-term governments were below those on treasury bills and three- to five-year notes.
7. Rates declined from 1959 to 1960, and again the spread widened.
8. Interest rates increased from 1960 to 1966, accompanied by the now familiar narrowing of the spread between short- and long-term governments. Again, short-term rates exceeded long-term rates at the 1966 peak.

This analysis of Figure A23–2 clearly reveals the cyclical nature of the term structure of interest rates. Toward the top of the business cycle, in periods such as 1953, 1957, 1959, and 1966, the monetary authorities tend to keep money in short supply. This drives rates up, especially short-term interest rates. At the termination of the boom, monetary authorities tend to ease up on the money supply; this has the most noticeable effect on short-term interest rates, which fall proportionately more than long-term rates. This relative decline, of course, increases the spread between long- and short-term rates. Over the course of the following business expansion, short-term rates rise relatively more than long-term rates. Thus, as the boom builds up, the spread between long- and short-term rates decreases.

The same statistics are shown in Figure A23–3, where panels A, B,

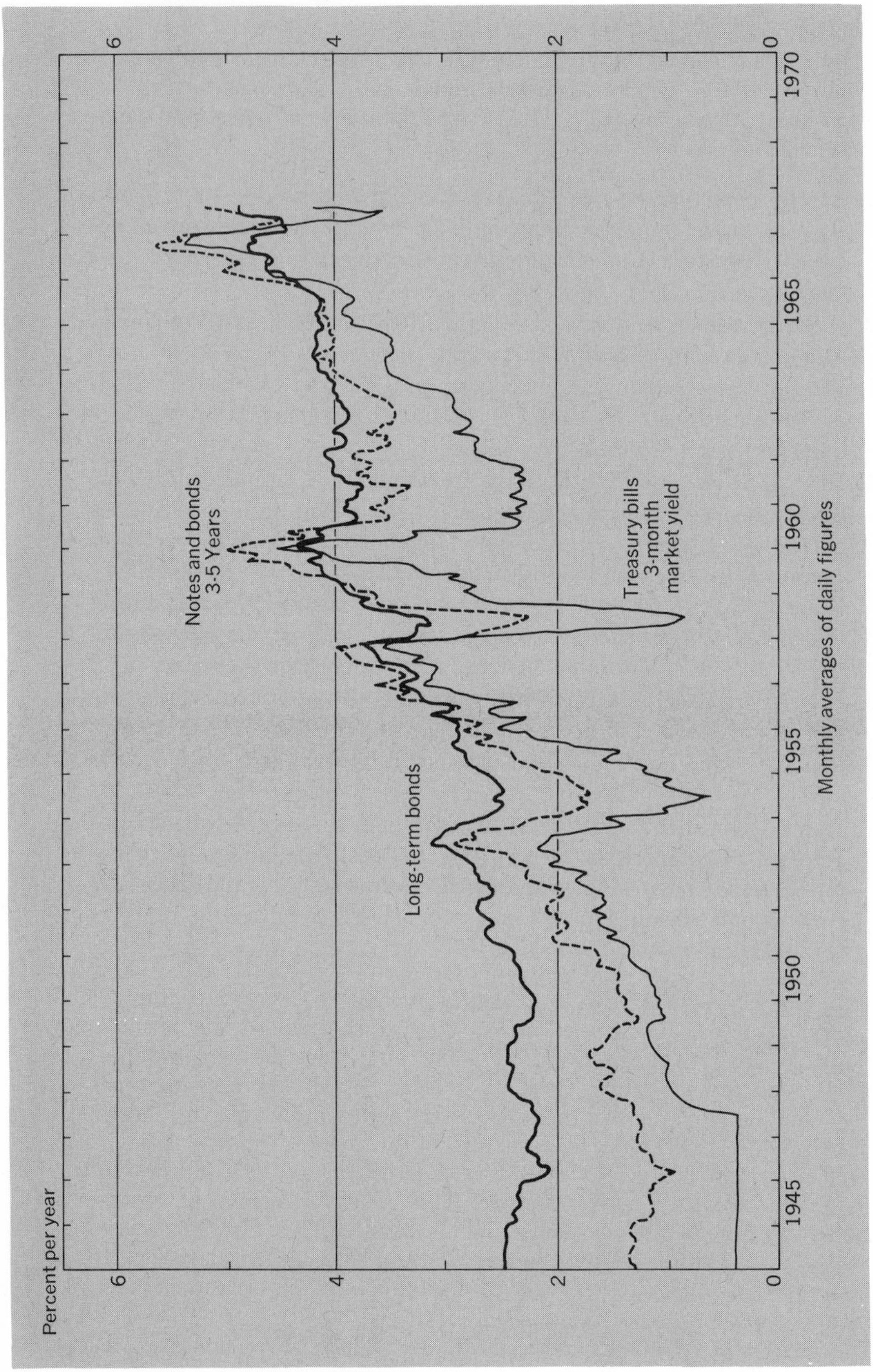

Figure A23–2 Yields on U.S. Government Securities

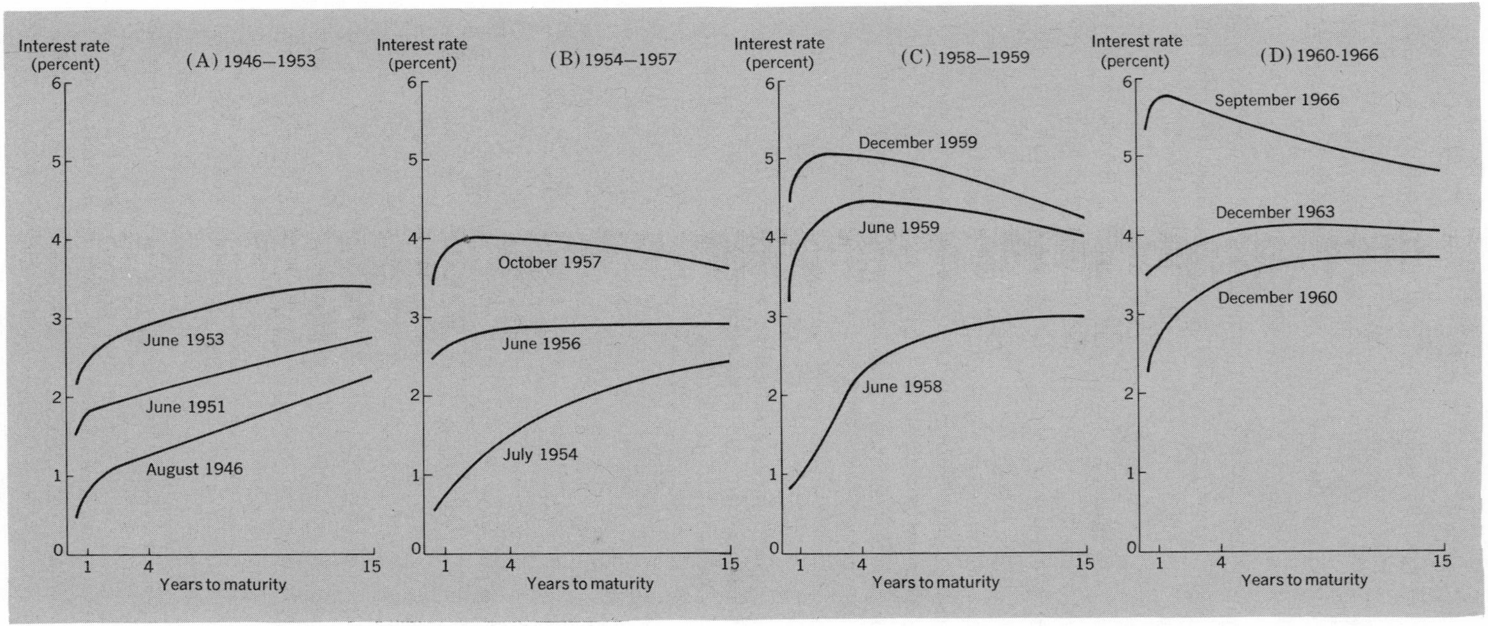

Figure A23–3 Term Structure of Interest Rates at Various Points in Time

C, and D represent each of the four major interest rate cycles: 1946–1953, 1954–1967, 1958–1959, and 1960–1966, respectively. Each panel shows a curve representing the term structure of interest rates at the low point on the interest cycle, at an intermediate point during the cycle, and at the interest rate peak. Three interesting observations can be made:

1. The panels reveal clearly the upward drift in the general level of interest rates. The successive interest rate troughs and peaks are always above the troughs and peaks in earlier cycles.
2. The term structure of interest rates always has a steep slope when the level of interest rates is low, but it is relatively flat or even downward sloping (after a little "hump") when rates are high. A humped yield curve shows relatively low rates for three-month treasury bills, higher rates for 9- to 12-month bills and three- to five-year notes, and lower yields for the long-term bonds.
3. Intermediate between the trough and the peak in the *level* of rates, the *term structure* also has an intermediate slope—flatter than at the trough but steeper (or less negative) than at the peak.

TABLE A23–1 HYPOTHETICAL RELATIONSHIP BETWEEN SHORT-TERM AND LONG-TERM INTEREST RATES

	SITUATION A— EXPECT RISING RATES			SITUATION B— EXPECT FALLING RATES		
Year	Long-Term* (5 year note)	Short-Term (1 year note)	Intermediate-Term (3 year note)†	Long-Term* (5 year note)	Short-Term (1 year note)	Intermediate-Term (3 year note)†
1	4	2	3	4	6	5
2		3	4		5	4
3		4	5		4	3
4		5	‡		3	‡
5		6	‡		2	‡

* Technically, the long-term rate should be a geometric average of short-term rates rather than the arithmetic average that we have used. This refinement may be ignored for present purposes.

† Intermediate term in this example could be anything between one and five years; for example, two-year notes, three-year notes, or four-year notes. Depending on the definition of intermediate term, different rates would emerge.

‡ Cannot be calculated on basis of given information; need to know expected rate in year 6. This same logic explains why long-term rates are shown only for the current year.

Theoretical Explanation for the Term Structure of Interest Rates

Expectations Theory. Two alternative theories are used to explain the term structure: the *expectations theory* and the *market segmentation theory*. The expectations theory states that the long-run interest rate is an average of expected short-term rates. According to this theory, if interest rates are expected to rise in the long run, the current short-term rate will be below the long-term rate.

The expectations theory is illustrated in Table A23–1, where "long term" is defined as five years. In section A, the expected trend in short-term rates is upward—from 2 percent to 6 percent over five years. The long-term rate is thus 4 percent; a lender could obtain an average yield of 4 percent on his investment either by lending long at 4 percent or by lending short at various increasing rates.

The situation is reversed in section B of Table A23–1. Here, the trend in short-term rates is expected to be downward. But again, the average of the short-term rates is 4 percent, so 4 percent is the effective long-term rate.

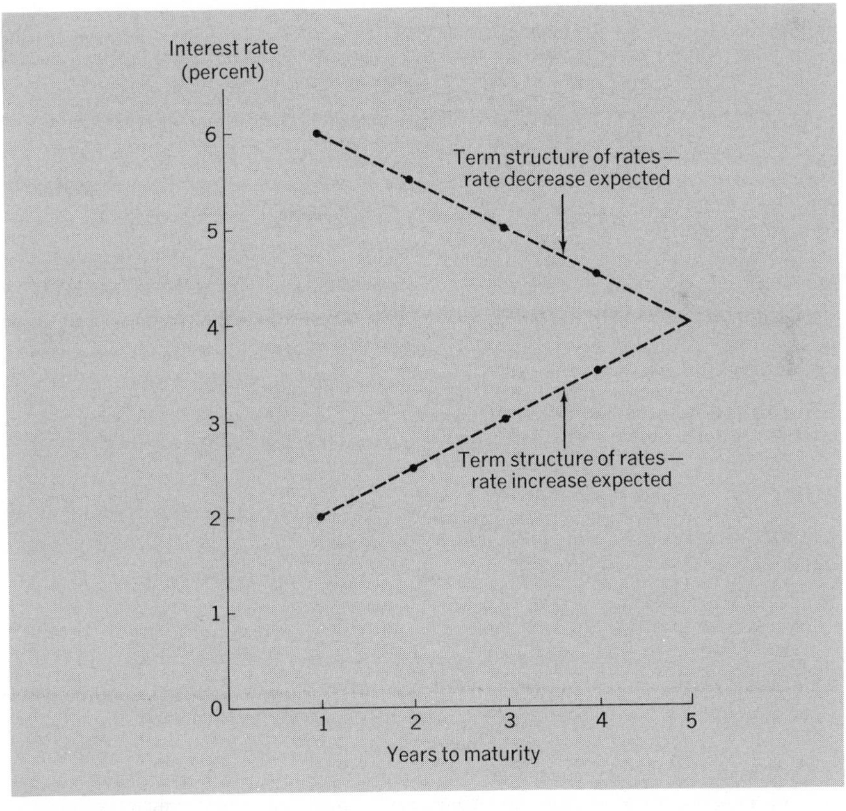

Figure A23–4 Term Structure of Rates under Hypothetical Situations A and B

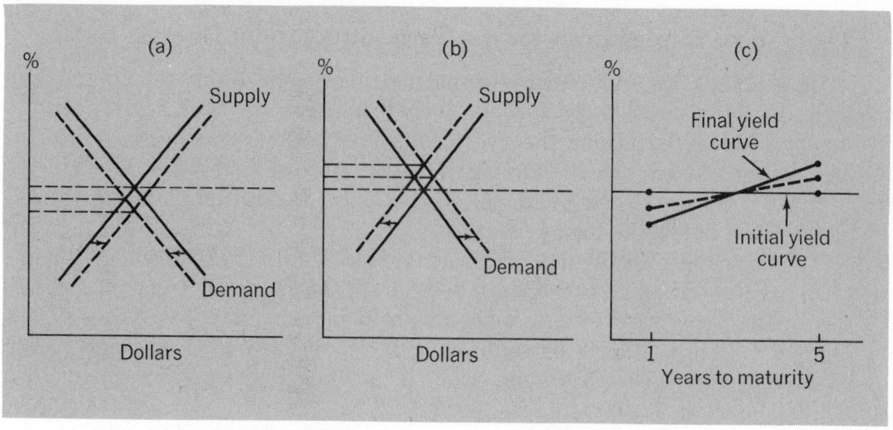

Figure A23–5 Explanation of Why Yield Curve Would Slope Up If Market Segmentation Theory Holds and Expectations Call for Constant Short-Term Rates
(a) Short-term market (1 year) (b) Long-term market (5 years) (c) Term structure of rates (yield curve)

1. *Basic Assumptions.* (a) Lenders prefer to lend short rather than long if they think short-term rates are equally likely to go up or down. Short-term securities are generally more liquid than long-term instruments, and they are better protected against capital losses (although they do not have much potential for capital gains). Moreover, if the loan is made to an individual or a business, frequent maturities give the lender a chance to reexamine the loan and to refuse renewals if the borrower's credit standing has deteriorated.

(b) Borrowers would, on balance, prefer to borrow long rather than short. Long-term borrowing minimizes the danger of being forced to renew a loan under unfavorable circumstances, or of being unable to renew the loan because of chaotic money market conditions or because of a deterioration in the borrower's credit rating.

(c) Short-term rates are about as likely to go up as they are to go down.

(d) There are only two maturities, 1-year and 5-year notes.

2. Initially, the supply-demand situation in the short- and long-term markets are as shown by the solid lines in panels a and b. Because expectations about short-term rates are constant, long- and short-term rates are equal and the yield curve is flat.

3. Because they prefer to borrow long term, borrowers shift markets. The demand curve shifts to the left in panel A and to the right in panel B. This causes short-term rates to fall, long-term rates to rise, and the yield curve to assume an upward slope.

4. Because they prefer to lend short, lenders also shift markets. The supply curve shifts to the right in panel A and to the left in panel B. This reinforces the drop in short-term rates and the rise in long-term rates, and increases the upward slope of the yield curve.

The term structure of rates in year 1 under situations A and B is graphed as Figure A23–4. With expectations of rising rates, the yield curve is upward sloping. With expectations of falling rates, the yield curve slopes down.

Market Segmentation Theory. The expectations theory assumes that, in the aggregate, lenders and borrowers are indifferent between long- and short-term investments except for any expected yield differentials between the types of securities.[2] The alternative hypothesis, the market

[2] In discussing the term structure of interest rates, we are holding constant the risk of default. This is done by using government securities, which presumably have no default risk.

segmentation theory, disputes this assumption about borrower and lender preferences.[3] Specifically, the market segmentation theory holds that most lenders prefer to lend short term, while most borrowers prefer to borrow long term. Lenders prefer short-term investments because of the decreased risk of interest rate fluctuations and the higher liquidity provided by short-term securities. Borrowers prefer long-term debt because this reduces the likelihood of their being unable to renew the loan on account of temporarily embarrassing conditions or temporary unavailability of credit (for example, as occurred in 1966). Because of these lender and borrower preferences, the market segmentation theory holds that the term structure of interest rates should normally be upward sloping (see Figure A23–5 and the explanation given there).

Recent empirical studies suggest that there is some validity to both of these theories. Specifically, the recent work indicates that if lenders and borrowers have no reason for expecting a change in the general level of interest rates, the yield curve will be upward sloping because of market segmentation. (Under the expectations theory, the term structure of interest rates would be flat if there were no expectations of a change in the level of short-term rates.) However, it is a fact that during periods of extremely high interest rates, the yield curve is downward sloping; this proves that the expectations theory also operates. In summary, both theories have an element of truth; both must be employed to explain the term structure of rates.

[3] What we call the market segmentation theory is sometimes divided into two parts—the segmentation part, which refers to legal restrictions limiting certain lenders and borrowers to particular maturities, and the liquidity part, which causes lenders and borrowers to prefer one maturity to another. We include both parts under "market segmentation."

24

The Financial Life Cycle of the Firm

The preceding chapter showed the importance of relating financial plans and policies to the underlying economic and financial environment. In addition, financing patterns should change as the characteristics of the firm itself evolve. Analogies are always dangerous, but the analogy to the life cycle of the individual is useful, if it is not taken too literally and is not carried too far. The individual finds, as the old saying has it, that certain things are appropriate to the behavior of a child, to the behavior of a young man, to the behavior of the head of a mature and established family, and to an aged person for his elder statesmanship and wisdom.

Just as the outside world changes, so the individual, regardless of his age or stage in life, must make adjustments. But further, even if the external environment does not change, the individual must adjust as the aging process goes on. In a similar fashion, the financial policies of a firm must be related to the stages of its development.

STAGES OF GROWTH AND FINANCING

The inspiration to view the financing of a firm over its life cycle comes from comments dealing with historical series on sources and uses of funds made by Professor George Evans at a National Bureau of Economic Research conference.[1]

Evans's Hypothesis

Evans states his hypothesis succinctly: "Asset financing during the early, rapid stages of growth is carried on largely through stock and bond issues; thereafter, retained earnings are likely to become very important and, finally, annual depreciation charges bulk large as a source of funds for gross additions to plant."[2] The hypothesis suggests that there are three stages of growth in a business firm, which might be referred to as (1) the early stage, (2) the maturity stage, and (3) the leveling-off stage. In stage one, the firm is said to rely on stock and bond issues; in stage two, on retained earnings; and in stage three, on depreciation charges.

A preliminary empirical basis for the generalizations is provided by Figure 24–1, which reproduces findings for the relative importance of different forms of financing over time for six steel companies and five chemical companies. The data are clearly consistent with the hypothesis set out.

A further corroboration of the Evans approach is suggested in the book by the Oxford financial economists analyzing the business financing of the firm. Their conclusion likewise was that for an understanding of the financial policies of business enterprise in the United Kingdom, it was much more important to group the firms by size and growth rate of sales rather than by industry.

> It is also highly significant that the contributors to the Oxford financial studies usually found it more illuminating to compare and contrast the companies in different size and growth groups than those in different industrial groups. This is not to say that any

[1] George Herbeston Evans, Jr., "Discussion: The Development of Historical Series on Sources and Uses of Corporate Funds," *Conference on Research in Business Finance* (New York: National Bureau of Economic Research, Inc., 1952), pp. 28–34.

[2] Evans, p. 23.

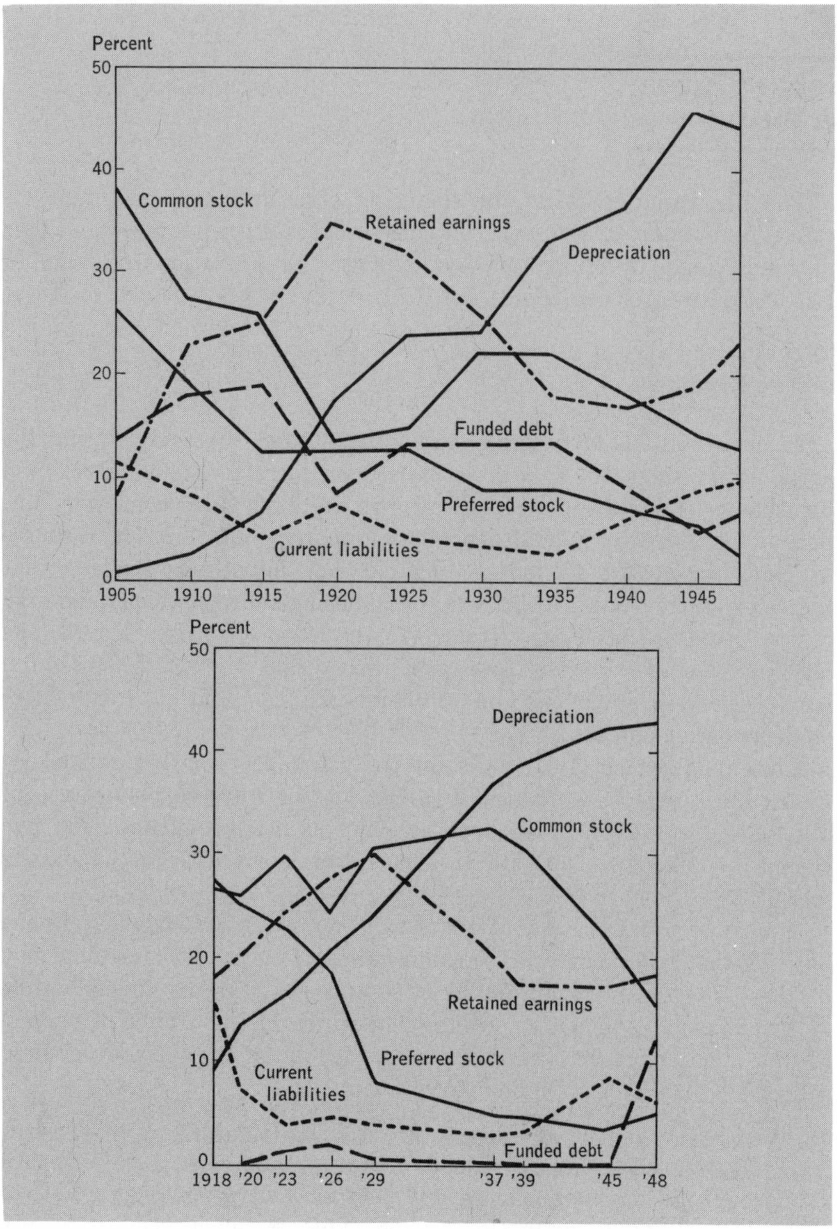

Figure 24–1 *upper:* **Chief Sources of Funds for Asset Financing: Six Steel Companies;** *lower:* **Five Chemical Companies. Medians of percentage of total are computed for each company on data accumulated to indicated dates**

SOURCE: G. H. Evans, Jr., "Discussion: The Development of Historical Series on Sources and Uses of Corporate Funds," *Conference on Research in Business Finance.* (New York: National Bureau of Economic Research, Inc., 1952), p. 33.

of the size groups or growth groups were homogeneous—far from it—but at least such groups were often found to be significantly different (and frequently in some systematic and explicable fashion) than were the twenty-one industrial groups.[3]

Rate of Growth

The influence of the rate of sales growth, referred to in the Oxford study, can be shown by the example in Table 24–1, which compares two manufacturing firms. One grows from $800,000 sales to $1.2 million in one year; the other grows by the same amount, but over a four-year period.[4] Each asset category increases by the same percentage as sales, as do accounts payable and accruals. Common stock is constant, and retained earnings do not increase at a constant rate. Any additional financing requirements are met by notes payable.

It will be observed that when firm 1 achieves a 50 percent sales growth in one year, the current ratio, which was weak in the beginning, deteriorates further. The debt ratio, which was 50 percent initially, moves beyond generally accepted prudent levels. The financial community always likes to feel that the owner has as much money in the business as the creditors have, but in the second year, the creditors have supplied over half the total funds. The profit rate has improved because the firm is using debt more heavily; that is, it is receiving the benefit of financial leverage.

The consequences may be contrasted when the firm uses four periods to achieve the same amount of growth. The financial ratios give a profile of what has happened. The current ratio has improved; it has risen above the 2-to-1 bankers' rule of thumb to 2.4 to 1. The debt ratio has dropped to 25 percent, very low compared with the average of 40 percent for all manufacturing (see Chapter 3). However, the profit-to-net-worth ratio has declined to the norm for all manufacturing.

A paradox is encountered. On the one hand, rapid sales growth means high profitability but a precariousness in the firm's financial position unless equity financing is obtained in relatively large amounts. On the other hand, slow growth can be encompassed by the plowback from retained earnings and depreciation charges. The example suggests that

[3] Brian Tew and R. F. Henderson (eds.), *Studies in Company Finance* (Cambridge, England: Cambridge University Press, 1959), p. 255.

[4] Parenthetically, it may be observed that a 50 percent sales growth rate is not at all unusual for a new firm starting out in the electronics industry or the plastics industry, or for almost any small firm in other than retail or wholesale trade. Even in the latter industries, in the early stages of the life cycle of the firm, if a firm is going to succeed, it must have a very rapid growth rate.

a firm growing by only 10 percent a year should not have serious financial problems if it obtains normal profits and retains a high percentage in the business. But owners of rapidly growing firms may find that

TABLE 24–1 FINANCIAL EFFECTS OF DIFFERENT RATES OF GROWTH
(in thouands of dollars)

	FIRM 1		FIRM 2				
	1	2	1	2	3	4	5
Sales	$800	$1,200	$800	$900	$1,000	$1,100	$1,200
Current assets (30%)	240	360	240	270	300	330	360
Fixed assets (20%)	160	240	160	180	200	220	240
Total assets	$400	$ 600	$400	$450	$ 500	$ 550	$ 600
Accounts payable (10%)	80	120	80	90	100	110	120
Notes payable	96	172	96	79	56	27	(8)
Other accruals (3%)	24	36	24	27	30	33	36
Current liabilities	$200	$ 328	$200	$196	$ 186	$ 170	$ 148
Common stock	100	100	100	100	100	100	100
Retained earnings*	100	172	100	154	214	280	352
Net worth	$200	$ 272	$200	$254	$ 314	$ 380	$ 452
Total claims	$400	$ 600	$400	$450	$ 500	$ 550	$ 600
Key ratios							
Current ratio (times)	1.2	1.1	1.2	1.4	1.6	1.9	2.4
Debt to assets (percentage)	50	55	50	44	37	31	25
Sales to total assets (times)	2	2	2	2	2	2	2
Profit to net worth (percentage)	24	26.5	24.0	21.3	19.1	17.3	15.9

* Profit is 6% of sales; retained earnings are equal to profit plus retained earnings from the previous year.

when their sales are growing at a high rate, they may have difficulty financing the required asset growth necessary to support the rising sales level. Alternatively, a firm that increasingly holds net earnings in the business as a substitute for the use of debt may find that with declining leverage its rate of return on net worth also declines. Both paradoxes are readily unraveled if one looks at the simple dynamics of this growth situation.

FINANCING IN RELATION TO A CROSS SECTION OF STAGES

The situation described in Table 24–1 is generally found when rapid growth is compared with the alternative of less rapid growth. We may generalize further by considering a summary of firms and their financial characteristics in terms of their different sizes and ages.

The relation between the growth of a firm and its requirements is exhibited by Figure 24–2, which presents the sales and the total assets of the Bethlehem Steel Corporation during the period 1910–1960. With the exception of the disruptions brought about by World War I and World War II and their aftermaths, the growth of sales of the Bethlehem Steel Corporation has roughly followed the S-shaped growth curve.

Financing requirements of the firm have paralleled the growth pattern in sales. After 1940, the firm has been able to achieve a sales-total-asset ratio exceeding 1 during most years. Yet the sales-total-asset ratio is substantially below the characteristic 2-to-1 ratio observed for manufacturing firms in less capital-intensive industries.

A relationship exists between a firm's growth in sales and the nature of its financing requirements. A general framework for obtaining perspective on the financial life cycle of the firm can be developed. Table 24–2 sets forth a summary of leading financial characteristics of manufacturing firms, classified by size and age. This panorama is based on a review of studies of the growth of individual firms and on the Financial Research Program of the National Bureau of Economic Research on capital formation and its financing in a number of industries.

The summary is idealized in that many exceptions can be found in actuality. It is not an ideal picture in the sense that each set of characteristics represents the optimal situation. It indicates how the age and the growth rate of a firm and the nature of its financial environment are reflected in its financial patterns over time. In the following sections, the table is discussed to convey the idea of how a firm is likely to move from one stage to another.

Small, Rapidly Growing Firm

The small, successful firm will typically have a high sales growth rate—20 to 30 percent a year. Its profit rate on sales will be somewhat higher than the average for large manufacturing companies. Compared with traditional and customary standards, its financial position is relatively weak. The current ratio is probably under 1 to 1. The sales-to-total-assets ratio will be high. The debt ratio is 67 percent.

TABLE 24–2 GENERAL SUMMARY OF FINANCIAL PATTERNS IN RELATION TO SIZE AND AGE OF FIRM*

	GROWTH RATE (IN PERCENTAGES)	PROFIT TO SALES	FINANCIAL POSITION		MAIN FORMS	MAIN SOURCES	DIVIDEND PAYOUT (IN PERCENTAGES)	MERGERS
Small								
Rapid growth	20–30	8	Current ratio Asset turnover Debt ratio	1 3 67%	Current liabilities	Trade credit	0–10	Need for full range of management capabilities
Moderate growth	5–8	5	Current ratio Asset turnover Debt ratio	2 2 33–50%	Long-term debt Common stock Retained earnings	Privately placed term loans	20–25	Cost reduction incentives
Medium								
Rapid growth	16–20	6–7	Current ratio Asset turnover Debt ratio	1.4 2.5 50%	Long-term debt Current liabilities Common stock	Privately placed term loans	5–15	Cost reduction, rounding out of sales lines
Moderate growth	4–7	5	Current ratio Asset turnover Debt ratio	2 2 33%	Long-term debt Common stock Retained earnings	Bonds, equity capital market	40–50	Diversification into new product lines
Large								
Moderate growth	4–6	5	Current ratio Asset turnover Debt ratio	2 2 33%	Retained earnings, Depreciation	Retained earnings	50–60	Diversification into new product lines

* Based on the institutional framework of the United States.

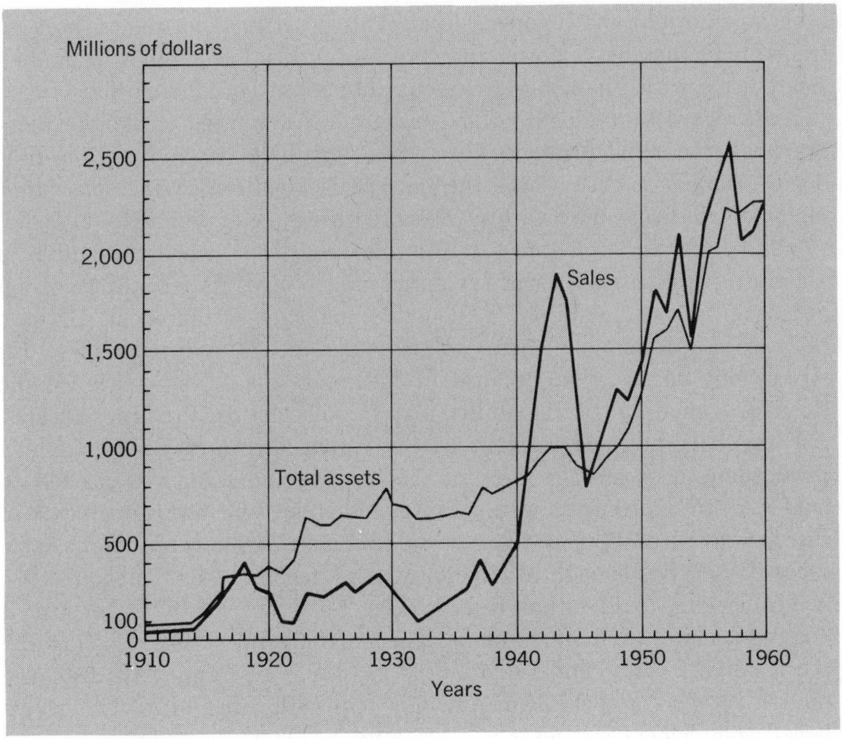

Figure 24–2 Bethlehem Steel Corporation, 1910–1916

Because Table 24–2 provides the profit on sales, the asset turnover, and the debt ratio, the return on net worth can be calculated. In the present instance, the return on total assets would be 24 percent, more than double the norm of about 10 to 12 percent for all manufacturing.[5] The return on net worth would be 72 percent (after taxes).[6] Because of its precarious financial position, the underfinanced small firm shows a high return on net worth. With a relatively normal profit on sales, the high turnover of total assets results in a favorable profit rate on total assets. The relatively high debt ratio further magnifies the return on net worth. The result is a profit rate on net worth of 72 percent after taxes—but with a good chance of bankruptcy!

Studies of new, small firms indicate that 80 to 90 percent of the initial financing comes from the funds of the owners of the business and their relatives and friends. As the sales grow, the major initial source of external financing is likely to be trade credit. Suppliers provide credit of

[5] Sales margin $\times$ turnover = $8 \times 3 = 24\%$ return on assets.

[6] $\frac{\text{return on assets}}{1.0 - \text{debt ratio}} = \frac{24\%}{1.0 - 0.67} = \frac{24}{0.33} = 72\%$ return on net worth (after taxes).

both an informal and a formal kind. This practice is fortunate, because trade credit thereby performs the very useful social function of providing small firms with financing that would otherwise be unavailable.

With regard to dividend policy (the term is here used to include withdrawals), the small firm should pay out very little, if anything, in dividends. Here is a case where the pattern is idealized in the sense that many small firms may fail to observe this rule or guide to action.

Small firms will sometimes sell out to large firms when they grow to a certain point. A small firm is created and receives its initial propulsion because of a specific ability of the owner-manager-entrepreneur. He may be a good salesman, a good engineer, or a good production man. He strikes out on his own because of his one strong competence. While the firm is small, a specific ability may be sufficient for the firm's success.

Very soon, however, a firm reaches "that awkward age" in which more than the dynamic force of one or two individuals is needed to enable it to continue to prosper. At this stage, the owner-manager of the firm realizes that it takes a full range of managerial abilities to succeed. It is not enough to have only sales, technical, or financial skills. A firm begins to find that it is making numerous mistakes because it does not have a full range of balanced managerial skills. Additionally, the small firm may find that limited capital is restraining its potential growth rate. As a consequence, it may join with other firms with which it can complement strengths and weaknesses. Or, more typically, a large firm sees that it can use the particular managerial talents of the small firm and can supply everything else lacking in the small firm. For these reasons, many small firms are likely to be merged into larger firms.

Small, Long-Established Firm

If a firm is small and old, it is probably not in a growing industry. Since manufacturing firms are being discussed, the long-established firm is probably producing a particular product to which large firms do not give much attention. Its growth rate in sales is probably no better than the over-all average of the industry. The profit rate is not likely to be more than normal.

Its financial position is likely to meet conventional standards. It meets the traditional standard for the current ratio, the bankers' rule of thumb of 2 to 1. Its sales-to-total-assets ratio approximates the 1.9 for all manufacturing. The debt ratio probably is from 33 to 50 percent, reflecting the fact that because it is small it may have difficulty raising equity funds.

Because the firm has been in existence for a time, its past performance record may have enabled it to obtain moderate amounts of long-term debt. Also, it probably has had time to build up fairly large retained earnings. As it meets the bankers' traditional financial standards, it qualifies for some bank financing.

Dividend payouts are probably still on the low side, because the small firm by nature has only limited access to the external financial markets. Hence, it relies on internal financing to a great degree.

The firm is likely to engage in mergers. It may be acquired by a large firm for its special product contribution. Large firms seek vertical integration as they reach the stage of maturity. In older firms, in the later stages of the life cycle of an industry, profit margins may decline. For this reason, such firms may engage in mergers to encompass an additional product stage or product splinter to broaden their product lines. If larger volume per dollar of investment can thereby be generated, improved profit margins may result.

Medium-Sized, Rapidly Growing Firm

The remainder of the firms in the summary table have some relation to the two categories already discussed. For the medium-sized firm, growth rates and net profit rates will not be so high as those for the new, small firm. The medium firm will be in a somewhat better financial position. Because it is medium-sized, although new, it probably has been in operation long enough to have established a performance record that gives it at least a degree of access to the external capital markets.

Such a firm's dividend payout is still relatively low because of its high profit rate and the need to finance further growth. It is likely to seek mergers to round out production or sales lines and thus to spread the relatively fixed costs of the sales organization or production organization over a large number of product lines, making it more able to compete effectively with the larger firms in its line of business.

Medium-Sized, Moderately Growing Firm

The firm of medium size with a moderate growth rate will have characteristics similar to those of small firms with moderate growth rates. The profit rate will approximate the profit rate of industry generally. The firm will satisfy the financial standards normally regarded as sound. It will doubtlessly achieve a current ratio of at least 2 to 1. It will have a normal sales-to-total-assets ratio of about 2. It will have reduced its debt ratio to about 33 percent of assets.

The medium-sized firm will have greater access to the capital markets than will the small firm of moderate growth rate. The fixed costs of capital flotations will bear less heavily on the larger firm than on the small firm. For this reason, the medium-sized firm of moderate growth and profitability will have a somewhat higher dividend payout than will the smaller firm.

The lower growth rate of the medium-sized firm may lead it to seek product diversification in an effort to enter new product-market areas with more favorable growth opportunities. It will seek to acquire smaller, rapidly growing firms which have products with favorable growth potentialities.

Large-Sized, Moderately Growing Firm

The large firm with a moderate growth rate is likely to be an established firm in an industry that has reached its maturity. The firm will generally exhibit the characteristics of a medium-sized firm. However, its larger size implies a higher fixed-assets-to-total-assets ratio. Thus the fixed assets will provide a throw-off of funds from depreciation charges. The large firm will therefore draw on the capital markets for financing to a smaller degree. Instead, it will rely to a greater extent on internal financing.

A large rapidly growing firm either will be the dominant factor in a growth industry (IBM) or will be engaged in mergers (the conglomerates). The first type of firm will have significant internal funds because of high rates of return, but will also use external financing. The second type of firm will use internal cash flows, debt, and exchanges of stock to finance its acquisitions.

Illustrative Patterns

The influence of industry, age, size, and rate of growth on financing of firms can also be indicated and is in Table 24–3. Firms in the textiles and shoe-manufacturing industries generally have a large peak seasonal investment in receivables. This seasonal investment does not justify a proportionate amount of permanent capital. Consequently, such firms are likely to make use of receivables to provide a secured basis for financing large temporary investment requirements during each year.

Similarly, a canning manufacturer is likely to experience a peak seasonal growth in inventories. Again, such large investments do not justify permanent capital sufficient to finance the seasonal peak inventories. Therefore, field warehousing or other types of commodity loans are the strategic financing requirements.

The many new scientifically oriented firms with rapid growth have a different financing requirement. Their investment in equipment is likely to be heavy, and their large outlays on research may require a number of years before a profitable series of products results. The initial outlays for research must require venture capital—capital willing to assume substantial risks. Permanent investment requirements for firms are reduced by the opportunities for leasing their heavy equipment needs.

The small, basic manufacturing company is likely to have its heaviest

TABLE 24–3 ILLUSTRATIVE FINANCING STRATEGIES

CHARACTERISTIC OF FIRM	CRITICAL FINANCING NEED	STRATEGIC FINANCING REQUIREMENT
Small		
Textiles and Shoes	Peak seasonal in receivables	Receivables financing
Scientific	Equipment and research outlays	Leasing, venture capital
Canning	Peak seasonal in inventories	Field warehousing, other commodity loans
Manufacturing	Equipment	Conditional sales contract, leasing, venture capital
Moderate Size		
Manufacturing	Plant and equipment	Long-term debt and equity financing
Rapid growth	Working capital and fixed assets	Convertible debt or debt with warrants
Large		
Moderate growth	Fixed asset replacement	Internal funds

investment in equipment. Conditional sales contracts or leasing may take care of this strategic financing requirement. In addition, the initial period of operations is likely to require an investment of venture capital. However, a manufacturing firm that has been in business for a number of years and has achieved moderate size is likely to have heavy investment in both plant and equipment. With a record of sales, profitability, and some stability of management, a moderate-sized manufacturing firm is likely to have access to the open capital market for both long-term debt and equity securities.

The rapidly growing, moderate-sized firm will probably have a record of reasonably stable and rising sales and profits, and it will experience a need to finance both assets and working capital. Such a firm is likely to use a certain amount of straight debt, supplemented by subordinated convertibles or debt with warrants that will, in time, provide additional equity capital.

The large firm in a mature industry is likely to be experiencing only moderate growth. With reasonably stable profits and a heavy investment in fixed assets (which contributes to cash flow due to depreciation charge-off), its main financing requirement is for replacement of fixed assets. Most of these needs will be met from internal sources.

The purpose of this review of some illustrative financing strategies has been to place characteristic financing needs in proper perspective and to relate them to financing forms and sources. It has not been possible to generalize on the financing patterns and requirements of every type of firm and every type of industry. However, these illustrations have served to indicate that some basic patterns emerge when firms are viewed analytically in terms of their industry characteristics, age, size, and growth rate. With a foundation based on an understanding of the basic patterns and relationships, in addition to a sound analytical framework, practical experience will develop the maturity and good judgment essential to making good financial decisions.

INFLUENCE OF ECONOMIC CLIMATE

These broad patterns and the financing of the firm over its life cycle are likely to be substantially modified by variations in money market conditions over time. During a strong bull market in equities, such as occurred in the late 1920s, the advantages of equity financing become substantial. During depressed periods like that of the 1930s the characteristic life-cycle pattern of growth and sales is likely to be seriously disturbed. The occurrence of wars will cause erratic disturbances in the growth cycle of a firm.

In addition, characteristics of the general economic environment are likely to influence the forms of financing employed. For example, during the post-World War II period, the fear of inflation, coupled with the danger of a postwar depression, made convertible securities popular. The convertible securities, of course, provided a hedge against deflation and at the same time offered some participation in the growth potentialities of firms and industries during a period characterized by attractive growth records among many firms.

FINANCIAL GUIDELINES

On the basis of the perspectives provided by a review of the financial life cycle of firms, some generalizations may be drawn. These generalizations summarize many of the topics discussed previously and provide a statement of guidelines for the financial manager.

1. Permanent needs should not be financed from short-term sources.
2. A substantial portion of current assets represents permanent investment and should be financed from long-term sources.
3. Financing should be arranged before needs become immediately pressing. "The best time to get money is the time it is not needed."
4. It is better to obtain financing in larger "chunks" than in a series of small amounts, because each financing transaction carries a large element of fixed costs.
5. Anticipate needs so that future needs will also be met.
6. Financing is a personal business. The financial manager should cultivate personal and professional contacts with credit men, bank loan officers, investment bankers, and financial executives of insurance companies and finance companies.
7. The financial manager should have some element of flexibility in his financing programs so that the unexpected does not find him in a vulnerable position.
8. The financial manager should be prepared to bargain strenuously on the terms of financial agreements. He should not permit his firm to be tied up in loan terms that will hamper its freedom of action in the future.
9. Especially in a new firm, the commitment of funds should be held to a minimum. Buildings and equipment should be rented initially, or used equipment should be employed to the extent permitted by fund-raising capacity.
10. Irrational aversion to debt reduces profits. Judicious use of debt provides valuable leverage.
11. Small and new firms, however, especially, must recognize that growth requires a large plowback of earnings if excessive debt is to be avoided or equity ownership is not to be shared. Growth of sales may lead to a feeling of prosperity and large withdrawals, which may hamper the healthy growth of a firm.

SUMMARY

The framework provided by the concept of the financial life cycle of the firm gives the perspective on the financing alternatives available to the firm. Acquisition of funds at one stage of a firm's development should be made with a view to establishing the best foundation for the forms of financing most likely to be required at subsequent stages.

The overview of the financial life cycle of firms also highlights the interrelationships between growth rates, financial position, forms and sources of financing, and dividend and merger policies. Understanding these relationships will prevent the firm from adopting such mutually inconsistent policies as setting a high target growth rate, a high dividend payout ratio, and a ban on external debt and equity financing.

A widespread fault of small firms in their early stages is excessive withdrawals of funds by owner-managers. Failure to recognize the financing requirements of rapid growth and the necessity for obtaining the major portion of such financing from internal sources during the early stages of a firm's development will lead to financial difficulties. As a firm establishes a performance record, the opportunities for financing are broadened. The possibilities for obtaining external sources of funds on favorable terms improve during the later stages of a firm's development. At the same time, the reduced rate of growth makes it probable that a larger proportion of needs will be provided from internal sources.

Application of the life-cycle framework can yield useful guidelines for financial decisions. The financial policies of the firm constitute an important area of managerial decisions required for successful operations.

QUESTIONS

24–1 Discuss the relationship between size of firm and the life-cycle concept.

24–2 Discuss the relationship between diversification and the life-cycle concept.

24–3 Should a firm always attempt to forestall the declining phase of the life cycle? What about a firm created for the purpose of exploiting a given mineral deposit, say an iron ore mine?

24–4 Explain how each of the following factors could be expected to influence the extent to which actual firms conform to the life-cycle hypothesis:

a) Development of the corporate form of organization
b) Corporate diversification
c) Research and development expenditures
d) Trend toward larger firms

24–5 If the average cost of capital is actually minimized when the firm has a certain amount of debt in its capital structure, is it logical for older, slower growing firms to retire all their debt by retaining earnings? If such a tendency is observed, what is the implication for the economists' notion that firms seek to maximize stockholder wealth?

24–6 A fast-growing firm usually has a higher profit rate than a firm growing more slowly. Yet the former will be less able to finance its growth from retained earnings. Explain.

24–7 A large, well-established firm typically retains a lower percentage of its earnings than does a smaller, faster growing firm.

Yet the larger firm finances a higher percentage of its financing needs from retained earnings than does the smaller firm. Explain.

24–8 Two firms each earn 6 percent on sales and have an asset turnover of 2 times. Firm A has a debt-to-total-assets ratio of one third. Firm B has a ratio of two thirds. What is the respective profit rate on net worth for each firm?

24–9 A firm has a 5 percent return on sales. It has a debt-to-net-worth ratio of 100 percent. What turnover of total assets is required for a 20 percent return on net worth?

24–10 Which firms are likely to have the higher asset turnover—new, small, rapidly growing firms or the largest firms in American industry?

24–11 What are the major sources of initial financing of new, small firms? Why?

24–12 Are large firms likely to have a higher or a lower ratio of trade receivables to trade payables than have smaller firms in the same line of business?

24–13 At what stage in its development is an industrial firm likely to make the greatest use of long-term debt? Explain.

24–14 Explain the characteristics of the economy and the stage of development of a firm and of its financial structure that will favor the use of convertible debt to raise funds equal to 20 percent of its present total assets.

PROBLEMS

24–1 Match each firm in list 1 with the most appropriate form of financing found in list 2. Present the key factors that determine your choice.

List 1

a) A medium-sized specialty steel company in Texas expects to double its sales in 12 years. Stock prices are expected to more than double over that period. Existing short-term debt is somewhat high, and the company has no long-term debt.
b) A laundromat plans expansion by the installation of ten additional washing machines and three new driers.
c) A plastics manufacturing company of $8 million sales volume 70 percent owned by the founder and chief engineer, sells 60 percent of its output to a small number of large aircraft firms and finds itself continually short of working capital.
d) An electronics company doing $25 million of sales needs $5 million to finance its expansion. It has a debt-to-total-assets ratio of 60 percent, and its common stock, which is widely held, has tripled in price during the past year.

e) A manufacturing company with steadily growing sales (currently at $20 million) needs $2 million to finance new equipment which will substantially increase sales 10 to 14 months after the investment is made. Profits are expected to increase more than proportionally to the sales increase. Its debt-to-total-assets ratio runs about 30 percent.

f) A finance company with good prospective sales growth, relatively low debt ratio, stock prices temporarily depressed, and very good banking relations seeks to finance a prospective 10 percent increase in assets during the forthcoming year.

g) A medium-sized electrical utility ($100 million total assets) with a debt ratio of 40 percent needs an additional $20 million to finance the growth taking place in the early stages of a business upswing.

h) A small chemical company producing many competitive lines has been growing on the average at about 10 percent a year—at a higher rate in good years and at a lower one in poor years. To finance growth, the firm is attempting to decide between a convertible debenture issue or debt with warrants to buy common stock. Its existing total debt ratio is 10 percent of total assets.

List 2

1) Common stock
2) Convertible preferred stock
3) Subordinated debentures
4) Conditional sales contract
5) Accounts receivables financing or factoring
6) Mortgage bonds
7) Debt with warrants
8) Convertible debentures

24–2 United Engineers, Inc., has experienced the following sales, profit, and balance sheet patterns. Identify the financial problem that has developed, and recommend a solution for it.

UNITED ENGINEERS, INC.
FINANCIAL DATA
1959–1968
(in millions of dollars)

Income Statements	*1959*	*1960*	*1961*	*1962*	*1963*	*1964*	*1965*	*1966*	*1967*	*1968*
Sales	$50	$70	$90	$100	$120	$200	$180	$220	$240	$340
Profits after tax	5	7	9	10	12	20	18	22	24	34
Dividends	4	5	6	6	7	10	10	14	18	24
Retained earnings	1	2	3	4	5	10	8	8	6	10
Cumulative retained earnings	1	3	6	10	15	25	33	41	47	57

Balance Sheets

Current assets	10	15	20	25	30	50	40	55	60	80
Net fixed assets	15	20	25	25	30	50	50	55	60	90
Total assets	$25	$35	$45	$ 50	$ 60	$100	$ 90	$110	$120	$170
Trade credit	4	6	8	9	10	18	15	20	20	60
Bank credit	4	6	10	10	13	29	14	20	20	20
Other	1	5	6	6	7	8	8	9	8	8
Total current liab.	9	17	24	25	30	55	37	49	48	88
Long-term debt	0	0	0	0	0	5	5	5	10	10
Total debt	9	17	24	25	30	60	42	54	58	98
Common stock	15	15	15	15	15	15	15	15	15	15
Retained earnings	1	3	6	10	15	25	33	41	47	57
Net worth	16	18	21	25	30	40	48	56	62	72
Total claims on assets	$25	$35	$45	$50	$60	$100	$ 90	$110	$120	$170

24–3 a) A firm with $20 million of assets judges that it is at the beginning of a three-year growth cycle. It is a manufacturing firm with a total-debt-to-assets ratio of 16 percent. It expects sales and net earnings to grow at a rate of 10 percent a year.

Stock prices are expected to rise 30 percent a year over the three-year period. The firm will need $2 million at the beginning of the three-year period and another $1 million by the middle of the third year. It is at the beginning of a general business upswing, when money and capital costs are what they generally are after about a year of recession and at the beginning of an upswing. By the middle of the third year, money and capital costs will have their characteristic pattern near the peak of an upswing.

How should the firm raise the $2 million and the $1 million?

b) An aerospace company with sales of $50 million a year needs $10 million to finance expansion. It has a debt-to-total-assets ratio of 65 percent. Its common stock, which is widely held, is selling at a price/earnings ratio of 25 times. It is comparing the sale of common stock and convertible debentures.

Which do you recommend? Why?

c) A chemical company has been growing steadily. To finance a growth of sales from $80 million a year to $100 million over a two-year period, it needs $4 million in additional equipment. When additional working capital needs are taken into account, the total additional financing required during the first year is $10 million. Profits will rise by 50 percent after the first 10 months. The stock is currently selling at 20 times earnings. It can borrow on straight debt at 5½ percent. It could borrow with a convertibility or warrant "sweetner" for

¾ percent less. The present debt-to-total-asset ratio is 25 percent.

Which form of financing should it employ?

Selected References

Dauten, C. A., "The Necessary Ingredients of a Theory of Business Finance," *Journal of Finance,* X (May 1955), 107–120.

Kuznets, Simon, *Capital in the American Economy—Its Formation and Financing* (Princeton, N.J.: Princeton University Press, 1961).

Marris, Robin, "A Model of the 'Managerial' Enterprise," *Quarterly Journal of Economics,* LXXVII (May 1963), 185–209.

McLean, J. G., and R. W. Haigh, "How Business Corporations Grow, *Harvard Business Review,* XXXII (November-December 1954), 81–93.

O'Neal, F. Hodge, "Minority Owners Can Avoid Squeeze-Outs," *Harvard Business Review,* XLI (March-April 1963), 150–160.

Schroeder, G. G., *The Growth of Major Steel Companies, 1900–1950* (Baltimore: Johns Hopkins, 1953).

Seltzer, L. H., *A Financial History of the American Automobile Industry* (Cambridge, Mass.: Houghton Mifflin, 1928).

Simon, H. A., and C. P. Bonini, "The Size Distribution of Business Firms," *American Economic Review,* XLVIII (September 1958), 607–617.

Weston, J. Fred, "Toward Theories of Financial Policy," *Journal of Finance,* X (May 1955), 130–143.

White, K. K., *Financing Company Expansion* (New York: American Management Association, 1964).

APPENDIX A

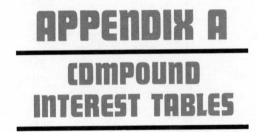

COMPOUND INTEREST TABLES

TABLE A–1 COMPOUND SUM OF $1

Year	1%	2%	3%	4%	5%	6%	7%
1	1.010	1.020	1.030	1.040	1.050	1.060	1.070
2	1.020	1.040	1.061	1.082	1.102	1.124	1.145
3	1.030	1.061	1.093	1.125	1.158	1.191	1.225
4	1.041	1.082	1.126	1.170	1.216	1.262	1.311
5	1.051	1.104	1.159	1.217	1.276	1.338	1.403
6	1.062	1.126	1.194	1.265	1.340	1.419	1.501
7	1.072	1.149	1.230	1.316	1.407	1.504	1.606
8	1.083	1.172	1.267	1.369	1.477	1.594	1.718
9	1.094	1.195	1.305	1.423	1.551	1.689	1.838
10	1.105	1.219	1.344	1.480	1.629	1.791	1.967
11	1.116	1.243	1.384	1.539	1.710	1.898	2.105
12	1.127	1.268	1.426	1.601	1.796	2.012	2.252
13	1.138	1.294	1.469	1.665	1.886	2.133	2.410
14	1.149	1.319	1.513	1.732	1.980	2.261	2.579
15	1.161	1.346	1.558	1.801	2.079	2.397	2.759
16	1.173	1.373	1.605	1.873	2.183	2.540	2.952
17	1.184	1.400	1.653	1.948	2.292	2.693	3.159
18	1.196	1.428	1.702	2.026	2.407	2.854	3.380
19	1.208	1.457	1.754	2.107	2.527	3.026	3.617
20	1.220	1.486	1.806	2.191	2.653	3.207	3.870
25	1.282	1.641	2.094	2.666	3.386	4.292	5.427
30	1.348	1.811	2.427	3.243	4.322	5.743	7.612

Year	8%	9%	10%	12%	14%	15%	16%
1	1.080	1.090	1.100	1.120	1.140	1.150	1.160
2	1.166	1.188	1.210	1.254	1.300	1.322	1.346
3	1.260	1.295	1.331	1.405	1.482	1.521	1.561
4	1.360	1.412	1.464	1.574	1.689	1.749	1.811
5	1.469	1.539	1.611	1.762	1.925	2.011	2.100
6	1.587	1.677	1.772	1.974	2.195	2.313	2.436
7	1.714	1.828	1.949	2.211	2.502	2.660	2.826
8	1.851	1.993	2.144	2.476	2.853	3.059	3.278
9	1.999	2.172	2.358	2.773	3.252	3.518	3.803
10	2.159	2.367	2.594	3.106	3.707	4.046	4.411
11	2.332	2.580	2.853	3.479	4.226	4.652	5.117
12	2.518	2.813	3.138	3.896	4.818	5.350	5.936
13	2.720	3.066	3.452	4.363	5.492	6.153	6.886
14	2.937	3.342	3.797	4.887	6.261	7.076	7.988
15	3.172	3.642	4.177	5.474	7.138	8.137	9.266
16	3.426	3.970	4.595	6.130	8.137	9.358	10.748
17	3.700	4.328	5.054	6.866	9.276	10.761	12.468
18	3.996	4.717	5.560	7.690	10.575	12.375	14.463
19	4.316	5.142	6.116	8.613	12.056	14.232	16.777
20	4.661	5.604	6.728	9.646	13.743	16.367	19.461
25	6.848	8.623	10.835	17.000	26.462	32.919	40.874
30	10.063	13.268	17.449	29.960	50.950	66.212	85.850

TABLE A–1 *(Continued)*

Year	*18%*	*20%*	*24%*	*28%*	*32%*	*36%*
1	1.180	1.200	1.240	1.280	1.320	1.360
2	1.392	1.440	1.538	1.638	1.742	1.850
3	1.643	1.728	1.907	2.067	2.300	2.515
4	1.939	2.074	2.364	2.684	3.036	3.421
5	2.288	2.488	2.932	3.436	4.007	4.653
6	2.700	2.986	3.635	4.398	5.290	6.328
7	3.185	3,583	4.508	5.629	6.983	8.605
8	3.759	4.300	5.590	7.206	9.217	11.703
9	4.435	5.160	6.931	9.223	12.166	15.917
10	5.234	6.192	8.594	11.806	16.060	21.647
11	6.176	7.430	10.657	15.112	21.199	29.439
12	7.288	8.916	13.215	19.343	27.983	40.037
13	8.599	10.699	16.386	24.759	36.937	54.451
14	10.147	12.839	20.319	31.691	48.757	74.053
15	11.974	15.407	25.196	40.565	64.359	100.712
16	14.129	18.488	31.243	51.923	84.954	136.97
17	16.672	22.186	38.741	66.461	112.14	186.28
18	19.673	26.623	48.039	85.071	148.02	253.34
19	23.214	31.948	59.568	108.89	195.39	344.54
20	27.393	38.338	73.864	139.38	257.92	468.57
25	62.669	95.396	216.542	478.90	1033.6	2180.1
30	143.371	237.376	634.820	1645.5	4142.1	10143.

Year	*40%*	*50%*	*60%*	*70%*	*80%*	*90%*
1	1.400	1.500	1.600	1.700	1.800	1.900
2	1.960	2.250	2.560	2.890	3.240	3.610
3	2.744	3.375	4.096	4.913	5.832	6.859
4	3.842	5.062	6.544	8.352	10.498	13.032
5	5.378	7.594	10.486	14.199	18.896	24.761
6	7.530	11.391	16.777	24.138	34.012	47.046
7	10.541	17.086	26.844	41.034	61.222	89.387
8	14.758	25.629	42.950	69.758	110.200	169.836
9	20.661	38.443	68.720	118.588	198.359	322.688
10	28.925	57.665	109.951	201.599	357.047	613.107
11	40.496	86.498	175.922	342.719	642.684	1164.902
12	56.694	129.746	281.475	582.622	1156.831	2213.314
13	79.372	194.619	450.360	990.457	2082.295	4205.297
14	111.120	291.929	720.576	1683.777	3748.131	7990.065
15	155.568	437.894	1152.921	2862.421	6746.636	15181.122
16	217.795	656.84	1844.7	4866.1	12144.	28844.0
17	304.914	985.26	2951.5	8272.4	21859.	54804.0
18	426.879	1477.9	4722.4	14063.0	39346.	104130.0
19	597.630	2216.8	7555.8	23907.0	70824.	197840.0
20	836.683	3325.3	12089.0	40642.0	127480.	375900.0
25	4499.880	25251.	126760.0	577060.0	2408900.	9307600.0
30	24201.432	191750.	1329200.	8193500.0	45517000.	230470000.0

TABLE A–2

PRESENT VALUE OF $1

Year	1%	2%	3%	4%	5%	6%	7%	8%	9%	10%	12%	14%	15%
1	.990	.980	.971	.962	.952	.943	.935	.926	.917	.909	.893	.877	.870
2	.980	.961	.943	.925	.907	.890	.873	.857	.842	.826	.797	.769	.756
3	.971	.942	.915	.889	.864	.840	.816	.794	.772	.751	.712	.675	.658
4	.961	.924	.889	.855	.823	.792	.763	.735	.708	.683	.636	.592	.572
5	.951	.906	.863	.822	.784	.747	.713	.681	.650	.621	.567	.519	.497
6	.942	.888	.838	.790	.746	.705	.666	.630	.596	.564	.507	.456	.432
7	.933	.871	.813	.760	.711	.665	.623	.583	.547	.513	.452	.400	.376
8	.923	.853	.789	.731	.677	.627	.582	.540	.502	.467	.404	.351	.327
9	.914	.837	.766	.703	.645	.592	.544	.500	.460	.424	.361	.308	.284
10	.905	.820	.744	.676	.614	.558	.508	.463	.422	.386	.322	.270	.247
11	.896	.804	.722	.650	.585	.527	.475	.429	.388	.350	.287	.237	.215
12	.887	.788	.701	.625	.557	.497	.444	.397	.356	.319	.257	.208	.187
13	.879	.773	.681	.601	.530	.469	.415	.368	.326	.290	.229	.182	.163
14	.870	.758	.661	.577	.505	.442	.388	.340	.299	.263	.205	.160	.141
15	.861	.743	.642	.555	.481	.417	.362	.315	.275	.239	.183	.140	.123
16	.853	.728	.623	.534	.458	.394	.339	.292	.252	.218	.163	.123	.107
17	.844	.714	.605	.513	.436	.371	.317	.270	.231	.198	.146	.108	.093
18	.836	.700	.587	.494	.416	.350	.296	.250	.212	.180	.130	.095	.081
19	.828	.686	.570	.475	.396	.331	.276	.232	.194	.164	.116	.083	.070
20	.820	.673	.554	.456	.377	.319	.258	.215	.178	.149	.104	.073	.061
25	.780	.610	.478	.375	.295	.233	.184	.146	.116	.092	.059	.038	.030
30	.742	.552	.412	.308	.231	.174	.131	.099	.075	.057	.033	.020	.015

Year	16%	18%	20%	24%	28%	32%	36%	40%	50%	60%	70%	80%	90%
1	.862	.847	.833	.806	.781	.758	.735	.714	.667	.625	.588	.556	.526
2	.743	.718	.694	.650	.610	.574	.541	.510	.444	.391	.346	.309	.277
3	.641	.609	.579	.524	.477	.435	.398	.364	.296	.244	.204	.171	.146
4	.552	.516	.482	.423	.373	.329	.292	.260	.198	.153	.120	.095	.077
5	.476	.437	.402	.341	.291	.250	.215	.186	.132	.095	.070	.053	.040
6	.410	.370	.335	.275	.227	.189	.158	.133	.088	.060	.041	.029	.021
7	.354	.314	.279	.222	.178	.143	.116	.095	.059	.037	.024	.016	.011
8	.305	.266	.233	.179	.139	.108	.085	.068	.039	.023	.014	.009	.006
9	.263	.226	.194	.144	.108	.082	.063	.048	.026	.015	.008	.005	.003
10	.227	.191	.162	.116	.085	.062	.046	.035	.017	.009	.005	.003	.002
11	.195	.162	.135	.094	.066	.047	.034	.025	.012	.006	.003	.002	.001
12	.168	.137	.112	.076	.052	.036	.025	.018	.008	.004	.002	.001	.001
13	.145	.116	.093	.061	.040	.027	.018	.013	.005	.002	.001	.001	.000
14	.125	.099	.078	.049	.032	.021	.014	.009	.003	.001	.001	.000	.000
15	.108	.084	.065	.040	.025	.016	.010	.006	.002	.001	.000	.000	.000
16	.093	.071	.054	.032	.019	.012	.007	.005	.002	.001	.000	.000	
17	.080	.060	.045	.026	.015	.009	.005	.003	.001	.000	.000		
18	.069	.051	.038	.021	.012	.007	.004	.002	.001	.000	.000		
19	.060	.043	.031	.017	.009	.005	.003	.002	.000	.000			
20	.051	.037	.026	.014	.007	.004	.002	.001	.000	.000			
25	.024	.016	.010	.005	.002	.001	.000	.000					
30	.012	.007	.004	.002	.001	.000	.000						

TABLE A–3 SUM OF AN ANNUITY OF $1 FOR *N* YEARS

Year	*1%*	*2%*	*3%*	*4%*	*5%*	*6%*
1	1.000	1.000	1.000	1.000	1.000	1.000
2	2.010	2.020	2.030	2.040	2.050	2.060
3	2.030	3.060	3.091	3.122	3.152	3.184
4	4.060	4.122	4.184	4.246	4.310	4.375
5	5.101	5.204	5.309	5.416	5.526	5.637
6	6.152	6.308	6.468	6.633	6.802	6.975
7	7.214	7.434	7.662	7.898	8.142	8.394
8	8.286	8.583	8.892	9.214	9.549	9.897
9	9.369	9.755	10.159	10.583	11.027	11.491
10	10.462	10.950	11.464	12.006	12.578	13.181
11	11.567	12.169	12.808	13.486	14.207	14.972
12	12.683	13.412	14.192	15.026	15.917	16.870
13	13.809	14.680	15.618	16.627	17.713	18.882
14	14.947	15.974	17.086	18.292	19.599	21.051
15	16.097	17.293	18.599	20.024	21.579	23.276
16	17.258	18.639	20.157	21.825	23.657	25.673
17	18.430	20.012	21.762	23.698	25.840	28.213
18	19.615	21.412	23.414	25.645	28.132	30.906
19	20.811	22.841	25.117	27.671	30.539	33.760
20	22.019	24.297	26.870	29.778	33.066	36.786
25	28.243	32.030	36.459	41.646	47.727	54.865
30	34.785	40.568	47.575	56.085	66.439	79.058

Year	*7%*	*8%*	*9%*	*10%*	*12%*	*14%*
1	1.000	1.000	1.000	1.000	1.000	1.000
2	2.070	2.080	2.090	2.100	2.120	2.140
3	3.215	3.246	3.278	3.310	3.374	3.440
4	4.440	4.506	4.573	4.641	4.770	4.921
5	5.751	5.867	5.985	6.105	6.353	6.610
6	7.153	7.336	7.523	7.716	8.115	8.536
7	8.654	8.923	9.200	9.487	10.089	10.730
8	10.260	10.637	11.028	11.436	12.300	13.233
9	11.978	12.488	13.021	13.579	14.776	16.085
10	13.816	14.487	15.193	15.937	17.549	19.337
11	15.784	16.645	17.560	18.531	20.655	23.044
12	17.888	18.977	20.141	21.384	24.133	27.271
13	20.141	21.495	22.953	24.523	28.029	32.089
14	22.550	24.215	26.019	27.975	32.393	37.581
15	25.129	27.152	29.361	31.772	37.280	43.842
16	27.888	30.324	33.003	35.950	42.753	50.980
17	30.840	33.750	36.974	40.545	48.884	59.118
18	33.999	37.450	41.301	45.599	55.750	68.394
19	37.379	41.446	46.018	51.159	63.440	78.969
20	40.995	45.762	51.160	57.275	72.052	91.025
25	63.249	73.106	84.701	98.347	133.334	181.871
30	94.461	113.283	136.308	164.494	241.333	356.787

TABLE A–3 (*Continued*)

Year	*16%*	*18%*	*20%*	*24%*	*28%*	*32%*
1	1.000	1.000	1.000	1.000	1.000	1.000
2	2.160	2.180	2.200	2.240	2.280	2.320
3	3.506	3.572	3.640	3.778	3.918	4.062
4	5.066	5.215	5.368	5.684	6.016	6.362
5	6.877	7.154	7.442	8.048	8.700	9.398
6	8.977	9.442	9.930	10.980	12.136	13.406
7	11.414	12.142	12.916	14.615	16.534	18.696
8	14.240	15.327	16.499	19.123	22.163	25.678
9	17.518	19.086	20.799	24.712	29.369	34.895
10	21.321	23.521	25.959	31.643	38.592	47.062
11	25.733	28.755	32.150	40.238	50.399	63.122
12	30.850	34.931	39.580	50.985	65.510	84.320
13	36.786	42.219	48.497	64.110	84.853	112.303
14	43.672	50.818	59.196	80.496	109.612	149.240
15	51.660	60.965	72.035	100.815	141.303	197.997
16	60.925	72.939	87.442	126.011	181.87	262.36
17	71.673	87.068	105.931	157.253	233.79	347.31
18	84.141	103.740	128.117	195.994	300.25	459.45
19	98.603	123.414	154.740	244.033	385.32	607.47
20	115.380	146.628	186.688	303.601	494.21	802.86
25	249.214	342.603	471.981	898.092	1706.8	3226.8
30	530.312	790.948	1181.882	2640.916	5873.2	12941.0

Year	*36%*	*40%*	*50%*	*60%*	*70%*	*80%*
1	1.000	1.000	1.000	1.000	1.000	1.000
2	2.360	2.400	2.500	2.600	2.700	2.800
3	4.210	4.360	4.750	5.160	5.590	6.040
4	6.725	7.104	8.125	9.256	10.503	11.872
5	10.146	10.846	13.188	15.810	18.855	22.370
6	14.799	16.324	20.781	26.295	33.054	41.265
7	21.126	23.853	32.172	43.073	57.191	75.278
8	29.732	34.395	49.258	69.916	98.225	136.500
9	41.435	49.153	74.887	112.866	167.983	246.699
10	57.352	69.814	113.330	181.585	286.570	445.058
11	78.998	98.739	170.995	291.536	488.170	802.105
12	108.437	139.235	257.493	467.458	830.888	1444.788
13	148.475	195.929	387.239	748.933	1413.510	2601.619
14	202.926	275.300	581.859	1199.293	2403.968	4683.914
15	276.979	386.420	873.788	1919.869	4087.745	8432.045
16	377.69	541.99	1311.7	3072.8	6950.2	15179.0
17	514.66	759.78	1968.5	4917.5	11816.0	27323.0
18	700.94	1064.7	2953.8	7868.9	20089.0	49182.0
19	954.28	1491.6	4431.7	12591.0	34152.0	88528.0
20	1298.8	2089.2	6648.5	20147.0	58059.0	159350.0
25	6053.0	11247.0	50500.0	211270.0	824370.0	3011100.0
30	28172.0	60501.0	383500.0	2215400.0	11705000.0	56896000.0

TABLE A–4 PRESENT VALUE OF AN ANNUITY OF $1

Year	1%	2%	3%	4%	5%	6%	7%	8%	9%	10%
1	0.990	0.980	0.971	0.962	0.952	0.943	0.935	0.926	0.917	0.909
2	1.970	1.942	1.913	1.886	1.859	1.833	1.808	1.783	1.759	1.736
3	2.941	2.884	2.829	2.775	2.723	2.673	2.624	2.577	2.531	2.487
4	3.902	3.808	3.717	3.630	3.546	3.465	3.387	3.312	3.240	3.170
5	4.853	4.713	4.580	4.452	4.329	4.212	4.100	3.993	3.890	3.791
6	5.795	5.601	5.417	5.242	5.076	4.917	4.766	4.623	4.486	4.355
7	6.728	6.472	6.230	6.002	5.786	5.582	5.389	5.206	5.033	4.868
8	7.652	7.325	7.020	6.733	6.463	6.210	6.971	5.747	5.535	5.335
9	8.566	8.162	7.786	7.435	7.108	6.802	6.515	6.247	5.985	5.759
10	9.471	8.983	8.530	8.111	7.722	7.360	7.024	6.710	6.418	6.145
11	10.368	9.787	9.253	8.760	8.306	7.887	7.499	7.139	6.805	6.495
12	11.255	10.575	9.954	9.385	8.863	8.384	7.943	7.536	7.161	6.814
13	12.134	11.348	10.635	9.986	9.394	8.853	8.358	7.904	7.487	7.103
14	13.004	12.106	11.296	10.563	9.899	9.295	8.745	8.244	7.786	7.367
15	13.865	12.849	11.938	11.118	10.380	9.712	9.108	8.559	8.060	7.606
16	14.718	13.578	12.561	11.652	10.838	10.106	9.447	8.851	8.312	7.824
17	15.562	14.292	13.166	12.166	11.274	10.477	9.763	9.122	8.544	8.022
18	16.398	14.992	13.754	12.659	11.690	10.828	10.059	9.372	8.756	8.201
19	17.226	15.678	14.324	13.134	12.085	11.158	10.336	9.604	8.950	8.365
20	18.046	16.351	14.877	13.590	12.462	11.470	10.594	9.818	9.128	8.514
25	22.023	19.523	17.413	15.622	14.094	12.783	11.654	10.675	9.823	9.077
30	25.808	22.397	19.600	17.292	15.373	13.765	12.409	11.258	10.274	9.427

Year	12%	14%	16%	18%	20%	24%	28%	32%	36%
1	0.893	0.877	0.862	0.847	0.833	0.806	0.781	0.758	0.735
2	1.690	1.647	1.605	1.566	1.528	1.457	1.392	1.332	1.276
3	2.402	2.322	2.246	2.174	2.106	1.981	1.868	1.766	1.674
4	3.037	2.914	2.798	2.690	2.589	2.404	2.241	2.096	1.966
5	3.605	3.433	3.274	3.127	2.991	2.745	2.532	2.345	2.181
6	4.111	3.889	3.685	3.498	3.326	3.020	2.759	2.534	2.339
7	4.564	4.288	4.039	3.812	3.605	3.242	2.937	2.678	2.455
8	4.968	4.639	4.344	4.078	3.837	3.421	3.076	2.786	2.540
9	5.328	4.946	4.607	4.303	4.031	3.566	3.184	2.868	2.603
10	5.650	5.216	4.833	4.494	4.193	3.682	3.269	2.930	2.650
11	5.988	5.453	5.029	4.656	4.327	3.776	3.335	2.978	2.683
12	6.194	5.660	5.197	4.793	4.439	3.851	3.387	3.013	2.708
13	6.424	5.842	5.342	4.910	4.533	3.912	3.427	3.040	2.727
14	6.628	6.002	5.468	5.008	4.611	3.962	3.459	3.061	2.740
15	6.811	6.142	5.575	5.092	4.675	4.001	3.483	3.076	2.750
16	6.974	6.265	5.669	5.162	4.730	4.033	3.503	3.088	2.758
17	7.120	5.373	5.749	4.222	4.775	4.059	3.518	3.097	2.763
18	7.250	6.467	5.818	5.273	4.812	4.080	3.529	3.104	2.767
19	7.366	6.550	5.877	5.316	4.844	4.097	3.539	3.109	2.770
20	7.469	6.623	5.929	5.353	4.870	4.110	3.546	3.113	2.772
25	7.843	6.873	6.097	5.467	4.948	4.147	3.564	3.122	2.776
30	8.055	7.003	6.177	5.517	4.979	4.160	3.569	3.124	2.778

APPENDIX B

GLOSSARY

Glossary

Accelerated Depreciation Depreciation methods that write off the cost of an asset at a faster rate than the write-off under the straight-line method. The three principal methods of accelerated depreciation are: (1) sum-of-years-digits, (2) double declining balance, and (3) units of production.

Accruals Continually recurring short-term liabilities. Examples are accrued wages, accrued taxes, and accrued interest.

Aging Schedule A report showing how long accounts receivable have been outstanding. It gives the percent of receivables not past due and the percent past due by, for example, one month, two months, or other periods.

Amortize To liquidate on an installment basis; an amortized loan is one in which the principal amount of the loan is repaid in installments during the life of the loan.

Annuity A series of payments of a fixed amount for a specified number of years.

Arrearage Overdue payment; frequently, omitted dividends on preferred stocks.

Assignment A relatively inexpensive way of liquidating a failing firm that does not involve going through the courts.

Balloon Payment When a debt is not fully amortized, the final payment is larger than the preceding payments and is called a "balloon" payment.

Benefit/Cost Ratio (*See* Profitability Index)

Bankruptcy A legal procedure for formally liquidating a business carried out under the jurisdiction of courts of law.

Bond A long-term debt instrument.

Book Value The accounting value of an asset. The book value of a share of common stock is equal to the net worth (common stock plus surplus) of the corporation divided by the number of shares of stock outstanding.

Break-even Analysis An analytical technique for studying the relation between fixed cost, variable cost, and profits. A break-even *chart* graphically depicts the nature of break-even analysis. The break-even *point* represents that volume of sales at which total costs equal total revenues (that is, profits equal zero).

Call (1) An option to buy (or "call") a share of stock at a specified price within a specific period. (2) The process of redeeming a bond or preferred stock issue before its normal maturity.

Call Premium The amount in excess of par value that a company must pay when it calls a security.

Call Price The price that must be paid when a security is called. The call price is equal to the par value plus the call premium.

Call Privilege A provision incorporated into a bond or a share of preferred stock that gives the issuer the right to redeem (call) the security at a specified price.

Calling The action of exercising the call privilege and redeeming securities prior to their maturity date.

Capital Asset An asset with a life of more than one year that is not bought and sold in the ordinary course of business.

Capital Budgeting The process of planning expenditures on assets whose returns are expected to extend beyond one year.

Capital Gains Profits on the sale of capital assets held for six months or more.

Capital Losses Losses on the sale of capital assets.

Capital Rationing A situation where a constraint is placed on the total size of the capital investment during a particular period.

Capital Structure The permanent long-term financing of the firm represented by long-term debt, preferred stock, and net worth (net worth consists of capital, capital surplus, and earned surplus). Capital structure is distinguished from *financial structure,* which includes short-term debt plus all reserve accounts.

Capitalization Rate A discount rate used to find the present value of a series of future cash receipts; sometimes called *discount rate.*

Carry-back; Carry-forward For income tax purposes, losses that can be carried backward or forward to reduce federal income taxes.

Cash Budget A schedule showing cash flows (receipts, disbursements, and net cash) for a firm over a specified period.

Cash Cycle The length of time between the purchase of raw materials and the collection of accounts receivable generated in the sale of the final product.

Certainty Equivalents The amount of cash (or rate of return) that someone would require *with certainty* to make him indifferent between this certain sum (or rate of return) and a particular uncertain, risky sum (or rate of return).

Chattel Mortgage A mortgage on personal property (not real estate). A mortgage on equipment would be a chattel mortgage.

Coefficient of Variation Standard deviation divided by the mean.

Collateral Assets that are used to secure a loan.

Commercial Paper Unsecured, short-term promissory notes of large firms, usually issued in denominations of $1 million or more. The rate of interest on commercial paper is typically somewhat below the prime rate of interest.

Commitment Fee The fee paid to a lender for a formal line of credit.

Compensating Balance A required minimum checking account balance that a firm must maintain with a commercial bank. The required balance is generally equal to 15 to 20 percent of the amount of loans outstanding. Compensating balances can raise the effective rate of interest on bank loans.

Composition An informal method of reorganization that voluntarily reduces creditors' claims on the debtor firm.

Compound Interest An interest rate that is applicable when interest in succeeding periods is earned not only on the initial principal but also on the accumulated interest of prior periods. Compound interest is contrasted to *simple interest,* in which returns are not earned on interest received.

Compounding The arithmetic process of determining the final value of a payment or series of payments when compound interest is applied.

Conditional Sales Contract A method of financing new equipment by paying it off in installments over a one- to five-year period. The seller retains title to the equipment until payment has been completed.

Consolidated Tax Return An income tax return that combines the income statement of several affiliated firms.

Continuous Compounding (Discounting) As opposed to discrete compounding, interest is added continuously rather than at discrete points in time.

Conversion Price The effective price paid for common stock when the stock is obtained by converting either convertible preferred stocks or convertible bonds. For example, if a $1,000 bond is convertible into 20 shares of stock, the conversion price is $50 ($1,000/20).

Conversion Ratio or Conversion Rate The number of shares of common stock that may be obtained by converting a convertible bond or share of convertible preferred stock.

Convertibles Securities (generally bonds or preferred stocks) that are exchangeable at the option of the holder for common stock of the issuing firm.

Cost of Capital The discount rate that should be used in the capital budgeting process.

Coupon Rate The stated rate of interest on a bond.

Covenant Detailed clauses contained in loan agreements. Covenants are designed to protect the lender and include such items as limits on total indebtedness, restrictions on dividends, minimum current ratio, and similar provisions.

Cut-off Point In the capital budgeting process, the minimum rate of return on acceptable investment opportunities.

Decision Tree A device for setting forth graphically the pattern of relationship between decisions and chance events.

Debt Ratio Total debt divided by total assets.

Debenture A long-term debt instrument that is not secured by a mortgage on specific property.

Default The failure to fulfill a contract. Generally, default refers to the failure to pay interest or principal on debt obligations.

Discount Rate The interest rate used in the discounting process; sometimes called *capitalization rate.*

Discounted Cash Flow Techniques Methods of ranking investment proposals. Included are (1) internal rate of return method, (2) net present value method, and (3) profitability index or benefit/cost ratio.

Discounting The process of finding the present value of a series of future cash flows. Discounting is the reverse of compounding.

Discounting of Accounts Receivable Short-term financing where accounts receivable are used to secure the loan. The lender *does not* buy the accounts receivable but simply uses them as collateral for the loan. Also called "pledging of accounts receivable."

Dividend Yield The ratio of the current dividend to the current price of a share of stock.

Earnings Multiplier The price/earnings ratio (the P/E ratio).

EBIT Abbreviation for "earnings before interest and taxes."

EPS Abbreviation for "earnings per share."

Economical Ordering Quantity (EOQ) The optimum (least cost) quantity of merchandise which should be purchased.

Equity The net worth of a business, consisting of capital stock, capital (or paid-in) surplus, earned surplus (or retained earnings), and, occasionally, certain net worth reserves. *Common equity* is that part of the total net worth belonging to the common stockholders. *Total equity* would include preferred stockholders. The terms "common stock," "net worth," and "equity" are frequently used interchangeably.

Excise Tax A tax on the manufacture, sale, or consumption of specified commodities.

Ex-dividend Date The date on which the right to the current dividend no longer accompanies a stock. (For listed stock, the ex-dividend date is four working days prior to the date of record.)

Exercise Price The price that must be paid for a share of common stock when it is bought with a warrant.

Expected Return The rate of return a firm expects to realize from an investment. The expected return is the mean value of the probability distribution of possible returns.

Extension An informal method of reorganization in which the creditors voluntarily postpone the date of required payment on past-due obligations.

Factoring A method of financing accounts receivable under which a firm sells its accounts receivable (generally without recourse) to a financial institution (the "factor").

Field Warehousing A method of financing inventories in which a "warehouse" is established at the place of business of the borrowing firm.

Financial Leverage The ratio of total debt to total assets. There are other measures of financial leverage, especially ones that relate cash inflows to required cash outflows. In this book, the debt/total asset ratio is generally used to measure leverage.

Financial Structure The entire right-hand side of the balance sheet—the way in which a firm is financed.

Fixed Charges Costs that do not vary with the level of output.

Float The amount of funds tied up in checks that have been written but are still in process and have not yet been collected.

Flotation Cost The cost of issuing new stocks or bonds.

Funded Debt Long-term debt.

Funding The process of replacing short-term debt with long-term securities (stocks or bonds).

Goodwill Intangible assets of a firm established by the excess of the price paid for the going concern over its book value.

Holding Company A corporation operated for the purpose of owning the common stocks of other corporations.

Improper Accumulation Earnings retained by a business for the purpose of enabling stockholders to avoid personal income taxes.

Income Bond A bond that pays interest only if the current interest is earned.

Indenture A formal agreement between the issuer of a bond and the bondholders.

Insolvency The inability to meet maturing obligations.

Interest Factor (IF) Numbers found in compound interest and annuity tables.

Internal Rate of Return (IRR) The rate of return on an asset investment. The internal rate of return is calculated by finding the discount rate that equates the present value of future cash flows to the cost of the investment.

Intrinsic Value That value that, in the mind of the analyst, is justified by the facts. It is often used to distinguish between the "true value" of an asset (the intrinsic value) and the asset's current market price.

Investment Banker One who underwrites and distributes new investment securities; more broadly, one who helps business firms to obtain financing.

Investment Tax Credit Business firms can deduct as a credit against their income taxes a specified percentage of the dollar amount of new investments in each of certain categories of assets.

Leverage Factor The ratio of debt to total assets.

Line of Credit An arrangement whereby a financial institution (bank or insurance company) commits itself to lend up to a specified maximum amount of funds during a specified period. Sometimes the interest rate on the loan is specified; at other times, it is not. Sometimes a commitment fee is imposed for obtaining the line of credit.

Liquidity Refers to a firm's cash position and its ability to meet maturing obligations.

Listed Securities Securities traded on an organized security exchange—for example, the New York Stock Exchange.

Lock-box Plan A procedure used to speed up collections and to reduc float.

Margin—Profit on Sales The *profit margin* is the percentage of profit after tax to sales.

Margin—Securities Business The buying of stocks or bonds on credit, known as *buying on margin.*

Margin Trading Buying securities on credit (margin).

Marginal Cost The cost of an additional unit. The *marginal cost of capital* is the cost of an additional dollar of new funds.

Marginal Efficiency of Capital A schedule showing the internal rate of return on investment opportunities.

Marginal Revenue The additional gross revenue produced by selling one additional unit of output.

Merger Any combination that forms one company from two or more previously existing companies.

Money Market Financial markets in which funds are borrowed or loaned for short periods. (The money market is distinguished from the capital market, which is the market for long-term funds).

Mortgage A pledge of designated property as security for a loan.

Net Present Value (NPV) Method A method of ranking investment proposals. The NPV is equal to the present value of future returns, discounted at the appropriate cost of capital, minus the present value of the cost of the investment.

Net Worth The capital and surplus of a firm—capital stock; capital surplus (paid-in capital); earned surplus (retained earnings); and, occasionally, certain reserves. For some purposes, preferred stock is included; generally, net worth refers only to the common stockholder's position.

Objective Probability Distributions Probability distributions determined by statistical procedures.

Operating Leverage The extent to which fixed costs are used in a firm's operation. Break-even analysis is used to measure the extent to which operating leverage is employed.

Opportunity Cost The rate of return on the best *alternative* investment that is available. It is the highest return that will *not* be earned if the funds are invested in a particular project. For example, the opportunity cost of *not* investing in common stocks yielding 8 percent might be 6 percent, which could be earned on bonds.

Ordinary Income Income from the normal operations of a firm. Operating income specifically excludes income from the sale of capital assets.

Organized Security Exchanges Formal organizations having tangible, physical locations. Organized exchanges conduct an auction market in designated ("listed") investment securities. For example, the New York Stock Exchange is an organized exchange.

Over-the-counter Market All facilities that provide for security transactions not conducted on organized exchanges. The over-the-counter market is typically a "telephone market," as most business is conducted over the telephone.

Over-the-counter Securities Securities that are not traded on an organized security exchange.

Par Value The nominal or face value of a stock or bond.

Payback Period The length of time required for the net revenues of an investment to return the cost of the investment.

Payout Ratio The percentage of earnings paid out in the form of dividends.

Perpetuity A stream of equal future payments expected to continue forever.

Pledging of Accounts Receivable Short-term borrowing from financial institutions where the loan is secured by accounts receivable. The lender may physically take the accounts receivable but typically has recourse to the borrower; also called *discounting of accounts receivable.*

Pooling of Interest An accounting method for combining the financial statements of two firms that merge. Under the pooling of interest procedure, the assets of the merged firms are simply added together to form the balance sheet of the surviving corporation. This method is different from the "purchase" method, where goodwill is put on the balance sheet to reflect a premium (or discount) paid in excess of book value.

Portfolio Effect The extent to which variations in returns on a combination of assets (a "portfolio") is less than the sum of the variations of the individual assets.

Pre-emptive Right A provision contained in the corporate charter and bylaws that gives holders of common stock the right to purchase on a pro rata basis new issues of common stock (or securities convertible into common stock).

Present Value (PV) The value today of a future payment, or stream of payments, discounted at the appropriate discount rate.

Price/earnings Ratio (P/E) The ratio of price to earnings. Faster growing or less risky firms typically have higher P/E ratios than slower growing or riskier firms.

Prime Rate The rate of interest commercial banks charge very large, strong corporations.

Pro Forma A projection. A *pro forma* financial statement is one that shows how the actual statement will look if certain specified assumptions are realized. *Pro forma* statements may be either future or past projections. An example of a backward *pro forma* statement occurs when two firms are planning to merge and show what their consolidated financial statements would have looked like had they been merged in preceding years.

Profit Margin The ratio of profits after taxes to sales.

Profitability Index (PI) The present value of future returns divided by the present value of the investment outlay.

Progressive Tax A tax that requires a higher percentage payment on higher incomes. The personal income tax in the United States, which is at a rate of 14 percent on the lowest increments of income to 70 percent on the highest increments, is progressive.

Prospectus A document issued for the purpose of describing a new security issue. The Securities and Exchange Commission (SEC) examines prospectuses to insure that statements contained therein are not "false and misleading."

Proxy A document giving one the authority or power to act for another. Typically, the authority in question is the power to vote shares of common stock.

Put An option to sell a specific security at a specified price within a designated period.

Rate of Return The internal rate of return on an investment.

Recourse Arrangement A term used in connection with accounts receivable financing. If a firm sells its accounts receivable to a financial institution under a recourse agreement, then, if the account receivable cannot be collected, the selling firm must repurchase the account from the financial institution.

Refunding The process of retiring an old bond issue and replacing it with a new debt or equity issue.

Regression analysis A statistical procedure for predicting the value of one variable (dependent variable) on the basis of knowledge about one or more other variables (independent variables).

Reinvestment Rate The rate of return at which cash flows from an investment are reinvested. The reinvestment rate may or may not be constant from year to year.

Reorganization When a financially troubled firm goes through reorganization, its assets are restated to reflect their current market value, and its financial structure is restated to reflect any changes on the asset side of the statement. Under a reorganization the firm continues in existence; this is contrasted to bankruptcy, where the firm is liquidated and ceases to exist.

Required Rate of Return The rate of return that stockholders expect to receive on common stock investments.

Residual Value The value of leased property at the end of the lease term.

Retained Earnings Profits after taxes that are retained in the business rather than being paid out in dividends.

Right A short-term option to buy a specified number of shares of a new issue of securities at a designated "subscription" price.

Rights Offering A securities flotation offered to existing stockholders.

Risk-adjusted Discount Rates The discount rate applicable for a particular risky (uncertain) stream of income: the riskless rate of interest plus a risk premium appropriate to the level of risk attached to the particular income stream.

Risk Index (RI) Calculated as a function of the present value interest factor for a riskless cash flow divided by the present value interest factor for the risky asset.

Risk Premium The difference between the expected rate of return on a particular risky asset and the rate of return on a riskless asset with the same expected life.

Salvage Value The value of a capital asset at the end of a specified period. It is the current market price of an asset being considered for replacement in a capital budgeting problem.

Selling Group A group of stock brokerage firms formed for the purpose of distributing a new issue of securities; part of the investment banking process.

Short-selling Selling a security that is not owned by the seller at the time of the sale. The seller borrows the security from a brokerage firm and must at some point repay the brokerage firm by buying the security on the open market.

Securities, Junior Securities that have lower priority in claims on assets and income than other securities (*senior securities*). For example, preferred stock is junior to debentures, but debentures are junior to mortgage bonds. Common stock is the most junior of all corporate securities.

Securities, Senior Securities having claims on income and assets that rank higher than certain other securities (*junior securities*). For example, mortgage bonds are senior to debentures, but debentures are senior to common stock.

Sinking Fund A required annual payment designed to amortize a bond or a preferred stock issue. The sinking fund may be held in the form of cash or marketable securities, but more generally the money put into the sinking fund is used to retire each year some of the securities in question.

Stock Dividend A dividend paid in additional shares of stock rather than in cash. It involves a transfer from earned surplus to the capital stock account; therefore, stock dividends are limited by the amount of earned surplus.

Stock Split An accounting action to increase the number of shares outstanding; for example, in a 3-for-1 split, shares outstanding would be tripled and each stockholder would receive three new shares for each one formerly held. Stock splits involve no transfer from surplus to the capital account.

Subjective Probability Distributions Probability distributions determined through subjective procedures without the use of statistics.

Subordinated Debenture A bond having a claim on assets only after the senior debt has been paid off in the event of liquidation.

Subscription Price The price at which a security may be purchased in a rights offering.

Surtax A tax levied in addition to the normal tax. For example, the normal corporate tax rate is 22 percent, but a surtax of 26 percent is added to the normal tax on all corporate income exceeding $25,000.

Tangible Assets Physical assets as opposed to such tangible assets as goodwill and the stated value of patents.

Tender Offers A situation wherein one firm offers to buy the stock of another, going directly to the stockholders, frequently over the opposition of the management of the firm whose stock is being sought.

Term Loan A loan generally obtained from a bank or insurance company with a maturity greater than one year. Term loans are generally amortized.

Trade Credit Interfirm debt arising through credit sales and recorded as an account receivable by the seller and as an account payable by the buyer.

Trust Receipt An instrument acknowledging that the borrower holds certain goods in trust for the lender. Trust receipt financing is used in connection with the financing of inventories for automobile dealers, construction equipment dealers, appliance dealers, and other dealers in expensive durable goods.

Underwriting (1) The entire process of issuing new corporate securities. (2) The insurance function of bearing the risk of adverse price fluctuations during the period in which a new issue of stock or bonds is being distributed.

Underwriting Syndicate A syndicate of investment firms formed to spread the risk associated with the purchase and distribution of a new issue of securities. The larger the issue, the more firms will typically be involved in the syndicate.

Utility Theory A body of theory dealing with the relationships among money income, utility (or "happiness"), and the willingness to accept risks.

Warrant A long-term option to buy a stated number of shares of common stock at a specified price. The specified price is generally called the "exercise price."

Working Capital Refers to a firm's investment in short-term assets—cash, short-term securities, accounts receivable, and inventories. *Gross working capital* is defined as a firm's total current assets. *Net working capital* is defined as current assets minus current liabilities. If the term "working capital" is used without further qualification, it generally refers to gross working capital.

Yield The rate of return on an investment—the internal rate of return.

Author Index

Subject Index